# XML and Java™
## Second Edition

DEVELOPING WEB APPLICATIONS

**Hiroshi Maruyama**
**Kent Tamura**
**Naohiko Uramoto**
**Makoto Murata**
**Andy Clark**
**Yuichi Nakamura**
**Ryo Neyama**
**Kazuya Kosaka**
**Satoshi Hada**

✦✦ Addison-Wesley

Boston • San Francisco • New York • Toronto
Montreal • London • Munich • Paris • Madrid
Capetown • Sydney • Tokyo • Singapore • Mexico City

The publisher offers discounts on this book when ordered in quantity for special sales. For more information, please contact:

Pearson Education Corporate Sales Division
201 W. 103rd Street
Indianapolis, IN 46290
(800) 428-5331
corpsales@pearsoned.com

Visit Addison-Wesley on the Web: www.aw.com/cseng/

*Library of Congress Cataloging in Publication Data*
XML and Java : developing Web applications / Hiroshi Maruyama . . . [et al.]. — 2nd ed.
    p.   cm.
  Includes bibliographical references and index.
  ISBN 0-201-77004-0 (alk. paper)
    1. XML (Document markup language)  2. Java (Computer program language)
  3. Web sites — Design.  I. Maruyama, Hiroshi, 1958–

  QA76.76.H94 X418    2002
  005.7'2—dc21                                                    2002018354

ISBN 0-201-77004-0
Text printed on recycled paper
1 2 3 4 5 6 7 8 9 10—CRS—0605040302
First printing, May 2002

# Contents

# Foreword

Hiroshi Maruyama, Kent Tamura, and Naohiko Uramoto released one of the first books that provided a practical introduction to developing XML applications using Java in early 1999. Three years later, much has happened in the XML community: Many new specifications have been released that were not discussed in the first edition, and some have been widely implemented in both commercial products and open source software, usually written in Java. Furthermore, the Java and XML communities have become more tightly integrated than they were in 1999, when many Java developers saw XML as more of a threat than an opportunity. Now the mantra "Java is portable code, XML is portable data" is repeated frequently.

The release of *XML and Java, Second Edition*, roughly coincides with the release of JDK 1.4, which incorporates XML technologies into the very core of Java. Sun has defined the Java API for XML Processing (JAXP), that incorporates both the de facto standard SAX API and the World Wide Web Consortium's Document Object Model (DOM) API. Also, JAXP fills in some of the gaps between these cross-platform standards to define JAXP APIs for loading, configuring, and invoking an XML parser and serializing DOM objects to XML text. Additional Java tools are being developed to assist in other XML-related tasks, such as the JAXM for XML messaging and JAXB to "compile" XML schemas into Java classes that automatically parse, validate, and serialize instances of them. Even more importantly, the basic XML functionality is automatically available to JDK and JRE 1.4 users without additional downloading or installation.

*XML and Java, Second Edition*, is an excellent resource for Java developers and system architects or advanced students needing to understand how to work with these new XML features being tightly bundled with Java. It assumes a basic working knowledge of XML and Java, so the experienced reader need not skip over widely covered introductory material. Furthermore, it exploits the combined expertise of the various authors while avoiding most of the discontinuity, redundancy, and inconsistency all too common in multiauthor books.

The book is organized into two parts, the first set of chapters (mostly written by Maruyama, Tamura, and Uramoto) effectively covers the core XML technologies, such as XML namespaces, SAX, DOM, schemas, and XSLT and how they can be used in Java programs. The second set primarily covers more experimental or Java-specific tools, such as application servers and EJB, messaging, data binding, and Web services tools such as SOAP, UDDI, and WSDL. In less knowledgeable hands, this wealth of material could be overwhelming, but the authors' deep expertise in these subjects allows them to handle it quite effectively, offering both concrete examples and high-level design guidance. Ryo Neyama's Chapter 10 provides a very useful overview of server-side Java XML programming using servlets, JSP, and Apache Cocoon. Yuichi Nakamura contributes two chapters on XML messaging and Web services that clearly show that Java developers have all the tools they need to participate in the Web services revolution. The principal authors contribute chapters describing the state of the art in using databases, security services, and the generation of Java classes from XML schema. The accompanying CD-ROM contains plenty of material for hands-on learning of the techniques covered in the book.

The emphasis throughout the book is on how to use the cross-platform standard tools from Java code; the authors do not succumb to the temptation to spend much time on those XML tools that exploit Java's strengths and idioms. This leaves the reader better equipped to work with XML on other platforms as well as from Java, and the knowledgeable Java programmer who understands the XML standards will have little trouble picking up the Java-specific tools.

This is not to say that the authors uncritically describe the Sun or W3C view of Java or XML. It provides an independent perspective, such as by illustrating how to use the Apache Xerces XML parser via the Java-standard JAXP interfaces instead of the Crimson parser included with JAXP. Likewise, Andy Clark's Chapter 6 on parser tricks shows how to use some of the more complex and obscure bits of XML (such as external parsed entities) effectively by using the features of the Apache Xerces parser. Other challenges we face in the *terra incognita* at the borders of XML and Java technology are described, and routes around the worst pitfalls mapped.

One especially valuable feature of *XML and Java, Second Edition,* is its treatment of the rather contentious subject of XML schemas and DTDs. XML 1.0 defines a Document Type Definition syntax describing constraints on XML structures that a validating parser must enforce, and the W3C has more recently produced a Recommendation defining an XML Schema Definition Language. The W3C schema language has not been particularly well received in the XML community, however, and several alternatives have been proposed. The International Organization for Standardization has undertaken an effort to define an international standard ISO/IEC JTC1/SC34 Document Schema Definition Language (DSDL), which covers XML DTDs, W3C schemas, the RELAX NG XML schema language, and the Schematron XPath-based tree pattern constraint language. It appears that XML users will have a menu of standard schema language options to choose from, some more appropriate than others for specific situations but none completely suitable for all scenarios.

This book has two chapters covering these subjects written by Makoto Murata, a coauthor of the RELAX NG specification and a researcher who has convincingly applied mathematical techniques to practical problems in the XML world. Chapter 9 presents information about XML schemas likely to be most useful to practitioners: it says what problems they are supposed to solve, presents the ways in which DTDs, W3C Schema, and RELAX NG address these problems, and summarizes the strengths and weaknesses of each. Chapter 16 addresses the larger principles at stake here in more depth, covering additional schema languages such as Schematron and RDF Schema. Together, these chapters provide a concise but rather profound summary of the state of the art in XML schema language theory and practice that should be of great use in guiding Java developers through the dynamic but confusing world of XML schemas.

The first edition of *XML and Java* played an important role in introducing Java developers to XML. The second edition not only brings this introduction up to date as Java and XML have evolved, but also shows the authors' deepening understanding of these technologies and how they fit together.

Michael Champion
Advisory Research and Development Specialist
Software AG, Darmstadt, Germany

# Preface

When we had the opportunity to write a book on XML in February 1998, which was just after we had released the first XML4J Parser from IBM's alphaWorks Web site, we discussed what we could achieve through publishing a book. We immediately concluded that a book on how to develop programs that deal with XML as data would be the most needed and that we could contribute through our experience in writing the parser. Several XML books were on the market, but most of them were either about the specifications or about creating XML documents. Few of them described how to write programs with XML as the input and output data format. Because Java was the implementation language of XML4J Parser and because many features (such as built-in Unicode character support) make XML and Java a perfect match, Java was a natural choice as the programming language. More importantly, Java was becoming the mainstream language for server-side programming. We believe that the first edition of the book satisfied, at least to a certain extent, the needs of developers who desperately needed to know the potential and limitations of these two emerging technologies and how they can be best applied to real-world situations.

We have the same goals in this edition with more new technologies—to show how the emerging technologies around XML and Java such as DOM Level 2, SAX2, XSLT, J2EE, XML Schema, and Web services—can be combined to solve real-world problems, and to discuss how these technologies will change the way future e-Business applications will be developed. The first edition of the book was not an introduction or a reference to each technology, and neither is the second edition. Each of these topics is worth an entire book. We do not list all the features of these technologies. Instead, we explain why you should be interested in them and how you can apply them to your problem by showing real-world examples.

This book has two parts. The first half covers basic tools for dealing with XML in Java. Here we concentrate only on the solid, stable technologies. XML technologies that were not W3C Recommendations at the time of writing are deliberately not included. That the beginning chapters are about "basic" technologies does not mean that these chapters are introductory. It simply means that these technologies and tools are the absolute minimum you need to understand in order to develop an XML-based application. Seasoned developers who trust only basic and proven tools will also find these chapters useful, because we covered a lot of programming techniques and hints for making the most of these tools. In the later chapters, on the other hand, we include emerging technologies, such as SOAP and Web services, that we believe are crucial for future e-Business solutions. Those who are looking for new technologies for their next projects and need to understand the potential and limitations of these technologies will find the chapters in the later chapters particularly useful.

All the sample programs in the book are available on the accompanying CD-ROM. Each sample has its own Readme file that describes how to set up and run it. It is our strong belief that knowledge about new software technologies can be acquired only through playing with them—running them, changing the configurations and modifying lines of code, and rerunning them to see the effects. We recommend that readers try the samples on the CD-ROM as much as possible. We made every effort to ensure that the samples are complete and run on most, if not all, platforms that support the latest Java runtimes. Any updates to the contents of the book can be downloaded from the publisher's Web site at `http://www.awl.com/cseng/`.

# Web Applications, XML, and Java

## 1.1 Introduction

This book is about how to design and develop Web applications based on Extensible Markup Language (XML), Java, and emerging technologies around XML and Java. The term "Web application" may be a little too restrictive here—the techniques described can be applied to any server-side system that manipulates content in XML. In particular, we focus heavily on business-to-business (B2B) applications—how such applications can send, receive, verify, and manipulate XML documents that are exchanged among companies. In addition to XML and Java, a number of emerging technologies will facilitate the design and implementation of B2B applications, such as Web application server, Simple Object Access Protocol (SOAP), Web services, and data binding. This book also explains the benefits and potential pitfalls of these new technologies.

This book is not intended to be an introduction to XML or Java. A number of books are available for those who need a quick understanding of XML or Java. We assume that readers have a basic understanding of XML and experience in writing simple Java programs. If you have already built one or more Web applications or you have a background in designing and building business applications, that will help you understand the material presented in this book. We recommend that you have both the XML and Java references that are listed in Appendix B handy when we walk you through the sample applications.

One of the wonderful things about Internet technologies is that many useful resources, such as tools, language processors, documents, and sample programs, can be downloaded from the Internet for free. Appendix B also contains a list of links that we are sure you will find useful. The following are two URLs that you *must know.* You should consult these links whenever you need in-depth information or to obtain the latest information on XML and Java. (Because the Internet is changing rapidly, there are many things that we could not include in this book simply because they were not available at the time of writing. It is the reader's responsibility to check whether the information in this book is current and compliant with the latest standards.)

- `http://www.w3.org/`—This is the official site of the World Wide Web Consortium (W3C). All the official documents on XML should be available from this site.

- `http://java.sun.com/`—This is the home of Java. The latest Java 2 Software Development Kit (SDK) is downloadable from this site.

We use a number of sample programs in this book in order to strengthen our discussion. Readers are encouraged to run these programs and understand how they work. Each program was designed and coded by one or more of the authors and tested with Java 2 SDK versions 1.2.2 and 1.3.1 running on Windows 2000/XP and Linux. They should also run on any other platform with an appropriate Java Runtime Environment (JRE). These programs are provided on the accompanying CD-ROM along with the source code. The CD-ROM also contains the latest versions of middleware that are required to run the sample programs. They include Xerces as an XML processor, Tomcat as a Java servlet engine, and DB2 as a database. The CD-ROM has one directory for each chapter, and each directory has a Readme file. Please refer to the detailed instructions on how to run the sample code on your platform.

## 1.1.1 Structure of This Book

This book is divided into two parts. Part 1, Chapter 1 through Chapter 9, covers the basic technologies, while Part 2, Chapter 10 through Chapter 16, deals with emerging technologies and more advanced topics.

The goal of Part 1 is to teach you the programming techniques that you absolutely need to know when dealing with XML—how you can parse, generate, and transform XML documents and how you can use the standard Application Program Interfaces (APIs) and tools during these processes. If you are asked to develop a Java application that reads and writes XML, you should be ready to take on the job using the knowledge acquired while reading Part 1.

Part 1 consists of the following chapters (the author who wrote the chapter is shown in parentheses).

**Chapter 1, Web Applications, XML, and Java** (Maruyama). The rest of this chapter reviews the history and the future of Web applications, describing the roles of XML and Java, and introduces some important concepts about the use of XML.

**Chapter 2, Parsing XML Documents** (Uramoto). This chapter introduces the most basic operation of XML processing, *parsing*, which analyzes XML documents and makes the contents available to application programs through a set of APIs.

**Chapter 3, Generating and Serializing XML Documents** (Uramoto). The reverse operation of parsing is *generating* XML documents. This chapter discusses how to generate XML documents from the application's internal structure.

**Chapter 4, Working with DOM** (Tamura). The **Document Object Model** (DOM) is a tree-based standard API for accessing the internal structure of XML documents. This chapter introduces the DOM Level 1 and DOM Level 2 APIs and gives advice on how to use these APIs in various situations.

**Chapter 5, Working with SAX** (Tamura). **Simple API for XML** (SAX) is another standard API for XML. Unlike DOM, it is based on an event model rather than the tree model. This chapter explains the use of SAX and compares it with the DOM API.

**Chapter 6, Parser Tricks** (Clark). XML processors are complex software having many features that can be used in many different scenarios. This chapter shows the most commonly used techniques for making the most use of existing XML processors.

**Chapter 7, XPath and XSLT** (Neyama). The DOM and SAX APIs are powerful and flexible enough to allow any complex operations on XML documents. However, simple tasks, such as extracting certain attribute values or renaming element names, can be done in a simpler way with the use of XPath and Extensible Stylesheet Language Transformations (XSLT). This chapter explains the capability of XPath and XSLT for DOM and SAX and discusses the use of XPath and XSLT in Java applications.

**Chapter 8, Bridging Application Data Structure and XML** (Maruyama). After an XML document is parsed, it is often necessary to convert the parsed result into an application-specific data structure. Chapter 8 addresses this topic by showing program examples of mapping XML into tree, table, and graph structures.

**Chapter 9, Working with Schemas: Datatypes and Namespaces** (Murata). The Document Type Definition (DTD) has been used to describe a permissible syntax for a set of XML documents for a particular application. However, there are a few drawbacks to the DTD, and attempts are underway to define new schema languages. In Chapter 9, we explain two concrete examples of such efforts, W3C XML

Schema and OASIS RELAX NG, focusing on the two practically important aspects: datatypes and namespace handling.

Part 2, consisting of Chapters 10 through 16, is organized around the major middleware technologies that enable XML- and Java-based Web application development. Unlike the basic XML tools, such as XML processors and XSLT processors, discussed in Part 1, these middleware technologies do not directly deal with XML but assist in the deployment of XML technologies in many different aspects of B2B systems, such as communicating using XML, storing and retrieving XML to and from databases, and securing B2B systems. The relationships between some of these technologies are depicted in Figure 1.1.

**Chapter 10, XML Application Server** (Neyama). The first middleware is the server platform for Java applications—Servlet. This chapter explains the basics of Servlet and the use of Servlet and JavaServer Pages (JSP) for XML applications.

**Chapter 11, XML and Databases** (Uramoto). Most Web applications are connected to some sort of backend database. XML data can be stored into or originated from such a database. This chapter describes APIs and techniques for interfacing XML-based applications with backend databases. It also touches on the use of Enterprise JavaBeans (EJB) for database transactions.

**Chapter 12, XML Messaging** (Nakamura). The most important use of XML is as the standard messaging format between applications. Simple Object Access Protocol

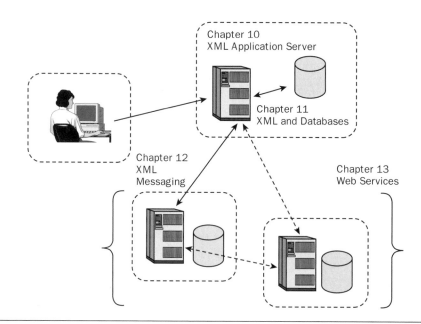

**Figure 1.1**  Chapters in Part 2

(SOAP) is becoming the foundation of Internet-based B2B communications. This chapter explores the basis of these protocols and shows how they can be used to integrate multiple systems in a decentralized manner.

**Chapter 13, Web Services** (Nakamura). XML, HTTP, and SOAP are giving rise to a new concept of **Web services**, where software functions are provided by Web applications through HTTP/XML-based protocols rather than traditional class libraries and software components. This chapter introduces the emerging technologies that enable the idea of Web services—including the Web Services Description Language (WSDL) and Universal Description, Discovery, and Integration (UDDI)—and discusses the application development processes within this new programming model.

**Chapter 14, Security** (Maruyama). When we conduct B2B communications on the Internet, one of our biggest concerns is security. This chapter covers the standard techniques for securing B2B applications and discusses design considerations.

In Chapters 15 and 16 we go back to XML itself, but on advanced topics that have recently gained attention.

**Chapter 15, Data Binding** (Maruyama). Although DOM and SAX provide generic APIs that can be used for any purpose, they do not reflect the application-specific data structure. The idea of **data binding** is to use XML Schema (or its equivalent) for bridging XML parsing with the application-specific data structure automatically. This chapter discusses the potential of this new technology.

**Chapter 16, Principles of Schema Languages** (Murata). Several ways of describing XML grammar are being proposed. They include RELAX, which was developed by one of the authors (Murata). These alternatives have their own distinctive features that would make building XML applications much easier in certain ways. Discussions in this chapter shed light on the possibilities of these new ideas.

It is not our intention to give you detailed information on each technology. Instead, the goal of Part 2 is to give you enough information so that you can make intelligent decisions about what technology you should pick in a given situation. We believe that a good system designer is one who always makes the right decisions about what middleware and technology should be used, by taking the customer's requirements and the environmental constraints into account. We hope the chapters in Part 2 help you to be a good system designer.

We provide some useful information in the appendixes.

**Appendix A, About the CD-ROM.** The contents of the associated CD-ROM and instructions for using it are described here.

**Appendix B, Useful Links and Books.** This is a useful but incomplete compilation of links on the Internet.

**Appendix C, XML-Related Standardization Activities.** A number of standards are being defined on top of XML. Appendix C covers the important ones.

**Appendix D, JDBC Primer.** The standard API for accessing relational databases from a Java program is Java Database Connectivity (JDBC). JDBC is used extensively in the sample programs in Chapter 11, XML and Databases. This primer will be a useful companion when you read Chapter 11, if you are not yet familiar with this API.

In the rest of this chapter, we first discuss Web applications and then give an overview of XML.

## 1.2  Web Applications

In this book, by **Web application** we mean a distributed application based on Web technology: HTTP, HTML, and the family of XML technologies.

### 1.2.1  From Static Contents to Dynamic Contents

The Web was originally designed as a mechanism to deliver static pages to clients on the Internet. When a browser sends a GET request to a Web server, the server fetches the requested file from its file system and returns it through the HTTP connection, as shown in Figure 1.2.

It is well known that the response to a GET request should not necessarily be a stored page that was created by a human author. The **Common Gateway Interface**, or CGI, is a mechanism in a Web server that invokes an external program upon

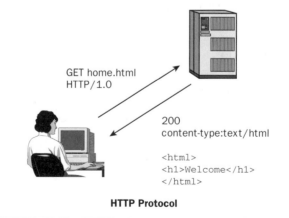

GET home.html
HTTP/1.0

200
content-type:text/html

```
<html>
<h1>Welcome</h1>
</html>
```

**HTTP Protocol**

**Figure 1.2**  HTTP protocol

receiving a request and returns the output of the program as the response as if it had been stored as a file. This is a powerful idea that allows the page to be created dynamically when a request arrives. For example, when a real-time stock quote service receives a request, it executes a database retrieval program to fetch the latest stock prices and returns them as an HTML page.

As the Web and browsers rapidly became popular through the efforts of Netscape Communications Corporation and others, people started to think about the possibility of using a browser as a universal user interface. Almost all modern application programs have a graphical user interface (GUI) so that they can be used without learning an application-specific command-line language. Programming with a Windows API or an X Window API requires a certain cost and a set of skills that are not readily available everywhere. The idea of the three-tier model was, instead of writing a GUI using these APIs, to use HTTP/HTML to interact with a user.[1] Two major merits of this idea are that (1) any client platform can be used as a user terminal and (2) the user can use the same look and feel as the accustomed Web interface.

In the three-tier model, an application program is built as a CGI program or one of its variations and is invoked by a request from a browser. Therefore, application programs run on a Web server, which in most cases is on the UNIX or Windows platform. For these applications to be useful, they are usually connected to existing database systems or transaction systems that usually run on large host systems. These are called **backend systems**.

Thus, **three-tier applications**, consisting of the following three functional units, gained popularity as the standard way of building a distributed application program in both the Internet and intranet environments.

- First tier—Browsers that act as a universal user interface
- Second tier—An application program running in a Web server as a CGI (or equivalent) program
- Third tier—Backend systems that provide database and transaction services

## 1.2.2 From B2C to B2B—From Web for Eyeballs to Web for Programs

One of the essential points of the three-tier model is the use of a browser for a *human* interface. The protocols designed for a human interface—that is, HTTP and

---

[1] The general idea of separating an application into three functional blocks precedes the browser-based three-tier model. These days, however, the term is used in the sense described here in most situations.

HTML—are used for this purpose. Isn't it possible to use the same protocols for communications between two applications?

Let us consider an example in which a program, instead of a human user, accesses a Web site and uses the results for its computation. Assume that there is a weather report service on the Web and we can get the current temperature in White Plains, New York, at the URL `http://www.example.com/White_Plains_NY_US.html`. When the Web is accessed with this URL, an HTML page such as that shown in Figure 1.3 is returned.

Suppose that we are asked by a site manager of a shopping mall in White Plains to develop an application program that monitors the temperature and issues a power overload warning if the city's temperature is above 100 degrees for more than three consecutive hours. The information necessary to develop this application is already on the Web at the previous URL.

The following code shows an HTML page that is returned from that URL. We need to obtain this page every hour, analyze and extract the temperature information from the page, and test whether the temperature exceeds 100 degrees for more than three hours.

```
<html>
<head>
<title>Weather Report</title>
</head>
<body>
```

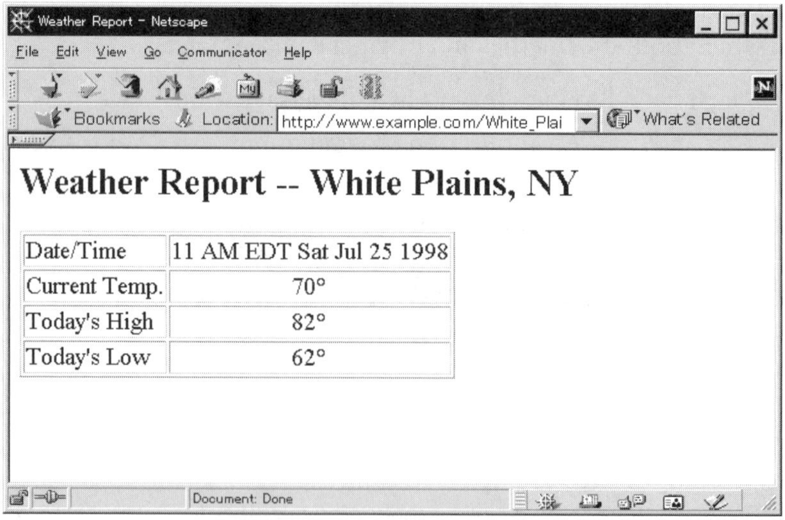

**Figure 1.3** Sample temperature page

```
     <h2>Weather Report -- White Plains, NY</h2>
     <table border=1>
         <tr><td>Date/Time</td><td align=center>11 AM EDT Sat Jul 25
         1998</td></tr>
[9]      <tr><td>Current Temp.</td><td align=center>70&#176;</td></tr>
         <tr><td>Today's High</td><td align=center>82&#176;</td></tr>
         <tr><td>Today's Low</td><td align=center>62&#176;</td></tr>
     </table>
     </body>
     </html>
```

A quick and dirty way to extract the current temperature of White Plains is to use the following strategy: *The current temperature of White Plains starts at line 9, column 45 of the page until the next ampersand.* Any experienced software engineer can point out problems with this strategy. For example, a slight change in the page, such as inserting a blank line or removing the whitespace on the left of the <tr> tags, will prevent our program from functioning properly even though these changes do not affect the usefulness for human readers of the page.

The second strategy is much better: *The temperature is in a <td> element of the second row and the second column of the first table in the page.* The latest browsers are equipped with an API to traverse the internal structure of a Web page, so it is possible to write a simple JavaScript program to implement this strategy. This strategy will withstand small changes that do not alter the appearance of the page. However, what happens if the page creator decided to include a "cool" masthead in this page, which uses a <table> tag to put many small GIF images together as is done in many other fancy pages? In such a case, the temperature will no longer be in the first table in the page.

HTML was originally designed to represent a logical structure of a *document*, where the natural components are header, title, paragraph, and so on, so tags are defined for expressing these. Notions such as current_temperature are defined nowhere in HTML. If we need to express data in an HTML page, we have to embed it into document-oriented tags. That is good enough for human users, but it is not good for programs to treat them as data.[2]

---

[2] The problem is further complicated by the fact that many of the currently available Web pages are not compliant with the HTML specification. Because HTML is simple and easy to understand, Web pages have been developed by many people with many different backgrounds. Casual Web page authors tend to become satisfied with a page once it is properly displayed with their browser and they publish it on a public Web site. Browser makers have put a lot of effort into tolerating errors as much as possible to allow these pages to be displayed without problems, but that also causes people to be less sensitive to the proper HTML syntax. Because of this, it is not easy to parse an HTML page to extract data. It is hoped that XML will restore order in this chaotic situation.

With XML, we can define a structure directly representing data. For example, the weather service URL might return the following XML document, instead of an HTML page, for the HTTP request for the URL `http://www.example.com/White_Plains_NY_US.xml`.

```
<?xml version="1.0" encoding="UTF-8"?>
<!DOCTYPE WeatherReport SYSTEM
"http://www.example.com/WeatherReport.dtd">
<WeatherReport>
    <City>White Plains</City>
    <State>NY</State>
    <Date>1998-07-25</Date>
    <Time>11:00:00-04:00</Time>
    <CurrTemp unit="Fahrenheit">70</CurrTemp>
    <High unit="Fahrenheit">82</High>
    <Low unit="Fahrenheit">62</Low>
</WeatherReport>
```

With this XML document, we can use the third strategy: *The current temperature is in the <CurrTemp> tag*. This XML document is a logical representation of the weather data—that is, it is independent from how the page is displayed for human users. Of course, we need to have agreed on the use of the <CurrTemp> tag in a weather report with the weather service provider, and this is done by publishing the specification of the XML document. The published specification can be considered as a sort of contract; it asserts the service provider's commitment that the required information can be consistently found at the stated position in a retrieved document. One way to describe the specification is to use a DTD, a syntactic specification of a class of XML documents. In our example, the DTD published by `www.example.com` would assert that a <CurrTemp> tag is always present as a direct child of the root element of a retrieved document.

Now our PowerWarning application has a more direct connection with the WeatherReport application. This is the first of many things that we can achieve by using XML. Suppose our PowerWarning system works well and becomes popular. We could decide to provide this service to other customers through our own Web site at `www.powerwarning.com`. Our subscribers (for example, a site management application) would connect to our site and set parameters such as the city to be monitored, the conditions for issuing a warning (for example, temperature and duration), and the method of notification (for example, pager or e-mail). Our generalized program running on our Web server would periodically poll the weather services of specified cities and issue a warning if a preset condition is met.

Our system, which is another Web application because it provides services through HTTP, can be called by other Web applications, as shown in Figure 1.4. This is no

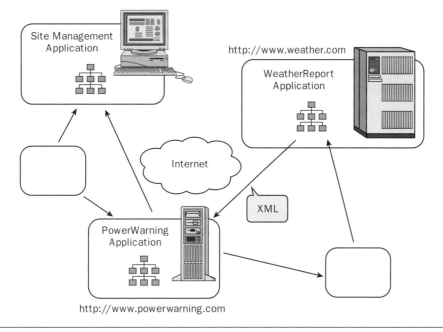

**Figure 1.4** XML enables a "Web of Web Applications."

longer the traditional three-tier model. It is more like a "Web of Web applications." Although the three-tier model connects human users and backend systems, the general Web application model may connect one Web application to another. XML is the data format of choice for such communication.

## 1.2.3 Interoperability Is Everything

Today, few new computer applications are developed from scratch; most are built by *integrating* other existing applications. These existing applications to be integrated frequently run on many different platforms and operating systems. Therefore, integration requires connecting them through a network. Some applications may even reside in a separate company because many companies today seek ways to outsource business processes that are not their core competency. Outsourced business processes have to be integrated with other business processes by connecting these applications using intercompany networks.

What are the requirements for intercompany integration? First and foremost, the applications must be able to talk to each other. In other words, they must be *interoperable* with each other. This means that they must agree on the common specifications of protocols and data formats. These agreements must be concise and clear. They must be based on open standards as much as possible. They must not be dependent on particular platforms, particular programming languages, and particular middleware. Can XML be a basis for such agreements?

The greatest advantage of XML as a data format language is that it is text-based and human-readable. If you use a binary data format instead and the specification is something like "The value of parameter X is represented as a 4-byte integer in network byte order, beginning at the twelfth octet from the top of the message," you would have to look at a this binary message's hexadecimal dump and understand the message content bit-by-bit for debugging, a tedious and time-consuming task.

By contrast, XML is a text-based format and therefore is human-readable. Further, XML messages can easily be read, created, and modified by using standard and common tools such as text editors or UNIX's string search tools, such as `grep`. This all makes understanding and analyzing XML messages much easier than any binary formats.

In XML, tags can be named with text strings composed of meaningful words. Suppose you have developed a decent Web application that you want to promote. As a Web application, it receives an HTTP request and returns an XML document as a response (rather than relying on more efficient methods such as Internet Inter-ORB Protocol, or IIOP). You provide your data in XML, so you also publish a DTD or a schema that describes its syntax. Assume that a potential partner would like to do business with you. By accessing your Web site, it learns that you provide an XML-based Web application for automatic B2B messaging. By studying your schema, it finds that it includes tags in plain English, such as `<purchaseOrder>` and `<date>`. Taking advantage of XML's simplicity, the company's engineers can develop "glue code" that connects its own business application to your Web application just by using off-the-shelf XML and Web application tools.

Another example of XML's simplicity is its ability to represent tree-structured data. But why would you want to use XML to represent tree-structured data instead of using an open standard such as **Abstract Syntax Notation One** (ASN.1)? ASN.1 is a binary data representation scheme for tree-structured data and is used in many communication protocols (one of its uses is for the X.509 digital certificate, which we discuss in Chapter 14).

ASN.1 is carefully designed so that it minimizes the size of data. A very efficient protocol handler can be realized by combining an ASN.1 message specification with a good ASN.1 parser implementation. In short, ASN.1 is optimized for efficiency. However, because of this, it has a complicated bit arrangement that makes understanding it hard. You can use automatic protocol generation tools to save some of the effort involved here, but good tools are expensive.

By contrast, XML has a similar ability to represent tree-structured data, but it is much simpler and is easier to understand and work with.

One lesson stands out from what we have learned from the history of the Internet: "Simplicity wins, efficiency loses."[3] On the Internet, the name of the game is *openness*—that is, accessibility and availability to the public. Even if you have an unparalleled technology, it will not win in the market without receiving wide support from most of the affected community. A technology that is relatively less efficient but open and easy to understand compared with its competitors will have a better chance to win on the Internet.

The second substantial benefit of using XML, which is frequently overlooked, is its capability to handle international character sets. Even if you are designing a simple message format, this point alone can be reason enough to adopt XML.

Today, business is often international in scope. This is especially true for Web applications because the Internet easily leaps national borders. It is only natural that business transactions will contain, for example, street names in Chinese and people's names in Arabic. The XML 1.0 Recommendation is defined based on the ISO 10646 (Unicode) character set, so virtually all the characters that are used daily all over the world are legal characters. We discuss character sets and internationalization more in Chapter 3.[4]

All the major IT vendors support XML. There have been many middleware technologies that enable integration between applications over a network, such as Common Object Request Broker Architecture (CORBA) and DCOM, but none of them have had support from *all* the major IT vendors, including IBM, Microsoft, Sun, Oracle, BEA, HP, and so on. This is probably the largest reason why XML is so popular now.

## 1.2.4 From Distributed Applications to Decentralized Applications

XML defines a data format but does not specify the middleware to process data. Any application that can read and write XML data can participate in integration regardless of the middleware the application uses. This contrasts with other distributed programming technologies, such as CORBA and DCOM, which require a

---

[3] From a talk given by Adam Bosworth, then of Microsoft, in May 1998 at IBM's Almaden Research Center in California.

[4] Do not confuse character sets with character encodings. A **character set** defines a set of characters regardless of how they are represented in a binary computer. A **character encoding** specifies a mapping between a character set and a particular binary representation of the characters. Therefore, one character set may have many different encodings.

certain middleware, programming language, or operating system to be used in each component application. Applications that use XML for their data exchange have a better chance of being integrated with other applications because of less dependency on their running environment. An integrated application whose components do not require a particular middleware, programming language, or operating system to be connected to other components is called **loosely coupled**. Components of a loosely coupled application typically run on a variety of operating systems and middleware located in widely scattered areas.

Integrating multiple Web applications over a network can be seen as *reusing* existing applications as software components. The history of software engineering is that of abstraction and reuse of software components. In the early days, we had **subroutines** to make one algorithm implementation be reused many times. The idea of **object-oriented programming**, which originated from Smalltalk-80, is to encapsulate the details of both algorithms and data structures in an object so that it is reusable even if its internals are changed. **Software components**, such as JavaBeans and Microsoft's Component Object Model (COM), enable reusing binary components without compiling.

Using a Web application as a software component encapsulates not only the details of the implementation of the Web application, but also the middleware, the programming language, and the operating system that the Web application uses. More importantly, it also hides the details of how this application is **managed**—that is, installation, configuration, updates, backups, and so on. This is particularly important when the cost associated with managing the component is high.

Consider a software component that calculates the optimum travel route from one city to another. This component is provided as a class library along with a set of header files and a database of the latest flight schedules of airline companies. The application developer uses the header files to compile the application, and the administrator installs and configures the component in the running environment. The problem here is that the flight schedule database should be updated whenever there is any change in its contents. The administrator must receive timely updates from the component vendor and incorporate these updates in the database. On the contrary, if this component is provided as a Web application, this management problem can be hidden from the administrator's view.

Encapsulating management is also desirable if the component requires special expertise to maintain. A component that requires high security, such as the one that manages customers' private data, is a good example.

### 1.2.5 The World of Web Services—More Dynamic Integration

The idea of integrating Web applications as very loosely coupled software components is now leading us to the next wave of software development, called **Web services**. Because these components are provided as services that are available from anywhere on the Internet without needing any installation or compilation to use them, the idea of *dynamically* integrating them at runtime (as opposed to integrating them at design time or compilation time) is becoming more realistic. A suite of new standards that make this idea possible are emerging. In Chapter 13, we discuss this movement in more detail.

## 1.3 Other Application Areas of XML

XML is so powerful and so flexible that many groups of people are considering using it for different purposes. Let us consider some of them.

- Metadata—Using XML to describe meta information about other documents or online resources
- Configuration files—Using XML to describe the configuration parameters of software
- Rich documents—Using XML to customize and enrich document description

### 1.3.1 Metadata

In the first half of 1997, XML was mainly thought of as the language for metadata. **Metadata** refers to information about data, such as title, author, file size, creation date, revision history, and keywords. Metadata can be used for searches, information filtering, document management, and so on.

To show the usefulness of explicit metadata, let us assume that we want to search documents that were written by Bill Clinton. We will get thousands of hits that contain the phrase "Bill Clinton" if we input "Bill Clinton" as the search keyword in current search engines. Most of the hits will be "noises" that merely mention Bill Clinton in the body of the article and will not be articles written by Bill Clinton. The search would be much more productive if we could express the search query as "find documents whose Author element contains the words 'Bill Clinton'."

Unfortunately, no such element, or tag, is defined in HTML, and it is unlikely that HTML will be extended to have a new Author tag in the near future. One reason is historical. HTML has been too rapidly extended as a result of the "browser war" between Netscape and Microsoft. W3C seems to have been more cautious about further extensions to HTML after HTML 4.0 was released in April 1998.

The second reason is that an HTML extension would not solve all the problems with metadata. Other resources, such as image files, audio and video files, and other content types, may require metadata extensions as well.

The third reason concerns performance. HTML has the TITLE and META tags, which can accommodate some metadata. Because these tags are inside an HTML document, search engines cannot refer to the information without downloading the entire HTML file. It is not efficient to download a 100KB HTML file just to check whether the TITLE tag contains a certain character string, particularly when hundreds of such files are available from a Web site. If we could put the metadata of all the documents available on the site into a single metafile, the search performance would greatly improve.

For these reasons, an external metadata description has received a lot of attention. Because of its extensibility, flexibility, and readability, XML is considered to be the best method for defining metadata syntax. RDF is an example of such metadata formats defined in XML.

### 1.3.2 Configuration Files

Another application area of XML is as a language for software configuration files. As software becomes complex, the configuration files also become complex. If a configuration file has multiple sections, or some fields require complex data, or support for international character sets is mandatory, it makes a lot of sense to use XML as the language for the configuration file. For example, Tomcat, an application server that we will use in Chapter 10, uses XML extensively in its configuration files.

### 1.3.3 Rich Documents

XML was originally developed as a simple subset of the Standard Generalized Markup Language, or SGML (ISO 8879), which was defined in 1986 as an international standard for document markup. Therefore, it is more than natural that XML is also used for document markup. Extensible Hypertext Markup Language (XHTML), an XML-compliant version of HTML, is one such example. The entire manuscript of this book was also written in XML.[5]

One popular use of XML as a document markup language is **Web publishing**, in which a content provider prepares original content marked up in XML and publishes it through Web sites. The content provider then transforms the content using a tool such as an XSLT processor into a set of HTML files with a customized design

---

[5] It is processed by a tool called SmartDoc (see http://www.asahi-net.or.jp/~dp8t-asm/java/tools/SmartDoc/index.html for details).

based on their customers' requirements. We briefly touch on a tool that automates this process in Chapter 10.

Although metadata and document markup are significant application areas of XML, in this book we concentrate mostly on the use of XML for B2B messaging.

# 1.4  Some XML Basics

As described in the power overload warning example in Section 1.2.2, XML is a key technology for B2B Web applications. Although we do not go into the details of the XML 1.0 Recommendation, several topics related to XML are helpful in reading and understanding the rest of the book. We discuss these topics in this section.

## 1.4.1  Standardization Process

Many of the Web-related standards are defined by W3C. Unlike ANSI and ISO, W3C is not an "official" standards body, so W3C issues its decisions as "recommendations," not as "international standards." Nonetheless, W3C recommendations effectively have the same authoritative standing as international standards issued by other standards bodies such as ISO and ANSI.

There are several levels in documents published by W3C. The less formal ones are called **Notes**. A Note is a submission by one organization or a group of organizations and is not the result of W3C formal discussions. If a formal proposal is submitted and it is determined to be important and worthy of discussion to reach a consensus, a Working Group is formed. A Working Group issues **Working Drafts** (WDs), which are published to the public so that they can receive receive feedback from anyone who is interested in the subject. Once the discussions converge on a set of common agreements and the Working Group feels that the Working Draft has become stable, the Working Group may issue a **Candidate Recommendation** (CR). The purpose of this document is to encourage implementations and to verify the specification through the implementation experiences. Once inconsistencies and ambiguities have been removed from the Candidate Recommendation, the Working Group issues a **Proposed Recommendation** (PR) as the basis for a vote. W3C member organizations cast votes for the proposal, and if it is approved, the proposal becomes a **Recommendation** (REC), which can be considered a standard in the normal sense.

In this book, we base our XML discussion on the XML 1.0 Recommendation. If we need to refer to other specifications, we will explicitly indicate which specification we are referring to. Any formal publication from W3C has a unique document name, whether it is a Note, Working Draft, Proposed Recommendation, or Recommendation. Readers are encouraged to check the latest publications at the W3C

Web site (`http://www.w3.org/`). Appendix C, XML-Related Standardization Activities, lists several important ones to keep an eye on.

## 1.4.2 Validity and Well-Formedness

Because this book is not intended to be an introduction to or a reference manual for XML, we do not discuss the details of the XML specification. However, we do want to explain one important concept: the difference between *validity* and *well-formedness*.

In XML, you can define your own tag set using a **Document Type Definition**, or DTD. The following is an example of a DTD.

```
<!ELEMENT WeatherReport (City, State, Date, Time, CurrTemp, High, Low)>
<!ELEMENT City (#PCDATA)>
<!ELEMENT State (#PCDATA)>
<!ELEMENT Date (#PCDATA)>
<!ELEMENT Time (#PCDATA)>
<!ELEMENT CurrTemp (#PCDATA)>
<!ELEMENT High (#PCDATA)>
<!ELEMENT Low (#PCDATA)>
<!ATTLIST CurrTemp unit  (Farenheight|Celsius) #REQUIRED>
<!ATTLIST High unit   (Farenheight|Celsius) #REQUIRED>
<!ATTLIST Low unit (Farenheight|Celsius) #REQUIRED>
```

Following the SGML tradition, the DTD has a different syntax from the XML syntax in the XML 1.0 Recommendation. We might want to use the same XML syntax for both documents and DTDs. This, in addition to a few other points (such as the introduction of data types into element specifications), is one of the hot topics being discussed by the XML community. Chapter 9 discusses two of these activities: the W3C XML Schema and RELAX NG.

An XML document with a `<!DOCTYPE>` declaration is said to be **valid** if it meets the constraints specified in the DTD. These constraints include the element content models (what child elements are allowed in what order) and attribute types. Validity constraints (VCs) are strictly defined in the XML 1.0 Recommendation. When an application receives an XML document, it should know the semantics of all the tags appearing in the document in order to process them correctly. Otherwise, the program has no clue how to handle an element with an unknown tag name even though it might look meaningful to human eyes (for example, `<Purchase_order>` may be understandable to English-speaking people, but it is as meaningless as `<seikyuusho>` to a program that does not know the semantics of the tag). Therefore, when processing XML documents with programs, we are usually interested in valid documents.

When a DTD is used as a schema language, an XML document must have a
`<!DOCTYPE>` declaration at the beginning of the document. This declaration
specifies a DTD against which an XML processor must validate the document.
For example, if an XML document has the following declaration, it should be
validated against a DTD available at `http://www.example.com/`
`WeatherReport.dtd`.[6]

```
<!DOCTYPE WeatherReport SYSTEM
 "http://www.example.com/WeatherReport.dtd">
```

On the other hand, XML is designed so that simple XML documents are parsable
without defining an explicit DTD as long as they contain no external entities.[7]
This is one of the big differences from SGML and HTML. In XML, every start tag
(for example, `<Body>`) must have a corresponding end tag (`</Body>`). Otherwise, a tag must be an empty tag that has an explicit slash at the end (for example,
`<City/>`). An XML document is said to be **well-formed** if it satisfies this constraint
as well as several others defined in the XML 1.0 Recommendation. A valid document is always well-formed, but there may be well-formed documents that are
not valid.

Why do we want to allow well-formed documents that may contain unknown
tags? Does it make sense at all to do such a thing? The answer is yes because not
all the tags must necessarily be understood by one program. For example, we may
want to allow text with HTML markups in a certain field, such as a comment.
Even though the content cannot be understood by the program that receives the
document, it can be submitted to an external browser upon request to display the
HTML-tagged comment on the screen. Rendering is another good example that
does not require DTD validity. Even if a browser encounters an unknown tag, usually it can simply be skipped without causing disastrous results.

## 1.4.3  Namespaces

The W3C Recommendation *Namespaces in XML* allows multiple tag sets (elements and attributes defined in schemas) in a single XML document. It is not
easy to design a good schema that is used by many people for a long time. Using
namespaces, you can reuse existing schemas to design more complex XML documents. In the following example, the tag `price` is defined in a namespace called
`http://ecommerce.org/edi` and is distinguished from a tag that has the same
name but belongs to a different namespace. Similarly, the tag `x` belongs to the
namespace `http://ecommerce.org/order`.

---

[6] How to specify the W3C XML Schema in an instance document is discussed in Chapter 9.
[7] An **external entity** is a unit in an XML document whose replacement string is to be retrieved
from a definition in a DTD.

```
<?xml version="1.0" encoding="UTF-8"?>
<order:x
    xmlns:order='http://ecommerce.org/order'
    xmlns:edi='http://ecommerce.org/edi'>
        <edi:price>14.95</edi:price>
</order:x>
```

In this example, edi in <edi:price> is called a **namespace prefix**. A namespace prefix must be declared at some ancestor element of the element where the prefix is used. The namespace declaration xmlns:edi='http://ecommerce.org/edi' declares that the namespace prefix edi is bound to the namespace http://ecommerce.org/edi, which is also called a namespace URI.

A **namespace URI** is the *name* of the tag set. In general, it has nothing to do with the location of the specification of the namespace. A namespace is often associated with a schema that dictates the syntax for the tags defined in the namespace. However, there is no standard way defined for validating an XML document against a namespace.

One of the original intentions of the namespace specification was to solve the problem of name collision. If the same element type, such as <price>, is defined in multiple namespaces, giving them different namespace prefixes can distinguish them in a single document. For this mechanism to work correctly, it must be able to rename namespace prefixes without modifying the contents of an XML document. Unfortunately, partly because XML documents lack a common data model, namespace prefixes are often fixed in an XML document.[8]

## 1.5  Summary

In this chapter, we first described the goals and the structure of this book. Then we discussed the evolution of Web applications that has led to the recent development of Web services technologies. Also, we touched briefly on a couple of topics related to XML that we feel you need to understand before reading the rest of the book. In the next chapter, we start exploring XML programming in Java.

---

[8] If there were a common XML data model that explicitly stated that namespace prefixes have no significance other than binding an element type or an attribute name to a namespace URI, this problem would never have happened. However, some XML specifications, most notably XPath and XSLT, allow namespace prefixes to be used in attribute values. For these substrings appearing in string content, XML processors will never know whether they are associated with some namespace URIs or they are just part of an application data string, even though they look like namespace prefixes.

# Parsing XML Documents

## 2.1 Introduction

In this chapter, we discuss the parsing of XML documents using an XML processor. **Parsing** is the process of reading a document and dissecting it into its elements and attributes, which can then be analyzed. In XML, parsing is done by an **XML processor**, the most fundamental building block of a Web application. In this book, Apache Xerces is used as an implementation of the XML processor, and we show how to design and develop Web applications. As the first step of this chapter, we begin to set up your programming environment in Xerces and Java. Next, we discuss how to read and parse a simple XML document. We use various examples, including well-formed and valid documents with Document Type Definitions (DTDs) or XML Schema, a document that contains namespaces. We finish by explaining how to do basic programming using common APIs: DOM and SAX.

### 2.1.1 XML Processors

As explained in Chapter 1, an XML processor is a software module that reads XML documents and provides application programs with access to their content and structure. The XML 1.0 specification from W3C precisely defines the functions of an XML processor. The behavior of a conforming XML processor is highly predictable, so using other conforming XML processors should not be difficult.

Figure 2.1 shows the role of an XML processor. An XML processor is a bridge between an XML document and an application. The XML processor parses and generates an XML document. The application uses an API to access objects that represent part of the XML document. DOM and SAX are well-known APIs for accessing the structure of an XML document. Throughout this book, you will learn the details of these APIs.

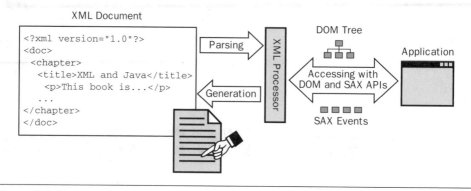

**Figure 2.1**  Using an XML processor

XML processors are categorized as *validating* and *non-validating* processors (see Section 1.4.2 for an explanation of validity and well-formedness). When reading an XML document, a **non-validating processor** checks the well-formedness constraints as defined in the XML 1.0 specification and reports any violations. A **validating processor** must check the validity constraints and the well-formedness constraints.

In this book, we use the Java version of Apache Xerces, a validating (and non-validating) XML processor. Xerces was developed by the Apache Xerces team (one of the authors is a main member of the development team) and is one of the most robust and faithful implementations of an XML processor. In the first edition of this book, the XML for Java Parser (aka XML4J), developed by another one of the authors, was used. XML for Java was donated to Apache, an open source community in 1999, and now it is called Xerces. If you want to use Xerces commercially, please read the license document on the Apache Xerces Web site (`http://xml.apache.org`).

The complete current release of Xerces is included on the accompanying CD-ROM. You can also download the latest version of Xerces from the Apache Xerces Web site.

## 2.1.2  Working with Xerces

Before installing Xerces, you need to set up your Java programming environment. All the programs used in this book have been tested against the Java 2 SDK (versions 1.2 and 1.3). The setup steps are as follows:

1. Install the Java 2 SDK (version 1.2 or 1.3).
2. Install Xerces version 1.4.3.
3. Add Xerces's jar files to the CLASSPATH environment variable.

Xerces is written in Java, so you first need to have Java 2 installed on your system. If needed, you can download the latest release from the Sun Microsystems Web site at `http://java.sun.com`. In this book, we assume you have installed the Java 2 SDK in `C:\jdk`.

The second step in setting up your programming environment is to install Xerces. In developing our sample programs, we used Xerces version 1.4.3. The CD-ROM that accompanies this book contains that version. To install Xerces:

1. Install Xerces on your system.
2. On the CD-ROM, move to the directory containing Xerces.
3. Unzip `Xerces-J-bin.1.4.3.zip`.

We assume you have installed Xerces in `C:\xerces-1_4_3`.

Note that because Xerces is written in Java, theoretically it can run on any operating system platform on any hardware that supports Java. However, platforms might differ, for example, in how to set the environment variable. We use Windows (95/98/Me/NT/2000) in our command-line input/output examples in this book. If your platform is other than these, you should replace the command prompts and certain shell commands with those appropriate for your platform.

The third step in setting up your programming environment is to set the `CLASSPATH` environment variable to tell the Java interpreter where to find the Java libraries. To execute the sample programs in this book, you must have in your `CLASSPATH` the jar files `c:\xerces-1_4_3\xerces.jar` and `c:\xerces-1_4_3\xercesSamples.jar`. You might also want to include the current directory (`.`) and the sample directory of the CD-ROM (`R:\samples`) in your `CLASSPATH`. You can set both of these in Windows 95/98/Me by using the following command:

```
c:\xerces-1_4_3>set CLASSPATH=".;c:\xerces-1_4_3\xerces.jar;c:\
xerces-1_4_3\xercesSamples.jar"
```

You might also want to add this command line to your profile to avoid having to type it every time you bring up a new command prompt. In Windows 95/98/Me, you add it to the `autoexec.bat` file. In Windows NT, you add it by right-clicking My Computer and then left-clicking System Properties and the Environment tab; then add the new variable `CLASSPATH` (similar operations are needed in Windows 2000).

> **NOTE:** When you are working with Xerces, you might want to know what the version is. The easiest way to find out is to type the following commands:
>
> ```
> R:\samples>java org.apache.xerces.framework.Version Xerces 1.4.3
> ```

If you are using the Java 2 SDK provided by IBM, you should be careful which version of Xerces you add in your CLASSPATH. Because in IBM's Java 2 SDK 1.3, Xerces is located in the directory jdk\jre\lib\ext, all the jar files in this directory are recognized by the Java interpreter before reading CLASSPATH. If the version of Xerces is old, you would face some errors. To avoid this, you can simply delete xerces.jar or replace it with the latest version. Another way to use an appropriate version of Xerces is to specify -Djava.ext.dirs=nulldir when you execute the Java command. This option tells the interpreter not to load the jar files in the ext directory.

To see whether the installation was successful, move to the installation directory (c:\xerces-1_4_3) and enter the following commands:

```
c:\xerces-1_X_X>java sax.Counter data/personal.xml
data/personal.xml: 2.160 ms (37 elems, 18 attrs, 140 spaces, 128 chars)
```

This program parses an XML document and reports the number of elements, attributes, and so on.

An alternative way to tell the Java interpreter where to find the jar files is to enter the following command:

```
c:\xerces-1_4_3>java -classpath "c:\xerces-1_4_3\xerces.jar;c:\
xerces-1_4_3\xercesSamples.jar" sax.SAXCount data/personal.xml data/
personal.xml: 260 ms (37 elems, 18 attrs, 140 spaces, 128 chars)
```

Now you are ready to try the sample programs on the CD-ROM. Go to the samples directory, which contains all the samples in this chapter. Note that in our samples we use "R" for the CD-ROM drive; you should substitute the correct letter for your own CD-ROM drive.

The samples directory contains sample programs for each chapter, and package names are assigned to the classes. For example, the SimpleParse class used in this chapter has the package name chap02.

Enter the following command to launch the program SimpleParse to read the document department.xml:

```
R:\samples>java chap02.SimpleParse chap02/department.xml
```

You will see nothing. However, this is expected because this sample program produces no output if successful.

All the sample programs in this book are included on the CD-ROM. Installation instructions for the tools used in the chapters are described in the readme.html file stored in directories for each chapter. Take a few moments to explore the CD-ROM before moving on to the next section.

## 2.2  Basics of Parsing Documents

This section describes how to parse well-formed and valid XML documents, and shows the differences between them.

### 2.2.1  Parsing Well-Formed Documents

In this section, we show how to read a simple XML document, called `department.xml`, using Xerces. This document represents a set of employee records in a department (see Listing 2.1). The meanings of the tags should be self-explanatory.

**Listing 2.1** Simple XML document, employee records for a department, `chap02/department.xml`

```
<?xml version="1.0" encoding="utf-8"?>
<department>
    <employee id="J.D">
        <name>John Doe</name>
        <email>John.Doe@foo.com</email>
    </employee>

    <employee id="B.S">
        <name>Bob Smith</name>
        <email>Bob.Smith@foo.com</email>
    </employee>

    <employee id="A.M">
        <name>Alice Miller</name>
        <url href="http://www.foo.com/~amiller/"/>
    </employee>
</department>
```

This is a well-formed XML document, and it should be parsed by a non-validating XML processor. The first task of this book is to read and parse the document by using Xerces. We run the sample program, `SimpleParse`, located in `samples\chap02` on the CD-ROM, using the following commands:

```
R:\samples>java chap02.SimpleParse chap02/department.xml
R:\samples>
```

This program, as in the previous section, produces no output. However, we know that Xerces did its job, because `SimpleParse` did the following:

- Opened the XML document `department.xml`
- Parsed it with an XML processor, which is described later

- Created a corresponding data structure in memory, a structure that can later be referred to or manipulated by application programs such as a Java object

The fact that you see no output means that there were no violations of well-formedness (missing end tags, improper nesting, and so on). Listing 2.2 gives the source code of SimpleParse. Although a very short program, it shows the basics of how you can use Xerces.

**Listing 2.2**  Parsing an XML document (non-validating), chap02/SimpleParse.java

```
        package chap02;
        /**
         *        SimpleParse.java
         **/
[5]     import org.w3c.dom.Document;
[6]     import org.apache.xerces.parsers.DOMParser;
        import org.xml.sax.SAXException;
        import java.io.IOException;

        public class SimpleParse {
            public static void main(String[] argv) {
                if (argv.length != 1) {
                    System.err.println(
                        "Usage: java chap02.SimpleParse <filename>");
                    System.exit(1);
                }
                try {
[18]        // Creates a parser object
[19]        DOMParser parser = new DOMParser();
[20]        // Parses an XML Document
[21]        parser.parse(argv[0]);
[22]        // Gets a Document object
[23]        Document doc = parser.getDocument();
[24]        // Does something
[25]            } catch (SAXException se) {
[26]                System.out.println("Parser error found: "
[27]                                    +se.getMessage());
[28]                System.exit(1);
                } catch (IOException ioe) {
                    System.out.println("IO error found: "
                            + ioe.getMessage());
                    System.exit(1);
                }
            }
        }
```

Now we'll look at the program `SimpleParse` line by line, referring to the numbers in square brackets on the left side of the program listing. First, this class imports some classes to use with Xerces:

- In line 5, the `Document` class, from the `org.w3c.dom` package, which is the interface that represents the whole XML document
- In line 6, the `DOMParser` class, from `org.apache.xerces.parsers`, which is a DOM-based XML processor

Also, two exception classes (`SAXException` and `IOException`) are imported.

The heart of this program is in lines 19–22.

```
[19]    DOMParser parser = new DOMParser();
```

Line 19 creates a DOM-based processor to parse an XML document.

```
[21]    parser.parse(argv[0]);
```

Next, line 21 parses an XML document specified by a command-line argument (`argv[0]`).

In this case, the `parse()` method takes the filename of the XML document. The method has the following argument patterns (signatures), and you can choose the appropriate one.

- `Document parse (String uri)`
- `Document parse (java.io.File f)`
- `Document parse (org.xml.sax.InputSource is)`
- `Document parse (java.io.InputStream is)`
- `Document parse (java.io.InputStream is, String systemId)`

The third one requires an object of the `org.xml.sax.InputSource` class, which is useful to wrap various input formats for an XML document to be parsed. Though it is originally from the SAX 1.0 API, it is widely used for a DOM parser as well as a SAX parser.

The class has four constructors:

- `InputSource ()`
- `InputSource (java.io.InputStream byteStream)`
- `InputSource (java.io.Reader characterStream)`
- `InputSource (java.lang.String systemId)`

If you want to write a method (say, `processWithParse()`) that takes an input filename as an argument, `processWithParse(InputSource is)` is more reusable than `processWithParse(File f)` or `processWithParse(String url)`.

```
[23]    Document doc = parser.getDocument();
```

Line 23 receives the `Document` instance. The `org.w3c.dom.Document` interface is specified by the DOM specification from W3C. The variable `doc` actually refers to an instance of an implementation class (`org.apache.xerces.dom.Document/mpl`) provided by Xerces. The instance represents the whole XML document and can contain (1) at most one `DocumentType` instance that represents a DTD, (2) one `Element` instance that represents a root element (which is called a document element), and (3) zero or more `Comment` and `ProcessingInstruction` instances. The interface provides methods to visit and modify child nodes of the root element. For example, an application can get the root (document) element of an XML document by using the `getDocumentElement()` method of the `Document` interface. This sample program is simple, but you can see many other programs in this book.

When something goes wrong, the program throws an exception. The program shown in Listing 2.2 catches the following two exceptions:

- `java.io.IOException`—Occurs when the XML processor failed to load the XML document (because the file was not found, for example)

- `org.xml.sax.SAXException`—Occurs when the input document violates the well-formedness constraints

You might think that this program has no practical value because it does not produce any output. However, it is useful as a syntax checker. It can tell you whether the input XML document is well-formed or not. To show you how this works, we give an XML document that is not well-formed, `department2.xml`, to `SimpleParse` in Listing 2.3.

**Listing 2.3** Not well-formed XML document, `chap02/department2.xml`

```
<?xml version="1.0" encoding="utf-8"?>
<department>
    <employee id="J.D">
        <name>John Doe</name>
        <email>John.Doe@foo.com</email1>
    </employee>

    <employee id="B.S">
        <name>Bob Smith</name>
        <email>Bob.Smith@foo.com</email>
    </employee>

    <employee id="A.M">
        <name>Alice Miller</name>
```

```
            <url href="http://www.foo.com/~amiller/"/>
        </employee>
    </department>
```

This document is not well-formed, because the end tag of the first `email` element is `</email1>`, not `</email>`. The result of parsing the document is as follows:

```
R:\samples>java chap02.SimpleParse chap02/department2.xml
Parser error found: The element type "email" must be terminated by
the matching end-tag "</email>".
```

The XML processor recognizes the mismatch of the start and end tags, and reports it to applications by an exception (`SAXException`). In Listing 2.2, the exception is caught in lines 25–28.

## 2.2.2  Parsing Valid Documents

In this section, we parse a valid XML document according to a DTD. An example called `department-dtd.xml` is shown in Listing 2.4. The `DOCTYPE` declaration (the second line) tells an XML processor the location of the DTD.

**Listing 2.4**  XML document with DTD, `chap02/department-dtd.xml`

```
<?xml version="1.0" encoding="utf-8"?>
<!DOCTYPE department SYSTEM "department.dtd">
<department>
    <employee id="J.D">
        <name>John Doe</name>
        <email>John.Doe@foo.com</email>
    </employee>

    <employee id="B.S">
        <name>Bob Smith</name>
        <email>Bob.Smith@foo.com</email>
    </employee>

    <employee id="A.M">
        <name>Alice Miller</name>
        <url href="http://www.foo.com/~amiller/"/>
    </employee>
</department>
```

The DTD for the document is shown in Listing 2.5.

**Listing 2.5**  DTD for XML document, `chap02/department.dtd`

```
<!ELEMENT department (employee)*>
<!ELEMENT employee (name, (email | url))>
<!ATTLIST employee id CDATA #REQUIRED>
<!ELEMENT name (#PCDATA)>
```

```
<!ELEMENT email (#PCDATA)>
<!ELEMENT url EMPTY>
<!ATTLIST url href CDATA #REQUIRED>
```

As shown in Section 1.4.2, a DTD specifies the structure of an XML document. For example, the first element declaration in Listing 2.5 says a `department` element must have zero or more `employee` elements. The second declaration says an `employee` element must have a `name` element as the first child element and an `email` or `url` element as the second child element. The third one indicates an `employee` element must have an `id` attribute. The word `#PCDATA` means characters, and the `url` element cannot have any children (it is an empty element). Refer to the XML 1.0 specification for the details.

Xerces is a validating processor, but it does not validate by default. So we must tell Xerces to validate an input XML document against the DTD. Listing 2.6 shows a sample program for the validation.

**Listing 2.6** Parsing an XML document (validating), `chap02/SimpleParseWith Validation.java`

```
package chap02;
/**
 *        SimpleParseWithValidation.java
 **/
import org.w3c.dom.Document;
import org.xml.sax.InputSource;
import org.xml.sax.SAXException;
import org.xml.sax.SAXParseException;
import org.xml.sax.ErrorHandler;
import org.apache.xerces.parsers.DOMParser;
import share.util.MyErrorHandler;
import java.io.IOException;

public class SimpleParseWithValidation {

    public static void main(String[] argv) {
        if (argv.length != 1) {
            System.err.println("Usage: java "+
                "chap02.SimpleParseWigthValidation <filename>");
            System.exit(1);
        }
        try {
            // Creates parser object
            DOMParser parser = new DOMParser();
[25]        // Sets an ErrorHandler
[26]        parser.setErrorHandler(new MyErrorHandler());
```

```
[27]              // Tells the parser to validate documents
[28]              parser.setFeature(
                      "http://xml.org/sax/features/validation",
                      true);
[31]              // Parses an XML Document
[32]              parser.parse(argv[0]);
[33]              // Gets a Document object
[34]              Document doc = parser.getDocument();
                  // Does something
           } catch (Exception e) {
              e.printStackTrace();
           }
        }
     }
```

Again, let's look at the program in detail. First, a DOMParser object is created.

In SimpleParse, shown in Listing 2.2, we caught a SAXException exception when an input XML document was not well-formed. An XML processor provides an **error handler** to handle errors more flexibly. The error handler recognizes fatal errors that prevent it from continuing a parsing process, errors that are defined in the XML 1.0 Recommendation, and warnings for other problems.

Error handlers should implement the org.xml.sax.ErrorHandler interface. To create an error handler, there are two well-known methods.

- An application itself implements org.xml.sax.ErrorHandler.
- A separate class implements the interface, and an application call the class.

If you can work with a general error handler that can be shared with other applications, the latter approach is good in terms of software reuse. If you want to use an application-specific handler, or you don't want to create a new class for the handler for some reason, the former approach may be better.

This book employs the latter approach. MyErrorHandler, shown in Listing 2.7, is a typical implementation of an error handler.

**Listing 2.7** Handling errors, share/util/MyErrorHandler.java

```java
package share.util;

import org.xml.sax.ErrorHandler;
import org.xml.sax.SAXException;
import org.xml.sax.SAXParseException;

public class MyErrorHandler implements ErrorHandler {
    /** Constructor. */
```

```
public MyErrorHandler(){
}
/** Warning. */
public void warning(SAXParseException ex) {
    System.err.println("[Warning] "+
                        getLocationString(ex)+": "+
                        ex.getMessage());
}
/** Error. */
public void error(SAXParseException ex) {
    System.err.println("[Error] "+
                        getLocationString(ex)+": "+
                        ex.getMessage());
}
/** Fatal error. */
public void fatalError(SAXParseException ex) {
    System.err.println("[Fatal Error] "+
                        getLocationString(ex)+": "+
                        ex.getMessage());
}
/** Returns a string of the location. */
private String getLocationString(SAXParseException ex) {
    StringBuffer str = new StringBuffer();

    String systemId = ex.getSystemId();
    if (systemId != null) {
        int index = systemId.lastIndexOf('/');
        if (index != -1)
            systemId = systemId.substring(index + 1);
        str.append(systemId);
    }
    str.append(':');
    str.append(ex.getLineNumber());
    str.append(':');
    str.append(ex.getColumnNumber());

    return str.toString();
}

}
```

The org.xml.sax.ErrorHandler interface defines fatalError(), error(), and warning(). The MyErrorHandler class implements these methods to show a filename, line and column numbers, and the content of an error.

In `SimpleParseWithValidation` (see Listing 2.6), `MyErrorHandler` is created in line 26 and set to a parser object.

```
[25]    // Sets an ErrorHandler
[26]    parser.setErrorHandler(new MyErrorHandler());
```

Next, we tell the XML processor to turn on validation by using the `setFeature()` method. This is a method of the `org.xml.sax.XMLReader` interface that is implemented by the `DOMParser` classes. The method is used to set various features of an XML processor. In this book, we use some of the features (see Section 6.3.1 for more on these features). Refer to `http://xml.apache.org/xerces-j/features.html` for the complete list of features. Note that the default value of the validation feature (`"http://xml.org/sax/features/validation"`) is false, so `SimpleParse` in the previous section did not check the validity of the XML document.

```
[27]    // Tells the parser to validate documents
[28]    parser.setFeature("http://xml.org/sax/features/validation", true);
```

Finally, we start parsing. This is the same process as in `SimpleParse`.

```
[31]    // Parses an XML Document
[32]    parser.parse(argv[0]);
[33]    // Gets a Document object
[34]    Document doc = parser.getDocument();
```

Now we run this program to parse a valid XML document, `department-dtd.xml`.

```
R:\samples>java chap02.SimpleParseWithValidation chap02/
department-dtd.xml
R:\samples>
```

Because `department-dtd.xml` shown in Listing 2.4 conforms to `department.dtd` (see Listing 2.5), it should be parsed without error. The next example is an invalid document, `department-dtd2.xml`, shown in Listing 2.8.

**Listing 2.8** Invalid XML document, `chap02/department-dtd2.xml`

```xml
<?xml version="1.0" encoding="utf-8"?>
<!DOCTYPE department SYSTEM "department.dtd">
<department>
    <employee>
        <name>John Doe</name>
        <email>John.Doe@foo.com</email>
    </employee>

    <employee id="B.S">
        <name>Bob Smith</name>
```

```
        <email>Bob.Smith@foo.com</email>
    </employee>

    <employee id="A.M">
        <name>Alice Miller</name>
        <url href="http://www.foo.com/~amiller/"/>
    </employee>
</department>
```

When we parse the document with `SimpleParseWithValidation`, we can see an error because the document does not conform to the DTD.

```
R:\samples>java chap02.SimpleParseWithValidation chap02/
department-dtd2.xml
[Error] 4:13 Attribute "id" is required and must be specified for
element type "employee".
```

As shown in the previous output, the fourth line of `department-dtd2.xml` has an error. The `email` element does not have an `id` attribute, although it is required. Errors and warnings with line numbers make it possible to recognize where and why they occurred.

> **NOTE:** The difference between an error and a fatal error is defined in the XML 1.0 specification. An error is a violation of the rules of the specification. A conforming XML processor may detect and report an error and may recover from it. That means an application may get the internal structure of parsed XML documents. Violations of validity constraints are errors. On the other hand, the XML processor must detect and report fatal errors to the application. Once a fatal error is detected, the processor must not continue normal processing. Violations of well-formedness constraints are fatal errors.

## 2.2.3 Design Point: Well-Formed versus Valid

In the previous sections, you learned how to parse well-formed and valid documents. In this section, we discuss which types of documents should be used when you design and develop real Web applications. In other words, what are the pros and cons of validation? This section discusses the design point from several viewpoints.

- If a document structure is strictly defined by a DTD, an application can skip a checking process for the structure. For example, suppose a DTD specifies a name element as a required element. Applications don't have to check the existence of the element, because if an XML document that conforms to the DTD is parsed by a validating XML processor, the element should appear in the document. If you use XML Schema (discussed in Chapter 9), data type checking is also done by a validating processor. This can prevent applications from stopping by receiving data that has an unexpected data type. That is, validation makes your applications simpler and safer.

- Validation is an expensive task when very large documents are to be parsed. Even if the documents are not so large, it is time-consuming when many documents must be parsed at the same time in a high-volume Web application. In such cases, we should think carefully if we need validation.

- When you consider a non-PC platform such as PDA devices, validation might be impossible in the limited-resource environment.

- It is an important point for design if we really need validation. For example, suppose two companies want to exchange an XML document. If both companies know the structure of the document and the sending company sends a valid document, the receiving company can expect the document to always be valid and thus validation is not needed. As discussed before, parsing with validation makes applications safe. However, if the transaction between the companies is very large, parsing without validation may be a good choice.

- If the structure of the document is not complex and applications do not require all the information in the document, validation might not be needed.

## 2.3 More about Parsing XML Documents

This section covers more parsing examples in various environments.

### 2.3.1 Parsing XML Documents with Namespaces

Namespaces allows us to use multiple tag sets in a single XML document. However, we need a trick when we want to use a DTD to specify the structure of the document. This section covers how to parse and validate XML documents with namespaces. Listing 2.9 shows an example of an XML document with a namespace.

**Listing 2.9** XML document with namespaces, chap02/department-ns.xml

```
<?xml version="1.0" encoding="utf-8"?>
<!DOCTYPE org:department SYSTEM "department-ns.dtd">
<org:department xmlns:org="http://www.schema.org/department/">
    <org:employee id="J.D">
        <org:name>John Doe</org:name>
        <org:email>John.Doe@foo.com</org:email>
```

```
    </org:employee>
    <org:employee id="B.S">
        <org:name>Bob Smith</org:name>
        <org:email>Bob.Smith@foo.com</org:email>
    </org:employee>

    <org:employee id="A.M">
        <org:name>Alice Miller</org:name>
        <org:url href="http://www.foo.com/~amiller/"/>
    </org:employee>
</org:department>
```

This document is valid, so we can parse it with a validating processor. However, if the processor is not namespace-aware, the element type name of the root element is org:department, and it is impossible to access the namespace prefix (org), local name (department), and namespace URI (http://www.schema.org/department/). To handle the namespace correctly, we should tell an XML processor to be aware of the namespace. In Xerces, we use the setFeature() method as we set the validation feature mentioned in the previous section.

The DTD for the document is shown in Listing 2.10. Because DTD does not support namespaces, we should embed the namespace prefix in the element declaration in order to validate the document, although the prefix do not have to be fixed. Refer to Section 6.2.1 for the trick of using parameter entities.

**Listing 2.10** XML document with DTD and namespaces, chap02/department-ns.dtd

```
<?xml version="1.0" encoding="utf-8"?>
<!ELEMENT org:department (org:employee)*>
<!ATTLIST org:department xmlns:org CDATA
            #FIXED "http://www.schema.org/department/">
<!ELEMENT org:employee (org:name, (org:email | org:url))>
<!ATTLIST org:employee id CDATA #REQUIRED>
<!ELEMENT org:name (#PCDATA)>
<!ELEMENT org:email (#PCDATA)>
<!ELEMENT org:url EMPTY>
<!ATTLIST org:url href CDATA #REQUIRED>
```

Listing 2.11 shows a sample program to validate an XML document with namespaces.

**Listing 2.11** Parsing an XML document with namespaces, chap02/SimpleParseWithNS.java

```
package chap02;
/**
```

```
 *         SimpleParseWithNS.java
 **/
import org.w3c.dom.Document;
import org.xml.sax.InputSource;
import org.xml.sax.SAXException;
import org.xml.sax.SAXParseException;
import org.xml.sax.ErrorHandler;
import org.apache.xerces.parsers.DOMParser;
import org.apache.xerces.parsers.SAXParser;
import org.w3c.dom.Document;
import share.util.MyErrorHandler;
import java.io.IOException;

public class SimpleParseWithNS {

    public static void main(String[] argv) {
  if (argv.length != 1) {
      System.err.println(
                    "Usage: java chap02.SimpleParseWithNS
<filename>");
      System.exit(1);
  }
  try {
      // Creates parser object
      DOMParser parser = new DOMParser();
      // Tells the parser to validate documents
      parser.setFeature(
          "http://xml.org/sax/features/validation", true);
[30]      // Tells the parser to be aware of namespaces
[31]      parser.setFeature(
[32]            "http://xml.org/sax/features/namespaces", true);
      // Sets an ErrorHandler
      parser.setErrorHandler(new MyErrorHandler());
      // Parses an XML Document
      parser.parse(argv[0]);
      // Gets a Document object
      Document doc = parser.getDocument();
      // Does something
  } catch (Exception e) {
      e.printStackTrace();
  }
    }
}
```

This program is very similar to `SimpleParseWithValidation`, shown in Listing 2.6. The difference is the following line:

```
[31] parser.setFeature("http://xml.org/sax/features/namespaces", true);
```

This tells the processor to recognize namespaces. As a result, an application can access the namespace prefix, the local part, and the URI with the method explained in Chapter 4. In the current version of Xerces, the default value of this feature is `true`. However, we recommend that you specify the feature explicitly. If you set the value to `false` in this feature, the parser does not recognize namespaces. For example, if the element type name is `ns1:root`, in which `ns1` is the namespace prefix, the prefix is just treated as a part of the element type name. Therefore, it is natural to keep the default value (`true`) if you have a strong reason not to use it (generally, namespace handling involves some cost). Further discussions on namespaces, the DTD, and XML Schema appear in Sections 6.2.1 and 9.2.

## 2.3.2  Parsing XML Documents with XML Schema

XML Schema is the specification to enhance the DTD and has some advantages over the DTD. It became a W3C Recommendation on May 2, 2001. Chapter 9 discusses XML Schema in detail. In this section, we show a basic technique to parse and validate an XML document with an XML Schema. Xerces supports most of the XML Schema specification, but the details are still under discussion (see `http://xml.apache.org/xerces-j/schema.html` for the limitations of the support), so you may be warned when parsing an XML document with XML Schema validation. Listing 2.12 shows an example of XML Schema that presents the same structure of the document.

**Listing 2.12** XML Schema example, `chap02/department.xsd`

```
<?xml version="1.0"?>
<schema xmlns="http://www.w3.org/2001/XMLSchema"
        xmlns:org="urn:department"
        targetNamespace="urn:department">

  <element name="department">
   <complexType>
    <sequence>
      <element ref="org:employee" minOccurs='0'
                                  maxOccurs='unbounded'/>
    </sequence>
   </complexType>
  </element>

  <element name="employee">
   <complexType>
    <sequence>
      <element ref="org:name"/>
```

```
        <choice>
         <element ref="org:email" minOccurs='0' maxOccurs='1'/>
         <element ref="org:url"   minOccurs='0' maxOccurs='1'/>
        </choice>
      </sequence>
      <attribute name="id"  type="ID" use='required'/>
     </complexType>
    </element>

    <element name="name" type='string'/>

    <element name="email" type='string'/>

    <element name="url">
     <complexType>
      <attribute name="href" type="string" use='required'/>
     </complexType>
    </element>

   </schema>
```

You can see an XML document with XML Schema in Listing 2.13. The location of the schema is specified by using the xsi:schemaLocation attribute at the root element of the document.

**Listing 2.13**  XML document with XML Schema, chap02/department-schema.xml

```
<?xml version="1.0" encoding="utf-8"?>
<org:department xmlns:org="urn:department"
        xmlns:xsi="http://www.w3.org/2001/XMLSchema-instance"
        xsi:schemaLocation="urn:department department.xsd">

  <org:employee id="J.D">
    <org:name>John Doe</org:name>
    <org:email>John.Doe@foo.com</org:email>
  </org:employee>

  <org:employee id="B.S">
    <org:name>Bob Smith</org:name>
    <org:email>Bob.Smith@foo.com</org:email>
  </org:employee>

  <org:employee id="A.M">
    <org:name>Alice Miller</org:name>
    <org:url href="http://www.foo.com/~amiller/"/>
  </org:employee>
</org:department>
```

This sets the feature for the support of XML Schema. The following is the output of the program.

```
R:\samples>java chap02.SimpleParseWithSchemaValidation chap02/
department-schema.xml
```

The program to validate the document is `SimpleSchemaWithSchemaValidation`, which is stored in the CD-ROM. The difference between this program and `SimpleParseWithNS` (see Listing 2.11) is the next line:

```
parser.setFeature
(http://apache.org/xml/features/validation/schema",true);
```

This set is the feature for the support of the XML Schema. The following is the output of the program:

```
R:\samples>java chap02.SimpleParseWithSchemaValidation
chap02/department-schema.xml
```

### 2.3.3  Design Point: The DTD versus XML Schema

At the time of this writing, several schema languages are available, including the DTD, XML Schema, and RELAX (see Chapter 16), to specify the structure of an XML document. This section describes the pros and cons of using a DTD and XML Schema.

If you want to define data types, you should use XML Schema. A DTD essentially has a single data type: `String`. It does not support numeric data types, for example.

If you want to use namespaces, using XML Schema is better, because the DTD does not support namespaces. If you want to use namespaces in a DTD, you can use the trick shown in Section 6.2.1.

If you don't need data types and namespaces, using a DTD is still a good decision for the following reasons. First, at this moment, the conformance levels of XML processors that support XML Schema depend on the implementations. However, all the processors can handle DTDs based on the XML 1.0 specification.

Second, the XML Schema specification does not specify how an XML processor should obtain a schema definition. That means it depends on the implementations. By contrast, the location of a DTD is always given in a `DOCTYPE` declaration.

### 2.3.4  Parsing XML Documents with JAXP

The Java API for XML Processing (JAXP) is a common API to handle (parse and transform) XML documents. As this book is being written, the current version of

JAXP is 1.1. The JAXP specification is available from `http://www.jcp.org/jsr/ detail/5.jsp` (you can also see a related specification in Appendix C). DOM and SAX are well known as APIs for accessing XML documents. JAXP provides an API that is not specified in DOM and SAX—an API for parsing and transforming XML documents. Xerces supports JAXP, and we can write highly interoperable source code that does not depend on the implementation of an XML processor.

Listing 2.14 shows an example of DOM-based parsing with JAXP.

**Listing 2.14** Parsing an XML document with the JAXP API, `chap02/ SimpleParseJAXP.java`

```
package chap02;
/**
 *          SimpleParseJAXP.java
 **/
import java.io.IOException;
import org.w3c.dom.Document;
import org.xml.sax.ErrorHandler;
import org.xml.sax.SAXException;
import org.xml.sax.SAXParseException;
import javax.xml.parsers.DocumentBuilderFactory;
import javax.xml.parsers.DocumentBuilder;
import javax.xml.parsers.FactoryConfigurationError;
import javax.xml.parsers.ParserConfigurationException;
import share.util.MyErrorHandler;

public class SimpleParseJAXP {

    public static void main(String[] argv) {
        if (argv.length != 1) {
            System.err.println(
                    "Usage: java chap02.SimpleParseJAXP <filename>");
            System.exit(1);
        }
        try {
            // Creates document builder factory
            DocumentBuilderFactory factory =
                        DocumentBuilderFactory.newInstance();
            // Tells the parser to validate documents
            factory.setValidating(true);
            // Tells the parser to be aware of namespaces
            factory.setNamespaceAware(true);
            // Creates builder object
            DocumentBuilder builder =
                        factory.newDocumentBuilder();
```

[28]
[29]
[30]
[31]
[32]
[33]

```
[35]                   // Sets an ErrorHandler
[36]                   builder.setErrorHandler(new MyErrorHandler());
[37]                   // Parses the document
[38]                   Document doc = builder.parse(argv[0]);
               } catch (ParserConfigurationException pe) {
                   pe.printStackTrace();
               } catch (SAXException se) {
                   se.printStackTrace();
               } catch (IOException ioe) {
                   ioe.printStackTrace();
               }
          }
     }
```

The main difference from `SimpleParse` shown in Listing 2.2 is the use of a factory method to create an instance of the parser. This technique is known as **Abstract Factory** and **Factory Method** design patterns. The `document` interface plays the role of an abstract factory that provides a factory method to create DOM nodes without considering implementation classes.

A number of these techniques have been found through development of large programs. The standard Java class library uses a lot of design patterns, so you may have already noticed it. In this book, we try to introduce various design patterns to develop reusable program code. We recommend *Design Patterns*, by Erich Gamma et al. (Addison-Wesley, ISBN 0201633612), for further reading.

Instead of creating the DOM parser instance, a special class called `factory` has the responsibility of creating the instance. It is based on design patterns to improve the reusability of software components, and they are used throughout this book. In the factory instance, features for supporting validation and namespaces are set. In the previous examples, these features were set to a parser instance. The JAXP approach is employed to abstract an XML processor.

```
[29]   factory.setValidating(true);
[31]   factory.setNamespaceAware(true);
```

The `setValidating()` method (line 29) tells the `DocumentBuilderFactory` object to be aware of the validation. Note that Xerces provides two separate features for the DTD and XML Schema validation. The current JAXP API provides only a single method. When you use Xerces, calling the method `factory.setValidating(true)` means setting both features for the DTD and XML Schema validation. If a JAXP-compliant XML processor does not support XML Schema, only the DTD validation is activated.

The `setNamespaceAware()` method (line 31) tells the `DocumentBuilder Factory` object to be aware of supporting namespaces. If you use Xerces, the default value is `true`.

A DOM parser instance is created from the factory instance.

```
[33]    DocumentBuilder builder = factory.newDocumentBuilder();
```

The method creates a `DocumentBuilder` instance. The mechanism to determine the implementation class of the `DocumentBuilder` interface is shown in Section 2.4.2.

An error handler is set to the parser instance and the program parses an input XML document.

```
[36]    builder.setErrorHandler(new MyErrorHandler());
[38]    Document doc = builder.parse(new File(argv[0]));
```

The following is the result of the program.

```
R:\samples>java chap02.SimpleParseJAXP chap02/department-dtd.xml
```

### 2.3.5  Design Point: JAXP and Xerces Native API

In the previous sections, you learned how to parse an XML document with the Xerces native and JAXP APIs. This section discusses their advantages and disadvantages.

Using JAXP provides a way to write highly reusable program code. For example, the small program shown in Listing 2.2 does not work without Xerces. Therefore, JAXP should be used whenever an application requires only basic parsing capability, because most XML processors, including Xerces, have supported or plan to support JAXP.

However, JAXP supports only a basic method for parsing, so it might not be enough when you want to do something special. Chapter 6 is devoted to the special but usable patterns (tricks) that can be used with Xerces. For example, if an application requires a custom DOM implementation, Xerces provides an easy way to accomplish it (see Section 6.3.2). So developers should consider the requirements of an XML processor before deciding which API is best.

# 2.4  Programming Interfaces
# for Document Structure

In the previous sections, we showed how to read and parse an XML document. Next, we explain how to process an XML document by accessing its internal structure through APIs.

The XML 1.0 Recommendation defines the precise behavior of an XML processor when reading and parsing a document, but it says nothing about which API to use. In this section, we discuss two widely used APIs.

The **Document Object Model (DOM)**, a tree structure–based API by W3C. The specification consists of Level 1 (Recommendation in October 1998), Level 2 (Recommendation in November 2000), and Level 3 (currently a Working Draft) documents. Xerces 1.4.3 supports most of DOM Level 2.

The **Simple API for XML (SAX)**, an event-driven API developed by David Megginson and a number of people on the xml-dev mailing list. Although not sanctioned by any standards body, SAX is supported by most of the available XML processors. Xerces 1.4.3 supports SAX and SAX2, which supports namespaces. In this book, the word "SAX" refers to SAX (version 1.0) and SAX2.

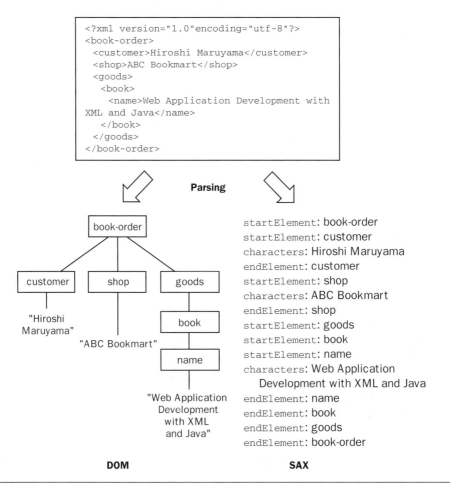

**Figure 2.2** DOM versus SAX

Figure 2.2 depicts the difference between the DOM and SAX APIs. When an application uses a DOM-based parser, it parses an XML document and passes a `Document` instance. The application should wait until it parses the whole XML document. When an application uses a SAX-based parser, it starts parsing an XML document and passes an event stream to the application in the course of parsing. The next sections discuss in detail the pros and cons of using these APIs.

> **NOTE:** In SAX2, some interfaces have been changed and renamed to support namespaces. Xerces supports both the SAX and SAX2 APIs, but the old SAX interfaces are now deprecated.

## 2.4.1 DOM: Tree-Based API

The term "document object model" has been used to refer to a model that defines the structure of an HTML document, thereby allowing scripting languages, such as JavaScript, to access the elements of the structure. You might have written JavaScript programs that manipulate the value of an input field in a form element in an HTML document. For example, `document.forms(1).username.value` refers to the value of the input field with the name `username` in the first form element in an HTML document. This expression is used to access the HTML DOM on HTML browsers like Microsoft Internet Explorer (IE) and Netscape Navigator.

However, current HTML object models and APIs to access them are browser-dependent (though the problem is being resolved). Thus you generally should prepare different pages suited for each type of browser that might execute your scripts. One goal of the DOM specification is to define a common, interoperable document object model for HTML as well as XML. The first edition of this book is based on the DOM Level 1 Recommendation. The DOM Level 2 Recommendation was published on November 13, 2000. Handling of namespaces, events, traversal range, and views were introduced in DOM Level 2. Standardization of DOM Level 3 is in progress. It will support load and save functions and other new functions. The details of using the DOM API are discussed in Chapter 4.

In DOM, an XML document is represented as a tree whose nodes are elements, text, and so on. An XML processor generates the tree and hands it to an application. A DOM-based XML processor (for example, `DOMParser` or `DocumentBuilder`) creates the entire structure of an XML document in memory (though Xerces defers the creation of DOM nodes until it is accessed).

XML is a language for describing tree-structured data. In XML, an element is represented by a start tag and a matching end tag (or an empty-element tag). An element may contain one or more other elements between its start and end tags. Thus

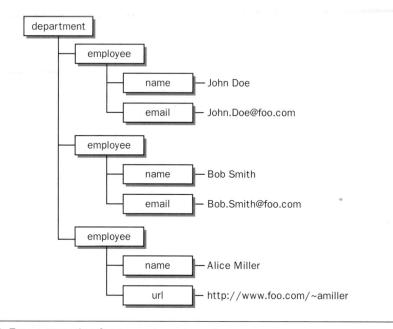

**Figure 2.3** Tree expression for `department.xml`

an entire document is represented as a nested tree. For example, our previous department example, `department.xml`, can be represented in a tree structure, as shown in Figure 2.3.

Each pair of start and end tags corresponds to an `Element` node, represented by the boxes in the figure, such as department and employee. Each chunk of text surrounded by two tags corresponds to a `Text` node, represented by the strings in the figure.

These nodes are defined as objects in DOM, and the DOM specification defines a platform- and language-neutral interface for application programs in terms of a standard set of the objects. To help interoperability, it defines APIs, called language bindings, for Java, ECMAScript (JavaScript), and the Interface Definition Language (IDL) from the Object Management Group (OMG).

From an object-oriented programming viewpoint, the DOM API is a set of interfaces that should be implemented by a particular DOM implementation. Table 2.1 shows the interfaces (and some classes) that define the DOM (Core) Level 1 specification. Figure 2.4 shows the class/interface hierarchy of the interfaces and classes. Note that `Node` is the primary data structure that constructs a tree structure. DOM tree constituents, such as `Element`, `Text`, and `Attr`, are all defined as interfaces derived from the `Node` interface.

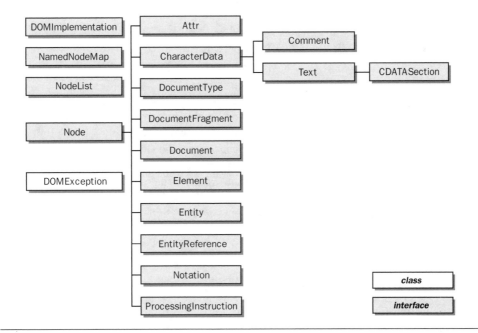

**Figure 2.4**  Class/interface hierarchy

**Table 2.1**  Interfaces in the `org.w3c.dom` Package

| INTERFACE NAME | DESCRIPTION |
| --- | --- |
| Node | The primary data type representing a single node in the document tree. |
| Document | Represents the entire XML document. |
| Element | Represents an element and any contained nodes. |
| Attr | Represents an attribute in an `Element` object. |
| ProcessingInstruction | Represents a processing instruction. |
| CDATASection | Represents a `CDATASection`. |
| DocumentFragment | A lightweight document object used for representing multiple subtrees or partial documents. |
| Entity | A lightweight document object used for representing multiple subtrees or partial documents. |
| EntityReference | Represents an entity reference, as it appears in the document tree. |
| DocumentType | Represents a DTD, which contains a list of entities. |
| Notation | Represents a notation declared in the DTD. A notation declares, by name, the format of an unparsed entity. |
| CharacterData | A parent interface of `Text` and others, which requires operations such as insert and delete string. |

(*continued*)

**Table 2.1** *continued*

| INTERFACE NAME | DESCRIPTION |
| --- | --- |
| `Comment` | Represents a comment. |
| `Text` | Represents text. |
| `DOMException` | An exception thrown when no further processing is possible. Normal errors are reported by return values. |
| `DOMImplementation` | Intended to be a placeholder of methods that are not dependent on specific DOM implementations. |
| `NodeList` | Represents an ordered collection of nodes. The items in the `NodeList` are accessible via an integral index, starting from 0. |
| `NamedNodeMap` | Represents a collection of nodes that can be accessed by name. |

## 2.4.2 SAX: Event-Driven API

In the previous section, we showed a method to access the structure and content of an XML document represented as a tree with the DOM API. An alternative to the tree-based API to access the document structure is an event-driven API. An application that wants information about document structure, such as element and attribute names/values in the document, can register *handlers,* a kind of callback function, to an XML processor. The processor notifies the handlers of events such as the start of a tag, an attribute, and the existence of data characters. Unlike when using the DOM API, which can traverse the structure of the document multiple times, the entire process of parsing with the SAX API is one-pass, and the event sequence is notified to an application in the process.

SAX is designed as a lightweight API that does not generate a tree structure of an input document. Applications must register event handlers to a parser instance that implements the `org.xml.sax.XMLReader` interface. SAX has several event handler interfaces, including `ContentHandler`, `DTDHandler`, and `ErrorHandler`. It also provides the default implementation class `org.xml.sax.helpers.DefaultHandler`, which implements all the interface methods that do nothing. You can implement the methods necessary for your application if you extend `DefaultHandler` as your event handler.

`ContentHandler` is the most often used interface because it is called whenever an element and an attribute are found. You can see how it is used in Listing 2.15, a simple program that reads an XML document and notifies events according to the document structure.

**Listing 2.15** Tracing SAX events, chap02/TraceEventsNS.java

```
        package chap02;
        /**
         * TraceEventsNS.java
         */
        import java.io.IOException;
        import org.xml.sax.helpers.XMLReaderFactory;
        import org.xml.sax.XMLReader;
        import org.xml.sax.SAXException;
        import org.xml.sax.Attributes;
        import org.xml.sax.helpers.DefaultHandler;

[12]    public class TraceEventsNS extends DefaultHandler {
[13]        public TraceEventsNS() {
[14]        }

        static public void main(String[] argv) {
            if (argv.length != 1) {
                System.err.println(
                        "Usage: chap02.TraceEventsNS <filename>");
                System.exit(1);
            }
            try {
[23]            // Creates SAX Parser object. When SAX2.0 is used,
[24]            // XMLReader class is used. Implementation class is
[25]            // specified by using
[26]            // System property org.xml.sax.driver
[27]            XMLReader parser =
[28]                XMLReaderFactory.createXMLReader();
[29]            // Tells the parser to be aware of namespace
[30]            parser.setFeature(
[31]                    "http://xml.org/sax/features/namespaces", true);
[32]            // Creates document handler and registers the handler
[33]            TraceEventsNS handler = new TraceEventsNS();
[34]            parser.setContentHandler(handler);
[35]            parser.setDTDHandler(handler);
[36]            parser.setErrorHandler(handler);

                // Parses input document
                parser.parse(argv[0]);

            } catch (SAXException se) {
                se.printStackTrace();
            } catch (IOException ioe) {
                ioe.printStackTrace();
```

```
            }
        }

        public void startDocument() throws SAXException {
            System.out.println("startDocument is called:");
        }

        public void endDocument() throws SAXException {
            System.out.println("endDocument is called:");
         }

        public void startElement(String uri, String localpart,
                            String name, Attributes amap) {
            System.out.println("startElement is called: localpart="
                            + localpart
                            + ", namespace URI="+uri);
            for (int i = 0; i < amap.getLength(); i++) {
                String attname = amap.getQName(i);
            String type   = amap.getType(i);
            String value  = amap.getValue(i);
            System.out.println("  attribute name="+attname+" type="
                            +type+" value="+value);
        }
        }

        public void endElement(String name) throws SAXException {
            System.out.println("endElement is called: " + name);
        }

        public void characters(char[] ch, int start, int length)
            throws SAXException {
            System.out.println("characters is called: " +
                            new String(ch, start, length));
        }
    }

[12]   public class TraceEventsNS extends DefaultHandler {...
        }
```

In Line 12, the TraceEventsNS class extends the DefaultHandler class, which is a helper class used to catch all the events provided the SAX API.

```
[27]   XMLReader parser = XMLReaderFactory.createXMLReader();
```

The org.xml.sax.XMLReader is an interface that represents a SAX-based parser, and an instance of the interface is given by the createXMLReader() method.

The object is associated with an implementation class of an XML processor (SAX parser) by using the following two methods.

- Specify the class name as the argument of the `createXMLReader()` method.
- Specify the class name as the value of the `org.xml.sax.driver` system property. In this case, `createXMLReader()` is called with no arguments.

```
java -Dorg.xml.sax.driver=org.apache.xerces.parsers.SAXParser
...
```

Using this property enables your program to be independent of specific parser implementations.

```
[30]   parser.setFeature("http://xml.org/sax/features/namespaces", true);
```

If you want the parser to be aware of namespaces, you can set a feature of the parser (see line 30). The feature `http://xml.org/sax/features/namespaces` is the same as for the DOM parser (see Section 2.3.1).

```
[33]   TraceEventsNS handler = new TraceEventsNS();
[34]   parser.setContentHandler(handler);
[35]   parser.setDTDHandler(handler);
[36]   parser.setErrorHandler(handler);
```

In lines 33–36, an instance of `TraceEventsNS` that implements `DefaultHandler` is created, and event handlers are set to the parser instance. Although the three handlers are set, methods for `ContentHandler` are actually implemented in `TraseEventsNS`, which extends the `DefaultHandler` class. The class provides "empty" method implementations for interfaces, and you do not have to prepare the other methods.

```
    parser.parse(argv[1]);
```

The `parse()` method starts parsing. The SAX parser reads an input XML document and sends events to the instance that implements the handler. Table 2.2 shows the methods defined in the `ContentHandler` interface.

**Table 2.2**  Methods of the `ContentHandler` Interface

| METHOD NAME | DESCRIPTION |
| --- | --- |
| startDocument() | Receives notification of the beginning of the document. |
| endDocument() | Receives notification of the end of the document. |
| startElement(String uri, String localpart, String name, Attributes amap) | Receives notification of the beginning of an element. |

*(continued)*

**Table 2.2**  *continued*

| METHOD NAME | DESCRIPTION |
| --- | --- |
| endElement(String name) | Receives notification of the end of an element. |
| characters(char ch[], int start, int length) | Receives notification of character data. |
| ignorableWhitespace(char ch[], int start, int length) | Receives notification of ignorable whitespace in element content. |
| processingInstruction (String target, String data) | Receives notification of a processing instruction. |
| setDocumentLocator(Locator locator) | Receives an object for locating the origin of SAX document events. The Locator object gives information on the location of the event, such as line number and column position. |

The following is the output of TraceEventsNS.

```
R:\samples>java chap02.TraceEventsNS org.apache.xerces.parsers.
   SAXParser department-ns.xml
startDocument is called:
startElement is called: localpart=department, namespace URI=http://
   www.schema.org/department/
startElement is called: localpart=employee, namespace URI=http://www.
   schema.org/department/attribute name=id type=CDATA value=J.D
startElement is called: localpart=name, namespace URI=http://www.
   schema.org/department/characters is called: John Doe
startElement is called: localpart=email, namespace URI=http://www.
   schema.org/department/characters is called: John.Doe@foo.com
startElement is called: localpart=employee, namespace URI=http://www.
   schema.org/department/attribute name=id type=CDATA value=B.S
startElement is called: localpart=name, namespace URI=http://www.
   schema.org/department/characters is called: Bob Smith
startElement is called: localpart=email, namespace URI=http://www.
   schema.org/department/characters is called: Bob.Smith@foo.com
startElement is called: localpart=employee, namespace URI=http://www.
   schema.org/department/attribute name=id type=CDATA value=A.M
startElement is called: localpart=name, namespace URI=http://www.
   schema.org/department/characters is called: Alice Miller
startElement is called: localpart=url, namespace URI=http://www.
   schema.org/department/attribute name=href type=CDATA value=http://
   www.foo.com/~amiller/
endDocument is called:
```

In Listing 2.13 we showed a DOM-based program with JAXP. In Listing 2.16, we show a SAX-based program with JAXP.

**Listing 2.16**  Tracing SAX events, chap02/TraceEventsJAXP.java

```java
package chap02;
/**
 * TraceEventsJAXP.java
 */
import java.io.File;
import java.io.IOException;
import javax.xml.parsers.SAXParser;
import javax.xml.parsers.SAXParserFactory;
import javax.xml.parsers.ParserConfigurationException;
import javax.xml.parsers.FactoryConfigurationError;
import org.xml.sax.SAXException;
import org.xml.sax.Attributes;
import org.xml.sax.helpers.DefaultHandler;

public class TraceEventsJAXP extends DefaultHandler {
  public TraceEventsJAXP() {
  }

  static public void main(String[] argv) {
    try {
      if (argv.length != 1) {
        System.err.println(
                   "Usage: chap02.java TraceEventsJAXP finename");
        System.exit(1);
      }
```
```java
      // Creates SAX Parser factory
      SAXParserFactory factory =
                            SAXParserFactory.newInstance();
      // Tells the parser to be aware of namespaces
      factory.setNamespaceAware(true);
      // Creates parser object
      SAXParser parser = factory.newSAXParser();
      DefaultHandler handler = new TraceEventsJAXP();
      // Parses input document
      parser.parse(new File(argv[0]), handler);
```
```java
      } catch (SAXException e) {
    e.printStackTrace();
      } catch (IOException ioe) {
    ioe.printStackTrace();
      } catch (ParserConfigurationException pce) {
    pce.printStackTrace();
      }
  }
```

The line numbers `[26]` through `[35]` appear in the left margin aligned with the following lines:

- [26] `// Creates SAX Parser factory`
- [27] `SAXParserFactory factory =`
- [28] `SAXParserFactory.newInstance();`
- [29] `// Tells the parser to be aware of namespaces`
- [30] `factory.setNamespaceAware(true);`
- [31] `// Creates parser object`
- [32] `SAXParser parser = factory.newSAXParser();`
- [33] `DefaultHandler handler = new TraceEventsJAXP();`
- [34] `// Parses input document`
- [35] `parser.parse(new File(argv[0]), handler);`

```
public void startDocument() throws SAXException {
  System.out.println("startDocument is called:");
}

public void endDocument() throws SAXException {
  System.out.println("endDocument is called:");
}

public void startElement(String uri, String localpart,
                        String name, Attributes amap) {
  System.out.println("startElement is called: localpart="
                    + localpart
                    + ", namespace URI="+uri);
  for (int i = 0; i < amap.getLength(); i++) {
    String attname = amap.getQName(i);
    String type = amap.getType(i);
    String value = amap.getValue(i);
    System.out.println("  attribute name="+attname+" type="
                                +type+" value="+value);
  }
}

public void endElement(String name) throws SAXException {
  System.out.println("endElement is called: " + name);
}

public void characters(char[] ch, int start, int length)
                                throws SAXException {
  System.out.println("characters is called: " +
                    new String(ch, start, length));
}
}
```

The output of this program is the same as in Listing 2.15.

```
[27]    SAXParserFactory factory = SAXParserFactory.newInstance();
```

Line 27 creates an instance of the factory class `SAXParserFactory` for the SAX API.

```
[30]    factory.setNamespaceAware(true);
```

Line 30 tells the factory to be aware of namespaces.

```
[32]    SAXParser parser = factory.newSAXParser();
```

Line 32 creates a `SAXParser` instance from the factory.

```
[33]    DefaultHandler handler = new TraceEventsJAXP();
[35]    parser.parse(new File(argv[0]), handler);
```

Lines 33 and 35 create an instance of an event handler (`DefaultHandler`) implementation (`TraceEventsJAXP` itself). The handler is given to the parser as an argument of the `parse()` method.

We described methods for parsing XML documents with the JAXP API. The `DocumentBuilderFactory` (for DOM) and `SAXParserFactory` (for SAX) factories hide the implementation of the XML processors. However, how do the factories call the factory implementations? How can developers use another implementation?

In DOM, `DocumentBuilderFactory.newInstance()` gives an instance of an implementation class. The JAXP 1.1 specification defines a procedure for determining the class name as follows (refer to the specification for details).

1. Use the `javax.xml.parsers.DocumentBuilderFactory` system property.
2. Use `lib/jaxp.properties` in the JRE directory.
3. Use the `META-INF/services/javax.xml.parsers.DocumentBuilder Factory` file in jars (provided by the Jar Services API).
4. Use the platform default.

For example, an implementation of `DocumentBuilderFactory` provided by Xerces is `org.apache.xerces.jaxp.DocumentBuilderFactoryImpl`. When you want to specify the class at runtime, do as follows:

```
R:\samples>java chap02.SimpleParseJAXP
-Djavax.xml.parsers.SAXParserFactory=org.apache.xerces.jaxp.
DocumentBuilderFactoryImpl
chap02/department-dtd.xml
```

In SAX, replace the string `"DocumentBuilderFactory"` with `"SAXParserFactory"`.

## 2.4.3 Design Point: DOM versus SAX

When you design and develop Web applications, the choice of the access API is very important.

The use of DOM is best suited for the following situations:

- When structurally modifying an XML document—for example, sorting elements in a particular order or moving some elements from one place in the tree to another.

- When sharing the document in memory with other applications. Applications can share a `Document` instance after the parsing process.

- When the size of the XML documents to be parsed is not so large. Generally, creation of Java objects has a performance penalty. Xerces is designed to delay the creation of element and text node objects until they are requested, but DOM-based programming is still more costly than using SAX.

- When applications want to start processing after finishing validation.

On the other hand, an XML processor with SAX does not create a tree structure. Instead, it scans an input XML document and generates events. Application programs receive these events and do whatever is appropriate for the task, such as getting an element type name and its text content. SAX is more efficient than DOM, therefore, it is good for the following occasions:

- When your task is performance and memory sensitive.

- When your task does not need to recognize the (complex) structure of an XML document. SAX scans the XML document at once, so you should keep the status of where you are processing during the parsing process. When the XML document represents a set of attribute/value pairs, you can get them very efficiently with SAX.

Listing 2.17 summarizes the programming patterns with the Xerces and JAXP APIs.

**Listing 2.17** Programming patterns for the Xerces and JAXP APIs

(1) Xerces: DOM parser

```
import org.w3c.dom.Document;
import org.apache.xerces.parsers.DOMParser;
import org.w3c.dom.Document;

String filename;
...
DOMParser parser = new DOMParser();
parser.parse(filename);
Document doc = parser.getDocument();
```

(2) Xerces: SAX parser

```
import org.xml.sax.helpers.XMLReaderFactory;
import org.xml.sax.XMLReader;
import org.xml.sax.helpers.DefaultHandler;
import org.w3c.dom.Document;
```

```
DefaultHandler handler;
String filename;
...
XMLReader parser = XMLReaderFactory.createXMLReader();
parser.setContentHandler(handler);
parser.setDTDHandler(handler);
parser.setErrorHandler(handler);
parser.parse(filename);
```

### (3) Xerces: handling namespaces

```
parser.setFeature("http://xml.org/sax/features/namespaces", true);
```

### (4) Xerces: Validation

```
parser.setFeature("http://xml.org/sax/features/validation", true);
```

### (5) Xerces: Schema validation

```
parser.setFeature("http://apache.org/xml/features/validation/schema",
true);
```

### (1) JAXP: DOM parser

```
import javax.xml.parsers.DocumentBuilderFactory;
import javax.xml.parsers.DocumentBuilder;
import org.w3c.dom.Document;

String filename;
...
DocumentBuilderFactory factory =
                DocumentBuilderFactory.newInstance();
DocumentBuilder builder =
                factory.newDocumentBuilder();
Document doc = builder.parse(filename);
```

### (2) JAXP: SAX parser

```
import javax.xml.parsers.SAXParser;
import javax.xml.parsers.SAXParserFactory;
import org.xml.sax.helpers.DefaultHandler;
import org.w3c.dom.Document;

DefaultHandler handler;
String filename;
...
SAXParserFactory factory =
                SAXParserFactory.newInstance();
SAXParser parser = factory.newSAXParser();
```

```
parser.parse(filename, handler);
```

(3) JAXP: Handling namespaces

```
factory.setNamespaceAware(true);
```

(4) JAXP: (Schema) validation

```
factory.setValidating(true);
```

## 2.5 Summary

In this chapter, we showed various approaches to parsing XML documents with Xerces and how to choose the appropriate ones for your application. For example, for the type of XML document, you should consider the following:

- Is it well-formed or valid? (See Section 2.2.3.)
- Does it contain namespaces? (See Section 2.3.1.)
- Is a DTD or XML Schema used? (See Section 2.3.2.)

For the API to access the structure of the document, you can choose an appropriate API based on the discussion in Section 2.4.3:

- Tree-based: DOM (see Section 2.4.1)
- Event-based: SAX (see Section 2.4.2)

Furthermore, for the API to parse XML documents, you have two choices (we discussed them in Section 2.3.4):

- Xerces native API
- JAXP API

To determine these choices, you should consider the characteristics of (1) the Web application you want to develop, (2) the XML documents, and (3) the platform where the application is running. Many examples in this book can help you to make decisions for your design and development tasks.

In the next chapter, we show you how to generate and serialize XML documents.

# Generating and Serializing XML Documents

## 3.1 Introduction

In the examples in Chapter 2, we assumed that there was an input XML document before any process began. If you are going to build an application program that takes a set of data from a backend database and generates an XML document based on the data, you might need to generate a document structure from scratch. The generated structure might be exchanged between applications by serializing the document structure to an XML document.

In this chapter, we present the basics of constructing a DOM tree from scratch. Once the structure is built, you can instruct an XML processor to output an XML document from it.

We first discuss generating a DOM tree without worrying about a DTD and validity (see Section 3.2). The DOM API described in Chapter 2 enables you to build a well-formed tree structure without relying on any particular implementation of XML processor. Applications that use the XML processor can create and modify a DOM tree in a very flexible way. This characteristic is useful for many applications (especially for document applications).

However, if you use XML for messaging, or exchanging structured data between business applications, validity is important. A validating XML processor checks the validity on the receiving side, but generally it is more desirable to generate a valid XML document where it is created. Section 3.3 shows how to build a valid DOM tree according to a given DTD. If the network is not reliable, we may need validation on both sides.

In the first edition of this book, we introduced **validating generation**, which enables developers to create DOM nodes incrementally according to a DTD. The function was provided by the XML for Java Parser versions 1 and 2. Unfortunately, the function is not implemented in Xerces (maybe because the DOM specification does not support it). However, we believe this function is essential for XML document generation. Therefore, we introduce an alternative approach—validating a DOM tree after creating it (see Section 3.3).

A generated DOM tree in memory can be stored as an XML document in a file system or database, or sent to other applications. The conversion from a DOM tree to an XML document is called **serialization**. The serialization is not a task for an XML processor based on XML 1.0, and the DOM API itself does not support serialization. However, the serialization is important in a practical sense because XML documents are exchanged among applications as text data on a network. In this book, you learn how to serialize a DOM tree by using functions provided by Xerces.

The rest of this chapter covers some miscellaneous but important topics on XML processing. The result of serialization of a generated DOM tree may sometimes look strange to readers. It is caused by processing whitespace in an XML document. We cover handling whitespace in Section 3.5. The last section is devoted to internationalization, which is also important for interoperability.

## 3.2  Creating a DOM Tree from Scratch

This section covers how to create DOM objects and how to construct a tree by using example programs.

### 3.2.1  Creating a Document Object

First, we show how to create a DOM tree without reading an XML document externally. The steps for the creation are as follows:

1. Create an `org.w3c.dom.Document` object.
2. Create a root element (document element).
3. Append the root element as a child of the `Document` object.
4. Create elements (with attributes), text, and comment nodes, and construct a DOM tree.

If you want to see a complete program in advance, refer to Listing 3.1. Recall that in the DOM tree structure, a document is represented by a `Document` object, so this is what you need to create first. There are several ways to create the object:

- Create an object of the implementation class for the Document interface directly.
- Get an object of the implementation class for the Document interface by using Java's reflection capability.
- Get an object of the implementation class for the Document interface by using the JAXP API.

The implementation class for the Document interface is org.apache.xerces. dom.DocumentImpl. In the first approach, the class is explicitly generated as follows:

```
import org.w3c.dom.Document;
import org.apache.xerces.dom.DocumentImpl;

. . .
// Creates Document object
Document doc = new DocumentImpl();

. . .
```

This program fragment is very simple, but you must modify the code if you want to use an XML processor other than Xerces, because the implementation class of the Document interface depends on the implementation of the XML processor.

If the DOM implementation is to be dynamically selected at runtime, you can use Java's reflection feature to create a class object and then create an instance of it as follows:

```
import org.w3c.dom.Document;
. . .
// Creates Document object
String documentImpl = "org.apache.xerces.dom.DocumentImpl";
Document doc = (Document)Class.forName(documentImpl).newInstance();

. . .
```

Note that the org.apache.xerces.dom.DocumentImpl class is not imported in the previous example. The class name can be specified by using a command-line argument, a system property, or an external file at runtime. The second approach is a little more complicated but preferable because it can compile without Xerces and is more XML processor–independent.

From the viewpoint of XML processor dependence, using the JAXP API is the best way to create a Document object. As described in Chapter 2, the javax.xml. parsers.DocumentBuilderFactory class is used as a DOM parser. This class provides the newDocument() method, which returns a Document object. This method makes it possible to get a Document object without depending on specific implementation classes. An example follows.

```
import org.w3c.dom.Document;
import javax.xml.parsers.DocumentBuilderFactory;
import javax.xml.parsers.DocumentBuilder;
...
// Creates Document object
DocumentBuilderFactory factory = DocumentBuilderFactory.newInstance();
DocumentBuilder builder = factory.newDocumentBuilder();
Document doc = builder.newDocument();
...
```

## 3.2.2  Creating and Appending Child Nodes

Other DOM objects, such as `Element` and `Text`, also need to be created as implementation-specific objects. However, the `Document` interface provides implementation-neutral methods for creating them. Therefore, after you get the `Document` object, you can create these nodes without specifying their implementation classes. This is based on the design patterns mentioned in Section 2.3.4.

Let's look at how we use the patterns. Suppose that we want to create a `person` element and set it as the root element `doc`. In Xerces, the `Element` interface is implemented by the class `org.apache.xerces.dom.ElementImpl`, so some simple code may look like this:

```
Element root = new ElementImpl((DocumentImpl)doc, "person");
doc.appendChild(root);
```

Unfortunately, this code is dependent on the specific implementation; Xerces. We can eliminate this kind of implementation dependency by using a factory method. Therefore the previous example can be rewritten as:

```
Element root = doc.createElement("person");
```

In this code, the `Element` node is not created directly by using a new function but is created with the `createElement()` method. Now the code is solely written in the DOM API and so is more portable. Listing 3.1 lists the factory methods provided by the `Document` interface. In the DOM Level 2 specification, two methods were added to support namespaces.

**Listing 3.1** Factory methods provided by the `Document` interface

```
public Element createElement(String tagName)
public Element createElementNS(String namespaceURI, String
qualifiedName) (Level 2)
public DocumentFragment createDocumentFragment()
public Text createTextNode(String data)
```

```
public Comment createComment(String data)
public CDATASection createCDATASection(String data)
public ProcessingInstruction createProcessingInstruction(String
target, String data)
public Attr createAttribute(String name)
public Attr createAttributeNS(String namespaceURI, String
qualifiedName) (Level 2)
public EntityReference createEntityReference(String name)
```

The following objects can be attached to a Document object as its children (remember that Document is also derived from Node):

- At most, one DocumentType object—this represents the DTD
- One Element object—this is the root element
- Zero or more Comment objects
- Zero or more ProcessingInstruction objects

We have already created the root element. Next, we add a new element named name as a child node of the root element (the person element just created).

```
Element item = doc.createElement("name");
item.appendChild(doc.createTextNode("John Doe"));
root.appendChild(item);
```

We created a name element that contains a Text node with the content string "John Doe" and appended the element as the (last) child of the root element.

An Element object can take the following objects as children:

- Any number of Element objects
- Any number of EntityReference objects
- Any number of Text objects
- Any number of CDATASection objects
- Any number of Comment objects
- Any number of ProcessingInstruction objects

At this point, we have created the DOM object tree shown in Figure 3.1.

Note that you can recursively add elements to build a complex tree structure.

**Figure 3.1** A generated DOM tree

Listing 3.2 shows a complete program that generates and outputs a simple XML document. This code creates a `Document` instance (lines 16–20), creates and appends the root element (line 23), and creates a comment (lines 25–26), an element and an attribute (lines 29–31), and a processing instruction (lines 32–34). The created DOM tree is output by using the serialization package from Xerces (lines 48–53). It is important to output a well-formed or valid XML document to be able to store it or pass it to other applications. We discuss serialization in Section 3.4.

**Listing 3.2** Creating a DOM tree, `chap03/MakeDocumentWithFactory.java`

```
       package chap03;
       /**
        *         MakeDocumentWithFactory.java
        **/
       import org.w3c.dom.Document;
       import org.w3c.dom.Element;
       import org.w3c.dom.Text;
       import org.w3c.dom.ProcessingInstruction;
[9]    import org.apache.xml.serialize.XMLSerializer;
[10]   import org.apache.xml.serialize.OutputFormat;

       public class MakeDocumentWithFactory {
           public static void main(String[] argv) {
               try {
[15]               // Creates Document object
[16]               String documentImpl =
[17]                   "org.apache.xerces.dom.DocumentImpl";
[18]               Document doc = (Document)Class.
[19]                   forName(documentImpl).newInstance();
[20]               // Creates <department> element as root
[21]               Element root = doc.createElement("department");
[22]               // Sets the element as root
[23]               doc.appendChild(root);
[24]               // Creates comment node
[25]               root.appendChild(doc.createComment(
[26]                   "The first employee description."));
[27]               // Creates <employee> elements and its text
[28]               // content, and adds it
[29]               Element employee = doc.createElement("employee");
[30]               employee.setAttribute("id", "J.D");
[31]               root.appendChild(employee);
[32]               // Create Processing Instruction
[33]               root.appendChild(doc.createProcessingInstruction(
[34]                                 "application", "commandForApp"));
                   // Creates <name> element and adds it
```

```
              Element name = doc.createElement("name");
              name.appendChild(doc.createTextNode("John Doe"));
              employee.appendChild(name);
              // Creates <email> element and adds it
              Element email = doc.createElement("email");
              email.appendChild(
                  doc.createTextNode("John.Doe@foo.com"));
              employee.appendChild(email);

              // Prepares output format
              OutputFormat formatter = new OutputFormat();
[47]          // Preserves whitespace
[48]          formatter.setPreserveSpace(true);
[49]          // The XML document is output to standard output
[50]          XMLSerializer serializer =
[51]              new XMLSerializer(System.out, formatter);
[52]          // Serializes the DOM tree as an XML document
[53]          serializer.serialize(doc);

          } catch (Exception e) {
              e.printStackTrace();
          }
      }
  }
```

Executing this program produces the following output.

```
R:\samples>java chap03.MakeDocumentWithFactory
<?xml version="1.0" encoding="UTF-8"?>
<department><!--The first employee description.--><employee id="J.D">
<name>
John Doe</name><email>John.Doe@foo.com</email></employee>
<?application commandForApp?></department>
```

Although the result is divided into multiple lines, it is actually output on one line (compare it with department.xml, which appeared in Chapter 2. This occurs because no whitespace for improving readability is contained in the program-generated XML document. Handling whitespace is discussed further in Section 3.5.

Listing 3.3 shows a JAXP version (MakeDocumentWithFactoryJAXP) to generate the same XML document. The Document object can be created by using the DocumentBuilder class. That means the class is a factory to create new Document objects, and newDocumentBuilder() is a factory method.

```
DocumentBuilderFactory factory = DocumentBuilderFactory.newInstance();
DocumentBuilder builder = factory.newDocumentBuilder();
Document doc = builder.newDocument();
```

Listing 3.3 contains no implementation class. If you want to use Listing 3.2 with an XML processor other than Xerces, the program should be modified (line 17) because the DOM specification does not provide an API to create a `Document` instance. When you use Listing 3.3, you can use it with other JAXP-aware XML processors without modification.

**Listing 3.3** Creating a DOM tree with the JAXP API, `chap03/` `MakeDocumentWithFactoryJAXP.java`

```
package chap03;
/**
 *        MakeDocumentWithFactoryJAXP.java
 **/
import javax.xml.parsers.DocumentBuilderFactory;
import javax.xml.parsers.DocumentBuilder;
import org.w3c.dom.Document;
import org.w3c.dom.Element;
import org.w3c.dom.Text;
import org.w3c.dom.ProcessingInstruction;
import org.apache.xml.serialize.OutputFormat;
import org.apache.xml.serialize.XMLSerializer;

public class MakeDocumentWithFactoryJAXP {
    public static void main(String[] argv) {
        try {
            // Creates document builder factory
            DocumentBuilderFactory
                factory = DocumentBuilderFactory.newInstance();
            DocumentBuilder
                builder = factory.newDocumentBuilder();
            Document doc = builder.newDocument();

            // Creates <department> element as root
            Element root = doc.createElement("department");
            // Sets the element as root
            doc.appendChild(root);
            // Creates comment node
            root.appendChild(doc.createComment(
                "The first employee description."));
            // Creates <employee> elements and its text content,
            // and adds it
            Element employee = doc.createElement("employee");
            employee.setAttribute("id", "J.D");
            root.appendChild(employee);
            // Create Processing Instruction
```

```
                    root.appendChild(doc.createProcessingInstruction(
                        "application", "commandForApp"));
                    // Creates <name> element and adds it
                    Element name = doc.createElement("name");
                    name.appendChild(doc.createTextNode("John Doe"));
                    employee.appendChild(name);
                    // Creates <email> element and adds it
                    Element email = doc.createElement("email");
                    email.appendChild(doc.createTextNode(
                        "John.Doe@foo.com"));
                    employee.appendChild(email);

                    // Prepares output format
                    OutputFormat formatter = new OutputFormat();
                    // Preserves whitespace
                    formatter.setPreserveSpace(true);
                    // The XML document is output to standard output
                    XMLSerializer serializer =
[55]                    new XMLSerializer(System.out, formatter);
                    // Serializes the DOM tree as an XML document
                    serializer.serialize(doc);

                } catch (Exception e) {
                    e.printStackTrace();
                }
            }
        }
```

### 3.2.3 Handling Namespaces

The DOM Level 2 specification introduced two new methods (see the following) to the Element and Attr nodes for supporting namespaces. Using these methods makes it possible to create XML documents with namespaces.

```
public Element createElementNS(String namespaceURI, String
qualifiedName) throws DOMException
public Attr    createAttributeNS(String namespaceURI, String
qualifiedName) throws DOMException
```

Both methods take two arguments. The first argument is a namespace URI. A "qualified" name is specified as the second argument. The format of a qualified name is "prefix:local-name," where "prefix" is the namespace prefix used in an XML document and "local-name" is the name of an element or attribute.

A special attribute named xmlns is used to associate a namespace URI and a prefix. This attribute is not created automatically when the methods are executed.

Developers should create this attribute and set it to an appropriate element. Listing 4.1 in Section 4.3.5 shows a sample program that checks namespaces in an XML document and adds `xmlns` attributes automatically.

Listing 3.4 shows a sample program to create an XML document with namespaces.

**Listing 3.4** Creating a DOM tree with namespaces, `chap03/MakeDocumentWithNS.java`

```
package chap03;
/**
 *       MakeDocumentWithNS.java
 **/
import javax.xml.parsers.DocumentBuilderFactory;
import javax.xml.parsers.DocumentBuilder;
import org.w3c.dom.Document;
import org.w3c.dom.Element;
import org.w3c.dom.Text;
import org.w3c.dom.ProcessingInstruction;
import org.apache.xml.serialize.XMLSerializer;
import org.apache.xml.serialize.OutputFormat;

public class MakeDocumentWithNS {
    public static void main(String[] argv) {
        final String NAMESPACE_URI
            = "http://www.foo.com/department";
        final String NAMESPACE_PREFIX_WITH_COLON = "ns:";
        final String NAMESPACE_SPEC
            = "http://www.w3.org/2000/xmlns/";
        try {
            // Creates document builder factory
            DocumentBuilderFactory
                factory = DocumentBuilderFactory.newInstance();
            DocumentBuilder
                builder = factory.newDocumentBuilder();
            Document doc = builder.newDocument();

            // Creates <department> element as root with namespace
            Element root = doc.createElementNS(NAMESPACE_URI,
                NAMESPACE_PREFIX_WITH_COLON+"department");
            // Sets xmlns attribute to specify namespace
            // prefix and uri
            root.setAttributeNS(NAMESPACE_SPEC, "xmlns:ns",
                NAMESPACE_URI);

            // Sets the element as root
```

```
        doc.appendChild(root);

        // Creates comment node
        root.appendChild(doc.createComment(
            "The first employee description."));

        // Creates <employee> elements and its text content,
        // and adds it
        Element employee = doc.createElementNS(NAMESPACE_URI,
            NAMESPACE_PREFIX_WITH_COLON+"employee");
        employee.setAttributeNS(NAMESPACE_URI,
            NAMESPACE_PREFIX_WITH_COLON+"id", "J.D");
        root.appendChild(employee);

        // Create Processing Instruction
        root.appendChild(doc.createProcessingInstruction(
            "application", "commandForApp"));

        // Creates <name> element and adds it
        Element name = doc.createElementNS(NAMESPACE_URI,
            NAMESPACE_PREFIX_WITH_COLON+"name");
        name.appendChild(doc.createTextNode("John Doe"));
        employee.appendChild(name);

        // Creates <email> element and adds it
        Element email = doc.createElementNS(NAMESPACE_URI,
            NAMESPACE_PREFIX_WITH_COLON+"email");
        email.appendChild(
            doc.createTextNode("John.Doe@foo.com"));
        employee.appendChild(email);

        // Prepares output format
        OutputFormat formatter = new OutputFormat();
        formatter.setPreserveSpace(true);
        // The XML document is output to standard output
        XMLSerializer serializer =
            new XMLSerializer(System.out, formatter);
        // Serializes the DOM tree as an XML document
        serializer.serialize(doc);

    } catch (Exception e) {
        e.printStackTrace();
    }
  }
}
```

Executing this program produces the following output.

```
R:\samples>java chap03.MakeDocumentWithNS
<?xml version="1.0" encoding="UTF-8"?>
<ns:department xmlns:ns="http://www.foo.com/department"><!--The first
employee description.--><ns:employee ns:id="J.D"><ns:name>John Doe</
ns:name><ns:email>John.Doe@foo.com</ns:email></ns:employee>
<?application commandForApp?></ns:department>
```

## 3.3 Validating a Generated DOM Tree

The DOM tree created in Section 3.2 is well-formed. However, suppose some applications require that the document be valid. How can we accomplish this?

In the first edition of this book, we introduced a programming example for checking validation incrementally while creating a DOM tree. XML for Java versions 1 and 2 provide the *validating generation* feature for the purpose. However, Xerces does not support validating generation, because the DOM specification does not support the function. However, we believe the feature is very important for developing Web applications. Therefore, in this book we provide another way to validate a generated document.

The program `ValidateCreatedTree`, shown in Listing 3.5, creates a DOM tree, serializes it as a string that represents an XML document, and validates it. Xerces provides the `DocumentType` interface and its implementation to represent `doctype` information. It is added in the creation phase. We know it is a quick and dirty way to validate a generated document, but it is useful.

**Listing 3.5** Validating a created DOM tree, `chap03/ValidateCreatedTree.java`

```
package chap03;
/**
 *        ValidateCreatedTree.java
 **/
import java.io.StringWriter;
import java.io.StringReader;
import javax.xml.parsers.DocumentBuilderFactory;
import javax.xml.parsers.DocumentBuilder;
import org.w3c.dom.Document;
import org.w3c.dom.DOMImplementation;
import org.w3c.dom.Element;
import org.w3c.dom.Text;
import org.w3c.dom.ProcessingInstruction;
```

```
            import org.w3c.dom.DocumentType;
            import org.apache.xml.serialize.Serializer;
            import org.apache.xml.serialize.XMLSerializer;
            import org.apache.xml.serialize.OutputFormat;
            import org.apache.xerces.dom.DocumentImpl;
            import org.apache.xerces.parsers.DOMParser;
            import org.xml.sax.SAXException;
            import org.xml.sax.InputSource;
            import share.util.MyErrorHandler;

            public class ValidateCreatedTree {
                public static void main(String[] argv) {
                    try {
                        // Creates document builder factory
                        DocumentBuilderFactory factory =
                            DocumentBuilderFactory.newInstance();
                        factory.setValidating(true);
                        // Tells the parser to be aware of namespaces
                        factory.setNamespaceAware(true);
                        // Creates builder object
                        DocumentBuilder builder =
                            factory.newDocumentBuilder();
                        // Sets an ErrorHandler
                        builder.setErrorHandler(new MyErrorHandler());

[39]                    // DOMImplementation is used to get doctype object
[40]                    DOMImplementation domImpl = builder.
                        getDOMImplementation();
[41]                    // Creates Document Type Definition
[42]                    DocumentType docType = domImpl.createDocumentType(
[43]                        "department",
[44]                        null,
[45]                        "chap03/department.dtd");
[46]                     Document doc = domImpl.createDocument(null, "department",
[47]                        docType);
[48]
                        // Gets <department> element as document element
                        Element root = doc.getDocumentElement();

                        // Creates comment node
                        root.appendChild(doc.createComment(
                            "The first employee description."));

                        // Creates <employee> elements and its text content,
                        // and adds it
                        Element employee = doc.createElement("employee");
```

```
            employee.setAttribute("id", "J.D");
            root.appendChild(employee);

            // Create Processing Instruction
            root.appendChild(doc.createProcessingInstruction(
                "application", "commandForApp"));

            // Creates <name> element and adds it
            Element name = doc.createElement("name");
            name.appendChild(doc.createTextNode("John Doe"));
            employee.appendChild(name);

            // Creates <email> element and adds it
            Element email = doc.createElement("email");
            email.appendChild(doc.createTextNode(
                "John.Doe@foo.com"));
            employee.appendChild(email);

[77]        // Serializes the DOM tree as an XML document
[78]        OutputFormat formatter = new OutputFormat();
[79]
[80]        // The XML document will be serialized as string
[81]        StringWriter out = new StringWriter() ;
[82]        XMLSerializer serializer =
[83]            new XMLSerializer(out, formatter);
[84]        formatter.setPreserveSpace(true);
[85]        serializer.serialize(doc);
[86]        out.flush();
[87]        out.close() ;
[88]
[89]        // Parses the document
[90]        try {
[91]            builder.parse(new InputSource(
[92]                new StringReader(out.getBuffer().toString())));
                System.out.println(out.getBuffer().toString());
            } catch (SAXException ex) {
                ex.printStackTrace();
            }
        } catch (Exception e) {
            e.printStackTrace();
        }
    }
}
```

The first half of the program is the same as MakeDocumentWithFactory, shown in Listing 3.2. Let's look at the original part, which begins with line 39.

First, we create a `DocumentType` object and append it as the child of the `Document` object. The `DocumentType` is specified in the DOM Level 2 specification, but a method to create the object is not specified. Therefore, we use a factory method defined by the `org.apache.xerces.dom.DocumentImpl` class, which comes from Xerces.

```
public DocumentType
createDocumentType(java.lang.String qualifiedName,
java.lang.String publicID,
                java.lang.String systemID)
throws DOMException
```

The first argument of this method is the name of the root element. It should be qualified with a prefix if the document contains namespaces. The second and third arguments take a public or system identifier, respectively (one should be specified and the other is `null`). In Listing 3.5, the name of the DTD file is specified as a system identifier.

```
[42]    DocumentType docType = domImpl.createDocumentType(
                            "department",
                            null,
                            "chap03/department.dtd");
```

In the next part, the generated DOM tree will be serialized as a string.

```
        // Serializes the DOM tree as an XML document
[78]    OutputFormat formatter = new OutputFormat();

        // The XML document will be serialized as string
[81]    StringWriter out = new StringWriter() ;
[82]    XMLSerializer serializer =
                    new XMLSerializer(out, formatter);
[84]    formatter.setPreserveSpace(true);
[85]    serializer.serialize(doc);
```

Note that a `StringWriter` object is set in the constructor for an `XMLSerializer` object (`System.out` is used in Listing 3.2).

Finally, the serialized XML document is parsed with the DTD (line 91).

```
[91]    builder.parse(new InputSource(
            new StringReader(out.getBuffer().toString()))));
```

The following is the execution result.

```
    R:\samples>java chap03.ValidateCreatedTree
    <?xml version="1.0" encoding="UTF-8"?>
    <!DOCTYPE department SYSTEM "department.dtd">
```

```
<department><!--The first employee description.--><employee id="J.D">
<name>John
Doe</name><email>John.Doe@foo.com</email></employee><?application
commandForApp?
></department>
```

## 3.4 Serializing a DOM Tree

In the previous sections, you learned how to create a DOM tree from scratch. To store the tree as a file or to send it to other applications, you should serialize the DOM object tree as an XML document. The serialization process depends on the XML processor because there is no standard API for serialization. Xerces provides a utility class, `org.apache.xml.serialize.XMLSerializer`, to output a DOM tree in various formats.

### 3.4.1 Using the XMLSerializer Package

Remember the `MakeDocumentWithFactory` class shown in Listing 3.2? In this program, the serialization process begins at line 46.

```
[9]    import org.apache.xml.serialize.XMLSerializer;
[10]   import org.apache.xml.serialize.OutputFormat;
       ...
       // Prepares output format
[46]   OutputFormat formatter = new OutputFormat();
       // Preserves whitespace
[48]   formatter.setPreserveSpace(true);
       // The XML document will be output to standard output
[50]   XMLSerializer serializer =
              new XMLSerializer(System.out, formatter);
       // Serializes the DOM tree as an XML document
[53]   serializer.serialize(doc);
```

The `OutputFormat` class is used to specify the format of serialization, and the class has four constructors.

- OutputFormat()
- OutputFormat(Document doc)
- OutputFormat(Document doc, String encoding, boolean indenting)
- OutputFormat(String method, String encoding, boolean indenting)

As you can see, you can specify an encoding and the indenting of a serialized document. In the previous example, the object was created with no argument.

For example, we can modify the first part of the program shown in Listing 3.2 as follows:

```
OutputFormat formatter = new OutputFormat(xml, "Shift_JIS", true);
```

In the second argument, an encoding named `"Shift_JIS"`, which is a Japanese encoding, is specified. The third argument is a boolean variable for Xerces to put appropriate indentations in the output document to make it easier to read. When the modified program is compiled and executed, this is the result.

```
R:\samples>java chap03.MakeDocumentWithFactoryModified
<?xml version="1.0" encoding="Shift_JIS"?>
<department><!--The first employee description.--><employee id="J.D">
        <name>John Doe</name>
        <email>John.Doe@foo.com</email>
    </employee><?application commandForApp?></department>
```

The `setPreserve()` method is used to specify whether any whitespace should be preserved. In this chapter, there is no need to specify this method, because a DOM tree is created by a program.

Let's continue to explain the previous code fragment. After creating an `OutputFormat` object, we create an `XMLSerializer` object with it.

```
// The XML document will be output to standard output
XMLSerializer serializer = new XMLSerializer(System.out, formatter);
```

In this case, the following constructor for the `XMLSerializer` class is used (refer to the Xerces API document for other constructors).

```
public XMLSerializer(OutputStream output, OutputFormat format)
```

The first argument takes the `java.io.Outputstream` object for output. In this program, the standard output (`System.out`) is used, but you can set other output stream objects to get a file or a string. The second argument takes the `OutputFormat` object created before.

Finally, we execute serialization with `serialize` method.

```
// Serializes the DOM tree as an XML document
serializer.serialize(doc);
```

## 3.4.2 Discussions about Serialization

We showed methods to create a DOM tree from scratch and serialize it as an XML document with sample programs. You can easily modify the programs for other purposes—for example, to connect to your database to automatically generate an employee list of your whole department in the form of XML. Another possibility is to create a DOM tree interactively by bringing up a series of dialogs (wizards, in Windows terminology) and asking the user to supply the data.

You may think that it might have been easier to generate an XML document directly using `System.out.println()` (or `printf()` in C or `cout` in C++, or . . .) as follows.

```
System.out.println("<?xml version=\"1.0\"?>");
System.out.println("<department>");
System.out.println("  <employee>");
System.out.println("    <name>John Doe</name>");
...
```

In fact, most current CGI programs and servlets generate HTML pages this way. Why do we bother creating a complex object structure rather than just using the `println()` method? We can give you two good reasons.

First, XML documents *must* be well-formed.

The current browsers are amazingly forgiving about errors in HTML markup. This is partly because even though some of the tags are ignored or handled incorrectly, nothing serious happens. The information will be displayed on a screen in a reasonable way, and the human user is responsible for making sense of it. On the other hand, XML tags are supposed to be interpreted by application programs. The well-formedness of XML documents is strictly defined in the XML 1.0 Recommendation, and all conforming XML processors are required to report errors to application programs if the parsed XML document is not well-formed. There should not be errors such as missing end tags, unknown entities, and unknown characters. Creating a toy program that generates very simple XML documents may be possible with the `println()` method. But for complex enterprise Web applications, you should let an XML processor be responsible for generating well-formed and valid documents.

Second, creating well-formed and valid XML documents is not as easy as it may seem.

XML is intended to be a simple, lightweight markup language. Yet, understanding every detail of the specification is not easy. For example, how can you distinguish between ignorable whitespace and unignorable whitespace? Or how can you include a newline character within an attribute value?

The XML 1.0 Recommendation precisely defines these details, and the XML processors in your business partner's application program expect that your XML document complies with them. Even though you are familiar with these details, it is not productive for you to develop code that takes care of them every time you call the `println()` method. One of the biggest values you can expect from an XML processor is that it can handle these details for you.

Third, generation by string processing using the `println()` method sometimes produces security holes.

Suppose we create an HTML document in which a person's name from an input form is embedded.

```
String name;
        . . .
out.println("<td>Name</td><td>" + name + "</td>");
    . . .
```

The previous code works correctly when the name variable refers to "John Doe" and outputs the following string.

```
<td>Name</td><td>John Doe</td>
```

However, if the name variable refers to a string that contains some special characters, like "<," it outputs an incorrect HTML document, because it is difficult to check whether the embedded string is a correct fragment of the HTML document.

A more serious problem occurs if someone embeds a string that conforms to HTML but contains a malicious program. Cross-site scripting (CSS), described in Section 10.2.1, is a typical example. You should make sure that printing an HTML or XML document doesn't cause a security hole. By creating and validating an HTML or XML document as a whole before printing, you can avoid including the illegal characters.

For these reasons, we recommend that you create an XML document from a DOM tree. It may involve a cost, but we believe it is a necessary investment.

XML processors are the result of intensive intellectual work. Using them frees you from worrying about the proper nesting of tags, escaping special characters such as an ampersand and a left angle bracket, and handling international character sets. So why not use XML processors?

Another important point when you want to generate an XML document is the encoding of the document. In this book, we recommend that you use UTF-8 or UTF-16 because any XML processor must handle these two encodings.

This is not so serious a problem if an application handles only English; however, there are many language-specific encodings for Japanese, for example. Some legacy systems may use these encodings, but even so, you should use UTF-8 or UTF-16 encoding when data in XML is exchanged between systems.

One reason why business applications employ XML is to keep the interoperability independent from implementations and platforms. Using widely accepted encodings makes it possible to improve interoperability.

## 3.5 Handling Whitespace

In previous sections, we showed programming examples to create and serialize XML documents. When the XML documents are created and serialized, there are a couple of things that should receive serious consideration, such as handling whitespace.

According to the XML 1.0 Recommendation, **whitespace** is one or more space (#x20) characters, carriage returns, line feeds, or tabs. Whitespace is used to delimit tokens. Many production rules in the XML 1.0 Recommendation explicitly also include *S*, the nonterminal symbol that represents whitespace.

In some applications, whitespace is meaningful (for example, poetry and program source code). However, whitespace is also used to improve the readability of XML documents. In this case, the whitespace itself is meaningless. To demonstrate how much we can improve the readability by inserting appropriate whitespace, we remove all the nonessential whitespace from our example in Chapter 2, `department.xml`. The result is a single long line shown in the file `departmentNoWS.xml` in Listing 3.6 (because of the page-width limitation, the line is wrapped, but notice that there are no newline characters between the lines). Obviously, this is much less readable than the original one, which contains appropriate newlines and indentations. As we have shown in previous sections, when an XML document is generated by a program with the DOM API, the generated document contains no whitespace for improved readability.

**Listing 3.6** XML document without indentation, `chap03/departmentNoWS.xml`

```
<?xml version="1.0"?>
<department><employee id="J.D"><name>John
Doe</name><email>John.Doe@foo.com</email></employee><employee id="B.S">
<name>Bob Smith</name><email>Bob.Smith@foo.com</email></employee>
<employee id="A.M"><name>Alice Miller</name><url href="http://www.foo.
com/~amiller/"/></employee></department>
```

An XML document without whitespace is difficult for humans to read. However, what about for computer programs? Figure 3.2 shows the DOM trees for `department.xml` and `departmentNoWS.xml` using the visualization tool `TreeWalker`, which is included in the Xerces distribution package.

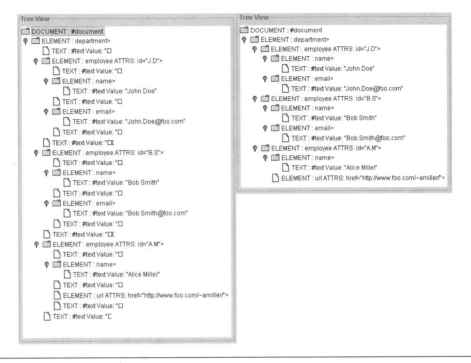

**Figure 3.2** Visualization of an XML document (`department.xml` on the left, `departmentNoWS.xml` on the right)

Note that in the DOM tree of `department.xml`, all the whitespace, including both newlines and space characters, is preserved. This is a required behavior of a conforming XML processor because some whitespace is in fact meaningful in some types of applications. Without knowing the semantics of the application, you do not know which whitespace is significant and which is not.

One of most frequent questions from developers about the DOM API is the use of the `getFirstChild()` method of the `org.w3c.dom.Node` interface. When developers want to get the first child element of an element, they simply call the `getFirstChild()` method. However, as you can see in Figure 3.2 (on the left), in many cases the first child node is a `Text` node that contains only whitespace.

In our `department.xml` example, whitespace is not explicitly stated in the content models in the DTD (`department.dtd`). For example, the content model of the element `department` allows only `name`, `email`, and `url` as possible child elements. Will whitespace (`Text` elements consisting of whitespace characters) violate the validity of the document?

To allow inserting whitespace for readability without explicitly specifying white-space in the content models in a DTD, the XML 1.0 Recommendation defines the following rule as one of the validity constraints.

*The declaration matches children and the sequence of child elements belongs to the language generated by the regular expression in the content model, with optional white space (characters matching the nonterminal S) between each pair of child elements.*

Thus, although the DOM tree may have extraneous whitespace, validation is done by ignoring whitespace that is not defined in the content model.

What you should care about is that if a DTD is not specified, it is impossible to determine whether the whitespace is ignorable or not. For example, if the content model of a department element is as follows, all the whitespace in the department element is meaningful.

```
<!DOCTYPE department (#PCDATA|employee|name|email|url)*>
```

If certain whitespace is significant, there are two ways to tell an XML processor or an application about it.

- Define the significant whitespace in the content models in the DTD.
- Specify the xml:space="preserve" attribute in an XML document in order to indicate the intent that applications preserve all whitespace.

The XML document shown in Listing 3.7 indicates that all whitespace within the department element is to be preserved. Note that it is a hint for an XML application, not for an XML processor.

**Listing 3.7** XML document with xml:space attribute, chap03/department-preserved.xml

```
<?xml version="1.0"?>
<!DOCTYPE department SYSTEM "department-preserved.dtd">
<department xml:space="preserve">
    <employee id="J.D">
        <name>John Doe</name>
        <email>John.Doe@foo.com</email>
    </employee>

    <employee id="B.S">
        <name>Bob Smith</name>
        <email>Bob.Smith@foo.com</email>
    </employee>

    <employee id="A.M">
        <name>Alice Miller</name>
```

```
            <url href="http://www.foo.com/~amiller/"/>
        </employee>
    </department>
```

Xerces provides the `getIsIgnorableWhitespace()` method in `org.apache.` `xerces.dom.TextImpl` to test whether a node is ignorable whitespace. The method is Xerces-specific. The program (`RemoveIgnorableWSNodes`) shown in Listing 3.8 removes all the ignorable whitespace from an input XML document.

**Listing 3.8** Removing ignorable whitespace, `chap03/RemoveIgnorableWSNodes.` `java`

```java
package chap03;
/**
 *          RemoveIgnorableWSNodes.java
 **/
import javax.xml.parsers.DocumentBuilderFactory;
import javax.xml.parsers.DocumentBuilder;
import java.io.IOException;
import org.w3c.dom.Document;
import org.w3c.dom.Element;
import org.w3c.dom.Node;
import org.w3c.dom.Document;
import org.apache.xerces.parsers.DOMParser;
import org.xml.sax.SAXException;
import org.apache.xml.serialize.XMLSerializer;
import org.apache.xml.serialize.OutputFormat;
import share.util.MyErrorHandler;

public class RemoveIgnorableWSNodes {

    public static void main(String[] argv) {
        if (argv.length != 1) {
            System.err.println(
                "Usage: java RemoveWSNodes <filename>");
            System.exit(1);
        }
        try {
            // Creates document builder factory
            DocumentBuilderFactory factory =
                DocumentBuilderFactory.newInstance();
            // Tells the parser to validate documents
            factory.setValidating(true);
            // Creates builder object
            DocumentBuilder builder =
                factory.newDocumentBuilder();
            // Sets an ErrorHandler
```

```
                builder.setErrorHandler(new MyErrorHandler());
                // Parses the document
                Document doc = builder.parse(argv[0]);
                // Removes ignorable whitespace
                removeIgnorableWSNodes(doc.getDocumentElement());
                // Prepares output format
                OutputFormat formatter = new OutputFormat();
                formatter.setPreserveSpace(true);
                // The XML document is output to standard output
                XMLSerializer serializer =
                    new XMLSerializer(System.out, formatter);
                // Serializes the DOM tree as an XML document
                serializer.serialize(doc);
            } catch (Exception e) {
                e.printStackTrace();
                System.exit(1);
            }
        }

        public static void removeIgnorableWSNodes(Element parent) {
            Node nextNode = parent.getFirstChild();
            for (Node child = parent.getFirstChild();
                nextNode != null;) {
                child = nextNode;
                nextNode = child.getNextSibling();
                if (child.getNodeType() == Node.TEXT_NODE) {
                    // Checks if the text node is ignorable
                    if (((org.apache.xerces.dom.TextImpl)child).
                        isIgnorableWhitespace()) {
                        parent.removeChild(child);
                    }
                } else if (child.getNodeType() == Node.ELEMENT_NODE) {
                    removeIgnorableWSNodes((Element )child);
                }
            }
        }
    }
```

Now we try to execute the program with an XML document with a DTD
(department-dtd.xml).

```
R:\samples>java chap03.RemoveIgnorableWSNodes department-dtd.xml
<?xml version="1.0" encoding="UTF-8"?>
<!DOCTYPE department SYSTEM "department.dtd">
<department><employee id="J.D"><name>John Doe</name><email>John.
Doe@foo.com</email></employee><employee id="B.S"><name>Bob Smith
```

```
</name><email>Bob.Smith@foo.com</email></employee><employee id="A.M">
<name>Alice Miller</name><url href="http://www.foo.com/~amiller/"/>
</employee></department>
```

Xerces recognizes a content model for an element in the DTD, checks whether whitespace is ignorable or not according to the content model, and removes ignorable whitespace.

## 3.6 Internationalization

XML is useful for internationalization. On the basis of Unicode, XML can represent text written in many natural languages. XML further supports many non-Unicode encodings by converting them to Unicode because such encodings have been already in use. In fact, Xerces supports more than 40 encodings.

However, XML programming still requires special care about internationalization. Here is a brief summary of what you should know.

### 3.6.1 XML Declarations

We recommend that XML documents and DTDs (as well as external DTD subsets, external parsed entities, and external parameter entities) always begin with an XML declaration.

```
<?xml version="1.0" encoding="charset-name"?>
```

Here `"charset-name"` announces which character-encoding scheme is used for representing the document. Depending on which natural language and which editor you use, you must specify a different `charset-name`.

If you use only those characters in US-ASCII (to be precise, ANSI X3.4-1986), specify `"us-ascii"` as the `charset-name` or omit `encoding="charset-name"` entirely. If you use European languages, you are probably using one of the ISO 8859 family (typically ISO-8859-1), then, specify `"iso-8859-1"`.

If your text editor allows Unicode, we strongly recommend it. Although XML supports legacy encodings, conversion of such an encoding to Unicode is implemented differently by different XML processors. For example, different implementations provide different conversions for Shift-JIS encoding. Such non-unique conversions to Unicode are very harmful for Web applications because a digital signature is performed after the conversion. In fact, one of the authors has experienced some errors because of such non-unique conversions. According to the XML 1.0 specification, any XML processor should support UTF-8 and UTF-16. Support of the encodings depends on the implementations of the XML processors.

Unicode provides many encodings, such as UTF-8, UTF-16, and UTF-32, and each encoding has variations. Although the details of such encodings are beyond the scope of this book, we can give you a rule of thumb. If you use Notepad in Windows 2000, choose UTF-16 and specify `"utf-16"` as the encoding name.

### 3.6.2 Charset Parameter

Although an encoding declaration can be specified within an XML document, it is used only when the XML document is stored in a file on your hard disk.

If an XML document is sent or received via some protocol such as SOAP or HTTP, the encoding of the document is determined differently. Together with the document, a collection of information about the document is transmitted via the protocol. This information collection is the MIME header of this document. The encoding of the document is specified by the `charset` parameter of the field `"Content-type"` in the MIME header.

We strongly recommend use of the MIME type `"application/xml"` together with an appropriate `charset` parameter when an XML document is exchanged via a protocol. When a DTD is exchanged, use the MIME type `application/xml-dtd` with a `charset` parameter. You can find further discussions on this topic in Chapter 10.

## 3.7 Summary

In this chapter, we covered how to build a DOM tree structure using a DOM-compliant XML processor. We also discussed the importance of making sure that the DOM tree being built is valid, and we showed a simple program to validate the generated DOM tree. The DOM tree was serialized as an XML document using methods provided by Xerces. Finally, we explained the treatment of whitespace when generating an XML document from a generated DOM tree.

This chapter concludes the coverage of the basic programming skills for parsing and generating XML documents using the standard APIs. The next chapter shows advanced topics about DOM tree manipulation and gives more complex examples.

# Working with DOM

## 4.1  Introduction

We discussed parsing in Chapter 2 and document generation in Chapter 3. These chapters covered many important aspects of processing XML documents. However, in the development of Web applications, parsing and generation are not sufficient. You also need to understand how to manipulate the internal representation of XML documents. If you use SAX, you need to design the internal structure yourself. If you use DOM, you need to understand techniques for dealing with DOM trees using the DOM API.

In this chapter, we discuss basic techniques for and some pitfalls of manipulating DOM structures. Because of space limitations, we cannot describe every detail of DOM. Please consult the latest DOM specification whenever you have further questions. The DOM specification consists of six parts: "Core," "HTML," "Views," "Events," "Style," and "Traversal and Range." We discuss the parts "Core" and "Traversal and Range." Other parts are used when a document has a user interface like Web browsers.

## 4.2  DOM Basics

We touched briefly on DOM in Chapter 2 and on generating a DOM tree from scratch in Chapter 3. This section gives you more tips on DOM programming.

DOM provides a set of methods to access DOM trees. A node in a DOM tree may be one of the following interfaces: `Document`, `ProcessingInstruction`, `Comment`, `DocumentType`, `Notation`, `Entity`, `Element`, `Text`, `CDATASection`, or `EntityReference`. All these interfaces are derived from the `Node` interface (see Figure 2.3 in Chapter 2). Therefore, the basic structural methods, such as accessing and updating parent and child nodes, are defined in the `Node` interface. In this section, we show how the methods defined in `Node` are used and we look at some specific interfaces.

## 4.2.1 Accessing and Updating the Status of a Node

First, we cover the four methods for obtaining and updating information about the node, such as the node type and the node name. In the following explanation, assume that node is a variable pointing to an object of the Node interface or a derived interface.

- node.getNodeType(): Obtains the node type.

  This method returns an integer that represents the type of this node. For example, if the node is an Element, an integer denoted by Node.ELEMENT_NODE is returned.

  If you want to check whether a node is a Text node, be sure to check not only Node.TEXT_NODE but also Node.CDATA_SECTION_NODE. In many cases, CDATASection nodes should be treated as Text nodes. So you should write something like this:

  ```
  if (node.getNodeType() == Node.TEXT_NODE
      || node.getNodeType() == Node.CDATA_SECTION_NODE) {
      :
  }
  ```

  You can use the runtime type identification (RTTI) mechanism, which is instanceof in Java. The following is equivalent to the previous fragment because CDATASection is derived from Text.

  ```
  if (node instanceof Text) {
      :
  }
  ```

- node.getNodeName(): Obtains the name of the node.
  This method returns the name of the node. The name depends on the node type: For Element, it is the tag name; for Attr, it is the attribute name; and so on. Table 4.1 summarizes the getNodeType() and getNodeName() methods.

- node.getNodeValue(): Obtains the value of the node.
  This method returns the value of the node. The value is type-dependent. If the node is an Attr, the value of the attribute is returned, and if it is a Text or a CDATASection, the value is the test string. The value is also defined for ProcessingInstruction and Comment. For other node types, the value is null.

- node.setNodeValue(newValue): Updates the node value.
  This method updates the value defined in getNodeValue().

**Table 4.1**  Summary of `getNodeType()` and `getNodeName()` Methods

| DOM INTERFACE | getNodeType() | getNodeType() |
|---|---|---|
| Element | Node.ELEMENT_NODE | Qualified name of element |
| Attr | Node.ATTRIBUTE_NODE | Qualified name of attribute |
| Text | Node.TEXT_NODE | "#text" |
| CDATASection | Node.CDATA_SECTOIN_NODE | "#cdata-section" |
| EntityReference | Node.ENTITY_REFERENCE_NODE | Entity name |
| Entity | Node.ENTITY_NODE | Entity name |
| ProcessingInstruction | Node.PROCESSING_INSTRUCTION_NODE | PI target |
| Comment | Node.COMMENT_NODE | "#comment" |
| Document | Node.DOCUMENT_NODE | "#document" |
| DocumentType | Node.DOCUMENT_TYPE_NODE | Name of the root element |
| DocumentFragment | Node.DOCUMENT_FRAGMENT_NODE | "#document-fragment" |
| Notation | Node.NOTATION_NODE | Notation name |

## 4.2.2  Accessing Structural Information

Because DOM is tree-structured, any structural information is given by parent-child relationships. The `Node` interface provides a set of methods to access this information:

- `node.getParentNode()`
- `node.hasChildNodes()`
- `node.getFirstChild()`
- `node.getLastChild()`
- `node.getPreviousSibling()`
- `node.getNextSibling()`

Throughout this subsection, we use the following small XML fragment as an example.

```
<name>
    <given>John</given>
    <family>Doe</family>
</name>
```

The `name` element has five children:

- Text node that has "\n    "
- Element node of the name `given`
- Text node that has "\n    "

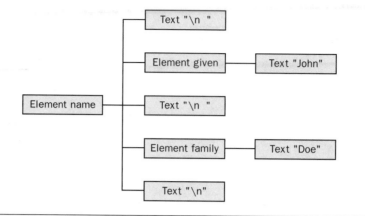

**Figure 4.1** DOM nodes representing the sample fragment

- `Element` node of the name `family`
- `Text` node that has `"\n"`

Note that whitespace for indentation is represented as a `Text` node and `"\n"` represents an end-of-line character. Each of the `given` elements and `family` elements has one `Text` node as its child. See Figure 4.1.

### Obtaining the Parent Node

The `node.getParentNode()` method returns the parent node of this node. If the `name` element is the root element in a document, `getParentNode()` applied to the `name` element returns the `Document` node. Figure 4.2 demonstrates how to use this method.

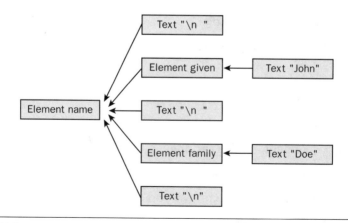

**Figure 4.2** Using `getParentNode()`

### Checking Whether a Node Has One or More Child Nodes

There are several ways to check whether a node has a child:

- `node.hasChildNodes()`
- `node.getFirstChild() != null`
- `node.getLastChild() != null`
- `node.getChildNodes().getLength() > 0`

Any of these work well for this purpose, but we recommend the first one for readability.

### Obtaining the Next and Previous Siblings

You can use the following two methods to go back and forth among child nodes:

- `node.getPreviousSibling()`: Returns the previous sibling
- `node.getNextSibling()`: Returns the next sibling

Figure 4.3 shows how to use these two methods.

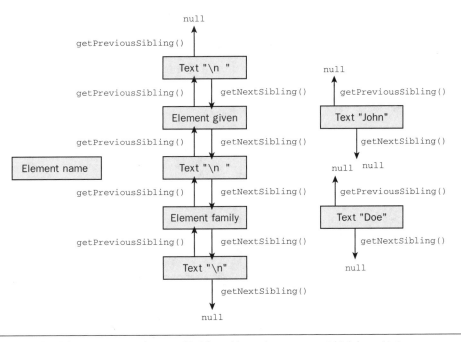

**Figure 4.3** Using `getPreviousSibling()` and `getNextSibling()` to move among siblings

### Processing Children in the Order in Which They Appear

Suppose you want to visit the five children of the name element in the order in which they appear:

1. Text node that has "\n   "
2. Element node of the name given
3. Text node that has "\n   "
4. Element node of the name family
5. Text node that has "\n"

To iterate on the children of a node, you have two choices:

- Use getFirstChild() and getNextSibling()—this is simple and straightforward.

```
for (Node child = node.getFirstChild();
    child != null;
    child = child.getNextSibling()) {
    ...process child
}
```

- Obtain a NodeList, and use an index to access the children.

```
NodeList nodeList = node.getChildNodes();
for (int i = 0;  i < nodeList.getLength();  i++) {
    Node child = nodeList.item(i);
    ...process child
}
```

Figure 4.4 illustrates how this is done.

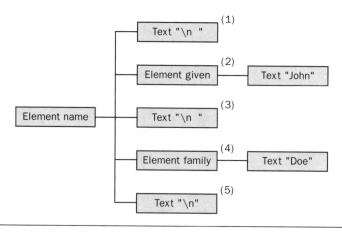

**Figure 4.4** Order of processing children

### Processing Children in Reverse Order

There are two ways to process children in reverse order:

- Use `getLastChild()` and `getPreviousSibling()`

```
for (Node child = node.getLastChild();
    child != null;
    child = child.getPreviousSibling()) {
    ...process child
}
```

- Obtain a `NodeList` by calling `getChildNodes()`, and use `item()` to access each item in the `NodeList`.

```
NodeList nodeList = node.getChildNodes();
for (int i = nodeList.getLength()-1;  i >= 0;  i−) {
    Node child = nodeList.item(i);
    ...process child
}
```

## 4.2.3 Inserting, Detaching, and Replacing a Child Node

We have looked at the ways to examine various parts of a DOM tree. Now we shift our attention to modifying the tree. Structural changes in a DOM tree are always made by inserting, detaching, or replacing a child node. In this section, we cover the following methods:

- `doc.createXXX(...)` (doc is an instance of `Document`)
- `node.insertBefore(newChild, refChild)`
- `node.appendChild(newChild)`
- `node.replaceChild(newChild, refChild)`
- `node.removeChild(oldChild)`

Some types of nodes—`Text`, `CDATASection`, `Comment`, `Notation`, and `ProcessingInstruction`—never have child nodes. Others may have constraints regarding allowed child node types. Violations of these rules generate `DOMExceptions`.

### Creating New Nodes

As described in Chapter 3, we use factory methods such as `createElement()` of the `Document` interface to create a new node.

```
Element newElement = doc.createElement("address");
newElement.appendChild(doc.createTextNode("1234 Orange Ave."));
// We discuss appendChild() later.
```

The `newElement` just created does not belong to a DOM tree rooted by `doc`. The owner of `newElement` is `doc`, and there is no parent of `newElement` because it is not yet appended to any node. Although `newElement.getOwnerDocument()` returns `doc`, `newElement.getParentNode()` returns `null`.

Another way to create a node is to duplicate other nodes.

```
Element newElement2 = newElement.cloneNode(false);
```

This statement creates a shallow copy. The node `newElement2` is a copy of `newElement`, including copies of its attributes, but descendants of `newElement` are not copied. Even if `newElement` is a child of some node, `newElement2` has no parent node.

```
Element newElement2 = newElement.cloneNode(true);
```

This statement performs a deep copy. The node `newElement2` is a copy of `newElement`, with the children of `newElement`. In this case, `newElement2` also has no parent node. Figure 4.5 shows the differences between a shallow copy and a deep copy.

### Inserting a Child Node

To insert a child node, use `node.insertBefore(newChild, refChild)`. It adds `newChild` to `node` as a child before `refChild`, which is a child of `node`. If `refChild` is `null`, `newChild` is added as the last child of `node`. Figure 4.6 illustrates how this is done.

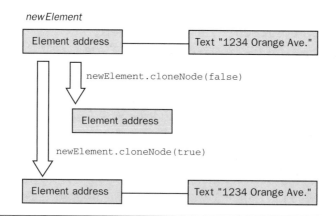

**Figure 4.5**  Behavior of `cloneNode()`

### Adding a Child Node

To add a child node, use `node.appendChild(newChild)` to add `newChild` as the last child of `node`. This is equivalent to `node.insertBefore(newChild, null)` and is illustrated in Figure 4.7.

### Replacing a Child Node

To replace an old child with a new child, use `node.replaceChild(newChild, oldChild)` to replace `oldChild`, which must be a child node of `node`, with `newChild`. The node `oldChild` will be deleted from the DOM tree—that is, `oldChild.getParentNode()` returns `null`. Figure 4.8 demonstrates its use.

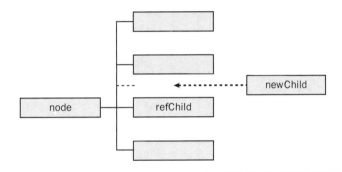

**Figure 4.6** Using `insertBefore()` to insert a new child

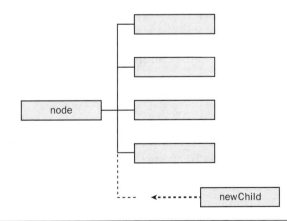

**Figure 4.7** Using `appendChild()` to add a child

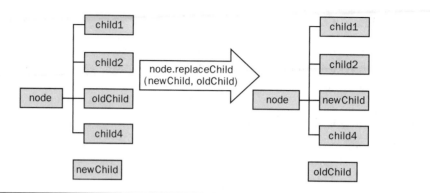

**Figure 4.8** Using `replaceChild()` to replace a child

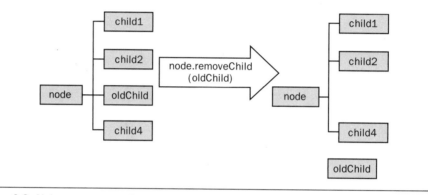

**Figure 4.9** Using `removeChild()` to detach a child

### Detaching a Child Node

Use `node.removeChild(oldChild)` to detach `oldChild`, which must be a child node of `node`, from the children of `node`. See Figure 4.9.

## 4.2.4 DOM Tree and Attributes

An `Element` node may have attributes in addition to child nodes. Attributes can be accessed through the `Attr` interface, which is derived from the `Node` interface. We now discuss how to obtain attribute values or `Attr` nodes.

The following are the attribute-manipulating methods defined as part of the `Element` interface.

- `NamedNodeMap getAttributes()`
- `String getAttribute(String name)`

- `void setAttribute(String name, String value)`
- `void removeAttribute(String name)`
- `Attr getAttributeNode(String name)`
- `void setAttributeNode(Attr newAttr)`
- `void removeAttributeNode(Attr oldAttr)`

To obtain an attribute whose name is already known, use `getAttribute(String name)` or `getAttributeNode(String name)`. The former returns the attribute value string of an attribute of the name `name`, and the latter returns the `Attr` node of the attribute. To obtain a list of all the attributes of an element, use `getAttributes()` as follows.

```
NamedNodeMap map = element.getAttributes();
for (int i = 0;  i < map.getLength();  i++) {
    Attr attr = (Attr)map.item(i);
    ...process attr
}
```

Alternatively, the `NamedNodeMap` interface has the `getNamedItem(String name)` method to get an attribute by its name.

### How to Check Whether an Element Has an Attribute

Observe that we cannot use the `getAttribute()` method of the `Element` interface to check whether an element has an attribute. As an example, suppose that we want to check the existence of an `id` attribute in the `elem` element.

```
String value = elem.getAttribute("id");
```

If the `elem` element has no `id` attribute, `getAttribute("id")` returns `""` (zero-length string) rather than returning `null`. The `getAttribute("id")` also returns `""` if the `id` attribute has a value of `""`. We cannot distinguish between these two cases.

To check the existence of an attribute, use "`elem.getAttributeNode(name) != null`," or "`elem.getAttributes().getNamedItem(name) != null`."

## 4.3  Advanced DOM

By now you should be able to create and manipulate any tree consisting of nodes. We discuss the advanced use and the pitfalls of DOM in this section.

### 4.3.1 How to Simplify Your Code by Removing Entity References

Special attention is needed when an XML document may contain general entity references, such as `&foo;`, which are to be replaced by their definitions. See the example in Table 4.2.

**Table 4.2** A Document without Entity References and a Document with an Entity Reference

| DOCUMENT A | DOCUMENT B |
|---|---|
| ```<root>``` <br> ```  <first>Ichibanme</first>``` <br> ```  <second>Nibanme</second>``` <br> ```</root>``` | ```<!DOCTYPE root [``` <br> ```  <!ENTITY first "<first>Ichibanme</first>">``` <br> ```]>``` <br> ```<root>``` <br> ```  &first;``` <br> ```  <second>Nibanme</second>``` <br> ```</root>``` |

Documents A and B are almost identical. In fact, validity should be checked after the entity reference `&first;` is replaced by its value, `<first>Ichibanme</first>`.

However, because the XML 1.0 Recommendation requires an XML processor to preserve entity references, the DOM trees for A and for B are different, as shown in Figure 4.10.

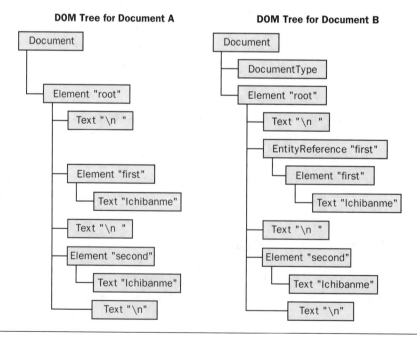

**Figure 4.10** DOM trees for documents A and B

In the DOM tree for document B, an `EntityReference` node is inserted where an entity reference appeared in the XML document. Therefore, if you do not take into account the possibility of entity references, you might miss elements. For instance, do not assume, when coding your program, that *the first element in the children of the* `root` *element must be a* `first` element because it is specified in the content model of the `root` element. *The first child element is a* `second` element in the case of document B.

If your application does not need information about whether entity references are used, you can simplify your code by avoiding `EntityReference` nodes. Then, with Xerces, you can turn off `EntityReference` creation with the following code.

```
DOMParser parser = new DOMParser();
parser.setFeature("http://apache.org/xml/features/dom/create-entity-
ref-nodes", false);
parser.parse(...);
Document doc = parser.getDocument();
// doc contains no EntityReference nodes.
```

With JAXP, you have to do nothing, because JAXP does not create `Entity Reference` nodes in parsing by default.

### 4.3.2 Tree Traversal

You might want to visit all the descendant nodes of a given node. A code fragment for such a visit is shown here.

```
public void processNodeRecursively(Node node) {
    ...process node
    for (Node child = node.getFirstChild();
            child != null;
            child = child.getNextSibling()) {
        processNodeRecursively(child);
    }
}
```

Starting at the `name` element in Figure 4.11, the code visits the nodes in this order:

1. `Element` node of the name `name`
2. `Text` node that has `"\n   "`
3. `Element` node of the name `given`
4. `Text` node that has `"John"`
5. `Text` node that has `"\n   "`
6. `Element` node of the name `family`

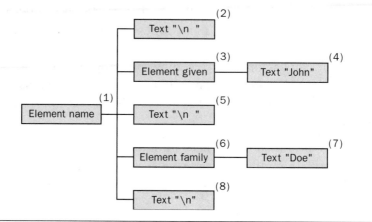

**Figure 4.11** Processing descendants

7. Text node that has `"Doe"`

8. Text node that has `"\n"`

The code uses only the methods described in Section 4.2. However, DOM Level 2, issued in November 2000, introduced new interfaces for traversing a tree. They are `NodeIterator`, `TreeWalker`, `NodeFilter`, and `DocumentTraversal`. The following code fragment behaves the same as the previous code fragment using recursion.

```
DocumentTraversal trav;
NodeIterator iter;
Node child;
trav = (DocumentTraversal)node.getOwnerDocument();
iterator = trav.createNodeIterator(node,
                                   NodeFilter.SHOW_ALL,
                                   null,
                                   false);
while ((child = iterator.nextNode()) != null) {
    ...process child
}
iterator.detach();
```

The advantages of these DOM Level 2 interfaces are:

- You can specify the node type that you are interested in before starting the loop.
- You can change the direction of traversal anytime.

Note that Crimson, the default parser of JAXP 1.1, does not have implementations of DOM traversal as of now. Xerces does have them.

### 4.3.3 DOM Collection Is Live

Given a node, how do we remove all its child nodes? You might think it is easy, but it is not.

Suppose you write the following code to remove all children of a node.

```
for (Node child = node.getFirstChild();
        child != null;
        child = child.getNextSibling()) {
    node.removeChild(child);
}
```

This looks like a straightforward implementation, but unfortunately, it does not work properly. It simply removes the first child of the node and exits the loop. Here is how it works—or more precisely, how it does not work.

1. In the initialization of the `for` loop, the first child of the node is assigned to `child` (if there are no children, this value is `null`).

2. The expression `child != null` is `true`, so this check passes and the body of the loop is executed.

3. The statement `node.removeChild(child)` removes the first child from node. As soon as the child is removed, its internal variables are updated and `child.getParentNode()`, `child.getPreviousSibling()`, and `getNextSibling()` all now return `null`.

4. In the third component of `for` (that is, `child = child.getNextSibling()`), `child` is set to `null` and the loop terminates.

Even if you use `getChildNodes()` and `NodeList` instead of `getNextSibling()`, as shown next, it still does not work. This is because `getChildNodes()` returns not the "snapshot" of the child nodes but a "live" data structure that will be updated immediately whenever any changes are made on the node from which it was created.

```
NodeList nodeList = node.getChildNodes();
for (int i = 0; i < nodeList.getLength(); i++) {
    node.removeChild(nodeList.item(i));
}
```

Thus, this code fails to remove the second child, fourth child, and so forth.

To remove all children properly, you can use either of the following code fragments. Both implement the strategy of "remove the first child node until there are no more child nodes."

```
while (node.hasChildNodes()) {
    node.removeChild(node.getFirstChild());
}
```

```
NodeList nodeList = node.getChildNodes();
while (nodeList.getLength() > 0) {
    node.removeChild(nodeList.item(0));
}
```

## 4.3.4 Moving Nodes over Documents

Each DOM node is *owned* by a `Document` node that created the node. We can use the `getOwnerDocument()` method of the `Node` interface to obtain the owner `Document` node. The `getOwnerDocument()` method for a `Document` node always returns `null`.

You cannot insert a DOM node into a document other than its owner. The following code throws a `DOMException`.

```
DOMParser parser = new DOMParser();
parser.parse(...);
Document doc1 = parser.getDocument();
parser.parse(...);
Document doc2 = parser.getDocument();

doc1.getDocumentElement().appendChild(doc2.getDocumentElement());
// DOMException is thrown at the above line.
```

To move nodes across the document boundary, use `doc.importNode(Node src, boolean deep)` of the `Document` interface. The `importNode()` method is a kind of factory method. It duplicates the specified `src` node (and its descendants if `deep` parameter is `true`) belonging to another document, for the `doc` document.

The following is a sample using `importNode()`.

```
DOMParser parser = new DOMParser();
parser.parse(...);
Document doc1 = parser.getDocument();
parser.parse(...);
Document doc2 = parser.getDocument();

Element root2 = doc2.getDocumentElement();
Node roo2forDoc1 = doc1.importNode(root2, true);
doc.getDocumentElement().appendChild(root2forDoc1);
```

In this case, `doc2` is not modified at all.

## 4.3.5 Namespaces in DOM

Some APIs in the previous sections are insufficient for processing documents using namespaces. Element names and attribute names in these APIs are actually treated as qualified names. The prefix in a qualified name is a placeholder for the namespace URI. Applications should use such URIs rather than prefixes.

DOM Level 2 introduces namespace-aware methods. They are named *xxx*NS(). Almost all methods take a namespace URI and a local name as parameters, though factory methods take a namespace URI and a qualified name.

`Element` nodes and `Attr` nodes created by namespace-aware methods support `getNamespaceURI()`, `getLocalName()`, `getPrefix()`, and `setPrefix()`. These methods for nodes created by namespace-unaware methods always return `null`.

If you parse a document and create a DOM tree by using the JAXP API, the resultant DOM tree is not namespace-aware by default. You can enable the namespace feature as follows:

```
DocumentBuilderFactory factory = DocumentBuilderFactory.
    newInstance();
factory.setNamespaceAware(true);
DocumentBuilder builder = factory.newDocumentBuilder();
builder.parse(...);
```

On the other hand, the Xerces native API creates a namespace-aware DOM tree by default. If you want to turn it off, call `setFeature()` like this:

```
DOMParser parser = new DOMParser();
parser.setFeature("http://xml.org/sax/features/namespaces", false);
parser.parse(...);
Document doc = parser.getDocument());
```

Next, we discuss two important points of namespace processing in DOM.

### DOM Creates No Namespace Declarations Automatically

For example:

```
Element elem = doc.createElementNS("urn:x-foo", "foo:root");
```

This code creates an element whose namespace URI is urn:x-foo and prefix is foo. But a namespace declaration like xmlns:foo="urn:x-foo" is not created automatically. If you need it, you have to add it by providing code similar to the following.

```
elem.setAttributeNS("http://www.w3.org/2000/xmlns/",
                    "xmlns:"+elem.getPrefix(),
                    elem.getNamespaceURI());
```

According to the "Namespaces in XML" specification, xmlns in a namespace dec-laration is not a prefix, and it has no corresponding namespace URI. In DOM, it is treated as a prefix and has a namespace URI, which is http://www.w3.org/2000/xmlns/.

### Adding Namespace Declarations Does Not Affect Other Nodes

You cannot modify the local name and the namespace URI of a node after creating the node. Take a look at the same example as in the last section.

```
Element elem = doc.createElementNS("urn:x-foo", "foo:root");
```

The local name of this elem element is root, and the namespace URI is urn:x-foo. Now we add a namespace declaration, xmlns:foo="urn:x-bar".

```
elem.setAttributeNS("http://www.w3.org/2000/xmlns/",
                    "xmlns:foo", "urn:x-bar");
```

In this operation, it seems as if we had the following fragment. Suppose that an ancestor element of elem already had a namespace declaration for the prefix foo.

```
<... xmlns:foo="urn:x-foo">
   <foo:root/>
</...>
```

We add a namespace declaration to the foo:root element.

```
<... xmlns:foo="urn:x-foo">
   <foo:root xmlns:foo="urn:x-bar"/>
</...>
```

In this lexical view, the namespace URI of foo:root should be changed to urn:x-bar. However, elem.getNamespaceURI() still returns urn:x-foo. You cannot change the namespace URI of a node by editing namespace declara-tions in DOM.

Unlike the local name and namespace URI, the prefix of a node is changeable with the setPrefix(newPrefix) method. Note that you have to add a namespace declaration for the new prefix when you change the prefix.

As described earlier, we can create incomplete DOM trees, such as those lack-ing the required namespace declarations or having inconsistent namespace declarations.

The program in Listing 4.1, NamespaceCorrector.java, is a utility class for these namespace problems. This class adds missing namespace declarations to the specified DOM tree; it also checks namespace inconsistencies and throws a DOMException if the DOM tree has inconsistencies.

**Listing 4.1** Utility to correct namespace problems, `chap04/NamespaceCorrector.`
`java`

```java
package chap04;

import org.w3c.dom.Attr;
import org.w3c.dom.DOMException;
import org.w3c.dom.Document;
import org.w3c.dom.Element;
import org.w3c.dom.Node;
import org.w3c.dom.NamedNodeMap;

/**
 * Add required namespace declarations.
 */
public class NamespaceCorrector {
    private static final String XMLNS_NS
        = "http://www.w3.org/2000/xmlns/";

    private NamespaceCorrector() {
    }

    /**
     * @param node The top node of target nodes
     */
    public static void correct(Node node) {
        switch (node.getNodeType()) {
        case Node.ELEMENT_NODE:
            correctElement((Element)node);
                            // Fall down
        case Node.DOCUMENT_NODE:
        case Node.DOCUMENT_FRAGMENT_NODE:
        case Node.ENTITY_REFERENCE_NODE:
            for (Node ch = node.getFirstChild();
                ch != null;
                ch = ch.getNextSibling()) {
                correct(ch);
            }
            break;
        }
    }

    /**
     * Check whether the prefixes and the namespaces of el and
     * its attributes are declared or not.
     * if not, add a namespace declaration to el.
     */
```

```java
private static void correctElement(Element el) {
    // Check el.
    String prefix = el.getPrefix();
    String current = el.getNamespaceURI();
    String declared = howDeclared(el, prefix);
    if (prefix == null) {
        if (current == null && declared == null) {
            // ok
        } else if (current == null || declared == null) {
            set(el, prefix, current == null ? "" : current);
        } else if (!current.equals(declared)) {
            set(el, prefix, current);
        }
    } else {
        if (current == null)
            throw new DOMException(DOMException.NAMESPACE_ERR,
                                   el.getNodeName()
                                   +" has no namespace");
        if (declared == null || !current.equals(declared))
            set(el, prefix, current);
    }

    // Check attributes of el.
    NamedNodeMap map = el.getAttributes();
    for (int i = 0;  i < map.getLength();  i++) {
        Attr attr = (Attr)map.item(i);
        prefix = attr.getPrefix();
        if (prefix == null || prefix.equals("xml")
            || prefix.equals("xmlns"))
            continue;
        current = attr.getNamespaceURI();
        declared = howDeclared(el, prefix);
        if (declared == null || !current.equals(declared)) {
            set(el, prefix, current);
            i = -1;            // map has changed.
                               // So restart the loop.
        }
    }
}

private static void set(Element el, String prefix, String ns) {
    String qname = prefix == null ? "xmlns" : "xmlns:"+prefix;

    if (el.getAttributeNode(qname) != null)
        throw new DOMException(DOMException.NAMESPACE_ERR,
                               "Namespace inconsistence");
```

```
                    el.setAttributeNS(XMLNS_NS, qname, ns);
        }

        /**
         * Search <var>context</var> and ancestors for declaration
         * of prefix.
         * @param prefix Prefix, or <code>null</code> for default ns.
         */
        private static String howDeclared(Element context,
                                          String prefix) {
            String qname = prefix == null ? "xmlns" : "xmlns:"+prefix;

            for (Node node = context; node != null;
                 node = node.getParentNode()) {
                if (node.getNodeType() == Node.ELEMENT_NODE) {
                    Attr attr = ((Element)node).getAttributeNode(qname);
                    if (attr != null) {
                        if (prefix == null &&
                                attr.getNodeValue().equals(""))
                            return null;
                        else
                            return attr.getNodeValue();
                    }
                }
            }
            return null;
        }
    }
```

The `correctElement()` method is the core of the program. Given an element, it searches ancestor elements containing the namespace declarations that are used for the given element and its attributes. If ancestors have no matching declaration, it checks the consistency of the declarations and adds `Attr` nodes representing the missing namespace declarations.

Listing 4.2 shows how `NamespaceCorrector` adds declarations correctly and checks namespace inconsistency.

**Listing 4.2**  An example to show how `NamespaceCorrector` works, `chap04/NCTest.java`

```
    package chap04;

    import javax.xml.parsers.DocumentBuilder;
    import javax.xml.parsers.DocumentBuilderFactory;
    import org.apache.xml.serialize.OutputFormat;
    import org.apache.xml.serialize.XMLSerializer;
```

```java
import org.w3c.dom.Document;
import org.w3c.dom.Element;

public class NCTest {
    static final String NS0 = "http://example.com/@";
    static final String NS1 = "http://example.com/a";
    static final String XML_NS =
            "http://www.w3.org/XML/1998/namespace";
    static final String XMLNS_NS = "http://www.w3.org/2000/xmlns/";

    public static void main(String[] argv) throws Exception {
        DocumentBuilderFactory dbfactory
                = DocumentBuilderFactory.newInstance();
        dbfactory.setNamespaceAware(true);
        DocumentBuilder builder = dbfactory.newDocumentBuilder();
        Document factory = builder.newDocument();
        OutputFormat format
                = new OutputFormat("xml", "UTF-8", true);
        XMLSerializer serializer
                = new XMLSerializer(System.out, format);

        Element top = factory.createElementNS(null, "Address");
        top.setAttributeNS(XMLNS_NS, "xmlns:p", NS0);

        // Add an element that has the namespace and no prefix.
        Element el1 = factory.createElementNS(NS1, "Zip");
        // el1 has an attribute of which namespace is
        // the same as el1.
        el1.setAttributeNS(NS1, "p:id", "");
        el1.appendChild(factory.createElementNS(null, "Zip2"));
        top.appendChild(el1);

        // Add an element that has the namespace and prefix.
        Element el2 = factory.createElementNS(NS1, "p:State");
        // el2 has an attribute. It has the same prefix
        // and the same NS.
        el1.setAttributeNS(NS1, "p:id", "");
        el2.setAttributeNS(XML_NS, "xml:lang", "en");
        top.appendChild(el2);

        Element el3 = factory.createElementNS(NS0, "p:City");
        top.appendChild(el3);

        // Prints the tree before correction.
        serializer.serialize(top);
        System.out.println("");
```

```
            // Correct
            NamespaceCorrector.correct(top);
            // Prints the tree after correction.
            serializer.reset();
            serializer.serialize(top);
            System.out.println("");

            // Another test:
            // p:Country and p:iso2 have the same prefix but
            // different namespaces.
            Element el4 = factory.createElementNS(NS0, "p:Country");
            el4.setAttributeNS(NS1, "p:iso2", "ja");
            // This should throw an exception.
            NamespaceCorrector.correct(el4);
        }
    }
```

First, this program builds a DOM tree that lacks some required namespace declarations, and serializes it to the console. The serialized XML document is broken. Then, NamespaceCorrector fixes the DOM tree and serializes it again. We can see the correct XML document on the console.

Finally, the program tests the behavior for namespace inconsistencies in the DOM tree. In this case, NamespaceCorrector detects inconsistencies such as an element and its attribute having the same prefix but different namespace URIs.

In Listing 4.2, the element el4 has the prefix "p" and the namespace NS0, and its attribute p:iso2 has the same prefix "p" and a different namespace, NS1. In this case, we cannot correct the DOM tree by adding namespace declarations. So NamespaceCorrector throws a DOMException.

```
R:\samples>java chap04.NCTest
<?xml version="1.0" encoding="UTF-8"?>
<Address xmlns:p="http://example.com/@">
   <Zip p:id="">
      <Zip2/>
   </Zip>
   <p:State xml:lang="en"/>
   <p:City/>
</Address>

<?xml version="1.0" encoding="UTF-8"?>
<Address xmlns:p="http://example.com/@">
   <Zip p:id="" xmlns="http://example.com/a"
xmlns:p="http://example.com/a">
      <Zip2 xmlns=""/>
```

```
      </Zip>
      <p:State xml:lang="en" xmlns:p="http://example.com/a"/>
      <p:City/>
</Address>

Exception in thread "main" org.w3c.dom.DOMException: Namespace
inconsistence
        at java.lang.Throwable.<init>(Throwable.java:96)
        at java.lang.Exception.<init>(Exception.java:44)
        at java.lang.RuntimeException.<init>(RuntimeException.java:49)
        at org.w3c.dom.DOMException.<init>(DOMException.java:34)
        at chap04.NamespaceCorrector.set(NamespaceCorrector.java:89)
        at
chap04.NamespaceCorrector.correctElement(NamespaceCorrector.java:78)
        at
chap04.NamespaceCorrector.correct(NamespaceCorrector.java:26)
        at chap04.NCTest.main(NCTest.java:67)
```

In this example, we could have changed the prefixes of the elements and attributes. However, `NamespaceCorrector` does not change the prefixes because such changes might cause other problems. If a changed prefix were used in attribute values or character data, we would have another problem.

## 4.4 Summary

In this chapter, we explained in detail the use of the `Node` interface, the most important interface for dealing with a DOM structure, and we showed several ways to use it. We also discussed some specific techniques of DOM.

> **Note:** W3C is working on DOM Level 3, which will define new schema access interfaces and load/save interfaces. With DOM Level 3, we will be able to refer to and modify schema information and achieve parser-independent parsing and generation.

# Working with SAX

## 5.1 Introduction

Unlike DOM, the SAX specification is not authorized by W3C. SAX was developed through the xml-dev mailing list, the largest community of XML-related developers. The development of SAX was finished in May 1998. SAX 2.0, which introduced namespace support and the feature/property mechanism, was completed in May 2000.

As described in Chapter 2, SAX is an event-based parsing API. Its methods and data structures are much simpler than those of DOM. This simplicity implies that application programs based on SAX are required to do more work than those based on DOM. On the other hand, SAX-based programs can often achieve high performance.

In this chapter, we describe some tips for using SAX. Then we compare DOM and SAX, and introduce sample programs using DOM and SAX.

## 5.2 Basic Tips for Using SAX

In Chapter 2, Sections 2.4 (see Figure 2.2) and 2.4.2 describe the basic concepts of SAX and the programming model for SAX. The concept of SAX is simple. A SAX parser reads an XML document from the beginning, and the parser tells an application what it finds by using the callback methods of `ContentHandler` or other interfaces.

However, there are some things you should know. We discuss them in this section.

### 5.2.1 ContentHandler

In this section, we discuss a major trap for beginning users of SAX and the parser feature mechanism, an important feature introduced in SAX2.

### Trap of the `characters()` Events

The `characters()` method of `ContentHandler` confuses SAX beginners. Consider the following document:

```
<root>
    Hello,
    XML &#x26; Java!
</root>
```

A programmer might expect the parsing of this document to throw five events:

- `startDocument()`
- `startElement()` for the `root` element
- `characters()`: "\n Hello,\n XML & Java!\n"
- `endElement()` for the `root` element
- `endDocument()`

Actually, the SAX parser of Xerces produces three `characters()` events between `startElement()` and `endElement()`. They are:

- `characters()`: "\n Hello,\n XML "
- `characters()`: "&"
- `characters()`: " Java!\n"

The SAX parser of Crimson produces eight `characters()` events:

- `characters()`: ""
- `characters()`: "\n"
- `characters()`: " Hello,"
- `characters()`: "\n"
- `characters()`: " XML "
- `characters()`: "&"
- `characters()`: " Java!"
- `characters()`: "\n"

These behaviors are not bugs in these parsers. The SAX specification allows splitting a text segment into several events. So take care when you write an application that processes character data.

Listing 5.1 is a program that checks whether the text in an element matches a given string. The program shows a way to solve the problem of split `characters()` events.

**Listing 5.1** A correct way to process text, chap05/TextMatch.java

```java
package chap05;

import java.io.IOException;
import java.util.Stack;
import org.xml.sax.Attributes;
import org.xml.sax.SAXException;
import org.xml.sax.XMLReader;
import org.xml.sax.helpers.DefaultHandler;
import org.xml.sax.helpers.XMLReaderFactory;

public class TextMatch extends DefaultHandler {
    StringBuffer buffer;
    String pattern;
    Stack context;

    public TextMatch(String pattern) {
        this.buffer = new StringBuffer();
        this.pattern = pattern;
        this.context = new Stack();
    }

    protected void flushText() {
        if (this.buffer.length() > 0) {
            String text = new String(this.buffer);
            if (pattern.equals(text)) {
                System.out.print("Pattern '"+this.pattern
                            +"' has been found around ");
                for (int i = 0; i < this.context.size();  i++) {
                    System.out.print("/"+this.context.elementAt(i));
                }
                System.out.println("");
            }
        }
        this.buffer.setLength(0);
    }

    public void characters(char[] ch, int start, int len)
        throws SAXException {
        this.buffer.append(ch, start, len);
    }
    public void ignorableWhitespace(char[] ch, int start, int len)
        throws SAXException {
        this.buffer.append(ch, start, len);
    }
    public void processingInstruction(String target, String data)
        throws SAXException {
```

```
            // Nothing to do because PI does not affect the meaning
            // of a document.
        }
        public void startElement(String uri, String local,
                                 String qname, Attributes atts)
            throws SAXException {
            this.flushText();
            this.context.push(local);
        }
        public void endElement(String uri, String local, String qname)
            throws SAXException {
            this.flushText();
            this.context.pop();
        }

        public static void main(String[] argv) {
            if (argv.length != 2) {
                System.out.println("TextMatch <pattern> <document>");
                System.exit(1);
            }
            try {
                XMLReader xreader = XMLReaderFactory.createXMLReader(
                        "org.apache.xerces.parsers.SAXParser");
                xreader.setContentHandler(new TextMatch(argv[0]));
                xreader.parse(argv[1]);
            } catch (IOException ioe) {
                ioe.printStackTrace();
            } catch (SAXException se) {
                se.printStackTrace();
            }
        }
    }
}
```

This program assumes that the start tags and end tags split the text and that the comments and processing instructions do not. Character data is saved to a buffer in the `characters()` method, and a matching process against the buffer is invoked in tag events.

Let's run `TextMatch` against the XML document shown in Listing 5.2.

**Listing 5.2** A sample document for `TextMatch`, chap05/match.xml

```
<?xml version="1.0" encoding="us-ascii"?>
<root>
    <movie>A 3x3 Matri<X/movie>
    <book>XM<!-- -->L &#x26; Jav<?target?>a</book>
</root>
```

```
R:\samples>java chap05.TextMatch "XML & Java" file:./chap05/match.xml
Pattern 'XML & Java' has been found around {}root/{}book
```

TextMatch finds "XML & Java" in the book element, the character data of which is split by a comment, an entity reference, and a processing instruction.

### Parser Features

The SAX2 specification defines two standard features: namespace and namespace-prefix. The default feature settings of SAX2-compliant parsers are as follows.

- Namespace feature, `http://xml.org/sax/features/namespaces`, is `true`.
- Namespace-prefix feature, `http://xml.org/sax/features/namespace-prefixes`, is `false`.

The default settings have these meanings.

- The parser provides information about namespace URIs and local names via `ContentHandler.startElement()`, `ContentHandler.endElement()`, `Attributes.getURI()`, and `Attributes.getLocalName()`.
- `ContentHandler.startPrefixMapping()` and `ContentHandler.endPrefixMapping()` are called when elements declaring namespaces are visited and left, respectively.
- An `Attributes` instance contains no namespace declarations.
- The availability of qualified names is implementation-dependent.

If the namespace feature is turned off, the availability of namespace URIs and local names is implementation-dependent, `start/endPrefixMapping()` are not called, and an `Attributes` instance contains namespace declarations.

If the namespace-prefix feature is turned on, qualified names are available, and an `Attributes` instance contains namespace declarations.

Table 5.1 shows a summary of these features.

**Table 5.1**  SAX Features

| NAMESPACE FEATURE | NAMESPACE-PREFIX FEATURE | NS URI/ LOCAL NAME | QUALIFIED NAME | CALLS *PrefixMapping() | NS DECLS IN Attributes |
|---|---|---|---|---|---|
| true | false | X | - | X | - |
| true | true | X | X | X | X |
| false | false | - | - | - | X |
| false | true | - | X | - | X |

Basically, you need not disable the namespace feature. Turn it off only when the slight overhead of this feature is unacceptable. Turn on the namespace-prefix feature if you need qualified names or namespace declarations as attributes.

According to the JAXP specification, a SAX parser created by `SAXParserFactory` is not namespace-aware by default. In the JAXP implementation of Xerces, `SAXParserFactory.setNamespaceAware()` affects the setting of the namespace feature. As for Crimson in the JAXP 1.1 reference implementation, `SAXParserFactory.setNamespaceAware()` seems to affect neither the namespace feature nor the namespace-prefix feature. We recommend that you always get an `XMLReader` instance by using `SAXParser.getXMLReader()` and that you set these features explicitly.

## 5.2.2 Using and Writing SAX Filters

A **SAX filter** receives SAX events from a SAX parser, modifies these events, and forwards them to a handler, as shown in Figure 5.1. As far as the SAX parser is concerned, the SAX filter can be seen as a handler. On the other hand, as far the handler is concerned, the SAX filter can be seen as a SAX parser.

The SAX2 specification provides the `XMLFilter` interface for SAX filters. This interface is derived from `XMLReader`, the interface for SAX parsers.

Typical uses of SAX filters are the following.

*Modifying XML documents*

When you write a program for modifying XML documents, you might want to reuse `XMLSerializer` for serializing SAX events to an XML document. Then you only have to write a SAX filter that modifies SAX events, and insert the filter between a SAX parser and `XMLSerializer`.

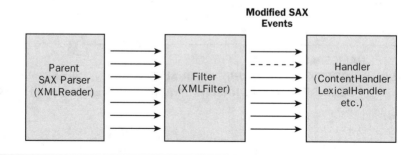

**Figure 5.1** SAX filter

*Convenience for the next handler*

You can simplify handlers for complicated tasks by creating preprocessing SAX filters. For example, suppose that you want to write a SAX handler that supports both `<book title="foobar">...</book>` and `<book><title>foobar </title>...</book>`. The SAX handler becomes simpler if you write a filter for canonicalizing events to one of the two formats. Another example is the `characters()` trap discussed in Section 5.2.1. You can avoid the trap by implementing a SAX filter that concatenates consecutive `characters()` events.

*Control of event flow*

Suppose that you want to use two handlers for a single XML document at the same time. Unfortunately, you cannot register two or more handlers of the same type to one `XMLReader` instance. So you implement a handler as a SAX filter (see Figure 5.2), or you make a filter that accepts the registration of two handlers and duplicates the input events (see Figure 5.3.)

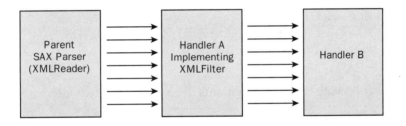

**Figure 5.2** A handler performs as a filter.

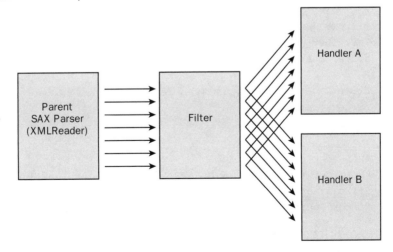

**Figure 5.3** A filter duplicates events.

## Using Filters

A typical code fragment for using a SAX parser follows.

```
XMLReader parser = XMLReaderFactory.createXMLReader();
// or parser = new SAXParser() if you use Xerces.
parser.setContentHandler(handler);
parser.parse(...);
```

If you want a filter between the parser and the handler, modify this code fragment to this:

```
XMLReader parser = ...
XMLFilter filter = new SomethingFilter();
filter.setParent(parser);
filter.setContentHandler(handler);
filter.parse(...);
```

or to this:

```
// If the constructor for the filter takes a parent
//(parser or filter) as a parameter.
XMLReader parser = ...
XMLReader filter = new SomethingFilter(parser);
filter.setContentHandler(handler);
filter.parse(...);
```

The following two code fragments use a parser and two filters.

First fragment:

```
XMLReader parser = ...
XMLFilter filter1 = new SomethingFilter();
filter1.setParent(parser);
XMLFilter filter2 = new OtherFilter();
filter2.setParent(filter1);

filter2.setContentHandler(handler);
filter2.parse(...);
```

Second fragment:

```
XMLReader parser = ...
XMLReader filter2 = new OtherFilter(new SomethingFilter(parser));
filter2.setContentHandler(handler);
filter2.parse(...);
```

These code fragments make an event chain, as shown in Figure 5.4.

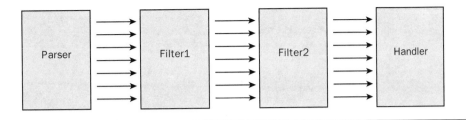

**Figure 5.4**  A parser, two filters, and a handler

## Writing Filters

The XMLFilter interface is derived from the XMLReader interface by adding getParent() and setParent(). The XMLFilter is merely an interface definition, and it does not help us to implement a filter. As a base class for implementing filters, SAX provides the XMLFilterImpl class.

As demonstrated earlier, if a filter constructor takes an XMLReader as an argument, the application code becomes simpler.

Listing 5.3 is an example of a SAX filter. It replaces elements like <email>foo@ example.com</email> with <uri>mailto:foo@example.com</uri>.

**Listing 5.3**  An example of a SAX filter, chap05/MailFilter.java

```java
package chap05;

import org.apache.xerces.parsers.SAXParser;
import org.apache.xml.serialize.OutputFormat;
import org.apache.xml.serialize.XMLSerializer;
import org.xml.sax.Attributes;
import org.xml.sax.ContentHandler;
import org.xml.sax.SAXException;
import org.xml.sax.XMLReader;
import org.xml.sax.helpers.AttributesImpl;
import org.xml.sax.helpers.XMLFilterImpl;
import org.xml.sax.helpers.XMLReaderFactory;

/**
 * <email>foo@bar.test</email>
 *    -> <uri>mailto:foo@bar.test</uri>
 */
public class MailFilter extends XMLFilterImpl {

    public MailFilter(XMLReader parent) {
        super(parent);
    }
```

```java
/**
 * Replace `email' with `uri',
 * and make a characters event for "mailto:".
 */
public void startElement(String uri, String local, String qname,
                         Attributes atts)
    throws SAXException {
    ContentHandler ch = this.getContentHandler();
    if (ch == null)
        return;
    if (uri.length() == 0 && local.equals("email")) {
        ch.startElement("", "uri", "uri", atts);
        String mailto = "mailto:";
        ch.characters(mailto.toCharArray(), 0, mailto.length());
    } else
        ch.startElement(uri, local, qname, atts);
}

/**
 * Replace `email' with `uri'.
 */
public void endElement(String uri, String local, String qname)
    throws SAXException {
    ContentHandler ch = this.getContentHandler();
    if (ch == null)
        return;
    if (uri.length() == 0 && local.equals("email")) {
        ch.endElement("", "uri", "uri");
    } else
        ch.endElement(uri, local, qname);
}

public static void main(String[] argv) throws Exception {
    OutputFormat format
            = new OutputFormat("xml", "UTF-8", false);
    format.setPreserveSpace(true);
    ContentHandler handler = new XMLSerializer(System.out, format);

    XMLReader parser = XMLReaderFactory.createXMLReader(
            "org.apache.xerces.parsers.SAXParser");
    XMLReader filter = new MailFilter(parser);
    filter.setContentHandler(handler);
    filter.parse(argv[0]);

    System.out.println("");
}
}
```

In the overriding methods of your filter, remember to forward (modified) SAX events to the appropriate methods of the registered handler. Note that get*Xxx*Handler() methods may return null. So you have to check whether the next handler is null before calling it.

To see how this program works, type the following:

```
R:\samples>type chap05\addresses.xml
<?xml version="1.0" encoding="us-ascii"?>
<addresses>
    <email>John.Doe@bar.test</email>
    <email>George.Smith@bar.test</email>
    <email>Anna.Millers@bar.test</email>
</addresses>

R:\samples> java chap05.MailFilter file:./chap05/addresses.xml
<?xml version="1.0" encoding="UTF-8"?>
<addresses>
    <uri>mailto:John.Doe@bar.test</uri>
    <uri>mailto:George.Smith@bar.test</uri>
    <uri>mailto:Anna.Millers@bar.test</uri>
</addresses>
```

## 5.2.3  New Features of SAX2

In this section, we summarize the new features of SAX2 for developers who have experience with SAX1.

### Namespace support

SAX1 was finalized before the "Namespace in XML" specification became a W3C Recommendation. So SAX1 has no namespace support. With SAX2, applications can receive namespace information as described in Section 5.2.1.

### SAX filters

SAX1 has no interface for filters, though we can write filters without such an interface. SAX2 introduced a standard XMLFilter interface. It makes writing and using filters easier.

### More information about an XML document

With SAX1, applications can know nothing about comments, CDATA sections, and many types of declarations in DTDs. SAX2 supports them with new interfaces.

*Feature/property mechanism*

SAX2 provides a generic mechanism to enable or disable the features of SAX parsers and to set or get extra information about SAX parsers.

*Name changes to classes and interfaces*

Some interfaces of SAX1 were made obsolete by SAX2. We recommend using the SAX2 interfaces even if you don't need the new features of SAX. Table 5.2 summarizes the name changes.

**Table 5.2** Interface Changes between SAX1 and SAX2

| SAX1 | SAX2 | CHANGES |
|------|------|---------|
| Parser | XMLReader | Support of new interfaces |
| ParserFactory | XMLReaderFactory | Support of new interfaces |
| DocumentHandler | ContentHandler | Support of namespace |
| HandlerBase | DefaultHandler | Support of new interfaces |
| AttributeList | Attributes | Support of namespace |
| AttributeListImpl | AttributesImpl | Support of new interfaces |
| N/A | DeclHandler | Receive declarations in DTDs |
| N/A | LexicalHandler | Receive lexical information such as comments and CDATA sections |
| N/A | XMLFilter | New filter interface |

# 5.3 DOM versus SAX

We discussed the basic concepts of DOM and tips for using DOM in Chapter 4 and discussed those of SAX in the previous section. In Section 2.4.3, we discussed points for deciding whether to use DOM or SAX. In this section, we compare the performance of DOM and SAX and study the conversion of DOM from and to SAX.

## 5.3.1 Performance: Memory and Speed

In this section, we compare the performance of DOM and SAX based on memory usage and on parsing speed.

### Memory Usage

First, we compare the memory usage of DOM and SAX. We can guess that SAX uses less memory than DOM.

We use the XML document shown in Listing 5.4. Its size is 348 bytes.

**Listing 5.4**  A sample document to test memory usage, `chap05/memtest10.xml`

```
<?xml version="1.0" encoding="us-ascii"?>
<root>
<child>Hello, XML! 1</child>
<child>Hello, XML! 2</child>
<child>Hello, XML! 3</child>
<child>Hello, XML! 4</child>
<child>Hello, XML! 5</child>
<child>Hello, XML! 6</child>
<child>Hello, XML! 7</child>
<child>Hello, XML! 8</child>
<child>Hello, XML! 9</child>
<child>Hello, XML! 10</child>
</root>
```

Listing 5.5 parses a given XML document ten times with a SAX parser and prints the memory usage for each iteration.

**Listing 5.5**  Print memory usage for SAX parsing, `chap05/MemoryUsageSAX.java`

```
package chap05;

import org.apache.xerces.parsers.SAXParser;

public class MemoryUsageSAX {
    static void printMemory() {
        System.gc();
        Runtime rt = Runtime.getRuntime();
        System.out.print(rt.totalMemory()-rt.freeMemory());
    }
    public static void main(String[] argv) throws Exception {
        String xml = argv[0];
        printMemory();
        System.out.println("");

        final int N = 10;
        SAXParser saxp = new SAXParser();
        printMemory();
        for (int i = 0; i < N; i++) {
            System.out.print(",");
            saxp.parse(xml);
            printMemory();
        }
        System.out.println("");
    }
}
```

```
R:\samples>java chap05.MemoryUsageSAX file:./chap05/memtest10.xml
104792,152912,208360,207712,247704,207712,247704,207712,247704,207712,
247704,207712
```

A SAX parser creates events and throws them to a handler. If the handler does nothing or there are no handlers, nothing is stored in memory. The result just shown confirms this observation. The amount of memory used did not increase after the first parsing. The memory consumed in the first parsing was for the classes and working area of the parser.

Next, let's do similar experiments for DOM. Listing 5.6 parses a given XML document with a DOM parser ten times and prints the memory usage for each iteration. To see how much memory is used for the DOM trees, the program keeps each of the created DOM trees in memory.

**Listing 5.6** Print memory usage for DOM parsing, `chap05/MemoryUsageDOM.java`

```java
package chap05;

import org.apache.xerces.parsers.DOMParser;
import org.w3c.dom.Document;

public class MemoryUsageDOM {
    static final String PROP_DOC =
        "http://apache.org/xml/properties/dom/document-class-name";
    static final String FEATURE_DEFER =
        "http://apache.org/xml/features/dom/defer-node-expansion";

    static void printMemory() {
        System.gc();
        Runtime rt = Runtime.getRuntime();
        System.out.print(rt.totalMemory()-rt.freeMemory());
    }

    public static void main(String[] argv) throws Exception {
        String className = argv[0];
        boolean defer = argv[1].equals("true");
        String xml = argv[2];
        printMemory();
        System.out.println("");

        final int N = 10;
        Document[] docs = new Document[N];
        DOMParser domp = new DOMParser();
        domp.setProperty(PROP_DOC, className);
        domp.setFeature(FEATURE_DEFER, defer);
```

```
            printMemory();
            for (int i = 0; i < N; i++) {
                System.out.print(",");
                domp.parse(xml);
                docs[i] = domp.getDocument();
                printMemory();
            }
            System.out.println("");
        }

    }
```

Xerces has two DOM implementations. One is fully compliant with all DOM
Level 2 specifications. Its `Document` implementation class is `org.apache.`
`xerces.dom.DocumentImpl`. Another implementation supports DOM Level 2
Core only. Its `Document` implementation class is `org.apache.xerces.dom.`
`CoreDocumentImpl`. In addition, `DocumentImpl` has the *Deferred DOM* feature,
which improves parsing speed. If Deferred DOM is enabled, the Xerces parser does
*not* create all DOM nodes during parsing. They are created only when an applica-
tion program attempts to access them.

In this section, we call `DocumentImpl` with Deferred DOM "Deferred DOM," we
call `DocumentImpl` without deferred DOM "Non-deferred DOM," and we call
`CoreDocumentImpl` "Core DOM."

Listing 5.6 can check the memory usage of these three implementations: Deferred
DOM, Non-deferred DOM, and Core DOM.

```
R:\samples>java chap05.MemoryUsageDOM org.apache.xerces.dom.
DocumentImpl true file:./chap05/memtest10.xml
104768,155576,334536,446816,563016,679216,795416,896928,1013128,
1129328,1245528,1347040

R:\samples> java chap05.MemoryUsageDOM org.apache.xerces.dom.
DocumentImpl false file:./chap05/memtest10.xml
104768,155576,278488,280832,324480,327120,329776,291456,335104,337744,
340400,302080

R:\samples> java chap05.MemoryUsageDOM org.apache.xerces.dom.
CoreDocumentImpl false file:./chap05/memtest10.xml
104776,155584,278472,280792,324416,327032,329664,291320,334944,337560,
340192,301848
```

The first command invokes Deferred DOM, which is the default setting of Xerces,
and uses approximately 110KB for one document. The second invokes Non-
deferred DOM and uses about 2.62KB for one document. The third invokes Core
DOM and uses about 2.60KB for one document.

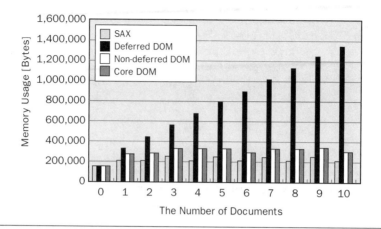

**Figure 5.5** Memory usage for SAX and DOM implementations

Figure 5.5 shows the memory usage of SAX, Deferred DOM, Non-deferred DOM, and Core DOM.

For Non-deferred DOM or Core DOM, the amount of memory used increases in proportion to the number of nodes in a document. For Deferred DOM, the amount of memory used is not proportional. It does not use 220KB for a document twice as large. Table 5.3 shows the memory usage for documents containing 10, 100, 200, 300, 400, or 500 child nodes.

This result indicates that Deferred DOM wastes much memory. In fact, Deferred DOM defers creating DOM nodes in order to improve not memory performance but parsing speed. In general, object creation in Java cost much time, and reducing object creation (`new` operators) is very effective for improving processing speed. By enabling Deferred DOM, Xerces keeps `char` arrays or `byte` arrays as often as possible, and defers `String` and DOM node creation.

It is obvious that the memory performance of SAX is better than that of DOM. We have learned that Deferred DOM, which is the default DOM in Xerces, uses a large amount memory for a small XML document and that there is little difference between Non-deferred DOM and Core DOM.

**Table 5.3** Memory Usage for Deferred DOM

| Number of Child Nodes | 10 | 100 | 200 | 300 | 400 | 500 |
|---|---|---|---|---|---|---|
| Memory for a Document (in KB) | 110 | 110 | 114 | 124 | 124 | 144 |

## Speed

We use the program shown in Listing 5.7 to compare parsing speeds.

**Listing 5.7** Print parsing times for SAX and DOM implementations, chap05/
SpeedTest.java

```java
package chap05;

import java.io.IOException;
import java.io.OutputStream;
import org.apache.xerces.parsers.SAXParser;
import org.apache.xerces.parsers.DOMParser;
import org.apache.xml.serialize.OutputFormat;
import org.apache.xml.serialize.XMLSerializer;
import org.w3c.dom.Document;

public class SpeedTest {
    static final String PROP_DOC =
        "http://apache.org/xml/properties/dom/document-class-name";
    static final String FEATURE_DEFER =
        "http://apache.org/xml/features/dom/defer-node-expansion";

    public static void main(String[] argv) throws Exception {
        int n = Integer.parseInt(argv[0]);
        boolean consume = argv[1].equals("true");
        String xml = argv[2];

        OutputFormat format;
        format = new OutputFormat("xml", "UTF-8", false);
        format.setPreserveSpace(true);
        OutputStream stream = new NullOutputStream();
        XMLSerializer serializer = new XMLSerializer(format);
        long start = 0, end;

        System.gc();
        SAXParser saxp = new SAXParser();
        if (consume)
            saxp.setDocumentHandler(serializer);
        for (int i = -1; i < n; i++) {
            if (i == 0)
                start = System.currentTimeMillis();
            if (consume) {
                serializer.reset();
                serializer.setOutputByteStream(stream);
            }
            saxp.parse(xml);
        }
        end = System.currentTimeMillis();
        System.out.println("SAX: "+(end-start)+"ms");
```

```
System.gc();
DOMParser domp = new DOMParser();
for (int i = -1; i < n; i++) {
    if (i == 0)
        start = System.currentTimeMillis();
    domp.parse(xml);
    Document doc = domp.getDocument();
    if (consume) {
    serializer.reset();
        serializer.setOutputByteStream(stream);
        serializer.serialize(doc);
    }

}
end = System.currentTimeMillis();
System.out.println("Deferred DOM: "+(end-start)+"ms");

System.gc();
domp.setFeature(FEATURE_DEFER, false);
for (int i = -1; i < n; i++) {
    if (i == 0)
        start = System.currentTimeMillis();
    domp.parse(xml);
    Document doc = domp.getDocument();
    if (consume) {
        serializer.reset();
        serializer.setOutputByteStream(stream);
        serializer.serialize(doc);
    }

}
end = System.currentTimeMillis();
System.out.println("Non-deferred DOM: "+(end-start)+"ms");

System.gc();
domp.setProperty(PROP_DOC,
                "org.apache.xerces.dom.CoreDocumentImpl");
for (int i = -1; i< n; i++) {
    if (i == 0)
        start = System.currentTimeMillis();
    domp.parse(xml);
    Document doc = domp.getDocument();
    if (consume) {
        serializer.reset();
        serializer.setOutputByteStream(stream);
```

```
                    serializer.serialize(doc);
                }


            }
            end = System.currentTimeMillis();
            System.out.println("Core DOM: "+(end-start)+"ms");
        }

        static class NullOutputStream extends OutputStream {
            public NullOutputStream() {
            }
            public void close() throws IOException {
            }
            public void flush() throws IOException {
            }
            public void write(byte[] b) throws IOException {
            }
            public void write(byte[] b, int off, int len)
                    throws IOException {
            }
            public void write(int b) throws IOException {
            }
        }
    }
```

Given a number for repeating parsing, the program repeatedly parses a document with SAX, Deferred DOM, Non-deferred DOM, and Core DOM, and then prints the time for parsing. This program also allows us to specify whether it serializes the parsed document.

The following shows the result of parsing a document 500 times. The document has about 500 elements. The first command does not serialize, and the second does.

```
R:\samples>java chap05.SpeedTest 500 false file:./chap05/memtest500.xml
SAX: 10114ms
Deferred DOM: 11237ms
Non-deferred DOM: 12748ms
Core DOM: 12648ms

R:\samples> java chap05.SpeedTest 500 true file:./chap05/memtest500.xml
SAX: 11036ms
Deferred DOM: 15462ms
Non-deferred DOM: 13760ms
Core DOM: 13850ms
```

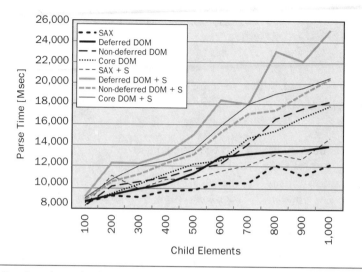

**Figure 5.6** Parsing times for SAX and DOM implementations

Figure 5.6 shows the time for parsing documents 500 times. The documents have 100 to 1,000 elements.

Roughly speaking, SAX is the fastest and Deferred DOM is not significantly slower than SAX. There is little difference between Non-deferred DOM and Core DOM.

Because a serializer accesses all nodes in the DOM tree, all nodes are eventually created even when Deferred DOM does not create them during parsing. In fact, Deferred DOM is the slowest in parsing combined with serialization.

## 5.3.2 Conversion from DOM to SAX and Vice Versa

As described earlier, the runtime performance of SAX is always better than that of DOM. However, application development with SAX only is a hard job. Converters from DOM to SAX and vice versa would be useful.

In this section, we introduce DOMReader, which throws SAX events from a DOM tree, and DOMConstructor, which creates a DOM tree from SAX events.

### Converting a DOM Tree to SAX Events

DOMReader traverses an input DOM tree and generates corresponding SAX events. It is derived from XMLReader, which is the SAX parser interface, because it generates SAX events. However, the input to DOMReader is a DOM node, though the input to XMLReader is InputSource or a URI. Thus, DOMReader ignores the parameters of the `parse()` method and receives the input DOM via the `setProperty()` method.

The core of `DOMReader` is the `processNode()` method, which generates corresponding SAX events from various types of DOM nodes. It is not difficult to understand this method if you are familiar with DOM and SAX. Because there are no ways to detect ignorable whitespace with the DOM API, `DOMReader` throws `characters()` events instead of `ignorableWhitespace()` events.

This program, shown in Listing 5.8, assumes that the input DOM tree has namespace information. The Xerces API enables namespaces by default. If you use JAXP, remember to enable the namespace feature explicitly. (See Section 4.3.5.)

**Listing 5.8** Convert a DOM tree to SAX events, `chap05/DOMReader.java`

```java
package chap05;

...[snip]...

public class DOMReader implements XMLReader {

    ... [snip] ...

    protected void parse() throws SAXException {
        this.processNode(this.current);
        this.current = null;
    }
    public void parse(InputSource input)
            throws IOException, SAXException {
        this.parse();
    }
    public void parse(String sysid)
            throws IOException, SAXException {
        this.parse();
    }

    protected void processNode(Node node) throws SAXException {
        char[] chars;

        this.current = node;
        switch (node.getNodeType()) {
        case Node.COMMENT_NODE:
            chars = node.getNodeValue().toCharArray();
            this.lhandler.comment(chars, 0, chars.length);
            break;
```

```
case Node.DOCUMENT_FRAGMENT_NODE:
    this.processChildren(node);
    break;

case Node.DOCUMENT_NODE:
    this.chandler.startDocument();
    this.processChildren(node);
    this.chandler.endDocument();
    break;

case Node.ELEMENT_NODE:
    // Preapares attributes
    if (this.attrs == null)
        this.attrs = new AttributesImpl();
    NamedNodeMap map = node.getAttributes();
    String[] prefixes = new String[map.getLength()];
    int nprefixes = 0;
    for (int i = 0; i < map.getLength(); i++) {
        Attr attr = (Attr)map.item(i);
        String qname = attr.getNodeName();
        if (this.namespaces
                && (qname.equals("xmlns") ||
                    qname.startsWith("xmlns:"))) {
            String prefix = "";
            int colon = qname.indexOf(':');
            if (colon >= 0)
                prefix = qname.substring(colon+1);
            this.chandler.startPrefixMapping(
                    prefix, attr.getNodeValue());
            prefixes[nprefixes++] = prefix;
            if (!this.namespaceprefixes)
                continue;
        }
        this.attrs.addAttribute(attr.getNamespaceURI(),
                        attr.getLocalName(),
                        qname,
                        "CDATA",
                        attr.getNodeValue());
    }

    String uri = node.getNamespaceURI();
    String lname = node.getLocalName();
    String qname = node.getNodeName();
    if (uri == null)
        uri = "";
    this.chandler.startElement(uri, lname, qname, attrs);
```

```
            this.attrs.clear();
            this.processChildren(node);
            this.chandler.endElement(uri, lname, qname);

            if (this.namespaces)
                while (nprefixes > 0)
                    this.chandler.endPrefixMapping(
                            prefixes[--nprefixes]);
            break;

        case Node.ENTITY_REFERENCE_NODE:
            this.lhandler.startEntity(node.getNodeName());
            this.processChildren(node);
            this.lhandler.endEntity(node.getNodeName());
            break;

        case Node.PROCESSING_INSTRUCTION_NODE:
            this.chandler.processingInstruction(node.getNodeName(),
                                            node.getNodeValue());

            break;

        case Node.CDATA_SECTION_NODE:
            chars = node.getNodeValue().toCharArray();
            this.lhandler.startCDATA();
            this.chandler.characters(chars, 0, chars.length);
            this.lhandler.endCDATA();
            break;

        case Node.TEXT_NODE:
            // DOM does not provide information whether
            // text is ignorable or not.
            chars = node.getNodeValue().toCharArray();
            this.chandler.characters(chars, 0, chars.length);
            break;

        case Node.DOCUMENT_TYPE_NODE:
            this.lhandler.startDTD(
                    node.getNodeName(),
                    ((DocumentType)node).getPublicId(),
                    ((DocumentType)node).getSystemId());
            // Ignore contents.
            this.lhandler.endDTD();
            break;

        case Node.ATTRIBUTE_NODE:
        case Node.ENTITY_NODE:
```

```
            case Node.NOTATION_NODE:
                throw new IllegalArgumentException
                    ("Internal Error: Non-supported node");
            }
        }

    protected void processChildren(Node parent)
            throws SAXException {
        for (Node child = parent.getFirstChild();
            child != null;
            child = child.getNextSibling()) {
            this.processNode(child);
        }
    }

    ... [snip] ...
}
```

Listing 5.9 is an example of using DOMReader. It prints SAX events directly created from an XML document by a SAX parser and also prints SAX events created from a DOM tree by DOMReader. SAXMonitor, used in this program, is a class to print SAX events to the console.

**Listing 5.9** An example using DOMReader, chap05/DOM2SAX.java

```java
package chap05;

import javax.xml.parsers.DocumentBuilder;
import javax.xml.parsers.DocumentBuilderFactory;
import org.w3c.dom.Document;
import org.xml.sax.XMLReader;
import org.xml.sax.helpers.XMLReaderFactory;

public class DOM2SAX {
    private static final String PROP_LEX
            = "http://xml.org/sax/properties/lexical-handler";
    private static final String PROP_DOM
            = "http://xml.org/sax/properties/dom-node";

    public static void main(String[] argv) {
        try {
            SAXMonitor mon = new SAXMonitor();

            System.out.println("--- SAX ---");
            XMLReader xreader = XMLReaderFactory.createXMLReader(
                    "org.apache.xerces.parsers.SAXParser");
            xreader.setContentHandler(mon);
            xreader.setProperty(PROP_LEX, mon);
```

```
            xreader.parse(argv[0]);

            System.out.println("--- DOM -> SAX ---");
            // Create namespace-aware DOM tree
            DocumentBuilderFactory factory
                = DocumentBuilderFactory.newInstance();
            factory.setNamespaceAware(true);
            DocumentBuilder builder = factory.newDocumentBuilder();
            Document doc = builder.parse(argv[0]);

            DOMReader reader = new DOMReader();
            // Register a monitor
            reader.setContentHandler(mon);
            reader.setProperty(PROP_LEX, mon);
            // Set the source DOM tree
            reader.setProperty(PROP_DOM, doc);
            // Start producing events
            reader.parse();
        } catch (Exception e) {
            e.printStackTrace();
        }
    }
}
```

The following is the result of running the program.

```
R:\samples>java chap05.DOM2SAX file:./chap05/nstest.xml
--- SAX ---
setDocumentLocator: line=1 column=1
startDocument
startPrefixMapping: foo=urn:x-foo
startElement: {urn:x-foo}root (foo:root),
characters: length=3 '\n  '
startPrefixMapping: foo=urn:x-foo
startElement: {}foo2 (foo2),
endElement: foo2
endPrefixMapping: foo
characters: length=3 '\n  '
startElement: {}bar (bar), foo:id='id'
comment: <!— foo foo —>
characters: length=11 '\n     aaa\n  '
endElement: bar
characters: length=3 '\n  '
processingInstruction: <?target ?>
characters: length=3 '\n  '
startCDATA: <![CDATA[
characters: length=11 '<foo></foo>'
```

```
endCDATA: ]]>
characters: length=1 '\n'
endElement: foo:root
endPrefixMapping: foo
endDocument
--- DOM -> SAX ---
startDocument
startPrefixMapping: foo=urn:x-foo
startElement: {urn:x-foo}root (foo:root),
characters: length=3 '\n   '
startPrefixMapping: foo=urn:x-foo
startElement: {}foo2 (foo2),
endElement: foo2
endPrefixMapping: foo
characters: length=3 '\n   '
startElement: {}bar (bar), foo:id='id'
comment: <!-- foo foo -->
characters: length=11 '\n      aaa\n   '
endElement: bar
characters: length=3 '\n   '
processingInstruction: <?target ?>
characters: length=3 '\n   '
startCDATA: <![CDATA[
characters: length=11 '<foo></foo>'
endCDATA: ]]>
characters: length=1 '\n'
endElement: foo:root
endPrefixMapping: foo
endDocument
```

The `setDocumentLocater()` method of the `ContentHandler` interface is not called because DOM nodes have no line or column information. However, apart from the events for `setDocumentLocater()`, the events from SAX and those from DOM-then-SAX are identical.

## Converting SAX Events to a DOM Tree

In contrast to `DOMReader`, the `DOMConstructor` class creates a DOM tree from SAX events.

Though the `processNode()` method is the core of `DOMReader`, `DOMConstructor` has no such core methods. Rather, all its event handler methods collectively create the DOM tree from the input events. This difference between `DOMReader` and `DOMConstructor` is caused by the differences in the programming models of DOM and SAX.

Because both normal character data and CDATA sections are represented by `characters()` events, we cannot distinguish CDATA sections from `characters()` events by examining `characters()` events only. To distinguish CDATA sections, we have to track the status of whether a parser is processing CDATA sections or not by checking `startCDATA()` and `endCDATA()`. As for entity references, we also have to check `startEntity()` and `endEntity()` to know whether or not a parser is processing an entity reference.

Methods such as `startCDATA()`, `startEntity()`, and `comment()` are methods of the `LexicalHandler` interface. So they are not called if a SAX parser does not support `LexicalHandler` or an application does not register a `DOMConstructor` instance as a `LexicalHandler()` to a SAX parser. In this case,

- No `Comment` nodes are generated.
- No `EntityReference` nodes are created and the contents of entity references are appended directly.
- `Text` nodes are generated instead of `CDATASection` nodes.

They do not change the meaning of an XML document, though they change the lexical representation of the XML document.

The type of an output node of `DOMConstructor` depends on the input SAX events. We get a `Document` node if the input SAX events start with `startDocument()` and end with `endDocument()`. Meanwhile, we get an `Element` node if the input SAX events start with `startElement()` and end with `endElement()`. To convert part of an XML document to a DOM tree, you can create a SAX filter to discard unnecessary events. See Listing 5.10.

**Listing 5.10** Convert SAX events to a DOM tree, `chap05/DOMConstructor.java`

```java
package chap05;

import org.xml.sax.Locator;
import org.xml.sax.Attributes;
import org.xml.sax.SAXException;
import org.xml.sax.ContentHandler;
import org.xml.sax.ext.LexicalHandler;
import java.util.Vector;
import java.util.Stack;
import org.w3c.dom.Attr;
import org.w3c.dom.Document;
import org.w3c.dom.Element;
import org.w3c.dom.Node;
import org.w3c.dom.ProcessingInstruction;
```

```java
public class DOMConstructor
        implements ContentHandler, LexicalHandler {

    public static final String XMLNS_NSURI
            = "http://www.w3.org/2000/xmlns/";

    Node contextNode = null;
    Stack contextStack;
    Document factory;
    boolean inCdata = false;
    Vector prefixes = null;
    StringBuffer buffer = null;

    /**
     * Create new DOMConstructor instance.
     * @param factory Factory instance to be used for creating nodes.
     */
    public DOMConstructor(Document factory) {
        this.factory = factory;
        this.contextStack = new Stack();
    }

    /**
     * Return created DOM node.
     */
    public Node getNode() {
        this.flushText();
        return this.contextNode;
    }

    protected void output(Node node) {
        if (this.contextNode == null) {
            this.contextNode = node;
        } else {
            this.contextNode.appendChild(node);
        }
    }

    protected void pushContext(Node newContext) {
        this.contextStack.push(this.contextNode);
        this.contextNode = newContext;
    }
    protected Node popContext() {
        Node ret = this.contextNode;
        this.contextNode = (Node)this.contextStack.pop();
        return ret;
    }
}
```

```
protected void flushText() {
    if (this.buffer == null || this.buffer.length() == 0)
        return;
    String text = new String(this.buffer);
    if (this.inCdata) {
        this.output(this.factory.createCDATASection(text));
    } else {
        this.output(this.factory.createTextNode(text));
    }
    this.buffer.setLength(0);
}


// Text and CDATA section
public void startCDATA() throws SAXException {
    this.flushText();
    this.inCdata = true;
}
public void endCDATA() throws SAXException {
    this.flushText();
    this.inCdata = false;
}
public void characters(char[] ch, int start, int length)
    throws SAXException {
    if (this.buffer == null)
        this.buffer = new StringBuffer();
    this.buffer.append(ch, start, length);
}
public void ignorableWhitespace(char[] ch, int start, int len)
    throws SAXException {
    this.characters(ch, start, len);
}


public void processingInstruction(String target, String data)
    throws SAXException {
    this.flushText();
    ProcessingInstruction pi;
    pi = this.factory.createProcessingInstruction(target, data);
    this.output(pi);
}
public void comment(char[] ch, int start, int length)
    throws SAXException {
    this.flushText();
    String data = new String(ch, start, length);
    this.output(this.factory.createComment(data));
}
```

```
public void startDocument() throws SAXException {
    this.pushContext(this.factory);
}
public void endDocument() throws SAXException {
    this.output(this.popContext());
}

public void startPrefixMapping(String prefix, String uri)
    throws SAXException {
    if (this.prefixes == null)
        this.prefixes = new Vector();
    else
        this.prefixes.removeAllElements();

    String qname = "xmlns";
    if (prefix.length() > 0)
        qname = "xmlns:"+prefix;
    Attr attr = this.factory.createAttributeNS(XMLNS_NSURI,
                                                qname);
    attr.setNodeValue(uri);
    this.prefixes.addElement(attr);
}
public void startElement(String uri, String local,
                    String qname, Attributes atts)
    throws SAXException {
    this.flushText();

    Element elem = this.factory.createElementNS(uri, qname);
    for (int i = 0; i < atts.getLength(); i++) {
        elem.setAttributeNS(atts.getURI(i),
                        atts.getQName(i),
                        atts.getValue(i));
    }
    if (this.prefixes != null && this.prefixes.size() > 0) {
        for (int i = 0; i < this.prefixes.size(); i++) {
            Attr attr = (Attr)this.prefixes.elementAt(i);
            elem.setAttributeNode(attr);
        }
        this.prefixes.removeAllElements();
    }
    this.pushContext(elem);
}
public void endElement(String uri, String local, String qname)
    throws SAXException {
    this.flushText();
    this.output(this.popContext());
```

```
    }
    public void endPrefixMapping(String prefix)
        throws SAXException {
    }


    // EntityReference
    public void startEntity(String name) throws SAXException {
        this.flushText();
        Node entityref = this.factory.createEntityReference(name);
        this.pushContext(entityref);
    }
    public void endEntity(String name) throws SAXException {
        this.flushText();
        this.output(this.popContext());
    }


    // DOCTYPE: ignored
    public void startDTD(String root, String p, String s)
        throws SAXException {
    }
    public void endDTD() throws SAXException {
    }

    public void setDocumentLocator(Locator locator) {
    }
    public void skippedEntity(String name) throws SAXException {
    }
}
```

The program SAX2DOM (see Listing 5.11) is an example of converting SAX events to a DOM tree with DOMConstructor. It prints the structure of a DOM tree parsed by a DOM parser and the structure of another DOM tree converted from SAX events. We must not disable the SAX namespace feature because DOMConstructor uses it. DOMMonitor, used in Listing 5.11, is a class for printing the structure of a DOM tree.

**Listing 5.11** An example using DOMConstructor, chap05/SAX2DOM.java

```
package chap05;

import javax.xml.parsers.DocumentBuilder;
import javax.xml.parsers.DocumentBuilderFactory;
import org.w3c.dom.Document;
import org.xml.sax.XMLReader;
import org.xml.sax.helpers.XMLReaderFactory;
```

```
public class SAX2DOM {
    private static final String PROP_LEX
            = "http://xml.org/sax/properties/lexical-handler";

    public static void main(String[] argv) {
        try {
            System.out.println("--- DOM ---");
            DocumentBuilderFactory factory
                    = DocumentBuilderFactory.newInstance();
            factory.setNamespaceAware(true);
            DocumentBuilder builder = factory.newDocumentBuilder();
            DOMMonitor.dump(builder.parse(argv[0]), 0);

            System.out.println("--- SAX -> DOM ---");
            // This builder is namespace-aware
            Document doc = builder.newDocument();
            DOMConstructor con = new DOMConstructor(doc);
            XMLReader xreader = XMLReaderFactory.createXMLReader(
                    "org.apache.xerces.parsers.SAXParser");
            // Register the DOMConstructor as
            // ContentHandler and LexicalHandler
            xreader.setContentHandler(con);
            xreader.setProperty(PROP_LEX, con);
            // Start construction
            xreader.parse(argv[0]);
            // Examine the result
            DOMMonitor.dump(con.getNode(), 0);
        } catch (Exception ex) {
            ex.printStackTrace();
        }
    }
}
```

The result of running SAX2DOM follows. We can see that two identical tree structures are created.

```
R:\samples>java chap05.SAX2DOM file:./chap05/nstest.xml
--- DOM ---
#document
    ELEMENT: foo:root xmlns:foo='urn:x-foo'
        #text
        ELEMENT: foo2 xmlns:foo='urn:x-foo'
        #text
        ELEMENT: bar foo:id='id'
            <!-- foo foo -->
            #text
```

```
        #text
        <?target ?>
        #text
        #cdata-section
        #text
--- SAX -> DOM ---
#document
    ELEMENT: foo:root xmlns:foo='urn:x-foo'
        #text
        ELEMENT: foo2 xmlns:foo='urn:x-foo'
        #text
        ELEMENT: bar foo:id='id'
            <!-- foo foo -->
            #text
        #text
        <?target ?>
        #text
        #cdata-section
        #text
```

## 5.4  Summary

In this chapter, we discussed some tips for using SAX and SAX filters. Then we compared the performance of DOM and SAX and described converting from DOM to SAX and from SAX to DOM.

In Chapter 6, we provide general tips on using XML processors and Xerces and discuss the new Xerces2 architecture.

# Parser Tricks

## 6.1 Introduction

Almost all XML parsers support the standard APIs, such as DOM and SAX, to allow application developers to parse XML documents and access the document information. However, the standard APIs don't directly help you solve common problems or take advantage of useful features unique to a specific parser. This chapter shows you how to tackle common problems and gives you some tricks specific to the Apache Xerces XML parser in Java (Xerces-J).

First we discuss how to solve common problems faced by XML application developers. These problems are independent of the parser implementation and affect all classes of XML applications. Therefore, there is no direct dependence on a specific parser version, and all the APIs used are standard and stable.

Next we show you how to take advantage of features that are specific to the Xerces parser. Using proprietary features and the API of any parser introduces an application dependency on that parser. Therefore, you should try to write your XML applications using standard APIs and use proprietary features and APIs only when you need the functionality. However, since the Xerces parsers are available under the Apache Open Source license, you can use the code, change it to suit your needs, and have the complete source code available if you need to add features or fix bugs in the future.

## 6.2 General Tricks

You can solve many XML application problems by using general tricks that are parser independent. This section teaches you how to solve some of the most common problems that XML developers encounter.

## 6.2.1 Namespace Validation with DTDs

The "Namepaces in XML" specification defines how to separate XML elements and attributes into separate namespaces to avoid name collisions when documents are mixed together. However, DTDs were not designed to validate documents with namespaces. But there is a trick you can use to add namespace support to DTDs. Although this trick isn't really a parser trick, it is useful enough to warrant its inclusion in this chapter.

We use an example to show how to add namespace support to a DTD. The following grammar defines an XML document that can be used to store a music collection.

```
<!ELEMENT collection (album)*>
<!ELEMENT album (artist,title)>
<!ATTLIST album cd-id CDATA #IMPLIED>
<!ELEMENT artist (#PCDATA)>
<!ELEMENT title (#PCDATA)>
```

The first step is to add three literal parameter entities to the DTD: a prefix, a suffix, and a namespace declaration. The names of the entities are not important, but remember that a name collision can occur if the DTD defines parameter entities with the same names.

```
<!ENTITY % prefix ''>
<!ENTITY % suffix ''>
<!ENTITY % xmlns 'xmlns%suffix;'>
```

The `prefix` and `suffix` parameter entities redefine the namespace prefix of the XML instance document. When you leave the value of these entities empty, your DTD retains the same element and attribute names by default. So existing documents that conform to the DTD can be used without modification. However, instance documents can redefine these values in the internal subset of the DTD to add a namespace prefix. To accommodate this new prefix, we defined the `xmlns` parameter entity, which we will use in an upcoming step.

Leaving the values of the `prefix` and `suffix` parameter entities blank allows existing documents that conform to the original DTD to be validated with the new namespace-aware DTD. However, this changes the information set for existing documents because elements and attributes gain namespace information.

The next step is to define literal parameter entities for the name of each element declared in the DTD. The value of each entity *must* be a reference to the namespace prefix you defined in the first step, followed immediately by the name of the element. For example:

```
<!ENTITY % collection '%prefix;collection'>
<!ENTITY % album '%prefix;album'>
<!ENTITY % artist '%prefix;artist'>
<!ENTITY % title '%prefix;title'>
```

Once you declare the entities for element names, modify all the element declarations to include the element names by reference. For example:

```
<!ELEMENT %collection; (%album;)*>
<!ELEMENT %album; (%artist;,%title;)>
<!ATTLIST %album; cd-id CDATA #IMPLIED>
<!ELEMENT %artist; (#PCDATA)>
<!ELEMENT %title; (#PCDATA)>
```

Next, add a namespace declaration attribute to all the elements that may be used as root elements in your instance documents. In our example, the `<collection>` element is the top-level element, so we declare the `xmlns` attribute for this element. The namespace URI that we've assigned as the default, fixed value was arbitrary, but you should choose your URI appropriately for your grammar.

```
<!ATTLIST %collection; %xmlns; CDATA #FIXED 'http://www.example.com/
music'>
```

Putting everything together, we have the modified DTD shown in Listing 6.1.[1]

**Listing 6.1**  Modified music collection DTD, `chap06/data/collection-ns.dtd`

```
<!ENTITY % prefix ''>
<!ENTITY % suffix ''>
<!ENTITY % xmlns 'xmlns%suffix;'>

<!ENTITY % collection '%prefix;collection'>
<!ENTITY % album '%prefix;album'>
<!ENTITY % artist '%prefix;artist'>
<!ENTITY % title '%prefix;title'>

<!ELEMENT %collection; (%album;)*>
<!ATTLIST %collection; %xmlns; CDATA #FIXED 'http://www.example.com/
music'>
<!ELEMENT %album; (%artist;,%title;)>
<!ATTLIST %album; cd-id CDATA #IMPLIED>
<!ELEMENT %artist; (#PCDATA)>
<!ELEMENT %title; (#PCDATA)>
```

Now both of the documents shown in Listings 6.2 and 6.3 can be validated using the same DTD grammar with our namespace modifications.

---

[1] Note that in all cases, parameter entities must be declared before they are referenced.

**Listing 6.2** Sample using default namespace

```
<!DOCTYPE collection SYSTEM 'collection-ns.dtd'>
<collection>
    <album cd-id='189EFCF'>
        <artist>They Might Be Giants</artist>
        <title>Flood</title>
    </album>
</collection>
```

**Listing 6.3** Sample using namespace prefixes

```
<!DOCTYPE a:collection SYSTEM 'collection-ns.dtd' [
    <!ENTITY % prefix 'a:'>
    <!ENTITY % suffix ':a'>
]>
<a:collection xmlns:a='http://www.example.com/music'>
    <a:album cd-id='2A77609'>
        <a:artist>Shonen Knife</a:artist>
        <a:title>Brand New Knife</a:title>
    </a:album>
</a:collection>
```

Notice the redefinition of the `prefix` and `suffix` parameter entities in the internal subset of the DTD in Listing 6.3. If the namespace is other than the default namespace (that is, a specific namespace prefix is bound to the namespace URI), the value of the `prefix` parameter entity *must* be the namespace prefix followed by a colon, and the `suffix` parameter entity value *must* be a colon followed by the namespace prefix. The added colons allow the DTD parser to correctly expand the element names and the namespace declaration attribute to contain the namespace prefix.

You can use this simple trick to update your old DTDs to be namespace-aware as a first step in your migration to using XML Schemas.

## 6.2.2 Entity Resolution

Entity resolution is perhaps the most useful feature of XML parsers that application developers often overlook. Simply stated, **entity resolution** allows the application to control how the parser locates parts of the document. Every separate part of the XML document is an entity—for example, the DTD external subset, external general entities referenced within the document, and external parameter entities referenced within the DTD. You can use an entity resolver to redirect the location of the declared entity.

Using entity resolution offers many advantages. One benefit is that you can improve application performance by redirecting system identifiers that specify resources located on the network to copies on the local file system. You can also use this feature to prevent a document from using an untrusted DTD grammar, which is especially important in a business-to-business scenario.

### Simple Entity Resolver

You can create an entity resolver by writing a simple class that implements the `org.xml.sax.EntityResolver` interface. The example in Listing 6.4 maps an entity with the system identifier `http://www.company.com/grammar.dtd` to a local copy of the DTD file. Notice that the code always sets the public and system identifiers on the new `InputSource` object. This is important to allow the parser to resolve other entities that may be declared relative to the resolved entity.

**Listing 6.4** Creating an entity resolver, chap06/`SimpleEntityResolver.java`

```java
package chap06.resolver;

import java.io.FileInputStream;
import java.io.InputStream;
import java.io.IOException;

import org.xml.sax.EntityResolver;
import org.xml.sax.InputSource;
import org.xml.sax.SAXException;

public class SimpleEntityResolver
    implements EntityResolver {

    public InputSource resolveEntity(String publicId, String
    systemId)
        throws SAXException, IOException {

        // resolve known entity using system identifier
        if (systemId.equals("http://www.example.com/grammar.dtd")) {
            // open local file
            InputStream inputStream = new
FileInputStream("c:\\xml\\grammar.dtd");

            // create input source and return
            InputSource inputSource = new InputSource(inputStream);
            inputSource.setPublicId(publicId);
            inputSource.setSystemId(systemId);
            return inputSource;
        }
```

```
                // don't know how to resolve entity, let parser resolve it
                return null;

            }

        }
```

To use your custom entity resolver, create an instance and register it with the parser of your choice. JAXP allows you to register an entity resolver on either a DocumentBuilder or a SAXParser.[2]

```
// import javax.xml.parsers.DocumentBuilder;
// import javax.xml.parsers.SAXParser;
// import org.xml.sax.EntityResolver;
// import chap06.resolver.SimpleEntityResolver;

// instantiate custom entity resolver
EntityResolver entityResolver = new SimpleEntityResolver();

// set entity resolver on document builder
DocumentBuilder documentBuilder = ...;
documentBuilder.setEntityResolver(entityResolver);

// set entity resolver on SAX parser
SAXParser saxParser = ...;
saxParser.getXMLReader().setEntityResolver(entityResolver);
```

This trick is an extremely powerful weapon and should be in every XML application developer's arsenal.

### Caching Common Entities in Memory

As stated in the previous section, an entity resolver can improve application performance by redirecting network access to a local copy of an entity. However, disk access is slower than memory access, so performance can be further improved by caching often-used entities (such as DTDs) in memory. The code in Listing 6.5 implements an entity resolver that caches entities in memory.

**Listing 6.5** Caching entities in memory, chap06/resolver/MemoryEntity Resolver.java

```
package chap06.resolver;

import java.io.ByteArrayInputStream;
import java.io.EOFException;
```

---

[2] We assume that you know how to instantiate a DocumentBuilder and a SAXParser using JAXP, as discussed in Chapter 2.

```
import java.io.File;
import java.io.FileInputStream;
import java.io.InputStream;
import java.io.IOException;
import java.util.Hashtable;

import org.xml.sax.EntityResolver;
import org.xml.sax.InputSource;
import org.xml.sax.SAXException;

public class MemoryEntityResolver
    implements EntityResolver {

    protected Hashtable cache = new Hashtable();

    public void put(String systemId, File file) throws IOException {

        // create array
        long length = (int)file.length();
        if (length > Integer.MAX_VALUE) {
            throw new IOException("file too large to cache");
        }
        int size = (int)length;
        byte[] array = new byte[size];

        // load file into array
        InputStream inputStream = new FileInputStream(file);
        while (size > 0) {
            int count = inputStream.read(array, array.length - size,
size);
            if (count == -1) {
                throw new EOFException("unexpected end of file");
            }
            size -= count;
        }
        inputStream.close();

        // add to cache
        cache.put(systemId, array);

    }

    public InputSource resolveEntity(String publicId, String systemId)
        throws SAXException, IOException {
```

```
                    // resolve known entity using system identifier
                    byte[] array = (byte[])cache.get(systemId);
                    if (array != null) {
                        // wrap array with input stream
                        InputStream inputStream = new ByteArrayInputStream(array);

                        // create input source and return
                        InputSource inputSource = new InputSource(inputStream);
                        inputSource.setPublicId(publicId);
                        inputSource.setSystemId(systemId);
                        return inputSource;
                    }

                    // don't know how to resolve entity, let parser resolve it
                    return null;

                }

            }
```

To use MemoryEntityResolver, create an instance, add files to the cache by call-ing the put() method, and register the entity resolver with your parser of choice. For example:

```
    // import java.io.File;
    // import javax.xml.parsers.SAXParser;
    // import org.xml.sax.EntityResolver;
    // import chap06.resolver.MemoryEntityResolver;
    // instantiate entity resolver and add files to cache

    MemoryEntityResolver memoryEntityResolver = new MemoryEntityResolver();
    memoryEntityResolver.put("http://www.example.com/music/collection.dtd",
                             new File("c:\\xml\\collection.dtd"));
    memoryEntityResolver.put("http://www.foobar.com/candy/chocolate.dtd",
                             new File("c:\\xml\\chocolate.dtd"));

    // set entity resolver on SAX parser
    SAXParser saxParser = ...;
    saxParser.getXMLReader().setEntityResolver(memoryEntityResolver);
```

### Enforcing Validation Using Specific Grammars

Resolving entities referenced in a document can improve application performance, but it can also be used to enforce that documents use a specific grammar deter-mined by the application. However, registering an entity resolver is not enough to force the document to use a specific grammar because certain things are beyond the entity resolver's control. For example, what if the instance document does not contain a DOCTYPE declaration or does not reference an external DTD using public or system identifiers? Then the registered entity resolver will not be called by the parser. At the very least, the instance document must contain a DOCTYPE declaration.

Even if the document contains the necessary information in the DOCTYPE declaration to allow the entity resolver to properly resolve the DTD grammar to be used, problems still exist. What if the document's DOCTYPE "lies" and references an invalid document grammar? In addition, a conformant XML parser must process the internal subset of the DTD, and these declarations take precedence over the declarations in the external subset. In either case, the document can "spoof" the application into using the wrong DTD grammar or the wrong declarations for validating the document.[3]

Entity resolution is not enough to enforce validation rules defined by the application. However, entity resolution can be used in conjunction with more advanced techniques to solve this problem. This problem is best solved by grammar caching performed by the parser implementation. Unfortunately, at the time of this writing, the Xerces parser does not have a grammar caching facility. You can use the Xerces Native Interface, described in Section 6.4, Advanced Xerces Tricks, to implement a solution to this problem, but the actual implementation is outside the scope of this book. Later, Xerces will incorporate a general grammar caching facility into the standard release of the parser.

Taking control of entity resolution is only one of the general tricks that you can use in your XML application. The next section presents a solution to a set of common problems developers experience when working with sockets.

### 6.2.3 Working with Sockets

Client-server applications are traditionally written to communicate via sockets using a proprietary binary format. Now existing applications as well as new client-server applications are being written to use XML as the communication medium to achieve data independence and greater flexibility. Therefore, XML documents are typically written and read using a socket stream, but problems occur when XML documents are transferred using a socket stream. This section provides a detailed description of these problems and presents a general solution.

---

[3] **Spoofing** is a trick used to capture or transmit incorrect information to make a receiver falsely believe the information is correct.

### The Problem

The primary problem with writing an XML document to a socket stream is that the stream usually doesn't close after the XML document is serialized. Because XML does not define a definitive *end* to the document stream, an XML parser will not stop parsing the document until the stream ends or closes.[4] Because neither is the case for a typical socket stream, the parser cannot know where the document ends.

Because opening and closing network connections is time-consuming, we want to avoid closing the socket and, instead, reuse the stream to write multiple documents (or other data). An XML parser must have a definitive end to the document, so we must find a way to separate the documents within the socket stream. First, we briefly look at some common attempts to solve this problem and the reasons they don't generally work. Then we present a solution that works regardless of the length or content of the document.

### Solutions with Problems

Several approaches to solving this problem are well intentioned but are naive in that they don't fully address the nature of the problem. Usually, these solutions are limited in their usefulness, don't perform well, and are ultimately doomed to fail for use with arbitrary XML documents.

One approach to solving this problem is to insert either a special non-XML character or a processing instruction to mark the end of a document. Then a specialized reader detects the marker and makes the document stream "appear" as if it has closed so that the parser can finish parsing the document. But this solution does not work for most XML files, and, depending on the implementation, does not perform well.

This solution doesn't work for most XML files for a variety of reasons. However, the primary reason this solution fails is due to the document's character encoding. XML is based on Unicode and can be encoded using different character encodings. Therefore, unless you can control the character encoding of the transmitted documents, inserting a special character or even a processing instruction cannot be done reliably. Additional code is needed to detect the encoding of the document and write the marker using the same character encoding.

---

[4] Section 2.1 of the XML 1.0 specification (second edition) states that a well-formed XML document matches the production:

```
[1] document ::= prolog element Misc*
```

This states that an XML document can be followed by zero or more comments or processing instructions. In short, the parser cannot know that a document ends until the stream closes!

Another solution with limitations uses a "superdocument." In this approach, a document is written to the socket stream in which the real transmitted documents appear as child elements of the new root element. This solution, however, is prohibitive because it requires extra processing on both the server and the client. In addition, arbitrary documents cannot be inserted into the superdocument as is, because the document may use a different character encoding or may contain an XML declaration (for example, `<xml version='1.0' ...>`) or `DOCTYPE` line that is not allowed to appear within the body of a document.

Although each of these solutions will work with limited success depending on how well you can control the environment and the XML document content, another solution must be found. So we will develop a solution that works regardless of the document's encoding and contents.

### A Stream within a Stream

Because the parser can't know the end of the document until the stream closes, we embed a stream *within* the socket stream. In short, we "wrap" the output stream so that we can write documents of arbitrary size and encoding, and "unwrap" the input stream at the other end for the parser. The embedded stream then correctly signals an end-of-file condition to the parser. For this solution to work, you must have access to both the server and client code.

To embed a stream within a stream, we use two I/O classes called `Wrapped OutputStream` and `WrappedInputStream`. The output stream is used by the program sending the data (which is an XML document, but it also works for arbitrary-length binary files), whereas the input stream is used by the receiver to read the data. By using the output and input stream in conjunction, we can hide from the application the details of how the inner stream is encoded.[5]

Listing 6.6 uses `WrappedOutputStream` to write an XML document to a socket stream.

---

[5] The `WrappedInputStream` and `WrappedOutputStream` classes are distributed as an Apache Xerces2 sample. The length of these classes prevents them from being listed in this text. Please refer to the accompanying CD-ROM for the complete source code.

   Here are some additional facts for the technically minded. `WrappedOutputStream` is a filter output stream that writes packets of data to the underlying stream. Each packet contains a data size followed by the bytes of the data. A packet size of zero "closes" the stream. On the other end, `WrappedInputStream` first reads the packet data size, followed by the bytes in the data. This operation is transparent to the application using the input stream. To the application, it appears as if the packet data is contiguous, with no header information to indicate the packet size.

**Listing 6.6** Wrapping an output stream

```
// import java.io.FileOutputStream;
// import java.io.OutputStream;
// import chap06.socket.WrappedOutputStream;

// assumed to have socket stream open
OutputStream socketOutputStream = ...;

// wrap output stream
OutputStream wrappedOutputStream =
    new WrappedOutputStream(socketOutputStream);

// write document to output stream
InputStream xmlInputStream = new
FileInputStream("c:\\xml\document.xml");
byte[] array = new bytes[2048];
int count = 0;
while ((count = xmlInputStream.read(array)) != -1) {
        wrappedOutputStream.write(array, 0, count);
}
xmlInputStream.close();

// "close" wrapped output stream
wrappedOutputStream.close();
```

When using WrappedOutputStream, the application is *required* to call the
close() method. This "closes" the wrapped output stream but does *not* close
the underlying stream. On the other end of the connection, the reader must use
WrappedInputStream to read the contents written by WrappedOutputStream.
Listing 6.7 shows how to wrap the incoming stream and parse its contents.

**Listing 6.7** Unwrapping an input stream for parsing

```
// import java.io.InputStream;
// import java.io.IOException;
// import javax.xml.parsers.SAXParser;
// import org.xml.sax.InputSource;
// import chap06.socket.WrappedOutputStream;

// assumed to have socket stream and parser
InputStream socketInputStream = ...;
SAXParser parser = ...;

// wrap input stream
InputStream wrappedInputStream =
    new WrappedInputStream(socketInputStream);
```

```
// parse document
try {
        InputSource inputSource = new InputSource(wrappedInputStream);
        parser.parse(inputSource);
}
finally {
        // "close" wrapped input stream
        wrappedInputStream.close();
}
```

Closing the wrapped input stream does *not* close the underlying stream. However, the application *must* call the `close()` method on `WrappedInputStream`. This is especially important for a fatal parsing error because the embedded stream will be left "open." Without an out-of-band method of communicating this error to the sender, the data stream will become corrupted. Closing the wrapped input stream skips to the end of the embedded document and leaves the underlying stream ready for reuse.

We have shown how to solve a few simple XML application problems, but many times the features provided by the standard interfaces are not sufficient. In those cases, options are available to application developers using the Xerces parser. We explore a few of these options in the next two sections.

## 6.3  Basic Xerces Tricks

You can use the general tricks to solve many common XML application problems, regardless of what parser implementation you use. However, at times you need to take advantage of the features of a specific parser. This section shows how to use the Xerces parser to solve problems that you cannot solve by using standard interfaces.

### 6.3.1  Extended Parser Options

SAX version 2 introduced a generic configuration mechanism to allow parser implementations to be extended without requiring the parser interface to be updated. Parser features and properties are set by name using the `setFeature()` and `setProperty()` methods. SAX defines a small set of core features and properties to be used with XML parsers that implement these methods. Most of the features and properties are supported by Xerces and other parsers.

In addition to the core settings, Xerces supports extra features and properties that you may find useful. The Xerces documentation contains a full list of the available features and properties, but here's a list of some of the more useful features.

`http://apache.org/xml/features/validation/dynamic`
This feature allows validation to be performed based on whether the document contains a `DOCTYPE` line. The standard validation feature must be turned on for this extended feature to work.

`http://apache.org/xml/features/allow-java-encodings`
This feature allows Java encoding names to be used in the `XMLDecl` and `TextDecl` lines of the XML document and external parsed entities, respectively. By default, only Internet Assigned Numbers Authority (IANA) encoding names are recognized (assuming that a decoder is available).

`http://apache.org/xml/features/validation/schema`
This feature allows the application to explicitly turn off support for validating documents against XML Schemas. By default, Xerces supports both DTD and XML Schema validation.

`http://apache.org/xml/features/nonvalidating/load-dtd-grammar`
This feature allows the application to prevent the parser from using the attribute declarations in the DTD to add default attribute values and attribute type information to elements in the document. This feature is *always* on when validation is enabled.

`http://apache.org/xml/features/nonvalidating/load-external-dtd`
This feature allows the application to prevent the parser from loading the external DTD referenced in the `DOCTYPE` line of the document. By default, the Xerces XML parser reads the external DTD even in non-validating mode so that default attribute values and attribute value normalization can be applied. This feature is *always* on when validation is enabled.

`http://apache.org/xml/features/dom/create-entity-ref-nodes`
This feature specifies whether entity reference nodes are created in the DOM document. By default, entity reference nodes are created.

This feature is only available for the Xerces DOM parser. The DOM Level 2 Views allow you to accomplish the same thing, but this Xerces feature allows you to avoid writing code.

`http://apache.org/xml/features/dom/include-ignorable-whitespace`
This feature specifies whether ignorable whitespace nodes are created in the DOM document. By default, all character content (even ignorable whitespace) is considered significant. This feature is only available for the Xerces DOM parser.

A grammar must be available and processed (even if not used for validation) in order to use this feature. Without a grammar, the parser has no way of determining what can be considered ignorable whitespace.

`http://apache.org/xml/features/dom/defer-node-expansion`
This feature allows the DOM parser to create a deferred document that is expanded as the application traverses the tree. The deferred document builds the full DOM document faster and saves memory when the application does not traverse the entire tree. This feature works only when the DOM document factory is set to the default Xerces DOM implementation.

Here is a list of a few of the extended properties.

`http://apache.org/xml/properties/dom/current-element-node`
This read-only property returns the current DOM element as the document tree is being constructed.

You may think that this property could be used to associate validation errors with their DOM nodes, but there are some caveats:

- Attribute errors will be reported before the element for the attribute is created.
- Because the parser validates an element's content at the end of the element's scope, the current element node returned by this property is the parent of the node that caused the validity error. Also, only the first child that causes the error will be reported.

`http://apache.org/xml/properties/dom/document-class-name`
This property allows the application to set the DOM document factory by name. The DOM parser will then use this factory to create the document nodes. The document class used must have a default, no-argument constructor.

## 6.3.2 Custom DOM Implementation

Application data is often organized in a hierarchical structure resembling a tree. Because an XML document is also a tree, it lends itself to being used to model application data. There are many benefits to using DOM: it is a convenient in-memory representation for the data; it provides an interface to XML processors such as Xalan for transformations; and it allows a platform- and application-independent serialization mechanism.

However, because DOM is a generic tree model, it is sometimes more convenient to provide a custom interface for the application. Therefore, in this section we create a DOM document that creates custom objects to model the music collection DTD defined in Section 6.2.1. The Xerces parser makes this easy by allowing the application to set the DOM document implementation by name.

First, as shown in Listings 6.8 through 6.11, we write custom classes to model the elements. To avoid having to write all the supporting DOM code, we extend the DOM implementation classes in the `org.apache.xerces.dom` package.

**Listing 6.8** Creating the `MusicCollection` class, `chap06/music/`
`MusicCollection.java`

```java
package chap06.music;

import java.io.IOException;
import java.util.Enumeration;

import chap06.util.DOMUtil;

import org.apache.xerces.dom.DocumentImpl;
import org.apache.xerces.dom.ElementImpl;
import org.apache.xerces.parsers.DOMParser;

import org.w3c.dom.DOMException;
import org.w3c.dom.Element;

import org.xml.sax.InputSource;
import org.xml.sax.SAXException;

public class MusicCollection
    extends ElementImpl {

    public MusicCollection(DocumentImpl ownerDoc) {
        super(ownerDoc, "collection");
    }

    public static MusicCollection loadCollection(String systemId)
        throws SAXException, IOException {
        return loadCollection(new InputSource(systemId));
    }

    public static MusicCollection loadCollection(InputSource inputSource)
        throws SAXException, IOException {

        DOMParser parser = new DOMParser();
        parser.setProperty("http://apache.org/xml/properties/dom/
        document-class-name",
                        MusicCollection.Document.class.getName());
        parser.parse(inputSource);
        return (MusicCollection)parser.getDocument().getDocumentElement();

    }
```

```java
public Enumeration getAlbums() {
    final MusicCollection collection = this;
    return new Enumeration() {
        private Element place =
            DOMUtil.getFirstChildElement(collection, "album");
        public boolean hasMoreElements() {
            return place != null;
        }
        public Object nextElement() {
            Element album = place;
            place = DOMUtil.getNextSiblingElement(place, "album");
            return album;
        }
    };
}

public static class Document
    extends DocumentImpl {

    public Element createElement(String name) {
        if (name.equals("collection")) {
            return new MusicCollection(this);
        }
        if (name.equals("album")) {
            return new Album(this);
        }
        if (name.equals("artist")) {
            return new Artist(this);
        }
        if (name.equals("title")) {
            return new Title(this);
        }
        throw new DOMException(DOMException.NOT_SUPPORTED_ERR, name);
    }

    public Element createElementNS(String uri, String name) {
        int index = name.indexOf(":");
        if (index != -1) {
            return createElement(name.substring(index + 1));
        }
        return createElement(name);
    }

}

}
```

**Listing 6.9**  Creating the `Album` class, `chap06/music/Album.java`

```java
package chap06.music;

import chap06.util.DOMUtil;

import org.apache.xerces.dom.DocumentImpl;
import org.apache.xerces.dom.ElementImpl;

import org.w3c.dom.Element;

public class Album
    extends ElementImpl {

    public Album(DocumentImpl ownerDoc) {
        super(ownerDoc, "album");
    }

    public Artist getArtist() {
        return (Artist)DOMUtil.getFirstChildElement(this, "artist");
    }

    public Title getTitle() {
        return (Title)DOMUtil.getFirstChildElement(this, "title");
    }

}
```

**Listing 6.10**  Creating the `Artist` class, `chap06/music/Artist.java`

```java
package chap06.music;

import chap06.util.DOMUtil;

import org.apache.xerces.dom.DocumentImpl;
import org.apache.xerces.dom.ElementImpl;

public class Artist
    extends ElementImpl {

    public Artist(DocumentImpl ownerDoc) {
        super(ownerDoc, "artist");
    }

    public void setName(String name) {
        DOMUtil.setNodeValue(this, name);
    }
```

```
        public String getName() {
            return DOMUtil.getNodeValue(this);
        }

    }
```

**Listing 6.11** Creating the `Title` class, `chap06/music/Title.java`

```
    package chap06.music;

    import chap06.util.DOMUtil;

    import org.apache.xerces.dom.DocumentImpl;
    import org.apache.xerces.dom.ElementImpl;

    public class Title
        extends ElementImpl {

        public Title(DocumentImpl ownerDoc) {
            super(ownerDoc, "title");
        }

        public void setName(String name) {
            DOMUtil.setNodeValue(this, name);
        }

        public String getName() {
            return DOMUtil.getNodeValue(this);
        }

    }
```

To keep the code simple and eliminate duplication, we use a simple DOM utility class called `DOMUtil`, as shown in Listing 6.12. This dramatically simplifies your application code and makes the DOM easier to program.

**Listing 6.12** Creating the DOM utility class, `chap06/util/DOMUtil.java`

```
    package chap06.util;

    import org.w3c.dom.Element;
    import org.w3c.dom.Node;

    public class DOMUtil {

        private DOMUtil() {}
```

```java
public static void setNodeValue(Node parent, String value) {
    Node child = parent.getFirstChild();
    while (child != null) {
        parent.removeChild(child);
        child = parent.getFirstChild();
    }
    Node text = parent.getOwnerDocument().createTextNode(value);
    parent.appendChild(text);
}

public static String getNodeValue(Node parent) {
    StringBuffer str = new StringBuffer();
    Node child = parent.getFirstChild();
    while (child != null) {
        if (child.getNodeType() == Node.TEXT_NODE) {
            str.append(child.getNodeValue());
        }
        child = child.getNextSibling();
    }
    return str.toString();
}

public static Element getFirstChildElement(Node parent, String name) {
    Node child = parent.getFirstChild();
    while (child != null) {
        if (child.getNodeType() == Node.ELEMENT_NODE) {
            if (child.getNodeName().equals(name)) {
                return (Element)child;
            }
        }
        child = child.getNextSibling();
    }
    return null;
}

public static Element getNextSiblingElement(Node node, String name) {
    Node sibling = node.getNextSibling();
    while (sibling != null) {
        if (sibling.getNodeType() == Node.ELEMENT_NODE) {
            if (sibling.getNodeName().equals(name)) {
                return (Element)sibling;
            }
        }
        sibling = sibling.getNextSibling();
    }
```

```
                return null;
        }

    }
```

The `MusicCollection` class has two important parts. The first part is the implementation of a document factory, as shown in Listing 6.13, to create our custom objects as the DOM tree is constructed by the parser.

**Listing 6.13** Document factory

```
public static class Document
    extends DocumentImpl {

    public Element createElement(String. name) {
        if (name.equals("collection")) {
            return new MusicCollection(this);
        }
        if (name.equals("album")) {
            return new Album(this);
        }
        if (name.equals("artist")) {
            return new Artist(this);
        }
        if (name.equals("title")) {
            return new Title(this);
        }
        throw new DOMException(DOMException.NOT_SUPPORTED_ERR, name);
    }

    public Element createElementNS(String uri, String name) {
        int index = name.indexOf(":");
        if (index != -1) {
            return createElement(name.substring(index + 1));
        }
        return createElement(name);
    }

}
```

The second part is constructing a Xerces `DOMParser` and using our custom document factory as the document class used to construct the tree when a file is parsed, as shown in the following code.

```
DOMParser parser = new DOMParser();
parser.setProperty("http://apache.org/xml/properties/dom/document-
class-name",
```

```
                    MusicCollection.Document.class.getName());
parser.parse(inputSource);
```

The sample program in Listing 6.14 uses the custom document implementation to load a music collection and display all the artists in the file to the standard output. Notice how there are no direct calls to DOM methods in the code.

**Listing 6.14** Program to display the artists, `chap06/music/DisplayArtists.java`

```java
package chap06.music;

import java.util.Enumeration;

public class DisplayArtists {

    public static void main(String[] argv) throws Exception {

        for (int i = 0; i < argv.length; i++) {
            MusicCollection collection = MusicCollection.
loadCollection(argv[i]);
            Enumeration albums = collection.getAlbums();
            while (albums.hasMoreElements()) {
                Album album = (Album)albums.nextElement();
                Artist artist = album.getArtist();
                System.out.println(artist.getName());
            }
        }

    }

}
```

Running this program with the following XML document, called `collection.xml`, produces the output shown after it.

```xml
<!DOCTYPE collection SYSTEM 'collection.dtd'>
<collection>
    <album cd-id='189EFCF'>
        <artist>They Might Be Giants</artist>
        <title>Flood</title>
    </album>
    <album cd-id='2A77609'>
        <artist>Shonen Knife</artist>
        <title>Brand New Knife</title>
    </album>
</collection>
```

```
R:\samples>java chap06.music.DisplayArtists
chap06/data/collection.xml
They Might Be Giants
Shonen Knife
```

In addition to implementing standard XML programming interfaces and providing special features for application developers, Xerces provides a modular parser framework. This new framework gives users more choices in configuring the parser and allows new parser components and configurations to be written. The next section describes this framework and provides a basis for advanced developers to start writing their own parser configurations.

## 6.4 Advanced Xerces Tricks

Xerces2 is a complete redesign of the Xerces parser, with the goal of making Xerces simpler, easier to maintain, and more modular. The foundation of the Xerces2 implementation is a set of interfaces known as the Xerces Native Interface (XNI). XNI is a framework for communicating the "streaming" document information set and constructing modular parser configurations.[7]

The modular framework provided by XNI and implemented by the Xerces2 parser components allows unprecedented flexibility and extensibility. XML application developers can mix and match existing parser components or write new components and configurations that better suit the needs of their applications. In the past, XML developers had to choose from a wide array of different (and often *incompatible*) parser implementations. With the advent of XNI, the all-or-nothing XML parser model no longer exists. Some example configurations might include the following.

*HTML parser*
An HTML scanner can be implemented and used in place of the default XML scanner in the parsing pipeline. This would allow existing HTML files to be parsed and processed by applications using standard XML APIs.

*Data binding parser*
DOM and SAX are not the only ways to access information from parsing an XML document. A parser implementation can be written that receives information from an XNI parser configuration and builds native Java objects, a process known as "data binding."[8] Because XNI defines a standard parser configuration interface, all existing (and future) parser configurations can be used to "drive" the data binding.

---

[7] The **streaming information set** is the set of document information that can be communicated by a serial, or as-you-see-it, XML processor.
[8] For more detailed information about data binding, refer to Chapter 15.

*XInclude processor*

A parser component can be added to the parser pipeline to automatically insert the external entities referred to by XInclude elements.

This is only a short list of what you can accomplish using the XNI framework. This section teaches you how to use the modularity of XNI and take full advantage of the features in the Xerces2 implementation.

## 6.4.1 The Xerces Native Interface

With several APIs already available for programming XML applications, why is the Xerces Native Interface needed? As the name implies, the interfaces are native (or internal) to the Xerces parsers. XNI is completely independent of existing APIs, such as DOM or SAX, so that parser implementations can be separated and layered by the user without introducing unneeded dependencies. In addition, the existing programming interfaces are "lossy" in that they do not contain valuable document information. XNI was designed to communicate as much document information as possible, within reason.

The Xerces Native Interface is divided between a set of core interfaces that define the streaming information set and a framework for building modular parser components and configurations. The core interfaces are contained within the `org.apache.xerces.xni` package, and the parser framework is defined in the `org.apache.xerces.xni.parser` package. Figure 6.1 shows the package hierarchy.

XNI parsers can be thought of as a series of components connected in a pipeline with separate pipelines for the document and DTD information. However, each pipeline is made by connecting a "source" to zero or more "filters"; the last stage of the pipeline is then connected to a "target" for the information flowing through the pipeline. Typically, a document or DTD scanner acts as the pipeline source. The information scanned from the XML document flows through the filters, which may augment or validate the document information. Finally, the events are received by the target, which generates some type of programming API, such as build a DOM tree or emit SAX events.

XNI contains several handler interfaces that define the document and DTD information that flows through the parser pipelines. The document information is defined in the `XMLDocumentHandler` interface. This handler is similar to a combination of the SAX `ContentHandler` and `LexicalHandler` interfaces but has different method prototypes and parameter values, where appropriate, to pass additional information. Listing 6.15 shows the entire interface.

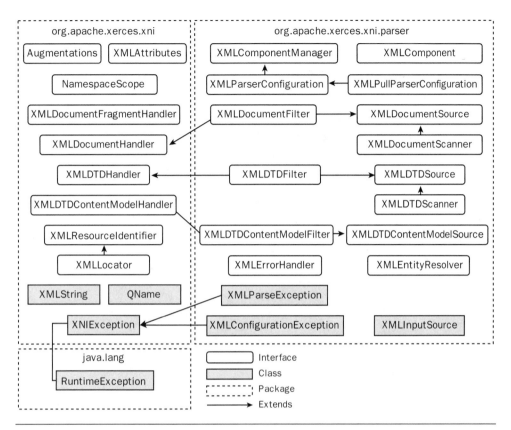

**Figure 6.1**  Hierarchy of XNI packages

**Listing 6.15**  XMLDocumentHandler interface

```
package org.apache.xerces.xni;

public interface XMLDocumentHandler {

    public void startDocument(XMLLocator locator, String encoding,
    Augmentations augs)
        throws XNIException;
    public void endDocument(Augmentations augs) throws XNIException;

    public void xmlDecl(String version, String encoding, String
    standalone, Augmentations augs)
        throws XNIException;
    public void doctypeDecl(String rootElement, String publicId,
                            String systemId, Augmentations augs)
                            throws XNIException;
```

```
public void comment(XMLString text, Augmentations augs) throws
XNIException;
public void processingInstruction(String target, XMLString data,
Augmentations augs)
    throws XNIException;

public void startPrefixMapping(String prefix, String uri,
Augmentations augs)
    throws XNIException;
public void endPrefixMapping(String prefix, Augmentations augs)
throws XNIException;

public void startElement(QName element, XMLAttributes attributes,
Augmentations augs)
    throws XNIException;
public void emptyElement(QName element, XMLAttributes attributes,
Augmentations augs)
    throws XNIException;
public void endElement(QName element, Augmentations augs) throws
XNIException;

public void characters(XMLString text, Augmentations augs) throws
XNIException;
public void ignorableWhitespace(XMLString text, Augmentations
augs) throws XNIException;

public void startGeneralEntity(String name,
                               XMLResourceIdentifier identifier,
                               String encoding,
                               Augmentations augs) throws
                               XNIException;
public void textDecl(String version, String encoding,
Augmentations augs)
    throws XNIException;
public void endGeneralEntity(String name, Augmentations augs)
throws XNIException;

public void startCDATA(Augmentations augs) throws XNIException;
public void endCDATA(Augmentations augs) throws XNIException;

}
```

Developers familiar with SAX should recognize the XMLDocumentHandler almost immediately. However, you'll notice a few differences between the SAX handlers and the XNI handlers. Some methods were changed to pass more information, whereas other methods were added when the SAX interface was lacking.

In addition to the document handler, there are two handler interfaces for DTD information. The `XMLDTDHandler` communicates the basic markup declarations defined in the internal and external subsets of a document's DTD, whereas the `XMLDTDContentModelHandler` is used only to break down element content models so that each stage in the DTD pipeline does not have to reproduce the work of parsing the element's content model.

Taken alone, the document and DTD handler interfaces don't communicate much more information than what is provided by the SAX interfaces. However, when these interfaces are combined with the XNI parser configuration framework, you can create a myriad of powerful configurations from an assortment of existing and custom modular components. In the following sections, we teach you how to take advantage of this powerful framework.

## 6.4.2 Components and the Component Manager

As stated earlier, XNI parsers are made from connecting a series of components to form an XML parsing pipeline. To make these (and other) parser components modular, XNI contains a component manager, which is responsible for storing features and properties that are common to the entire parser configuration. Although there may be many configurable components, there is only one component manager for any given parser configuration, as shown in Figure 6.2.

The `XMLComponent` interface contains methods that allow the component manager to initialize the state of each component and notify the components of changes that occur in the configuration. Before a document is parsed, each component is initialized by calling the `reset` method with an instance of the component manager, which implements the `XMLComponentManager` interface. The component then queries the component manager for any features and properties that it requires for its operation. For example, a document scanner needs to know whether namespace processing is enabled so that it can properly scan element names as qualified names.

Components in the parser configuration do not need to be directly related to the parsing pipeline, though. A parser configuration may contain other components

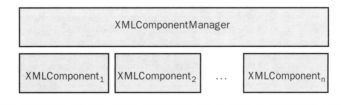

**Figure 6.2** Component manager framework

that are responsible for reporting errors, maintaining a list of commonly used symbols, and so on. What task the components perform is completely up to the parser configuration implementer. However, the Xerces2 reference implementation contains a number of shared components, which are discussed in more detail in Section 6.4.4, Building Parser Configurations from Xerces2 Components.

### 6.4.3 Parser Configurations

The actual work of parsing XML documents is done within the parser configuration defined by the `XMLParserConfiguration` interface. In this section, we give an overview of this interface and then implement a complete parser configuration as an example.

**Overview**

In the XNI parser configuration framework, the parser-processing pipeline is separate from parser instances. Whereas the parser configuration maintains the parser state and constructs the XML parsing pipelines, the parser merely receives the document and DTD information from the parser configuration to generate some type of programming model such as DOM or SAX. This separation allows the same API generating parser class to be used with any parser configurations so that the API generation code never needs to be duplicated. This separation is shown more clearly in Figure 6.3.

The parser configuration appears as a black box to the parser that uses it. Therefore, the configuration can be implemented as a single unit or can consist of any number of components connected as a processing pipeline, as shown in Figure 6.3. The only thing required is for the class to implement the `XMLParserConfiguration` interface.

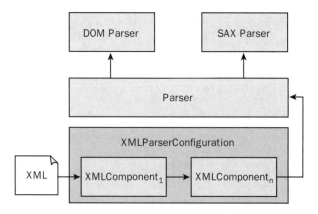

**Figure 6.3** Parser configuration framework

Because a parser configuration can be implemented as a single unit, there is no requirement that it use the XNI component and component manager framework. That framework is provided only as a convenience when reusing existing Xerces2 components or creating an entirely new modular configuration. In the following example, we implement the entire parser configuration as a single class.

### A Simple Example

In addition, there is no requirement that the parser configuration be used to parse XML documents. The parser configuration can parse any type of information as long as it exposes it to the parser as a series of XNI events. To demonstrate this, we create a simple parser configuration that is capable of parsing a text file of the following form:

```
They Might Be Giants:189EFCF:Flood
Shonen Knife:2A77609:Brand New Knife
```

Each line in this file is a separate record containing any number of fields separated by colons.

Listing 6.16 shows the source code that implements such a parser configuration.

**Listing 6.16**  Creating a parser configuration, `chap06/xni/SimpleConfiguration.java`

```java
package chap06.xni;

import java.io.*;
import java.util.*;
import org.apache.xerces.util.XMLAttributesImpl;
import org.apache.xerces.util.XMLStringBuffer;
import org.apache.xerces.xni.QName;
import org.apache.xerces.xni.XMLDocumentHandler;
import org.apache.xerces.xni.XMLDTDHandler;
import org.apache.xerces.xni.XMLDTDContentModelHandler;
import org.apache.xerces.xni.XNIException;
import org.apache.xerces.xni.parser.XMLConfigurationException;
import org.apache.xerces.xni.parser.XMLEntityResolver;
import org.apache.xerces.xni.parser.XMLErrorHandler;
import org.apache.xerces.xni.parser.XMLInputSource;
import org.apache.xerces.xni.parser.XMLParserConfiguration;

public class SimpleConfiguration
    implements XMLParserConfiguration {

    protected static final QName ROOT = new QName(null, "root",
    "root", null);
```

```
protected static final QName ROW = new QName(null, "row", "row",
null);
protected static final QName COL = new QName(null, "col", "col",
null);

protected static final XMLStringBuffer NEWLINE = new
XMLStringBuffer("\n");
protected static final XMLStringBuffer SPACE1 = new
XMLStringBuffer(" ");
protected static final XMLStringBuffer SPACE2 = new
XMLStringBuffer("  ");

private final XMLStringBuffer text = new XMLStringBuffer();
private final XMLAttributesImpl attributes = new
XMLAttributesImpl();

protected XMLDocumentHandler documentHandler;

public void setDocumentHandler(XMLDocumentHandler handler) {
    documentHandler = handler;
}

public XMLDocumentHandler getDocumentHandler() {
    return documentHandler;
}

public void parse(XMLInputSource source)
    throws IOException, XNIException {

    Reader reader = source.getCharacterStream();
    boolean openedStream = false;
    if (reader == null) {
        InputStream stream = source.getByteStream();
        if (stream == null) {
            openedStream = true;
            stream = new FileInputStream(source.getSystemId());
        }
        reader = new InputStreamReader(stream, "UTF8");
    }

    documentHandler.startDocument(null, "UTF8", null);
    documentHandler.startElement(ROOT, attributes, null);
    documentHandler.ignorableWhitespace(NEWLINE, null);

    BufferedReader in = new BufferedReader(reader);
    String line;
```

```
        while ((line = in.readLine()) != null) {
            StringTokenizer tokenizer = new StringTokenizer(line, ":");
            documentHandler.ignorableWhitespace(SPACE1, null);
            documentHandler.startElement(ROW, attributes, null);
            documentHandler.ignorableWhitespace(NEWLINE, null);
            if (tokenizer.hasMoreTokens()) {
                while (tokenizer.hasMoreTokens()) {
                    documentHandler.ignorableWhitespace(SPACE2, null);
                    documentHandler.startElement(COL, attributes, null);
                    text.clear();
                    text.append(tokenizer.nextToken());
                    documentHandler.characters(text, null);
                    documentHandler.endElement(COL, null);
                    documentHandler.ignorableWhitespace(NEWLINE, null);
                }
                documentHandler.ignorableWhitespace(SPACE1, null);
                documentHandler.endElement(ROW, null);
                documentHandler.ignorableWhitespace(NEWLINE, null);
            }
        }

        documentHandler.endElement(ROOT, null);
        documentHandler.endDocument(null);
        if (openedStream) {
            in.close();
        }

    }

    public void addRecognizedFeatures(String[] featureIds) {}
    public void setFeature(String featureId, boolean state) {}
    public boolean getFeature(String featureId) { return false; }

    public void addRecognizedProperties(String[] propertyIds) {}
    public void setProperty(String propertyId, Object value) {}
    public Object getProperty(String propertyId) { return null; }

    public void setDTDHandler(XMLDTDHandler handler) {}
    public XMLDTDHandler getDTDHandler() { return null; }
    public void setDTDContentModelHandler(XMLDTDContentModelHandler
handler) {}
    public XMLDTDContentModelHandler getDTDContentModelHandler() {
        return null;
    }
```

```
public void setErrorHandler(XMLErrorHandler handler) {}
public XMLErrorHandler getErrorHandler() { return null; }
public void setEntityResolver(XMLEntityResolver resolver) {}
public XMLEntityResolver getEntityResolver() { return null; }

public void setLocale(Locale locale) {}
public Locale getLocale() { return null; }


}
```

This parser configuration parses text files that are in the specified form and emits XNI events *as if* the following document were parsed by a normal XML parser:

```
<root>
 <row>
  <col>They Might Be Giants</col>
  <col>189EFCF</col>
  <col>Flood</col>
 </row>
 <row>
  <col>Shonen Knife</col>
  <col>2A77609</col>
  <col>Brand New Knife</col>
 </row>
</root>
```

Now let's examine in more detail how this parser configuration works. To start, we created a class that implements the XMLParserConfiguration interface. Because the format of our file is so simple, we don't care about resolving external entities or communicating DTD information. Therefore, we can provide empty implementations for most of the parser configuration methods. The only methods we need to implement are setDocumentHandler, so that our parser configuration knows which handler should receive the document information, and the parse method, which does the actual work.

The first thing we do in the parse method is to retrieve the input source stream or open it, if needed. For simplicity, we assume that the text file is encoded using only UTF-8.

```
Reader reader = source.getCharacterStream();
boolean openedStream = false;
if (reader == null) {
    InputStream stream = source.getByteStream();
    if (stream == null) {
        openedStream = true;
        stream = new FileInputStream(source.getSystemId());
```

```
    }
    reader = new InputStreamReader(stream, "UTF8");
}
```

Next we start sending document events with the following code:[9]

```
documentHandler.startDocument(null, "UTF8", null);
documentHandler.startElement(ROOT, attributes, null);
documentHandler.ignorableWhitespace(NEWLINE, null);
```

Notice that the `startElement` call makes reference to `ROOT` and `attributes`. Because we use the same element qualified names repeatedly, we have defined some convenient constants at the beginning of the class. In addition, we've defined some convenient whitespace padding buffers and created an empty `attributes` instance to pass to the document handler when we call `startElement`. The following code shows these constants and local variables that we use:

```
protected static final QName ROOT = new QName(null, "root", "root",
null);
protected static final QName ROW = new QName(null, "row", "row",
null);
protected static final QName COL = new QName(null, "col", "col",
null);

protected static final XMLStringBuffer NEWLINE = new
XMLStringBuffer("\n");
protected static final XMLStringBuffer SPACE1 = new XMLStringBuffer("
");
protected static final XMLStringBuffer SPACE2 = new XMLStringBuffer("
");

private final XMLStringBuffer text = new XMLStringBuffer();
private final XMLAttributesImpl attributes = new XMLAttributesImpl();
```

Now the real work of the `parse` method is done. Using `BufferedReader`, we read each line, tokenizing it with a Java `StringTokenizer`, and create the appropriate XNI events for the registered document handler. This code is pretty straightforward.

```
BufferedReader in = new BufferedReader(reader);
String line;
while ((line = in.readLine()) != null) {
    StringTokenizer tokenizer = new StringTokenizer(line, ":");
```

---

[9] Because this is a simple example, we're taking some shortcuts to keep the code short and manageable. When you implement a custom parser component or configuration, we *highly* recommend that you check that the handler references are non-null before calling methods.

```
documentHandler.ignorableWhitespace(SPACE1, null);
documentHandler.startElement(ROW, attributes, null);
documentHandler.ignorableWhitespace(NEWLINE, null);
if (tokenizer.hasMoreTokens()) {
    while (tokenizer.hasMoreTokens()) {
        documentHandler.ignorableWhitespace(SPACE2, null);
        documentHandler.startElement(COL, attributes, null);
        text.clear();
        text.append(tokenizer.nextToken());
        documentHandler.characters(text, null);
        documentHandler.endElement(COL, null);
        documentHandler.ignorableWhitespace(NEWLINE, null);
    }
    documentHandler.ignorableWhitespace(SPACE1, null);
    documentHandler.endElement(ROW, null);
    documentHandler.ignorableWhitespace(NEWLINE, null);
}
}
```

Once we reach the end of the input file, the only thing that remains is to send the end of the document and close the input stream if it was opened within the `parse` method.[10]

```
documentHandler.endElement(ROOT, null);
documentHandler.endDocument(null);
if (openedStream) {
    in.close();
}
```

We can test our parser configuration using one of the sample programs that come with Xerces2. Most of the command-line XNI samples have a -p option, which allows you to specify a parser configuration by name to use to run the sample. Using the `xni.Writer` sample with our sample configuration, we see the following output on the console:

```
R:\samples>java xni.Writer -p chap06.xni.SimpleConfiguration
chap06/data/collection.txt
<?xml version="1.0" encoding="UTF-8"?>
<root>
    <row>
        <col>They Might Be Giants</col>
        <col>189EFCF</col>
```

---

[10] We recommend that you always close the stream that you explicitly open, even if an exception is raised. Therefore, enclose the entire block of code within a `try-finally` block, which then attempts to close the stream if it was opened within the method.

```
        <col>Flood</col>
    </row>
    <row>
        <col>Shonen Knife</col>
        <col>2A77609</col>
        <col>Brand New Knife</col>
    </row>
</root>
```

We have implemented almost the simplest parser configuration possible. However, a real-world implementation of a parser configuration requires more work. Next, we give an overview of the responsibilities of a full parser configuration.

### Parser Configuration Responsibilities

In general, a parser configuration is responsible for the following:

- Maintaining feature and property settings
- Configuring the parser pipeline(s)
- Initializing parser components before parsing
- Notifying parser components of changes to features and properties during parsing

We take a quick look at each of these responsibilities in turn.

First, the parser configuration is responsible for maintaining feature and property settings. What does this mean? Simply put, the parser configuration must keep track of which features and properties are recognized and the values set for these features and properties so that they may be queried by the parser components when initialized. Because the parser configuration is responsible for holding all (or at least most) of the parser state, the parser class using the parser configuration may call the addRecognizedFeatures method and the addRecognized Properties method to add features and properties that should be accepted and stored by the parser configuration.

Also, when a new component is added to the configuration, the features and properties that it recognizes should be added to the list of those already recognized by the parser component. The parser configuration can query the features and properties recognized by a component by calling the getRecognized Features and getRecognizedProperties methods on the component. This list of recognized features and properties is important because when the parser configuration is queried for features or properties, the configuration should signal unrecognized ones by throwing a configuration exception that indicates this fact.

Next, the parser configuration must configure the parser pipeline, if appropriate. This simply means that the document sources, filters, and the registered document handler are chained together to form a pipeline for the document information.

Last, before parsing the input document, the parser configuration must initialize the state of each configurable component by calling the `reset` method, passing a reference to itself as the component manager. This gives each component an opportunity to query those features and properties that are required for its proper operation. In addition, anytime *during* parsing, if a feature or property changes state, each configurable component should be notified of the change by calling `setFeature` or `setProperty`.

Fortunately, most of this work is done for you by the default parser configuration implementations that come with the Xerces2 reference implementation. We take a little closer look at the basic parser configuration implementation in the next section.

## 6.4.4  Building Parser Configurations from Xerces2 Components

The Xerces2 parser is built on the XNI parser framework to handle all the common parser tasks as a series of separable modules. There are components to scan documents and DTDs, components to perform validation, components to bind namespace, and parser classes to generate DOM and SAX for all XNI parser configurations.

### Standard Xerces2 Components

The standard set of parser components in Xerces2 includes the following:

- Package `org.apache.xerces.impl`:
  - Class `XMLDocumentScannerImpl` implements `XMLComponent`, `XMLDocumentScanner`.
  - Class `XMLDTDScannerImpl` implements `XMLComponent`, `XMLDTDScanner`.
  - Class `XMLEntityManager` implements `XMLComponent`.
  - Class `XMLErrorReporter` implements `XMLComponent`.
  - Class `XMLNamespaceBinder` implements `XMLComponent`, `XMLDocumentHandler`, `XMLDocumentSource`.
- Package `org.apache.xerces.impl.dtd`:
  - Class `XMLDTDValidator` implements `XMLComponent`, `XMLDocumentHandler`, `XMLDocumentSource`, `XMLDTDHandler`, `XMLDTDSource`, `XMLDTDContentModelHandler`, `XMLDTDContentModelSource`.

- Package `org.apache.xerces.impl.xs`:
  - Class `XMLSchemaValidator` implements `XMLComponent`, `XMLDocumentHandler`, `XMLDocumentSource`.

- Package `org.apache.xerces.util`:
  - Class `SymbolTable`.

This library of parser components allows you to rearrange the default components as needed or combine them with custom components to create new types of parsers and parser configurations. When doing this, however, you should know the dependencies among the Xerces2 components. This section lists those dependencies and gives an example that builds a parser configuration using the Xerces2 components.

### Component Dependencies

The Xerces2 reference implementation that is required by most configurable components uses two standard components: the symbol table and the error reporter. For performance reasons, commonly used strings are stored within a symbol table to allow string comparisons to be done directly using the string references. Also, each component needs a common way to report errors to the application. The error reporter is used for this purpose. These components are stored within the parser configuration as properties using the property identifiers shown in Table 6.1.

In addition to depending on the symbol table and the error reporter, the document and DTD scanners both depend on an entity manager, which is responsible for starting and stopping entities. The entity manager makes this process transparent so that the scanners don't have to worry about the low-level scanning and management of entities; the scanners can just implement code to parse the document and DTD structures. The entity manager is also stored in the parser configuration using the property identifier shown in Table 6.1.

And the document scanner depends on the DTD scanner in order to scan the internal and external subsets of the DTD. The DTD scanner is stored using the property identifier shown in Table 6.1.

### Xerces2 Parser Configurations

The Xerces2 reference implementation contains a couple of parser configuration classes to simplify the construction of new parser configurations. The `BasicParser Configuration` class provides an abstract skeleton for implementing new parser configurations. This class manages components and parser configuration feature

**Table 6.1** Components Stored as Properties

| COMPONENT TYPE | PROPERTY IDENTIFIER |
| --- | --- |
| Symbol table, `org.apache.xerces.util.SymbolTable` | `http://apache.org/xml/properties/ internal/symbol-table` |
| Error reporter, `org.apache.xerces.impl.XMLErrorReporter` | `http://apache.org/xml/properties/ internal/error-reporter` |
| Entity manager, `org.apache.xerces.impl.XMLEntityManager` | `http://apache.org/xml/properties/ internal/entity-manager` |
| DTD scanner, `org.apache.xerces.impl.XMLDTDScannerImpl` | `http://apache.org/xml/properties/ internal/dtd-scanner` |

and property settings. To use this base class properly, the subclass is required to do the following:[11]

- Call the `addComponent` method for each configurable component in the configuration
- Override the `configurePipeline` method, if needed, to connect the document and DTD pipelines
- Implement the `setLocale` method
- Implement the `parse` method, which needs to do the following in order:
  1. Call the `reset` method
  2. Call the `configurePipeline` method
  3. Initiate the parsing of the document

In addition to the basic parser configuration, Xerces2 contains the `Standard ParserConfiguration` class, which constructs the standard configuration used by the default Xerces2 parsers. This configuration instantiates, registers, and configures the standard parser component pipeline. Figure 6.4 illustrates the standard configuration pipeline.

The standard parser configuration uses protected factory methods for constructing the standard set of parser components. This allows the user to create a configuration based on the standard configuration very quickly and easily. These factory methods are the following:

```
protected XMLErrorReporter    createErrorReporter();
protected XMLEntityManager    createEntityManager();
```

---

[11] Even though Xerces2 provides a base parser configuration, you can still create new parser configurations from scratch. The `BasicParserConfiguration` class is provided just for convenience.

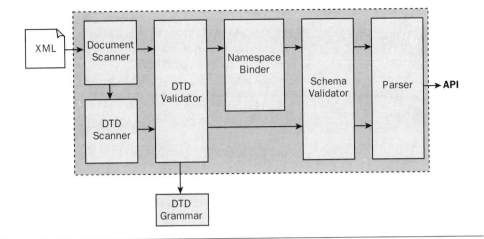

**Figure 6.4** Standard configuration pipeline

```
protected XMLDocumentScanner createDocumentScanner();
protected XMLDTDScanner       createDTDScanner();
protected XMLDTDValidator     createDTDValidator();
protected XMLNamespaceBinder createNamespaceBinder();
```

## Non-Validating Parser Configuration Example

We now proceed to build a non-validating parser configuration by building a parsing pipeline that does not contain the XMLDTDValidator component.[12]

For this parser configuration, we extend the BasicParserConfiguration to simplify the implementation. The code for this configuration is shown in Listing 6.17.

**Listing 6.17** Non-validating parser configuration, chap06/xni/
NonValidatingConfiguration.java

```
package chap06.xni;

import java.io.IOException;
import java.util.Locale;
import org.apache.xerces.impl.XMLDocumentScannerImpl;
import org.apache.xerces.impl.XMLDTDScannerImpl;
import org.apache.xerces.impl.XMLEntityManager;
```

---

[12] Even without the DTD validator, the internal and external subsets of the DTD will be processed by default. However, the attribute declarations will not be used to add default attribute values or attribute type information to the document's information set during parsing. In addition, there will be no indication of what character content can be considered ignorable whitespace—all element text will be considered character content.

```java
import org.apache.xerces.impl.XMLErrorReporter;
import org.apache.xerces.impl.XMLNamespaceBinder;
import org.apache.xerces.parsers.BasicParserConfiguration;
import org.apache.xerces.xni.XNIException;
import org.apache.xerces.xni.parser.XMLInputSource;

public class NonValidatingConfiguration
    extends BasicParserConfiguration {

    public static final String ERROR_REPORTER =
        "http://apache.org/xml/properties/internal/error-reporter";
    public static final String ENTITY_MANAGER =
        "http://apache.org/xml/properties/internal/entity-manager";
    public static final String DOCUMENT_SCANNER =
        "http://apache.org/xml/properties/internal/document-scanner";
    public static final String DTD_SCANNER =
        "http://apache.org/xml/properties/internal/dtd-scanner";
    public static final String LOCALE =
        "http://apache.org/xml/properties/internal/locale";

    protected XMLErrorReporter errorReporter = new XMLErrorReporter();
    protected XMLEntityManager entityManager = new XMLEntityManager();
    protected XMLDocumentScannerImpl docScanner = new
    XMLDocumentScannerImpl();
    protected XMLDTDScannerImpl dtdScanner = new XMLDTDScannerImpl();
    protected XMLNamespaceBinder namespaceBinder = new
    XMLNamespaceBinder();

    public NonValidatingConfiguration() {
        String[] recognizedProperties = {
            ERROR_REPORTER,      ENTITY_MANAGER,
            DOCUMENT_SCANNER,    DTD_SCANNER,
            LOCALE,
        };
        addRecognizedProperties(recognizedProperties);
        setProperty(ERROR_REPORTER, errorReporter);
        setProperty(ENTITY_MANAGER, entityManager);
        setProperty(DOCUMENT_SCANNER, docScanner);
        setProperty(DTD_SCANNER, dtdScanner);
        addComponent(errorReporter);
        addComponent(entityManager);
        addComponent(docScanner);
        addComponent(dtdScanner);
        addComponent(namespaceBinder);
    }
```

```
public void parse(XMLInputSource source)
    throws IOException, XNIException {
    reset();
    configurePipeline();
    docScanner.setInputSource(source);
    docScanner.scanDocument(true);
}

public void setLocale(Locale locale) {
    setProperty(LOCALE, locale);
}

protected void configurePipeline() {
    docScanner.setDocumentHandler(namespaceBinder);
    namespaceBinder.setDocumentHandler(fDocumentHandler);
    dtdScanner.setDTDHandler(fDTDHandler);
    dtdScanner.setDTDContentModelHandler(fDTDContentModelHandler);
}

}
```

First, we create the components that we will use in our parser configuration. Some of the components comprise the document and DTD pipelines and other components are required by the pipeline components.[13]

```
protected XMLErrorReporter errorReporter = new XMLErrorReporter();
protected XMLEntityManager entityManager = new XMLEntityManager();
protected XMLDocumentScannerImpl docScanner = new
XMLDocumentScannerImpl();
protected XMLDTDScannerImpl dtdScanner = new XMLDTDScannerImpl();
protected XMLNamespaceBinder namespaceBinder = new
XMLNamespaceBinder();
```

The basic parser configuration manages the feature and property settings as long we call the correct methods. Therefore, in the constructor, we add the set of configurable components, set the properties for our components so that they are accessible by other components in the system, and then add the configurable components to the configuration.

```
String[] recognizedProperties = {
    ERROR_REPORTER,      ENTITY_MANAGER,
    DOCUMENT_SCANNER,    DTD_SCANNER,
    LOCALE,
```

---

[13] Note that we do not explicitly create a symbol table. The basic parser configuration assumes that this is a common component, and constructs one and registers it with the appropriate property identifier by default.

```
    };
    addRecognizedProperties(recognizedProperties);
    .
    setProperty(ERROR_REPORTER, errorReporter);
    setProperty(ENTITY_MANAGER, entityManager);
    setProperty(DOCUMENT_SCANNER, docScanner);
    setProperty(DTD_SCANNER, dtdScanner);
    .
    addComponent(errorReporter);
    addComponent(entityManager);
    addComponent(docScanner);
    addComponent(dtdScanner);
```

Next, we implement a `configurePipeline` method to connect the document and DTD pipelines.

```
protected void configurePipeline() {
    docScanner.setDocumentHandler(namespaceBinder);
    namespaceBinder.setDocumentHandler(fDocumentHandler);
    dtdScanner.setDTDHandler(fDTDHandler);
    dtdScanner.setDTDContentModelHandler(fDTDContentModelHandler);
}
```

Finally, we implement the `parse` method to reset the components, configure the pipeline, and start the document scanner.

```
public void parse(XMLInputSource source)
    throws IOException, XNIException {
    reset();
    configurePipeline();
    docScanner.setInputSource(source);
    docScanner.scanDocument(true);
}
```

Using the `xni.Writer` sample with our sample configuration, we see the following output on the console:

```
R:\samples>java xni.Writer -p chap06.xni.NonValidatingConfiguration
chap06/data/collection-ns1.xml
<?xml version="1.0" encoding="UTF-8"?>
<collection>
    <album cd-id="189EFCF">
        <artist>They Might Be Giants</artist>
        <title>Flood</title>
    </album>
</collection>
```

Compare this with the output from the default configuration that has a DTD validator in the pipeline:

```
R:\samples>java xni.Writer chap06/data/collection-ns1.xml
<?xml version="1.0" encoding="UTF-8"?>
<collection xmlns="http://www.company.com/">
    <album cd-id="189EFCF">
        <artist>They Might Be Giants</artist>
        <title>Flood</title>
    </album>
</collection>
```

Notice that the non-validating parser configuration did not add the default `xmlns` attribute specified in the DTD.

The XNI examples presented here are simple in scope but demonstrate the flexibility of the framework in constructing new parser components and configurations. Because the Xerces2 parser is designed around this framework, a whole new class of XML applications can be built. Although the DOM and SAX parsers are sufficient for most developers, advanced application programmers will appreciate the power and robustness of the XNI framework.

## 6.5  Summary

You can use many tricks to tackle even the toughest XML application programming problems. And many of these tricks work with any generic XML parser, as shown in Section 6.2. But if you're a power programmer and cannot solve your application problems by using a generic parser, perhaps the power and flexibility provided by the Apache Xerces parser is suited to the task. With a little experimentation, you'll be surprised how much you can accomplish with the Xerces parsers—you may even discover a few tricks of your own.

# CHAPTER 7

# XPath and XSLT

In Chapters 4 and 5, we described DOM and SAX as generic APIs in Java to handle XML documents. DOM and SAX are powerful and flexible enough to do complex operations on an XML document. However, XPath is useful when we select just part of an XML document. Also, Extensible Stylesheet Language Transformations (XSLT) can convert an XML document to another format much more easily than DOM or SAX can in some cases. In this chapter, we describe the functions of XPath and XSLT and then explain how you can use them in Java. We also discuss the pros and cons of using XPath and XSLT compared with DOM and SAX.

## 7.1  XPath

The hyperlink concept of HTML made a significant impact on the Internet. People created a huge number of hyperlinks from their HTML files to others, even to those they did not know. It worked unexpectedly well. People finally created the largest distributed database ever seen. It is now called the Web.

XML was designed for the Web by nature. It has a hyperlink concept to point to another XML document. A URL is useful to specify the physical location of an XML document the way HTML does; however, it is not sufficient to specify the location of elements or attributes in an XML document. For example, if you want to specify a link to select Section 7.1 of this book, how can you do it?[1]

The answer is XPath. XPath provides a mechanism for specifying part of an XML document.

### 7.1.1  What Is XPath?

XPath is a W3C Recommendation used to specify part of an XML document. It also has useful functions to handle various data types, such as strings, numbers, and

---

[1] The source of this book is written as an XML document.

booleans. Unlike other XML-related languages (for example, XML Schema), XPath does not have a syntax defined by XML. Instead, XPath can be written in a very short form in a single line. You can embed an XPath in a Uniform Resource Identifier (URI) or an attribute in an XML document thanks to the design of XPath.[2]

XPath does not handle an XML document as a string form but as an abstract tree generated by an XML parser. XPath can specify a set of nodes (a *node set*) in an XML document, in which element nodes, attribute nodes, and text nodes are included. Thanks to this design decision, XPath is easy for humans to understand. Also, there is a possibility that we can formalize the nature of XPath from a mathematical point of view.

Even though XPath can be used as an independent tool, it was originally designed for use in another language, such as XSLT and XPointer. XSLT, described in Section 7.2, uses XPath not only to specify a node set in a target XML document but also to check whether a specified node set is empty or not. XPointer is built on top of XPath and defines some extensions to XPath. For example, XPointer defines the way to embed XPath into URI references. We do not describe XPointer in this book, however.

## 7.1.2 Syntax and Semantics of XPath

Let's look at the details of XPath. In this section, we give an overview of the syntax and semantics of XPath.

### Overview of the Syntax

UNIX and Windows have the notion of a file path to specify a file or a directory in a tree-structured file system. XPath also defines path notations to specify a node set in an XML document the way the file system does. Paths in XPath are called *location paths*. A parent element and its child element are separated using a slash (/) as in the UNIX file system. For example, the following XPath selects `Signature` elements of child elements of `Header` elements of child elements of the document element `Envelope` in an XML document.

```
/Envelope/Header/Signature
```

Each element separated by a slash is called a *location step* in XPath. In this example, `Envelope`, `Header`, and `Signature` are location steps.

There is a difference between a file path and an XPath. An XPath specifies not a single node but a node set. Even if an XPath selects only one node, the result is

---

[2] Embedding XPath into a URI is an extension to XPath defined by XPointer, which is based on XPath.

regarded as a set that has only one node. Similarly, if an XPath does not select any node, the result is regarded as an empty set. The previous example may not uniquely specify an element; that is, there may be more than one `Signature` element under a `Header` element. In such a case, XPath selects a set of `Signature` elements.

You can specify a file path in two ways: as an absolute path and as a relative path. Similarly, an XPath can be written in either an absolute or a relative way, as an *absolute location path* or as a *relative location path*. The origin node of an absolute location path is the document root of an XML document. The origin node of a relative location path is called the *context node,* just like the concept of the current working directory in UNIX and Windows. The context node is determined when an XPath is evaluated.

XPath provides an abbreviated notation for convenience in addition to a general notation for exactness. The previous XPath example is an abbreviated notation of the following general notation:

```
/child::Envelope/child::Header/child::Signature
```

The general notation of an XPath explicitly specifies the relationship between the context node and the nodes selected by the location step by using an *axis,* such as `child::`*element-name* and `attribute::`*attribute-name.*

Figure 7.1 illustrates what axes mean for a given context node. The figure shows a subtree of an XML document. Here, the central node is the context node, and the arrows represent axes referring to the other nodes. For example, the `parent` axis refers to the parent node of the context node.

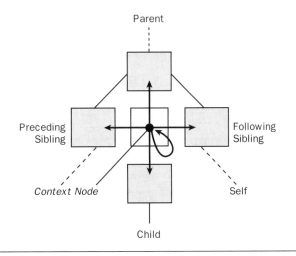

**Figure 7.1** Axes and a context node in XPath

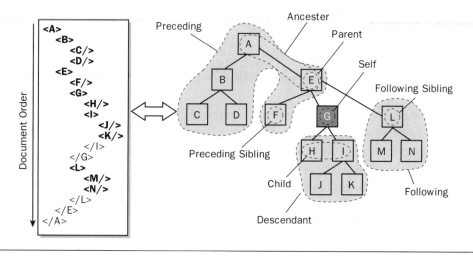

**Figure 7.2** Typical axes in XPath

Figure 7.2 shows more details of axes. Note that we still omit some axes defined by the XPath specification. There is an ordering in XPath called *document order*. The document order is the order in which the start tag of each node appears in the literal XML document. The axes are defined based on the document order. For example, the `preceding` axis selects all the nodes appearing before the context node in the document order.

The abbreviation notations, such as *element-name* and @*attribute-name*, correspond to the general notations we mentioned earlier—that is, `child::`*element-name* and `attribute::`*attribute-name*. Both a general notation and its corresponding abbreviated notation have the same meaning.

Table 7.1 shows typical examples that are often used in XPath programming. The description of the detailed syntax of XPath is beyond the scope of this book. For more information, refer to the XPath specification.

**Table 7.1**   XPath Examples

| XPATH EXAMPLE | ABBREVIATION | DESCRIPTION |
| --- | --- | --- |
| / | / | Selects the document root. Note that this is not the document element. |
| child::person | person | Selects the `person` element(s) among child elements under the context node. |
| child:person \| / | person \| / | Selects `person` element(s) or the document root. "\|" stands for a union (logical OR). |

**Table 7.1** *continued*

| XPATH EXAMPLE | ABBREVIATION | DESCRIPTION |
|---|---|---|
| `/child::Address Book` | `/AddressBook` | Selects the `AddressBook` element under the document root. That is, `AddressBook` is selected if it is the document element; otherwise, no element is selected. |
| `child::*` | `*` | Selects all the child elements under the context node. Note that this does not select any text nodes or attributes. |
| `child::text()` | `text()` | Selects all the text nodes under the context node. Note that if text nodes appear before and after an element, they are not concatenated but are selected as a set of text nodes. |
| `attribute::type` | `@type` | Selects the `type` attribute of the context node. |
| `/descendant-or-self::node()/child::email` | `//email` | Selects all the `email` elements in a document. Note that `//` is short for `/descendant-or-self::node()/`. The node () function selects all nodes, whatever their node type. |
| `child::person/child::email[position()=1]` | `person/email[1]` | Selects the first `email` element under all the `person` child elements in a context node. You can specify additional (or detail) conditions in "`[ ]`." This part is called the *predicate* in XPath. |
| `child::person[child::email and attribute::id="12345"]` | `person[email and @id="12345"]` | Selects all the `person` elements in a context node that have at least one `email` element and an `id` attribute with the value `12345`. |
| `child::name[attribute::family="neyama"][position()=last()]` | `name[@family="neyama"][last()]` | Selects the last `name` element in a context node that has a `family` attribute and the value `neyama`. |

## Objects and Types

The result of evaluating an XPath is called an *object*. An object has one of the following *primitive types*:

- *Node-set*—an unordered collection of nodes without duplications
- *String*—a sequence of characters
- *Boolean*—true or false
- *Number*—a floating-point number

Note that the tree representing a target XML document is processed as an ordered tree, but a node-set as a result object is unordered by definition.

XPath provides various functions that are used in location steps. The functions are categorized in four groups corresponding to the primitive types. Table 7.2 shows typical functions in XPath.

**Table 7.2** Typical Functions in XPath

| FUNCTION GROUP | CONVERSION FUNCTION | FUNCTIONS | DESCRIPTION |
|---|---|---|---|
| Node-set | None | *number* last( ) | Returns the number of the selected nodes (*context size*). |
| | | *number* position( ) | Returns the index of the selected node (*context position*). |
| | | *number* count (*node-set*) | Returns the number of nodes in the argument node-set. |
| String | *string* string (*object?*) | *string* local-name (*node-set?*) | Returns the local part of the node. The first node in the argument node-set in document order is used as the target node. |
| | | *string* namespace-uri(*node-set?*) | Returns the namespace URI of the node. The first node in the argument node-set in document order is used as the target node. |
| | | *string* concat(*string, string, string\**) | Returns the concatenation of its arguments. |
| Boolean | *boolean* boolean (*object*) | *boolean* starts-with (*string, string*) | Checks that the first argument string starts with the second argument string. |
| | | *boolean* contains (*string, string*) | Checks that the first argument string contains the second argument string. |
| | | *number* string-length (*string?*) | Returns the length of the argument. |
| | | *string* normalize-space(*string?*) | Normalizes the whitespace in the argument string by stripping leading and trailing whitespace characters and by replacing a sequence of whitespace characters with a single space. |
| | | *boolean* not(*boolean*) | Negates the argument boolean. |
| | | *boolean* true( ) | Always returns `true`. |
| | | *boolean* false( ) | Always returns `false`. |
| Number | *number* number (*object?*) | *number* sum (*node-set*) | Returns the sum of the argument node-set. Each node in the node-set is converted to a number through its string representation. |

In general, a function in a function group takes the arguments of the type that corresponds to the primitive type of the group—for example, boolean type for the boolean function group. If a function is called with arguments of types that do not match the function, the arguments are converted to the appropriate types by calling the conversion functions implicitly. For example, a nonempty node-set is converted to true of boolean type by the boolean() function. In this sense, the conversion functions are regarded as defining the conversion rules in XPath. Note that the conversion from string, boolean, and number to node-set is not supported.

### 7.1.3 XPath and Namespaces

To make the explanation easy in Section 7.1.2, we intentionally did not cover an important relationship between XPath and XML Namespaces (hereafter referred to as "namespaces"). Namespaces are becoming very important and are already used widely in many XML documents. For example, every element must be qualified by a namespace in a SOAP message (described in Chapter 12). In this section, we describe how to specify an XPath if the target XML document uses namespaces.

XPath supports namespaces if an XML processor used with an XPath processor supports namespaces. If the XML processor does not support namespaces, we do not need to care about the issues described in this section.[3] Hereafter, we assume that namespaces are supported.

The following example, shown previously in Section 7.1.2, specifies elements with an unqualified namespace.

```
/Envelope/Header/Signature
```

How can we specify namespace-qualified elements? The simplest way to do so is as follows:

```
/SOAP-ENV:Envelope/SOAP-ENV:Header/dsig:Signature
```

This example tries to select the `Signature` element qualified by the `dsig` namespace prefix by navigating first an `Envelope` element and then a `Header` element qualified by the `SOAP-ENV` namespace prefix from the document root.

The previous XPath works only when a target document always uses the same namespace prefixes (`SOAP-ENV` and `dsig` in this example). However, namespace

---

[3] If the processor does not support namespaces, it recognizes the `SOAP-ENV:Envelope` as a whole as an element name because it does not recognize the `SOAP-ENV` as a namespace prefix. Therefore, this works only when a target document always uses the same namespace prefixes as specified in an XPath.

prefixes are not always the same in general, and we should not assume it. Therefore, we do not recommend this kind of fixed prefix use for a general XPath notation.[4]

Furthermore, this simplest way has a problem in that the namespace scope depends on the context node. For example, as shown in the following example, the scope of the dsig namespace is limited under the Signature element. If the context node is the SOAP-ENV:Envelope element, the previous XPath cannot select the Signature element.

```
<SOAP-ENV:Envelope xmlns:SOAP-ENV="http://...">
  <SOAP-ENV:Header>
    <dsig:Signature xmlns:dsig="http://...">
    ... omitted ...
    </dsig:Signature>
  </SOAP-ENV:Header>
  <SOAP-ENV:Body>
  ... omitted ...
  </SOAP-ENV:Body>
</SOAP-ENV:Envelope>
```

This causes an XPath parsing error because the prefix, dsig, cannot be resolved within the scope of the SOAP-ENV:Envelope element. It works only if the dsig prefix is declared within the scope of the SOAP-ENV:Envelope element.

Finally, we show the correct use of an XPath that can handle namespaces without fixing namespace prefixes. For example, if you want to select all the Signature elements associated with the namespace http://www.w3.org/2000/09/xmldsig# (in fact, these are the Signature elements in the XML Digital Signature specification), you can specify an XPath as follows:

```
//*[namespace-uri()="http://www.w3.org/2000/09/xmldsig#" and
    local-name()="Signature"]
```

Note that the following two XPaths do not select the Signature elements as expected. These are typical mistakes that many people tend to make.

```
//Signature
//Signature[namespace-uri()="http://www.w3.org/2000/09/xmldsig#"]
```

---

[4] This works if an XPath is used in an XSLT stylesheet. As described in Section 7.2, namespaces declared in an XSLT stylesheet affect the evaluation of XPaths.

    As described in the next section, Xalan provides an XPath API that resolves application-specific namespaces by creating an instance of the NamespaceResolver interface. This is useful but not sufficient because an application must provide a fixed set of namespace prefixes beforehand.

In the first XPath, no elements will be selected because it selects all the `Signature` elements that are namespace-unqualified, but the `Signature` element of the XML Signature is namespace-qualified. In the second XPath, no elements will be selected because it selects all the `Signature` elements that are not only namespace-unqualified but also namespace-qualified by `http://www.w3.org/2000/09/xmldsig#`. Of course, no element can be both namespace-qualified and namespace-unqualified.

We want to emphasize again that once the namespace is introduced in an XML document, the simple notation of an XPath explained in Section 7.1.2 (for example, separating element names by a "/") is no longer valid in general. You should use the complicated notation just described.

## 7.1.4 XPath Programming in Java

In this section, we explain how to write a Java program using XPath. We use Apache Xalan-Java 2.1.0 (hereafter referred to as Xalan) as an XPath processor. Xalan is a popular XPath processor from the Apache Software Foundation.[5]

### A Simple Example

The source code for an example, `XPathTest`, is shown in Listing 7.1. This program outputs the selected nodes and their appearance count by applying the XPath given as the second argument to the target XML document given as the first argument.

**Listing 7.1** A simple Java program using XPath, `chap07/XPathTest.java`

```
package chap07;

// For JAXP
import javax.xml.parsers.DocumentBuilder;
import javax.xml.parsers.DocumentBuilderFactory;
import org.xml.sax.InputSource;

// For Xalan XPath API
import org.apache.xpath.XPathAPI;
import org.w3c.dom.traversal.NodeIterator;
import org.w3c.dom.Node;
import org.w3c.dom.Document;
```

---

[5] The API of Xalan version 2.*x* has been drastically changed from that of Xalan version 1.*x*. Therefore, a program using the Xalan 1.*x* API will not work with Xalan 2.*x*.

```
        public class XPathTest {
            public static void main(String[] args) throws Exception {
[16]            String xmlFilePath = args[0];
[17]            String xPath = args[1];
[18]
[19]            System.out.println("Input XML File: " + xmlFilePath);
[20]            System.out.println("XPath: " + xPath);
[21]
[22]            DocumentBuilderFactory factory =
[23]                DocumentBuilderFactory.newInstance();
[24]            factory.setNamespaceAware(true);
[25]            DocumentBuilder parser = factory.newDocumentBuilder();
[26]
[27]            InputSource in =
[28]                new InputSource(xmlFilePath);
                Document doc = parser.parse(in);
[30]
[31]            Node contextNode = doc.getDocumentElement();
[32]            NodeIterator i =
[33]                XPathAPI.selectNodeIterator(contextNode, xPath);
[34]            int count = 0;
[35]            Node node;
[36]            // For each node
[37]            while ((node = i.nextNode()) != null) {
[38]                // Outputs the node to System.out
[39]                System.out.println(node.toString());
[40]                count++;
[41]            }
                System.out.println("" + count + " match(es)");
            }
        }
```

The first half of the program (lines 17–30) creates a DOM tree from the target XML document by using an XML parser, and the last half (lines 32–43) invokes the XPath API provided by Xalan.

The most important part of this program is XPathAPI.selectNodeIterator (Node, String) (line 34). This method takes two arguments: a node as the beginning context node and an XPath string. The result has the type NodeIterator, which is a collection of the selected nodes. Each invocation of nextNode() returns the next selected element in the result list. This program simply outputs the selected nodes by using the toString() method. You can replace this portion with application-specific code as appropriate.

Let's run `XPathTest` using the sample XML document shown in Listing 7.2.

**Listing 7.2** A sample XML document for `XPathTest`, `chap07/data/sample.xml`

```
<?xml version="1.0" encoding="UTF-8"?>
<W3Cspecs xmlns="http://www.example.com/xmlbook2/chap07/">
  <spec title="XML Path Language (XPath) Version 1.0"
        url="http://www.w3.org/TR/xpath">
    <date type="REC">16 November 1999</date>
    <editors>
      <editor>
        <name>James Clark</name>
        <email>jjc@jclark.com</email>
      </editor>
      <editor>
        <name>Steve DeRose</name>
        <email>Steven_DeRose@Brown.edu</email>
      </editor>
    </editors>
  </spec>
  <spec title="XSL Transformations (XSLT) Version 1.0"
        url="http://www.w3.org/TR/xslt">
    <date type="REC">16 November 1999</date>
    <editors>
      <editor>
        <name>James Clark</name>
        <email>jjc@jclark.com</email>
      </editor>
    </editors>
  </spec>
</W3Cspecs>
```

To run the program, type the following command:

```
R:\samples\>java chap07.XPathTest
    file:./chap07/data/sample.xml "//*[local-name()='email']/text()"
```

In this example, the XPath selects all text nodes whose parent node's local name is `email`. In short, it collects all e-mail addresses in the XML document. The result appears as follows:

```
[#text: jjc@jclark.com]
[#text: Steven_DeRose@Brown.edu]
[#text: jjc@jclark.com]
3 match(es)
```

Three e-mail addresses are found.

## Handling Objects and Types

In Section 7.1.2, we explained that the result of evaluating an XPath is an object and that objects have these primitive types: node-set, string, boolean, and number. If you just want to select a set of DOM nodes with an XPath, the `XPathAPI.selectNodeIterator()` method, whose return type is the `Node Iterator` class, is powerful enough. Unfortunately, the `NodeIterator` class does not represent objects in XPath exactly. In other words, it does not contain XPath type information.

Type information provides the polymorphism for the objects. We can convert an object that has a specific type to another object that has another type according to the conversion rule defined in XPath. This functionality is useful when we reuse the semantics of XPath in applications of XPath. One of the most famous applications of XPath is XSLT, which is described in Section 7.2. In XSLT, XPath is used to test whether the specified nodes actually exist in the input XML document. In this case, XSLT reuses the result from converting the selected node-set to boolean—that is, if the XPath selects a nonempty node-set, the result is true; otherwise, it is false.

Accordingly, when we need to exactly handle objects and types as the result of evaluating an XPath, the `XPathAPI.selectNodeIterator()` method is not sufficient. Xalan provides an API for handling objects and types: the `XPathAPI.eval()` method. The method returns the instances of the following classes:

- `org.apache.xpath.objects.XObject`
- `org.apache.xpath.objects.XNodeSet`
- `org.apache.xpath.objects.XString`
- `org.apache.xpath.objects.XBoolean`
- `org.apache.xpath.objects.XNumber`

`XObject` is a common superclass for the other four classes corresponding to each type in XPath: node-set, string, boolean, and number. You can get an `XObject` object as a result of evaluating an XPath by calling the `XPathAPI.eval()` method. It is actually an instance of the subclasses of the `XObject` class: `XNodeSet`, `XString`, `XBoolean`, and `XNumber`.

Listing 7.3 shows part of `XObjectTest.java`, which is basically a variation of `XPathTest.java`. `XObjectTest` calls the `XPathAPI.eval()` method instead of the `XPathAPI.selectNodeIterator()` method. The Java object returned by the method, `xobject`, has the `bool()` method, which converts the object into boolean. The program finally prints the result of whether matching nodes are found.

**Listing 7.3** Part of the program `chap07/XObjectTest.java`

```
[31]            XObject xobject = XPathAPI.eval(contextNode, xPath);
[32]            boolean match = xobject.bool();
[33]            System.out.println("match found?: " + match);
```

For more details about these classes, please consult the Xalan API document.

In this section, we introduced XPath and its programming in Java. We hope you understand the powerful and useful capability of XPath. You will see another use of XPath in Chapter 11, Section 11.5.2, in retrieving XML documents stored into relational databases. You can write a program with XPath much more simply than with DOM or SAX. Also with XPath, you can easily and flexibly protect your program against small changes in the target XML document structure (DTD) or node selection logic. You can just modify the XPath in that case, while you need to modify the application logic when you are using DOM or SAX.

In Section 7.2, we introduce XSLT. Then we compare the pros and cons of DOM, SAX, XPath, and XSLT in Section 7.3 and discuss which one is better for what type of application.

## 7.2 XSLT

There is a criticism that the design of HTML is not very sophisticated because it does not separate a logical document structure from its presentation design.

Suppose that you are the CEO of a newspaper company and plan to publish news on the Web. News writers create source articles but they do not touch on the design of their presentation on the Web. Usually, Web designers create HTML documents based on the input from the news writers. If an HTML document contains both the content of news articles and their presentation (this is usually the case), a problem occurs when both designers and news writers want to modify the same HTML at the same time.

Furthermore, to differentiate your news site from those of your competitors, you may want to revise the overall design of your news site to capture the interest of more mobile users who are using Personal Digital Assistants (PDAs). For that purpose, you may decide to prepare two page designs, one for PC users and another for PDA users. How can you do that? You could first create a page for PC users and then copy it and modify the copy for PDA readers. However, it is easy to imagine that these steps would create a serious problem; for example, when a writer wants to update an article after the page design is final, it is hard to always modify both copies consistently.

As many of you may know, there is a famous software architecture model called the *Model-View-Controller (MVC) Model*. It is very useful when you design a graphical user interface (GUI). It clearly separates the role of the components in a GUI program into a model (M) for the structure of the data, a view (V) for presentation of the model, and a controller (C) for operations on the model. This separation makes it easy to minimize the side effect of each component; for example, changes on a view do not affect a model.

The proper design of HTML could, ideally, be the same as described earlier; that is, it could separate a model and its views.[6] In contrast to HTML, XML has the concept of model-view separation. A model is specified by an XML document, and a view is represented as an HTML document. It would be convenient to have a tool that converts an XML document to an appropriate HTML document based on a set of translation rules. XSLT is designed to provide the basis for such a translation.

## 7.2.1 What Is XSLT?

XSLT is a W3C Recommendation that converts an XML document to something else. In many cases, the result of the conversion is another XML document, but in some cases, it may be an HTML document or Comma-Separated Value (CSV), or even Portable Document Format (PDF). In this section, we describe only the XML-to-XML conversion.

In XSLT, a *template* is used to represent a fragment of a *result tree*. With XSLT, some parts of an input XML document—typically a value of an element or an attribute—are inserted into the template, and then the result tree is created. XSLT uses XPath and its additional functions to select or test nodes.

## 7.2.2 Syntax and Semantics of XSLT

A detailed explanation of XSLT syntax and semantics goes beyond the scope of this book because the XSLT specification is very big. Instead, we describe some typical techniques by using concrete examples that translate an XML document to various XHTML documents. Even though it does not fully cover all the capabilities provided by XSLT, we think it is still enough to give you the flavor of XSLT. We refer you to the following book for more detail: *XSLT: Working with XML and HTML*, by Khun Yee Fung (Addison-Wesley, ISBN 0-201-71103-6).

---

[6] Such M-V separation makes the concept of HTML complicated; however, HTML could not have become very popular if it had very complicated syntax.

### XSLT Stylesheets

A document that defines XSLT translation rules is called a *stylesheet*. Listing 7.4 is an example of a stylesheet (`sample-1.xsl`) that translates the XML document `sample.xml` (see Listing 7.2) into an XHTML document.

**Listing 7.4** Stylesheet for translating XML to XHTML, `chap07/data/sample-1.xsl`

```
[1]     <?xml version="1.0" encoding="UTF-8"?>
[2]     <xsl:stylesheet
[3]       version="1.0"
[4]       xmlns:xsl="http://www.w3.org/1999/XSL/Transform"
[5]       xmlns="http://www.w3.org/TR/xhtml1"
[6]       xmlns:ch7="http://www.example.com/xmlbook2/chap07/"
          exclude-result-prefixes="ch7">
          <xsl:output method="xml" encoding="UTF-8"/>
          <xsl:template match="/">
            <html>
            <head><title>XSLT Sample</title></head>
              <body>
                <ul>
                  <li>
        <xsl:value-of select="ch7:W3Cspecs/ch7:spec[1]/@title"/>
                  </li>
                  <li>
        <xsl:value-of select="ch7:W3Cspecs/ch7:spec[2]/@title"/>
                  </li>
                </ul>
              </body>
            </html>
          </xsl:template>
        </xsl:stylesheet>
```

A stylesheet is an XML document. For example, you can specify an `encoding` attribute in an XML declaration (line 1) just as in other XML documents. The document element of a stylesheet is the `xsl:stylesheet` element.[7] The value of the `version` attribute (line 3) is the XSLT version number (1.0). Usually, the namespaces used in a stylesheet are declared in the `xsl:stylesheet` element. In this example, three namespaces are declared: for the stylesheet itself (line 4), XHTML 1.0 as the output document (line 5), and the input XML document, `sample.xml` (line 6). The `exclude-result-prefixes` attribute specifies the namespace prefixes that should not be included in the result XML document.

---

[7] You can use `xsl:transform` instead of `xsl:stylesheet`. It is an alias of `xsl:stylesheet` and has the same meaning. In this book, we use `xsl:stylesheet`.

Child elements of the xsl:stylesheet element are parameters to the stylesheet (for example, xsl:output) and templates (xsl:template). We describe templates in the next section, XSLT Templates.

As shown in this example, xsl:output specifies the output format of this stylesheet. The method attribute specifies the overall format of the result tree. Possible values of the method attribute are xml (XML output), html (HTML output), text (text output), and so on. The XSLT processor, which is a component that processes an XSLT stylesheet, changes its behavior according to the method.

Listing 7.5 is the output XHTML document (sample-1.xhtml) translated from sample.xml by applying sample-1.xsl. The actual output does not contain any spaces, but we indented it for readability.

**Listing 7.5**  Translated XHTML document, chap07/data/sample-1.xhtml

```
<?xml version="1.0" encoding="UTF-8"?>
<html xmlns="http://www.w3.org/TR/xhtml1">
  <head>
    <title>XSLT Sample</title>
  </head>
  <body>
    <ul>
      <li>XML Path Language (XPath) Version 1.0</li>
      <li>XSL Transformations (XSLT) Version 1.0</li>
    </ul>
  </body>
</html>
```

In summary, elements in the template under the html element are first written, and then the values of the title attributes in sample.xml are embedded. In this way, XSLT is very powerful in extracting values from an input XML document and embedding them into an output template. To do the same task, you can write a program using DOM or SAX, but you need much more effort than when using XSLT.

In case of the sample-1.xsl, the xsl:output element and the xsl:template are only the child elements of the xsl:stylesheet element. However, you can specify more child elements. Table 7.3 summarizes the typical child elements under the xsl:stylesheet element.

Listing 7.6 is an overview of the XSLT stylesheet structure. Please refer the XSLT specification for the details.

**Table 7.3**  Child Elements of `xsl:stylesheet`

| ELEMENT | DESCRIPTION |
| --- | --- |
| `xsl:include` and `xsl:import` | Embed another stylesheet specified by the `href` attribute into the current stylesheet. Unlike with `xsl:include`, XSLT scans the stylesheet embedded by the `xsl:import` element before the current stylesheet. |
| `xsl:output` | Specifies the format of an output document; for example, an output is an XML document with the XML declaration. |
| `xsl:variable` and `xsl:param` | Declare a variable with a name specified by the `name` attribute and a value specified as its text value. With `xsl:param`, unlike with `xsl:variable`, the text is regarded as a default value of the variable; that is, it is overwritten by the variable with the same name. Variable declarations can be written in a template (described later). |
| `xsl:template` | Specifies a template. As you have seen in `sample.xsl`, you can write more than one `xsl:template` in `xsl:stylesheet`. The details are described in the section XSLT Templates. |

**Listing 7.6** An overview of the stylesheet structure

```
<xsl:stylesheet version="1.0"
                xmlns:xsl="http://www.w3.org/1999/XSL/Transform">
  <xsl:include href="..."/>
  <xsl:import href="..."/>
  <xsl:strip-space elements="..."/>
  <xsl:preserve-space elements="..."/>
  <xsl:variable name="...">...</xsl:variable>
  <xsl:param name="...">...</xsl:param>
  <xsl:output method="..." />
  <xsl:key name="..." match="..." use="..."/>
  <xsl:decimal-format name="..."/>
  <xsl:namespace-alias stylesheet-prefix="..." result-prefix="..."/>
  <xsl:attribute-set name="...">
    ...
  </xsl:attribute-set>

  <xsl:template match="...">
    ...
  </xsl:template>
  <xsl:template match="...">
    ...
  </xsl:template>
</xsl:stylesheet>
```

## XSLT Templates

A template is the most important part of a stylesheet. Each `xsl:template` element has a `match` attribute, which is an XPath to specify the part of an input XML document where the template is to be applied. For the stylesheet `sample-1.xsl`, for example, `match="/"` indicates that the template is to be applied to the document root of an input XML document. An `xsl:template` element contains a mixture of *literal strings* as fragments in the output document and *instructions*. The namespace prefix `xsl` distinguishes instructions from literal strings. When a template is applied, literal strings in the template are copied to the output document as they are, while instructions are executed. The template in the following example always outputs a fixed XHTML document regardless of its input document because it contains only literal strings.

```
<xsl:template match="/">
  <html xmlns="http://www.w3.org/TR/xhtml1">
    <head><title>XSLT sample 1</title></head>
    <body>
      <ul>
        <li>XML Path Language (XPath) Version 1.0</li>
        <li>XSL Transformations (XSLT) Version 1.0</li>
      </ul>
    </body>
  </html>
</xsl:template>
```

A literal string can be any sequence of characters that are allowed by XML, although the stylesheet as a whole must be a well-formed XML document. For example, an XSLT processor reports a syntax error if an end tag is missing but its start tag is specified. If you want to output such a fragment of XML, you must escape the start tag or use a CDATA section. Note that it is not always true that the output XML document is well-formed. For example, if you write an inappropriate string, such as "foo", outside the `html` tag in the previous example, the output document is no longer well-formed. In general, it is a very hard problem to make sure the output XML document is valid against a given DTD or an XML Schema. At this moment, one of the best ways to solve this problem is to parse the generated XML documents by using an XML parser as we discussed in Chapter 3, Section 3.4.2.

An instruction may apply a template to the selected nodes or the output values of the selected nodes. For example, the `xsl:value-of` instruction outputs the values of the nodes selected by an XPath specified in the `select` attribute. An XPath can be absolute or relative from the target node that an XSLT processor is working on (called the *current node,* to be described later). There are two XPaths in `sample-1.xsl` (see Listing 7.4): `ch7:W3Cspecs/ch7:spec[1]/@title` and ch7:W3Cspecs/ch7:spec[2]/@title. Their values are shown in sample-1.xhtml (see Listing 7.5) as "XML Path Language (XPath) Version 1.0" and "XSL Transformations (XSLT) Version 1.0," respectively.

Note that the namespace declaration for the namespace prefix ch7 in the xsl:stylesheet element affects the evaluation of the XPath. In this case, the namespace prefix ch7 in the XPath is associated with the namespace http://www.example.com/xmlbook2/chap07/ declared in the stylesheet. In XSLT, a namespace scope in a stylesheet is effective even in the evaluation of XPaths. This indicates that we do not need to follow the consideration on namespaces we describe in Section 7.1.3; that is, we should not use fixed namespace prefixes in XPath as long as XPath is used in XSLT.

The stylesheet sample-1.xsl assumes that there must be two title attributes in an input XML document. To make it more flexible, in Listing 7.7 we show you an improved stylesheet (sample-2.xsl) that can accept any number of title attributes.

**Listing 7.7** Improved stylesheet, chap07/data/sample-2.xsl

```
<?xml version="1.0" encoding="UTF-8"?>
<xsl:stylesheet
  version="1.0"
  xmlns:xsl="http://www.w3.org/1999/XSL/Transform"
  xmlns="http://www.w3.org/TR/xhtml1"
  xmlns:ch7="http://www.example.com/xmlbook2/chap07/"
  exclude-result-prefixes="ch7">
  <xsl:output method="xml" encoding="UTF-8"/>

  <!-- Template 1 -->
  <xsl:template match="/">
    <html>
      <head><title>XSLT Sample</title></head>
      <body>
        <ul>
<xsl:apply-templates select="ch7:W3Cspecs/ch7:spec"/>
        </ul>
      </body>
    </html>
  </xsl:template>

  <!-- Template 2 -->
  <xsl:template match="ch7:W3Cspecs/ch7:spec">
    <li><xsl:value-of select="@title"/></li>
  </xsl:template>

</xsl:stylesheet>
```

Two templates are defined in `sample-2.xsl` (Templates 1 and 2), while there is only one template in `sample-1.xsl`. Template 1 is almost the same as the one in `sample-1.xsl`. The only difference is that the child element of the `ul` element is the `xsl:apply-templates` element. Template 2 is newly added. The result of applying `sample-2.xsl` to `sample.xml` is identical to that of applying `sample-1.xsl` (see Listing 7.6). However, `sample-2.xsl` can accept any number of `title` attributes in `sample.xml`.

The `xsl:apply-templates` element is an instruction to apply templates to the nodes selected by the XPath expression specified in the `select` attribute. This instruction lets an XSLT processor first select templates that match nodes specified by an XPath expression in the `match` attribute, and then apply the selected templates to specified nodes. If more than one node is selected, an XSLT processor applies templates to all the selected nodes. In `sample-2.xsl`, an XSLT processor first selects two `ch7:spec` elements in `sample.xml`. Selected elements are specified by the XPath expression `ch7:W3Cspecs/ch7:spec` in the `select` attribute of the `xsl:apply-templates` element. Then it applies the second template to the selected elements. The second template is selected because the selected elements also match the `match` attribute `ch7:W3Cspecs/ch7:spec`. For each selected element, the second template outputs the value of the `title` attribute of the `ch7:spec` element as an `li` element.

In general, an XSLT processor recursively traverses an input XML tree structure as shown in Figure 7.3. The node that an XSLT processor is working with is called

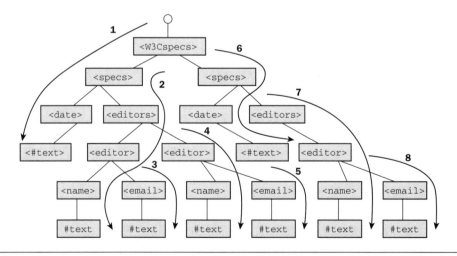

**Figure 7.3** Traversing an input XML document with an XSLT processor

the current node. An XSLT processor may change the current node to a different part of the tree structure depending on the instructions. Even so, control is finally returned to the previous current node, like a function call in a programming language.

There are several built-in templates to determine the default processing behavior of an XSLT processor. The priorities of built-in templates are lower than those written explicitly by a programmer. Therefore, a template written in a stylesheet is always selected when the template matches the same node that a built-in template also matches. Some typical built-in templates follow.[8]

```
<!-- Built-in template 1 -->
<xsl:template match="*|/">
  <xsl:apply-templates/>
</xsl:template>

<!-- Built-in template 2 -->
<xsl:template match="text()|@*">
  <xsl:value-of select="."/>
</xsl:template>

<!-- Built-in template 3 -->
<xsl:template match="processing-instruction()|comment()"/>
```

Built-in template 1 matches all the elements and the document root, and applies templates to all their child elements. If an `apply-templates` element does not have a `select` attribute, all the child elements under the current node are selected. Note that the `apply-templates` element changes the current node. Built-in template 2 matches all the text nodes and attribute nodes, and outputs their values. Built-in template 3 matches all the processing instructions (PIs) and comment nodes. The template does not output anything because it has no child elements. Therefore, it removes PIs and comments from the output document.

If you do not write any template—that is, you just use these built-in templates— all the tags, PIs, and comments are removed from an input XML document, and only the text and attribute values remain in the output document.

Using `sample-2.xsl` as an example, we can explain how templates are to be applied to an input XML document. To make the explanation simple, we omit the processing of whitespace. Table 7.4 shows the stylesheet processing steps in order.

---

[8] There are other built-in templates, which are not listed here.

**Table 7.4** Stylesheet Processing Steps

| STEP NO. | CURRENT NODE | TEMPLATE IN PROCESS | OUTPUT | DESCRIPTION |
|---|---|---|---|---|
| 1 | / | N/A | N/A | Selects a template in the stylesheet that matches /. In this case, template 1 is selected. |
| 2 | / | 1 | `<html><head> <title>XSLT sample 1</title> </head><body> <ul>` | Outputs the first literal string. |
| 3 | / | 1 | N/A | Selects `ch7:W3Cspecs[1]/ ch7:spec[1]` and `ch7: W3Cspecs/ch7:spec[2]` according to the `select` attribute in the `apply-templates` element. |
| 4 | `/ch7:W3C specs[1]/ ch7:spec[1]` | N/A | N/A | Selects a template in the stylesheet that matches `ch7:W3Cspecs[1]/ch7:spec [1]`. In this case, template 2 is selected. |
| 5 | `/ch7:W3C specs[1]/ ch7:spec[1]` | 2 | `<li>` | Outputs the first literal string in template 2. |
| 6 | `/ch7:W3C specs[1]/ ch7:spec[1]` | 2 | `XML Path Language (XPath) Version 1.0` | Outputs the value of the attribute selected by the XPath (@title) in the `select` attribute of the `xsl:value-of` element. |
| 7 | `/ch7:W3C specs[1]/ ch7:spec[1]` | 2 | `</li>` | Outputs the remaining literal string in template 2. |
| 8 | `/ch7:W3C specs[1]/ ch7:spec[2]` | N/A | `<li>XSL Transformations (XSLT) Version 1.0</li>` | Repeats steps 4 through 7 with `/ch7:W3Cspecs[1]/ ch7:spec[2]`. |
| 9 | / | 1 | `</ul></body> </html>` | Outputs the remaining literal string in the first template. |
| 10 | N/A | N/A | N/A | Ends |

The last example, shown in Listing 7.8, is `sample-3.xsl`, which generates an XHTML table from `sample.xml` (see Listing 7.2).

**Listing 7.8** More complex example of stylesheets, `chap07/data/sample-3.xsl`

```xml
<?xml version="1.0" encoding="UTF-8"?>
<xsl:stylesheet
  version="1.0"
  xmlns:xsl="http://www.w3.org/1999/XSL/Transform"
  xmlns="http://www.w3.org/TR/xhtml1"
  xmlns:ch7="http://www.example.com/xmlbook2/chap07/"
  exclude-result-prefixes="ch7">
  <xsl:output method="xml" encoding="UTF-8"/>

  <!-- Template 1 -->
  <xsl:template match="/">
    <html>
      <head><title>XSLT Sample</title></head>
      <body>
        <table border="1">
          <thead>
            <tr>
              <th>Title</th>
              <th>Status</th>
              <th>Date</th>
            </tr>
          </thead>
          <tbody><xsl:apply-templates/></tbody>
        </table>
      </body>
    </html>
  </xsl:template>

  <!-- Template 2 -->
  <xsl:template match="ch7:spec">
    <tr>
      <td><xsl:value-of select="@title"/></td>
      <td><xsl:apply-templates select="ch7:date/@type"/></td>
      <td><xsl:value-of select="ch7:date"/></td>
    </tr>
  </xsl:template>

  <!-- Template 3 -->
  <xsl:template match="@type">
    <xsl:variable name="type" select="."/>
    <xsl:choose>
      <xsl:when test='$type="REC"'>Recommendation</xsl:when>
      <xsl:when test='$type="PR"'>Proposed Recommendation</xsl:when>
```

```
      <xsl:when test='$type="WD"'>Working Draft</xsl:when>
      <xsl:otherwise>Other</xsl:otherwise>
    </xsl:choose>
  </xsl:template>

</xsl:stylesheet>
```

Listing 7.9, `sample-3.xhtml`, is the output XHTML file. We show the result with appropriate indentations for readability, but the actual result is not indented.

**Listing 7.9** The output XHTML document generated by `sample-3.xsl`, `chap07/data/sample-3.xhtml`

```
<?xml version="1.0" encoding="UTF-8"?>
<html xmlns="http://www.w3.org/TR/xhtml1">
  <head>
    <title>XSLT Sample</title>
  </head>
  <body>
    <table border="1">
      <thead>
        <tr>
          <th>Title</th>
          <th>Status</th>
          <th>Date</th>
        </tr>
      </thead>
      <tbody>
        <tr>
          <td>XML Path Language (XPath) Version 1.0</td>
          <td>Recommendation</td><td>16 November 1999</td>
        </tr>
        <tr>
          <td>XSL Transformations (XSLT) Version 1.0</td>
          <td>Recommendation</td><td>16 November 1999</td>
        </tr>
      </tbody>
    </table>
  </body>
</html>
```

In this example, for each `ch7:spec` element in `sample.xml`, its `title` and `type` attributes and its child element, `ch7:date`, are extracted and inserted as a record of the output XHTML table. There are three templates: Template 1 matches the root node and outputs an outer structure of the XHTML table; template 2 matches `ch7:spec` elements and outputs the contents of the matched element as a table record; and template 3 matches each `@title` attribute and outputs its value.

An xsl:choose element, which appeared in the third template, is similar to the switch-case statement in a programming language. It tests the value of the test attribute in each xsl:when element and outputs the contents of the xsl:when element that first passes the test. This template translates shorthand notations (for example, "REC") to their corresponding full notations (for example, "Recommendation").

The type is a variable declared as an attribute of the xsl:variable element, with the initial value of the @type attribute. It is referred to as $type in a when element.

In Table 7.5 we show some typical instructions that can be used in a template. There are other instructions in XSLT. Refer to the XSLT specification for the details.

**Table 7.5**   Instructions in XSLT

| INSTRUCTION/EXAMPLE | DESCRIPTION |
|---|---|
| `<xsl:value-of select="`*expression*`"/>`<br>`<xsl:value-of`<br>`select="ch7:W3Cspecs/ch7:spec[1]/@title"/>` | Outputs the result of evaluating the expression. |
| `<xsl:text>`*content*`</xsl:text>`<br>`<xsl:text>XSLT sample 1</xsl:text>` | Outputs the content. |
| `<xsl:if test=` **expression** `>` **template** `</xsl:if>`<br>`<xsl:if test="position()=1">first one</xsl:if>` | Evaluates the expression and if true, evaluates the template. |
| `<xsl:choose>`<br>  `<xsl:when test=`**expression**`>`**template**`</xsl:when>`<br>  `<xsl:otherwise>`**template**`</xsl:otherwise>`<br>`</xsl:choose>` | |
| `<xsl:choose>`<br>   `<xsl:when test='node()="US"'>United States`<br>   `</xsl:when>`<br>   `<xsl:when test='node()="CA"'>Canada</xsl:when>`<br>   `<xsl:when test='node()="JP"'>Japan</xsl:when>`<br>   `<xsl:otherwise>Other</xsl:otherwise>`<br>`</xsl:choose>` | Evaluates the expression and if true, evaluates the template. |
| `<xsl:variable name="`*qname*`" select="`*expression*`"/>`<br>`<xsl:variable name="type" select="."/>` | Declares a variable and initializes with the expression. |

## 7.2.3  XSLT Programming in Java

In this section, we use Xalan as an XSLT processor; it was also used as an XPath processor in Section 7.1.4. However, we do not use Xalan's API (the org.apache.xalan package); we use the Java API for XML Processing (JAXP). JAXP is a standard API for XML processing that is defined by the Java Community Process (JCP) and will be shipped with Java Development Kit (JDK) 1.4, which is the next version of JDK. It provides the API for XSLT processing as the `javax.xml.transform` package. The JAXP package is also included in `xalan.jar`, which is Xalan's jar file.

## Overview of JAXP API for Processing XSLT

Here we give an overview of the JAXP API for processing XSLT.

To absorb the differences between the underlying XSLT processors, JAXP provides two classes for processing XSLT: One is the `Transformer` class for the abstraction of an XSLT processor, and the other is the `TransformerFactory` class for the `Transformer`'s factory class. This design is similar to JAXP for XML processors, such as the `DocumentBuilder` and `DocumentBuilderFactory` classes. To abstract the I/O, JAXP provides two interfaces: the `Source` interface and the `Result` interface. The `Source` interface is used for both stylesheets and input XML documents.

JAXP supports three types of I/O interfaces: stream, DOM, and SAX. There are three packages, `javax.xml.transform.{stream, dom, sax}`, provided for that purpose. Each package contains two classes (for example, `StreamSource` and `StreamResult`) to implement the `Source` and the `Result` interfaces.

## Calling the XSLT Processor

Listing 7.10, `XSLTStreamTest.java`, shows a very simple example program to call the XSLT processor with streaming I/O.

**Listing 7.10** Calling XSLT with streaming I/O, chap07/XSLTStreamTest.java

```
package chap07;

import javax.xml.transform.TransformerFactory;
import javax.xml.transform.Transformer;
import javax.xml.transform.stream.StreamSource;
import javax.xml.transform.stream.StreamResult;

public class XSLTStreamTest {
    public static void main(String[] args) throws Exception {
        // args[0] specifies the path to the input XSLT stylesheet
        String xsltURL = args[0];
        // args[1] specifies the path to the input XML document
        String xmlURL = args[1];

        // Creates instances of StreamSource for the stylesheet
[16]    StreamSource xslt = new StreamSource(xsltURL);
        // Creates instances of StreamSource for the input document
[18]    StreamSource xml = new StreamSource(xmlURL);
```

```
              // Creates an instance of TransformerFactory
[21]          TransformerFactory factory =
[22]              TransformerFactory.newInstance();
              // Creates an instance of Transformer
[24]          Transformer transformer = factory.newTransformer(xslt);
              // Executes the Transformer
[26]          transformer.transform(xml, new StreamResult(System.out));
        }
    }
```

The XSLTStreamTest program accepts two arguments: an XSLT stylesheet and an input XML document. It applies the XSLT stylesheet to the input XML document and then outputs the result to the standard output.

You can run the program as follows:

```
R:\samples\>java chap07.XSLTStreamTest
    file:./chap07/data/sample-1.xsl file:./chap07/data/sample.xml
```

The result is shown in Listing 7.5. Let's run XSLTStreamTest for sample-2. xsl and sample-3.xsl, too. We get the results shown in Listings 7.5 and 7.9, respectively.

Next we explain the details of XSLTStreamTest.

First, it creates StreamSource objects from the URIs of a stylesheet and an input XML document (lines 16 and 18). A StreamSource object can also be created from either an InputStream object or a Reader object. The XSLT processor calls an XML processor. Applications do not need to call the XML processor by themselves. Next, it creates a TransformerFactory object (lines 21 and 22) and a Transformer object (line 24).

Note that this program uses TransformerFactory#newTransformer (Source). In this way, JAXP creates a Transformer object associated with a particular stylesheet. The Transformer object is reusable for multiple calls of the transform() method. Therefore, it is useful to apply the same stylesheet object to multiple XML documents. Care should be taken that the Transformer is not thread-safe.

Finally, a transformation is executed (line 26). The translation result is written to the standard output.

### Working with DOM

Listing 7.11, XSLTDOMTest.java, is an example using DOM for its I/O.

**Listing 7.11** Using DOM for I/O, chap07/XSLTDOMTest.java

```java
package chap07;

import javax.xml.transform.TransformerFactory;
import javax.xml.transform.Transformer;
import javax.xml.transform.dom.DOMSource;
import javax.xml.transform.dom.DOMResult;
import javax.xml.parsers.DocumentBuilder;
import javax.xml.parsers.DocumentBuilderFactory;
import org.apache.xml.serialize.OutputFormat;
import org.apache.xml.serialize.XMLSerializer;
import org.w3c.dom.Node;
import org.w3c.dom.Element;
import org.w3c.dom.Document;
import org.w3c.dom.DocumentFragment;

public class XSLTDOMTest {
    public static void main(String[] args) throws Exception {
```
```
[18]            // args[0] specifies the path to the input XSLT stylesheet
[19]            String xsltURL = args[0];
[20]            // args[1] specifies the path to the input XML document
[21]            String xmlURL = args[1];
[22]
[23]            // Creates an instance of DocumentBuilderFactory.
[24]            DocumentBuilderFactory dFactory =
[25]                DocumentBuilderFactory.newInstance();
[26]            dFactory.setNamespaceAware(true);
[27]            // Creates an instance of DocumentBuilder
[28]            DocumentBuilder parser = dFactory.newDocumentBuilder();
[29]
[30]            // Creates a DOM instance of the stylesheet
[31]            Document xsltDoc = parser.parse(xsltURL);
[32]            // Creates a DOM instance of the input document
[33]            Document xmlDoc = parser.parse(xmlURL);

                // Creates an instance of TransformerFactory
                TransformerFactory tFactory =
                    TransformerFactory.newInstance();
                // Checks if the factory supports DOM or not
[39]            if(!tFactory.getFeature(DOMSource.FEATURE) ||
[40]                !tFactory.getFeature(DOMResult.FEATURE))
[41]                 throw new Exception("DOM is not supported");

                // Creates instances of DOMSource and DOMResult
[44]            DOMSource xsltDOMSource = new DOMSource(xsltDoc);
[45]            DOMSource xmlDOMSource = new DOMSource(xmlDoc);
[46]            DOMResult domResult = new DOMResult();
```

```
                    // Creates an instance of Transformer
                    Transformer transformer =
                        tFactory.newTransformer(xsltDOMSource);

                    // Executes the Transformer
                    transformer.transform(xmlDOMSource, domResult);

                    // Gets the result
[56]                Node resultNode = domResult.getNode();

[58]                // Prints the response
[59]                OutputFormat formatter = new OutputFormat();
[60]                formatter.setPreserveSpace(true);
[61]                XMLSerializer serializer =
[62]                    new XMLSerializer(System.out, formatter);
[63]                switch (resultNode.getNodeType()) {
[64]                case Node.DOCUMENT_NODE:
[65]                    serializer.serialize((Document)resultNode);
[66]                    break;
[67]                case Node.ELEMENT_NODE:
[68]                    serializer.serialize((Element)resultNode);
[69]                    break;
[70]                case Node.DOCUMENT_FRAGMENT_NODE:
[71]                    serializer.serialize((DocumentFragment)resultNode);
[72]                    break;
[73]                default:
[74]                    throw new Exception("Unexpected node type");
[75]                }
                }
            }
```

Refer to XSLTStreamTest to run the program. The only thing you need to change is the class name.

Let's see the details of the program.

The first half of the program translates an input XML document into a DOM tree with an input stylesheet (lines18–33). Then it tests whether the JAXP implementation supports DOM (lines 39–41) because DOM support may not be provided in some JAXP implementations. The rest of the program is almost the same as XSLTStreamTest. The only difference is that it uses DOMSource and DOMResult instead of StreamSource and StreamResult (lines 44–46). Finally, it gets the result node set by using DOMResult#getNode() (line 56), serializes it, and outputs it (lines 58–75).

## Translating SAX Events to Other SAX Events

In Chapter 5, Section 5.2.2, we showed how to use a SAX event filter to translate SAX events. In this section, we create a program with a similar behavior using XSLT and JAXP. We discuss the pros and cons of using SAX, DOM, XPath, and XSLT in Section 7.3.

Figure 7.4 illustrates the concept of SAX event translation using XSLT. In the following discussion, the numbers in parentheses refer to the numbered areas in the figure. In the figure, `TransformerHandler` is a specialized `Transformer` that implements the `ContentHandler` interface. Similar to `Transformer`, `TransformerHandler` is associated with a stylesheet (1).

`SAXParser`, `TransformerHandler`, and the application are connected as a pipeline; that is, the `ContentHandler` interface of `TransformerHandler` is registered to `SAXParser` (2), and similarly the application's `ContentHandler` interface is registered to `TransformerHandler` (3). In this way, each `Content Handler` of a right-hand component is registered to its left-hand component to make a pipeline.

Once an XML document is given to the SAX parser (4), it is translated into SAX events and passed to the next component (5, 7). `TransformerHandler` translates SAX events by applying the stylesheet (6).

What is the advantage of this approach? Suppose that an application already has a SAX event handler for processing XML documents that are compliant with a particular DTD or an XML Schema. This approach provides the ability to process similar but different XML documents by preparing a stylesheet for this particular translation. A similar example is shown in Chapter 8, Section 8.3.

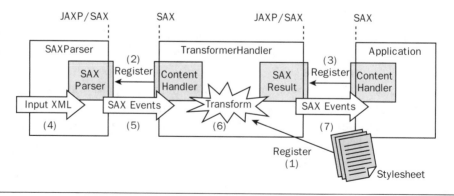

**Figure 7.4** Translating SAX events using XSLT

Suppose that an application developer has a SAX event handler like the one shown in Listing 7.12.

**Listing 7.12** SAX event handler, `chap07/BookHandler.java`

```java
package chap07;

import java.util.Vector;
import org.xml.sax.Attributes;
import org.xml.sax.SAXException;
import org.xml.sax.helpers.DefaultHandler;

public class BookHandler extends DefaultHandler {
    // An array to store the results
    final Vector books;
    public BookHandler() {
        this.books = new Vector();
    }

    // Instance variables temporarily used for processing
    Book currentBook = null;
    Author currentAuthor = null;
    StringBuffer buf = new StringBuffer();

    class Book {
        String publishedDate;
        Vector authors = new Vector();
        public String toString() {
            return ("Book(publishedDate=" + publishedDate +
                    ", authors=" + authors+")");
        }
    }
    class Author {
        String authorName;
        String contactTo;
        public String toString() {
            return ("Author(authorName=" + authorName +
                    ", contactTo=" + contactTo + ")");
        }
    }

    public void endDocument() throws SAXException {
        System.out.println(books);
    }

    public void startElement(String uri,
                             String localName,
                             String qName,
                             Attributes attributes)
```

```
                    throws SAXException
        {
            if ("Book".equals(localName)) {
                currentBook = new Book();
                return;
            }
            if ("Author".equals(localName)) {
                currentAuthor = new Author();
                return;
            }
            buf.setLength(0);
        }

        public void endElement(String uri,
                               String localName,
                               String qName)
            throws SAXException
        {
            if ("Book".equals(localName)) {
                books.addElement(currentBook);
                return;
            }
            if ("Author".equals(localName)) {
                currentBook.authors.addElement(currentAuthor);
                return;
            }
            if ("PublishedDate".equals(localName))
                currentBook.publishedDate = buf.toString();
            else if ("AuthorName".equals(localName))
                currentAuthor.authorName = buf.toString();
            else if ("ContactTo".equals(localName))
                currentAuthor.contactTo = buf.toString();
            buf.setLength(0);
        }

        public void characters(char[] ch, int start, int length)
            throws SAXException
        {
            buf.append(new String(ch, start, length));
        }
    }
```

BookHandler is designed to process Books.xml (shown in Listing 7.13). It reads Books.xml as an input XML document, stores each book entry in the array variable books in the Book object, and finally outputs the values of books to the standard output.

**Listing 7.13** The `Books.xml` document

```
<?xml version="1.0" encoding="UTF-8"?>
<Books xmlns="http://www.example.com/xmlbook2/chap07/">
  <Book>
    <PublishedDate>16 November 1999</PublishedDate>
    <Author>
      <AuthorName>James Clark</AuthorName>
      <ContactTo>jjc@jclark.com</ContactTo>
    </Author>
    <Author>
      <AuthorName>Steve DeRose</AuthorName>
      <ContactTo>Steven_DeRose@Brown.edu</ContactTo>
    </Author>
  </Book>
  <Book>
    <PublishedDate>16 November 1999</PublishedDate>
    <Author>
      <AuthorName>James Clark</AuthorName>
      <ContactTo>jjc@jclark.com</ContactTo>
    </Author>
  </Book>
</Books>
```

If you remember the document `sample.xml`, you will find similarities between `Books.xml` and `sample.xml`. For example, a `spec` element in `sample.xml` corresponds to a `Book` element in `Books.xml`. Even though these two have semantically the same contents, `BookHandler` cannot handle `sample.xml` correctly because they have different tag names.

In such a case, it is useful to have a preprocessing mechanism to translate `sample.xml` to another XML document having the same DTD for `Books.xml`. Once such a mechanism has been provided, just by preparing an XSLT stylesheet, an application can handle a similar but different XML document without any modification to the application itself. If we assume the existence of such a transformer between a SAX parser and an application at design time, the application becomes very flexible toward various input XML documents.

The program `XSLTSAXTest.java` (shown in Listing 7.14) is an example program for the translation purpose described earlier. It accepts two URI arguments (an XSLT stylesheet and an input XML document), applies the stylesheet to the input XML document, and then generates SAX events to be passed to `BookHandler`.

**Listing 7.14** Translating SAX events using XSLT, chap07/XSLTSAXTest.java

```
package chap07;

import javax.xml.parsers.SAXParser;
import javax.xml.parsers.SAXParserFactory;
import javax.xml.transform.TransformerFactory;
import javax.xml.transform.sax.SAXSource;
import javax.xml.transform.sax.SAXResult;
import javax.xml.transform.sax.SAXTransformerFactory;
import javax.xml.transform.sax.TransformerHandler;
import javax.xml.transform.stream.StreamSource;
import org.xml.sax.InputSource;
import org.xml.sax.XMLReader;

public class XSLTSAXTest {
    public static void main(String[] args) throws Exception {
        // args[0] specifies the URI for the XSLT stylesheet
        String xsltURL = args[0];
        // args[1] specifies the URI for the input XML document
        String xmlURL = args[1];

        // Creates a stream source for the stylesheet
        StreamSource xslt = new StreamSource(xsltURL);
        // Creates an input source for the input document
        InputSource xml = new InputSource(xmlURL);

        // Creates a SAX parser
[27]    SAXParserFactory pFactory = SAXParserFactory.newInstance();
[28]    SAXParser parser = pFactory.newSAXParser();
[29]    XMLReader xmlReader = parser.getXMLReader();

        // Creates an instance of TransformerFactory
[32]    TransformerFactory tFactory =
[33]        TransformerFactory.newInstance();

        // Checks if the TransformingFactory supports SAX or not
[36]    if (!tFactory.getFeature(SAXSource.FEATURE))
[37]        throw new Exception("SAX is not supported");

        // Casts TransformerFactory to SAXTransformerFactory
[40]    SAXTransformerFactory stFactory =
[41]        ((SAXTransformerFactory)tFactory);
        // Creates a TransformerHandler with the stylesheet
[43]    TransformerHandler tHandler =
[44]        stFactory.newTransformerHandler(xslt);
        // Sets the TransformerHandler to the SAXParser
        xmlReader.setContentHandler(tHandler);
        // Sets the application ContentHandler
```

```
                   // to the TransformerHandler
[49]               tHandler.setResult(new SAXResult(new BookHandler()));

                   // Parses the input XML
[52]               xmlReader.parse(xml);
               }
           }
```

Let's examine XSLTSAXTest in detail by referencing Figure 7.4.

First, we create a SAXParser by using JAXP API (lines 27–28) and get an XMLReader by calling SAXParser#getXMLReader() (line 29). Second, we create a TransformerFactory (lines 32–33) and test whether it supports the SAX API (lines 36–37). If the API is supported, we cast the type of Transformer Factory to the SAXTransformerFactory type (lines 40–41). Third, we create a TransformerHandler associated with a stylesheet (lines 43–44). This corresponds to step (1) in Figure 7.4. Fourth, we register the TransformerHandler to the XMLReader (2). Fifth, we register BookHandler, which is a ContentHandler prepared by the application, to SAXResult (line 49) (3). Finally, we call XMLReader#parse() to perform the pipeline (line 52); that is, the input XML document is translated into SAX events and passed to TransformerHandler (5), TransformerHandler performs the conversion (6), and the converted SAX events are passed to BookHandler (7).

Let's run XSLTSAXTest with sample.xml as an input XML document (see Listing 7.2) and sample-4.xsl as an XSLT stylesheet (see Listing 7.15). The stylesheet sample-4.xsl matches each element in sample.xml and translates it to the corresponding element in Books.xml. It outputs every attribute and context string as is. The final result is the same as Books.xml (see Listing 7.13).

**Listing 7.15** A stylesheet that translates sample.xml into Books.xml, chap07/data/sample-4.xsl

```
<?xml version="1.0" encoding="UTF-8"?>
<xsl:stylesheet
  version="1.0"
  xmlns:xsl="http://www.w3.org/1999/XSL/Transform"
  xmlns="http://www.example.com/xmlbook2/chap07/">
  <xsl:output method="xml" encoding="UTF-8"/>

  <xsl:template match="*[local-name()='W3Cspecs']">
    <Books><xsl:apply-templates/></Books>
  </xsl:template>

  <xsl:template match="*[local-name()='spec']">
    <Book><xsl:apply-templates/></Book>
  </xsl:template>
```

```
  <xsl:template match="*[local-name()='date']">
    <PublishedDate><xsl:apply-templates/></PublishedDate>
  </xsl:template>

  <xsl:template match="*[local-name()='editor']">
    <Author><xsl:apply-templates/></Author>
  </xsl:template>

  <xsl:template match="*[local-name()='name']">
    <AuthorName><xsl:apply-templates/></AuthorName>
  </xsl:template>

  <xsl:template match="*[local-name()='email']">
    <ContactTo><xsl:apply-templates/></ContactTo>
  </xsl:template>

  <xsl:template match="@*">
    <xsl:value-of select="name()"/>=<xsl:value-of select="."/>
  </xsl:template>
</xsl:stylesheet>
```

Running XSLTSAXTest in the console generates the output shown in Listing 7.16. The output is appropriately indented for readability although the original output is just a single line.

```
R:\samples\>java chap07.XSLTSAXTest file:./chap07/data/sample-4.xsl
file:./chap07/data/sample.xml
```

**Listing 7.16** Output of XSLTSAXTest

```
[Book(
  publishedDate=16 November 1999,
  authors=[
    Author(
      authorName=James Clark,
      contactTo=jjc@jclark.com),
    Author(
      authorName=Steve DeRose,
      contactTo=Steven_DeRose@Brown.edu)
  ]),
Book(
  publishedDate=16 November 1999,
  authors=[
    Author(
      authorName=James Clark,
      contactTo=jjc@jclark.com)
  ])
]
```

You will find that the contents of `sample.xml` are stored into the `Book` objects correctly.

### A Simple Way to Translate SAX Events

Now you can translate SAX events to other SAX events and pass them to another application's event handler. However, the drawback is that the programming style of `XSLTSAXTest` is far from the standard style of using JAXP.

For example, the standard way to use the JAXP API is to call `SAXParser#parse()`. On the other hand, `XSLTSAXTest` calls the `XMLReader#parse()` method of the `XMLReader` object, which is created by the `SAXParser#getXMLReader()` method call to a `SAXParser` instance. Another example is that the use of the JAXP API becomes tricky. In this way, this approach requires significant changes to an application if it is written in the standard JAXP programming style. Therefore, we do not recommend this approach.

We want to make JAXP invocation as transparent as possible; that is, we want to minimize the modification of an application as much as possible. For that purpose, as shown in Figure 7.5, we provide wrapper classes (`Transforming SAXParserFactory`, `TransformingSAXParser`, `XMLReaderWrapper`) to the corresponding JAXP classes (`SAXParserFactory`, `SAXParser`, and `XMLReader`).

Each wrapping class implements the same interface that the corresponding wrapped class does. Therefore, an application can call JAXP transparently through these wrapper classes. The application program is shown in Listing 7.17.

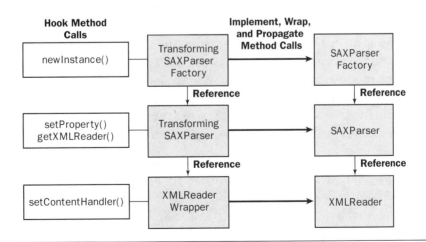

**Figure 7.5** A mechanism for transforming `SAXParser`

**Listing 7.17** Calling JAXP transparently, chap07/TransformingSAXParserTest.java

```java
package chap07;

import javax.xml.parsers.SAXParser;
import javax.xml.parsers.SAXParserFactory;
import javax.xml.transform.stream.StreamSource;
import org.xml.sax.InputSource;

public class TransformingSAXParserTest {
    public static void main(String[] args) throws Exception {
        // args[0] specifies the path to the input XSL file
        String xslURL = args[0];
        // args[1] specifies the path to the input XML file
        String xmlURL = args[1];

        // Creates a stream source for the XSL stylesheet
        StreamSource xsl = new StreamSource(xslURL);
        // Creates an input source for XML document
        InputSource xml = new InputSource(xmlURL);

        SAXParserFactory factory =
            TransformingSAXParserFactory.newInstance();
        SAXParser parser = factory.newSAXParser();
        parser.setProperty(TransformingSAXParser.PROPERTY_URI, xsl);
        parser.parse(xml, new BookHandler());
    }
}
```

Refer to XSLTSAXTest to run the program. You only need to change the class name.

This wrapper approach reduces the necessary changes to an application. In fact, only two lines must be changed from the original: The first change, when creating an instance of the SAXParserFactory class, is to explicitly call TransformingSAXParserFactory.newInstance() instead of SAXParserFactory.newInstance(); the second change is to specify a stylesheet by calling TransformingSAXParser#setProperty(String, Object) with a property name (http://www.example.com/xmlbook2/chap07/) and its value (the StreamSource object format of a stylesheet).

In this section, we explained XSLT programming through examples. We hope this helps you understand the powerful capability of XSLT. However, certain classes of applications cannot take advantage of XSLT. In some cases, it is not easy to determine whether it is better to use DOM, SAX, XPath, or XSLT for a particular application. We discuss this issue in Section 7.3.

# 7.3  Pros and Cons of XSLT, XPath, DOM, and SAX

Earlier in this chapter, we described XPath and XSLT. Also we showed how to use DOM and SAX. Now you have four ways to write a program to deal with XML documents. Which is the best way to write what kind of program in terms of rapid development, easy maintenance, and time and space efficiency? In this section, we discuss this issue.

## 7.3.1  Execution Efficiency

In general, it is not very easy to discuss time and space efficiency in Java because it highly depends on many factors, such as a developer's programming style, the behavior of a just-in-time compiler and garbage collection, and the implementation of libraries. These are some other factors specific to XML processing.

- The comparison between DOM and SAX, shown in Chapter 5, Section 5.3, covers performance and conversion issues.

- The DOM implementation of Xerces defers instantiation of a DOM object until it is really needed. Therefore, using DOM may not be much slower than using SAX if an application accesses only part of an entire DOM tree.

- The XPath implementation of Xalan is based on the DOM API.

- XSLT has a hidden overhead to process a stylesheet itself; however, a JAXP `Transformer` object, which abstracts a stylesheet, can be reusable but not thread-safe.

- Various optimization techniques are applied to XSLT and XPath implementation in the Saxon XSLT processor.[9]

- Xalan provides XSLTC, a compiler to generate Java byte code from an XSLT stylesheet.

Now you can understand that it is really difficult to predict time and space efficiency before you develop an application. Therefore, if you are not experienced in XML and Java programming, we recommend that you focus on how rapidly you can develop a program or how easily you can maintain it rather than on how fast or compact it is. If your program is designed simply and flexibly, it is relatively easy to switch to the other approach. The rest of this section focuses on development efficiency rather than time and space efficiency.

---

[9] Refer to `http://www-106.ibm.com/developerworks/library/x-xslt2/`.

## 7.3.2 Development Efficiency

Here are some questions you should consider when you want to improve development efficiency.

- How easy is it to write a typical application?
- How flexible is it to modify an existing program to meet future requirements?
- How easy is it to read and understand a program?
- How easy is it to determine problems and bugs?
- How easy is it to share the development of a large program?

Because quantitative analysis is not always easy, we discuss the pros and cons of development efficiency through two typical cases of XML processing. We first review the case in which the combination of XPath and DOM works better than using only DOM for traversing and modifying an XML document. Then we compare the use of SAX and DOM and the use of XSLT to translate an XML document to another XML document. We hope these discussions give you a clear view of development efficiency.

### Combination of XPath and DOM

A DOM tree faithfully represents the tree structure of an XML document. One approach to finding a target element in a DOM tree is to write a recursive program or use the `org.w3c.dom.traversal` package, but this is not very simple.

In this case, a combination of XPath and DOM not only makes a program simple but also improves the readability of the program because it becomes compact. This approach may be slower than the previous approach. However, it is worth taking this approach when you don't need to traverse the tree many times or when performance is not critical.

Let's look at the XML document in Listing 7.18. It is a SmartDoc format of Section 1.3.1 in the first edition of this book.

**Listing 7.18** `SmartDoc` example showing keywords, `chap07/data/XMLandJava_1_3_1.sdoc`

```
<?xml version='1.0' encoding="UTF-8"?>
<doc>
  <head>
    <author locale="en">Hiroshi Maruyama</author>
    <date><time/></date>
  </head>
  <body>
    <subsection>
```

```
      <title locale="en">1.3.1 Background of XML</title>
      <p locale="en">
HyperText Markup Language (<em>HTML</em>) has been widely used in
describing Web contents since it was defined in 1992. It has a simple
syntax, it is easy to create multimedia documents by incorporating
images, audio and so on, and it allows many other documents to be
linked together. With free browsers being deployed universally, it
has become one of the primary means to deliver information via the
Internet.
      </p>
      <p locale="en">
<em>HTML</em> has been enhanced many times in its history. Because
HTML has a fixed set of tags, the only way to add new functionality
into HTML is to bring it to <em>W3C</em> and put it on the discussion
table. This may be a lengthy process, and not all the tags are
general enough to be included in HTML.
      </p>
      <p locale="en">
With Extensible Markup Language (<em>XML</em>), one can define his or
her own tag set by means of document type definition (<em>DTD</em>).
At this moment, not many Web pages are authored in XML, but many
emerging proposals in the fields of document processing, meta
contents, database, and messaging are based on XML.
      </p>
    </subsection>
    </body>
</doc>
```

In this document, a keyword is enclosed by an em tag only when it first appears in each paragraph (enclosed by p element). Using this feature, we can make a keyword index.

First, we add an id attribute to each em element in the input XML document. Each id attribute has a sequence number. For example, the em element in the first paragraph will be changed as follows:

```
      <p locale="en">
HyperText Markup Language (<em id="id-0">HTML</em>) has been widely
used in ...
      </p>
```

Listing 7.19 is a keyword index file. Each keyword in the input XML document is associated with a keyword element, with the keyword itself in its id attribute. A keyword element has one or more ref elements. Each ref element corresponds to each keyword enclosed by an em tag. The href attribute of the ref element has a reference to the id attribute of the em element in the document.

**Listing 7.19**  Keyword index file, `XMLandJava_1_3_1-glossary.xml`

```
<?xml version="1.0" encoding="UTF-8"?>
<glossary>
  <keyword id="HTML">
    <ref href="#id-0"/>
    <ref href="#id-1"/>
  </keyword>
  <keyword id="W3C">
    <ref href="#id-2"/>
  </keyword>
  <keyword id="XML">
    <ref href="#id-3"/>
  </keyword>
  <keyword id="DTD">
    <ref href="#id-4"/>
  </keyword>
</glossary>
```

We use `MakeSmartDocGlossary.java` to perform the process just described. The following command displays the input document after it is processed, the keyword index, and list of XPath expressions that refer to the em elements in the input document.

```
R:\examples\>java chap07.MakeSmartDocGlossary
file:./chap07/data/XMLandJava_1_3_1.xml
```

Here are the processing steps of `MakeSmartDocGlossary.java`.

1.  Read an input XML document and generate a DOM tree, `sdoc`.
2.  Create a DOM tree, `gdoc`, for the keyword index by using the JAXP API.
3.  Find all the em elements in `sdoc` by using XPath.
4.  For each em element found in step 3, add an `id` attribute, register it to the keyword index if it is not registered yet, and create a `ref` element as a reference to the em element.
5.  Output `sdoc`.
6.  Output `gdoc`.
7.  For each `ref` element in the find-all-the-keywords index, find all the em elements referred by the `ref` element by using XPath, and output its XPath expression.

The following code fragment performs step 3. It finds all the em elements in `sdoc` by using XPath with the XPath expression `//em`. In this particular case, you can use the `Element#getElementsByTagNameNS()` method of the DOM API to get the same result, but XPath is more appropriate if you consider the flexibility or extensibility of the program.

```
        // Finds all "em" elements from the input DOM-tree
        NodeIterator ni = XPathAPI.selectNodeIterator(sdoc, "//em");
```

The following three code fragments perform step 4. The first code fragment is a loop to process each em element found in step 3.

```
        int nextID = 0;
        // For each node found
        while ((node = ni.nextNode()) != null) {
            ...
        }
```

Then, we add an id attribute to each em element. This is a good example of the combination of DOM and XPath.

```
        // Sets an id for the node
        String id = "id-"+ nextID++;
        ((Element)node).setAttribute("id", id);
```

The following code fragment extracts a keyword from each em element and checks whether its associated keyword element is already registered to gdoc. We use XPath for the check because it will not be simple to use the DOM API. Then, we register the keyword to gdoc if it is not found there. Finally, we create a ref element with a reference to the em element and register it to gdoc.

```
        // Gets the keyword
        String keyword = node.getFirstChild().getNodeValue();
        // Checks if the keyword is already registered
        String xpath = ("//keyword[@id=normalize-space('" +
                        keyword + "')]");
        Element elemKeyword =
            (Element)XPathAPI.selectSingleNode(gdoc, xpath);
        if (elemKeyword == null) {
            // If it has not been registered yet,
            // registers it
            elemKeyword = gdoc.createElement("keyword");
            elemKeyword.setAttribute("id", keyword);
            groot.appendChild(elemKeyword);
        }
        Element ref = gdoc.createElement("ref");
        ref.setAttribute("href", "#" + id);
        elemKeyword.appendChild(ref);
```

The following code fragment performs step 7. It extracts all the references from gdoc and finds the em elements referred to by the references. We use XPath to find all the href attributes of the ref elements and em elements.

```
// Finds all "keyword" elements in the glossary DOM-tree
ni = XPathAPI.selectNodeIterator(gdoc, "//keyword/ref/@href");
// For each node found
while ((node = ni.nextNode()) != null) {
    String id = node.getNodeValue().substring(1);
    // Finds all "em" elements match with the keyword
    String xpath = "//em[@id='" + id + "']";
    Node node2 = XPathAPI.selectSingleNode(sdoc, xpath);
    // Prints its XPath expression
    System.out.println("The ID '" + id +
                       "' found  at " + getXPath(node2));
}
```

The following is the full source code of getXPath().

```
// Creates XPath expression from Node
public static String getXPath(Node node) {
    Node localNode = node;
    switch (localNode.getNodeType()) {
    case Node.ELEMENT_NODE:
        // Finds all previous nodes that have the same node name
        int index = 1;
        String nodeName = node.getNodeName();
        while ((localNode = localNode.getPreviousSibling()) != null)
            if (localNode.getNodeName().equals(nodeName))
                index++;

        return (getXPath(node.getParentNode()) + "/" +
                node.getNodeName() + "[" + index + "]");
    case Node.TEXT_NODE:
        return (getXPath(node.getParentNode()) + "/text()");
    case Node.DOCUMENT_NODE:
        return "";
    default:
        throw new UnknownError("Unexpected node type");
    }
}
```

The getXPath() method builds an XPath expression to uniquely identify a node in a DOM tree. An example of such an XPath expression is:

```
/doc[1]/body[1]/subsection[1]/p[2]/em[2]
```

The getXPath() method is a typical example of traversing a DOM tree recursively.

Because there are one or more XPath expressions to a node in a DOM tree, there is no standard library to perform such an operation even though it is often needed.

This implementation traverses from the given node up to the document root. To determine the position of the target node, this program scans all the sibling nodes between the target node and its parent node. Therefore, the performance may not be very good.

Another implementation example is `IndexCreator`, described in Section 11.5.2. It recursively traverses a DOM tree from a parent down to its child nodes. While processing a parent node, it uses an XPath expression to uniquely identify a child node. This approach is efficient if you need to build XPath expressions for all the nodes in a DOM tree.

Now you have learned that a combination of the XPath API and the DOM API allows you to traverse a DOM tree simply and flexibly.

### Comparison of SAX/DOM and XSLT for XML Document Conversion

A SAX event handler can generate another XML document from input SAX events. In this book, you have learned two ways to convert an XML document to another using SAX. One way is to use a SAX filter to convert SAX events (shown in Section 5.2.2). The other way is to use a SAX event converter using XSLT. We discuss which way is better in what situations.

In general, a SAX event handler extracts document contexts from input SAX events and saves them in instance variables. As dependencies between the contexts become complex, a SAX event handler becomes hard to implement. For example, as shown in Figure 7.6, if element A has dependencies with elements B, C, and D, the context that the SAX event handler has to manage becomes quite complicated.

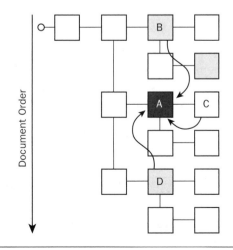

**Figure 7.6** Context dependencies in a SAX event handler

In the case of a SAX filter, it has to generate SAX events to be passed on to the following event handler in a pipeline. For example, because the processing of element A depends on element D, the handler holds all the events in a queue until element D appears to process element A. It may need more than one queue if there are other dependencies, and the program may become unrealistically complicated and hard to maintain.

Let's reconsider the `MailFilter` example in Section 5.2.2, which converts this:

```
<email>foo@bar.test</email>
```

to this:

```
<uri>mailto:foo@bar.test</uri>
```

In this example, the only dependency of the `email` element is its child text node. This dependency is easy to handle because the dependent nodes appear very close.

Another simple example shown in Section 5.2.2 converts between `<book title="foobar">...</book>` and `<book><title>foobar</title>...</book>`. The conversion from the former to the latter can be performed right after receiving the event of the `book` element because it has no dependency with any other elements. The reverse direction has a dependency, and the `book` element cannot be converted until receiving the `title` event.

The final example is a SAX filter program to sort sibling elements by their attribute values in alphabetical order. The program has to save all the events of the sibling elements in a buffer and then sort the elements in the buffer. It may become complicated if each sibling element has child elements. This example could imply the limitation of SAX's ability for XML document conversion. Because the SAX API is known as a faster API, it is worth using if the conversion rule is simple enough and the rule is not subject to change.

The DOM API is appropriate for complicated examples in which the SAX API is hard to use. If memory efficiency is not a serious issue, as we described in this section, it is a good idea to use the combination of the XPath API and the DOM API for traversing a DOM tree and getting the resulting XML document or SAX events.

We haven't described any issues here with XSLT because it is a high-level language designed for such conversions. It is powerful enough to perform a conversion, a sort, or an evaluation even if there is a complex dependency between any elements specified as XPath expressions. The advantage of using XSLT is that you can write a conversion program using a reasonably simple stylesheet that makes a program flexible for future specification changes or functional enhancements. With XSLT, for example, a position change of the dependent element requires only a change to the corresponding XPath expression. It is much easier than using DOM or SAX.

Another advantage is that it is possible to generate an XSLT stylesheet by using a tool or a runtime library because a stylesheet is an XML document. One example is a Web services scenario described in Chapter 13. Suppose that a service provider publishes a WSDL, and a service requester has an interface based on a different but similar WSDL. In such a case, it may be possible to generate a stylesheet to convert a service requester's WSDL to a service provider's WSDL so that they can communicate with each other. Another example is a data binding scenario described in Chapter 8. It may be possible to generate a stylesheet for unidirectional or bidirectional conversion between two different XML document fragments mapped from Java objects. These are promising areas in which XSLT can play an important role in the future.

The limitation of XSLT's ability is in writing complicated logic other than pattern matching. As the logic becomes complicated, a stylesheet becomes complicated and hard to read.[10] XSLT uses XPath expressions in a search patterns. This is another limitation of XSLT because XPath cannot express computations, such as date calculations and currency conversion. In this case, DOM or SAX is more appropriate than XSLT.

In this section, we discussed the pros and cons of using DOM, SAX, XPath, and XSLT from the aspect of execution and development efficiency.

## 7.4  Summary

In this chapter, we described XPath and XSLT as useful alternative methods to DOM and SAX to process XML documents.

In Section 7.1, we showed how easy it is to specify part of an XML document as a node set with XPath and how to use XPath in Java applications. XPath is robust in handling the change of input XML documents (DTD) in some cases, compared to using DOM or SAX. Another admirable point we did not mention is that XPath can be used even by nonprogrammers such as Web designers. If you are developing an application that processes XML documents and want to let end users customize the behavior of the application, you may want to use XPath for that purpose. Obviously, XSLT should be one such application.

In Section 7.2, we explained how to convert an XML document to another with XSLT and how to call an XSLT processor in Java applications. XSLT can be applied to many applications, such as filtering information for backend applications and publishing HTML documents converted from XML documents. XSLT will be used

---

[10] One reason is that a stylesheet is defined as an XML document.

more frequently not only in standalone applications but also in server-side and client-side applications. We describe how XSLT can be used in Web applications in Part 2 of this book.

In Section 7.3, we discussed when you should use XPath and XSLT and when you should not. They are very powerful in the area that they naturally target. However, they cannot describe some complex application logic, such as date calculations and currency conversion. You should use SAX or DOM to describe such complex application logic that is beyond the expressive power of XPath and XSLT.

Finally, we described how you can abstract XML documents in Java applications. For example, SAX and DOM give Java applications a stream view and a tree view of XML documents, respectively. XPath also provides a tree view of XML documents. In the next chapter, we describe another approach to abstracting XML documents in Java applications—a data binding technique to map between XML and Java data structures.

CHAPTER 8

# Bridging Application Data Structure and XML

## 8.1 Introduction

The theme of this book is how XML and Java interact with each other. In Chapter 2 (parsing) we explained how to transform an XML document into a Java data structure based on DOM and SAX. Chapter 3 (generation) showed how to generate an XML document from a Java program. Chapter 4 (DOM/DOM2) and Chapter 5 (SAX/SAX2) dealt with standard APIs to access an XML document from a Java program. Common to these techniques is the concept of mapping between XML documents and Java data structures. However, these are not the only ways to do mapping between XML and Java. This chapter introduces various mapping patterns and techniques.

As we discussed in Chapter 1, and as we will see in Chapters 12 (messaging) and 13 (Web services), XML is a data format suitable for *data exchange* and is not necessarily suitable for *processing*. From an application programmer's point of view, XML documents exist in an external data format only, and once they are read into memory, the programmer deals with the internal data structure—that is, Java objects for implementing application-specific logic. XML processors are responsible for converting XML documents into Java data in the form of DOM or SAX, but these data structures rarely represent your application's data structure. For example, suppose that you parse a purchase order document and receive a DOM structure. You need the customer's name and the serial number to process the data. From a `<customer>` element, you may need to scan its child nodes to find a `<name>` node and a `<serialNumber>` node and then convert them into appropriate Java data types. Instead of a DOM tree, what the application programmer really wants is Java objects reflecting the application data structure, such as class `Customer`. This class has the `name` and `serialNumber` fields, and these fields are to be filled with the data extracted from the XML document. This eliminates the extra code of scanning a DOM tree and simplifies the application code. Therefore, it is common that application programmers convert a DOM tree or a SAX event stream into an application-specific data representation before any application-specific process is executed.

In the programming language literature, the concept of mapping between internal data structures and external octet sequences is common, and the terms marshal and unmarshal are used for describing the mapping processes (see Figure 8.1). An XML document is an octet stream. Therefore, parsing an XML document can be considered to be unmarshaling, while generating an XML document can be considered as marshaling.

In this chapter, we explain that there are certain patterns in mappings between XML documents and application data. In Section 8.2, we consider mappings where the application data structure and the XML document structure are isomorphic. If the application data structure is slightly different from the input XML document structure, the use of XSLT to adjust the structure is a standard technique. We explain this technique in Section 8.3. Two-dimensional arrays, or tables, are also a common data structure. In Section 8.4, we briefly discuss tables as the application data structure. The general technique of mapping between XML documents and relational tables is covered in detail in Chapter 11, XML and Databases. However, we explain mapping for one special type of table—*hash tables,* in this chapter. Section 8.5 shows a useful technique of representing an XML document as a hash table. In more complex cases, the application data structure may be represented

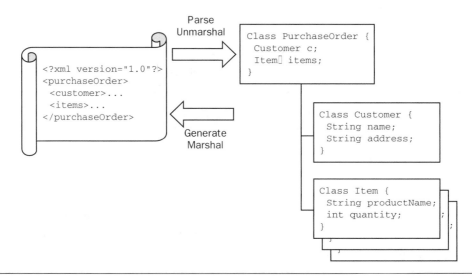

**Figure 8.1** Marshaling and unmarshaling

as a graph. We give an example of mapping an XML document into a graph structure in Section 8.6. In Chapter 15, Data Binding, we revisit mappings and explore how to automate mappings between the application data structure and the XML document structure.

## 8.2  Mapping to Almost Isomorphic Tree Structures

The most typical mapping occurs when the structure of XML documents reflects the application data structure and thus the mapping is almost isomorphic.[1] We use the hypothetical purchase order document, `po.xml`, in Listing 8.1 as our example.

**Listing 8.1** Purchase order document, `chap08/isomorphic/po.xml`

```
<?xml version="1.0" encoding="UTF-8"?>
<!DOCTYPE purchaseOrder SYSTEM "PurchaseOrder.dtd">
<purchaseOrder>
    <customer>
        <name>Robert Smith</name>
        <customerId>788335</customerId>
        <address>8 Oak Avenue, New York, US</address>
    </customer>
    <comment>Hurry, my lawn is going wild!</comment>
    <items>
        <item partNum="872-AA">
            <productName>Lawnmower</productName>
            <quantity>1</quantity>
            <USPrice>148.95</USPrice>
            <shipDate>2002-09-03</shipDate>
        </item>
        <item partNum="926-AA">
            <productName>Baby Monitor</productName>
            <quantity>1</quantity>
            <USPrice>39.98</USPrice>
            <shipDate>2002-08-21</shipDate>
        </item>
    </items>
</purchaseOrder>
```

Our application reads in this purchase order document, calculates the price, and generates an invoice. One natural modeling of this program is to represent each of the concepts, such as purchase order, customer, and item, as a Java object. Hence, the three classes shown in Listings 8.2, 8.3, and 8.4 are to be prepared.

---

[1] The data binding tools that we describe in Chapter 15 are most useful in such cases.

**Listing 8.2** `PurchaseOrder` class, `chap08/isomorphic/PurchaseOrder.java`

```java
public class PurchaseOrder {

    Customer customer;
    String comment;
    Vector items = new Vector();
    ...
    }
```

**Listing 8.3** `Customer` class, `chap08/isomorphic/Customer.java`

```java
public class Customer {

    String name;
    int customerId;
    String address;
    ...
}
```

**Listing 8.4** `Item` class, `chap08/isomorphic/Item.java`

```java
public class Item {

    String partNum;
    String productName;
    int quantity;
    float usPrice;
    String shipDate;
    ...
}
```

How can we map an input XML document into instances of these classes? For simplicity, let us assume that we have already parsed an XML document and have a DOM tree. What we need to do is recursively scan this DOM tree, and for each element that represents a concept to be represented as a Java object, generate an instance of the corresponding class. For example, upon encountering a `<purchaseOrder>` element during the DOM tree scan, create a new instance of the `PurchaseOrder` class, as shown in Figure 8.2.

To do this, we provide a static method called `unmarshal()` in the class `PurchaseOrder` (see Listing 8.5). This method takes a DOM node representing a `<purchaseOrder>` element as an input parameter and returns a new `PurchaseOrder` instance.

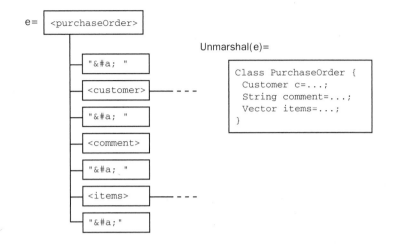

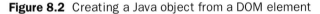

**Figure 8.2**  Creating a Java object from a DOM element

**Listing 8.5**  unmarshal() method for PurchaseOrder class, chap08/isomorphic/ PurchaseOrder.java (continued)

```
       static PurchaseOrder unmarshal(Element e) {
           PurchaseOrder po = new PurchaseOrder();
           for (Node c1=e.getFirstChild(); c1!=null; c1=c1.getNextSibling()) {
               if (c1.getNodeType()==Node.ELEMENT_NODE) {

[48]               if (c1.getNodeName().equals("customer")) {
[49]                   // <customer> subelement
[50]                   po.setCustomer(Customer.unmarshal((Element)c1));

[52]               } else if (c1.getNodeName().equals("comment")) {
[53]                   // <comment> subelement
[54]                   po.setComment(TypeConversion.toString(c1));

[56]               } else if (c1.getNodeName().equals("items")) {
[57]                   // <items> subelement
[58]                   for (Node c2 = c1.getFirstChild();
[59]                       c2 != null;
[60]                       c2 = c2.getNextSibling()) {
[61]                       if (c2.getNodeType()==Node.ELEMENT_NODE) {
[62]                           Element childElement2 = (Element)c2;
[63]                           if (c2.getNodeName().equals("item")) {
[64]                               po.addItem(Item.unmarshal((Element) c2));
[65]                           }
[66]                       }
[67]                   }
[68]               }
```

```
            }
        }
        return po;
    }
```

Parameter e of this method points to a `<purchaseOrder>` element in a DOM tree. This method first creates an instance of the `PurchaseOrder` class and then scans the child nodes of the element e to fill in the fields of the `PurchaseOrder` instance. For example, when the method encounters a `<customer>` element, it creates a `Customer` object by calling the static method `unmarshal()` of the class `Customer` and sets the created object to the `customer` field of the `PurchaseOrder` object (lines 48–50).

When seeing a `<comment>` element, the method converts the contents of the element into a `String` object and assigns it to the `comment` field (lines 52–54).

Child nodes of an `<items>` element are a repetition of `<item>` elements, so the method goes further down to its subelements and for each `<item>` element, the method creates an instance of the `Item` class and adds it to the `item` field of the `PurchaseOrder` (lines 56–68). As a helper class for handling a type conversion from a DOM node to a Java primitive type, we write a simple class called `TypeConversion`, shown in Listing 8.6.

**Listing 8.6**  `TypeConversion` class, `chap08/isomorphic/TypeConversion.java`

```java
package chap08.isomorphic;

import org.w3c.dom.Node;

public class TypeConversion {

    static String toString(Node n) {
        String content = n.getFirstChild().getNodeValue();
        return content;
    }

    static int toInteger(Node n) {
        String content = n.getFirstChild().getNodeValue();
        return Integer.parseInt(content);
    }

    static float toFloat(Node n) {
        String content = n.getFirstChild().getNodeValue();
        return Float.parseFloat(content);
    }

}
```

What about unmarshaling of the `Customer` class? As we did for our `PurchaseOrder` class, we write a static method called `unmarshal()` that is to be called whenever a `<customer>` element is found. The implementation of this method is shown in Listing 8.7. You may notice that it has exactly the same pattern as the `unmarshal()` method of our `PurchaseOrder` class.

**Listing 8.7** `unmarshal()` method for `Customer` class, `chap08/isomorphic/Customer.java` (continued)

```
static Customer unmarshal(Element e) {
    Customer co = new Customer();
    for (Node c1=e.getFirstChild(); c1!=null; c1=c1.getNextSibling()) {
        if (c1.getNodeType()==Node.ELEMENT_NODE) {

            if (c1.getNodeName().equals("name")) {
                // <name> subelement
                co.setName(TypeConversion.toString(c1));

            } else if (c1.getNodeName().equals("customerId")) {
                // <customreId> subelement
                co.setCustomerId(TypeConversion.toInteger(c1));

            } else if (c1.getNodeName().equals("address")) {
                // <address> subelement
                co.setAddress(TypeConversion.toString(c1));
            }
        }
    }
    return co;
}
```

Similarly, we can build the `unmarshal()` method for the class `Item`. In this code, shown in Listing 8.8, we also extract the value of the attribute `partNum` (line 57).

**Listing 8.8** `unmarshal()` method for `Item` class, `chap08/isomorphic/Item.java` (continued)

```
       static Item unmarshal(Element e) {
           Item item = new Item();
[57]       item.setPartNum(e.getAttribute("partNum"));
           for (Node c1=e.getFirstChild(); c1!=null; c1=c1.getNextSibling()) {
               if (c1.getNodeType()==Node.ELEMENT_NODE) {

                   if (c1.getNodeName().equals("productName")) {
                       // <productName> subelement
                       item.setProductName(TypeConversion.toString(c1));
```

```
                } else if (c1.getNodeName().equals("quantity")) {
                    // <quantity> subelement
                    item.setQuantity(TypeConversion.toInteger(c1));

                } else if (c1.getNodeName().equals("USPrice")) {
                    // <USPrice> subelement
                    item.setUSPrice(TypeConversion.toFloat(c1));

                } else if (c1.getNodeName().equals("shipDate")) {
                    // <shipDate> subelement
                    item.setShipDate(TypeConversion.toString(c1));
                }
            }
        }
        return item;
    }
```

Now we are ready to convert a whole DOM tree into our application data model.
We need to parse an input XML document and give the resulting DOM tree to one
of the unmarshal() methods that we programmed. The main() method, shown
in Listing 8.9, does exactly that.

**Listing 8.9** main() method for PurchaseOrder class, chap08/isomorphic/
PurchaseOrder.java (continued)

```
     public static void main(String[] argv) throws Exception {
         if (argv.length < 1) {
             System.err.println("Usage: java chap08.PurchaseOrder file");
             System.exit(1);
         }
[79]     DocumentBuilderFactory factory =
[80]         DocumentBuilderFactory.newInstance();
[81]     DocumentBuilder builder = factory.newDocumentBuilder();
[82]     builder.setErrorHandler(new MyErrorHandler());
[83]     Document doc = builder.parse(argv[0]);

         Element root = doc.getDocumentElement();
         if (root.getNodeName().equals("purchaseOrder")) {
[87]         PurchaseOrder po = unmarshal(root);
             Customer co = po.getCustomer();
             System.out.println("*********** Invoice **************  ");
             System.out.println("Date:"+ new java.util.Date());
             System.out.println("");
             System.out.println("To: "+co.getName());
             System.out.println("    "+co.getAddress());
             System.out.println("    Customer#:"+co.getCustomerId());
```

```
System.out.println("");
System.out.println("----------------------");
int i=0;
float total = (float)0.0;
for (Iterator itr=po.getItems(); itr.hasNext(); i++) {
    Item item = (Item)itr.next();
    System.out.println("Item #"+i+" : "+item.getPartNum()+
                        ", Quantity="+item.getQuantity()+
                        ", UnitPrice="+item.getUSPrice()+
                        ", ShipDate="+item.getShipDate());

    total += item.getUSPrice();
}
System.out.println("----------------------");
System.out.println("total = $"+total);
    }
}
```

Lines 79–83 parse the input and obtain a DOM tree. After checking that the root element is in fact a `purchaseOrder` element, we create a `PurchaseOrder` instance by calling the static method `unmarshal()` in line 87. The rest of the code is pure application logic that is responsible for generating an invoice.

What can we learn from this manual mapping? We have seen that if the mapping preserves the structural similarity between the XML document and the Java data structure, writing unmarshaling codes can be a fairly automatic task. You prepare one class for one complex element type (for example, `<purchaseOrder>`, `<customer>`, or `<item>`) that has a static method, `unmarshal()`, for scanning a DOM tree and creating a corresponding Java instance.

The question is, then, is it possible to automatically generate such mapping codes from a schema of input XML documents? The answer is yes. In Chapter 15, we describe a few of these tools.

## 8.3  Structure Adjustment by XSLT

In the previous section, we assumed that our XML documents and application data share the same structure. Sometimes this assumption does not hold in the real world, and the technique we just saw cannot be directly applied.

Consider our purchase order application. We use the same XML document, `po.xml`, (see Listing 8.1) as the input to our application. In this format, one purchase order can have multiple items in it. Suppose that we are asked to feed the XML documents into a legacy application whose data model allows only one

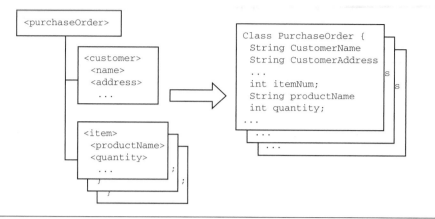

**Figure 8.3** Structural mismatch

item per purchase order.[2] The mapping we need is something like that shown in Figure 8.3.

There is an apparent mismatch between the input XML structure and the application data structure, so the technique we used in the previous section cannot be directly applied. How can we write a program that creates the desired Java data structure, as shown in Figure 8.3, from this input? Modifying the program in the previous section is one possibility. To do that, however, you need to temporarily store the customer data that will later be assigned to the PurchaseOrder objects. This is not a big deal in terms of the number of lines of additional code, but you may need either a global variable or additional parameters in the unmarshal() methods.

Another way to solve this nonstraightforward mapping is to use XSLT to adjust the XML structure *before* processing. Suppose that the input XML has the form shown in Listing 8.10 instead of Listing 8.1. This time, the mapping is isomorphic and the technique in the previous section can be directly applied.

**Listing 8.10** Transformed purchase order, chap08/mismatch/po1.xml

```
<?xml version="1.0" encoding="UTF-8"?>
<purchaseOrders>
    <purchaseOrder>
        <name>Robert Smith</name>
        <customerId>788335</customerId>
        <address>8 Oak Avenue, New York, US</address>
        <partNum>872-AA"</partNum>
        <productName>Lawnmower</productName>
```

---

[2] We encountered such an application when we were building an order entry system for IBM.

```
        <quantity>1</quantity>
        <USPrice>148.95</USPrice>
        <shipDate>2002-09-03</shipDate>
    </purchaseOrder>
    <purchaseOrder>
        <name>Robert Smith</name>
        <customerId>788335</customerId>
        <address>8 Oak Avenue, New York, US</address>
        <partNum>926-AA</partNum>
        <productName>Baby Monitor</productName>
        <quantity>1</quantity>
        <USPrice>39.98</USPrice>
        <shipDate>2002-08-21</shipDate>
    </purchaseOrder>
</purchaseOrders>
```

How can we obtain Listing 8.10 from Listing 8.1? The answer is to use XSLT. XSLT is designed for this sort of transformation. It is a powerful language to do such things as:

- Extracting `<item>` elements from inside a `purchaseOrder/items` element
- Adding child elements of the `<customer>` element to each `<item>` element

The XSLT script `mismatch/flatten.xsl` (see Listing 8.11) does this transformation. Note that this transformation can be called from a Java program using the JAXP API, as we discussed in Section 7.2.2 of Chapter 7, so the extra generation and parsing are eliminated.

**Listing 8.11**  XSLT transformation script, `chap08/mismatch/flatten.xsl`

```
<?xml version="1.0" encoding="UTF-8"?>
<xsl:stylesheet
    version="1.0"
    xmlns:xsl="http://www.w3.org/1999/XSL/Transform">
    <xsl:output indent="yes" encoding="UTF-8"/>

    <xsl:template match="/">
        <purchaseOrders>
            <xsl:apply-templates select="purchaseOrder/items"/>
        </purchaseOrders>
    </xsl:template>

    <xsl:template match="item">
        <purchaseOrder>
            <xsl:copy-of select="/purchaseOrder/customer/name"/>
            <xsl:copy-of select="/purchaseOrder/customer/customerId"/>
```

```
            <xsl:copy-of select="/purchaseOrder/customer/address"/>
            <partNum><xsl:value-of select="@partNum"/></partNum>
            <xsl:copy-of select="productName"/>
            <xsl:copy-of select="quantity"/>
            <xsl:copy-of select="USPrice"/>
            <xsl:copy-of select="shipDate"/>
        </purchaseOrder>
      </xsl:template>

    </xsl:stylesheet>
```

Can you see the usefulness of XSLT in mapping from XML to an application-specific data structure? This technique also applies to applications that need to process logically equivalent but different DTD documents. For example, if your application is required to process both types of purchase orders as in Listings 8.1 and 8.10, a single application program, combined with an appropriate XSLT stylesheet, will be enough for processing both. This situation frequently occurs when there are multiple versions of DTDs for essentially the same set of documents.

So far we focused on cases where mappings are relatively straightforward. In other words, your application data structure has essentially a tree shape, and it reflects the structure of marshaled XML documents fairly well. Some developers argue that 80% of all application development is indeed of this type, so 80% of the time you can have a straightforward mapping as we saw in Section 8.2, especially when we use the XSLT technique for adjusting the structure. Having a straightforward mapping is even more important if you use a software tool that does the mapping automatically. In Chapter 15, we will see such software tools.

Of course, there is always the remaining 20%. When we are told to develop such an application, we need to write our own custom mapping code. Even in such cases, there are certain patterns that may be useful to you. The next three sections show some of these patterns that we encounter most frequently.

## 8.4  Mapping to Tables

Mapping to tables is one of the most common patterns. Even in our purchase order application, the content of an `<items>` element is a repetition of the same element type, `item`, so this part can be naturally represented as a table (see Figure 8.4). From an application programming point of view, a table is a data structure that is suitable for operations such as searching, sorting, and totaling specific columns. In addition, table-represented data can be easily exported into and imported from applications such as databases and spreadsheets.

```
<items>                                    partNum  productName  Quantity  USPrice  shipDate
  <item partNum="872-AA">
    <productName>Lawnmower</productName>   872-AA   Lawnmower    1         148.95   2002-09-03
    <quantity>1</quantity>
    <USprice>148.95</USprice>              926-AA   Baby Monitor 1         39.98    2002-08-21
    <shipDate>2002-09-03</shipDate>
  </item>                                    :          :          :        :         :
  <item partNum="926-AA">
    <productName>BabyMonitor</productName>
    <quantity>1</quantity>
    <USPrice>39.98</USPrice>
    <shipDate>2002-08-21</shipDate>
  </item>
</items>
```

| partNum | productName | Quantity | USPrice | shipDate |
|---------|-------------|----------|---------|----------|
| 872-AA  | Lawnmower   | 1        | 148.95  | 2002-09-03 |
| 926-AA  | Baby Monitor | 1       | 39.98   | 2002-08-21 |
| :       | :           | :        | :       | :        |

**Figure 8.4**  Table data

In Chapter 11, we discuss how to store XML documents into a relational database and how to retrieve relational database contents as XML documents. In Section 11.5, refer to Listing 11.6, which decomposes XML documents and stores them into relational tables, and Listing 11.8, which generates XML documents from these tables. These programs correspond to unmarshaling and marshaling of table data. In both cases, we define mapping based on the database schema and the schema of XML documents. Some commercial database management systems have tools to generate such mappings automatically.

Mapping to tables is most suitable when your data consists of a set of records that all have a common structure. If your data is semistructured—that is, it is essentially tree-structured—mapping to hash tables (described next) is another candidate to consider.

## 8.5  Mapping to Hash Tables

Another interesting mapping is to map XML documents to hash tables. Frequently, XML is used as the format of software configuration files. For example, Tomcat, the servlet container we explain in Chapter 10, uses a number of configuration files (such as `server.xml`) in XML. You may think that many configuration files are simple enough so that flat text files are good enough. However, in our experience, we know that configuration files keep growing as program development continues. At some point we are forced to segment a configuration file into several logical sections. We must also define a basic syntax of delimiter characters and escape characters. We will also face deciding what international character encoding to use. Considering all this, it is worth using XML for configuration files in the first place.

Let us consider a configuration file (see Listing 8.12) of a hypothetical application program for generating sales reports.

**Listing 8.12** Configuration file, `chap08/hashtable/config.xml`

```
<?xml version="1.0" encoding="UTF-8"?>
<config>
    <productData locationType="file">
        <defaultFileName>c:/productMarketing/products.xml
        </defaultFileName>
    </productData>
    <customerData locationType="db">
        <databaseURL>jdbc:db2:sales.ibm.com/customer</databaseURL>
        <userId>maruyama</userId>
        <passWord>montelac</passWord>
    </customerData>
    <reportFormat locationType="file">
        <defaultFileName>c:/CEO/monthlyReport.xml</defaultFileName>
        <reportTo>M. Murata</reportTo>
        <reportTo>K. Kosaka</reportTo>
    </reportFormat>
</config>
```

How can our application program access this configuration file? It is not likely that we want to scan the entire file and do some specific task (for example, summing numbers). Instead, each piece of data in the configuration file will be accessed whenever a specific component of our application needs that particular piece of data, using the name of the configuration parameter as the key. Therefore, a hash table with configuration parameters as its keys is a natural choice of data structure to hold the configuration data. If our program needs the value of a configuration parameter called `defaultFileName`, we can efficiently look up the hash table with this name as the key. In XML-based configuration files, parameter names can be expressed as path expressions, such as `/config/productData/defaultFileName`.[3]

Our configuration file can be expressed as the following hash table.

| KEY | VALUE |
| --- | --- |
| /config/productData/@locationType | [file] |
| /config/productData/defaultFileName | [c:/productMarketing/products.xml] |
| /config/customerData/@locationType | [db] |
| /config/customerData/databaseURL | [jdbc:db2:sales.abc.com/customer] |
| /config/customerData/userId | [maruyama] |

---

[3] In Section 11.5.2, we discuss storing XML data as a pair of an XPath expression and its value. We do the same here, except that instead of using XPath's positional parameter to ensure the uniqueness of a path's value (as in `/purchaseOrder[1]/shipTo[1]/street[1]`), we use path expressions without positional predicates (as in `/config/productData/defaultFileName`) and allow their values to have multiple values in a `Vector` object.

| | |
|---|---|
| /config/customerData/passWord | [montelac] |
| /config/reportFormat/@locationType | [file] |
| /config/reportFormat/defaultFileName | [c:/CEO/monthlyReport.xml] |
| /config/reportFormat/reportTo | ["M. Murata", "K. Kosaka"] |

Now let us consider how we can map an XML file into such a hash table. We use a
common technique of generating path expressions using SAX. Look at the SAX
handler in Listing 8.13.[4]

**Listing 8.13**  `Config` class, `chap08/hashtable/Config.java`

```
       package chap08.hashtable;
       import java.io.IOException;
       import org.xml.sax.SAXException;
       import org.xml.sax.Attributes;
       import org.xml.sax.helpers.DefaultHandler;
       import javax.xml.parsers.SAXParser;
       import javax.xml.parsers.SAXParserFactory;
       import javax.xml.parsers.ParserConfigurationException;
       import java.util.Hashtable;
       import java.util.Vector;
       import java.util.Enumeration;

       public class Config extends DefaultHandler {

           private StringBuffer path;
           private StringBuffer textContent;
[17]       private Hashtable hashtable;

           public Config(String fn) throws SAXException, IOException,
           ParserConfigurationException {
               SAXParserFactory factory = SAXParserFactory.newInstance();
               SAXParser parser = factory.newSAXParser();

               this.path = new StringBuffer();
[24]           this.hashtable = new Hashtable();
               parser.parse(fn, this);
           }

           public void startElement(String uri, String local, String qname,
           Attributes atts) throws SAXException {
               // Update path
               path.append('/');
```

---

[4] In a similar program in Section 11.5.2, we first parse the input to obtain a DOM tree and then
compute a path expression for each node.

```
                  path.append(qname);
                  int nattrs = atts.getLength();
                  for (int i=0; i<nattrs; i++) {
[34]                  addValue(path.toString()+"/@"+atts.getQName(i), atts.
                      getValue(i));
                  }
[36]              this.textContent = new StringBuffer();
              }

          public void endElement(String uri, String local, String qname)
          throws SAXException {
              if (this.textContent != null) {
[41]              addValue(path.toString(), this.textContent.toString());
                  this.textContent = null;
              }
              // Restore path
              int pathlen = path.length();
[46]          path.delete(pathlen-qname.length()-1,pathlen);
          }

          public void characters(char[] ch, int start, int length) throws
          SAXException {
              if (this.textContent != null) {
                  this.textContent.append(ch, start, length);
              }
          }

      Hashtable getHashtable() {
          return this.hashtable;
      }

      void addValue(String key, String value) {
          Vector v = (Vector)this.hashtable.get(key);
          if (v == null) {
              v = new Vector();
              this.hashtable.put(key,v);
          }
          v.add(value);
      }

      public static void main(String[] args) throws Exception {
          if (args.length < 1) {
              System.err.println("Usage: java chap08.hashtable.Config
              file");
              System.exit(1);
          }
```

```
        Config theConfig = new Config(args[0]);
        Hashtable ht = theConfig.getHashtable();
        for (Enumeration e = ht.keys(); e.hasMoreElements(); ){
            String key = (String)e.nextElement();
            System.out.println(key+"="+ht.get(key));
        }
    }

}
```

The hash table that we are going to build is declared in line 17 and initialized in line 24. A new entry is added to the hash table when an attribute (line 34) or an element with some text content (line 41) is found. The text content of an element is accumulated in a `StringBuffer` in a variable named `textContent`. This buffer is initialized when a start tag is found (line 36) and discarded when an end tag is found. Therefore, any characters in SAX events that occur before a start element or after an end element are ignored. This is OK because our XML documents have no MIXED content models.

Another interesting point of this program is the way to build path expressions. During the parsing process, the current path expression is kept in a `StringBuffer` in a variable named `path`. We do not need to keep track of this path expression in a stack because when we see an end tag, we can always recover the parent path expression by removing the element name plus one character (for the separator "/"), as we do in line 46.

Once an XML configuration file is mapped into a hash table, configuration parameters can be efficiently accessed from any part of our program. A great advantage of this approach is that because our mapping code does not hardcode any particular element names or attribute names, there is no need to modify the code when new configuration parameters are added. In fact, this mapping code works universally regardless of the schema of input XML documents.

This mapping is optimized for keyed access by path expressions. Mapping to hash tables does not make sense for applications that have different access patterns, such as traversing the entire document.

## 8.6  Mapping to Graph Structures

Trees, tables, and hash tables are optimized for different access patterns. Here, we consider another frequently used data structure: graphs. Graphs are convenient when the access pattern of your program involves following links between shared data.

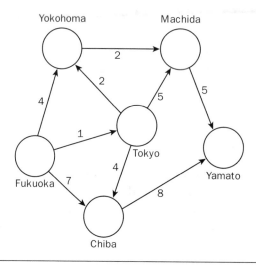

**Figure 8.5** Graph data

Let us take an application that computes the shortest path between two cities as our example. Figure 8.5 shows our problem. Circles represent cities, and arrows between them represent connections between cities. The numbers associated with the arrows are the cost of moving to one city from another. What is the shortest path from Fukuoka to Yamato? What is the cost of the shortest path? There is a well-known, simple but efficient algorithm known as *Dijkstra's algorithm* to solve this problem.

We want to express this problem as an XML document and map it into a graph data structure, as shown in Figure 8.5, that is needed for implementing Dijkstra's algorithm efficiently. One natural XML encoding of the problem is something like cities.xml, shown in Listing 8.14.

**Listing 8.14** Graph represented as XML, chap08/graph/cities.xml

```
<?xml version="1.0" encoding="UTF-8"?>
<FindShortestPath xmlns="urn:shortest-path">
    <StartCity>Fukuoka</StartCity>
    <TargetCity>Yamato</TargetCity>
    <Paths>
        <Path from="Fukuoka" to="Tokyo" cost="1"/>
        <Path from="Fukuoka" to="Yokohama" cost="4"/>
        <Path from="Fukuoka" to="Chiba" cost="7"/>
        <Path from="Tokyo" to="Chiba" cost="4"/>
        <Path from="Tokyo" to="Yokohama" cost="2"/>
        <Path from="Tokyo" to="Machida" cost="5"/>
        <Path from="Yokohama" to="Machida" cost="2"/>
        <Path from="Machida" to="Yamato" cost="5"/>
```

```
            <Path from="Chiba" to="Yamato" cost="8"/>
        </Paths>
    </FindShortestPath>
```

We will develop code to convert this XML document into a graph structure, whose vertexes are represented by `Vertex` objects and whose edges are represented by `Edge` objects.

Part of the `Vertex` class is shown in Listing 8.15. A `Vertex` instance has a string, `label`, for the city's name and a list, `outgoingEdges`, that holds all the edges pointing to other cities (lines 12–13). In addition, it has two variables, `bestScore` and `bestPath`, to keep track of working values during the computation. All the vertexes are kept in a single hash table named `vertexList`. When a vertex is needed, we call the static method `register()` instead of creating a new instance. This method checks whether there is already a vertex for the city and returns it if there is.

**Listing 8.15** `Vertex` class, `chap08/graph/Vertex.java`

```
      class Vertex  {
[12]     private String label;
[13]     private List outgoingEdges;
         private int bestScore;
         private Edge bestPath;
         private static Hashtable vertexList = new Hashtable();

         static Vertex register(String label) {
            Vertex v = (Vertex)vertexList.get(label);
            if (v==null) {
               v = new Vertex(label);
               vertexList.put(label,v);
            }
            return v;
         }

         Vertex(String label) {
            this.label = label;
            this.outgoingEdges = new LinkedList();
            this.bestScore = Integer.MAX_VALUE;
            this.bestPath = null;
         }

         void addEdge(Edge e) {
            this.outgoingEdges.add(e);
         } /* end excerpt1 */
         ...
      }
```

The Edge class has `fromVertex` and `toVertex` to keep both ends of the connection (see Listing 8.16). When a new edge is created, it registers itself in `outgoingEdges` of `fromVertex`.

**Listing 8.16** Edge class, `chap08/graph/Edge.java`

```
class Edge {
    private Vertex fromVertex;
    private Vertex toVertex;
    private int cost;

    Edge(Vertex from, Vertex to, int c) {
        this.fromVertex = from;
        this.toVertex = to;
        this.cost = c;
        this.fromVertex.addEdge(this);
    }
    ...
}
```

Now that we have both our application data structure and the input XML structure, we are ready to consider the mapping between them. Our strategy is this. We will scan an input XML document. Whenever we encounter a city, whether it appears in a `Path` element or in `TargetCity` or `StartCity`, we register it using `Vertex.register()`. When we see a `Path` element, we also need to create an `Edge` instance. Because the constructor of the `Edge` class takes care of updating the appropriate variables in the structure being built, we do not need to do anything other than create a new instance of `Edge`.

We implement our strategy in a SAX handler, `ShortestPath.java`, shown in Listing 8.17.

**Listing 8.17** ShortestPath class, `chap08/graph/ShortestPath.java`

```
package chap08.graph;
import java.io.IOException;
import org.xml.sax.SAXException;
import org.xml.sax.Attributes;
import org.xml.sax.helpers.DefaultHandler;
import javax.xml.parsers.SAXParser;
import javax.xml.parsers.SAXParserFactory;
import java.util.*;

public class ShortestPath extends DefaultHandler {

    static final String SHORTEST_PATH_URI = "urn:shortest-path";
    StringBuffer buffer = null;
```

```
        static Vertex startCity;
        static Vertex targetCity;

        public void startElement(String uri, String local, String qname,
        Attributes atts) throws SAXException {
            if (!uri.equals(SHORTEST_PATH_URI)) return;
            if ( local.equals("StartCity") || local.equals("TargetCity")) {
                this.buffer = new StringBuffer();
            } else if (local.equals("Path")) {

[23]            String fromString = atts.getValue("from");
[24]            if (fromString==null) throw new SAXException("Attribute
                'from' missing");
[25]            Vertex from = Vertex.register(fromString);
[26]
[27]            String toString = atts.getValue("to");
[28]            if (toString==null) throw new SAXException("Attribute 'to'
                missing");
[29]            Vertex to = Vertex.register(toString);

                String costString = atts.getValue("cost");
                if (costString==null) throw new SAXException("Attribute
                'cost' missing");
[33]            new Edge(from,to,Integer.parseInt(costString));
            }
        }

        public void endElement(String uri, String local, String qname)
        throws SAXException {
            if (!uri.equals(SHORTEST_PATH_URI)) return;
            if (local.equals("StartCity")) {
[40]            this.startCity = Vertex.register(new String(this.buffer));
                buffer = null;
            } else if (local.equals("TargetCity")) {
[43]            this.targetCity = Vertex.register(new String(this.buffer));
                buffer = null;
            }
        }

        public void characters(char[] ch, int start, int length) throws
        SAXException {
            if (this.buffer != null) {
                this.buffer.append(ch, start, length);
            }
        }
        /* end excerpt1 */
```

For the `StartCity` and `TargetCity` elements, we need to accumulate possibly fragmented characters in text content using a `StringBuffer`. This is the same technique we have seen repeatedly in this book. These city names are registered when end tags are processed (lines 40 and 43).[5] When a `path` element is found, its three attributes are extracted, the from city and the to city are registered (lines 23–29), and an `Edge` object is created (line 33). In this way, we can map an input XML document into our application data structure.

For completeness, we show the rest of our main class, `ShortestPath`, in Listing 8.18.

**Listing 8.18** `main()` method for `ShortestPath` class, `chap08/graph/ShortestPath.java` (continued)

```
      public static void main(String[] argv) throws Exception {
          if (argv.length < 1) {
              System.err.println("Usage: java chap08.graph.ShortestPath
              file");
              System.exit(1);
          }

          SAXParserFactory factory = SAXParserFactory.newInstance();
          factory.setNamespaceAware(true);
          SAXParser parser = factory.newSAXParser();
          ShortestPath handler = new ShortestPath();

          parser.parse(argv[0],handler);

[68]      SortedSet open = new TreeSet(new VertexComparator());
[69]      startCity.update(0,null,open);
[70]
[71]      while (!open.isEmpty()) {
[72]          Vertex v = (Vertex) open.first();
[73]          open.remove(v);
[74]          for (Iterator i = v.getEdges(); i.hasNext(); ) {
[75]              Edge e = (Edge)i.next();
[76]              e.getToVertex().update(v.getBestScore()+e.getCost(),e,
                  open);
[77]          }
[78]      }

          Vertex.showAll();
      }
```

---

[5] Dijkstra's algorithm computes the shortest paths from a given vertex to *all* vertexes simultaneously. Therefore, the value of `TargetCity` is not used in this program.

Lines 68–78 implement Dijkstra's algorithm. It uses a helper class, `VertexComparator`, to compare the current cost values between two `Vertex` objects. Its source is included on the CD-ROM.

As we have done in this example, if you need to map XML documents into a graph structure, you need to give labels to each node and refer to these labels to express the links between nodes. Having a hash table to record the mapping between node labels and node objects is essential in this process.

## 8.7 Summary

In this chapter, we have considered the general problem of mapping between XML documents and application data structures. In particular, we looked at mapping to trees, tables, and graphs. These are not the only techniques for mapping—if you have written more than a few XML applications, you should have already accumulated a list of useful "patterns" of mapping. If and when these patterns become sufficiently frequent, it will be worth developing a tool for automating the mapping. Chapter 15 covers such tools.

# Working with Schemas: Datatypes and Namespaces

## 9.1 Introduction

XML allows users to choose appropriate names (such as `WeatherReport` and `department`) for tags and attributes. By using a collection of appropriate names for elements and attributes, the user can create XML documents appropriate for a particular application.

A *schema* formally describes permissible XML documents for a particular application. That is, a schema describes permissible names for tags and attributes and permissible structural relationships between such tags and attributes. In other words, a schema provides a markup vocabulary. The DTD of XML 1.0 provides such schemas. DTDs have been used for many years to specify markup vocabularies based on XML and its predecessor, SGML.

However, with the dramatic progress of XML, the following disadvantages of DTDs have come to be widely recognized.

*Peculiar syntax*

The syntax of DTDs is very different from that of XML documents. In fact, a DTD consists of `<!ELEMENT ... >`, `<!ATTLIST ...>`, and `<!ENTITY ... >` declarations, which are neither tags nor attributes. Moreover, *parameter entities,* which are macros for DTDs, are often used to represent such declarations. Many people believe that this peculiar syntax makes DTDs harder to learn.

The peculiar syntax of DTDs also makes it difficult to develop software tools for handling DTDs. In comparison with tools for handling XML documents, those for handling DTDs are few, and their quality and price are not very satisfactory.

*Insufficient datatypes*

XML inherits DTDs from SGML, which has been used primarily for representing human-readable documents rather than representing data interchanged between programs. For this reason, the datatypes of DTDs are totally insufficient for data interchange and interwork with Java or a relational database.

For example, suppose that we want to introduce the tag name `<age>` to represent the age of a person. If a person is ten years old, we write `<age>10</age>`. However, because of the limitations of DTDs, we cannot specify that only integers are permitted. As a result, we cannot automatically detect inappropriate descriptions such as `<age>unknown</age>`.

*Inconsistencies with namespaces*

An important extension to XML 1.0 is the introduction of namespaces. Unfortunately, DTDs cannot handle namespaces properly. In particular, schema authors are forced to define namespace prefixes for namespace names (URIs); documents cannot use other namespace prefixes.

To overcome the problems of DTDs, several schema languages have been developed. In this chapter, we consider two notable languages: XML Schema of W3C and RELAX NG of OASIS and ISO/IEC JTC1. These schema languages use the XML syntax to represent schemas, and they support namespaces and datatypes.

## 9.2 W3C XML Schema

After the XML Working Group (WG) successfully created XML 1.0, W3C formed the XML Schema WG in 1998. W3C XML Schema is the fruit of the three-year activity of this working group. Parts 0, 1, and 2 of W3C XML Schema were published as a W3C Recommendation in May 2001.

Although W3C XML Schema is a powerful language, it is also a complicated language. Both proponents and opponents of W3C XML Schema exist in the XML community. It is hard to understand the full set of W3C XML Schema, and conformant implementations do not exhibit interoperability as of this writing. Moreover, since RELAX NG has been published by OASIS and then ISO/IEC JTC1, W3C XML Schema is *not* the only schema language for XML.

However, W3C XML Schema does have some advantages over DTDs. Among them, we concentrate on datatypes and namespaces. This chapter does not try to cover all the features of W3C XML Schema. Those readers who are ambitious enough to try the full set of W3C XML Schema are referred to other books and to the W3C XML Schema Recommendation.

## 9.2.1 Mimicking DTDs

This section shows how DTD features can be mimicked in W3C XML Schema. Features specific to W3C XML Schema are covered later in this chapter.

### Element Type Declarations of DTDs

We use the simple XML document `itemList.xml`, shown in Listing 9.1, as an example. This document represents an item list (`itemList`) of items (`item`). Each `item` has two child elements: `name` and `quantity`.

**Listing 9.1** An item list document, `chap09/itemList.xml`

```
<?xml version="1.0" encoding="utf-8"?>
<itemList>
  <item>
    <name>pen</name>
    <quantity>5</quantity>
  </item>
  <item>
    <name>eraser</name>
    <quantity>7</quantity>
  </item>
  <item>
    <name>stapler</name>
    <quantity>25</quantity>
  </item>
</itemList>
```

We can create a DTD to formally describe which document represents item lists. Listing 9.2 shows an example of such a DTD called `itemList.dtd`.

**Listing 9.2** An item list DTD, `chap09/itemList.dtd`

```
        <?xml version="1.0" encoding="utf-8"?>

        <!-- A DTD describing list of items. -->
[4]     <!ELEMENT itemList   (item*)>
[5]     <!ELEMENT item       (name, quantity)>
[6]     <!ELEMENT name       (#PCDATA)>
[7]     <!ELEMENT quantity   (#PCDATA)>
```

This DTD has four element type declarations. The first element type declaration (line 4) specifies that elements of the tag name `itemList` contain zero or more elements of the tag name `item`. The second declaration (line 5) specifies that elements of the tag name `item` contain an element of the tag name `name` followed by an element of the tag name `quantity`. The other element type declarations (lines 6 and 7) specify the elements of the tag name `name` or `quantity`. The keyword `#PCDATA` shows that the contents of such elements are strings.

Listing 9.3 shows a schema, `itemList.xsd`, written in W3C XML Schema that mimics the DTD `itemList.dtd`.

**Listing 9.3** A simple schema, chap09/itemList.xsd

```
        <?xml version="1.0" encoding="utf-8"?>
[2]     <xsd:schema xmlns:xsd='http://www.w3.org/2001/XMLSchema'>

[4]         <xsd:element name="itemList">
[5]             <xsd:complexType>
[6]                 <xsd:sequence>
[7]                     <xsd:element ref="item"
[8]                             minOccurs="0" maxOccurs="unbounded"/>
[9]                 </xsd:sequence>
[10]            </xsd:complexType>
            </xsd:element>

[13]        <xsd:element name="item">
[14]            <xsd:complexType>
[15]                <xsd:sequence>
[16]                    <xsd:element ref="name"/>
[17]                    <xsd:element ref="quantity"/>
[18]                </xsd:sequence>
[19]            </xsd:complexType>
            </xsd:element>

[22]        <xsd:element name="name" type="xsd:string"/>

[24]        <xsd:element name="quantity" type="xsd:string"/>

        </xsd:schema>
```

The root element (line 2) for a schema is `xsd:schema`. This element belongs to the namespace `http://www.w3.org/2001/XMLSchema`.[1] This schema contains four `xsd:element` elements (lines 4, 13, 22, and 24). The first and second `xsd:element` elements declare `itemList` and `item`, respectively. The content model

---

[1] An earlier version of W3C XML Schema used `http://www.w3.org/2000/10/XMLSchema`, but this URI is obsolete.

(lines 14–19) of item is represented by xsd:complexType, xsd:sequence, and one xsd:element for name and another for quantity. The content model (lines 5–10) of itemList further uses the attributes minOccurs="0" and maxOccurs="unbounded". These attributes specify that an itemList can have zero or more item elements. The third and fourth xsd:element elements declare name and quantity, respectively. The attribute type="xsd:string" specifies that any string can be used as the value of name and quantity.

This schema can be referenced from a document, as shown in Listing 9.4, by specifying the attribute noNamespaceSchemaLocation, which belongs to the namespace "http://www.w3.org/2001/XMLSchema-instance". This attribute is merely a hint and is ignored when parsers are explicitly instructed to use another schema.

**Listing 9.4** Referencing a schema from a document, chap09/itemList-xsd.xml

```xml
<?xml version="1.0" encoding="utf-8"?>
<itemList
  xmlns:xsi='http://www.w3.org/2001/XMLSchema-instance'
  xsi:noNamespaceSchemaLocation="itemList.xsd">
  <item>
    <name>pen</name>
    <quantity>5</quantity>
  </item>
  <item>
    <name>eraser</name>
    <quantity>7</quantity>
  </item>
  <item>
    <name>stapler</name>
    <quantity>25</quantity>
  </item>
</itemList>
```

Even when W3C XML Schema is used, application programmers using Xerces can write programs as usual. The only difference is that programmers have to specify the use of W3C XML Schema by invoking setFeature for DOM or SAX parsers. The following three statements specify the use of validation, namespaces, and W3C XML Schema, respectively.

```
parser.setFeature(
    "http://xml.org/sax/features/validation",
    true);
parser.setFeature(
    "http://xml.org/sax/features/namespaces",
    true);
```

```
parser.setFeature(
    "http://apache.org/xml/features/validation/schema",
    true);
```

If we run the program `SimpleParseWithSchemaValidation` (shown in Chapter 2, Listing 2.6), it parses this document and further validates it against `itemList.xsd`. Because the document is valid against the schema, this program reports no errors.

Rather than specifying the attribute `noNamespaceSchemaLocation` in an XML document, we can explicitly instruct Xerces to reference certain schemas. We only have to invoke `setProperty` for DOM or SAX parsers.[2]

```
parser.setProperty(
    "http://apache.org/xml/properties/schema/" +
        "external-noNamespaceSchemaLocation",
    "itemList.xsd");
```

Such programs do not require the attribute `noNamespaceSchemaLocation` in XML documents. Even if this attribute is specified, it is simply ignored. The schema specified by `setProperty` (in this example, `itemList.xsd`) is used.

## Attribute-List Declarations of DTDs

Next, we introduce an attribute to this document. The `item` elements have the attribute `number`, as shown in Listing 9.5.

**Listing 9.5** Adding attributes to a document, `chap09/itemList-attribute.xml`

```
<?xml version="1.0" encoding="utf-8"?>
<itemList>
  <item number="003">
    <name>pen</name>
    <quantity>5</quantity>
  </item>
  <item number="004">
    <name>eraser</name>
    <quantity>7</quantity>
  </item>
  <item number="009">
    <name>stapler</name>
    <quantity>25</quantity>
  </item>
</itemList>
```

---

[2] Note that this property is specific to Xerces. JAXP 1.1 does not provide any standard mechanisms yet.

We have to update the DTD accordingly, as shown in Listing 9.6. An attribute-list declaration <!ATTLIST ....> for item is introduced (line 6). CDATA implies that any string may be used as a value of this attribute.

**Listing 9.6**  An attribute-list declaration, chap09/itemList-attribute.dtd

```
        <?xml version="1.0" encoding="utf-8"?>

        <!-- A DTD describing list of items. -->
        <!ELEMENT itemList  (item*)>
        <!ELEMENT item      (name, quantity)>
[6]     <!ATTLIST item      number CDATA #REQUIRED>
        <!ELEMENT name      (#PCDATA)>
        <!ELEMENT quantity  (#PCDATA)>
```

We then revise our schema, itemList.xsd, and declare the attribute number for the item elements. The attribute-list declaration in the DTD is captured by <attributeGroup name="*name*" ...> and is referenced by <attributeGroup ref="*name*"/> within <complexType ...>, shown in Listing 9.7.

**Listing 9.7**  Referencing the attribute-list declaration, chap09/itemList-attribute.xsd

```
        <?xml version="1.0" encoding="utf-8"?>
        <xsd:schema xmlns:xsd='http://www.w3.org/2001/XMLSchema'>

        <xsd:element name="itemList">
          <xsd:complexType>
            <xsd:sequence>
              <xsd:element ref="item"
                           minOccurs="0" maxOccurs="unbounded"/>
            </xsd:sequence>
          </xsd:complexType>
        </xsd:element>

        <xsd:element name="item">
          <xsd:complexType>
            <xsd:sequence>
              <xsd:element ref="name"/>
              <xsd:element ref="quantity"/>
            </xsd:sequence>
[19]        <xsd:attributeGroup ref="item"/>
          </xsd:complexType>
        </xsd:element>

        <xsd:element name="name" type="xsd:string"/>

        <xsd:element name="quantity" type="xsd:string"/>
```

```
[27]        <xsd:attributeGroup name="item">
[28]          <xsd:attribute name="number" type="xsd:string"
                    use="required"/>
          </xsd:attributeGroup>

      </xsd:schema>
```

Within `<attributeGroup name="name" ...>`, we declare attributes with
`<attribute ...>`. Their `name` attribute specifies the attribute name, and the
`type` attribute specifies a datatype. In this example, we have an `attributeGroup`
(line 27), which is referenced at line 19. An `attribute` (line 28) declares an
attribute. It specifies `number` and `xsd:string` as the attribute name and datatype,
respectively, and further specifies that the declared attribute is required with
`use="required"`.

## Comments in Schemas

Comments contribute to the readability of schemas. Because it is very hard to
guess the intention of schema authors, it is desirable to have many comments
in a schema.

W3C XML Schema provides `<annotation><documentation>...`
`</documentation></annotation>` as a mechanism for representing
comments. Almost all elements constructing schemas can have a comment as the
first child. Unlike XML comments (that is, `<!--...-->`), it is clear that an
`<annotation><documentation>...</documentation></annotation>`
element applies to its parent. The previous schema, to which we have introduced
many comments, is shown in Listing 9.8.

**Listing 9.8** Adding comments to a schema, chap09/itemList-attribute-
annotation.xsd

```
<?xml version="1.0" encoding="utf-8"?>
<xsd:schema xmlns:xsd='http://www.w3.org/2001/XMLSchema'>
  <xsd:annotation>
    <xsd:documentation>The root of a schema</xsd:documentation>
  </xsd:annotation>

  <xsd:element name="itemList">
    <xsd:annotation>
      <xsd:documentation>&lt;!ELEMENT itemList (item*)&gt;
      </xsd:documentation>
    </xsd:annotation>

    <xsd:complexType>
      <xsd:sequence>
        <xsd:annotation>
```

```
            <xsd:documentation>This xsd:sequence is required.
            </xsd:documentation>
        </xsd:annotation>

        <xsd:element ref="item"
                    minOccurs="0" maxOccurs="unbounded">
          <xsd:annotation>
            <xsd:documentation>reference to item elements
              </xsd:documentation>
              <xsd:documentation>minOccurs="0" and
                maxOccurs="unbounded" mimics "*"</xsd:documentation>
          </xsd:annotation>
        </xsd:element>
      </xsd:sequence>
    </xsd:complexType>
</xsd:element>

<xsd:element name="item">
  <xsd:annotation>
    <xsd:documentation>&lt;!ELEMENT item (name, quantity)&gt;
    </xsd:documentation>
  </xsd:annotation>

  <xsd:complexType>
    <xsd:sequence>
      <xsd:element ref="name"/>
      <xsd:element ref="quantity"/>
    </xsd:sequence>
    <xsd:attributeGroup ref="item"/>
  </xsd:complexType>
</xsd:element>

<xsd:element name="name" type="xsd:string">
  <xsd:annotation>
    <xsd:documentation>&lt;!ELEMENT name (#PCDATA)&gt;
    </xsd:documentation>
  </xsd:annotation>
</xsd:element>

<xsd:element name="quantity" type="xsd:string">
  <xsd:annotation>
    <xsd:documentation>&lt;!ELEMENT quantity (#PCDATA)&gt;
    </xsd:documentation>
  </xsd:annotation>
</xsd:element>

<xsd:attributeGroup name="item">
  <xsd:annotation>
```

```
            <xsd:documentation>&lt;!ATTLIST item number CDATA #IMPLIED&gt;
            </xsd:documentation>
         </xsd:annotation>

         <xsd:attribute name="number" type="xsd:string">
           <xsd:annotation>
             <xsd:documentation>number CDATA #IMPLIED&gt;
             </xsd:documentation>
           </xsd:annotation>
         </xsd:attribute>

      </xsd:attributeGroup>

   </xsd:schema>
```

Table 9.1 summarizes how each construct of DTD can be mimicked in W3C XML Schema. We assume that the prefix xsd refers to the namespace http://www.w3.org/2001/XMLSchema.

**Table 9.1**   Mimicking DTD Constructs in W3C XML Schema

| DTD | W3C XML SCHEMA |
|---|---|
| `<!ELEMENT name (#PCDATA)>`<br>*without attribute-list declarations* | `<xsd:element name="name"`<br>`        type="xsd:string"/>` |
| `<!ELEMENT name (#PCDATA)>`<br>*with attribute-list declarations* | `<xsd:element name="name">`<br>`  <xsd:complexType>`<br>`    <xsd:simpleContent>`<br>`      <xsd:extension base="xsd:string">`<br>`        <xsd:attributeGroup ref="foo"/>`<br>`      </xsd:extension>`<br>`    </xsd:simpleContent>`<br>`  </xsd:complexType>`<br>`</xsd:element>` |
| `<!ELEMENT name (#PCDATA | foo1`<br>`    | foo2 | ...)*>`<br>*without attribute-list declarations* | `<xsd:element name="name">`<br>`  <xsd:complexType mixed="true">`<br>`    <xsd:choice minOccurs="0"`<br>`                maxOccurs="unbounded">`<br>`      <xsd:element ref="foo1"/>`<br>`      <xsd:element ref="foo2"/>`<br>`      ...`<br>`    </xsd:choice>`<br>`  </xsd:complexType>`<br>`</xsd:element>` |

**Table 9.1**  *continued*

| DTD | W3C XML SCHEMA |
|---|---|
| `<!ELEMENT` *name* `(#PCDATA \| foo1`<br>   `\| foo2 \| ...)*>`<br>*with attribute-list declarations* | `<xsd:element name="`*name*`">`<br>  `<xsd:complexType mixed="true">`<br>    `<xsd:choice minOccurs="0"`<br>            `maxOccurs="unbounded">`<br>     `<xsd:element ref="foo1"/>`<br>     `<xsd:element ref="foo2"/>`<br>     `...`<br>    `</xsd:choice>`<br>    `<xsd:attributeGroup ref="`*name*`"/>`<br>  `</xsd:complexType>`<br>`</xsd:element>` |
| `<!ELEMENT` *name* `(`*element-content-model*`)>`<br>*without attribute-list declarations* | `<xsd:element name="`*name*`">`<br>  `<xsd:complexType>`<br>    *element-content-model*<br>  `</xsd:complexType>`<br>`</xsd:element>` |
| `<!ELEMENT` *name* `(`*element-content-model*`)>`<br>*with attribute-list declarations* | `<xsd:element name="`*name*`">`<br>  `<xsd:complexType>`<br>    *element-content-model*<br>    `<xsd:attributeGroup ref="`*name*`"/>`<br>  `</xsd:complexType>`<br>`</xsd:element>` |
| *reference to*<br> *other elements in content models* | `<xsd:element ref="`*name*`"/>` |
| `,` *in content models* | `<xsd:sequence>` ... `</xsd:sequence>` |
| `\|` *in content models* | `<xsd:choice>` ... `</xsd:choice>` |
| `*` *in content models* | `minOccurs="0" maxOccurs="unbounded"` |
| `+` *in content models* | `minOccurs="1" maxOccurs="unbounded"` |
| `?` *in content models* | `minOccurs="0" maxOccurs="1"` |
| `<!ATTLIST` *name*<br>   *attribute-declarations*`>` | `<xsd:attributeGroup name="`*name*`">`<br>   *attribute-declarations*<br>`</xsd:attributeGroup>` |
| *attribute declaration* | `<attribute name="..." ...>...`<br>`</attribute>` |
| `#IMPLIED` | `use="optional"` (*default*) |
| `#REQUIRED` | `use="required"` |
| `CDATA` | `type="xsd:string"` |

**Table 9.1** *continued*

| DTD | W3C XML SCHEMA |
|---|---|
| `<!-- ... -->` | `<annotation><documentation>...`<br>`</documentation></annotation>` |
| `<!ENTITY % param-ent-name`<br>    `attribute-declarations>` | `<xsd:attributeGroup`<br>   `name="param-ent-name">`<br>   `attribute declarations`<br>   `</xsd:attributeGroup>` |
| `<!ENTITY % param-ent-name`<br>    `element-content-model>` | `<xsd:modelGroup`<br>    `name="param-ent-name">`<br>    `element content model`<br>    `</xsd:modelGroup>` |
| `%name;` (*reference to parameter*<br> *entities in content models*) | `<xsd:modelGroup ref="name"/>` |
| `%name;` (*reference to parameter*<br> *entities in content models*) | `<xsd:attributeGroup ref="name"/>` |
| `<!ENTITY name ...>`<br>(*parsed or unparsed entity*<br>*declarations*) | *Not applicable* |

## 9.2.2 Datatypes

Strings in XML documents are often used to represent data such as integers, decimals, names, and dates. Such a string may appear as the content of an element or the value of an attribute. The datatypes of W3C XML Schema can ensure that element contents and attribute values correctly represent the data of specified datatypes.

### Using Datatypes

A `quantity` element in the previous example represents the quantity of a type of item. Thus, permissible values are integers. Because DTDs do not provide any mechanisms for representing integers, it is impossible to specify that such elements contain integers rather than mere strings. On the other hand, W3C XML Schema provides very rich datatypes. For example, the datatype `short` provides integers greater than or equal to –32768 and less than or equal to 32767. To specify that permissible values of `quantity` elements are `short`, we specify `type="xsd:short"` for the `xsd:element` for `quantity`, modifying line 24 of `itemList.xsd` as follows:

```
<xsd:element name="quantity" type="xsd:short"/>
```

Let us replace 5 in the first `quantity` element in Listing 9.4 with `five`. Then, `SimpleParseWithSchemaValidation` reports an error as follows:

```
R:\samples>java chap02.SimpleParseWithSchemaValidation
                           chap09/itemList-nonDigit-xsd.xml
 [Error] 7:30 Datatype error: In element 'quantity' : 'five'
 is not a decimal.
```

When a document is found to be invalid against a schema, a `SAXParseException` is raised. The use of W3C XML Schema does not cause any differences from the use of DTDs.

However, declaring the datatype as `short` does *not* make the methods of DOM or SAX return integers. Their return values are of the datatype `java.lang.String`. For example, when the method `getData()` is applied to a `Text` node representing the content of the first `quantity` element, the return value is an instance of the class `java.lang.String`. It is *not* an integer.

Application programmers thus have to explicitly convert strings to instances of appropriate classes. For example, we obtain an integer from a string by evaluating `Int.parseInt(str)`, where `str` is the return value of the DOM or SAX method. Because the XML document has been validated against `itemList.xsd`, it is guaranteed that no exceptions occur during the conversion.

It is planned that future versions of DOM will provide mechanisms for returning instances of specified datatypes rather than strings. It is unclear whether future versions of SAX will provide such mechanisms.

Table 9.2 summarizes those built-in datatypes of W3C XML Schema that we consider particularly useful. For each datatype, we show which datatypes of Java and SQL roughly correspond to it.

**Table 9.2**  Comparison of Datatypes

| TAXONOMY | W3C XML SCHEMA | JAVA | SQL |
|---|---|---|---|
| Strings | string, normalizedString, and token | java.lang.String | CHAR, VARCHAR, NCHAR, NATOINAL VARCHAR |
| Numeric | byte | java.lang.Byte | TINYINT |
| | int | java.lang.Integer | INTEGER |
| | long | java.lang.Long | BIGINT |
| | short | java.lang.Short | SMALLINT |
| | float | java.lang.Float | REAL |
| | double | java.lang.Double | DOUBLE |
| | decimal | java.math.BigDecimal | NUMERIC |

**Table 9.2** *continued*

| TAXONOMY | W3C XML SCHEMA | JAVA | SQL |
| --- | --- | --- | --- |
| Date and time | `time` | `java.sql.TIME` | TIME |
| | `dateTime` | `java.sql.Timesamp` | TIMESTAMP or TIMESTAMP WITH TIME ZONE |
| | `date` | `java.sql.Date` | DATE |
| URI | `anyURI` | | |
| DTD compatibility | `ID, IDREF, IDREFS, ENTITY, ENTITIES, NOTATION, NMTOKEN, NMTOKENS` | | |

## Using Facets

In the previous example, we allowed any string as a value of `name` and allowed any integer from –32768 to 32767 as a value of `quantity`. However, we often want to specify further constraints. For example, we might want to change `itemList.xsd` so that permissible values of `name` are strings up to 5 characters and permissible values of `quantity` are integers greater than or equal to 0 and less than or equal to 20. In W3C XML Schema, such constraints are represented by *facets*.

A modified version of `itemList.xsd` is shown in Listing 9.9. Although `xsd:element` elements in the previous subsection specified the attribute `type`, they do not have this attribute this time. Instead, they have child elements named `xsd:simpleType` (lines 23 and 31).

**Listing 9.9** Using facets, `chap09/itemList-facet.xsd`

```
<?xml version="1.0" encoding="utf-8"?>
<xsd:schema xmlns:xsd='http://www.w3.org/2001/XMLSchema'>

 <xsd:element name="itemList">
   <xsd:complexType>
     <xsd:sequence>
       <xsd:element ref="item"
            minOccurs="0" maxOccurs="unbounded"/>
     </xsd:sequence>
   </xsd:complexType>
 </xsd:element>

 <xsd:element name="item">
   <xsd:complexType>
```

```
            <xsd:sequence>
              <xsd:element ref="name"/>
              <xsd:element ref="quantity"/>
            </xsd:sequence>
          </xsd:complexType>
        </xsd:element>

        <xsd:element name="name">
[23]        <xsd:simpleType>
[24]          <xsd:restriction base="xsd:token">
[25]            <xsd:maxLength value="5"/>
            </xsd:restriction>
          </xsd:simpleType>
        </xsd:element>

        <xsd:element name="quantity">
[31]        <xsd:simpleType>
[32]          <xsd:restriction base="xsd:short">
[33]            <xsd:maxInclusive value="20"/>
[34]            <xsd:minInclusive value="0"/>
            </xsd:restriction>
          </xsd:simpleType>
        </xsd:element>

      </xsd:schema>
```

An xsd:simpleType element represents an anonymous user-defined datatype. In this example, two xsd:simpleType elements occur. Both contain xsd: restriction elements (lines 24 and 32). In the description of name, the attribute base of the xsd:restriction element specifies xsd:token (line 24). This implies that this user-defined datatype is created by imposing restrictions on the built-in datatype xsd:token. The restriction is represented by the xsd:maxLength facet (line 25), which specifies that the string length is up to 5.

In the description for quantity, the attribute base of the xsd:restriction element (line 32) specifies xsd:short. This implies that this user-defined datatype is created by imposing restrictions on the built-in datatype xsd:short. The xsd:maxInclusive and xsd:minInclusive facets (lines 33 and 34) provide these restrictions. The former shows that permissible integers are less than or equal to 20, while the latter shows that permissible integers are greater than or equal to 0.

In itemList-xsd.xml (see Listing 9.4), the second and third name elements contain a string of more than 5 characters, and the third quantity element contains

an integer greater than 20. Thus, `SimpleParseWithSchemaValidation` reports
an error as follows:

```
R:\samples>java chap02.SimpleParseWithSchemaValidation
                                      chap09/itemList-facet-xsd.xml
[Error] 10:24 Datatype error: In element 'name' : Value 'eraser'
with length '6' exceeds maximum length facet of '5'..
[Error] 14:25 Datatype error: In element 'name' : Value 'stapler'
with length '7' exceeds maximum length facet of '5'..
[Error] 15:28 Datatype error: In element 'quantity' : 25 is out
of bounds:[ 0 <= X <= 20 ].
```

Next, we explicitly specify a list of permissible values. For example, suppose that
we want to specify that the permissible values of name are pen and eraser. We do
this by adding the `xsd:enumeration` facet (lines 25 and 26) to the declaration of
name in `itemList.xsd` as shown in Listing 9.10.

**Listing 9.10** Part of `itemList-enum.xsd`

```
        <xsd:element name="name">
          <xsd:simpleType>
            <xsd:restriction base="xsd:token">
[25]          <xsd:enumeration value="pen"/>
[26]          <xsd:enumeration value="eraser"/>
            </xsd:restriction>
          </xsd:simpleType>
        </xsd:element>
```

Let us create a new document, `itemList-enum-xsd.xml`, by modifying
`itemList-xsd.xml`. This document references `itemList-enum.xsd` and
contains 20 rather than 25. Since `itemList-enum-xsd.xml` contains <name>
stapler</name>, the following error is reported.

```
R:\samples>java chap02.SimpleParseWithSchemaValidation
                                      chap09/itemList-enum-xsd.xml
[Error] 14:25 Datatype error: In element 'name' : Value 'stapler'
must be one of [pen, eraser].
```

Finally, we show the use of a regular expression for specifying permissible values.
Suppose that we want to allow all strings ending with er. We do this by adding the
`xsd:pattern` facet (line 25), as shown in Listing 9.11.

**Listing 9.11** Part of `itemList-pattern.xsd`

```
        <xsd:element name="name">
          <xsd:simpleType>
            <xsd:restriction base="xsd:token">
[25]          <xsd:pattern value=".*er"/>
            </xsd:restriction>
```

```
        </xsd:simpleType>
      </xsd:element>
```

Let us create a new document, `itemList-pattern-xsd.xml`, by modifying `itemList-enum-xsd.xml`. This document references `itemList-pattern.xsd`. Since `itemList-pattern-xsd.xml` contains `<name>pen</name>`, the following error is reported.

```
R:\samples>java chap02.SimpleParseWithSchemaValidation
                              chap09/itemList-pattern-xsd.xml
[Error] 6:21 Datatype error: In element 'name' : Value 'pen'
does not match regular expression facet '.*er'..
```

Table 9.3 summarizes the facets of W3C XML Schema.

**Table 9.3**   Facets in W3C XML Schema

| TAXONOMY | FACET NAME | SUMMARY EXAMPLE |
|---|---|---|
| General | `enumeration` | Specifies a permissible value. To permit multiple values, specify this facet multiple times. |
| | | Permit `foo` and `bar`. |
| | | ```<br><xsd:simpleType><br>  <xsd:restriction base="xsd:token"><br>    <xsd:enumeration value="foo"/><br>    <xsd:enumeration value="bar"/><br>  </xsd:restriction><br></xsd:simpleType><br>``` |
| Strings | `length`, `minLength`, and `maxLength` | A non-negative integer indicating constraints on the length, and used mainly for `string` and datatypes derived from it. The measurement unit is a Unicode character. The facets `minLength` and `maxLength` impose restrictions on the minimum and maximum length, while `length` specifies the exact length. |
| | | Equal to or more than 5 characters, and equal to or less than 10 characters. |
| | | ```<br><xsd:simpleType><br>  <xsd:restriction base="xsd:string"><br>    <xsd:minLength value="5"/><br>    <xsd:maxLength value="10"/><br>  </xsd:restriction><br></xsd:simpleType><br>``` |
| | `pattern` | Regular expressions for strings, and used mainly for `string` and datatypes derived from it. |

(*continued*)

**Table 9.3** *continued*

| TAXONOMY | FACET NAME | SUMMARY EXAMPLE |
|---|---|---|
| | | A sequence of five digits (0–9). |

```
<xsd:simpleType>
 <xsd:restriction base="xsd:string">
    <xsd:pattern value='[0-9]{5}'/>
  </xsd:restriction>
 </xsd:simpleType>
```

| TAXONOMY | FACET NAME | SUMMARY EXAMPLE |
|---|---|---|
| Numeric | maxInclusive, maxExclusive, minExclusive, and minInclusive | Used mainly for numerical datatypes. The prefixes max and min mean maximum and minimum. The suffixes Inclusive and Exclusive mean whether or not the indicated value is permitted. |
| | | Greater than or equal to 100, and less than 1000. |

```
<xsd:simpleType>
  <xsd:restriction base="xsd:short">
    <xsd:minInclusive value="100"/>
    <xsd:maxExclusive value="1000"/>
  </xsd:restriction>
 </xsd:simpleType>
```

| TAXONOMY | FACET NAME | SUMMARY EXAMPLE |
|---|---|---|
| | totalDigits and fractionDigits | Used for the datatype decimal. The facet totalDigits indicates the maximum number of digits, including the decimal point, while fractionDigits indicates the maximum number of digits following the decimal point. |
| | | Two fraction digits (for example, "???.23") and two other digits (for example, "24.56") |

```
<xsd:simpleType>
  <xsd:restriction base="xsd:decimal">
    <xsd:totalDigits value="5"/>
    <xsd:fractionDigits value="2"/>
  </xsd:restriction>
 </xsd:simpleType>
```

## 9.2.3 Using Namespaces

Although the XML Namespace Recommendation was published in 1998, it did not provide namespace-aware validation. To create a DTD for documents containing namespaces, we have been forced to choose a particular namespace prefix for a namespace.[3] The choice of a particular namespace prefix conflicts with the original

---

[3] However, there is a trick for easily changing namespace prefixes in DTDs. For more about this, see Chapter 6.

intention of the XML Namespace Recommendation. Furthermore, there are no standard ways to construct DTDs containing multiple namespaces.

W3C XML Schema supports namespaces. A schema written in W3C XML Schema specifies a namespace as the target. Components declared in this schema belong to that target namespace. A document containing multiple namespaces is validated against a collection of schemas, each of which specifies one of these namespaces as the target. Namespace prefixes used in documents or schemas are merely proxies for namespace names (URIs). Those in documents do not have to coincide with those used in schemas.

As an example, consider the XML document shown in Listing 9.12. This document contains the namespaces `http://www.example.net/foo` and `http://www.w3.org/1999/xhtml`.

**Listing 9.12** A document with multiple namespaces, `chap09/multiNS.xml`

```
<?xml version="1.0" encoding="utf-8"?>
<foo xmlns="http://www.example.net/foo">
  <p xmlns="http://www.w3.org/1999/xhtml"/>
  <ol xmlns="http://www.w3.org/1999/xhtml">
    <li>bullet 1</li>
    <li>bullet 2</li>
  </ol>
</foo>
```

Let us construct a schema for this document. The namespace for the root element `foo` is `http://www.example.net/foo`. A schema for this element is shown in Listing 9.13

**Listing 9.13** A schema for the root element, `chap09/foo.xsd`

```
      <?xml version="1.0" encoding="utf-8"?>
      <xsd:schema xmlns:xsd="http://www.w3.org/2001/XMLSchema"
[3]       targetNamespace="http://www.example.net/foo"
          xmlns:xhtml="http://www.w3.org/1999/xhtml">

[6]   <xsd:import namespace="http://www.w3.org/1999/xhtml"/>

       <xsd:element name="foo">
         <xsd:complexType>
           <xsd:choice
               minOccurs="0" maxOccurs="unbounded">
[12]         <xsd:element ref="xhtml:p" />
[13]         <xsd:element ref="xhtml:ol" />
           </xsd:choice>
```

```
      </xsd:complexType>
    </xsd:element>
  </xsd:schema>
```

The instruction `targetNamespace="http://www.example.net/foo"` (line 3) shows that this schema is concerned with the namespace `http://www.example.net/foo`. `xsd:import` (line 6) shows that this schema references declarations from the namespace `"http://www.w3.org/1999/xhtml/"`. Observe that `p` and `ol` of the namespace `http://www.w3.org/1999/xhtml` are referenced from the content model for `foo` (lines 12 and 13).

The namespace for the child elements `p` and `ol` is `http://www.w3.org/1999/xhtml`. The element `ol` in turn has the child element `li`. A schema for these elements is shown in Listing 9.14.

**Listing 9.14**  A schema for child elements, `chap09/xhtml.xsd`

```
<?xml version="1.0" encoding="utf-8"?>
<xsd:schema xmlns:xsd="http://www.w3.org/2001/XMLSchema"
  xmlns:xhtml="http://www.w3.org/1999/xhtml"
  targetNamespace="http://www.w3.org/1999/xhtml">

 <xsd:element name="p" type="xsd:string"/>

 <xsd:element name="ol">
   <xsd:complexType>
     <xsd:sequence>
       <xsd:element ref="xhtml:li"
                    minOccurs="0" maxOccurs="unbounded"/>
     </xsd:sequence>
   </xsd:complexType>
 </xsd:element>

 <xsd:element name="li" type="xsd:string"/>

</xsd:schema>
```

Finally, we have to reference these schemas from the XML document. To specify `foo.xsd` for the namespace `http://www.example.net/foo` and specify `xhtml.xsd` for the namespace `http://www.w3.org/1999/xhtml`, we add the attribute `schemaLocation`, as shown in Listing 9.15. Again, this attribute is merely a hint.

**Listing 9.15**  Referencing the schemas, `chap09/multiNS-xsd.xml`

```
<?xml version="1.0" encoding="utf-8"?>
<foo xmlns="http://www.example.net/foo"
     xmlns:xsi="http://www.w3.org/2001/XMLSchema-instance"
     xsi:schemaLocation= "http://www.example.net/foo
```

```
                        foo.xsd
                http://www.w3.org/1999/xhtml
                        xhtml.xsd">
    <p xmlns="http://www.w3.org/1999/xhtml"/>
    <ol xmlns="http://www.w3.org/1999/xhtml">
      <li>bullet 1</li>
      <li>bullet 2</li>
    </ol>
  </foo>
```

Namespace prefixes in documents do not have to coincide with those in schemas. For example, the XML document in Listing 9.16 also conforms to the two schemas just shown.

**Listing 9.16** Using a different namespace prefix, chap09/multiNS-different Prefix-xsd.xml

```
    <?xml version="1.0" encoding="utf-8"?>
    <foo:foo xmlns:foo="http://www.example.net/foo"
          xmlns:xsi="http://www.w3.org/2001/XMLSchema-instance"
          xsi:schemaLocation= "http://www.example.net/foo
                                  foo.xsd
                        http://www.w3.org/1999/xhtml
                            xhtml.xsd">
      <xhtml1:p xmlns:xhtml1="http://www.w3.org/1999/xhtml"/>
      <xhtml2:ol xmlns:xhtml2="http://www.w3.org/1999/xhtml">
        <xhtml2:li>bullet 1</xhtml2:li>
        <xhtml2:li>bullet 2</xhtml2:li>
      </xhtml2:ol>
    </foo:foo>
```

Rather than specifying the attribute schemaLocation, we can write programs that explicitly reference schemas. We only have to invoke setProperty for DOM or SAX parsers as follows:[4]

```
    parser.setProperty(
      "http://apache.org/xml/properties/schema/external-schemaLocation",
      "http://www.example.net/foo    foo.xsd" +
      "http://www.w3.org/1999/xhtml   xhtml.xsd ");
```

Such programs do not require the use of the attribute schemaLocation in XML documents. Even if this attribute is specified, it is simply ignored. The schemas specified by setProperty (in this example, foo.xsd and xhtml.xsd) are always used.

---

[4] Note that this property is specific to Xerces. JAXP 1.1 does not provide any standard mechanisms yet.

## 9.2.4  Advanced Features

In this chapter, we have considered W3C XML Schema as DTD + datatypes + namespaces and only covered the relevant features of W3C XML Schema. Such restricted use of W3C XML Schema is not difficult and provides significant advantages.

However, W3C XML Schema provides far more advanced features than those covered in this chapter. The following list is a very brief summary of such features.

*Complex type*

A complex type describes permissible contents (elements and text) and attributes. Complex types are used by element declarations.

*Simple type*

A simple type describes permissible character strings, which lexically represent values in that simple type. Simple types are used for attribute declarations or element declarations.

*Derivation by extension*

Derivation by extension is to create a complex type from an existing type by adding child elements or attributes.

*Derivation by restriction*

Derivation by restriction is to create a (simple or complex) type from another (simple or complex) type by imposing further restrictions.

*Model group definitions*

A model group mimics a parameter entity describing a content model fragment. Model groups do not describe attributes.

*Attribute group definitions*

An attribute group mimics a parameter entity describing a group of attributes. Attribute groups do not describe child elements.

*Wildcards*

A wildcard matches elements and attributes dependent on their namespace names independently of their local names.

*Element substitution groups*

An element substitution group allows elements in content models to be substituted with different elements.

*Identity constraints*

Identity constraints are generalizations of ID/IDREF for ensuring uniqueness of elements or attribute values and using such values as keys.

### 9.2.5 Further Information

The details of W3C XML Schema are described by the following W3C Recommendations.

*XML Schema Part 0: Primer*

This document introduces the W3C XML Schema facilities through numerous examples.

*XML Schema Part 1: Structures*

This document specifies the W3C XML Schema definition language, which offers facilities for describing the structure and constraining the contents of XML 1.0 documents.

*XML Schema Part 2: Datatypes*

This document defines facilities for defining datatypes to be used in W3C XML Schema.

Xerces supports W3C XML Schema, and other implementations are also available. However, some of them are beta releases and do not really conform to the W3C XML Schema Recommendation. In particular, they might not correctly support those features covered in this section.

Further information, including the recommendations just listed, is available at the Web page of the XML Schema WG (`http://www.w3.org/XML/Schema`).

## 9.3 RELAX NG

RELAX NG is a simple yet powerful alternative to W3C XML Schema. RELAX NG was created by an international standardization organization, the Organization for the Advancement of Structured Information Standards (OASIS). RELAX NG was later published as a committee specification of ISO/IEC JTC1 SC34.

RELAX NG was created by unifying two schema languages: TREX and RELAX Core. RELAX Core has been published as a Technical Report (ISO/IEC TR 22250-1:2001) by ISO/IEC JTC1 and was originally submitted to ISO/IEC JTC1 by Japan. Under the influence of RELAX Core, James Clark (the technical lead of the original XML WG, the editor of W3C XML XSLT, and the implementer of reference implementations of XML and XSLT) designed TREX. The RELAX NG technical committee of OASIS unified these two schema languages and published RELAX NG version 1.0 as a committee specification in December 2001.

## 9.3.1 Mimicking DTDs

This subsection demonstrates how to mimic DTD features in RELAX NG by rewriting the schemas shown in Section 9.2.1. Features specific to RELAX NG are not covered.

### Mimicking Element Type Declarations

Recall that we rewrote a simple DTD (see Listing 9.2) in W3C XML Schema (see Listing 9.3). Listing 9.17 is a rewrite in RELAX NG.

**Listing 9.17** A simple schema, `chap09/itemList0.rng`

```
[1]      <?xml version="1.0" encoding="utf-8"?>
         <grammar xmlns="http://relaxng.org/ns/structure/1.0">
[3]        <start>
             <ref name="itemList"/>
           </start>

           <define name="itemList">
             <element name="itemList">
[9]            <zeroOrMore>
[10]             <ref name="item"/>
               </zeroOrMore>
             </element>
           </define>

           <define name="item">
             <element name="item">
[17]           <ref name="name"/>
[18]           <ref name="quantity"/>
             </element>
           </define>

           <define name="name">
             <element name="name">
```

```
[24]              <text/>
              </element>
          </define>

          <define name="quantity">
            <element name="quantity">
[30]              <text/>
            </element>
          </define>

        </grammar>
```

The root `grammar` (line 1) declares the namespace `http://relaxng.org/ns/structure/1.0`. This schema has four `define` elements, each of which has an `element` child element. These `element` elements specify the permissible tag names `itemList`, `item`, `name`, and `quantity`. The `zeroOrMore` element (line 9) and its child `ref` (line 10) specify that an `itemList` element can contain zero or more `item` elements. The two `ref` elements (lines 17 and 18) specify that an `item` element has a `name` element followed by a `quantity` element. The `text` elements (lines 24 and 30) specify that a `name` element and a `quantity` element can have any string as their contents. The `start` element (line 3) specifies that the root is an `itemList` element.

We can make this schema more compact. First, we can eliminate `ref` and `define`. The schema in Listing 9.18 is created by replacing each `ref` with the body of the corresponding `define`.

**Listing 9.18**  A compact schema, chap09/itemList1.rng

```
<?xml version="1.0" encoding="utf-8"?>
<grammar xmlns="http://relaxng.org/ns/structure/1.0">
  <start>
    <element name="itemList">
      <zeroOrMore>
        <element name="item">
          <element name="name">
            <text/>
          </element>
          <element name="quantity">
            <text/>
          </element>
        </element>
      </zeroOrMore>
    </element>
  </start>
</grammar>
```

Because this grammar no longer contains `define`, we can eliminate `grammar` and `start` (and move the namespace declaration to the root element), as shown in Listing 9.19.

**Listing 9.19** An even more compact schema, chap09/itemList2.rng

```
<?xml version="1.0" encoding="utf-8"?>
<element name="itemList"
  xmlns="http://relaxng.org/ns/structure/1.0">
  <zeroOrMore>
    <element name="item">
      <element name="name">
        <text/>
      </element>
      <element name="quantity">
        <text/>
      </element>
    </element>
  </zeroOrMore>
</element>
```

Let us validate `itemList.xml` against `itemList0.rng`. As a RELAX NG validator, we use Jing by James Clark. Version 2001-12-03 of `jing.jar` is included on the accompanying CD-ROM. The latest version is available from `http://www.thaiopensource.com/relaxng/jing.html`.

In preparation, add the jar file of Jing to your CLASSPATH. For example:

```
set CLASSPATH=".;c:\relaxng\jing.jar;c:\xerces-1_4_3\xerces.jar"
```

We can invoke Jing by specifying `com.thaiopensource.relaxng.util.Driver` as the main class. The first argument is a schema and the second is an instance document.

```
R:\samples>java com.thaiopensource.relaxng.util.Driver
                       chap09/itemList0.rng chap09/itemList.xml
```

Because no errors are found, Jing does not report anything.

## Mimicking Attribute-List Declarations

Recall that we added an attribute-list declaration to `itemList-attribute.dtd` (see Listing 9.6). To capture this attribute-list declaration, we only have to introduce an `attribute` element, as shown in Listing 9.20.

**Listing 9.20** A schema with an attribute declaration, `chap09/itemList-attribute.rng`

```
      <?xml version="1.0" encoding="utf-8"?>
      <element name="itemList"
        xmlns="http://relaxng.org/ns/structure/1.0">
        <zeroOrMore>
          <element name="item">
[6]         <attribute name="number"/>
            <element name="name">
              <text/>
            </element>
            <element name="quantity">
              <text/>
            </element>
          </element>
        </zeroOrMore>
      </element>
```

The only difference from `itemList2.rng` (see Listing 9.19) is the addition of `attribute` (line 6). It declares `number` as a mandatory attribute.

To make the attribute `number` optional, we wrap the `attribute` with an `optional` element as follows:

```
[6]      <optional><attribute name="number"/></optional>
```

## Comments in Schemas

As a representation of comments, RELAX NG provides `documentation` elements in the namespace `http://relaxng.org/ns/compatibility/annotations/1.0`, as shown in Listing 9.21. Elements or attributes of foreign namespaces such as <p> of XHTML can also be used for representing comments.

**Listing 9.21** A schema with annotations, `chap09/itemList-attribute-annotation.rng`

```
      <?xml version="1.0" encoding="utf-8"?>
      <element name="itemList"
        xmlns="http://relaxng.org/ns/structure/1.0"
        xmlns:a="http://relaxng.org/ns/compatibility/annotations/1.0">

[6]      <a:documentation>The root of a schema</a:documentation>

        <zeroOrMore>
          <element name="item">
[10]        <a:documentation>Attributes and child elements can be
                            described together.</a:documentation>
            <attribute name="number">
```

```
[13]                  <a:documentation>Describes an attribute.</a:documentation>
                 </attribute>
                 <element name="name">
[16]                  <a:documentation>Describes a child element.</a:documentation>
                   <text/>
                 </element>
                 <element name="quantity">
[20]                  <a:documentation>Describes another child element.</a:documentation>
                   <text/>
                 </element>
               </element>
             </zeroOrMore>
           </element>
```

This schema is similar to `itemList-attribute.rng` (see Listing 9.20), but five `documentation` elements (lines 6, 10, 13, 16, and 20) are added.

Table 9.4 summarizes how each construct of DTD can be mimicked in RELAX NG. We assume that unqualified elements are in the namespace `http://relaxng.org/ns/structure/1.0`, and the prefix a refers to the namespace `http://relaxng.org/ns/compatibility/annotations/1.0`.

**Table 9.4**   Mimicking DTD Constructs in RELAX NG

| DTD | RELAX NG |
| --- | --- |
| `<!ELEMENT name (#PCDATA)>`<br>*and optional attribute-list*<br>*declarations* | `<define name="name">`<br>  `<element name="name">`<br>    *attribute-declarations*<br>    `<text/>`<br>  `</element>`<br>`</define>` |
| `<!ELEMENT name (#PCDATA | foo1`<br>   `| foo2 | ...)*>`<br>*with optional attribute-list*<br>*declarations* | `<define name="name">`<br>  `<element name="name">`<br>    *attribute-declarations*<br>    `<mixed>`<br>      `<zeroOrMore>`<br>        `<choice>`<br>          `<ref name="foo1"/>`<br>          `<ref name="foo2"/>`<br>          `...`<br>        `</choice>`<br>      `</zeroOrMore>`<br>    `</mixed>`<br>  `</element>`<br>`</define>` |

**Table 9.4**  *continued*

| DTD | RELAX NG |
|---|---|
| `<!ELEMENT name (element-content-model)>`<br> *with optional attribute-list declarations* | `<define name="name">`<br>  `<element name="name">`<br>    *attribute-declarations*<br>    *element-content-model*<br>  `</element>`<br> `</define>` |
| *reference to*<br> *other elements in content models* | `<ref name="name"/>` |
| `,` *in content models* | `<group> ... </group>`<br>(*If an* element, define, *or* optional *element has more than one child, an intervening* group *element is implicitly introduced.*) |
| `|` *in content models* | `<choice> ... </choice>` |
| `*` *in content models* | `<zeroOrMore> ... </zeroOrMore>` |
| `+` *in content models* | `<oneOrMore> ... </oneOrMore>` |
| `?` *in content models or* `#IMPLIED` *in attribute-list declarations* | `<optional> ... </optional>` |
| *attribute declarations* | `<attribute name="...">...</attribute>` |
| CDATA | `<text/>` |
| `<!-- ... -->` | `<a:documentation>...`<br>`</a:documentation>` |
| `<!ENTITY % param-ent-name`<br>    `attribute-declarations>` | `<define name="param-ent-name">`<br>    *attribute declarations*<br>`</define>` |
| `<!ENTITY % param-ent-name`<br>    `element-content-model>` | `<define name="param-ent-name">`<br>    *element content model*<br>`</define>` |
| `%name;` (*reference to parameter entities in content models*) | `<ref name="name"/>` |
| `%name;` (*reference to parameter entities in attribute declarations*) | `<ref name="name"/>` |
| `<!ENTITY name ...>`<br> (*parsed or unparsed entity declarations*) | *Not applicable* |

## 9.3.2 Using Datatypes and Facets of W3C XML Schema

RELAX NG does not have a fixed set of datatypes. Rather, it utilizes datatype libraries defined elsewhere. In particular, RELAX NG can use datatypes and facets of W3C XML Schema.

The schema in Listing 9.22 is equivalent to `itemList-facet.xsd` (see Listing 9.9), which specifies datatypes and facets.

**Listing 9.22** Using datatypes and facets, `chap09/itemList-facet.rng`

```
         <?xml version="1.0" encoding="utf-8"?>
         <element name="itemList"
           xmlns="http://relaxng.org/ns/structure/1.0"
           xmlns:a="http://relaxng.org/ns/compatibility/annotations/1.0"
[5]        datatypeLibrary="http://www.w3.org/2001/XMLSchema-datatypes">
           <zeroOrMore>
             <element name="item">
               <attribute name="number"/>
               <element name="name">
[10]             <data type="token">
                   <a:documentation>Tokens up to 5 characters</a:documentation>
[12]               <param name="maxLength">5</param>
                 </data>
               </element>

               <element name="quantity">
[17]             <data type="short">
                   <a:documentation>Short numbers between 0 and 20
                   </a:documentation>
[19]               <param name="maxInclusive">20</param>
[20]               <param name="minInclusive">0</param>
                 </data>
               </element>
             </element>
           </zeroOrMore>
         </element>
```

The attribute `datatypeLibrary` (line 5) specifies which datatype library is used. The value `http://www.w3.org/2001/XMLSchema-datatypes` indicates the use of W3C XML Schema datatypes. The first `data` (line 10) specifies that the content of a `name` element is of the datatype `token`, which is a datatype of W3C XML Schema. The first `param` (line 12) specifies that tokens are up to 5 characters. This is done by specifying the facet `maxLength` of W3C XML Schema. The second `data` (line 17) specifies that the content of a `quantity` element is of the datatype `short`, which is a datatype of W3C XML Schema. The second `param` (line 19) specifies that the value is less than or equal to 20, while the third `param` (line 20) specifies that the value is greater than or equal to 0. This is done by specifying the facets `maxInclusive` and `minInclusive` of W3C XML Schema.

### 9.3.3 Using Namespaces

Handling of namespaces in RELAX NG is quite different from that in W3C XML Schema. In RELAX NG, one-to-one correspondence between namespaces and schemas is not required. Rather, a single RELAX NG schema can handle multiple namespaces. When we declare an element or attribute, we can indicate the namespace name by specifying or inheriting the attribute `ns`.

Recall `multiNS.xml` (see Listing 9.12) and `multiNS-differentPrefix-xsd.xml` (see Listing 9.16). Because these XML documents have two namespaces, we had to create two W3C XML Schema schemas, `foo.xsd` (see Listing 9.13) and `xhtml.xsd` (see Listing 9.14). However, RELAX NG allows us to create a single RELAX NG schema as shown in Listing 9.23.

**Listing 9.23**  A schema for two namespaces, `chap09/multiNS.rng`

```
        <?xml version="1.0" encoding="utf-8"?>
[2]     <element
          name="foo"
          ns="http://www.example.net/foo"
          xmlns="http://relaxng.org/ns/structure/1.0"
          datatypeLibrary="http://www.w3.org/2001/XMLSchema-datatypes">

          <zeroOrMore>
            <choice>

[11]          <element name="p"  ns="http://www.w3.org/1999/xhtml">
                <data type="string"/>
              </element>

[15]          <element name="ol" ns="http://www.w3.org/1999/xhtml">
                <zeroOrMore>
[17]              <element name="li">
                    <data type="string"/>
                  </element>
                </zeroOrMore>
              </element>

            </choice>
          </zeroOrMore>
        </element>
```

Among the four `element` elements in this schema, the first (line 2) specifies the attribute `ns` and announces the namespace `http://www.example.net/foo`. The second (line 11) announces the namespace `http://www.w3.org/1999/xhtml`. The third (line 15) announces the same namespace, which is inherited by the fourth one (line 17).

### 9.3.4  Co-occurrence Constraints

Co-occurrence constraints are interdependencies between attributes and elements. An example of co-occurrence constraints is that *either the attribute `foo` or an element `foo` shall be specified, but not both*. W3C XML Schema cannot capture co-occurrence constraints, although many users require them.

RELAX NG is very powerful in handling co-occurrence constraints. To demonstrate, we use the schema shown in Listing 9.24.

**Listing 9.24**  A schema for co-occurrence constraints, `chap09/bookList.rng`

```
        <?xml version="1.0" encoding="utf-8"?>
        <element name="bookList"
          ns="http://www.example.org"
          xmlns="http://relaxng.org/ns/structure/1.0"
          datatypeLibrary="http://www.w3.org/2001/XMLSchema-datatypes">
          <zeroOrMore>
            <element name="book">
[8]            <interleave>
[9]              <choice>
[10]               <element name="title"><data type="string"/></element>
[11]               <attribute name="title"><data type="string"/></attribute>
[12]             </choice>
[13]             <choice>
[14]               <oneOrMore>
[15]                 <element name="author"><data type="string"/></element>
[16]               </oneOrMore>
[17]               <attribute name="author"><data type="string"/></attribute>
[18]             </choice>
[19]             <optional>
[20]               <choice>
[21]                 <element name="price"><data type="decimal"/></element>
[22]                 <attribute name="price"><data type="decimal"/></attribute>
[23]               </choice>
[24]             </optional>
[25]           </interleave>
            </element>
          </zeroOrMore>
        </element>
```

Lines 8 through 25 describe the content and attributes of book elements. The first choice element (line 9) specifies that a title is represented by either a child element (line 10) or an attribute (line 11). Either a single child element or an attribute exists, but not both.

The second choice element (line 13) specifies that authors are represented either by child elements (lines 14–16) or an attribute (line 17). More than one author element may exist. The attribute author is present only if there are no author elements.

The third choice element (line 20) specifies that prices are represented by a child element (line 21) or an attribute (line 22). Because we have optional (line 19), there might not be any price information.

These three choice elements are combined by interleave (line 8) rather than group. As a result, the child elements title, author, and price (if any) may occur in *any* order.

The bookList document, shown in Listing 9.25, is valid against this schema. This document contains three book elements. They represent title, author, and price information differently.

**Listing 9.25** A document with book information, chap09/bookList.xml

```xml
<?xml version="1.0" encoding="utf-8"?>
<bookList xmlns="http://www.example.org">

  <book price="81.94">
    <title>The Java (tm) Programming Language, Third Edition</title>
    <author>Ken Arnold</author>
    <author>James Gosling</author>
    <author>David Holmes</author>
  </book>

  <book title="The Java Tutorial Second Edition">
    <author>Mary Campione</author>
    <price>45.95</price>
    <author>Kathy Walrath</author>
  </book>

  <book author="Peter Holman" title="Dowland, Lachrimae"/>

</bookList>
```

To represent titles, the first book element uses an element, while the second and third use the title attribute. To represent authors, the first and second use author elements, while the third uses the attribute author. To represent prices, the first uses the attribute price, and the second uses a price element. The third does not have price information. Observe that the second `book` element has an `author` element, a `price` element, and another `author` element in that order. This sequence will be disallowed if we replace `interleave` (line 8 in Listing 9.24) with `group`.

## 9.3.5 Further Information

Although we have seen most of the keywords of RELAX NG, we have not quite covered all its features. The details of RELAX NG are described by the official documents in the following list.

*RELAX NG Tutorial*

This tutorial demonstrates most of the features of RELAX NG with ample examples.

*RELAX NG Specification*

This is the definitive specification of RELAX NG and is intended to be used in conjunction with the next two specifications.

*RELAX NG DTD Compatibility*

This specification defines datatypes and annotations for use in RELAX NG schemas to support some of the features of XML 1.0 DTDs that are not supported directly by RELAX NG.

*Guidelines for using W3C XML Schema Datatypes with RELAX NG*

This document specifies guidelines for using the datatypes and facets of W3C XML Schema from RELAX NG.

In parallel to the language design, RELAX NG has been actively implemented. As of this writing, three validators for RELAX NG have been developed. They are Jing, Multi-Schema Validator, and VBRELAXNG. Jing and VBRELAXNG are included on the accompanying CD-ROM.

- Jing was developed by James Clark, the chair of the RELAX NG technical committee and a co-editor of the specifications.
- Multi-Schema Validator was developed by Kohsuke Kawaguchi of Sun Microsystems. Besides supporting RELAX NG, it supports RELAX Namespace, RELAX Core, TREX, and a subset of W3C XML Schema.
- VBRELAXNG was developed by Koji Yonekura of NEC. It is written in Visual Basic and provides an interactive tutorial.

Further information, including these specifications, is available at the Web page of the OASIS RELAX NG technical committee (`http://relaxng.org/`).

## 9.4 Summary

In this chapter, we have seen the problems associated with DTDs and introduced W3C XML Schema and RELAX NG through numerous examples. DTDs have three problems: a peculiar syntax, a lack of datatypes, and the inability to handle namespaces. W3C XML Schema is a powerful schema language: It provides many datatypes and facets, and supports namespaces. However, W3C XML Schema is also a complicated schema language, and we have merely covered a DTD-mimicking subset with namespaces and datatypes added. On the other hand, RELAX NG is a simple yet powerful alternative to W3C XML Schema. In particular, RELAX NG can support co-occurrence constraints. RELAX NG can borrow datatype libraries, including W3C XML Schema Part 2, and also support namespaces.

It is not easy to compare schema languages. If we merely create a list of supported features, complicated schema languages will look better. However, deliberate omission of features is often crucial because some features violate layering of XML parsers, validators, and application programs. In Chapter 16, we study the principles of schema languages and compare XML Schema and RELAX NG.

For impatient readers, here is a piece of advice. This author (Murata) believes that RELAX NG is technically superior to W3C XML Schema. However, it is true that W3C XML Schema is supported by W3C, Microsoft, and IBM. If you need a simple yet powerful language and reliable implementations, it is a good idea to use RELAX NG. If you care about authorization by W3C and support from large companies, you might want to use a DTD-mimicking subset of W3C XML Schema together with datatypes and namespaces.

# XML Application Server

In Chapter 1, we overviewed how Web applications have emerged and Internet technology has evolved. When the Web began, HTML files were statically prepared and the target audience was mostly humans using Web browsers. People world-wide have quickly adopted the Web. Thus, the role of the Web has changed from being a means of information sharing to providing a more business-oriented services infrastructure. To process business deals, the Web first enabled interactive access to backend business applications; that is, business-to-consumer (B2C) Web applications emerged. In many cases, the central data format was HTML. Servlet and JavaServer Pages (JSP) were originally designed for building such Web applications in Java. However, as business deals have become more dynamic and automated, the central data format has become XML; that is, business-to-business (B2B) Web applications have emerged.

In this section, we discuss Web applications from an XML and B2B point of view. In Section 10.1, we describe the background of the XML application server. Then we introduce three important technologies that are related to an XML application server: Servlet in Section 10.2, JavaServer Pages in Section 10.3, and Apache Cocoon in Section 10.4. Finally, we describe how to develop Web applications by using and combining these technologies.

## 10.1 The Background of the XML Application Server

Most readers have heard of commercial Web application servers such as IBM's WebSphere, BEA's WebLogic, and Sun's iPlanet. These are Java-based middleware, so developers can write Web applications in Java on top of them. If a Web application server can process XML as a first-class data format, we call it an *XML application server*.

In this section, we describe what an XML application server is and why it is needed.

## 10.1.1 The Need for a Common Framework for Building Web Applications

When we develop Web applications in Java, we need to consider an enormous number of requirements—for example, HTTP protocol handling at the transport layer, XML-based protocol handling such as SOAP at the messaging layer, storing XML into relational databases and vice versa, transactions, authentication, and authorization. These are not all the requirements but are the major ones.

It is not an easy job for average developers to collect and combine all the necessary technologies to build a Web application by themselves. For example, ensuring the security of an application server is quite difficult for those who are not security experts if many libraries and many types of middleware are installed. Furthermore, it may increase the total cost to maintain these underlying technologies. In the worst case, some technology may not work with another technology at the same time. Another type of issue is that we may lose the portability of our applications. Specifically, it becomes very difficult to deploy an application from one computer environment to another depending on the requirements of various libraries and middleware.

Accordingly, we want a single and sound framework for building Web applications that can integrate all the required technologies into a single server or a cluster of servers. For portability, such a framework should not depend on a particular vendor's product; it should be vendor-neutral. Portability is one of the most important factors for Java applications.

What is the most common framework for building Web applications in Java? *Java 2 Enterprise Edition (J2EE)*. J2EE is a set of standard architectures and APIs. Many companies, including IBM and Sun, are participating in defining the J2EE standard in the open organization called *Java Community Process (JCP)*. IBM's WebSphere, BEA's WebLogic, and Sun's iPlanet are the most famous J2EE-compliant application servers. Needless to say, an application written for a J2EE-compliant application server should work with another J2EE-compliant application server.

J2EE adopts existing Java and Internet technologies—for example, Servlet, JSP, and Enterprise JavaBeans (EJB) as legacy technologies; and SOAP and Web services as emerging technologies. We describe EJB in Chapter 11, SOAP in Chapter 12, and Web services in Chapter 13. Therefore, we focus on Servlet and JSP in this section. J2EE will continue to involve various Internet standards and provide rich functions for building enterprise Web applications, keeping its vendor-neutral characteristics.

*Servlet* is an API and application framework to write application logic that runs on the server side. A server-side component called a *servlet container* that runs on one or more Java virtual machines (VMs) launches a servlet instance as a thread for handling HTTP requests. It is faster and more efficient than a CGI script because it is instantiated as a long-term, semipermanent process in an operating system.

JavaServer Pages allows us to embed application logic that runs on the server side into a text document, such as an HTML document or an XML document. The concept is not new; we see the same concept in Server-Side Include (SSI), Active Server Pages (ASP), and the PHP scripting language.

J2EE adopts XML as a data format for describing a portable application, such as Web Application Archive (WAR) and Enterprise Application Archive (EAR). For example, a "web.xml" in WAR is used to configure servlets and JSPs.

## 10.1.2 What Is an XML Application Server?

When we develop a B2B application using XML, we need to consider how to handle XML at the server side—that is, receiving an XML document as a request from the client, analyzing it, and processing it according to an XML-based protocol such as SOAP. In many cases, the application needs to send back a response to the client as an XML document.

Many application servers bundle an XML parser for processing XML documents, but most of them do not provide any support for XML-based protocols as of this writing.[1] One reason is that an XML-based protocol is an emerging technology and is still under discussion at the World Wide Web Consortium (W3C).

Even if a standard XML-based protocol (most likely SOAP) matures, there may be a need for an application-specific XML-based protocol in some cases, depending on an industry-specific requirement. Therefore, it is worthwhile that we discuss a typical way to handle an XML-based protocol using Java programs. Thus we describe how to handle and generate XML documents by using Servlet in Section 10.2 and JSP in Section 10.3.

As we mentioned, J2EE will include support for Web services and SOAP in the near future. For example, "Java Specification Request (JSR) 109: Implementing Enterprise

---

[1] IBM's WebSphere Application Server is the first commercial one to bundle Apache SOAP, which is a SOAP engine developed by Apache Software Foundation. However, it is offered as a servlet application and is not deeply incorporated into the heart of the application server itself.

Web Services," which is a specification for supporting Web services in the next version of the J2EE framework, is being defined by JCP. When application servers support JSR 109, building SOAP and Web services will become much easier than it is today. To learn what functions are required for processing SOAP and building Web services with SOAP, refer to Chapters 12 and 13.

We typically want to store incoming XML documents into a relational database management system (RDBMS) if they contain important information for the business—for example, an XML document that requests a purchase order and an invoice for the request. We may also want to retrieve the data from the RDBMS as an XML document. Although J2EE does not support such functions now, we can do it by combining the database connectivity and XML processing API that J2EE does support. We discuss how to accomplish such functions in Chapter 11.

B2B seems to be well supported by the J2EE framework. How about B2C? If we assume we already have some data source as XML documents on the server side, we may want to provide a service that targets not only a business but also a consumer. For example, the weather report application in Chapter 1 may want to support both machine clients and human clients at the same time. In other words, we may want to integrate B2B and B2C applications. How do we support such requirements? With Apache Cocoon, an XML publishing framework developed by Apache Software Foundation. We describe an example in which both machine clients and human clients are supported by Cocoon in Section 10.4.

As we mentioned, most common functions for processing XML in Web applications will be integrated into the J2EE framework. It will drastically increase the portability of XML-based Web applications and decrease the effort required for building XML-based Web applications. We believe it should be the final goal of XML application servers.

In this section, we discussed the needs of XML application servers from the J2EE point of view. J2EE is a Java standard framework for building Web applications. XML-based protocols are still undergoing standardization and are subject to change. Therefore, we do not describe any specific XML-based protocol in this section. Rather, we describe a generic way of handling XML-based protocols.

Next, we explain the basics of XML processing on the server side by using Servlet.

## 10.2 Servlet

More and more XML documents are likely to be exchanged in business transactions among companies in the near future. Let's consider a dynamic XML-based service that exchanges XML documents by replacing HTML with XML. As the first step, we introduce Servlet to process XML documents.[2]

First, in Section 10.2.1, we describe a stock quote servlet as an example of one-way service, which returns an XML document as an HTTP GET response. Then, in Section 10.2.2, we describe a bookstore servlet as an example of a request-and-response service, which receives an XML document from an HTTP POST request and then returns an XML document as its response. Finally, in Section 10.2.3, we discuss state management in servlets as a generic programming issue. In this section, we use application-specific XML documents. As you read this chapter, take into account that these techniques can be naturally extended to XML messaging (see Chapter 12) and Web services (see Chapter 13).

## 10.2.1 Returning XML Documents from a Servlet

Assume you are a CEO of a small start-up company that wants to begin a B2B service using the Web as soon as possible to defeat its rival companies. What is the easiest and quickest way to start such a service?

One possibility is to provide a one-way service that returns an XML document as an HTTP response. Specifically, the service receives a request as an HTTP GET request, which does not contain an XML document but contains some HTTP request parameters. Then it processes the request parameters and finally returns an XML document as its response. This kind of one-way service is very easy to build and does not require a large effort for writing clients to connect to this service. For example, we could write a Java client for this service very easily. This easiness may increase the business opportunities of the company.

### Stock Quote Service

Figure 10.1 shows a simple example of one-way services. This is a stock quote service that returns the current stock price of a specified company in an XML document. The company's name, such as IBM, is given as the request parameter of HTTP GET (a non-XML request).[3]

The `StockQuoteServlet.java` servlet, shown in Listing 10.1, is an example implementation of the stock quote service running as a servlet.

---

[2] We assume Servlet specification v2.2 in this book. Although Servlet does not restrict its transport protocol to HTTP, in this book, we assume only HTTP as the transport protocol. Also note that Java Servlet specification v2.3 was released in September 2001.

[3] Note that a similar service actually exists. See `http://www.xmltoday.com/examples/ stockquote/` for more details.

**Figure 10.1** Stock quote service

**Listing 10.1** A servlet for a stock quote service, `chap10/stockquote/StockQuoteServlet.java`

```java
package chap10.stockquote;

import java.io.Writer;
import java.io.IOException;
import java.io.StringReader;
import java.io.OutputStreamWriter;
import javax.servlet.ServletException;
import javax.servlet.http.HttpServlet;
import javax.servlet.http.HttpServletRequest;
import javax.servlet.http.HttpServletResponse;
import javax.xml.parsers.SAXParser;
import javax.xml.parsers.SAXParserFactory;
import javax.xml.parsers.ParserConfigurationException;
import org.xml.sax.InputSource;
import org.xml.sax.SAXException;
import org.xml.sax.helpers.DefaultHandler;
import chap10.EscapeString;

public class StockQuoteServlet extends HttpServlet {
    private static final String NAMESPACE_URI =
        "http://www.example.com/xmlbook2/chap10/stockquote";

    SAXParserFactory factory;
    public void init() throws ServletException {
        // Creates an instance of SAXParserFactory
        factory = SAXParserFactory.newInstance();
        factory.setNamespaceAware(true);
    }

    public void doGet(HttpServletRequest req,
                      HttpServletResponse res)
        throws ServletException, IOException
    {
        // Gets the parameter named "company"
        String company = req.getParameter("company");
```

```
        // Escapes the string to prevent cross-site scripting attack
        company = EscapeString.escape(company);
        // Gets the stock price of the company
        int price = getPrice(company);

        // Creates a response XML document from a template
        String xml =
            ("<?xml version=\"1.0\" encoding=\"UTF-8\"?>" +
             "<StockQuote" +
             "  company=\"" + company + "\"" +
             "  xmlns=\"" + NAMESPACE_URI + "\">" +
             "  <price>" + price + "</price>" +
             "</StockQuote>");

        // Checks the response XML is well-formed
        // by calling the parser
        try {
            SAXParser parser = factory.newSAXParser();
            InputSource input =
                new InputSource(new StringReader(xml));
            parser.parse(input, new DefaultHandler());
        } catch (ParserConfigurationException e) {
            throw new ServletException(e);
        } catch (SAXException e) {
            throw new ServletException(e);
        }

        // Sets the Content-Type header
        res.setContentType("application/xml; charset=utf-8");
        // Creates a writer with the encoding parameter as "UTF-8"
        Writer out = new OutputStreamWriter(res.getOutputStream(),
                                            "UTF-8");
        // Sends the response XML to the client
        out.write(xml);
        out.flush();
    }

    int getPrice(String company) {
        // Pseudo implementation of getPrice
        byte[] data = (company == null ? "" : company).getBytes();
        int price = 0;
        for (int i = 0; i < data.length; i++)
            price += data[i] & 0xff;
        price = 150 - price % 100;
        return price;
    }
}
```

Note that we will describe the cross-site scripting attack, which is mentioned in the comment, later in this section.

Let's run `StockQuoteClient`, a standalone Java client for `StockQuoteServlet`, with the following command:

```
R:\samples>java chap10.stockquote.StockQuoteClient
   http://demohost:8080/xmlbook2/chap10/StockQuoteServlet?company=IBM
```

Listing 10.2 shows the result. The actual output may not contain line breaks, but we inserted them for readability.

**Listing 10.2** The result of `StockQuoteServlet`

```
<?xml version="1.0" encoding="UTF-8" ?>
<StockQuote
  company="IBM"
  xmlns="http://www.example.com/xmlbook2/chap10/stockquote">
  <price>134</price>
</StockQuote>
```

This is an example of a one-way service that is implemented as a servlet. Regarding how a servlet works on the server side, see The Mechanism of a Servlet Container. Let's see the details of the program.

### The Mechanism of a Servlet Container

A servlet container manages servlets on one or a few Java VM processes running on a server machine (see Figure 10.2).

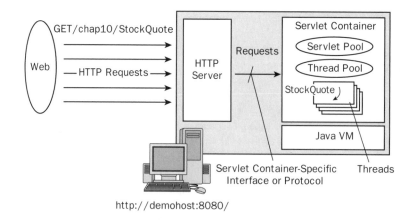

**Figure 10.2** The mechanism of a servlet container

Once the Java VM process starts, it lasts as long as the server is working. Thus, servlets do not have the overhead of CGI, which starts a new process for every HTTP request.

An HTTP server and a servlet container are connected by a container-specific interface or protocol. A servlet container dispatches a thread to handle an HTTP request. Then a servlet is called as an application program to handle the request. The overhead to start a thread is less than that of a process. Also, a servlet container stores instances of servlets and threads into a pool and reuses them whenever needed.

## Program Details

Let's take a closer look at `StockQuoteServlet.java`. A servlet is defined as a subclass of the `HttpServlet` class.

```
public class StockQuoteServlet extends HttpServlet {
```

Servlet's `init()` method is called only once, when the instance of the servlet is initialized. The developer of a servlet can describe whatever they want to be called when the servlet is initialized—for example, creating a database connection for later use. As for the lifecycle of a servlet, see Lifecycle of a Servlet.

In this servlet, the `init()` method creates an instance of the `SAXParserFactory` class for later use for creating `SAXParser` objects. The coding is not very different from that of standalone Java applications.

```
SAXParserFactory factory;
public void init() throws ServletException {
    // Creates an instance of SAXParserFactory
    factory = SAXParserFactory.newInstance();
    factory.setNamespaceAware(true);
}
```

The `doGet()` method is called whenever an HTTP GET request arrives. There are two parameters for this method: the `HttpServletRequest` object and the `Http ServletResponse` object. These are abstractions of HTTP request and response. For example, the `HttpServletRequest` object has a `getReader()` method to get a `Reader` object from which a servlet reads the content of an HTTP request.

```
public void doGet(HttpServletRequest req, HttpServletResponse res)
    throws ServletException, IOException
{
...
}
```

A servlet provides a `doPost()` method to handle HTTP POST requests as well. If you want to write a servlet that can handle both GET and POST requests, you can provide a common method called by both the `doGet()` and `doPost()` methods, or override the `service()` method. Note that the `service()` method calls the `doGet()` and `doPost()` methods according to the type of HTTP request as the default behavior.

Let's see the details of the `doGet()` method of `StockQuoteServlet`.

First, the servlet gets the value of the parameter named `company`. This value represents the name of a company, such as IBM, to get its stock price. Then, the value is *escaped* as an XML string to prevent cross-site scripting attacks. Finally, the servlet gets a stock price for the specified company by calling the `getPrice()` method.

```
// Gets the parameter named "company"
String company = req.getParameter("company");
// Escapes the string to prevent cross-site scripting attack
company = EscapeString.escape(company);
// Gets a stock price of the company
int price = getPrice(company);
```

In a real application, the `getPrice()` method should have the code to get a stock price online—for example, by connecting to the backend database system. In this sample, however, the method returns a pseudo stock price.

```
int getPrice(String company) {
    // Pseudo implementation of getPrice
    byte[] data = (company == null ? "" : company).getBytes();
    int price = 0;
    for (int i = 0; i < data.length; i++)
        price += data[i] & 0xff;
    price = 150 - price % 100;
    return price;
}
```

Next, the servlet creates a response XML document by embedding the values into a template XML document.

```
// Creates a response XML document from a template
String xml =
    ("<?xml version=\"1.0\" encoding=\"UTF-8\"?>" +
    "<StockQuote" +
    "  company=\"" + company + "\"" +
    "  xmlns=\"" + NAMESPACE_URI + "\">" +
    "  <price>" + price + "</price>" +
    "</StockQuote>");
```

Before sending back the XML document as an HTTP response, we make sure that the XML document is well-formed according to the discussion in Chapter 3, Section 3.4.2. We use a SAXParser object for the check. If the document is not well-formed, the SAXParser object throws a SAXException exception. Thus, the servlet can detect that the generated XML document is wrong. The servlet rethrows the exception caused by parsing, enclosing it with a ServletException exception, and sends back an error report to the client. Note that a more appropriate way of reporting the error to the client is to use an XML document that represents the error. It may increase the opportunity that the machine client can handle the error automatically. However, we do not adopt this idea here to keep the example as simple as possible.

```
// Checks the response XML is well-formed
// by calling a parser
try {
    SAXParser parser = factory.newSAXParser();
    InputSource input =
        new InputSource(new StringReader(xml));
    parser.parse(input, new DefaultHandler());
} catch (ParserConfigurationException e) {
    throw new ServletException(e);
} catch (SAXException e) {
    throw new ServletException(e);
}
```

If the XML document is well-formed, the servlet sets the HTTP Content-Type header as application/xml; charset=utf-8 and then creates a writer object by specifying the encoding parameter as UTF-8. Finally, the servlet sends the XML document back to the client as an HTTP response.

```
// Sets the Content-Type header
res.setContentType("application/xml; charset=utf-8");
// Creates a writer with the encoding parameter as "UTF-8"
Writer out = new OutputStreamWriter(res.getOutputStream(),
                                    "UTF-8");
// Sends the response XML to the client
out.write(xml);
out.flush();
```

Now that we have shown the details of StockQuoteServlet, we hope you understand how easy it is to write such a one-way service. Next let's look at cross-site scripting, one of the typical security vulnerabilities in Web applications and one that most developers are not aware of.

### Lifecycle of a Servlet

A servlet is generated, executed, and destroyed according to the following lifecycle.

1. An instance of a servlet is created when the servlet container is started or when the first request that should be processed by the servlet arrives. The servlet container creates an instance of a servlet according to the information described in a deployment descriptor. For more about the deployment descriptor, see Deployment of Servlets.

2. Once an instance of a servlet is created, the servlet enters the initializing state, and the `init()` method is called only once. The servlet performs its initialization—for example, allocating and initializing resources.

3. After the initialization, the servlet enters the running state, which can serve requests. Each request for the servlet is handled by the predefined callback methods, such as the `doGet()` and the `doPost()` methods. These methods are repeatedly called for each HTTP request.

4. When a system administrator or the servlet container stops the servlet, it enters the destroyed state. At this time, the `destroy()` method is called only once. In this state, the servlet performs the necessary finalization before it is actually destroyed—for example, releasing the resources allocated in the `init()` method.

### Deployment of Servlets

Servlets should be deployed to a servlet container before they are in use. A file called a *deployment descriptor* is used to give the servlet container the information about how to deploy the servlets. A deployment descriptor defines a *Web application*, which is a set of servlets and JSPs that are typically related to each other. Servlets and JSPs in the same *Web application* are deployed under the same URL. Note that this *Web application* is not a generic term used in other parts of this book. The *Web application* used here is Servlet-specific terminology. We use *italic* for the Servlet-specific *Web application* to make a clear distinction.

A deployment descriptor consists of a servlet name (which corresponds to a servlet definition), a class name for the servlet, init parameters, and mapping to URLs. A mapping to URLs is given by a URL pattern, which is a URL or a regular expression. Here is an example deployment descriptor:

| SERVLET NAME | CLASS NAME | INIT PARAMETERS | MAPPING TO URLS |
| --- | --- | --- | --- |
| snoop | chap10.SnoopServlet | foo="var" | /snoop |
| hello | chap10.HelloServlet | *None* | *.xml |

This deployment descriptor indicates that a servlet named snoop is created from
the chap10.SnoopServlet class, and the corresponding *Web application*'s URL
followed by /snoop is mapped to this servlet. In the same manner, the *Web application*'s URL followed by any string ending with .xml is mapped to the servlet
named hello—for example, http://www.example.com/xmlbook2/chap10/
index.xml, where http://www.example.com/xmlbook2/chap10/ is the
*Web Application*'s URL.

### Countermeasure for Cross-Site Scripting

Listing 10.1 contained a comment about cross-site scripting. *Cross-site scripting* is
one of the security vulnerabilities of Web applications caused by an embedded
script as a parameter of an HTTP request.

The CrossSiteScriptingServlet.java servlet, shown in Listing 10.3, is an
example of such a vulnerability. Care should be taken because the CrossSite
ScriptingServlet class has the cross-site scripting vulnerability. Therefore, the
servlet example is disabled on the accompanying CD-ROM by default. Although
you can try the example by enabling the definition of the servlet CrossSite
ScriptingServlet in web.xml, you must not put the servlet on a public
Web server.

**Listing 10.3** A servlet that has a cross-site scripting vulnerability, chap10/
CrossSiteScriptingServlet.java

```
package chap10;

import java.io.IOException;
import javax.servlet.ServletException;
import javax.servlet.http.HttpServlet;
import javax.servlet.http.HttpServletRequest;
import javax.servlet.http.HttpServletResponse;

/**
 * *** WARNING ***
 * Care should be taken when you deploy this servlet on your server.
 * This servlet demonstrates the cross-site scripting attack,
 * therefore it has a security vulnerability by nature.
 */
public class CrossSiteScriptingServlet extends HttpServlet {
    public void doGet(HttpServletRequest req,
                      HttpServletResponse res)
        throws ServletException, IOException
    {
        // Gets the parameter named "parameter"
        String parameter = req.getParameter("parameter");
```

```
            // Creates a response HTML document from a template
            String html =
                ("<!DOCTYPE html PUBLIC " +
                "\"-//W3C//DTD HTML 4.01//EN\">" +
                "<HTML lang=\"en\">" +
                "<HEAD>"+
                "<TITLE>An example of cross-site" +
                " scripting vulnerability</TITLE>"+
                "<META http-equiv=\"Content-Type\"" +
                "content=\"text/html; charset=us-ascii\">" +
                "</HEAD>" +
                "<BODY><P>" +
                // Includes the parameter here
                parameter +
                "</P></BODY>" +
                "</HTML>");
            // Sends the response HTML to the client
            res.setContentType("text/html; charset=utf-8");
            res.getWriter().print(html);
        }
    }
```

The servlet `CrossSiteScriptingServlet` embeds the value of `parameter`, obtained from a GET request, into a response HTML document as is.

The developer of this servlet assumes the following URL is used to access the servlet. In this case, there is no problem because the string `Hello!` is just shown on the Web browser.

```
http://demohost:8080/xmlbook2/chap10/CrossSiteScriptingServlet?
parameter=Hello!
```

However, if someone accesses the servlet with the following URL and the Web browser supports the `SCRIPT` tag such as JavaScript does, what happens? Note that the original URL is just one line but is wrapped for printing.

```
http://demohost:8080/xmlbook2/chap10/CrossSiteScriptingServlet
?parameter=<SCRIPT%20language="JavaScript">alert('Hello!')</SCRIPT>
```

The Web browser will pop up a window with the message `Hello!` This is the result of executing the script as follows. Needless to say, the script originally came from the HTTP request and was embedded in the response HTML document.

```
<SCRIPT language="JavaScript">alert('Hello!')</SCRIPT>
```

You may wonder why this is a problem because in this case, a script embedded by a user is just executed on the user's Web browser. It seems to be the user's responsibility.

The essence of the cross-site scripting problem is that the script is executed under the context that you are browsing this page. Let us assume that a malicious attacker publishes a Web page with a URL link to a Web site that you trust and the URL contains a malicious script. If you click the URL link on the malicious Web page, the script is executed under the context of the Web page you trust.

Such a malicious script has a privilege to access Web browser's cookies, which should be accessed only by the Web server that provides the Web page. Therefore, if a cookie has critical information from a security point of view, an attacker may steal the information. On many shopping Web sites, once a user logs on to the server, the session information is stored in a cookie. A malicious attacker can capture the session and steal the user's personal information. This type of security vulnerability is called cross-site scripting, a serious attack for end users.

You might think that the cross-site scripting attack does not affect the servlet described in this section because the servlet does not process any HTML documents, only XML documents. However, the XML documents created by the servlet can be embedded as a part of other HTML documents generated by other servlets or JSPs. Also, some Web browsers can execute the scripts in the XML documents without checking that the Content-Type header indicates not an HTML document but an XML document. Therefore, we show how to prevent a cross-site scripting attack.

One of the simplest ways to prevent a cross-site scripting attack is to escape the characters having a special meaning in HTML and XML, like "<" in parameter values.

Listing 10.4 shows `EscapeString.java`, which escapes the characters.

**Listing 10.4** Escaping special characters, `chap10/EscapeString.java`

```java
package chap10;

final public class EscapeString {
    private EscapeString() {}

    public static String escape(String string) {
        StringBuffer buf = new StringBuffer();
        int length = string.length();
        for (int i = 0; i < length; i++) {
            char ch;
            switch (ch = string.charAt(i)) {
            case '<':
                buf.append("&lt;");
                break;
            case '>':
```

```
                            buf.append("&gt;");
                            break;
                    case '"':
                            buf.append("&quot;");
                            break;
                    case '\'':
                            buf.append("&apos;");
                            break;
                    case '&':
                            buf.append("&amp;");
                            break;
                    default:
                            buf.append(ch);
                            break;
                }
            }
        return buf.toString();
    }
}
```

You can see that this code replaces the special characters with an equivalent string. For example, the "<" is replaced by "&lt;". By replacing the special characters, a Web browser receiving an HTML or XML document treats the malicious script as a string that is embedded in another tag instead of executing it as a script.

We can improve `CrossSiteScriptingServlet` by replacing the code to get parameters with the following code:

```
// Gets the parameter named "parameter", escaping the characters
String parameter = EscapeString.escape(req.getParameter("parameter"));
```

Even though the way to prevent the cross-site scripting vulnerability is quite easy, a lot of servlets, JSPs, and CGIs in the world still have this vulnerability. Application developers need to be more careful about the cross-site scripting attack in programming.

## 10.2.2 Receiving XML Documents

In this section, we describe a request-and-response service that receives XML documents. Specifically, the service receives an XML document in an HTTP POST request, processes it, and returns an XML document as its response. We introduce this service in this section because it should be a natural extension of the one-way service described in Section 10.2.1.

In general, an XML document is embedded in the payload of an HTTP POST request and is transferred to others. Alternatively, an XML document can be sent as a parameter of an HTML form. However, the former approach is better than the latter because a Multipurpose Internet Mail Extensions (MIME) media type can be written in a Content-Type header according to the type of the document (in this case, the type should be `application/xml` or something appropriate). This approach improves interoperability between a Web client and a servlet.

### A Bookstore Service

We use an online bookstore service like Amazon.com as an example in this section. Unlike Amazon.com, we assume this is an example of B2B instead of B2C; therefore, we do not use a Web browser as a Web client that sends a purchase order to this bookstore service. We use a Java program instead.

The `BookStoreServlet` class is a servlet implementation of the bookstore service. It provides a virtual shopping cart so that a client can order books interactively. We also provide the `BookStoreClient` class as a client for the servlet.

The `BookStoreServlet` and `BookStoreClient` objects communicate with each other to order books, as shown in Figure 10.3.

Listings 10.5 and 10.6 are the XML documents processed by the servlet `BookStoreServlet`.

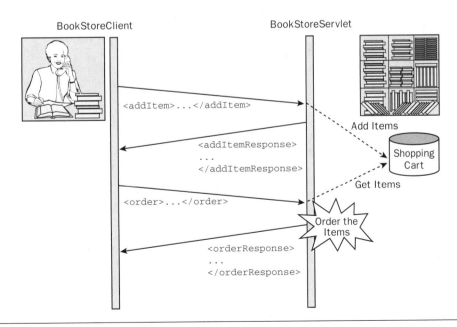

**Figure 10.3** `BookStoreServlet` and `BookStoreClient` in the bookstore service

**Listing 10.5** XML document, `chap10/data/addItem.xml`

```
<?xml version="1.0" encoding="UTF-8"?>
<addItem
xmlns="http://www.example.com/xmlbook2/chap10/bookstore/BookStore">
    <item id="0201123456" count="3"/>
    <item id="0209876543" count="2"/>
</addItem>
```

**Listing 10.6** XML document, `chap10/data/order.xml`

```
<?xml version="1.0" encoding="UTF-8"?>
<order
    xmlns="http://www.example.com/xmlbook2/chap10/bookstore/BookStore"
/>
```

The `addItem` element is used to add a book order request to a shopping cart. Its child element, `item`, contains a book's ISBN and the number of books to order. The `order` element is used to issue an actual order for the books in the shopping cart.

Listing 10.7 shows the result of calling the servlet `BookStoreServlet` by running the `BookStoreClient` class. The first argument of the `BookStoreClient` class indicates the URL of the servlet `BookStoreServlet`, the second argument indicates the URL of the `addItem.xml` file, and the third argument indicates the URL of the `order.xml` file.

**Listing 10.7** The result of running the `BookStoreClient` class

```
R:\samples>java chap10.bookstore.BookStoreClient
 http://demohost:8080/xmlbook2/chap10/bookstore/BookStoreServlet
 data\addItem.xml data\order.xml
REQUEST: data\addItem.xml
<?xml version="1.0" encoding="UTF-8"?>
<addItem
  xmlns="http://www.example.com/xmlbook2/chap10/bookstore/BookStore">
  <item id="0201123456" count="3"/>
  <item id="0209876543" count="2"/>
</addItem>

The client will send the above request.
Hit enter to proceed==>RESPONSE:
<?xml version="1.0" encoding="UTF-8"?>
<addItemResponse
  xmlns="http://www.example.com/xmlbook2/chap10/bookstore/BookStore">
  <item count="3" id="0201123456"/>
  <item count="2" id="0209876543"/>
</addItemResponse>
```

```
The client has received the above response
Hit enter to proceed==>
REQUEST: data\order.xml
<?xml version="1.0" encoding="UTF-8"?>
<order
  xmlns="http://www.example.com/xmlbook2/chap10/bookstore/BookStore"
/>

The client will send the above request.
Hit enter to proceed==>
RESPONSE:
<?xml version="1.0" encoding="UTF-8"?>
<orderResponse
  xmlns="http://www.example.com/xmlbook2/chap10/bookstore/BookStore">
  <item count="2" id="0209876543"/>
  <item count="3" id="0201123456"/>
</orderResponse>
The client has received the above response
Hit enter to proceed==>
```

Two kinds of book orders are added to the shopping cart by the `addItem` request. They are actually ordered by the `order` request.

Here are three major functions to implement `BookStoreServlet`:

1. Receiving a request XML document from a client
2. Returning a response XML document to a client
3. Managing a shopping cart

The second function has already been described in Section 10.2.1. In the rest of this section, we describe how to implement the first and third functions.

### Receiving Request XML Documents from Clients

You may wonder why receiving request XML documents is so difficult that it is worth describing here. It may seem that you could just feed an input stream object, which can be obtained by calling the `HttpServletRequest#getReader()` method, to an XML processor. Actually, such a simple way of reading XML documents works in most applications. The problem, however, is not so simple as we might expect when we consider handling international character sets. In more general terms, we need to consider the interoperability issues.

In the rest of this section, we describe a general way of maintaining interoperability, providing a set of generic libraries to receive XML documents contained in HTTP requests according to a standard way prescribed in Requests For Comments (RFCs).

We need to handle an HTTP Content-Type header appropriately to receive an XML document from a Web client. Otherwise, we cannot ensure the interoperability between a Web client and a servlet. This process is more difficult than you would expect if you want to be exact.

The HTTP Content-Type header is specified in the MIME specification. *RFC 3023: XML Media Types* specifies media types for XML documents.[4] We describe the right way to handle media types and `charset` parameters compliant with RFC 3023.

We overview what RFC 3023 specifies just to help you understand it. See the RFC for the exact and detailed specification.

- The media type for a document entity can be either `text/xml`, `application/xml`, or `*/*+xml`, where `*/*+xml` represents a type associated with an XML application, such as `image/svg+xml`. The document entity that belongs to these media types is called an XML MIME entity.

- Most XML documents belong not to `text/xml` but to `application/xml`.

- Using the `charset` parameter and `utf-8` or `utf-16` as a `charset` is strongly recommended.

A `charset` can be specified in an HTTP Content-Type header as well as an encoding declaration in an XML document in the HTTP payload. You may feel that it is redundant or confusing. RFC 3023 shows how to resolve `charset`s when both of them or one of them is specified.

We use the following examples to describe how to resolve `charset`s.

1. `text/xml` with UTF-8 `charset`

   ```
   Content-type: text/xml; charset="utf-8"
   <?xml version="1.0" encoding="utf-8"?>
   ```

   In this case, the `charset` is `utf-8`. If the `charset` parameter specified in an HTTP Content-Type header, it is adopted before anything else.

2. `text/xml` without `charset`

   ```
   Content-type: text/xml
   <?xml version="1.0" encoding="utf-8"?>
   ```

   In this case, the `charset` is `us-ascii` despite the encoding declaration being `utf-8`. The value `us-ascii` is used as, so to speak, *the greatest common divisor,* which can be handled by the all applications that process `text/xml`.

---

[4] Makoto Murata, one of the authors of this book, is one of the authors of RFC 3023.

3. `application/xml` with UTF-16 `charset`

```
Content-type: application/xml; charset="utf-16"
{BOM}<?xml version="1.0" encoding="utf-16"?>
```

In this case, the `charset` is `UTF-16`. BOM is an acronym for Byte Order Mark.
`{BOM}` indicates a special 2-byte data indicating that the subsequent octet
strings are encoded, whether in big endian or little endian. Because Java's
`InputStreamReader` class and `OutputStreamWriter` class can handle
BOM by themselves, you do not need to be careful about BOM as long as you
use this reader and writer.

4. `application/xml` without `charset` and BOM

```
Content-type: application/xml
<?xml version='1.0' encoding="Shift_JIS"?>
```

In this case, the charset cannot be determined by just looking at the Content-
Type header. Instead, an XML processor determines the charset based on the
encoding declaration in an XML document, according to the XML specification.
Therefore, the `charset` is `Shift_JIS`.

When we implement a servlet that handles media types compliant with the
RFC 3023 specification, we need to consider how to create a SAX `InputSource`
object from an `InputStream` of an HTTP request and pass it to the XML processor.

`XmlMimeEntityHandler.java`, shown in Listing 10.8, is a generic library to
handle the processing described earlier. The `getInputSource()` method creates
an `InputSource` object from an `InputStream` object according to a Content-
Type header in the HTTP POST request received by the servlet. Also, the method
confirms that the media type in a Content-Type header is an XML media type.

**Listing 10.8** A library class that handles XML MIME entities, `chap10/`
`XmlMimeEntityHandler.java`

```
package chap10;

import java.io.Reader;
import java.io.InputStream;
import java.io.InputStreamReader;
import java.io.UnsupportedEncodingException;
import javax.mail.internet.ContentType;
import javax.mail.internet.ParseException;
import org.xml.sax.InputSource;

final public class XmlMimeEntityHandler {
    private XmlMimeEntityHandler() {}

    public static InputSource getInputSource(String ctype,
                                             InputStream in)
```

```
                        throws XmlMimeEntityException
            {
                        // Creates ContentType
                        ContentType contentType = null;
                        try {
[21]                        contentType = new ContentType(ctype);
                        } catch (ParseException e) {
                            throw new XmlMimeEntityException(e.getMessage());
                        }

[26]                    // Checks primitive type
[27]                    String primaryType = contentType.getPrimaryType();
[28]                    if (!"text".equals(primaryType) &&
[29]                        !"application".equals(primaryType))
[30]                        throw new XmlMimeEntityException(ctype);
[31]
[32]                    // Checks sub type
[33]                    String subType = contentType.getSubType();
[34]                    if (!"xml".equals(subType) && !subType.endsWith("+xml"))
[35]                        throw new XmlMimeEntityException(ctype);

                        // Gets charset parameter
                        String charset = contentType.getParameter("charset");
[39]                    if (charset == null) { // no charset
[40]                        // MIME type "text/*" omitted charset should be treated
[41]                        // as us-ascii
[42]                        if ("text".equals(contentType.getPrimaryType()))
[43]                            charset = "us-ascii";
[44]                    }

                        InputSource input;
                        if (charset == null) { // application/xml omitted charset
[48]                        input = new InputSource(in);
                        } else {
                            // Creates a reader with java charset
                            Reader reader = null;
                            try {
[53]                            reader = new InputStreamReader(in, charset);

                            } catch (UnsupportedEncodingException e) {

                                throw new XmlMimeEntityException(e.getMessage());

                            }
[57]                        input = new InputSource(reader);
                        }

                        return input;
            }
        }
```

First, the method creates an instance of the ContentType class from a given
Content-Type header value (line 21). The ContentType class, which is part of
the JavaMail API, is an abstraction of the value of the Content-Type header. Then,
the method checks the ContentType object (lines 26–35). At this moment, if the
charset parameter is omitted and the primary type is text, us-ascii is used as
the charset (lines 39–44). If the charset cannot be determined eventually, an
InputSource object is created from the InputStream object (line 48). In this
case, the XML processor determines the charset according to the encoding declaration in the XML document. Once the charset is determined, an
InputStreamReader object is created from the charset (line 53), and then an
InputSource object is created from the InputStreamReader object (line 57).
In this case, the XML processor handles the input as a Unicode string.

Before looking at how a servlet invokes the XmlMimeEntityHandler.getInput
Source() method, let's see GenericDOMServlet.java, shown in Listing 10.9.

**Listing 10.9** A generic servlet that handles an input XML document as a DOM tree,
chap10/GenericDOMServlet.java

```
package chap10;

import java.io.InputStream;
import java.io.IOException;
import javax.xml.parsers.DocumentBuilder;
import javax.xml.parsers.DocumentBuilderFactory;
import javax.xml.parsers.ParserConfigurationException;
import javax.servlet.ServletException;
import javax.servlet.http.HttpServlet;
import javax.servlet.http.HttpServletRequest;
import javax.servlet.http.HttpServletResponse;
import org.w3c.dom.Document;
import org.w3c.dom.Element;
import org.w3c.dom.Node;
import org.xml.sax.InputSource;
import org.xml.sax.SAXException;
import org.apache.xml.serialize.OutputFormat;
import org.apache.xml.serialize.XMLSerializer;
import chap10.XmlMimeEntityHandler;
import chap10.XmlMimeEntityException;

public abstract class GenericDOMServlet extends HttpServlet {
    static final String NAMESPACE_URI =
        "http://www.example.com/xmlbook2/chap10/GenericDOMServlet";

    DocumentBuilderFactory factory;
    public void init() throws ServletException {
```

```
        factory = DocumentBuilderFactory.newInstance();
        factory.setNamespaceAware(true);
}

public void doPost(HttpServletRequest req,
                   HttpServletResponse res)
    throws ServletException, IOException
{
    DocumentBuilder parser = newDocumentBuilder();
    Document resDoc;
    try {
        // Gets Content-Type header
        String ctypeValue = req.getContentType();
        // Gets an input source
        InputStream in = req.getInputStream();
        InputSource input =
            XmlMimeEntityHandler.getInputSource(ctypeValue, in);
        // Parses the input here
        Document reqDoc = parse(input);

        // Creates an output document
        resDoc = doProcess(req, res, reqDoc);
    } catch (XmlMimeEntityException e) {
        e.printStackTrace();

        // Creates an output document
        resDoc = newDocument();
        Element root =
            resDoc.createElementNS(NAMESPACE_URI, "error");
        root.setAttribute("xmlns", NAMESPACE_URI);
        String name = e.getClass().getName();
        String message = e.getMessage();
        Node node =
            resDoc.createTextNode(name + ": " + message);
        root.appendChild(node);
        resDoc.appendChild(root);
    }

    if (resDoc != null) {
        // Sets the Content-Type header
        res.setContentType("application/xml; charset=utf-8");
        // Serializes the DOM into bytes,
        // and then sends it back to the client
        OutputFormat formatter = new OutputFormat();
        formatter.setPreserveSpace(true);
        XMLSerializer serializer =
            new XMLSerializer(res.getOutputStream(), formatter);
```

```
            serializer.serialize(resDoc);
        }
    }

    protected DocumentBuilder newDocumentBuilder()
        throws ServletException
    {
        try {
            return factory.newDocumentBuilder();
        } catch (ParserConfigurationException e) {
            throw new ServletException(e);
        }
    }

    protected Document newDocument()
        throws ServletException
    {
        DocumentBuilder parser = newDocumentBuilder();
        return parser.newDocument();
    }

    protected Document parse(InputSource in)
        throws ServletException, IOException
    {
        try {
            DocumentBuilder parser = newDocumentBuilder();
            return parser.parse(in);
        } catch (SAXException e) {
            throw new ServletException(e);
        }
    }

    public abstract Document doProcess(HttpServletRequest req,
                                       HttpServletResponse res,
                                       Document reqDoc)
        throws ServletException, IOException;
}
```

GenericDOMServlet is a generic servlet to receive XML documents from
HTTP requests in a correct way by calling the XmlMimeEntityHandler.
getInputSource() method. This servlet abstracts the application logic by defining an abstract method, doProcess(). An application of this servlet, such
as BookStoreServlet, is expected to extend this servlet and implement the
doProcess() method. (The source code for BookStoreServlet is shown later
in this section.) After processing the received XML document in the doPost()
method, GenericDOMServlet calls the doProcess() method of its subclass.

The `doProcess()` method takes three arguments: `HttpServletRequest`, `HttpServletResponse`, and `Document`. The first and second arguments are the same as the arguments for the `doPost()` method. The third argument, `Document`, is the result of parsing the input XML document, which can be accessed as a DOM object. The return value of the `doProcess()` method is also `Document`, which is sent back to the client as a response from the application.

Let's take a closer look at the code fragment that is processing a received XML document in the `doPost()` method of `GenericDOMServlet`.

```
// Gets Content-Type header
String contentTypeValue = req.getContentType();
// Gets an input source
InputStream in = req.getInputStream();
InputSource input =
    XmlMimeEntityHandler.getInputSource(contentTypeValue, in);
// Parses the input here
Document reqDoc = parser.parse(input);
```

First, the servlet gets the value of the Content-Type header by calling the `HttpServletRequest#getContentType()` method. Second, it gets an `InputStream` object by calling the `HttpServletRequest#getInputStream()` method to read raw bytes from the stream. Note that we do not use a `Reader` object by calling the `HttpServletRequest#getReader()` method because the encoding selected for this reader object depends on the implementation of a servlet container. Third, it creates an `InputSource` object to be passed to the XML processor by calling the `XmlMimeEntityHandler.getInputSource()` method. Finally, it creates a DOM tree by passing the `InputSource` object to the XML processor.

In this way, a subclass of this servlet can obtain a node value as Unicode string from the DOM tree; that is, the servlet can accept multilanguage XML documents.

### Processing a Shopping Cart

To implement a shopping cart, the servlet needs to hold a state across more than one HTTP request. The servlet can use the `HttpSession` class for that purpose. The `HttpSession` class is an API to manage HTTP sessions that are typically implemented by using cookies.

Figure 10.4 shows the mechanism to manage an HTTP session in Tomcat.

Tomcat adds the Set-Cookie header in an HTTP response to the first HTTP request from a client. Set-Cookie is a directive for the client to set the Cookie header in the subsequent HTTP requests. Tomcat also adds Set-Cookie2, which is an extension of

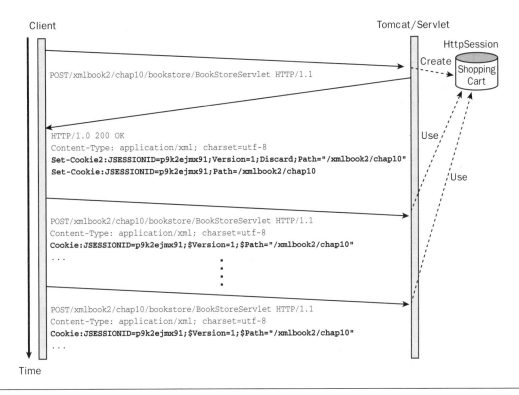

**Figure 10.4** A servlet session using cookies

Set-Cookie. Set-Cookie contains a value of JSESSIONID, which uniquely identifies the HttpSession object managed by Tomcat on the server side. The client sends the received as the Cookie header in subsequent HTTP requests. When Tomcat receives an HTTP request, it gets the value of JSESSIONID from the Cookie header and retrieves the HttpSession object associated with JSESSIONID from its local storage or memory. An HttpSession object can hold one or more objects (for example, a shopping cart object) as its attributes by using the HttpSession#setAttribute() method. This mechanism allows the servlet to use the same shopping cart object in subsequent HTTP requests.

Before looking at how the servlet accesses the HttpSession object, let's see the source code for BookStoreServlet.java, shown in Listing 10.10.

**Listing 10.10** A servlet class for the bookstore service, chap10/bookstore/BookStoreServlet.java

```
package chap10.bookstore;

import java.io.IOException;
import java.util.Iterator;
```

```
          import javax.servlet.ServletException;
          import javax.servlet.http.HttpServletRequest;
          import javax.servlet.http.HttpServletResponse;
          import javax.servlet.http.HttpSession;
          import org.w3c.dom.Node;
          import org.w3c.dom.Element;
          import org.w3c.dom.Document;
          import org.w3c.dom.NodeList;
          import chap10.GenericDOMServlet;

          public final class BookStoreServlet extends GenericDOMServlet
              implements BookStoreApplication
          {
              public Document doProcess(HttpServletRequest req,
                                        HttpServletResponse res,
                                        Document reqDoc)
                  throws ServletException, IOException
              {
                  // Gets a shopping cart from a session if it already exists.
                  // If it does not exist, a shopping cart is newly created.
                  ShoppingCartBean shoppingCart;
                  HttpSession session = req.getSession();
                  synchronized (session) {
                      shoppingCart = (ShoppingCartBean)
[29]                      session.getAttribute(SHOPPING_CART_BEAN);
[30]                  if (shoppingCart == null) {
[31]                      shoppingCart = new ShoppingCartBean();
[32]                      session.setAttribute(SHOPPING_CART_BEAN,
[33]                                           shoppingCart);
                      }
                  }

[37]              // Gets the root element of reqDoc
[38]              Element reqRoot = reqDoc.getDocumentElement();
[39]              // Gets the local name of the root element
[40]              String localName = reqRoot.getLocalName();

                  // Prepares a DOM object for the response
                  Document resDoc = newDocument();

[45]              // If the input XML document is "addItem"
[46]              if ("addItem".equals(localName)) {
[47]                  Element resRoot =
[48]                      resDoc.createElementNS(NAMESPACE_URI,
[49]                                             localName + "Response");
[50]                  resRoot.setAttribute("xmlns", NAMESPACE_URI);
[51]
```

```
[52]                    // For each "item" element in the request
[53]                    NodeList list =
[54]                        reqRoot.getElementsByTagNameNS(NAMESPACE_URI,
[55]                                                        "item");
[56]                    int length = list.getLength();
[57]                    for (int i = 0; i < length; i++) {
[58]                        Element elemItem = (Element)list.item(i);
[59]                        ItemBean item = new ItemBean(elemItem);
[60]                        // Adds the item into the shopping cart
[61]                        shoppingCart.addItem(item);
[62]                        Node node = resDoc.importNode(elemItem, true);
[63]                        resRoot.appendChild(node);
[64]                    }
[65]                    resDoc.appendChild(resRoot);
[66]                    return resDoc;
[67]                }
[68]                // If the input XML document is "order"
[69]                if ("order".equals(localName)) {
[70]                    Element resRoot =
[71]                        resDoc.createElementNS(NAMESPACE_URI,
[72]                                        localName + "Response");
[73]                    resRoot.setAttribute("xmlns", NAMESPACE_URI);
[74]
[75]                    // For each item in the shopping cart
[76]                    Iterator iterator = shoppingCart.getItems();
[77]                    while (iterator.hasNext()) {
[78]                        ItemBean item = (ItemBean)iterator.next();
[79]                        //
[80]                        // Orders the items here
[81]                        //
[82]                        Element elemItem =
[83]                            resDoc.createElementNS(NAMESPACE_URI, "item");
[84]                        elemItem.setAttribute("id", item.getId());
[85]                        elemItem.setAttribute("count", ""+item.getCount());
[86]                        resRoot.appendChild(elemItem);
[87]                    }
[88]                    resDoc.appendChild(resRoot);
[89]                    return resDoc;
[90]                }
                    throw new ServletException("Unknown request: " + localName);
                }
            }
```

As we stated earlier, `BookStoreServlet` is a subclass of `GenericDOMServlet` and implements the `doProcess()` method, which is an abstract method of `GenericDOMServlet`.

The servlet gets an `HttpSession` object by calling the
`HttpServletRequest#getSession()` method.

```
HttpSession session = req.getSession();
```

The handler first gets a shopping cart object from the `HttpSession` object by
calling its `getAttribute()` method (line 29). At the first HTTP request, the
shopping cart object is newly created and stored into the `HttpSession` object
because it does not exist (lines 30–33). Second, it gets the local part of the document element of the request DOM tree (lines 37–40). The local part is either
`addItem` or `order`. Third, it handles the request according to the local name. In
case of `addItem`, the handler converts an `item` element in the request DOM tree
into an `ItemBean` object and adds it into the shopping cart object (lines 45–67).
As described earlier, the handler can access the `ItemBean` object in subsequent
HTTP requests. In case of `order`, the handler gets all the `ItemBean` objects in the
shopping cart object and orders the items (lines 68–90). (This example does not
actually order books, of course.) Finally, the handler returns the response DOM
tree (lines 66 and 89).

We described how a servlet can hold a state, such as a shopping cart, across multiple HTTP requests by using the `HttpSession` object.

### The Client Communicating with the Servlet

The `BookStoreClient` class is a client program to communicate with the servlet
`BookStoreServlet`.

The `BookStoreClient` class assumes a URL for the target servlet as the first argument, and URLs for XML files to be sent as the subsequent arguments. It waits for
keyboard input from a user before and after sending HTTP requests so that it can
send the requests interactively.

The following code fragment shows how the client creates a `BookStoreClient`
object in the `main()` method.

```
// Creates an HTTP client,
// using the first parameter as the target URL
String url = args[0];
BookStoreClient domClient = new BookStoreClient(url);
```

The following code fragment shows how the client sends a request XML
document. The `BookStoreClient#send()` method has two arguments: the
media type, `application/xml`, and the charset parameter, `utf-8`. They are to be
set as the Content-Type header in the HTTP request.

```
// Sends the XML document
InputSource request = new InputSource(new FileReader(args[i]));
Document resDoc =
    domClient.send(request, "application/xml", "utf-8");
```

Let's look at the details of the `BookStoreClient#send()` method. First, the client creates a DOM tree from the `InputSource` object.

```
// Creates a DOM tree from the InputSource
Document reqDoc = factory.newDocumentBuilder().parse(request);
```

Then, the client converts the DOM tree into an octet stream encoded in the specified charset. For information about the serialization of a DOM tree, refer to Chapter 3, Section 3.4.

```
// Converts the reqDoc into the specified charset
OutputFormat formatter = new OutputFormat("xml", charset, false);
formatter.setPreserveSpace(true);
ByteArrayOutputStream bout = new ByteArrayOutputStream();
XMLSerializer serializer = new XMLSerializer(bout, formatter);
serializer.serialize(reqDoc);
InputStream bin = new ByteArrayInputStream(bout.toByteArray());
```

Finally, the client sends the XML document, receives a response XML document, and converts it into a DOM tree. These steps are almost the same as those of the servlet `BookStoreServlet`.

```
// Sends the data to the servlet
HttpURLConnection con = httpClient.send(bin, mimeType, charset);

// Receives a response from the server
String contentTypeValue = con.getContentType();
InputStream in = con.getInputStream();
InputSource input =
    XmlMimeEntityHandler.getInputSource(contentTypeValue, in);

// Parses the response XML, and returns it
return factory.newDocumentBuilder().parse(input);
```

In the `send()` method, the client uses the `HttpClient` object as an HTTP client. The Content-Type header in the HTTP response can be obtained by calling the `HttpURLConnection#getContentType()` method.

Listing 10.11 shows `HttpClient.java`, to be used by the `BookStoreClient` object.

**Listing 10.11** A generic HTTP client that sends HTTP POST requests, `chap10/HttpClient.java`

```
package chap10;

import java.io.IOException;
import java.io.InputStream;
import java.io.OutputStream;
import java.io.BufferedOutputStream;
import java.net.URL;
import java.net.HttpURLConnection;

final public class HttpClient {
    // The target URL
    final String url;
    // On-memory storage for cookies
    Cookie cookie = null;
    // A constructor
    public HttpClient(String url) { this.url = url; }

    public HttpURLConnection send(InputStream in,
                                  String mimeType,
                                  String charset)
        throws IOException
    {
        // Creats an HTTP connection
        URL objURL = new URL(url);
        HttpURLConnection con =
            (HttpURLConnection)objURL.openConnection();

        // Sets HTTP method
        con.setRequestMethod("POST");
        // Sets Content-Type header
        if (mimeType != null) {
            String value =
                mimeType +
                (charset == null ? "" : "; charset=" + charset);
            con.setRequestProperty("Content-Type", value);
        }

        // Sets the received cookie
        if (cookie != null)
            con.setRequestProperty("Cookie",
                                   cookie.getCookieValue());

        con.setDoOutput(true);

        // Sends a request to the server
        OutputStream out =
```

The line numbers shown in the left margin: [30], [31], [32], [33], [34], [35], [36], [38], [39], [40], [41].

```
                      new BufferedOutputStream((con.getOutputStream())));
                  byte[] buf = new byte[2048];
                  int length;
                  while ((length = in.read(buf)) != -1)
                      out.write(buf, 0, length);
                  out.flush();
                  out.close();
[55]              // Creates Cookie from Set-Cookie header
[56]              String value;
[57]              if ((value = con.getHeaderField("Set-Cookie2")) != null)
[58]                  cookie = new Cookie(value);
[59]              else if ((value = con.getHeaderField("Set-Cookie")) != null)
[60]                  cookie = new Cookie(value);

                  // Returns the HTTP response
                  return con;
          }
      }
```

The HttpClient object sends the data as an HTTP POST request by calling the HttpURLConnection object. It also adds the Content-Type header in the HTTP request according to the given media type and the charset parameter (lines 30–36).

By the way, the standard Java API, the HttpURLConnection class, does not have a function to handle a Cookie, which is required to implement the shopping cart. In general, a Cookie needs to be managed carefully from a privacy and security point of view. The reason the HttpURLConnection class does not provide the Cookie function is the policy that Cookie management is the application's responsibility.

We prepare the Cookie class that abstracts the Cookie header. This class gets the value of the Set-Cookie header and creates the Cookie value to be set to the Cookie header. We do not show the source code for the Cookie class because space is limited. Refer to the full source code on the CD-ROM.

The HttpClient object uses the Cookie object as follows.

1. When it sends an HTTP request, it adds the Cookie header if the instance variable cookie is not null (lines 38–41).

2. When it receives an HTTP response with either the Set-Cookie or Set-Cookie2 header, it creates a Cookie object and stores it into a cookie instance variable (lines 55–60).

Because the HttpClient is just a sample program, we did not pay attention to privacy and security. However, when you develop a real application, you are responsible for implementing a policy to decide whether the client can send a cookie or not.

In this section, we described how to implement a request-and-response service as a servlet, using a bookstore service as an example.

## 10.2.3 Considerations for State Management

Care should be taken for stateful servlet programming because multiple threads may simultaneously call a method of a servlet, and a servlet instance is not always identical across the method calls. In this section, we discuss considerations for state management for servlet programming. This is not an XML-specific topic, but we believe it is helpful for readers.

Generally speaking, servlets need to hold their states for various reasons. If you write a multithreaded servlet, you must be careful how you manage shared resources. In such a case, we often use the `synchronized` block and the `synchronized` method to prevent simultaneous access of a shared resource. However, it would be difficult for application programmers to consider which part of a program should be protected.

Is there any technique to hold a shared state across multiple requests or multiple instances without using the `synchronized` block?

A servlet's states are categorized into the following five patterns, according to the scope of the state (a scope is the range in which an object is accessible):

1. A state for each HTTP request
2. A state for each servlet definition
3. A state for each HTTP client
4. A state for each *Web application*
5. A persistent state

In pattern 1, a state is held in a local variable. In this case, the state is the object obtained from the `HttpServletRequest` object (except for the `HttpSession` object) or newly created in a method. A typical example of the former is a parameter value of an HTTP request. In either case, objects are created and discarded in a method call. In other words, state objects must not be accessible outside the scope of the method call. Needless to say, this state does not need to be protected.

In pattern 2, a state is held in an instance variable of the servlet. Mutual exclusion is required for this pattern, as we described earlier. Furthermore, the number of servlet instances could be more than one for the same servlet definition in some cases (for the details, refer to The Number of Instances of Servlets). In this case, holding the state as an instance variable is meaningless.

In pattern 3, a state is held in an `HttpSession` object. In this case, a servlet can use the state without any care because more than one HTTP request does not arrive simultaneously during the same session. Note that the state is discarded when the HTTP session finishes.

In pattern 4, a state is held in a `ServletContext` object, which corresponds to a *Web application*. In this case, mutual exclusion is required because an object stored in the `ServletContext` object can be simultaneously accessed by the instances of the servlets and JSPs that belong to the same *Web application*. The state held in the `ServletContext` object is discarded when the corresponding *Web application* terminates.

In pattern 5, a state is held in external storage, such as a database. Also, an entity bean in EJB is available for this purpose (see Chapter 11, Section 11.7). With this pattern, the state is held persistently; that is, the state can survive after the server terminates. However, there is significant overhead in accessing the state and in management cost. Therefore, this pattern is appropriate when the number of accesses to the state is relatively smaller than those of patterns 1 through 4.

As a result, it is easy and safe to use a combination of patterns 1 (`HttpServlet Request`), 3 (`HttpSession`), and 5 (database) according to the requirement level. The decision points for choosing the pattern could be how long the state is used, how often the state is to be updated, how critical it would be if the state were lost, and so on. If the state is temporarily used, frequently updated, and not critical, you may choose pattern 1 or 3 instead of 5, and vice versa.

Another typical case is to use pattern 1 or 3 while a user is editing the state and move it to the pattern 5 after the editing is done. For example, in typical B2C applications, user information and order information are held in a database while pending user information or virtual shopping carts are held in HTTP request parameters or `HttpSession` objects.

### The Number of Instances of Servlets

Usually, only one servlet instance is created for each servlet definition except for the following two cases:

1. When a servlet implements the `SingleThreadModel` interface. The servlet container makes sure that a single thread is assigned to the instance of the servlet to handle one HTTP request at a time, or it may create more than one servlet instance to handle simultaneous HTTP requests.
2. When a servlet is marked as *distributable* in the deployment descriptor. The servlet can be deployed onto one or more Java VMs at the same time, and servlet instances are created on each Java VM.

In this section, we described a one-way servlet and a request-and-response servlet as basic techniques for exchanging XML documents among companies. Also, we discussed considerations for multiple threads in servlet programming. We can apply the same techniques to database access (see Chapter 11), XML messaging (see Chapter 12), and Web services (see Chapter 13).

You might feel that returning an XML document using Servlet is somewhat rigid. We described two ways to generate an XML document using Servlet in the examples: one is using a string template of an XML document embedded in the program, as shown in Listing 10.1; the other is serializing a DOM tree that is generated by the servlet, as shown in Listing 10.9. In either case, we need to recompile the servlet when we want to change the XML document that is generated.

In the next section, we describe JavaServer Pages as a more flexible way to generate XML documents.

## 10.3 JavaServer Pages

A servlet writing an XML document tends to be hard to maintain and reuse because XML fragments, which are typically placed using the `println()` method, are embedded in the program. If we can use a template for an XML document in which some values can be inserted, the program becomes maintainable and reusable. JavaServer Pages (JSP) is the best fit for this purpose.

In this section, we introduce JSP and then show example JSPs that process XML documents. We use both the informational service and the transactional service, as described in Section 10.2.

### 10.3.1 What Is JSP?

In this section, we provide a brief introduction to JSP.

#### A Simple Example of JSP

Listing 10.12 shows a simple example of JSP called `hello.jsp`.

**Listing 10.12** A simple example of JSP, `hello.jsp`

```
<!DOCTYPE html PUBLIC "-//W3C//DTD HTML 4.01//EN">
<HTML lang="en">
  <HEAD>
    <TITLE>The first sample of JavaServer Pages</TITLE>
    <META http-equiv="Content-Type"
      content="text/html; charset=us-ascii">
```

**Figure 10.5** The result of `hello.jsp`

```
    </HEAD>
    <BODY>
      <H1>Hello!</H1>
      <P>It's <%=new java.util.Date()%> now.</P>
    </BODY>
  </HTML>
```

The JSP `hello.jsp` outputs an HTML document. Open the following URL with a Web browser to see the Web page shown in Figure 10.5.

```
    http://demohost:8080/xmlbook2/chap10/hello.jsp
```

The JSP `hello.jsp` looks like an HTML file, but it has the following line, which is to be replaced by the string representing the current date, as shown in Figure 10.5.

```
    <P>It's <%=new java.util.Date()%> now.</P>
```

JSP outputs a string as the result of evaluating Java expressions enclosed by `<%=` and `%>`. As you can see, JSP allows you to embed dynamic contents in a document template.

### Syntax of JSP

Table 10.1 shows some well-known JSP expressions. There are other useful JSP expressions; refer to the JSP specification for the details. As for how JSP works on an XML application server, see The Mechanism of a JSP Container.

### The Mechanism of a JSP Container

A JSP runtime is called a *JSP container*. Figure 10.6 illustrates how a JSP is executed in a JSP container. (The following numbers in parentheses refer to the numbered

**Table 10.1** Well-Known JSP Expressions

| SYNTAX/EXAMPLE/RESULT | DESCRIPTION |
|---|---|
| <% *Java program fragment %>* | |
| ```<%for (int i = 0; i < 3; i++) {%>``` <br> Hello! <br> ```<%}%>``` <br><br> Hello!Hello!Hello! | This is called a *scriptlet*. You can write any Java program between the symbols <% and %>. Note that a Java statement must not be completed in one scriptlet, as shown in the example. |
| <%=*Expression*%> | |
| ```<%=new java.util.Date()%>``` <br><br> Sat Sep 15 19:00:13 JST 2001 | The expression is evaluated as a Java string, and the result is written to the output. |
| ```<%@ page```<br>  ```[import="{Class Name}, ..."]```<br>  ```[contentType="MediaType[; charset=Charset]"]```<br>```%>```<br><br>```<%@ page```<br>  ```import='java.util.Vector, java.io.*"%>```<br>```<%@ page```<br>  ```charset="application/xml; charset=UTF-8"%>```<br><br>N/A | You can specify attributes of the entire page that JSP outputs. The classes specified in the import attribute are imported. The contentType attribute specifies the value of the Content-Type header in the HTTP response to be sent back to the client. |

sections of Figure 10.6.) Once the HTTP server receives an HTTP request to JSP, it requests that a JSP container process the request (1). The JSP container reads a JSP file associated with the URL from the server's local disk (2).

The JSP file is eventually converted into a servlet instance. First, the JSP container converts the JSP file into Java source code that contains a servlet class definition (3). Second, it compiles the source code and generates a .class file (4). Third, it loads the .class file onto a Java VM (5) and creates a servlet instance for the JSP (6). Finally, the instance handles an HTTP request, just like the other servlets (7).

We recommend that you compare some JSP files with the generated source code to understand how JSP works. With Tomcat, the generated source code files are placed under the *<jakart-tomcat>*\work directory.

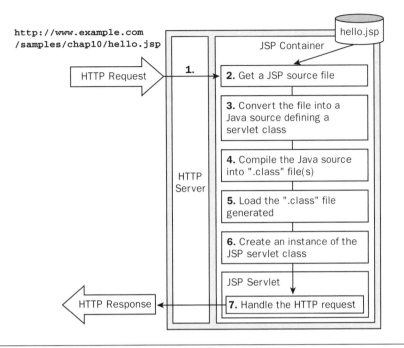

**Figure 10.6**   The mechanism of a JSP container

## 10.3.2  An Informational JSP Returning XML Documents

The JSP `hello.jsp` generates an HTML document. JSP, however, can generate not only HTML documents but also XML documents.[5] In this section, we describe JSPs that return XML documents.

### Stock Quote Service

In Section 10.2.1, we described the stock quote service servlet. In such kinds of applications, typically, a template for the result XML document is finalized in advance and we only need to embed values in the template later. JSP is the best fit for such applications.

`StockQuote.jsp`, shown in Listing 10.13, is the JSP implementation of a stock quote service.

---

[5] You will understand the reason if you recall the process in which a JSP is converted into a servlet.

**Listing 10.13** A JSP for a stock quote service, `StockQuote.jsp`

```
<%@ page contentType="application/xml; charset=UTF-8"%>
<jsp:useBean
  id="stockQuote"
  scope="request"
  class="chap10.stockquote.StockQuoteBean" />
<jsp:setProperty name="stockQuote" property="*" />
<?xml version="1.0" encoding="UTF-8"?>
<StockQuote
  company="<jsp:getProperty name="stockQuote" property="company"/>"
  xmlns="http://www.example.com/xmlbook2/chap10/stockquote">
  <price>
    <jsp:getProperty name="stockQuote" property="price"/>
  </price>
</StockQuote>
```

With JSP, it is easy to implement a one-way service that only returns XML documents.

### Countermeasure for Cross-Site Scripting

Before we go into the details of `StockQuote.jsp`, we emphasize that this JSP also has a cross-site scripting vulnerability, as we discussed for the servlet in Section 10.2.1.

More specifically, the following portion is vulnerable. The `jsp:setProperty` tag sets the parameter value of `company` in the HTTP request to the property that has the same name as the `stockQuote` bean as is. The value of `company` is written to the output as is by `jsp:getProperty`. This is the cross-site scripting vulnerability.

```
<jsp:setProperty name="stockQuote" property="*" />
...
<?xml version="1.0" encoding="UTF-8"?>
<StockQuote
  company="<jsp:getProperty name="stockQuote" property="company"/>"
...
```

Therefore, even the typical combination of `jsp:setProperty` and `jsp:get Property` has the cross-site scripting vulnerability. You should remember to escape the string to prevent cross-site scripting attacks, although it makes JSP programs slightly complicated.

`StockQuote.jsp` should be replaced by `StockQuote2.jsp`, as shown in Listing 10.14. It writes the value of `company` after explicitly escaping the string.

**Listing 10.14**  A revised JSP for a stock quote service, `StockQuote2.jsp`

```
<%@ page import="chap10.EscapeString"
        contentType="application/xml; charset=UTF-8"%>
<jsp:useBean
  id="stockQuote"
  scope="request"
  class="chap10.stockquote.StockQuoteBean" />

<jsp:setProperty name="stockQuote" property="*" />
<%
String company = EscapeString.escape(stockQuote.getCompany());
%>

<?xml version="1.0" encoding="UTF-8"?>
<StockQuote
  company="<%=company%>"
  xmlns="http://www.example.com/xmlbook2/chap10/stockquote">
  <price>
    <jsp:getProperty name="stockQuote" property="price"/>
  </price>
</StockQuote>
```

We access the following URL by running `StockQuoteClient`. The command is almost the same. The only difference is the URL. The result is the same as in Listing 10.2.

```
http://demohost:8080/xmlbook2/chap10/StockQuote2.jsp?company=IBM
```

### A Consideration for Serializing XML Documents

Serializing an XML document in JSP is not a good idea based on the points we described in Section 3.4.2 because it does not check the well-formedness of XML documents with an XML processor.

However, we can narrow the variety of the XML documents to be generated if we escape all the strings to be embedded in the template in the way we described in the cross-site scripting attack section. The reason is that at least we can exclude the possibility that XML tags will be contained in the parameterized strings. For JSP, we recommend that you check the well-formedness of the XML documents generated by the JSP at development time. By doing so, you can avoid generating XML documents that are not well-formed.

Therefore, we recommend that you escape the strings to be output in advance.

### Program Details

Next, we describe the details of `StockQuote2.jsp` step by step.

The following specifies the attributes (import class and Content-Type header) about the whole page to be generated by StockQuote2.jsp.

```
<%@ page import="chap10.EscapeString"
         contentType="application/xml; charset=UTF-8"%>
```

The following code fragment is a declaration of a bean named stockQuote. The bean is instantiated from the chap10.stockquote.StockQuoteBean class with a scope of the HTTP request.

```
<jsp:useBean
  id="stockQuote"
  scope="request"
  class="chap10.stockquote.StockQuoteBean" />
```

Listing 10.15 shows the source code for the bean used by StockQuote.jsp. This bean has two properties: company and price. The stock price is calculated the same way as in StockQuoteServlet in Section 10.2.1.

**Listing 10.15** A bean class that holds the information for a stock quote service, chap10/stockquote/StockQuoteBean.java

```
package chap10.stockquote;

public class StockQuoteBean {
    private String company = null;
    private int price = 0;
    public StockQuoteBean() { }
    public void setCompany(String company) {
        this.company = company;
    }
    public String getCompany() { return company; }
    public void setPrice(int price) { this.price = price; }
    public int getPrice() {
        // Pseudo implementation of getPrice
        byte[] data = (company == null ? "" : company).getBytes();
        price = 0;
        for (int i = 0; i < data.length; i++)
            price += data[i] & 0xff;
        price = 150 - price % 100;
        return price;
    }
}
```

The following code fragment sets the property of the stockQuote bean to "*", which means that all properties of the bean are set from the corresponding parameters in an HTTP request. Then the value is escaped to prevent the cross-site scripting attack.

```
<jsp:setProperty name="stockQuote" property="*" />
<%
String company = EscapeString.escape(stockQuote.getCompany());
%>
```

The following code fragment generates a response XML document. There are JSP expressions, `company` and `price`, embedded in the template. Even though we use `jsp:getProperty` to embed a price as is, there is no problem because the type of `price` is integer. Therefore, we do not need to care about cross-site scripting and well-formedness.

```
<?xml version="1.0" encoding="UTF-8"?>
<StockQuote
  company="<%=company%>"
  xmlns="http://www.example.com/xmlbook2/chap10/stockquote">
  <price><jsp:getProperty name="stockQuote" property="price"/></price>
</StockQuote>
```

## 10.3.3  The Combination of Servlet and JSP

In this section, we describe how to combine Servlet and JSP so that we can take advantage of both technologies.

### A Component Model Combining Servlet and JSP

Servlet complements the weak point of JSP and vice versa. Servlet has a *programming language–centric* model and document fragments are embedded in a program, while JSP has a *document-centric* model and program code fragments are embedded in a document.

Does this imply that we have to tolerate their weak points in developing applications with Servlet or JSP? The answer is no. We can combine Servlet and JSP—that is, use Servlet to implement complicated application logic and use JSP to generate an output document.

Figure 10.7 shows a *chaining model* of Servlet and JSP as one of the application development models that combine Servlet and JSP.

A servlet processes an input XML document and stores the result as a bean's property values so that JSP can use them easily. Then, JSP embeds the property values in the template of an XML document. The servlet uses the `HttpSession` object, described in Section 10.2, to pass the bean to the JSP. Finally, the servlet forwards the client to the JSP to delegate the output generation.

Figure 10.8 shows another combination of Servlet and JSP, called a *cascading model*. In this model, a servlet includes the output of a JSP within the servlet's output and sends it back to a Web client as if all the content were generated by the servlet. In

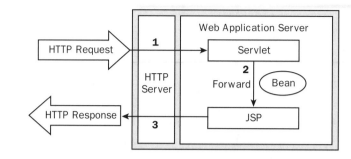

**Figure 10.7** A chaining model of Servlet and JSP

this sense, this model is very similar to the Server-Side Include. We typically use beans to pass some values to the JSP like the chaining model. Note that the servlet needs to set HTTP headers such as Content-Type by itself in this model. In other words, the headers in the HTTP response from the JSP do not affect the servlet's HTTP response.

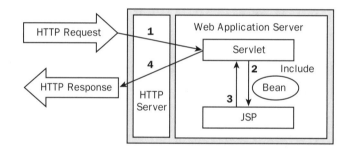

**Figure 10.8** A cascading model of Servlet and JSP

You can take advantages of both Servlet and JSP by combining them. For example, if you want to modify an output XML document, you can just modify the JSP file.

This development model can be clearly mapped to the Model-View-Controller (MVC) Model: Bean as Model, JSP as View, and Servlet as Controller. This indicates the possibility that we can provide different views for different clients by providing customized JSPs for each client.

### Improving BookStoreServlet Using JSP

`BookStoreServlet2` is an example application that implements the chaining model shown in Figure 10.7. It is an improved version of `BookStoreServlet`, shown in Section 10.2. We use a servlet to process an input XML document contained in an HTTP request and generate an output XML document in an HTTP response by using JSP.

You can run `BookStoreServlet2` by using the following command. The result is the same as in Listing 10.7. This is almost the same as for `BookStoreServlet`. The only difference is to change the URL to `BookStoreServlet2`.

```
R:\samples>java chap10.bookstore.BookStoreClient
 http://demohost:8080/xmlbook2/chap10/bookstore/BookStoreServlet2
 data\addItem.xml data\order.xml
```

### Program Details

Listing 10.16 shows the source code for `BookStoreServlet2.java`.

**Listing 10.16** Improved servlet class for the bookstore service, `chap10/bookstore/BookStoreServlet2.java`

```
package chap10.bookstore;

import java.io.IOException;
import java.util.Iterator;
import javax.servlet.ServletException;
import javax.servlet.http.HttpSession;
import javax.servlet.http.HttpServletRequest;
import javax.servlet.http.HttpServletResponse;
import org.w3c.dom.Element;
import org.w3c.dom.Document;
import org.w3c.dom.NodeList;
import chap10.GenericDOMServlet2;

public final class BookStoreServlet2 extends GenericDOMServlet2
    implements BookStoreApplication
{
    public void doProcess2(HttpServletRequest req,
                           HttpServletResponse res,
                           Document reqDoc)
        throws ServletException,
               IOException
    {
        // Gets a shopping cart from a session if it already exists.
        // If it does not exist, a shopping cart is newly created.
        ShoppingCartBean shoppingCart;
        HttpSession session = req.getSession();
        synchronized (session) {
            shoppingCart = (ShoppingCartBean)session
                .getAttribute(SHOPPING_CART_BEAN);
            if (shoppingCart == null) {
                shoppingCart = new ShoppingCartBean();
                session.setAttribute(SHOPPING_CART_BEAN,
                                     shoppingCart);
```

```
        }
    }

    // Gets the root element of reqDoc
    Element reqRoot = reqDoc.getDocumentElement();
    // Gets the local name of the root element
    String localName = reqRoot.getLocalName();

    // If the input XML document is "addItem"
    if ("addItem".equals(localName)) {
        // Creates an instance of BeansArrayBean
        // so that this servlet can store objects
        BeansArrayBean array = new BeansArrayBean();

        // For each "item" element in the request
        NodeList list = reqRoot
            .getElementsByTagNameNS(NAMESPACE_URI, "item");
        int length = list.getLength();
        for (int i = 0; i < length; i++) {
            ItemBean item = new ItemBean((Element)list.item(i));
            // Adds the item into the shopping cart
            shoppingCart.addItem(item);
            array.addBean(item);
        }
        session.setAttribute("result", array);
        String url = "/bookstore/" + localName + "Response.jsp";
        req.getRequestDispatcher(url).forward(req, res);
        return;
    }
    // If the input XML document is "order"
    if ("order".equals(localName)) {
        // Creates an instance of BeansArrayBean
        // so that this servlet can store objects
        BeansArrayBean array = new BeansArrayBean();

        // For each item in the shopping cart
        Iterator iterator = shoppingCart.getItems();
        while (iterator.hasNext()) {
            ItemBean item = (ItemBean)iterator.next();
            //
            // Orders the items here
            //
            array.addBean(item);
        }
        session.setAttribute("result", array);
        String url = "/bookstore/" + localName + "Response.jsp";
        req.getRequestDispatcher(url).forward(req, res);
        return;
```

```
            }
            throw new ServletException("Unknown request: " + localName);
        }
    }
```

The major change from `BookStoreServlet.java` is that `BookStoreDOM`
`Handler2` does not return the response DOM tree, unlike `BookStoreDOM`
`Handler`. In `BookStoreDOMHandler2`, a JSP generates the response XML documents instead.

`BookStoreDOMHandler2` is almost same as `BookStoreDOMHandler` except for
the following three points.

1.  It adds `ItemBean`, which represents the item to be processed by the `addItem`
    or `order` function, into `BeansArrayBean` instead of returning a DOM tree.
    For example, the following code is a part of the `addItem` function.

    ```
    // If the input XML document is "addItem"
    if ("addItem".equals(localName)) {
        // Creates an instance of BeansArrayBean
        // so that this servlet can store objects
        BeansArrayBean array = new BeansArrayBean();

        // For each "item" element in the request
        NodeList list =
            reqRoot.getElementsByTagNameNS(NAMESPACE_URI, "item");
        int length = list.getLength();
        for (int i = 0; i < length; i++) {
            ItemBean item = new ItemBean((Element)list.item(i));
            // Adds the item into the shopping cart
            shoppingCart.addItem(item);
            array.addBean(item);
        }
    ...
    }
    ```

2.  It stores `BeanArrayBean` in the `HttpSession` object with the name `result`
    as follows:

    ```
    session.setAttribute("result", array);
    ```

3.  It delegates the output of XML documents to the JSP by calling the `Request-`
    `Dispatcher#forward()` method. The `RequestDispatcher` object can be
    obtained by calling the `HttpServletRequest#getRequestDispatcher()`
    method. The following code corresponds to that process.

    ```
    String url = "/bookstore/" + localName + "Response.jsp";
    req.getRequestDispatcher(url).forward(req, res);
    ```

For a cascading model, a servlet calls the `RequestDispatcher#include()` method instead of the `forward()` method.

`BookStoreDOMHandler2` stores the result as a bean in step 2, and then it forwards the client to the JSP to return the output XML documents in step 3.

Listing 10.17 shows `BeansArrayBean.java`, which is a bean to store the results. This bean can contain any number of beans.

**Listing 10.17** A bean class that holds an array of beans, `chap10/bookstore/BeansArrayBean.java`

```
package chap10.bookstore;

import java.util.ArrayList;

public class BeansArrayBean {
    private ArrayList list = new ArrayList();
    public int getCount() { return list.size(); }
    public Object getBean(int i) { return list.get(i); }
    public void addBean(Object object) { list.add(object); }
}
```

Listing 10.18 shows the JSP `addItemResponse.jsp`, which generates the output XML documents for the `addItem` request.

**Listing 10.18** A JSP that creates a response for the `addItem` request, `addItemResponse.jsp`

```
<%@ page import="chap10.bookstore.ItemBean, chap10.EscapeString"
        contentType="application/xml; charset=utf-8"%>
<jsp:useBean id="result"
            class="chap10.bookstore.BeansArrayBean"
            scope="session"/>
<addItemResponse
  xmlns="http://www.example.com/xmlbook2/chap10/bookstore/BookStore"
>
<%
for (int i = 0; i < result.getCount(); i++) {
    ItemBean item = (ItemBean)result.getBean(i);
    String id = EscapeString.escape(item.getId());
%>
<item id="<%=id%>" count="<%=item.getCount()%>"/>
<%
}
%>
</addItemResponse>
```

The following code fragment specifies the classes to be imported and the Content-Type header of this page.

```
<%@ page import="chap10.bookstore.ItemBean, chap10.EscapeString"
          contentType="application/xml; charset=utf-8"%>
```

Then, the following code declares the `result` bean to be passed by the servlet. Note that the scope of this bean is the HTTP session (`session`). This corresponds to the servlet used by an `HttpSession` object to carry the bean.

```
<jsp:useBean id="result"
            class="chap10.bookstore.BeansArrayBean"
            scope="session"/>
```

The following code outputs the start tag of the `addItemResponse` element.

```
<addItemResponse
  xmlns="http://www.example.com/xmlbook2/chap10/bookstore/BookStore"
>
```

Then, the following code fragment outputs all the `item` elements that correspond to the books to be added to the shopping cart. Each book item is obtained from the corresponding `ItemBean` in the `result` bean, declared earlier by `jsp:useBean`. Furthermore, it escapes the value of `id` to prevent cross-site scripting attacks.

```
<%
for (int i = 0; i < result.getCount(); i++) {
    ItemBean item = (ItemBean)result.getBean(i);
    String id = EscapeString.escape(item.getId());
%>
<item id="<%=id%>" count="<%=item.getCount()%>"/>
<%
}
%>
```

Finally, the following code outputs the end tag of the `addItemResponse` element.

```
</addItemResponse>
```

The JSP `orderResponse.jsp` is almost the same as `addItemResponse.jsp`. The full source code for both is available on the CD-ROM.

We hope you understand that the combination of Servlet and JSP makes an application more flexible for changes to the output XML documents.

In this section, we described JSP, which allows you to easily generate an XML document. In addition, the combination of Servlet and JSP gives great flexibility to Web applications for changes to the output documents.

We describe Apache Cocoon in the next section.

## 10.4  Apache Cocoon

In Sections 10.2 and 10.3, we described a B2B approach to processing XML documents by using Servlet and JSP. In the future, more and more services on the Web will accept and provide XML documents. We can regard such an XML-based service as an XML data source that can be accessed via HTTP. This indicates that there can be many XML data sources on the Web.

Under such circumstances, we may want to support both B2B (a machine client) and B2C (a human client) with a single XML-based service in some cases. In one case, we may need to provide an XML document as it is for a machine client and a human-readable document, such as an HTML document, for a human client. In another case, we may want to integrate multiple data sources provided as XML documents.

We believe one of the possibilities is to use Cocoon. Apache Cocoon is commonly regarded as middleware for XML-based Web publishing. We believe, however, that it can be a solution for the goals just described. In this section, we describe Cocoon, revealing the reason why we believe so.

We are not providing a general view of Cocoon in this section because this is not an introduction to it. Rather, we focus on how to achieve our two goals by using Cocoon.

### 10.4.1  Having Well-Grounded Goals

**The Need for Document Distribution for Various Web Clients**

Today, the Web is globally popularized and various kinds of Web clients are used: PCs, mobile phones, application programs, and so on. They have different CPU speeds, memory limitations, I/O devices, and the expected data format, such as HTML and XML. For example, an HTML document (if it is the expected data format) is displayed differently on each client, and sometimes a client may not be able to display the whole document.

So far, we have to provide different documents for different types of clients. However, as types of clients become diverse, this kind of ad hoc approach becomes difficult.

One solution to handling such an issue is to generate various documents from a single XML document, as shown in Figure 10.9. Here, the XML document is

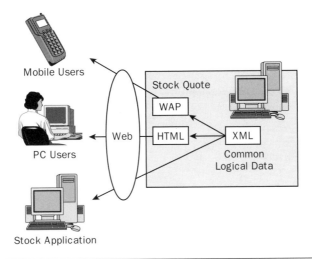

**Figure 10.9**  Multichanneling using Cocoon

regarded as common logical data that should be maintained as first-class data for an application. We call this approach *multichanneling* of an XML document.

### Integrating Multiple XML Documents

Figure 10.10 illustrates multiple XML data sources at different locations. In this case, we may want to output a single XML document to clients by integrating these XML documents.

The XML document shown in Listing 10.19 is an aggregation of the stock prices of different companies. Each stock price is collected from different stock quote services, described in Sections 10.2 and 10.3.

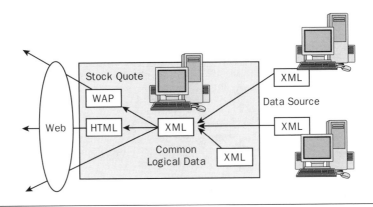

**Figure 10.10**  Merging multiple XML documents

**Listing 10.19** Integrating multiple XML documents

```
<?xml version="1.0" encoding="UTF-8"?>
<StockQuotes
  xmlns:xmlns="http://www.example.com/xmlbook2/chap10/stockquote">
  <StockQuote company="IBM">
    <price>134</price>
  </StockQuote>
  <StockQuote company="ABC">
    <price>52</price>
  </StockQuote>
  <StockQuote company="XYZ">
    <price>83</price>
  </StockQuote>
</StockQuotes>
```

### The Need for XML-Based Content Management

As we described, there are certain needs for managing XML documents as a common logical data source, integrating and transforming them if necessary, and finally sending them to Web clients. We call this *XML-based content management.*

## 10.4.2 Integrating and Multichanneling XML Documents Using Cocoon

In this section, we describe how to integrate the multiple data sources into a single XML document and transform them for the Web client if necessary by using Cocoon.

### Stock Quote Aggregation Service

We use the example of the stock quote service shown in the previous section. First, we prepare StockQuote.xml, shown in Listing 10.20.

**Listing 10.20** An XML document that aggregates response XML documents from multiple stock quote services using Cocoon, StockQuote.xml

```
<?xml version="1.0" encoding="UTF-8"?>

<!-- Stylesheet for Web browsers -->
<?xml-stylesheet href="StockQuote-HTML.xsl"
  type="text/xsl"?>
<!-- Stylesheet for Java clients -->
<?xml-stylesheet href="StockQuote-XML.xsl"
  type="text/xsl" media="java"?>
```

```
<!-- Processing instructions for Cocoon  -->
<?cocoon-process type="xsp"?>
<?cocoon-process type="xslt"?>

<!-- XSP (eXtensible Server Pages)  -->
<xsp:page
  xmlns:xsp="http://www.apache.org/1999/XSP/Core"
  xmlns:util="http://www.apache.org/1999/XSP/Util">
  <StockQuotes
    xmlns="http://www.example.com/xmlbook2/chap10/stockquote">
    <util:include-uri href=
"http://demohost:8080/xmlbook2/chap10/StockQuote3.jsp?company=IBM"/>
    <util:include-uri href=
"http://demohost:8080/xmlbook2/chap10/StockQuote3.jsp?company=ABC"/>
    <util:include-uri href=
"http://demohost:8080/xmlbook2/chap10/StockQuote3.jsp?company=XYZ"/>
  </StockQuotes>
</xsp:page>
```

`StockQuote.xml` aggregates the stock prices for IBM, ABC, and XYZ, transforms them, and returns the result to Web clients. It returns an HTML table to Web browsers, while it returns an XML document as is to Java clients.

You can open the following URL for `StockQuote.xml` with a Web browser and see an HTML table, as shown in Figure 10.11.

```
http://demohost:8080/xmlbook2/chap10/cocoon/StockQuote.xml
```

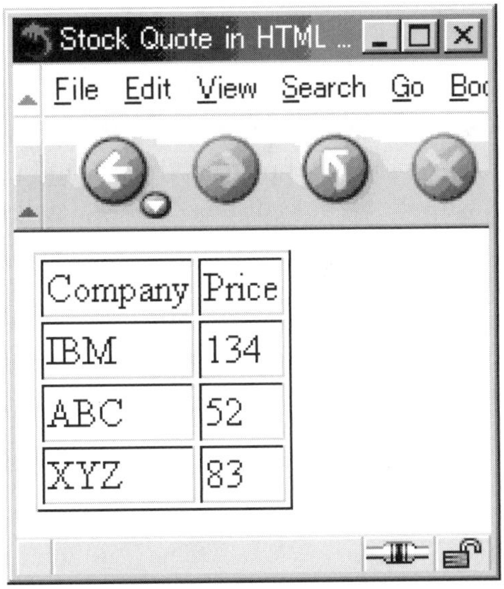

**Figure 10.11** A screenshot of the Web browser showing `StockQuote.xml`

You can access the same URL with a Java client by running the following command. Note that the command is actually a single line but is wrapped for printing.

```
R:\samples>java chap10.stockquote.StockQuoteClient
  http://demohost:8080/xmlbook2/chap10/cocoon/StockQuote.xml
```

StockQuoteClient is a simple program that sends an HTTP GET request to the specified URL and returns the response. You will see the same XML document shown in Listing 10.20 as the result.[6]

As we described, Cocoon allows you not only to collect stock prices from the multiple XML document sources but also to transform the information to generate different output for different types of clients.

### Program Details

Next we describe the details of StockQuote.xml.

The following code fragment associates this XML document with XSLT stylesheets. Processing instruction (PI) xml-stylesheet is defined in the W3C Recommendation "Associating Style Sheets with XML Documents Version 1.0."

```
<!-- Stylesheet for Web browsers -->
<?xml-stylesheet href="StockQuote-HTML.xsl"
  type="text/xsl"?>
<!-- Stylesheet for Java clients -->
<?xml-stylesheet href="StockQuote-XML.xsl"
  type="text/xsl" media="java"?>
```

The first xml-stylesheet associates this document with the StockQuote-HTML.xsl stylesheet. It is used to convert this document to an HTML document as the default stylesheet for Web browsers. The second xml-stylesheet associates this document with the StockQuote-XML.xsl stylesheet. It is used to output this document as is to Java clients. Cocoon selects an appropriate stylesheet by distinguishing the clients by checking the User-Agent header in an HTTP request. Then it applies the selected stylesheet to this document to generate the output. Note that if more than one stylesheet matches the same client, a more specific stylesheet is adopted. In this case, StockQuote-XML.xsl is adopted for the Java client, although it matches both StockQuote-HTML.xsl and StockQuote-XML.xsl.

Listing 10.21 shows StockQuote-HTML.xsl.

---

[6] Note that some redundant namespace declarations will be embedded in the XML document.

**Listing 10.21** An XSLT stylesheet that converts a response XML document from a stock quote service into an HTML document, `StockQuote-HTML.xsl`

```
<?xml version="1.0" encoding="UTF-8"?>

<xsl:stylesheet
  version="1.0"
  xmlns:xsl="http://www.w3.org/1999/XSL/Transform"
  xmlns:sq="http://www.example.com/xmlbook2/chap10/stockquote"
  exclude-result-prefixes="sq">

  <!-- Specifies the output format as HTML -->
  <xsl:output
    method="html"
    media-type="text/html"
    encoding="UTF-8"/>

  <!-- Templates -->
  <xsl:template match="/">
    <HTML lang="en">
      <HEAD>
        <TITLE>Stock Quote in HTML</TITLE>
      </HEAD>
      <BODY>
        <TABLE border="1">
          <TR><TD>Company</TD><TD>Price</TD></TR>
          <xsl:apply-templates select="//sq:StockQuote"/>
        </TABLE>
      </BODY>
    </HTML>
  </xsl:template>

  <xsl:template match="sq:StockQuote">
    <TR>
      <TD><xsl:value-of select="@company"/></TD>
      <TD><xsl:value-of select="sq:price"/></TD>
    </TR>
  </xsl:template>
</xsl:stylesheet>
```

The `xsl:output` element specifies the output format as HTML and the Content-Type as a META element in the HTML document (lines 12–13). The template that matches the document root "/" outputs the whole HTML document containing a table (lines 15–28). The template that matches the `StockQuote` element outputs each row of the table (lines 30–35).

Listing 10.22 shows `StockQuote-XML.xsl`.

**Listing 10.22** An XSLT stylesheet that returns a response XML document from a stock quote service as is, `StockQuote-XML.xsl`

```
       <?xml version="1.0" encoding="UTF-8"?>

       <xsl:stylesheet
         version="1.0"
         xmlns:xsl="http://www.w3.org/1999/XSL/Transform"
         xmlns="http://www.example.com/xmlbook2/chap10/stockquote">
         <xsl:output
[8]        method="xml"
[9]        media-type="application/xml"
[10]       encoding="UTF-8"/>

       <xsl:template match="/">
[13]       <xsl:processing-instruction name="cocoon-format">
[14]         type="application/xml"
           </xsl:processing-instruction>
[16]       <xsl:apply-templates/>
         </xsl:template>

       <xsl:template match="*">
         <xsl:copy>
           <xsl:apply-templates select="@*|*|text()"/>
         </xsl:copy>
       </xsl:template>

       <xsl:template match="@*">
         <xsl:copy/>
       </xsl:template>
     </xsl:stylesheet>
```

The `xsl:output` element specifies the output format as XML (line 8), the media type (line 9), and encoding (line 10). The template that matches the document root "/" outputs PI `cocoon-format` as a directive for Cocoon. It indicates that the media type of the document generated by using this stylesheet is `application/xml` (line 13-14). The `xsl:apply-templates` instruction applies templates to the document element (line 16). The remaining templates output the input XML documents as is.

The following part of `StockQuote.xml` calls the stock quote JSP service dynamically using Extensible Server Pages (XSP).[7] XSP is similar to JSP and generates

---

[7] Note that we used `StockQuote3.jsp`, which is a variant of `StockQuote2.jsp`. It does not output the XML declaration because of the requirement from Cocoon.

dynamic content being developed by the Apache Cocoon project. It is still in draft form and is subject to change. See the Cocoon Web site (`http://xml.apache.org/cocoon1/`) for details.

The results of the JSP calls are embedded in `StockQuote.xml`.

```
<!-- XSP (eXtensible Server Pages)  -->
<xsp:page
   xmlns:xsp="http://www.apache.org/1999/XSP/Core"
   xmlns:util="http://www.apache.org/1999/XSP/Util">
   <StockQuotes xmlns="http://www.example.com/xmlbook2/chap10/stockquote">
     <util:include-uri
href="http://demohost:8080/xmlbook2/chap10/StockQuote3.jsp?company=IBM"/>
     <util:include-uri
href="http://demohost:8080/xmlbook2/chap10/StockQuote3.jsp?company=ABC"/>
     <util:include-uri
href="http://demohost:8080/xmlbook2/chap10/StockQuote3.jsp?company=XYZ"/>
   </StockQuotes>
</xsp:page>
```

In this section, we introduced Cocoon because we believe the concept of XML-based content management will become more popular in the near future. We described such a concept of content management by using Cocoon, although there are many features of Cocoon that we did not describe.

## 10.5 Summary

In this chapter, we described Servlet, JSP, and Cocoon as technologies for XML application servers. We hope you understand the basic techniques for handling XML documents on the server side and how you can implement Web applications that process XML documents.

The technologies we described in this chapter are placed at the frontend of a Web application. In Chapter 11, we describe the relationship between XML and databases as the backend of a Web application.

CHAPTER

# XML and Databases

## 11.1  Introduction

In Chapter 10, we discussed the basics of Servlet, JSP, and Cocoon and learned how to develop a practical and secure Web application. In this chapter, we focus on how to represent structured data using XML, store it in a relational database management system (RDBMS), and search for it.

The three tier-model of application development that we discussed in Chapter 1 consists of a Web browser or a client application as tier 1, a Web server or an application server as tier 2, and a database system or a transaction system as tier 3, as shown in Figure 11.1. An RDBMS is most frequently used as tier 3 in three-tier systems.

The debut of Java applets for client-side application development had a big impact in the world. Now, Java has become a very important technology for server-side application development (see Section 10.1.1). XML is also becoming a common format for data exchange among Web applications, and XML Schema languages

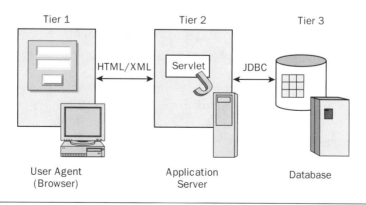

**Figure 11.1**  A three-tier Web application

make it possible to define datatypes and associate them with database tables. This chapter discusses how to design Web applications that access a database and shows many working examples.

Java provides a common API for accessing a database system known as Java Database Connectivity (JDBC). It is a part of the Java standard library, and many database vendors supply JDBC drivers that implement this API for accessing their own implementation of database products. Thus JDBC provides a high-level interface to Java programmers and relieves them from dealing with the low-level details of database access. Appendix D explains the basics of JDBC; they are used in most of the sample programs in this chapter.

Section 11.3 describes how to map an XML document to relational tables, and Section 11.4 describes how to map relational tables to an XML document. Section 11.5 covers some working examples. Section 11.6 introduces a servlet that accesses a database. We show an approach using Enterprise JavaBeans (EJB) that can reduce programming costs and can develop highly scalable Web applications in Section 11.7. Before moving to these topics, we start with general discussions on storing and searching for an XML document.

## 11.2 Storing and Searching for XML Documents

Database management systems such as RDBMS are very efficient in dealing with a large amount of data, and they provide the essential characteristics for mission-critical applications that require robustness, integrity, consistency, and availability. The three-tier model shown in Figure 11.1 is widely used for applications such as purchase orders, ticket reservations, and electronic form application systems. However, most data stored in these systems is not in XML format.

There are three approaches to storing data represented in XML into database systems:

1. Store an XML document as a structured document.
2. Store an XML document as a DOM tree object.
3. Store an XML document as a set of relational tables.

The first approach came into use for storing and retrieving structured documents by using an SGML/XML native database. For example, OpenText (LiveLink) is a full-text search engine (see `http://www.opentext.com/livelink`). An XML database server called Tamino, from Software AG, also employs this approach (see `http://www.softwareag.com/tamino`). LiveLink associates an XML element with a region and realizes structure-aware searching. Tamino provides a searching capability by using an (extended) XPath expression and manages indexes for schemas to optimize the search process. The advantage of using the native database is that there is no need to design mapping between an XML document and tables, which is nontrivial work, as discussed in this chapter. An XML document can just be stored in the database and retrieved with XPath, XQuery, and other standards-based technologies. The native database also provides a full-text search capability that can be useful when complex documents (rather than data) are to be stored.

The second approach can be realized by using an Object-Oriented Database (OODB). In the OODB framework, a data object is stored as a persistent object, and an application can address the object via a pointer. In an XML-based OODB, an XML document can be represented as a DOM tree object and is stored in its persistent data store. A well-known implementation of this approach is eXcelon (see `http://www.exceloncorp.com`). The product is based on a general OODB called ObjectStore. It stores a collection of DOM objects and provides searching functions by using XPath with some extensions. The main advantage of this approach is the same as for the native database.

The last approach is the topic of this chapter. In this approach, an XML document is stored in an RDBMS. It can manage a set of relational tables and their schemas, which are strictly defined. On the other hand, an XML document is *semistructured* data, which is one of the most important characteristics of XML; therefore, it is not easy to map an XML document with one or more tables.

This chapter focuses on the third approach for the following two reasons. First, most existing business applications store data in RDBMS. To develop an XML-based Web application integrated with existing resources, it is natural to store an XML document sent from clients in RDBMSs.

Second, most commercial RDMBS products, such as Oracle and DB2, provide high availability against large data volume and huge numbers of accesses to them. They also provide various management capabilities, including data backup and recovery. These features have a significant meaning when you develop large-scale and reliable business applications. Furthermore, many techniques to optimize a system and a query have already been established, so users can benefit from them.

How to retrieve stored XML documents is another big issue. There are four well-known approaches for retrieving.

- *An application-specific query language,* such as OpenText. For example, when you want to search `TITLE` elements that contain the string "XML" with OpenText, you can use a query like `region TITLE including "XML"` (assuming that the `TITLE` element is associated with the `TITLE` region, which is an OpenText-specific topic). The syntax of the query is application-specific.

- *XPath* (see Chapter 7). XPath and its (application-specific) extension can be used as a query language because parts of XML document can be addressable by using XPath. It is also possible to convert an XPath expression to Structured Query Language (SQL) to search a database in which XML documents are decomposed into tables by using JDBC.

- *XQuery*, the W3C standard in progress. XQuery is a standard of query language for XML documents specified by W3C. It is based on SQL, and XPath is used to address part of an XML document. XQuery can specify the format of the result in a flexible way. The latest Working Draft was published on June 7, 2001. This specification may change before becoming a Recommendation; therefore, the details of XQuery are not covered in this book. If you want to know more about it, visit the W3C Web site (`http://www.w3.org/XML/Query`). The advantages of XQuery are as follows.

  - It provides a common query language for XML documents. It does not depend on a particular type of database (native, OODB, and RDB).

  - It can be applicable to a set of XML documents.

  - It provides powerful syntax to search and transform the result.

  The following is an example of a query appearing in the XQuery 1.0 specification.

```
FOR $p IN distinct(document("bib.xml")//publisher)
LET $a := avg(document("bib.xml")//book[publisher = $p]/price)
RETURN
    <publisher>
        <name> {$p/text()} </name>
        <avgprice> {$a} </avgprice>
    </publisher>
```

  The words FOR, LET, WHERE, and RETURN are the main building blocks of XQuery, and the query is called an "FLWR expression." The previous query lists for each publisher the average price of its books. You may have heard that the concept of the query is similar to SQL. That's true. A FOR clause specifies a target part of an XML document. It corresponds to SELECT in SQL. A LET clause is used to bind a variable to the result of a function (to get an average of multiple values, in this case). A WHERE clause specifies the condition of the query. The result of applying the condition is returned with the RETURN clause. It is a kind of template for output. The variables in the template are bound in the query process. XQueryX is a syntax for representing the FLWR expression in XML. The draft of XQueryX is also available at W3C (`http://www.w3.org/TR/xqueryx`).

- *Structured Query Language* (SQL). SQL is a common language to access an RDBMS. If an XML document is decomposed into data to be stored in a table as a column value or it is generated from data stored in a database, it can be accessed by using SQL. We discuss more about this approach in the next section.

In this chapter, we focus on storing XML documents in an RDBMS. Furthermore, we should consider the opposite direction, creating XML documents from a set of relational tables. This is very important because most existing business data is stored in RDBMSs in the form of tables, not XML documents. The next section covers mapping between XML documents and relational tables.

## 11.3  Mapping from an XML Document to Tables

One of the most important characteristics of XML is that it is semistructured data. It is difficult to define this word precisely, but it means data for which a strict schema cannot be defined, or for which it is difficult to define a strict schema. XML allows an iteration of an arbitrary number of elements. This flexibility of XML makes it difficult to map an XML document to one or more relational tables because a table has a strict schema. This section concentrates on mapping a semistructured XML document with relational tables. Chapter 15 covers a broader topic on data binding.

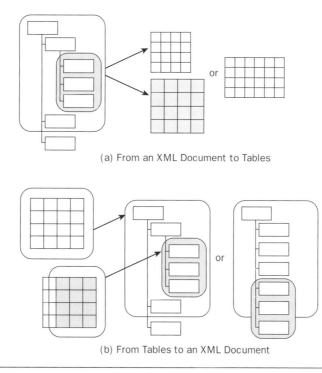

(a) From an XML Document to Tables

(b) From Tables to an XML Document

**Figure 11.2**  Mapping between an XML document and relational tables

Figure 11.2 shows the mapping between an XML document and relational tables. The upper part of the figure (a) shows a mapping from an XML document to a set of tables. An XML document is decomposed into one or more tables. In this case, we need a technique to convert structured (and ordered) data to table (and unordered) data. We should determine what information should be stored (some information may not be needed). We also should determine how many tables are required to cover the XML document based on a given XML schema. There is no established strategy for the decomposition at this moment. We introduce some approaches in this section.

The lower part of Figure 11.2 (b) shows the mapping from relational tables to an XML document. In this case, table data is converted to structured data. Most techniques are common with the opposite direction, but there is a design choice for representing the table data as a structured XML document. The figure shows two possibilities for the mapping, which are covered in the next section.

For example, how can we define the schema of an XML document (po.xml) to store it in a database? Listing 11.1 shows the XML document.

**Listing 11.1**  A DTD for a purchase order, chap11/po.xml

```
<?xml version="1.0"?>
<!DOCTYPE purchaseOrder [
<!ELEMENT purchaseOrder (shipTo, items)>
<!ATTLIST purchaseOrder invoiceNo CDATA #REQUIRED>
<!ELEMENT shipTo (name, street?)>
<!ATTLIST shipTo country CDATA #REQUIRED>
<!ELEMENT name (#PCDATA)>
<!ELEMENT street (#PCDATA)>
<!ELEMENT items (item*)>
<!ELEMENT item (#PCDATA)>
<!ATTLIST item qty CDATA #REQUIRED>
]>
<purchaseOrder invoiceNo="2001-08-31-12345">
    <shipTo country="US">
        <name>Alice Smith</name>
        <street>123 Maple Street</street>
    </shipTo>
    <items>
        <item qty="2">ThinkPad X21</item>
        <item qty="1">ThinkPad T22</item>
    </items>
</purchaseOrder>
```

If a schema (or a DTD) for the document is finalized and a program knows the details of the schema, we can define a schema that depends on the document to be stored. The schemas for two tables to store the document `po.xml` are shown in Tables 11.1 and 11.2.

Data items appearing once in a document (such as `invoiceNo` and `name`) can be represented in a table (see Table 11.1). Items appearing multiple times (such as `item`) should be defined in separate tables (see Table 11.2). That means XML documents are semistructured data so that it is impossible to map a single table in most cases. When you want to submit a query to find "people who ordered the ThinkPad X21," the two tables must be joined, because the `name` and `item` elements are mapped in different tables. However, if the structure of an XML document is not very complex and its schema can be defined, this approach is worth trying.

If an XML document can be decomposed into tables, the data can be accessed via SQL. It can be integrated with other (non-XML) data stored in databases and existing applications, which is an advantage for managing XML documents in an RDBMS.

As mentioned before, the mapping between an XML document and tables is a nontrivial work. Database vendors like IBM and Oracle provide tools to help developers (see `http://www.ibm.com/software/data/db2/extenders/xmlext/`). For example, DB2 XML Extender provides an XML-based mapping language. Users can create the mapping file with a wizard-like GUI. Oracle provides XML Developer's Kit (XDK) (see `http://otn.oracle.com/tech/xml/xdkhome.html`) that contains an XML processor that supports XML Schema and useful classes to develop real applications by using XML and databases. Using these tools can reduce the cost of schema design and mapping. Though some tools

**Table 11.1**   Relational Tables for `po.xml` (1): `PO_TBL`

| invoiceNO VARCHAR(32) | country VARCHAR(32) | name VARCHAR(128) | street VARCHAR(128) |
|---|---|---|---|
| 2001-08-31-12345 | US | Alice Smith | 123 Maple Street |

**Table 11.2**   Relational Tables for `po.xml` (2): `ITEM_TBL`

| itemID VARCHAR(32) | item VARCHAR(128) | qty INTEGER | invoice_ID VARCHAR(32) |
|---|---|---|---|
| 2001-08-31-12345-1 | ThinkPad X21 | 2 | 2001-08-31-12345 |
| 2001-08-31-12345-2 | ThinkPad T22 | 1 | 2001-08-31-12345 |

for mapping are available, there is no tool that maps them automatically. Some design points are covered in the next section.

### 11.3.1  Designing Relational Tables

Most practical XML documents (for example, a purchase order or a contract) are represented with multiple tables. The structure of a typical XML document consists of the following components:

- Elements that appear once (for example, total price and contract date) in a document
- Elements that appear repeatedly (for example, goods)
- An identifier that is unique to each document

First, we can create a table for a top-level concept represented by the root element of an XML document. Generally speaking, an XML document can depict a contract, a purchase order, a technical report, and so on. It can be represented as a single table called the *parent table*. For the document `po.xml`, a table shown in Table 11.1 is the parent table. The table defines the `invoice_ID`, `country`, `name`, and `street` elements.

### 11.3.2  Defining the Primary Keys in a Table

The parent table contains a column whose value is unique, so it can be used as a primary key. A primary key is a value or a set of values that can uniquely identify a row in a table. In `po.xml`, the value of the `invoice_ID` attribute can be used as the primary key. RDBMS prohibits storing multiple records that have the same primary key value, so we should make sure the value is actually unique. If an XML document contains no such unique identifier, a primary key should be generated and added to the table to join with other tables. In Listings 11.6 and 11.11 later in this chapter, we define a column name that does not appear in `po.xml`. Its value is generated as a unique value by using the `java.rmi.UID` class.

Some of the constraints defined for XML schema languages can be mapped to the constraints for tables. For example, if an element is not optional, the `NOT NULL` constraint should be applied to the corresponding column name.

### 11.3.3  Designing a Table for Multiply Occurring Elements

Elements iterated in an XML document (defined by using "*" and "+" in a DTD) can be represented in a separate table. In `po.xml`, the element `item` is represented in a table called a *child table*. A parent table and child tables are joined when an

RDBMS receives a query. For child tables, defining the primary key is important, though in most cases the original XML document contains the identifier for the element.

RDMBSs provide various types of constraints among tables. For example, if a record in a parent table is deleted, related records should be deleted from child tables. The following constraint does this automatically.

```
FOREIGN KEY ("invoice_ID") REFERENCES PO_TBL ("invoice_ID")
                         ON DELETE CASCADE) ;
```

This constraint indicates that the `invoice_ID` column in the item table shown in Table 11.2 (`ITEM_TBL`) is the foreign key associated with the `invoice_ID` column in the purchase order table shown in Table 11.1 (`PO_TBL`). And if a record that has a certain `invoice_ID` value is deleted from the `PO_TBL` table, all the records that have same `invoice_ID` value are automatically deleted from the `ITEM_TBL` table.

### 11.3.4 Datatype Mapping

A database schema strictly defines datatypes for each column. On the other hand, a DTD does not support datatypes such as numerical and fixed-length character types. Therefore, to express datatype information in a DTD, you should represent them explicitly in an XML document by using the `dtype` attribute, for example. In the first edition of this book, Chapter 6 introduced a sample program using this approach. Now XML Schema has come into play, and it makes it possible to define datatypes in schemas (see Chapter 9). RELAX, another XML schema language described in Chapter 16, also employs the datatype specification the same as XML Schema. Section 9.2.2 discusses mapping among the datatypes of Java, XML Schema, and SQL.

A DTD does not constrain the length of characters (though XML Schema does support it). You should take care when you extract a string from an element's content and store it into a database. For example, if a column is defined as `CHARACTER(32)`, it is impossible to store any string exceeding this limitation. If the maximum length of the data cannot be estimated, you should use the `VARCHAR` type, which allows you to change the maximum size after you create a table. If the length of characters is very long, use the Character Large Object (`CLOB`) or the Binary Large Object (`BLOB`) datatype.

### 11.3.5 Semantics of Data

All elements that appear once are not always represented as a single table. When a relational table is designed, there are many techniques for data modeling. Creating an Entity-Relationship Diagram (ER diagram) is one well-known method of modeling. The table design essentially depends on what an XML document represents, and this fact causes difficulty for automatic mapping between an XML document and tables without knowing the semantics of the data to be stored.

Next we introduced some points for designing relational schemas for a given XML document.

### 11.3.6 Two Approaches

In Section 11.2, we showed how to map between an XML document and database tables. When we know the schema of an XML document, we can define tables that can store the XML document. In this section, we call this approach the *mapping method*. However, if we don't know the schema for the document, how can we store the document?

One solution is to decompose XML documents by using XPath and store a pair of an XPath expression and the content addressed by the expression. We call this approach the *XPath method*. By using the XPath method, we can store po.xml in the table shown in Table 11.3.

Figure 11.3 depicts the two approaches. The mapping method requires a DTD or XML Schema to associate a node value with a column value in a table with an appropriate datatype. On the other hand, the XPath method does not require a schema, but all node values are stored in a column with a single datatype.

In Section 11.5, we further discuss these two methods using sample programs.

**Table 11.3**   Relational Tables for po.xml (1c)

| Node_ID | XPath_String | content_string | document_ID |
|---|---|---|---|
| 1 | /purchaseOrder[1]/@invoiceNo | 2001-08-31-12345 | 2001-08-31-12345 |
| 2 | /purchaseOrder[1]/shipTo[1]/@country | US | 2001-08-31-12345 |
| 3 | /purchaseOrder[1]/shipTo[1]/name[1] | Alice Smith | 2001-08-31-12345 |
| 4 | /purchaseOrder[1]/shipTo[1]/street[1] | 123 Maple Street | 2001-08-31-12345 |
| 5 | /purchaseOrder[1]/items[1]/item[1]/@qty | 2 | 2001-08-31-12345 |
| 6 | /purchaseOrder[1]/items[1]/item[1] | ThinkPad X21 | 2001-08-31-12345 |
| 7 | /purchaseOrder[1]/items[1]/item[2]/@qty | 1 | 2001-08-31-12345 |
| 8 | /purchaseOrder[1]/items[1]/item[2] | ThinkPad T22 | 2001-08-31-12345 |

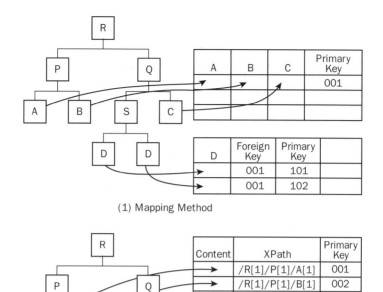

**Figure 11.3** The mapping and XPath methods

# 11.4 Mapping from Tables to an XML Document

In the previous sections, we discussed conversions from an XML document to relational tables. However, conversions from tables to an XML document are often required when data is originally stored in a database as table records. The discussions in the previous sections are useful for such conversions. For example, if multiple tables represent a certain concept, such as a purchase order, it can be represented in an XML document. It is possible to map an XML document to a table one by one with links that correspond to foreign keys. However, in many cases it causes problems because it is not easy to manage multiple XML documents. If primary keys in the table are not necessary in an XML document, they can be ignored.

## 11.4.1 Nested and Flat Representation

Let's look at how to convert the tables shown in Tables 11.4, 11.5, and 11.6 by using the two approaches. The tables store information for purchase orders. This example is more complex than we saw before in Tables 11.1 and 11.2 so that we can explain the two approaches. The tables show information about addresses, quantities, and products, respectively. The `invoice_ID` column in Table 11.4 is referred to as a foreign key in Table 11.5. The `productID` column in Table 11.6 is also referred to from Table 11.5.

**Table 11.4** Relational Tables for Purchase Orders (1): `PO_TBL`

| invoice_ID<br>VARCHAR(32) | country<br>VARCHAR(32) | name<br>VARCHAR(128) | street<br>VARCHAR(128) |
|---|---|---|---|
| 2001-08-31-12345 | US | Alice Smith | 123 Maple Street |
| 2001-08-31-12346 | US | Bob Miller | 1365 Tree Street |

**Table 11.5** Relational Tables for Purchase Orders (2): `ITEM_TBL`

| itemID<br>VARCHAR(32) | productID<br>VARCHAR(128) | qty<br>INTEGER | invoice_ID<br>VARCHAR(32) |
|---|---|---|---|
| 000001 | ibm0010 | 2 | 2001-08-31-12345 |
| 000002 | ibm0011 | 1 | 2001-08-31-12345 |
| 000003 | ibm0010 | 8 | 2001-08-31-12346 |
| 000004 | ibm0011 | 10 | 2001-08-31-12346 |

**Table 11.6** Relational Tables for Purchase Orders (3): `PRODUCT_TBL`

| ProductID<br>VARCHAR(32) | Name<br>VARCHAR(128) | Company<br>VARCHAR(64) |
|---|---|---|
| ibm0010 | ThinkPad X21 | IBM |
| ibm0011 | ThinkPad T22 | IBM |

Let's look at how to convert from the tables to an XML document by using the two methods.

Listing 11.2 shows a list of purchase orders with the nesting method. In this example, product information is represented with the `product` element, which is a child element of an `item` element. The structure is quite natural, and it is easy for humans to read. However, it is redundant because the same product information appears in multiple purchase orders. Relationships between invoices and products use many-to-many mapping, so using the nesting method may not be the best solution.

**Listing 11.2** Constructed XML document (nesting method), `chap11/po2.xml`

```
<?xml version="1.0"?>
<purchaseOrderList
  <invoice invoiceNo="2001-08-31-12345">
    <shipTo country="US">
        <name>Alice Smith</name>
        <street>123 Maple Street</street>
    </shipTo>
    <items>
      <item qty="2">
        <product>
          <name>ThinkPad X21</name>
        </product>
      </item>
      <item qty="1">
        <product>
          <name>ThinkPad T22</name>
        </product>
      </item>
    </items>
  </invoice>
  <invoice invoiceNo="2001-08-31-12346">
    <shipTo country="US">
      <name>Bob Miller</name>
      <street>1365 Tree Street</street>
    </shipTo>
    <items>
      <item qty="8">
        <product>
          <name>ThinkPad X21</name>
        </product>
      </item>
      <item qty="10">
        <product>
          <name>ThinkPad T22</name>
        </product>
      </item>
    </items>
  </invoice>
</purchaseOrderList>
```

Listing 11.3 shows an XML document using the flat method. Information for
each product appears once in the document. Multiple invoices refer to the information by using the `ID` and `IDREF` type attributes. The `product` element has the
`productID` attribute, which is referred to by the `productIDRef` attribute of an

item element. Multiple item elements can share product information. The flat method has a compact representation unlike the nesting approach. However, to get product information for an item, you should write code to relate the ID and IDREF type attributes.

**Listing 11.3** Constructed XML document (flat method), chap11/po3.xml

```
<?xml version="1.0"?>
<purchaseOrderList>
  <invoice invoiceNo="2001-08-31-12345">
    <shipTo country="US">
        <name>Alice Smith</name>
        <street>123 Maple Street</street>
    </shipTo>
    <items>
      <item qty="2" productIDRef="ibm0011"/>
      <item qty="1" productIDRef="ibm0011"/>
    </items>
  </invoice>
  <invoice invoiceNo="2001-08-31-12346">
    <shipTo country="US">
        <name>Bob Miller</name>
        <street>1365 Tree Street</street>
    </shipTo>
    <items>
      <item qty="8" productIDRef="ibm0010"/>
      <item qty="10" productIDRef="ibm0011"/>
    </items>
  </invoice>
  <products>
    <product productID="ibm0010">
      <name>ThinkPad X21</name>
    </product>
    <product productID="ibm0011">
      <name>ThinkPad T22</name>
    </product>
  </products>
</purchaseOrderList>
```

We introduced the nesting and flat methods for representing data stored in relational tables. You can choose the appropriate approach according to the original table data. The book titled *Professional XML Database*, by Kevin Williams et al. (Wrox Press, ISBN 1-86003-58-7) shows a set of many useful rules for mapping from tables to an XML document. In that book, the two approaches are called the containment and pointered approaches.

You can convert an XML document to another XML document by using XSLT. In the first edition of this book, we first created an XML document that contained `row` elements that had multiple `col` subelements, which is a very naive representation of a table. The XML document was next converted to an HTML document. It is possible to get a non-HTML document—for example, a PDF document.

### 11.4.2 Element versus Attribute Representation

The next design point is how to represent data by using an attribute or an element. For example, we can use an element to represent a product name as follows:

```
<!-- Represents a product name as an element -->
<product productID="ibm0010">
  <name>ThinkPad X21</name>
</product>
```

And it is also possible to represent it by using an attribute as follows:

```
<!-- Represents a product name as an attribute -->
<product productID="ibm0010" name="ThinkPad X21"/>
```

There have been long discussions on this topic before XML was created. You can see a survey of the discussions, edited by Robin Cover, at `http://xml.coverpages.org/elementsAndAttrs.html`.

For example, one says we should use an element if the data represents an essential part of a whole concept. Another says it depends on whether the data represents content or markup. Yet another says we should employ the attribute approach, because it reflects the characteristics of tables (for example, a list of attributes is unordered), and it may be efficient.

There is no general answer that is better than another. It should depend on the semantics of the data. Two attributes may be related so that it is natural to represent them in a structured way. Therefore, when you design an XML schema for a given table schema, you should consider multiple viewpoints, such as data modeling, efficiency, and the applications that receive the XML documents.

## 11.5 Program Examples

In Section 11.3.6, we discussed two approaches for mapping from an XML document to relational tables. This section introduces the examples for these approaches. The techniques described in this section are also useful for mapping relational tables to an XML document.

## 11.5.1 Mapping Method

Listing 11.4 shows a sample program to decompose an XML document (po.xml, shown in Listing 11.1) into predefined tables. This is a typical program for the mapping approach.

**Listing 11.4** Archiving an XML document, chap11/XMLTableArchiver

```
package chap11;
/**
 * XMLArchiver.java
 *
 *  This program assumes the following database schema
 *
 *  TABLE "PO_TBL"  (
 *                  "invoice_ID"    VARCHAR(32)    NOT NULL,
 *                  "country"       VARCHAR(32)    NOT NULL,
 *                  "name"          VARCHAR(128)   NOT NULL,
 *                  "street"        VARCHAR(128)   NOT NULL,
 *                  PRIMARY KEY     ("invoice_ID") ) ;
 *
 *  TABLE "ITEM_TBL"  (
 *                  "item_ID"       VARCHAR(32)    NOT NULL,
 *                  "item"          VARCHAR(128)   NOT NULL,
 *                  "qty"           INTEGER        NOT NULL,
 *                  "invoice_ID"    VARCHAR(32)    NOT NULL,
 *                  PRIMARY KEY     ("item_ID"),
 *                  FOREIGN KEY     ("invoice_ID")
 *                          REFERENCES PO_TBL ("invoice_ID")
 *                                  ON DELETE CASCADE) ;
 */

import java.sql.Connection;
import java.sql.Statement;
import java.sql.PreparedStatement;
import java.sql.ResultSet;
import java.sql.DriverManager;
import java.sql.SQLException;
import java.rmi.server.UID;
import java.util.Hashtable;
import java.io.File;
import javax.xml.parsers.DocumentBuilderFactory;
import javax.xml.parsers.DocumentBuilder;
import org.apache.xml.serialize.XMLSerializer;
import org.apache.xml.serialize.OutputFormat;
import org.w3c.dom.Element;
import org.w3c.dom.Node;
```

```
import org.w3c.dom.Document;
import org.w3c.dom.NodeList;
import share.util.MyErrorHandler;

public class XMLTableArchiver {

    // Names of database, tables, and elements
    static final String XML_DB              = "XMLDB";
    static final String PO_TBL              = "PO_TBL";
    static final String ITEM_TBL            = "ITEM_TBL";
    static final String JDBC_DRIVER_CLASS   =
                            "COM.ibm.db2.jdbc.app.DB2Driver";

    static final String ELT_PO              = "purchaseOrder";
    static final String ELT_SHIPTO          = "shipTo";
    static final String ELT_STREET          = "street";
    static final String ELT_NAME            = "name";
    static final String ELT_ITEMS           = "items";
    static final String ELT_ITEM            = "item";
    static final String ATTR_COUNTRY        = "country";
    static final String ATTR_QTY            = "qty";
    static final String ATTR_INVOICE_ID     = "invoiceNo";
    static final String COLUMN_INVOICE_ID   = "INVOICE_ID";
    static final String COLUMN_QTY          = "QTY";
    static final String COLUMN_ITEM         = "ITEM";

    // Connection with database
    private Connection con = null;
    // Prepared statement for storing data into PO_TBL
    private Statement stmt = null;
    // Prepared statement for storing data into ITEM_TBL
    private PreparedStatement stmtForItem  = null;

    // Register the driver with DriverManager
    static {
        try {
            Class.forName(JDBC_DRIVER_CLASS);
        } catch (Exception e) {
            e.printStackTrace();
        }
    }

    /**
     * Constructor
     *
     */
    public XMLTableArchiver (String userid, String password) {
        try {
```

```
                        // Creates connection
[89]                    con = DriverManager.getConnection("jdbc:db2:"+XML_DB,
                                              userid,
                                              password);
[92]                    con.setAutoCommit(false);
[93]                    stmt = con.createStatement();
[94]                    stmtForItem = con.prepareStatement(
                          "INSERT INTO " + ITEM_TBL + " VALUES (?, ?, ?, ?)");

                    } catch (java.sql.SQLException e) {
                        e.printStackTrace();
                    }
                }

                /**
                 * Store data into database
                 *
                 * @param doc a <code>Document</code> to be stored
                 */
                public void store(Document doc) {
                    try {
                        String invoiceNo = null;
                        String country   = null;
                        String name      = null;
                        String street    = null;

                        // Gets information for PO_TBL
                        Element poElt =
                        (Element)doc.getElementsByTagName(ELT_PO).item(0);
                        invoiceNo = poElt.getAttribute(ATTR_INVOICE_ID);
                        Element shipToElt = (Element)
                            doc.getElementsByTagName(ELT_SHIPTO).item(0);
                        country = shipToElt.getAttribute(ATTR_COUNTRY);
                        Element nameElt = (Element)
                            doc.getElementsByTagName(ELT_NAME).item(0);
                        name = nameElt.getFirstChild().getNodeValue();
                        Element streetElt = (Element)
                            doc.getElementsByTagName(ELT_STREET).item(0);
                        street = streetElt.getFirstChild().getNodeValue();
                        // Submits an insert query
                        String query = "INSERT INTO " + PO_TBL +
                                    " VALUES ('" + invoiceNo + "', '" +
                                    country + "', '" + name + "', '" +
                                    street + "')";

                        // Submits query
[134]                   stmt.executeUpdate(query);
                        // Gets information for ITEM_TBL
```

```
[136]                  Element itemsElt =
                       (Element)doc.getElementsByTagName(ELT_ITEMS).item(0);
                       NodeList nl = itemsElt.getChildNodes();
                       Element itemElt = null;
                       try {
                           for (int i = 0; i < nl.getLength(); i++) {
                               if (nl.item(i).getNodeType() ==
                                   Node.ELEMENT_NODE) {
                                   // Gets item node
                                   itemElt = (Element)nl.item(i);
                                   String qty  =
                                           itemElt.getAttribute(ATTR_QTY);
                                   String itemName =
                                           itemElt.getFirstChild().
                                           getNodeValue();
                                   String itemID = new UID().toString();
[152]                              stmtForItem.setString(1, itemID);
                                   stmtForItem.setString(2, itemName);
                                   stmtForItem.setInt(3,
                                                   Integer.parseInt(qty));
                                   stmtForItem.setString(4, invoiceNo);
[157]                              stmtForItem.executeUpdate();
                               }
                           }
                       } catch (SQLException se) {
                           // Rolls back the first insertion
                           System.out.println("Insertion Error: all the " +
                                       "operation to database is canceled");
[164]                      con.rollback();
                       }
                       // Commits the insertions to tables
[167]                  con.commit();
                       System.out.println("Stored with ID "+invoiceNo);

                   } catch (Exception e) {
                       e.printStackTrace();
                   }
               }
           public static void main(String[] argv) {
               if (argv.length != 1) {
                   System.err.println("Usage: XMLTableArchiver " +
                                       "filename");
                   System.exit(1);
               }
               try {
                   // Userid and password are specified as
```

```
                              // System properties
[183]                         String userid = System.getProperty("chap11.userid");
                              String password =
                                            System.getProperty("chap11.password");
                              XMLTableArchiver arc =
                                            new XMLTableArchiver(userid, password);
                              // Parses input document
[189]                         DocumentBuilderFactory factory =
                                            DocumentBuilderFactory.newInstance();
                              DocumentBuilder builder =
                                            factory.newDocumentBuilder();
                              // Sets an ErrorHandler
                              builder.setErrorHandler(new MyErrorHandler());
                              // Parses the document
                              Document doc = builder.parse(new File(argv[0]));
                              // Stores the document
                              arc.store(doc);
                        } catch (Exception e) {
                              e.printStackTrace();
                        }
                  }
            }
```

This program, XMLTableArchiver, assumes that the two tables PO_TBL and ITEM_TBL have been defined. Samples of the tables are shown in Tables 11.1 and 11.2.

This program works as follows:

1. Creates a connection to a database (named XML_DB, line 89).
2. Creates a Statement object for the PO_TBL table (line 93).
3. Creates a PreparedStatement object for the ITEM_TBL table to handle the multiple-insert process (line 94).
4. Parses an input XML document and extracts information for the PO_TBL table (line 189).
5. Submits an insertion request to PO_TBL (line 134).
6. Extracts information for the ITEM_TBL table from the XML document (line 136).
7. Submits an insertion request to ITEM_TBL. If the process fails, cancels the insertion operation for PO_TBL by calling the rollback() method (line 164).
8. After the insertion operations succeed, commits all the operations (line 167).

We have already shown how to parse an XML document (see Chapter 2), how to extract information from a DOM tree (see Chapter 2), and how to connect to a database with JDBC (see Appendix D). Now we describe some important techniques that appeared for the first time in this program.

### Prepared Statement

In the first sample program shown in Section D.5 of Appendix D, a `Statement` object is first created to submit an SQL query. Then, the query string is passed to the method `executeQuery()` and compiled into an internal representation when the method is invoked. On the other hand, as shown in Listing 11.4, the `PreparedStatement` object is created with a template for an SQL query. The template contains placeholders represented by "?". The actual values for the placeholders are determined at runtime; therefore, the template can be reused for multiple queries.

The related code fragment in Listing 11.4 is as follows:

```
[71]    private PreparedStatement stmtForItem  = null;
...
[94]    stmtForItem = con.prepareStatement(
            "INSERT INTO " + ITEM_TBL + " VALUES (?, ?, ?, ?)");
```

First, a `PreparedStatement` object is created by using the `preparedStatement()` method of the `Connection` class. A template SQL query with four placeholders is passed to the method to precompile the template.

```
[152]   stmtForItem.setString(1, itemID);
        stmtForItem.setString(2, itemName);
        stmtForItem.setInt(3,    Integer.parseInt(qty));
        stmtForItem.setString(4, invoiceNo);

[157]   stmtForItem.executeUpdate();
```

Before the query is submitted, the placeholders are filled with the content of the `ITEM_ID`, `ITEM`, `QTY`, and `INVOICE_ID` elements. The `PreparedStatement` class provides a set of methods for setting values with the appropriate datatypes (for example, the `setString()` and `setInt()` methods). Finally, the query is submitted. In the example in Listing 11.4, the `executeUpdate()` method is used, while the `executeQuery()` method is used in Appendix D. The former method does not return the `ResultSet` object and can be used for INSERT and DELETE operations. For SELECT operations, the latter method is used to get the search result.

In the program shown in Listing 11.4, the insertion for the `PO_TBL` is called once. However, the insertion for the `ITEM_TBL` tables is called multiple times. When the same type of query is called repeatedly, using the `PreparedStatement` object is efficient.

## Rollback of Operations

In this program, the insertion operation is applied to two tables. If the insertion operation to the first table succeeds but the insertion to the second table fails, it causes an inconsistency between the tables.

The sequence of the insertion process can be called as a *transaction*. A transaction should be atomic, consistent, isolated, and durable (these features are abbreviated as ACID). To learn more about transaction processing, see the references in Appendix B. If a process in a transaction fails, the transaction as whole should fail and the state should be returned to the point before starting the transaction. For example, if the insertion to the second table failed, the insertion to the first table should be canceled. The cancellation process is called as a *rollback*, which is very important for developing a reliable business system (for example, the two tables might show bank accounts for money transfer).

Most RDBMSs provide a rollback mechanism. In JDBC, the `rollback()` method in the `Connection` class is prepared. In the program shown in Listing 11.4, the `rollback()` command is called when the insertion process for the `ITEM_TBL` table fails after the insertion process for the `PO_TBL` table (line 164). After the insertion to the two tables succeeds, the `commit()` method is called (line 167). To enable this function, you should execute the `setAutoCommit(false)` method before starting the insertion process (line 92).

Now it is time to execute the program. First, we should create a database and tables by loading the `setupXPathDB.ddl` script, shown in Listing 11.5. The script is written in Data Definition Language (DDL) format, which is a common syntax to define database schemas. Assume that we can execute the DB2 command (see the Readme file on the CD-ROM).

**Listing 11.5** DDL file for creating tables (mapping method), chap11/ setupMappingDB.ddl

```
--------------------------------------------------
-- Create database "XMLDB"
--------------------------------------------------
CREATE DATABASE XMLDB;
CONNECT TO XMLDB user db2admin using db2admin;


--------------------------------------------------
-- Create table "PO_TBL"
--------------------------------------------------
```

```
CREATE TABLE "PO_TBL"  (
                "INVOICE_ID"        VARCHAR(32)    NOT NULL,
                "COUNTRY"           VARCHAR(32)    NOT NULL,
                "NAME"              VARCHAR(128)   NOT NULL,
                "STREET"            VARCHAR(128)   NOT NULL,
                PRIMARY KEY         ("INVOICE_ID") ) ;

-----------------------------------------------
-- Create table "ITEM_TBL"
-----------------------------------------------

CREATE TABLE "ITEM_TBL"  (
                "ITEM_ID"           VARCHAR(32)    NOT NULL,
                "ITEM"              VARCHAR(128)   NOT NULL,
                "QTY"               INTEGER        NOT NULL,
                "INVOICE_ID"        VARCHAR(32)    NOT NULL,
                PRIMARY KEY    ("ITEM_ID"),
                FOREIGN KEY    ("INVOICE_ID") REFERENCES PO_TBL
                                    ("INVOICE_ID") ON DELETE
                                    CASCADE) ;

R:\samples>db2 -tvf chap11\setupMappingDB.ddl
...
```

The script creates a database (XMLDB) and two tables (PO_TBL and ITEM_TBL).
Next, we execute the following command. A userid and a password are specified as
system property values (line 183 in Listing 11.4). If the properties are not specified,
the default userid (logon userid) and password are used.

```
R:\samples>java -Dchap11.userid="db2admin" -Dchap11.password=
"db2admin" chap11.XMLTableArchiver chap11\po.xml
Stored with ID 2001-08-31-12345
```

The output indicates that the document po.xml has been stored in the database
with the primary key 2001-08-31-12345.

The next example, shown in Listing 11.6, is the program XMLTableRetriever,
which searches for and deletes purchase order documents with invoice_ID (the
primary key).

**Listing 11.6** Retrieving an XML document, chap11/XMLTableRetriever

```
package chap11;
/**
 * XMLRetriever.java
 *
 */
import java.sql.Connection;
```

```java
import java.sql.Statement;
import java.sql.PreparedStatement;
import java.sql.ResultSet;
import java.sql.DriverManager;
import java.sql.SQLException;
import java.rmi.server.UID;
import java.util.Hashtable;
import java.util.Enumeration;
import org.apache.xml.serialize.XMLSerializer;
import org.apache.xml.serialize.OutputFormat;
import org.w3c.dom.Element;
import org.w3c.dom.Node;
import org.w3c.dom.Document;
import javax.xml.parsers.DocumentBuilderFactory;
import javax.xml.parsers.DocumentBuilder;
import java.io.StringWriter;

public class XMLTableRetriever {

    // Names of database, tables, and elements
    static final String XML_DB           = "XMLDB";
    static final String PO_TBL           = "PO_TBL";
    static final String ITEM_TBL         = "ITEM_TBL";
    static final String JDBC_DRIVER_CLASS =
                        "COM.ibm.db2.jdbc.app.DB2Driver";
    static final String ELT_PO           = "purchaseOrder";
    static final String ELT_SHIPTO       = "shipTo";
    static final String ELT_STREET       = "street";
    static final String ELT_NAME         = "name";
    static final String ELT_ITEMS        = "items";
    static final String ELT_ITEM         = "item";
    static final String ATTR_COUNTRY     = "country";
    static final String ATTR_QTY         = "qty";
    static final String ATTR_INVOICE_ID  = "invoiceNo";
    static final String COLUMN_INVOICE_ID = "INVOICE_ID";
    static final String COLUMN_QTY       = "QTY";
    static final String COLUMN_ITEM      = "ITEM";

    // Connection with database
    Connection con = null;
    // Query statement
    Statement stmt = null;

    static {
        try {
            // Register the driver with DriverManager
            Class.forName(JDBC_DRIVER_CLASS);
        } catch (Exception e) {
```

```
                    e.printStackTrace();
            }
    }

    /**
     * Constructor
     *
     */
    XMLTableRetriever(String userid, String password) {
        try {
            // Creates connection
            con = DriverManager.getConnection("jdbc:db2:"+XML_DB,
                                              userid,
                                              password);
            // Creates statement
            stmt = con.createStatement();
        } catch (SQLException e) {
            e.printStackTrace();
        }
    }

    /**
     * Search an XML document with document id
     *
     * @param docId document ID assigned at registration process
     * @see XMLArchiver
     */
    public Document searchByDocumentID(String docId) {
        String queryForPOTbl = "SELECT * FROM " +
            PO_TBL + " WHERE " + COLUMN_INVOICE_ID + "='" +
            docId + "'";
        String invoiceID = null;
        String country   = null;
        String name      = null;
        String street    = null;
        try {
            // Get result of the query
            ResultSet rs = stmt.executeQuery(queryForPOTbl);
            if (rs.next()) {
                invoiceID = rs.getString(1);
                country   = rs.getString(2);
                name      = rs.getString(3);
                street    = rs.getString(4);
            } else {
                System.out.println("Not found");
                return null;
            }
```

[82]

```
                      // Creates DOM tree from PO_TBL
                      Document doc =
                            createPoTree(invoiceID, country, name, street);
                      // Appends items to the tree
                      doc = appendItems(invoiceID, doc);
                      // Serializes it
                      System.out.println(toString(doc));
                      rs.close();
                      return doc;
                  } catch (Exception e) {
                      e.printStackTrace();
                  }
                  return null;
              }

              /**
               * Create DOM Tree from PO_TBL
               *
               * @param invoiceID invoiceID
               * @param country country
               * @param name name
               * @param street street
               * @return generated <code>Document</code> object
               */
[127]         Document createPoTree(String invoiceID,
                                    String country,
                                    String name,
                                    String street) {
                  Document doc = null;
                  try {
                      // Creates document object
                      DocumentBuilderFactory factory =
                                      DocumentBuilderFactory.newInstance();
                      DocumentBuilder builder =
                                      factory.newDocumentBuilder();
                      doc = builder.newDocument();

                      // Constructs DOM tree
                      Element rootElt = doc.createElement(ELT_PO);
                      rootElt.setAttribute(ATTR_INVOICE_ID, invoiceID);
                      doc.appendChild(rootElt);

                      Element shipToElt = doc.createElement(ELT_SHIPTO);
                      rootElt.appendChild(shipToElt);
                      rootElt.appendChild(doc.createElement(ELT_ITEMS));

                      Element nameElt = doc.createElement(ELT_NAME);
                      shipToElt.setAttribute(ATTR_COUNTRY, country);
```

```
                    shipToElt.appendChild(nameElt);
                    nameElt.appendChild(doc.createTextNode(name));

                    Element streetElt = doc.createElement(ELT_STREET);
                    shipToElt.appendChild(streetElt);
                    streetElt.appendChild(doc.createTextNode(street));
            } catch (Exception e) {
                e.printStackTrace();
            } finally {
                return doc;
            }
    }


    /**
     * Delete an XML document with document id
     *
     * @param docId document ID assigned at registration process
     * @see XMLArchiver
     */
    public void deleteByDocumentID(String docId) {
        String SQLquery = "DELETE " + " FROM " +
                            PO_TBL + " WHERE " + COLUMN_INVOICE_ID
                            + " = '" + docId + "'";

        try {
            int deletedLineNo = stmt.executeUpdate(SQLquery);
            // Only one document should be deleted since
            // document id is unique
            if (deletedLineNo == 1) {
                System.out.println("Document " +docId +
                                    " has been deleted");
            } else {
                System.out.println("deletion failed");
            }
        } catch (Exception e) {
            e.printStackTrace();
        }
    }

    public Document appendItems(String invoiceID, Document doc) {
        String item = null;
        int     qty = 0;
        String queryForItemTbl = "SELECT * FROM " +
            ITEM_TBL + " WHERE " + COLUMN_INVOICE_ID + "='" +
            invoiceID + "'";
        Element itemsElt =
            (Element)doc.getElementsByTagName(ELT_ITEMS).item(0);
        try {
```

```
            ResultSet rs = stmt.executeQuery(queryForItemTbl);
            while (rs.next()) {
                item      = rs.getString(COLUMN_ITEM);
                qty       = rs.getInt(COLUMN_QTY);
                Element itemElt = doc.createElement(ELT_ITEM);
                itemElt.setAttribute(ATTR_QTY,
                                     new Integer(qty).toString());
                itemElt.appendChild(doc.createTextNode(item));
                itemsElt.appendChild(itemElt);
            }
        } catch (Exception e) {
            e.printStackTrace();
        }
        return doc;
    }
    /**
     * Convert <code>Document</code> object to string
     *
     * @param doc a <code>Document</code> object
     * @return its serialization
     */
    public static String toString(Document doc) {
        // Serializes the DOM tree as an XML document
        OutputFormat formatter = new OutputFormat();
        formatter.setPreserveSpace(true);

        // The XML document will be serialized as string.
        StringWriter out = new StringWriter() ;
        XMLSerializer serializer =
                        new XMLSerializer(out, formatter);
        try {
            serializer.serialize(doc);
        } catch (Exception e) {
            e.printStackTrace();
        }
        out.flush();
        return out.toString();
    }

    public static void main(String[] argv) {
        if (argv.length != 2) {
            System.err.println("Usage: XMLTableRetriever [-s|-d]"
                              +" docid");
            System.exit(1);
        }
            // Userid and password are specified as
            // System properties
```

```
            String userid = System.getProperty("chap11.userid");
            String password =
                            System.getProperty("chap11.password");
            XMLTableRetriever arc =
                        new XMLTableRetriever(userid, password);
        if (argv[0].equals("-s"))
            arc.searchByDocumentID(argv[1]);
        else if (argv[0].equals("-d"))
            arc.deleteByDocumentID(argv[1]);
        else
            System.out.println("Not supported: " + argv[1]);
    }

}
```

Comments embedded in the program show its procedure. It takes two arguments: a flag that means search (-s) or delete (-d) and an invoice ID. The method searchByDocumentID() (line 82) constructs an SQL query for the PO_TBL table. For example, if invoice_ID is 2001-08-31-12345, the SQL query is as follows:

```
SELECT * FROM PO_TBL WHERE invoice_ID='2001-08-31-12345'
```

The createPoTree() method (line 127) generates a purchase order document from the search result for the query. Recall that we showed various techniques to generate a DOM tree and serialize it in Chapter 3.

This program submits two queries to PO_TBL and ITEM_TBL. We can get all the needed data with a single call by joining the tables. The SQL query looks like this.

```
SELECT A.COUNTRY, A.NAME, A.STREET, B.ITEM, B.QTY
from PO_TBL AS A, ITEM_TBL AS B where (A.invoice_ID='2001-08-31-12345')
AND (A.invoice_ID = B.invoice_ID)
```

The result for the query contains the data for two tables. However, each record for items contains duplicated COUNTRY, NAME, and STREET information. Furthermore, the join operation involves a cost in general. Therefore, we should determine which method is better based on the actual environment where this kind of program runs. For example, if our database is located on a remote machine and network latency is serious, the cost for two query submissions is more than the cost for the table joining and the redundant data transmission.

Note that in the deletion process, a record is deleted only from the PO_TBL table. We defined a constraint for the tables in the schema shown in Listing 11.5. The constraint automatically deletes related records in ITEM_TBL. If there is no such constraint, you should manage the deletion processes for the two tables.

The following is the result for the searching and deletion processes.

```
R:\samples>java -Dchap11.userid="db2admin" -Dchap11.password="db2admin"
chap11.XMLTableRetriever -s 2001-08-31-12345
<?xml version="1.0" encoding="UTF-8"?>
<purchaseOrder invoiceNo="2001-08-31-12345"><shipTo country="US">
<name>Alice Smith</name><street>123 Maple Street</street></shipTo>
<items><item qty="2">ThinkPad
X21</item><item qty="1">ThinkPad T22</item></items></purchaseOrder>

R:\samples>java chap11.XMLTableRetriever -d 2001-08-31-12345
Document 2001-08-31-12345 has been deleted
```

## 11.5.2 XPath Method

Section 11.5.1 described a sample program that decomposed an XML document and stored data in two tables by mapping schemas for XML and a database (the mapping method). In this section, we introduce another approach (the XPath method). In this approach, a set of an XPath expression and its contents is stored in a table. In the mapping method, we defined a table for a specific schema. In the XPath approach, the table is independent from any specific schema, so any XML document can be stored in the table. We use the following three classes.

- IndexCreator extracts a set of an XPath expressions and text contents, and attribute values. It is called from XPathArchiver.

- XPathArchiver stores the set into the database.

- XPathRetriever extracts and deletes the set from the database.

Listing 11.7 shows the source code for IndexCreator.

**Listing 11.7** Creating an XPath index, chap11/IndexCreator.java

```java
package chap11;
/**
 * IndexCreator.java
 *
 */
import java.util.Hashtable;
import org.apache.xerces.parsers.DOMParser;
import org.w3c.dom.Element;
import org.w3c.dom.Node;
import org.w3c.dom.Document;
import org.w3c.dom.Attr;
import org.w3c.dom.NodeList;
import org.w3c.dom.NamedNodeMap;
```

```
          public class IndexCreator {

              // Stores xpath-content relationship
              private Hashtable pathValueTbl = new Hashtable();

              public Hashtable getTable() {
                  return pathValueTbl;
              }

              /**
               * Constructor
               *
               */
              public IndexCreator () {
              }

              /**
               * Search text nodes with XPath and store them to hash table
               *
               * @param node node to be indexed
               */
              public void makeIndexTbl (Node node) {
               makeIndexTbl(node, "/"+node.getNodeName()+"[1]");
              }
```
[41]
```
              public void makeIndexTbl (Node node, String xpath) {
                  // Searches Text nodes and stores them with xpath
```
[43]
```
                  if (node.getNodeType() == Node.TEXT_NODE) {
                      if (!isWhitespaces(node.getNodeValue())) {
                          pathValueTbl.put(xpath, node.getNodeValue());
                          System.out.println(xpath+"="+node.getNodeValue());
                      }
                      // Searches attribute values and stores them with xpath
                  } else if (node.getNodeType() == Node.ELEMENT_NODE) {
                      NamedNodeMap nmap = node.getAttributes();
                      for (int i = 0; i < nmap.getLength(); i++) {
                          String attrXpath = xpath + "/@" +
          nmap.item(i).getNodeName();
                          System.out.println(attrXpath+"="+
                                              nmap.item(i).getNodeValue());
                          pathValueTbl.put(xpath, nmap.item(i).getNodeValue());
                      }
                  }
                  // Called recursively
                  for (Node child = node.getFirstChild();
                       child != null;
                       child = child.getNextSibling()) {
```

```
                if (child.getNodeType() == Node.ELEMENT_NODE) {
                    makeIndexTbl(child, xpath + "/" + child.getNodeName()
                    + "[" +
                                getPosition(child) + "]");
                } else if (child.getNodeType() == Node.TEXT_NODE) {
                    makeIndexTbl(child, xpath);
                }
            }
    }
    /**
     * Return the position of the node.
     *
     * @param node <code>Node</code>
     * @return The position of the node in the all siblings
     * that has same element name
     */
    int getPosition(Node node) {
        if (node.equals(node.getOwnerDocument())) {
            return 0;
        }
        NodeList nl = node.getParentNode().getChildNodes();
        int j = 1;
        for (int i = 0; i < nl.getLength(); i++) {
            if (node.getNodeName().equals(
                                nl.item(i).getNodeName())) {
                if (node.equals(nl.item(i))) {
                    return j;
                } else {
                    j++;
                }
            }
        }
        return 0;
    }

    boolean isWhitespaces (String str) {
        for (int i = 0; i < str.length(); i++) {
            if (str.charAt(i) != '\n' &&
                str.charAt(i) != '\t' &&
                str.charAt(i) != '\r' &&
                str.charAt(i) != ' ') {
                return false;
            }
        }
        return true;
    }
}
```

The procedure of this program is as follows:

1.  Gets a DOM tree and traverses the nodes of the tree (line 41).
2.  When a text element or an attribute is found, calculates the XPath and stores it with the content in a hash table (line 43).

The method `makeIndexTable()` (line 41) is the heart of this program. The method visits all child nodes for a given node and checks whether they are text or attribute nodes.

When a text node or an attribute node is found, the method stores an XPath expression with the text content or attribute value in the hash table `pathValue Table`. The `makeIndexTable()` method is called recursively to construct an XPath expression. Section 7.3.2 in Chapter 7 introduces another method to get an XPath expression for a given node.

The class `XMLPathArchiver` extracts a set of the XPath expression and its contents from the hash table. Before explaining the program, we define a schema for two tables used for the program. We use the `XMLDB` database used in the previous section and create two tables: `DOCUMENT_TBL` and `NODE_VALUE_TBL`.

Listing 11.8 shows a configuration file to create the tables and set constraints.

**Listing 11.8**  DDL file for creating tables (XPath method), `chap11/setupXPathDB.ddl`

```
-------------------------------------------------
-- Create database "XMLDB"
-------------------------------------------------
CREATE DATABASE XMLDB;
CONNECT TO XMLDB user db2admin using db2admin;

-------------------------------------------------
-- Create table "DOCUMENT_TBL"
-------------------------------------------------

CREATE TABLE "DOCUMENT_TBL"   (
               "DOCUMENT_ID"      VARCHAR(32)   NOT NULL,
               "STORED_TIME"      TIMESTAMP     NOT NULL WITH
                                                DEFAULT CURRENT
                                                TIMESTAMP,
               "ROOT_ELEMENT"     VARCHAR(128)  NOT NULL,
               "DOCUMENT_CONTENT" BLOB(102400)  LOGGED COMPACT NOT
                                                NULL,
               PRIMARY KEY        ("DOCUMENT_ID") ) ;

-------------------------------------------------
-- Create table "NODE_VALUE_TBL"
-------------------------------------------------
```

```
CREATE TABLE "NODE_VALUE_TBL"  (
            "NODE_ID"         VARCHAR(32) NOT  NULL,
            "PATH_STRING"     VARCHAR(2048) NOT NULL,
            "CONTENT_STRING" VARCHAR(256)  NOT NULL,
            "DOCUMENT_ID"     VARCHAR(32)   NOT NULL,
            PRIMARY KEY       ("NODE_ID"),
            FOREIGN KEY       ("DOCUMENT_ID")  REFERENCES
                                               DOCUMENT_TBL
                                               ("DOCUMENT_ID")
                                               ON DELETE CASCADE) ;
```

The DOCUMENT_TBL table contains the following columns.

- DOCUMENT_ID(VARCHAR) represents an identifier of an XML document (the column is used for the primary key). Because the schema for the XML document is unknown, it is impossible to use data that appeared in the document. Therefore, a unique value is generated and inserted.

- STORED_TIME(TIMESTAMP) represents a stored date. The value is automatically generated by the database (see the constraint to do so in Listing 11.8).

- ROOT_ELEMENT(VARCHAR) represents the root element of an XML document.

- DOCUMENT_CONTENT(BLOB) represents an XML document as a whole.

In the schema shown in Listing 11.8, the BLOB type is used for storing an XML document. CLOB is another solution for a datatype in which to store an XML document. When the CLOB type is used, the string to be stored is converted with a predefined encoding. It sometimes causes a problem, as mentioned in Chapter 3, Section 3.6. The advantage of using CLOB is that it can search with an SQL query or other vendor-specific searching methods. The DB2 XML Extender provides a special datatype called XMLCLOB that can be searched for by using an XPath expression.

The NODE_VALUE_TBL table contains the PATH_STRING column for an XPath expression, CONTENT_STRING for its content, DOCUMENT_ID for the foreign key of DOCUMENT_TBL, and NODE_ID for the unique identifier (the primary key). An example of NODE_VALUE_TBL is shown in Table 11.3.

To create the tables, we need to load the script file setupXPathDB.ddl.

```
R:\samples>db2 -tvf chap11\setupXPathDB.ddl
...
```

The source code for XMLPathArchiver, which extracts XPath expressions by using the IndexCreator class and stores them, is shown in Listing 11.9.

**Listing 11.9** Archiving XPath expressions, `chap11/XPathArchiver.java`

```java
package chap11;
/**
 * XPathArchiver.java
 *
 */
import java.sql.Connection;
import java.sql.Statement;
import java.sql.PreparedStatement;
import java.sql.ResultSet;
import java.sql.DriverManager;
import java.sql.SQLException;
import java.rmi.server.UID;
import java.util.Hashtable;
import java.util.Enumeration;
import java.io.File;
import javax.xml.parsers.DocumentBuilderFactory;
import javax.xml.parsers.DocumentBuilder;
import org.apache.xml.serialize.XMLSerializer;
import org.apache.xml.serialize.OutputFormat;
import org.w3c.dom.Element;
import org.w3c.dom.Node;
import org.w3c.dom.Document;
import java.io.StringWriter;
import share.util.MyErrorHandler;

public class XPathArchiver {

    // Names of database, tables, and elements
    static final String JDBC_DRIVER_CLASS =
                            "COM.ibm.db2.jdbc.app.DB2Driver";
    static final String XML_DB            = "XMLDB";
    static final String DOCUMENT_TBL      = "DOCUMENT_TBL";
    static final String NODE_VALUE_TBL    = "NODE_VALUE_TBL";
    static final String COL_DOCUMENT_ID   = "DOCUMENT_ID";
    static final String COL_DOCUMENT_CONTENT= "DOCUMENT_CONTENT";
    static final String COL_ROOT_ELEMENT  = "ROOT_ELEMENT";

    // Connection with database
    Connection con = null;
    // Prepared statement for storing data into DOCUMENT_TBL
    PreparedStatement stmtForDocTbl  = null;
    // Prepared statement for storing data into NODE_VALUE_TBL
    PreparedStatement stmtForNodeTbl = null;

    // Register the driver with DriverManager
```

```
static {
    try {
        Class.forName(JDBC_DRIVER_CLASS);
    } catch (Exception e) {
        e.printStackTrace();
    }
}

/**
 * Constructor
 *
 */
public XPathArchiver (String userid, String password) {
    try {
        // Creates connection
        con = DriverManager.getConnection("jdbc:db2:"+XML_DB,
                                          userid,
                                          password);
        // Explicit commit should be needed
        con.setAutoCommit(false);
        // Creates prepared statement to insert data to
        // DOCUMENT_TBL
        // A Timestamp (STORED_DATE) will be set at database.
        stmtForDocTbl  = con.prepareStatement(
                        "INSERT INTO " + DOCUMENT_TBL +
                        "(" + COL_DOCUMENT_ID      + ", "
                            + COL_DOCUMENT_CONTENT + ", "
                            + COL_ROOT_ELEMENT
                            + ") VALUES(?, ?, ?)");
        // Creates prepared statement to insert data to
        // NODE_TBL
        stmtForNodeTbl = con.prepareStatement("INSERT INTO "
                            + NODE_VALUE_TBL +
                            " VALUES(?, ?, ?, ?)");
    } catch (java.sql.SQLException e) {
        e.printStackTrace();
    }
}

/**
 * Store data into database
 *
 * @param doc a <code>Document</code> to be stored
 */
public void store(Document doc) {
    try {
        // Generates an unique id
```

[90]

```
                      UID documentId = new UID();
                      // Sets data to the prepared statement for
                      // DOCUMENT_TBL
                      stmtForDocTbl.setString(1, documentId.toString());
[97]                  stmtForDocTbl.setBytes (2, toString(doc).getBytes());
                      stmtForDocTbl.setString(3, doc.getDocumentElement().
                                        getTagName());
                      // Executes it
                      try {
[102]                     stmtForDocTbl.executeUpdate();
                          System.out.println("Stored with ID " +
                                        documentId.toString());
                          // Sets data to the prepared statement
                          // for NODE_TBL
                          IndexCreator idx = new IndexCreator();
                          // Creates XPath-content table
[109]           idx.makeIndexTbl(doc.getDocumentElement());
[110]                     Hashtable tbl = idx.getTable();
                          Enumeration enum = tbl.keys();
                          // For all xpath expressions with contents,
                          while (enum.hasMoreElements()) {
                              String path = (String)enum.nextElement();
                              String content = (String)tbl.get(path);
                              // Generates an unique id for each xpath
[117]                         UID nodeId = new UID();
                              // Sets data
                              stmtForNodeTbl.setString(1,
                                            nodeId.toString());
                              stmtForNodeTbl.setString(2, path);
                              stmtForNodeTbl.setString(3, content);
                              stmtForNodeTbl.setString(4,
                                            documentId.toString());
                              // Executes it
[126]                         stmtForNodeTbl.executeUpdate();
                          }
                      } catch (SQLException e) {
                          // Rolls back the insertion processes
                          System.out.println("SQL Error: all the operation"
                                            + "to database is canceled");
                          con.rollback();
                          System.exit(1);
                      }
                      // Commits all operation
                      con.commit();
                  } catch (SQLException e) {
                      e.printStackTrace();
```

```
            }
        }

        /**
         * Convert <code>Document</code> object to string
         *
         * @param doc a <code>Document</code> object
         * @return its serialization
         */
        public static String toString(Document doc) {
            // Serializes the DOM tree as an XML document
            OutputFormat formatter = new OutputFormat();
            formatter.setPreserveSpace(true);
            // The XML document will be serialized as string
            StringWriter out = new StringWriter() ;
            XMLSerializer serializer =
                                new XMLSerializer(out, formatter);
            try {
                serializer.asDOMSerializer().serialize(doc);
            } catch (Exception e) {
                e.printStackTrace();
            }
            out.flush();
            return out.toString();
        }

        public static void main(String[] argv) {
            if (argv.length != 1) {
                System.err.println("Usage: XPathArchiver filename");
                System.exit(1);
            }
            try {
                // Userid and password are specified as
                // System properties
                String userid = System.getProperty("chap11.userid");
                String password =
                                System.getProperty("chap11.password");
                XPathArchiver arc =
                                new XPathArchiver(userid, password);
                IndexCreator  idx = new IndexCreator();
                // Parses input document
                DocumentBuilderFactory factory =
                                DocumentBuilderFactory.newInstance();
                DocumentBuilder builder =
                                factory.newDocumentBuilder();
                // Sets an ErrorHandler
                builder.setErrorHandler(new MyErrorHandler());
```

[180]

```
                    // Parses the document
                    Document doc = builder.parse(new File(argv[0]));
                    // Stores the document
                    arc.store(doc);
                } catch (Exception e) {
                    e.printStackTrace();
                }
            }
        }
```

The program works as follows:

1. Parses an XML document and creates a DOM tree (line 180).
2. Passes the root element in the document to the `makeIndexTbl()` method of the `IndexCreator` class (line 109).
3. Stores an XML document (line 102).
4. Stores a set of an XPath expression and its content in the tables (line 126).

The most important process in this program is storing the set to the tables (`DOCUMENT_TBL` and `NODE_VALUE_TBL`).

First, two prepared statement objects are created for the two tables. The reason the object is used for the (single) insertion operation to the `DOCUMENT_TBL` table is that a `BLOB` datatype should be embedded in the query. This is done by using the `setBytes()` method (line 97).

The `store()` method first extracts information from a DOM tree to submit an insertion query to the `DOCUMENT_TBL` table (line 90). It is similar to the process shown in Listing 11.4.

```
[117]  UID nodeId = new UID();
       // Sets data
       stmtForNodeTbl.setString(1, nodeId.toString());
       stmtForNodeTbl.setString(2, path);
       stmtForNodeTbl.setString(3, content);
       stmtForNodeTbl.setString(4,
       documentId.toString());
       // Executes it
       stmtForNodeTbl.executeUpdate();
```

To generate a unique ID, the `java.rmi.UID` class is used. The `UID` object generates a string value that is unique on a machine where JVM is running. The XML document itself is converted to a byte array and set in the `PreparedStatement` object. After values in the object are set, the `executeUpdate()` method is called (line 126).

Next, the `store()` method creates an `IndexCreator` object and calls the `makeIdxTbl()` method (line 109), and gets a hash table that contains a set of an XPath and its contents (line 110). By using data in the hash table, an SQL query for the `NODE_VALUE_TBL` table is created and submitted (line 126).

The following is the result of executing `XPathArchiver`. The userid and password for accessing the database `XMLDB` are specified as system properties.

```
R:\samples>java -Dchap11.userid="db2admin" -Dchap11.password=
"db2admin" chap11.XPathArchiver chap11\po.xml
Stored with ID 35b39e75:e8b91faee7:-8000
/purchaseOrder[1]/@orderDate=1999-10-20
/purchaseOrder[1]/shipTo[1]/@country=US
/purchaseOrder[1]/shipTo[1]/name[1]=Alice Smith
/purchaseOrder[1]/shipTo[1]/street[1]=123 Maple Street
/purchaseOrder[1]/items[1]/item[1]/@qty=2
/purchaseOrder[1]/items[1]/item[1]=ThinkPad X21
/purchaseOrder[1]/items[1]/item[2]/@qty=1
/purchaseOrder[1]/items[1]/item[2]=ThinkPad T22
```

The value "35b39e75:e8b91faee7:-8000" is the identifier for the XML document (`po.xml`) generated by the `java.rmi.UID` class.

After we execute the program, the database contains an XML document (`po.xml`). The next program, shown in Listing 11.10, retrieves it.

**Listing 11.10** Retrieving an XML document, `chap11/XPathRetriever.java`

```java
package chap11;
/**
 * XPathRetriever.java
 *
 */
import java.sql.*;
import java.rmi.server.UID;
import java.util.Hashtable;
import java.util.Enumeration;
import java.io.File;
import javax.xml.parsers.DocumentBuilderFactory;
import javax.xml.parsers.DocumentBuilder;
import org.apache.xml.serialize.XMLSerializer;
import org.apache.xml.serialize.OutputFormat;
import org.w3c.dom.Element;
import org.w3c.dom.Node;
import org.w3c.dom.Document;
import org.xml.sax.InputSource;
```

```
import java.io.StringWriter;
import share.util.MyErrorHandler;

public class XPathRetriever {

    // Names of database, tables, and elements
    static final String XML_DB              = "XMLDB";
    static final String LOGIN_USER_ID       = "db2admin";
    static final String LOGIN_PASSWORD      = "db2admin";
    static final String DOCUMENT_TBL        = "DOCUMENT_TBL";
    static final String NODE_VALUE_TBL      = "NODE_VALUE_TBL";
    static final String COL_DOCUMENT_ID     = "DOCUMENT_ID";
    static final String COL_DOCUMENT_CONTENT = "DOCUMENT_CONTENT";
    static final String JDBC_DRIVER_CLASS   =
                                "COM.ibm.db2.jdbc.app.DB2Driver";
    // Connection with database
    Connection con = null;
    // Query statement
    Statement stmt = null;

    static {
        try {
            // Register the driver with DriverManager
            Class.forName(JDBC_DRIVER_CLASS);
        } catch (Exception e) {
            e.printStackTrace();
        }
    }

    /**
     * Constructor
     *
     */
    XPathRetriever(String userid, String password) {
        try {
            // Creates connection
            con = DriverManager.getConnection("jdbc:db2:"+XML_DB,
                                              userid,
                                              password);
            // Creates statement
            stmt = con.createStatement();
        } catch (java.sql.SQLException e) {
            e.printStackTrace();
        }
    }

    /**
```

```
          * Search an XML document with document id
          *
          * @param docId document ID assigned at registration process
          * @see XMLArchiver
          */
[71]      public void searchByDocumentID(String docId) {
              String SQLquery = "SELECT "+ COL_DOCUMENT_CONTENT +
                              " FROM " + DOCUMENT_TBL + " WHERE " +
                              COL_DOCUMENT_ID +" = '" + docId + "'";
                  try {
                      // Get result of the query
                      ResultSet rs = stmt.executeQuery(SQLquery);
                      // Checks the existence of result
                      if (!rs.next()) {
                          System.out.println("Not found");
                          return;
                      }
                      // Display Result
                      // Parses input document
                      DocumentBuilderFactory factory =
                                  DocumentBuilderFactory.newInstance();
                      DocumentBuilder builder =
                                  factory.newDocumentBuilder();
                      // Sets an ErrorHandler
                      builder.setErrorHandler(new MyErrorHandler());
                      // Only one document should be retrieved since
                      // document id is unique
                      // Gets data stream from results set
                      Document doc = builder.parse(
                                  new InputSource(rs.getBinaryStream(1)));
                      System.out.println(toString(doc));
                      rs.close();
                  } catch (Exception e) {
                      e.printStackTrace();
                  }
          }

          /**
          * Delete an XML document with document id
          *
          * @param docId document ID assigned at registration process
          * @see XMLArchiver
          */
[109]     public void deleteByDocumentID(String docId) {
              String SQLquery = "DELETE " + " FROM " +
                              DOCUMENT_TBL + " WHERE "+
```

```
                              COL_DOCUMENT_ID +" = '" + docId + "'";
        try {
            int deletedLineNo = stmt.executeUpdate(SQLquery);
            // Only one document should be deleted since document
            // id is unique
            if (deletedLineNo == 1) {
                System.out.println("Document " +docId +
                                    " has been deleted");
            } else {
                System.out.println("deletion failed");
            }
        } catch (Exception e) {
            e.printStackTrace();
        }
    }

    /**
     * Convert <code>Document</code> object to string
     *
     * @param doc a <code>Document</code> object
     * @return its serialization
     */
    public static String toString(Document doc) {
        // Serializes the DOM tree as an XML document
        OutputFormat formatter = new OutputFormat();
        formatter.setPreserveSpace(true);

        // The XML document will be serialized as string.
        StringWriter out = new StringWriter() ;
        XMLSerializer serializer = new XMLSerializer(out,
                                formatter);
        try {
            serializer.asDOMSerializer().serialize(doc);
        } catch (Exception e) {
            e.printStackTrace();
        }
        out.flush();
        return out.toString();
    }

    public static void main(String[] argv) {
        if (argv.length != 2) {
            System.err.println("Usage: XPathRetriever " +
                    "[-s|-d] docid");
            System.exit(1);
        }
        try {
```

```
            // Userid and password are specified as
            // System properties
            String userid = System.getProperty("chap11.userid");
            String password =
                            System.getProperty("chap11.password");
            XPathRetriever arc = new XPathRetriever(userid,
                                                    password);

            if (argv[0].equals("-s"))
                arc.searchByDocumentID(argv[1]);
            else if (argv[0].equals("-d"))
                arc.deleteByDocumentID(argv[1]);
            else
                System.out.println("Not supported: "
                                    + argv[1]);
        } catch (Exception e) {
            e.printStackTrace();
        }
    }
}
```

The XPathRetriever program retrieves or deletes an XML document with an identifier assigned when it is stored. The program retrieves an XML document from the DOCUMENT_TBL table and returns it. The following is the result of the searching and deletion process.

```
R:\samples>java -Dchap11.userid="db2admin" -Dchap11.password=
"db2admin" chap11.XPathRetriever -s 35b39e75:e8b91faee7:-8000
<purchaseOrder orderDate="1999-10-20">
    <shipTo country="US">
        <name>Alice Smith</name>
        <street>123 Maple Street</street>
    </shipTo>
    <items>
    <item qty="2">ThinkPad X21</item>
    <item qty="1">ThinkPad T22</item>
    </items>
</purchaseOrder>

R:\samples>java -Dchap11.userid="db2admin" -Dchap11.password=
"db2admin" chap11.XPathRetriever -d 35b39e75:e8b91faee7:-8000
Document 35b39e75:e8b91faee7:-8000 has been deleted
```

The searching process is handled by searchByDocumentID() (line 71) and the deletion process is done by the deleteByDocumentID() method (line 109). The details are not covered here, but it is easy to read the source code and determine what these methods do.

The last sample program in this section searches for an XML document in a database with XPath. The program, `XMLRetrieverWithXPath`, is included on the CD-ROM.

The class takes two arguments. The first is (a subset of) an XPath expression, and the second is its value. For example, a pair of `"/purchaseOrder/items/item"` and `"ThinkPad X21"` means the program should search an XML document that has an `item` element that contains `"ThinkPad X21"`, and the element is the child of an `item` element that is a child of a `purchaseOrder` element.

In the `NODE_VALUE_TBL` table, an XPath expression is stored with a position index like `/purchaseOrder[1]/shipTo[1]/name[1]`. It is included by the expression `/purchaseOrder/items/item`, but it is not matched literally. Our program converts an XPath expression into an SQL string. For example:

1. `/purchaseOrder/items/item` is converted to `/purchaseOrder[%]/items[%]/item[%]`. "%" is a wildcard, so any string can appear in this position. The expression is used with the `LIKE` operator in an SQL query.
2. `//item` is converted to `%/item`.
3. `item` is converted to `%/item`.

The following is an example of using this program.

```
R:\samples>java -Dchap11.userid=db2admin -Dchap11.password=db2admin
chap11.XPathArchiver chap11\po.xml
Stored with ID 35b3a6e1:e8b961b433:-8000
/purchaseOrder[1]/@orderDate=1999-10-20
/purchaseOrder[1]/shipTo[1]/@country=US
/purchaseOrder[1]/shipTo[1]/name[1]=Alice Smith
/purchaseOrder[1]/shipTo[1]/street[1]=123 Maple Street
/purchaseOrder[1]/items[1]/item[1]/@qty=2
/purchaseOrder[1]/items[1]/item[1]=ThinkPad X21
/purchaseOrder[1]/items[1]/item[2]/@qty=1
/purchaseOrder[1]/items[1]/item[2]=ThinkPad T22

R:\samples>java -Dchap11.userid=db2admin -Dchap11.password=db2admin
chap11.XPathArchiver chap02\department.xml
Stored with ID 3a6c26ef:e8b961df3b:-8000
/department[1]/employee[1]/@id=J.D
/department[1]/employee[1]/name[1]=John Doe
/department[1]/employee[1]/email[1]=John.Doe@foo.com
/department[1]/employee[2]/@id=B.S
/department[1]/employee[2]/name[1]=Bob Smith
/department[1]/employee[2]/email[1]=Bob.Smith@foo.com
/department[1]/employee[3]/@id=A.M
/department[1]/employee[3]/name[1]=Alice Miller
/department[1]/employee[3]/url[1]/@href=http://www.foo.com/~amiller/
```

```
R:\samples>java -Dchap11.userid=db2admin -Dchap11.password=db2admin
chap11.XMLRetrieverWithXPath "/purchaseOrder/items/item" "ThinkPad
X21" 35b3a6e1:e8b961b433:-8000

R:\samples>java -Dchap11.userid=db2admin -Dchap11.password=db2admin
chap11.XMLRetrieverWithXPath "@id" "J.D" 3a6c26ef:e8b961df3b:-8000

R:\samples>java -Dchap11.userid=db2admin -Dchap11.password=db2admin
chap11.XMLRetrieverWithXPath "/department[1]/employee[3]/name[1]"
"Alice Miller" 3a6c26ef:e8b961df3b:-8000
```

## 11.6 A Servlet for Accessing a Database

In previous sections, we showed how to map between an XML document and
tables and store and search for an XML document. All the programs we showed
are standalone programs. As shown in Figure 11.1, a practical three-tier application
implements business logic on an application server with Servlet or Enterprise
JavaBeans. In this section and the next, we explain how to accomplish such a
scenario.

The program XMLDBServlet, shown in Listing 11.11, is a servlet that calls the
XMLTableRetriever class, shown in Listing 11.6. The servlet receives an XML
document that contains an invoice ID via HTTP, searches the database with the
ID, and returns the result document. This class is a subclass of chap10.
GenericDOMServlet.java, shown in Listing 10.9 in Chapter 10.

**Listing 11.11** A Java servlet to access the database, chap11/XMLDBServlet.java

```java
package chap11;
/**
 * XMLDBServlet.java
 *
 */
import javax.servlet.*;
import javax.servlet.http.*;
import java.io.*;
import java.net.*;
import java.util.*;

import org.w3c.dom.Document;
import org.w3c.dom.Element;
import org.xml.sax.InputSource;
import org.apache.xml.serialize.XMLSerializer;
import org.apache.xml.serialize.OutputFormat;
```

```
        import javax.xml.parsers.DocumentBuilderFactory;
        import javax.xml.parsers.DocumentBuilder;
        import chap10.GenericDOMServlet;

        public class XMLDBServlet extends GenericDOMServlet {

            XMLTableRetriever arc;

[25]        public void init() throws ServletException {
        // Gets userid and password
        String userid   = getInitParameter("USERID");
        String password = getInitParameter("PASSWORD");
        // This constructor initiate connection to database
        arc = new XMLTableRetriever(userid, password);
            }

            /**
             * Handle request using GenericDOMServlet
             */
[36]        public Document doProcess(HttpServletRequest req,
                        HttpServletResponse res,
                        Document reqDoc) {
[39]    Document resDoc = null;
        try {
                Element root = reqDoc.getDocumentElement();
                String invoiceID = root.getFirstChild().getNodeValue();
                // Searches for documents with id
                resDoc = arc.searchByDocumentID(invoiceID);
                if (resDoc == null) {
            // Creates an XML document for the error
            DocumentBuilder builder =
                    DocumentBuilderFactory.newInstance().
                    newDocumentBuilder();
            resDoc = builder.newDocument();
            resDoc.appendChild(resDoc.createElement("Error"));
                }
            } catch (Exception e) {
                e.printStackTrace();
            }
[56]        return resDoc;
            }

            public String getServletInfo() {
                return "A XMLDB servlet";
            }
            public void destroy(){
            }

        }
```

We described basic Servlet programming in Chapter 10, Section 10.2. We discuss some important points here.

- Connection to a database is processed in the `init()` method (line 25). In this method, an `XMLTableArchiver` object is created, and the connection is initiated. The connection is kept until the servlet is destroyed. If the process is implemented by CGI, the connection process is invoked for each CGI execution. As shown the previous section, a connection pool can be used in the `init()` method. Some application servers provide a vendor-specific way to connect to a database. Section 10.2.3 shows some things to consider when you use multithreaded programming in servlets.

- The `doProcess()` method (line 36) gets two streams for input and output, and a `Document` object. The class is a subclass of the `chap10.GenericDOM Servlet` class used to handle the `charset` and MIME type of the input XML document correctly (see the discussion in Section 10.2.2). The input document is parsed, and an ID for an XML document to be searched is extracted (line 56). The `searchByDocumentID()` method of the `XMLTableArchiver` class (see Listing 11.6) is called to submit a query to a database. The retrieved document is returned with the return value of the `doProcess()` method. By using the `chap10.GenericDOMServlet` class, you do not care about the handling of the `charset` and MIME type, and you can keep your program compact and safe.

Assume that this program is registered to an application server or a servlet engine and is accessible with the URL `http://demohost:8080/xmlbook2/chap11/XMLDBServlet`. The following is an XML document for input named `test.xml`.

```
<?xml version="1.0" encoding="UTF-8"?>
<invoiceNo>2001-08-31-12345</invoiceNo>
```

The program `SendXML` sends an XML document to a URL and outputs the result. It is also included on the CD-ROM. The program produces the following result.

```
R:\samples>java chap11.SendXML    < chap11\test.xml
<?xml version="1.0" encoding="UTF-8"?>
<purchaseOrder invoiceNo="2001-08-31-12345"><shipTo country="US">
<name>Alice Smith</name><street>123 Maple Street</street></shipTo>
<items><item qty="2">ThinkPad X21</item><item qty="1">ThinkPad T22
</item></items></purchaseOrder>
```

## 11.7 Working with EJB

### 11.7.1 The Importance of EJB

As discussed in Section 11.1, the three-tier model (see Figure 11.1) consists of the following components:

- Client: a Web browser or a client application
- Presentation: a servlet or JSP that handles interaction with the client
- Business logic: program code for application-specific processes
- Data store: a database that manages business data

For example, the classes shown in Section 11.5 include business logic, and the servlet shown in Section 11.6 is a component for the presentation.

However, in these classes, the program code for presentation, business logic, and data store is not cleanly separated, as shown in Figure 11.4. Furthermore, a process for transaction control, which should be a common service, is written by developers and embedded in the program.

When a large-scale Web application is being developed, we developers want to concentrate on business logic, and common services such as transaction control and database connection management should be provided from the middleware that we use. That can reduce the cost of design, development, and management of the Web application.

Java 2 Enterprise Edition (J2EE) and EJB enable such an environment. This section briefly covers J2EE and EJB and compares them with the approaches we showed earlier in this chapter. If you are interested in this topic, many books are available on J2EE and EJB.

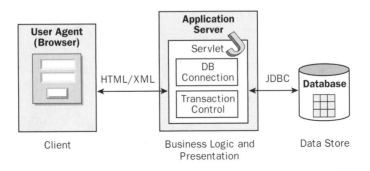

**Figure 11.4** A three-tier Web application with embedded processes

J2EE is a set of server-side Java technologies. Before J2EE was available, many vendors provided their own ways to develop large-scale Web applications. J2EE aims to integrate these technologies as a set of standard technologies. J2EE contains Java Servlet, JDBC, EJB, Java Message Service (JMS), Java Naming and Directory Interface (JNDI), Java Transaction API (JTA), Remote Method Invocation (RMI), and other technologies. Many vendors support J2EE and provide J2EE-compliant middleware. For example, IBM's WebSphere 4.0 is a J2EE-compliant application server. EJB plays a key role in these technologies.

Figure 11.5 shows a three-tier Web application with J2EE/EJB. There are two clear differences from Figure 11.4. First, a Web container and EJB container are introduced in Figure 11.5. The *Web container* contains servlets and JSPs. The *EJB container* contains business logic and provides the following system services:

- Transaction management
- Security (only a client that has a permission can execute business logic)
- Communication with a remote client/EJB
- Lifecycle (session) management
- Database connection management

Developers can develop EJBs that contain business logic and not have to worry about implementing the services just listed by using standard technologies.

There are two types of EJBs.

- An *entity bean* represents a persistent business object. It is associated with a record in a database, and it is possible to automatically store the object values in a table as column data. Entity beans are categorized into two types.
    - Container-Managed Persistence (CMP). In a CMP, the EJB container handles EJB objects' persistence and accesses database. CMP Developers do not have

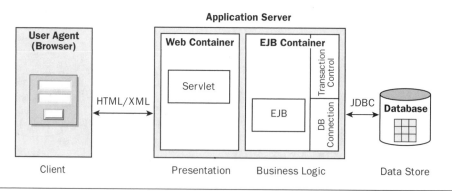

**Figure 11.5** A three-tier Web application with J2EE/EJB

to write a program code for database access. A CMP basically corresponds to a record in a database table; therefore, join processes among multiple tables are required.

- Bean-Managed Persistence (BMP). A BMP can provide flexibility. A BMP contains a program code for database access. It similar to the code shown in the previous sections, but developers can manage multiple tables.

- A *session bean* is used for describing business logic that does not relate to persistent data. There are also two types of section beans.

  - *Stateful* session bean. A stateful bean can keep the status (instance values) in the interaction between a client and an EJB.

  - *Stateless* session bean. A stateless bean does not keep the status and can be used for describing business logic that does not require a state control.

The EJB 2.0 specification, published in October 2000, introduces a new type of enterprise bean—the Message Driven Bean (MDB). J2EE 1.2 itself includes JMS so that you can develop asynchronous processing in large-scale Web applications (described in Chapter 12). However, JMS and EJB are not properly integrated in the sense that you cannot access an EJB container via JMS. In J2EE 1.3 (based on EJB 2.0), MDB provides an EJB container with asynchronous processing functions. Messages sent via JMS are dispatched to an MDB object within the EJB container.

### 11.7.2  A Simple EJB

Next, we show a simple example of EJB. Information on J2EE and EJB is available at `http://java.sun.com/j2ee`. The Web site provides the EJB 2.0 specification and a comprehensive tutorial.

The following four classes are required to develop an EJB:

- An EJB bean class that contains business logic
- A home interface for the EJB container to create the EJB bean object
- An EJB client that accesses the EJB bean
- A remote interface for the EJB client to call the methods of the EJB bean

Listing 11.12 shows an entity bean (CMP) that corresponds to a record in the `NODE_VALUE_TBL` table, shown in Section 11.5.2.

**Listing 11.12**  A simple entity bean, `chap11/NodeValueBean.java`

```
package chap11;

import java.util.*;
import javax.ejb.*;
import javax.naming.*;
```

```
// This is a CMP bean based on EJB 2.0
public abstract class NodeValueBean implements EntityBean {

    private EntityContext context;

    // Access methods for persistent fields.
    // EJB container associates each field with
    // column of a table
    public abstract String getNodeId();
    public abstract void setNodeId(String nodeId);

    public abstract String getPathString();
    public abstract void setPathString(String pathString);

    public abstract String getContentString();
    public abstract void setContentString(String contentString);

    public abstract String getDocumentId();
    public abstract void setDocumentId(String documentId);

    // Implements EntityBean methods
    public String ejbCreate (String nodeId,
                    String pathString,
                    String contentString,
                    String documentId)
        throws CreateException {
        setNodeId(nodeId);
        setPathString(pathString);
        setContentString(contentString);
        setDocumentId(documentId);
        return nodeId;
    }

    public void ejbPostCreate (String nodeId,
                    String pathString,
                    String contentString,
                    String documentId)
        throws CreateException {
    }

    public void setEntityContext(EntityContext ctx) {
        context = ctx;
    }

    public void unsetEntityContext() {
        context = null;
    }
```

```
        public void ejbRemove() {}
        public void ejbLoad() {}
        public void ejbStore() {}
        public void ejbPassivate() {}
        public void ejbActivate() {}

        // Defining Business methods

        // Suppose NodeValueInfo is a class that contains column data
        public NodeValueInfo getNodeValueInfo() {
        return new NodeValueInfo(getNodeId(),
                                 getPathString(),
                                 getContentString(),
                                 getDocumentId());
        }

        public void updateContent(String content) {
        setContentString(content);
        }
    }
```

You might be surprised that this program does not contain any program code for database access. There are not even any instance variables that represent column names (which is a new feature introduced in EJB 2.0). This means that the program is very robust against the modification of the database. Program code for transaction control is also not required. This class is deployed in a J2EE-compliant application server with home and remote interfaces (the details of the interfaces are not covered in this book.)

An EJB client program calls the methods defined in the EJB bean class, such as getNodeValueInfo() and setContent() in Listing 11.12. The former method returns information stored in the database (the class NodeValueInfo is included on the CD-ROM). The latter method updates a value of the persistent data. If this method is called, an SQL query is submitted to a database. However, the EJB bean does not know the database (table) name and the actual SQL query. The EJB container manages the process.

The information to associate an entity bean and a database is stored in an XML document called a *deployment descriptor*. It can be created by a Wizard-like GUI or other tools.

EJBs are deployed as distributed objects based on Java RMI-IIOP. That means an EJB object in an EJB container can call other EJBs in other containers located somewhere in the network. It is a big weapon for load balancing large-scale Web applications. On the other hand, if our system is local and relatively small, using

EJB may be expositive. For example, although a CMP bean automates database access, it is sometimes not effective because it may retrieve unused values.

The simple example shown in Listing 11.12 is an entity bean that relates a record in a single database table. However, as we have shown with examples in previous sections, multiple tables are required to represent an XML document. They are often in a one-to-many relationship. Some techniques to handle the relationships with CMP and BMP are in the EJB 2.0 tutorial available at `http://java.sun.com/j2ee`.

We briefly introduced EJB and a sample program. One big question is when to use EJB. Suppose we have an existing system or we are designing a new Web application. Should we use the EJB framework for the application?

A simple answer depends on the scalability and extensibility of the system. If it is large or it will be extended in the near future, there is no doubt about using EJB. EJB reduces the cost of developing transaction control, database connection, security, and so on. It is easy to run multiple servers for accepting a large number of requests by combining EJBs in a distributed environment. If an existing system is developed by using Java beans, it is easy to move to an EJB environment.

Another key factor is the reusability of business logic. We can distribute the logic as EJB beans that can work on any J2EE-compliant application server.

## 11.8  Summary

This chapter described how to develop a Web application with database access. Because XML has become a first-class format for exchanging business data, it is very important to determine the method for storing an XML document in and retrieving it from a database—in particular, RDMBS. This chapter also discussed how to develop a three-tier Web application with Servlet and EJB. They are becoming a common framework for developing highly scalable and reliable Web applications.

This chapter described how to integrate databases in a three-tier architecture. As you know, the Web is distributed and very dynamic. A huge amount of Web pages and (HTML-based) services are on the Web. Recently, a new architecture to provide services in a very dynamic way on the Web is receiving attention. The next two chapters describe it—Web services.

# XML Messaging

## 12.1 Introduction

As we explained in Chapter 1, XML messaging is one of the most important and promising application areas of XML. In particular, XML messaging is expected to play a central role in business-to-business (B2B) collaborations in the exchange of XML documents between applications of the businesses. Furthermore, even within large businesses where Enterprise Application Integration (EAI) is concerned, their legacy applications are being integrated with XML messaging in a loosely coupled manner. In this section, we review why XML messaging is receiving considerable attention, relating it to distributed computing. We also show how to structure XML messaging and discuss why the Simple Object Access Protocol (SOAP) is so important in XML messaging. SOAP itself will be reviewed in great detail in Section 12.2.

### 12.1.1 Distributed Computing and Interoperability

When the computer was introduced in the industry, each company tried to computerize its in-house business operations independently from the others. Until only a decade ago, most of these in-house application systems were not connected with each other. As a result, people had to perform daily B2B operations with a phone or fax. Obviously, this way of doing business is not cost-effective, and businesses can easily lose opportunities or risk increased costs because of human error. Since then, computerizing B2B operations has become one of the most important goals for both industry and computer vendors. For example, the automobile industry has tried to computerize its supply chain management system to reduce labor costs, lead time for product supply, and simple wrong operations. Such an effort was started independently by some advanced groups of companies, and therefore there was an increasing need for a standardized means of integrating their efforts.

In the early 1990s, the idea of Electronic Data Interchange (EDI) emerged for standardizing data formats to be exchanged among companies in the same group. The idea was successful and accepted by many enterprise companies. People, however, started to be aware of the limitation that once EDI was used in daily operations, it was not very easy to modify a binary data format for the extension requirements caused by changes in business environments. EDI was not widely accepted by medium-size and small companies because the cost of introducing EDI technology was sometimes very expensive.

Distributed computing technology became mature in the mid-1990s and applicable for B2B transactions. One of the most important technologies was Remote Procedure Call (RPC), which allows a program residing in a remote computer to be invoked, just like a local program. The Object Management Group (OMG) was formed to standardize RPC for the interoperability of heterogeneous application systems. It was named the Common Object Request Broker Architecture (CORBA) based on object-oriented programming, which allows remote objects to exchange messages. The OMG defines the Interface Definition Language (IDL) to specify APIs for each object. IDL is designed independently of any other language, and language bindings are defined to map between IDL and specific programming languages. The OMG also defines many useful services, including Object Services such as Transaction and Security Services, so that they cover most of the technologies needed for B2B system integration. More than 500 companies have joined the OMG. Many people regarded CORBA as a promising technology to overcome the technical limitations of EDI. Even though the OMG still continues to revise CORBA and enrich Object Services, unfortunately CORBA seems to be losing the interest of developers. One of the most serious problems is the size of the CORBA specification. The core specification has over a thousand pages, which is beyond the capacity of human understanding and thus prevents casual programmers from using it. Another problem is that the language-binding mechanism does not always work well enough to absorb the heterogeneity between different programming languages.

As for interoperability, although the efforts previously described focused on it for enterprise applications, we cannot ignore the big movement that happened in the late 1990s—the Internet and the Web. With the Internet, not only developers but also casual computer users could freely access documents distributed throughout the world by using any Web browser and could exchange e-mail by using any mailer. Most of these people do not have to know what the computer system is, how the network configuration is used in the target server, what kind of operating system is running, and which programming language is used to write such an application. Even though the network protocols (for example, HTTP and SMTP) and data-encoding methods (for example, Base64) used in the Internet and the

Web are simpler and less efficient than those used in EDI and CORBA, the significant fact is that simplicity and interoperability (or connectivity) are much more important than efficiency. We learned that as the Internet and the Web changed the world just as the telephone and fax did.

As part of the discussion of interoperability, we may want to integrate applications by means of standard Internet technologies. The concept of "Web services," recently promoted by many software vendors, addresses such a requirement. One of the most generic definitions is "Web services are applications that can be accessed via standard technologies such as XML and HTTP." In this sense, the XML-processing servlets discussed in Chapter 10 can be considered Web services. However, it is often insufficient to exchange XML documents merely between businesses for application integration.

In this chapter, we clarify the issues for XML-based application integration, paying attention to XML messaging, and see how such issues are solved with SOAP. Then, in the next chapter, we provide an overall picture of Web services, showing the building blocks for Web services architecture.

## 12.1.2  Overview of XML Messaging

Although the term "XML messaging" indicates that XML documents are exchanged between applications, it is a good idea to introduce a communication stack concept, as in the OSI seven-layer model, to understand the term more precisely. Figure 12.1 illustrates a three-layer model for an XML messaging stack. Let us remember the examples in Chapter 10 in which XML documents were transmitted over HTTP. Such an approach is considered a mere combination of HTTP at the transport layer and XML documents at the application layer. You might be required to adopt other transports, such as the Simple Mail Transfer Protocol (SMTP) and Java Message Service (JMS), instead of HTTP. However, you may have some questions: Why do we need an intermediate layer called the messaging layer? How is

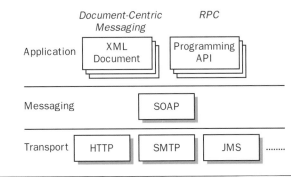

**Figure 12.1**  XML messaging stack

RPC related to XML messaging in more detail? What is the difference between RPC and document-centric messaging? We are here to help.

One of the motivations for the messaging layer stems from end-to-end communication. As we showed in Chapter 11, recent enterprise systems have a multilayer structure. Even in the simplest case, you have an HTTP server, a servlet engine, an EJB container and a database. In addition, you may have a firewall, a network dispatcher, and a reverse proxy in front of the HTTP server, and you may have legacy applications to be accessed via JMS from the servlet engine. If we take an HTTP-based approach in Chapter 10 for B2B collaboration, we can only reach the servlet engine in some cases because backend applications are often accessible only via other transports, such as the Internet Inter-ORB Protocol (IIOP) and IBM MQSeries. Such configuration is very common in enterprise companies. If the target of your XML document is a backend application behind IBM MQSeries, you have to prepare an intermediary application by hand. The messaging layer solves such problems by defining a concept of the end-to-end message path in a transport-agnostic manner. We review this concept in more detail in the Header Processing and Intermediary section.

At the messaging layer, an *envelope* is defined to include application-specific XML documents. It seems redundant at first glance but is convenient because you can add various functions in a flexible manner. Let us consider some real-world examples.

- You can easily add information on the envelope. Assume that you want to send a purchase order document, which describes only the names of the company and the department. You may include the document within an envelope, adding the address of the company, the person who should receive the envelope, and so on. Note that you can add information without changing the contents.

- Physical envelopes are not transparent, unlike a digital envelope. Therefore, others cannot see the contents. Furthermore, if the recipient of the envelope is required to show identification, we can ensure that the envelope is delivered to the correct person. In summary, envelopes serve as security and privacy.

- An envelope can contain more than one document and can contain other types of attachments other than documents, such as images and videos.

These examples show that envelopes are useful for additional facets. Let us shift our focus to envelopes as digital data. Typically, an envelope consists of two parts: a *body,* or *payload,* containing application-specific data and a *header* containing additional facets. Based on this structure, you can include application-independent facets within the header, such as security, routing, and transaction information.

The concept of the envelope is not new. But it is used in many new ways. For example, in electronic mail, various headers are defined in addition to the main text, such as a receiver address, sender address, subject, character encoding, and routing. As for HTTP, typically used by Web browsers, various headers are defined, such as a target address, requestor address, and cache information. These headers are automatically processed at the transport layer, and applications do not have to worry about such details. In the same manner, it seems worthwhile to define such an envelope structure at the messaging layer in a transport-agnostic manner.

### 12.1.3 New-Generation Distributed Programming

So far, we have discussed the messaging layer, addressing how to exchange XML documents. In other words, applications send and receive XML documents, understanding the semantics of the documents. As shown in Figure 12.1, this kind of XML messaging is called document-centric messaging (DCM). It is very usual that the format of exchanged XML documents is provided for B2B collaboration. For example, a business defines an XML format for a purchase order, and its trading partners have to submit purchase order documents conforming to the format. In such typical cases, DCM should be used.

On the other hand, XML is considered as a data format for performing RPC, as shown in Figure 12.1. With RPC, applications can invoke procedures located on other nodes as if they were located on the same machine. In contrast to using DCM, applications are not concerned with XML documents when using RPC; instead, they are concerned with the API of the remote procedures (see Figure 12.1). In that case, XML is used only on the wire to encode data for RPC.

RPC is a fairly old concept, and many RPC technologies exist. However, there are some problems with the existing technologies when we use them for B2B collaboration over the Internet. First, some of them depend on a particular language, and the client and server applications have to use the same programming language. Java Remote Method Invocation (RMI) and Distributed Common Object Model (DCOM) are typical examples. This *tightly coupled* approach is advantageous in performance but disadvantageous in interoperability. To improve interoperability, CORBA provides IDL for programming-language independence. The concept of IDL is simple, but a CORBA platform tends to become big because CORBA specifies an integrated architecture for IDL, protocol, API, message format, and services. In a B2B situation, it is difficult to assume that both businesses have such a fairly big platform. As a result, CORBA is rarely used for B2B collaboration.

How can we develop an RPC technology that can be used over the Internet? What should be standardized for highly interoperable RPC? The answer could be a *loosely coupled* RPC.[1] Existing tightly coupled RPCs are concerned with the standardization of the API that is accessed by applications. On the other hand, the loosely coupled RPC is concerned only with the data format for communicating RPC data. In other words, how to provide the application with an API should be platform-dependent but should not be shared between platforms. This approach clearly contributes to the improvement of interoperability.

It is not worthwhile to discuss which is more important, DCM or RPC. If you are concerned with XML documents in your applications, you have to take the DCM approach. On the other hand, if you have applications and want to publish on the Internet as soon as possible, RPC should be easier. Throughout this chapter and the next, you should keep in mind that DCM and RPC are complementary.

## 12.2 Simple Object Access Protocol

SOAP is a messaging layer protocol, as shown in Figure 12.1, and is the most broadly accepted open standard at that layer. The SOAP specification defines the Envelope structure, which wraps application-specific XML contents, a set of encoding rules for expressing instances of application-defined data types, and a convention for representing RPCs.

Here, we first review briefly the birth of SOAP (in Section 12.2.1). Then we introduce a simple example for travel reservations (in Section 12.2.2) and review various aspects of SOAP in more detail with the example (in Section 12.2.3). Finally, we discuss when we should use SOAP (in Section 12.2.4).

### 12.2.1 The Birth of SOAP

SOAP was recognized as an "open standard" when SOAP 1.1 was submitted as a Note to W3C jointly with Microsoft, IBM, Lotus, UserLand, and DevelopMentor. Although SOAP existed before as specifications 0.9 and 1.0, those specifications were considered proprietary to Microsoft. For example, previous SOAP specifications were based on XML Data Reduced (XDR) instead of XML Schema, were too RPC-oriented, and were not extensible. Furthermore, because Microsoft played a central role, some people thought that SOAP was Windows-specific technology.

On the other hand, people have been demanding XML messaging for application integration because XML-based B2B collaboration is increasing. Although

---

[1] The term "loosely coupled" concerns interoperability rather than performance and is discussed in terms of Web services in Chapter 13.

SOAP 1.0 was enough for that purpose, people were reluctant to adopt it because it was considered Microsoft proprietary. Therefore, IBM and Lotus joined Microsoft to come up with SOAP 1.1, incorporating W3C standards. The companies submitted SOAP 1.1 as a Note to W3C. This indicates that W3C is going to recognize SOAP as a standard. W3C also started the XML Protocol Working Group based on SOAP 1.1. The working group recently announced SOAP 1.2, clarifying ambiguous portions of SOAP 1.1.[2] Apart from the standardization, the collaboration of IBM and Microsoft contributes to the broad acceptance of SOAP.

## 12.2.2 Travel Reservation Example

Here, we introduce a travel reservation example. We assume that the example programs are used to reserve a package tour after a user has searched the tour based on their requirements, such as destination, date, and budget. The main tasks of the example are to receive a reservation request, including a package tour code, date, and user ID; to check the input data; and to return an acceptance message if appropriate. We prepare two kinds of programs for the example. One has an ordinary Java API and is used later for showing how SOAP-RPC works. The other has an XML-in/XML-out–style API; that is, it receives an XML document for a reservation request and returns an XML document for an acceptance. It is used for showing how document-centric messaging works in SOAP.

Listing 12.1 shows a travel service program that can be accessed via Java method calls and is accessed via SOAP-RPC. The Java class `TravelServiceRPC` has only one method, called `reserve`, which accepts three parameters, a user ID, a tour ID, and the departure date. The logic of the method is simplified to check only whether the specified departure date is later than the current time. The method returns the object `Reservation`, shown in Listing 12.2, which includes member variables for a reservation, such as a user ID, a tour ID, a departure date, and a reservation ID. As you can see, the class defines only setter and getter methods for these member variables. As we will show later, SOAP defines encoding rules for expressing such objects in XML.

**Listing 12.1** The travel service program for RPC, `chap12/travel/provider/TravelServiceRPC.java`

```
package chap12.travel.provider;

import java.util.Date;
import chap12.travel.Reservation;
```

---

[2] SOAP 1.2 is being updated as we write this book. Furthermore, most SOAP engines are based on SOAP 1.1 for now. Considering the situation, we use SOAP 1.1 in this chapter and the next.

```
public class TravelServiceRPC {
    public Reservation reserve(String user,
                                String tourId,
                                Date departure)
        throws Exception
    {
        long currentTime = System.currentTimeMillis();
        // Only check if the departure is after today
        if ( currentTime > departure.getTime() ) {
            throw new Exception("Date is wrong: " + departure);
        }
        Reservation resv=new Reservation();
        resv.setUser(user);
        resv.setTourId(tourId);
        resv.setDate(departure);
        resv.setReservationId(tourId+currentTime);
        return resv;
    }
}
```

**Listing 12.2** The class for maintaining travel reservation information, `chap12/travel/Reservation.java`

```
package chap12.travel;

import java.util.Date;

public class Reservation {
    private String user;
    private String tourId;
    private Date date;
    private String reservationId;

    public String getUser() {
        return user;
    }
    public String getTourId() {
        return tourId;
    }
    public Date getDate() {
        return date;
    }
    public String getReservationId() {
        return reservationId;
    }
    public void setUser(String newUser) {
        user = newUser;
```

```
        }
        public void setTourId(String newTourId) {
            tourId = newTourId;
        }
        public void setDate(Date newDate) {
            date = newDate;
        }
        public void setReservationId(String newReservationId) {
            reservationId = newReservationId;
        }
        public String toString() { // This is just a utility
            String str ="Reservation: ";
            str = str + "user/"+ user + " ";
            str = str + "tourId/"+ tourId + " ";
            str = str + "date/"+ date + " ";
            str = str + "reservationId/"+ reservationId + " ";
            return str;
        }
    }
```

Listing 12.3 shows another program, which performs the reservation task in an XML-in/XML-out manner. The method `reserve` in the `TravelServiceXML` class receives an XML document, which is represented in a DOM object, for a reservation request and returns a DOM object for a reservation acceptance. The `reserve` method invokes the `insertValues` method, within which the `insertValue` method is invoked to copy a property, such as user ID, tour ID, and departure date; and finally a generated acceptance ID is included in the response document.

**Listing 12.3** The travel service program with an XML-in/XML-out interface, `chap12/travel/provider/TravelServiceXML.java`

```
    package chap12.travel.provider;

    import java.io.IOException;
    import java.io.StringReader;
    import javax.mail.MessagingException;
    import org.w3c.dom.Document;
    import org.w3c.dom.Element;
    import org.w3c.dom.Node;
    import org.w3c.dom.NodeList;
    import org.w3c.dom.Text;
    import org.apache.xerces.dom.DocumentImpl;
    import org.apache.soap.util.xml.DOM2Writer;

    import chap12.simplesoap.util.EnvelopeUtil;
    import chap12.simplesoap.MessageConsumer;
```

```
public class TravelServiceXML {
    public Document reserve(Document req) throws Exception {
        Document res=
            EnvelopeUtil.createDOM(new StringReader(RESP_TMP));
        insertValues(res, req);
        return res;
    }
    private void insertValues(Document res, Document req) {
        // just copy from request to response
        insertValue(USER, res, req);
        insertValue(TOUR_ID, res, req);
        insertValue(YEAR, res, req);
        insertValue(MONTH, res, req);
        insertValue(DAY, res, req);

        long currentTime = System.currentTimeMillis();
        Element accept=
            (Element)
                res.getElementsByTagNameNS(TOUR_NS,
                                           "accepted")
                    .item(0);
        Element resv=res.createElement("reservation-id");
        accept.appendChild(resv);
        accept.appendChild(res.createTextNode("\n    "));
        resv.appendChild(
            res.createTextNode(getTourID(req)+currentTime));
    }
    private void insertValue(String tagName,
                             Document res,
                             Document req) {
        Element el_out=
            (Element)res.getElementsByTagNameNS(TOUR_NS,tagName)
                    .item(0);
        Element el_in=
            (Element)req.getElementsByTagNameNS(TOUR_NS,tagName)
                    .item(0);
        NodeList list = el_in.getChildNodes();
        for(int i=0; i<list.getLength(); i++) {
            Node node = res.importNode(list.item(i), true);
            el_out.appendChild(node);
        }
    }
    private String getTourID(Document doc) {
        Element el=
            (Element)doc.getElementsByTagNameNS(TOUR_NS,TOUR_ID)
                    .item(0);
```

```
        NodeList list = el.getChildNodes();
        String tourId="";
        for(int i=0; i<list.getLength(); i++) {
            if (list.item(i).getNodeType()==Node.TEXT_NODE) {
                Text textNode = (Text)list.item(i);
                tourId += textNode.getData();
            }
        }
        return tourId;
    }
    final static private String USER="user";
    final static private String TOUR_ID="tourId";
    final static private String YEAR="year";
    final static private String MONTH="month";
    final static private String DAY="day";
    final static private String TOUR_NS="urn:reserve-tour-msg";
    final static private java.lang.String RESP_TMP=
        "    <ns1:accepted xmlns:ns1=\"urn:reserve-tour-msg\">\n"+
        "      <ns1:user></ns1:user>\n"+
        "      <ns1:tourId></ns1:tourId>\n"+
        "      <ns1:depature>\n"+
        "        <ns1:year></ns1:year>\n"+
        "        <ns1:month></ns1:month>\n"+
        "        <ns1:day></ns1:day>\n"+
        "      </ns1:depature>\n"+
        "    </ns1:accepted>\n";
}
```

Listings 12.4 and 12.5 show examples of XML documents for the program
`TravelServiceXML`. When you look at them closely, you should notice that the
request and response XML documents are similar. Accordingly, in the program, all
parameters in the request are copied to the response, and only a reservation ID is
created to be included in the response.

**Listing 12.4** Request XML document for travel reservation

```
<ns1:reserve xmlns:ns1="urn:reserve-tour-msg">
    <ns1:user>nakamury</ns1:user>
    <ns1:tourId>hawaii55</ns1:tourId>
    <ns1:departure>
        <ns1:year>2001</ns1:year>
        <ns1:month>9</ns1:month>
        <ns1:day>15</ns1:day>
    </ns1:departure>
</ns1:reserve>
```

**Listing 12.5** Response XML document for travel reservation

```
<ns1:accepted xmlns:ns1="urn:reserve-tour-msg">
    <ns1:user>nakamury</ns1:user>
    <ns1:tourId>hawaii55</ns1:tourId>
    <ns1:departure>
        <ns1:year>2001</ns1:year>
        <ns1:month>9</ns1:month>
        <ns1:day>15</ns1:day>
    </ns1:departure>
    <ns1:reservation-id>hawaii55988028016497</ns1:reservation-id>
</ns1:accepted>
```

In this section, we showed two kinds of travel reservation programs: `TravelServiceRPC` and `TravelServiceXML`. In the following sections, we describe two kinds of SOAP messaging styles with these programs: RPC and document-centric messaging.

## 12.2.3  Basic Concepts of SOAP

Next we cover the key aspects of SOAP. First we introduce the SOAP Envelope. Besides describing its syntax, we take a close look at a unique concept in SOAP called "intermediary," and we explain header processing. Also, we discuss another important feature of SOAP, SOAP encoding rules.

### SOAP Envelopes

SOAP defines a means to envelop application-specific XML documents. A *SOAP Envelope* specifies a framework within which you can include both application-specific and application-independent information in an XML document. SOAP also defines a set of rules for processing each entry of the XML document.

Figure 12.2 depicts the structure of a SOAP Envelope. A SOAP Envelope is an XML document that has a required *Body* element and an optional *Header* element as its children. Header is intended to include application-independent information and can include multiple header entries. In the SOAP 1.1 specification, a transaction ID is shown as an example of a header entry. In addition, we may also include security information in a header entry, as detailed in Chapter 14. On the other hand, Body includes application-specific information, such as the travel reservation request in our example. Like the Header element, Body also can have multiple body entries, as shown in Figure 12.2.

An example of a SOAP message is shown in Listing 12.6. This message comes from a combination of two things: a request message for `TravelServiceXML` and a transaction ID, described in the SOAP specification. The namespace URI for SOAP

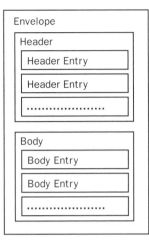

**Figure 12.2** Structure of a SOAP Envelope

Envelopes is `http://schemas.xmlsoap.org/soap/envelope/`, and it is found in the `xmlns:SOAP-ENV` attribute of the `Envelope` element.[3]

**Listing 12.6** Example of a SOAP message

```
<SOAP-ENV:Envelope
    xmlns:SOAP-ENV="http://schemas.xmlsoap.org/soap/envelope/">
    <SOAP-ENV:Header>
        <t:Transaction xmlns:t="some-URI"
                       SOAP-ENV:mustUnderstand="1">
            5
        </t:Transaction>
    </SOAP-ENV:Header>
    <SOAP-ENV:Body>
        <ns1:reserve xmlns:ns1="urn:reserve-tour-msg">
            <ns1:user>nakamury</ns1:user>
            <ns1:tourId>hawaii55</ns1:tourId>
            <ns1:departure>
                <ns1:year>2001</ns1:year>
                <ns1:month>9</ns1:month>
                <ns1:day>15</ns1:day>
            </ns1:departure>
        </ns1:reserve>
    </SOAP-ENV:Body>
</SOAP-ENV:Envelope>
```

---

[3] You can access `http://schemas.xmlsoap.org/soap/envelope/` via a Web browser to see the actual schema definition of the SOAP Envelope.

The transaction ID in a header entry serves as a correlation of multiple SOAP messages, according to the specification. In our travel reservation example, a customer may first search a package tour, reserve it, and finally pay with a credit card. Assuming that these three steps are performed via SOAP messaging, we may be able to correlate these three messages with the transaction ID. The `mustUnderstand` attribute in the header entry indicates that the recipient of the message must process the header entry. Because the processing rule for the attribute is tightly related to the intermediary, further details are discussed in the section Header Processing and the Intermediary. As for the body entry, you can see that the XML document in Listing 12.4 is embedded as it is in the Body element.

As for errors, the SOAP Fault element is defined to include information such as a fault code, string, and details. Assume that a past date is specified in a travel reservation request. In that case, a receiver application can return a SOAP message including the SOAP Fault element to the requestor. In addition, the SOAP Fault can also be used when a program encounters an error during header entry processing.

You may ask, why is the SOAP Envelope necessary? You could develop a travel reservation program as in Chapter 10, making the program exchange XML documents without the Envelope. However, such a program would not be flexible and extensible. Assume that you take the non-Envelope approach. Although it would be enough, you later would be required to insert a digital signature into the XML documents. Such modification should be performed easily. If you develop your applications with SOAP, you do not have to modify a module that processes SOAP body entries—that is, XML documents for travel reservation requests. Instead, you can extend your applications by adding a digital signature–processing module. As for error handling, because the SOAP engine processes application-independent errors, you can focus on only application-specific errors.

## Header Processing and the Intermediary

One of the most interesting features of SOAP is the concept of the *intermediary*. And the processing rules for the SOAP Envelope take account of the intermediary explicitly. As shown in Figure 12.3, a SOAP message is sent by an initial sender, travels through potentially multiple intermediaries, and arrives at the final destination. The path on which a SOAP message travels is called the *message path*. Even if we combine multiple transports, we have only a *single* message path. Such an intermediary concept seems redundant in some cases. However, it is very flexible because you can place additional processing components on intermediaries without modifying the applications of the initial sender and the ultimate destination.

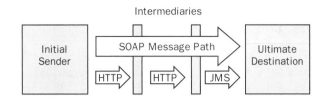

**Figure 12.3**  SOAP intermediaries and transports.

In reality, enterprises often have two firewalls between the intranet and the Internet. The area between two firewalls is called the Demilitarized Zone (DMZ). One typical configuration is that an application server is located in the DMZ, and it communicates with backend servers via IBM MQSeries. Even when you are required to handle a digital signature in the DMZ, you may not have to update your backend applications, thanks to the transport-agnostic nature and the intermediary concept of SOAP.

The definition of the SOAP Envelope includes two attributes for header entries: `actor` and `mustUnderstand`. The processing rules for them are specified based on the message path concept, as shown in Figure 12.3. The `actor` attribute is used to indicate who must process the header entry. Referring to Figure 12.3, we assume that the first intermediary is `http://xmlbook/inter1`, and the second is `http://xmlbook/inter2`. In this assumption, the following header entry is targeted at the second intermediary, but not the first one.

```
<t:Transaction xmlns:t="some-URI"
               SOAP-ENV:actor="http://xmlbook/inter2">
    5
</t:Transaction>
```

Note that when the `actor` attribute is omitted, the header entry is targeted at the final destination.

The `mustUnderstand` attribute indicates whether the application specified by the `actor` attribute must process the header entry. The following example indicates that the header entry is targeted at the second intermediary, and the intermediary must process the header entry.

```
<t:Transaction xmlns:t="some-URI" SOAP-ENV:actor="http://xmlbook/
inter2"
    SOAP-ENV:mustUnderstand="1">
    5
</t:Transaction>
```

If the `mustUnderstand` attribute is not specified, its default value is 0, and the intermediary does not have to process the header entry.

The concept of intermediaries is interesting and is expected to be useful in many cases. However, there are some ambiguities about the `actor` and `mustUnderstand` attributes. For example, SOAP does not prescribe what entity should be indicated by the URI of the `actor` attribute. Although we assume that `actor` attributes indicate particular nodes, it is possible that an `actor` indicates a particular handler, assuming that multiple handlers are located at each node. In that case, we would adopt `http://foo-vendor/transaction-handler` as the value of the `actor` attribute. As for `mustUnderstand`, some people are criticizing the fact that there is no definition of "processing" in the specification.

In spite of such issues, the concept of the SOAP intermediary is extremely important and demanded. Recently, enterprise systems have been located within firewalls, so they are accessed via intermediary nodes such as routers and proxies. Accordingly, XML messages travel to a final destination via multiple intermediary nodes. We can expect that we will have requirements for processing XML messages at intermediary nodes very often.

### SOAP Encoding

How can we access the `TravelServiceRPC` class in Listing 12.1 from a remote host? According to the concept of RPC, we can remotely invoke such a program as if it were a local call. To implement the RPC mechanism, we have to somehow encode the method invocation of the requestor, transmit the encoded data over the network, and decode it to invoke a method at the destination. As for encoding, XML can be used to express method invocations, as you can imagine. Now, how can we encode method invocations?

As illustrated in Figure 12.1, XML messaging is used two different ways: through document-centric messaging and RPC. The SOAP Envelope is not intended either; only body entries are concerned with what the purpose is. SOAP encoding rules especially concern RPC, prescribing how to encode application-specific data in XML format. In the SOAP Envelope, the attribute `encodingStyle` is defined to specify a particular encoding rule, and `http://schemas.xmlsoap.org/soap/encoding/` is substituted when you use SOAP encoding rules. However, note that the SOAP encoding URI is *not* a default value of the attribute. In other words, you can take or define another encoding rule to specify in the attribute. Here we discuss only SOAP encoding. Other encoding approaches are discussed in Chapter 15.

Let us begin by showing examples of SOAP encoding. Assume that you access our `TravelServiceRPC` program (see Listing 12.1). In that case, the invocation of the `reserve` method should be represented in XML to transmit to the destination. And as for the response, the `Reservation` object should be represented in XML to reply to the requestor. SOAP encoding serves such a purpose. Listing 12.7 shows the request SOAP message, and Listing 12.8 shows the response SOAP message. They are both generated from Apache SOAP, which we describe later. In Listing 12.7, a method invocation, `reserve(nakamury,hawaii55,2001-08-15T00:00:00Z)`, is encoded. The method invocation is represented in XML, viewing it as structured data; that is, the method name is a parent element, and the parameters are its child elements. In this encoding, we have to specify a parameter name to represent a parameter as an XML element, but we do not have to specify its type if there is some agreement between the requestor and the provider. Listing 12.8 shows a response SOAP message, which encodes the `Reservation` object. The value `xsi:type="ns2:reservation"` in the `return` element indicates that an object of the type `ns2:reservation` is encoded here. Furthermore, child elements of the `return` element correspond to member variables of the `Reservation` class. Note that there is no definition of the correspondence relationship between `ns2:reservation` and the `Reservation` class in the message itself. Such mapping is platform-dependent. In Apache SOAP, such mapping is specified in a deployment descriptor, described in the Apache SOAP section.

**Listing 12.7**  SOAP-RPC request message

```
<SOAP-ENV:Envelope
    xmlns:SOAP-ENV="http://schemas.xmlsoap.org/soap/envelope/"
    xmlns:xsi="http://www.w3.org/1999/XMLSchema-instance"
    xmlns:xsd="http://www.w3.org/1999/XMLSchema">
    <SOAP-ENV:Body>
        <ns1:reserve xmlns:ns1="urn:reserve-tour-rpc"
            SOAP-ENV:encodingStyle=
                "http://schemas.xmlsoap.org/soap/encoding/">
            <user xsi:type="xsd:string">nakamury</user>
            <tourId xsi:type="xsd:string">hawaii55</tourId>
            <departure xsi:type="xsd:timeInstant">
                2001-08-15T00:00:00Z
            </departure>
        </ns1:reserve>
    </SOAP-ENV:Body>
</SOAP-ENV:Envelope>
```

**Listing 12.8**  SOAP-RPC response message

```
<SOAP-ENV:Envelope
    xmlns:SOAP-ENV="http://schemas.xmlsoap.org/soap/envelope/"
    xmlns:xsi="http://www.w3.org/1999/XMLSchema-instance"
    xmlns:xsd="http://www.w3.org/1999/XMLSchema">
```

```
<SOAP-ENV:Body>
    <ns1:reserveResponse xmlns:ns1="urn:reserve-tour-rpc"
        SOAP-ENV:encodingStyle=
            "http://schemas.xmlsoap.org/soap/encoding/">
        <return xmlns:ns2="urn:xml-soap-travel-demo"
            xsi:type="ns2:reservation">
        <tourId xsi:type="xsd:string">hawaii55</tourId>
        <user xsi:type="xsd:string">nakamury</user>
        <date xsi:type="xsd:timeInstant">
            2001-08-15T00:00:00Z
        </date>
        <reservationId xsi:type="xsd:string">
            hawaii55987928919559
        </reservationId>
        </return>
    </ns1:reserveResponse>
    </SOAP-ENV:Body>
</SOAP-ENV:Envelope>
```

SOAP encoding rules assume an abstract type system and define a mapping
between the type system and XML syntax. The type system consists of a set of basic
types such as integer and string, complex types, array types, and so on. With these
constructs, we can define data models. For example, our `Reservation` class can
be viewed as a complex type that has four properties, such as `user` of type `string`
and `date` of type `timeInstant`. Listing 12.9 shows XML Schema and a XML document for the `Reservation` class.

**Listing 12.9**  XML Schema and document for `Reservation` class

```
<complexType name="Reservation">
    <element name="tourId" type="xsd:string"/>
    <element name="user" type="xsd:string"/>
    <element name="date" type="xsd:timeInstant"/>
    <element name="reservation" type="xsd:string"/>
</complexType>

<Reservation>
    <tourId xsi:type="xsd:string">hawaii55</tourId>
    <user xsi:type="xsd:string">naka</user>
    <date xsi:type="xsd:timeInstant">2001-08-15T00:00:00Z</date>
    <reservationId xsi:type="xsd:string">hawaii55987928919559
    </reservationId>
</Reservation>
```

The mapping between the `Reservation` class and the schema must be obvious.
Accordingly, you can imagine how the `Reservation` object is translated into an

XML document via the `Reservation` class and XML Schema. Now you may ask, how can very complicated Java objects be encoded? The issue involved is called data binding, explained in Chapter 15 in detail. Instead, here we consider one complicated example, as shown in Figure 12.4.

Figure 12.4 shows that two objects refer to a common object, and this is called a multi-reference. In this case, it is not sufficient to encode each object separately; we have to encode objects by including the relationship between them. According to SOAP encoding rules, objects that are referred to by multiple objects should be separated and be placed at the top level. Then the reference is represented by the `href` and `id` attributes. Figure 12.4 is encoded as follows:

```
<AirTicketReservation>
   <airline>United</airline>
   <customer href="#customer-1"/>
</AirTicketReservation>
<HotelReservation>
   <hotel>Hilton</hotel>
   <customer href="#customer-1"/>
</HotelReservation>
<Customer id="customer-1">
   <name>Henry Ford</name>
</Customer>
```

If you look at the `customer` element under `AirTicketReservation` and `HotelReservation`, you notice that each of them has an `href` attribute whose value is `#customer-1`. On the other hand, the `Customer` element has an `id` attribute, `customer-1`, which can be referred by `#customer-1`.

With SOAP encoding rules, you can specify what kind of XML documents are transmitted over the network for RPC invocation. However, we also have to allow users to invoke remote methods as if they were local methods. To provide such a function, you have to define an IDL and generate a client stub from it. We discuss that in more detail in Chapter 13, Section 13.2.

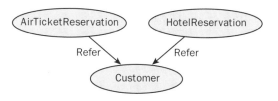

**Figure 12.4**  An object model with multi-references

## 12.2.4  To Use SOAP or Not?

As we have seen, SOAP provides various functions and is convenient in many cases. On the other hand, its performance should be much worse than traditional tightly coupled technologies such as CORBA. Here, we discuss in which situations we should use SOAP. We can summarize that we should use SOAP for B2B and use existing technologies like CORBA and EJB for application integration within an intranet. Here is a list of situations in which SOAP could be useful.

*Supporting different types of clients*

Assume that you have server applications developed with Java, and they are running in a UNIX environment. And for some reason, you have to develop client applications with Visual Basic in Windows. In this case, SOAP is the most appropriate alternative. We already have SOAP for both platforms, so you can start developing now.

*Supporting multiple transports*

Even if you use a single transport now, you may have to adopt multiple transports in the future. In this case, with SOAP you can minimize the changes to your application when you have to use multiple transports.

*End-to-end security*

End-to-end security is one of the most appropriate reasons for using SOAP. Security information can be placed within a SOAP header; accordingly, it can travel through multiple hosts. Such security information can be handled by SOAP platforms.

*A gateway for the enterprise*

Enterprises can provide many services. In this case, you have a gateway server, which plays the role of SOAP intermediary. The SOAP intermediary can perform "intermediate" tasks such as routing, security, and session management. From the requestor side, customers do not have to manage access points for services. At the provider side, you can even change the transport without more coding. The concepts of SOAP header and actor are useful in this situation.

## 12.3  SOAP Engines

### 12.3.1  Prototyping a SOAP Engine

Here, we prototype a SOAP engine that supports a subset of the SOAP specification. Once we start, you may notice the meaning of "Simple" in the name SOAP; that is, you can get an initial implementation working soon. First we develop a minimal function for the SOAP engine and then improve it, adding features like transport agnostic, intermediary, and header processing. For simplicity, we stick to document-centric messaging. SOAP-RPC is exemplified in the section Apache SOAP, showing other functions for product-level quality.

**SOAP Application for Travel Reservation**

Let us begin by developing requestor and provider programs that exchange SOAP messages over HTTP. Figure 12.5 illustrates the architecture. SOAPHTTPRequestor0 constructs a SOAP message for a travel reservation request, transmits with HttpURLConnection, and then receives a SOAP message for an acceptance response. A servlet engine receives the request SOAP message transmitted by HttpURLConnection and dispatches it to TravelServiceXML. Note that TravelServiceXML cannot consume a SOAP message. Therefore, we prepare TravelServiceSOAP, which extracts a body entry from the request SOAP message and hands it to TravelServiceXML. TravelServiceSOAP also constructs a response SOAP message, including a response XML document from TravelServiceXML as a body entry. The constructed response SOAP message is returned to the requestor by the servlet engine.

We showed some programs to send XML documents over HTTP in Chapter 10. Reusing the idea in them, we could describe the SOAPHttpRequestor0 class, as shown in Listing 12.10. This program reads an XML document from a file and

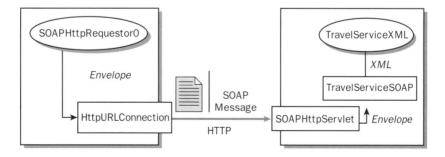

**Figure 12.5**  Initial architecture for the SOAP engine

includes the document in a SOAP Envelope only if the document is not a SOAP Envelope. Furthermore, SOAPHttpRequestor0 sends the SOAP message with HttpURLConnection, processing the character code set properly, as in the Chapter 10 examples.[4]

**Listing 12.10** Initial SOAP-over-HTTP requestor, chap12/travel/requestor/ SOAPHttpRequestor0.java

```java
package chap12.travel.requestor;

import java.io.FileReader;
import java.io.InputStream;
import java.io.OutputStream;
import java.net.URL;
import java.net.HttpURLConnection;
import javax.xml.parsers.DocumentBuilder;
import javax.xml.parsers.DocumentBuilderFactory;
import org.w3c.dom.Document;
import org.xml.sax.InputSource;
import org.apache.xml.serialize.OutputFormat;
import org.apache.xml.serialize.XMLSerializer;

import chap10.XmlMimeEntityHandler;
import chap12.simplesoap.util.EnvelopeUtil;

public class SOAPHttpRequestor0 {
    public static String SOAP_ENV="SOAP-ENV:Envelope";
    public static String CONTENT_TYPE_VALUE=
                        "text/xml; charset=UTF-8";
    public static void main(java.lang.String[] args)
        throws Exception
    {

        Document doc;

        // Parses the request XML with the specified charset (utf-8)
        DocumentBuilderFactory factory
            = DocumentBuilderFactory.newInstance();
        factory.setNamespaceAware(true);
        InputSource input =
            new InputSource(new FileReader(args[0]));
```

---

[4] According to the SOAP specification, in case of a SOAP error while processing the request, the SOAP HTTP server must issue an HTTP 500 "Internal Server Error" response and include a SOAP message in the response containing a SOAP Fault element. However, when the HttpURLConnection class recognizes the HTTP 500 error code, it does not read the contents of the HTTP response anymore. Accordingly, we cannot read the SOAP Fault. Therefore, SOAP engines such as Apache SOAP do not use HttpURLConnection but implement equivalent functions based on Socket classes.

```
doc = factory.newDocumentBuilder().parse(input);
OutputFormat formatter =
    new OutputFormat(doc, "utf-8", false);
formatter.setPreserveSpace(true);

// SOAP-ENV:Envelope is added if needed
if (!doc.getDocumentElement().
        getTagName().equals(SOAP_ENV))
{
    Document env = EnvelopeUtil.createEmptyEnvelope();
    doc = EnvelopeUtil.addBodyEntry(env, doc);
}

// Print out the request message
System.out.println("******** Request Message ********");
XMLSerializer serializer =
    new XMLSerializer(System.out, formatter);
serializer.serialize(doc);

// Set up HTTP transport
URL url = new URL(args[1]);
HttpURLConnection con =
    (HttpURLConnection)url.openConnection();
con.setRequestMethod("POST") ;
con.setRequestProperty("Content-Type",
                    "text/xml; charset=UTF-8") ;
con.setRequestProperty("SOAPAction", "\"\"") ;
con.setDoOutput(true) ;

// Serialize and send the request message
OutputStream out = con.getOutputStream() ;
serializer = new XMLSerializer(out, formatter);
serializer.serialize(doc);

// You may get error
if (con.getResponseCode() != HttpURLConnection.HTTP_OK)
    throw new Exception("Error in HttpURLConnection: "
                    + con.getResponseMessage()) ;

// Receive response message
InputStream in = con.getInputStream();
input =
    XmlMimeEntityHandler
        .getInputSource(con.getContentType(), in);

Document resp = factory.newDocumentBuilder().parse(input);

System.out.println("\n\n******** Response Message ********");
formatter = new OutputFormat();
```

```
                    formatter.setPreserveSpace(true);
                    serializer = new XMLSerializer(System.out, formatter);
                    serializer.serialize(resp);
                    System.out.println("\n\n******** Succeeded *******");
            }
    }
```

Let us move on to the server side. Listing 12.11 shows a servlet that processes SOAP messages. For initialization, the `init` method looks at an initial parameter, `ConsumerClass`, to find a class name. Note that such parameter/value pairs are defined in the `web.xml` file. The class specified here is instantiated and substituted to a member variable `consumer`. For example, the `TravelServiceSOAP` class is found and instantiated, and then the object is substituted to `consumer`. Note that other parameter/value pairs defined in `web.xml` are also handed to the `consumer` object. Incoming SOAP messages are processed in the `post` method. The method constructs a DOM object and dispatches to `consumer`. Then it gets a response DOM from `consumer` and returns it to the requestor, serializing the DOM object. As in the Chapter 10 examples (see Listing 10.8), the character code set is properly processed with the `XmlMimeEntityHandler`, `XMLSerializer`, and `OutputFormat` classes. The `doGet` method is provided to check whether this servlet is properly deployed with a Web browser.

**Listing 12.11** A servlet for processing SOAP messages, `chap12/simplesoap/`
`transport/SOAPHttpServlet.java`

```
package chap12.simplesoap.transport;

import java.io.PrintWriter;
import java.io.InputStream;
import java.io.ByteArrayOutputStream;
import java.io.IOException;
import java.util.Properties;
import java.util.Enumeration;
import javax.xml.parsers.DocumentBuilder;
import javax.xml.parsers.DocumentBuilderFactory;
import javax.xml.parsers.ParserConfigurationException;
import javax.servlet.ServletException;
import javax.servlet.http.HttpServlet;
import javax.servlet.http.HttpServletRequest;
import javax.servlet.http.HttpServletResponse;
import org.w3c.dom.Document;
import org.w3c.dom.Element;
import org.w3c.dom.Node;
import org.xml.sax.SAXException;
import org.xml.sax.InputSource;
```

```
import org.apache.xml.serialize.OutputFormat;
import org.apache.xml.serialize.XMLSerializer;

import chap10.XmlMimeEntityHandler;
import chap12.simplesoap.util.EnvelopeUtil;
import chap12.simplesoap.MessageConsumer;

public class SOAPHttpServlet extends HttpServlet {
    private MessageConsumer consumer=null;
    static public String CONSUMER_CLASS = "ConsumerClass";

    public void init() throws ServletException {
        try {
            // Find a consumer class name, and instatiate it
            String cname =
                getServletConfig().getInitParameter(CONSUMER_CLASS);
            Class cls = Class.forName(cname);
            this.consumer = (MessageConsumer)cls.newInstance();
            // Collect other properties
            Enumeration enum =
                getServletConfig().getInitParameterNames();
            Properties props = new Properties();
            while(enum.hasMoreElements()) {
                String propName = (String)enum.nextElement();
                props.put(propName,
                        getServletConfig().
                            getInitParameter(propName));
            }
            // Set properties to the consumer
            this.consumer.setProperties(props);
        } catch(Exception ex) {
            ex.printStackTrace();
            throw new ServletException(ex.getMessage());
        } finally {
            System.out.println(this.consumer.toString());
        }
    }
    public void doPost(HttpServletRequest req,
                    HttpServletResponse res)
        throws ServletException, java.io.IOException
    {
        try {
            // Gets Content-Type header
            String contentTypeValue = req.getContentType();
            // Gets an input source
            InputStream in = req.getInputStream();
```

```
                    InputSource input =
                        XmlMimeEntityHandler
                            .getInputSource(contentTypeValue, in);

                    // Parses the input here
                    DocumentBuilderFactory factory =
                        DocumentBuilderFactory.newInstance();
                    factory.setNamespaceAware(true);
                    DocumentBuilder parser = factory.newDocumentBuilder();
                    Document reqMsg = parser.parse(input);

                    // Invoke the main logic and get a response
                    Document resMsg = consumer.invoke(reqMsg);

                    //Serialize and send back the response
                    res.setContentType("text/xml; charset=utf-8");
                    // Serializes the response to return
                    OutputFormat formatter =
                        new OutputFormat(resMsg, "utf-8", false);
                    formatter.setPreserveSpace(true);
                    XMLSerializer serializer =
                        new XMLSerializer(res.getWriter(),
                                          formatter);
                    serializer.serialize(resMsg);
                } catch (Exception e) {
                    throw new ServletException(e);
                }
            }
            public void doGet(HttpServletRequest req,
                              HttpServletResponse res)
                throws ServletException, IOException
            {
                // Utility to check if this servlet is properly deployed
                // via Web browser
                PrintWriter out = res.getWriter ();
                res.setContentType("text/html");
                out.println("<html><head>");
                out.println("<title>XML and Java Edition 2</title></head>");
                out.println ("<body><h1>Chaptor 11</h1>");
                out.println ("<p>I am SOAPHttpServlet</p></body></html>");
            }
        }
```

Although SOAPHttpServlet can dispatch the DOM of a SOAP message to an object specified by a consumer member variable, our TravelServiceXML does not consume the SOAP message, but only consumes the XML document for the travel reservation request. Listing 12.12 is a program that extracts a body entry to feed it to `TravelServiceXML`. `TravelServiceSOAP` plays the role of adapter between `SOAPHttpServlet` and `TravelServiceXML`. This class also constructs a response SOAP Envelope enveloping a response from `TravelServiceXML`. In this program, you may notice the `EnvelopeUtil` class, which provides a collection of operations on SOAP Envelope, such as adding a body entry and removing a header entry. Refer to the accompanying CD-ROM for its implementation details.

**Listing 12.12** SOAP adapter for `TravelServiceXML`, `chap12/travel/provider/` `TravelServiceSOAP.java`

```
package chap12.travel.provider;

import org.w3c.dom.Document;

import chap12.simplesoap.util.EnvelopeUtil;
import chap12.simplesoap.MessageConsumer;

public class TravelServiceSOAP implements MessageConsumer {

    private TravelServiceXML xmlService = new TravelServiceXML();

    public Document invoke(Document req) throws Exception {
        try {
            Document reqMsgBody = EnvelopeUtil.removeEnvelope(req);
            Document resMsgBody = xmlService.reserve(reqMsgBody);
            Document resMsg = EnvelopeUtil.createEmptyEnvelope();
            resMsg = EnvelopeUtil.addBodyEntry(resMsg, resMsgBody);
            return resMsg;
        } catch(Exception ex) {
            ex.printStackTrace();
            throw ex;
        }
    }
    public void setProperties(java.util.Properties props)
        throws java.lang.Exception {}
}
```

`SOAPHttpServlet`, `TravelServiceSOAP`, and `TravelServiceXML` run on Tomcat. We have a configuration file, `web.xml`, on the CD-ROM to run these classes. Refer to the CD-ROM for information on how to run Tomcat, making the configuration effective.

Let us execute `SOAPHttpRequestor0`. This class takes two parameters: a path for the input XML document file and a servlet URL. A sample XML document for the travel reservation request shown in Listing 12.4 is located at `\samples\` `chap12\travel\requestor\request0.xml` on the CD-ROM. And the servlet

URL is `http://demohost:8080/xmlbook2/chap12/servlet/SOAPTravelServlet`. You can execute the program as follows:

```
R:\samples>java chap12.travel.requestor.SOAPHttpRequestor0
          chap12\travel\requestor\request0.xml
          http://demohost:8080/xmlbook2/chap12/servlet/
          SOAPTravelServlet
******** Request Message *******
<?xml version="1.0" encoding="utf-8"?>
<SOAP-ENV:Envelope xmlns:SOAP-ENV="http://schemas.xmlsoap.org/soap/
envelope/">
  <SOAP-ENV:Body>
  <ns1:reserve xmlns:ns1="urn:reserve-tour-msg">
  <user>nakamury</user>
  <tourId>hawaii55</tourId>
  <departure>
    <year>2002</year>
    <month>9</month>
    <day>15</day>
  </departure>
</ns1:reserve></SOAP-ENV:Body>
</SOAP-ENV:Envelope>

******** Response Message *******
<?xml version="1.0" encoding="UTF-8"?>
<SOAP-ENV:Envelope xmlns:SOAP-ENV="http://schemas.xmlsoap.org/soap/
envelope/">
  <SOAP-ENV:Body>
  <ns1:accepted xmlns:ns1="urn:reserve-tour-msg">
      <user>nakamury</user>
      <tourId>hawaii55</tourId>
      <departure>
        <year>2002</year>
        <month>9</month>
        <day>15</day>
      </departure>
    <reservation-id>hawaii551001421318551</reservation-id>
    </ns1:accepted></SOAP-ENV:Body>
</SOAP-ENV:Envelope>

******** Succeeded *******
```

### Abstracting the Transport to Support JMS

SOAP is inherently transport-independent. However, `SOAPHttpRequestor0` tightly depends on HTTP. Here, we abstract the transport layer, simultaneously supporting JMS. With this improvement, applications are independent of a particular transport protocol. As we will see later, applications can employ various transports without changing the code.

Figure 12.6 shows the architecture that we will develop next. On the requestor side, we have TransportSender instead of HttpURLConnection. Transport Sender is an abstract of transport-specific classes, such as HttpTransportSender and JMSTransportSender, and encapsulates a function for sending and receiving SOAP messages. On the provider side, we have TransportListener instead of SOAPHttpServlet. TransportListener is an abstraction of SOAPHttpServlet and JMSTransportListener, which we will see later. Also, we have the MessageConsumer interface, which should be implemented by classes such as TransportSender and TravelServiceSOAP. The commonality here is that both classes receive a request SOAP message and return a response SOAP message. This idea is especially useful when we develop intermediaries later.

Let us look at the implementation of JMS support. Listing 12.13 shows the JMSTransportListener class. In the main method, an instance of this class is created, and setup is invoked to perform basic configuration. The setup method first creates an object of the Queue class, creates a QueueReceiver object to receive messages from the queue, and finally register itself to the QueueReceiver object. JMSTransportListener implements MessageListener. Messages placed on the queue are received by the QueueReceiver object and are fed to JMSTransportListener via the onMessage method of the MessageListener interface. Processing in onMessage is similar to the post method of SOAPHttp Servlet. The onMessage method first extracts a SOAP message from a given JMS message to construct a DOM object for it and then invokes an object referred by

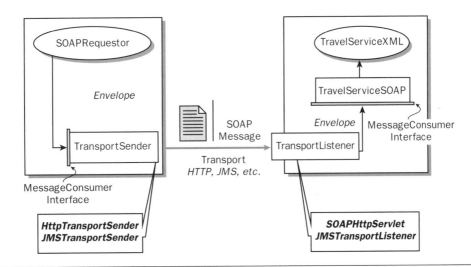

**Figure 12.6** Abstracting the transport layer of a SOAP engine

the `consumer` member variable. The incoming JMS message includes information about the reply queue, and `onMessage` creates a `QueueSender` object for the reply queue to return a response SOAP message to the requestor.

**Listing 12.13** Program for receiving SOAP messages over JMS, `chap12/simplesoap/transport/JMSTransportListener.java`

```
package chap12.simplesoap.transport;

import java.io.StringReader;
import java.io.StringWriter;
import javax.jms.DeliveryMode;
import javax.jms.JMSException;
import javax.jms.MessageListener;
import javax.jms.Queue;
import javax.jms.QueueConnection;
import javax.jms.QueueConnectionFactory;
import javax.jms.QueueReceiver;
import javax.jms.QueueSender;
import javax.jms.QueueSession;
import javax.jms.Session;
import javax.jms.TemporaryQueue;
import javax.jms.TextMessage;
import javax.naming.InitialContext;
import org.w3c.dom.Document;
import org.apache.xml.serialize.OutputFormat;
import org.apache.xml.serialize.XMLSerializer;

import chap12.simplesoap.util.EnvelopeUtil;
import chap12.simplesoap.MessageConsumer;

public class JMSTransportListener implements MessageListener {
    private java.lang.String queue;
    private QueueConnection connection;
    private QueueSession session;
    private MessageConsumer consumer;

    public static void main(String[] args) throws Exception {
        // set up initial configuration of this class
        JMSTransportListener listener = new JMSTransportListener();
        listener.queue = args[1];
        listener.consumer =
            (MessageConsumer)Class.forName(args[0]).newInstance();

        try {
            // initial setup for JMS
            listener.setup();
        } catch( JMSException ex ) {
            Exception e = ex.getLinkedException();
            ex.printStackTrace();
```

```
                System.exit(1);
        } catch( Exception ex ) {
            ex.printStackTrace();
            System.exit(1);
        }

        synchronized(listener) {
            listener.wait();
        }

        listener.close();
    }

    public void setup() throws Exception{
        try {
            System.out.println("Server Started");
            System.out.println("QueueName: " + this.queue);
            //  get connection factory via JNDI
            InitialContext jndiContext = new InitialContext();
            QueueConnectionFactory factory =
                (QueueConnectionFactory)
                    jndiContext.lookup("QueueConnectionFactory");

            //  create connection and session
            this.connection = factory.createQueueConnection();
            this.connection.start();
            this.session =
                this.connection
                    .createQueueSession(false,
                                        Session.AUTO_ACKNOWLEDGE);
            //  look up a queue via JNDI
            Queue queue = (Queue) jndiContext.lookup(this.queue);
            //  create a queue receiver
            QueueReceiver receiver =
                this.session.createReceiver(queue);
            //  register itself so as to receive messages
            receiver.setMessageListener(this);
        } catch (JMSException je) {
            System.out.println("Server caught "+je);
            throw je;
        } catch (Exception je) {
            System.out.println("Server caught "+je);
            throw je;
        }
    }

    public void onMessage(javax.jms.Message jmsMessage) {
        System.out.println("JMS onMessage invoked:" +
                            jmsMessage.toString());
```

```java
QueueSession replySession = null;
QueueSender sender=null;
try {
    // extract SOAP message from JMS message
    String requestString = null;
    if (jmsMessage instanceof TextMessage) {
        requestString = ((TextMessage)jmsMessage).getText();
    } else {
    }

    // if "terminate" is received, terminate this program
    if ( requestString.equalsIgnoreCase("terminate") ) {
        synchronized(this){
            this.notify();
        }
        return;
    }

    // create a JMS sender for reply queue
    Queue replyTo = (Queue)jmsMessage.getJMSReplyTo();
    replySession = this.connection.createQueueSession(false,
            Session.AUTO_ACKNOWLEDGE);
    sender = replySession.createSender(replyTo);
    sender.setDeliveryMode(DeliveryMode.NON_PERSISTENT);

    if (jmsMessage instanceof TextMessage) {
        // create DOM for SOAP message and invoke the next
        // consumer
        Document reqMsg =
            EnvelopeUtil
                .createDOM(new StringReader(requestString));
        Document resMsg = this.consumer.invoke(reqMsg);

        // serialize response message,
        // and send via a reply queue
        TextMessage replyMessage =
            replySession.createTextMessage();
        StringWriter writer = new StringWriter();
        OutputFormat formatter =
            new OutputFormat(resMsg, "utf-8", false);
        formatter.setPreserveSpace(true);
        XMLSerializer serializer =
            new XMLSerializer(writer, formatter);
        serializer.serialize(resMsg);
        replyMessage.setText(writer.toString());
        replyMessage
            .setJMSCorrelationID(
```

```
                          jmsMessage.getJMSMessageID());
                sender.send(replyMessage);
            } else {
            }
        } catch (JMSException je) {
            Exception e = je.getLinkedException();
            if ( e != null ) je.printStackTrace();
        } catch (Exception je) {
            je.printStackTrace();
        }

        try {
            if ( sender != null ) sender.close();
        } catch( JMSException ex ) {
        };
        try {
            if ( replySession != null ) replySession.close();
        } catch( JMSException ex ) {
        };
    }

    public void close() {
        try {
            if ( this.session != null ) this.session.close();
        } catch( JMSException ex ) {
            System.out.println(
                "JMSServerEndpoint: Could not close Session.");
        }
        try {
            this.connection.close();
        } catch( JMSException ex ) {
            System.out.println(
                "JMSServerEndpoint: Could not close Connection.");
        }
    }
}
```

On the requestor side, we develop HttpTransportSender and JMSTransport
Sender, defining a common interface. With this abstraction, requestor applications can send and receive SOAP messages without worrying about transport
details. Listing 12.14 shows HttpTransportSender, which encapsulates SOAP
messaging over HTTP. Its core portion stems from SOAPHttpRequestor0; that is,
we extracted only an HTTP-specific portion and wrapped it, defining a DOM-in/
DOM-out API.

**Listing 12.14** Program component for sending SOAP messages over HTTP, chap12/
simplesoap/transport/HttpTransportSender.java

```
package chap12.simplesoap.transport;

import java.io.InputStream;
import java.io.OutputStream;
import java.net.HttpURLConnection;
import java.net.URL;
import javax.xml.parsers.DocumentBuilder;
import javax.xml.parsers.DocumentBuilderFactory;
import org.w3c.dom.Document;
import org.xml.sax.InputSource;
import org.apache.xml.serialize.OutputFormat;
import org.apache.xml.serialize.XMLSerializer;
import chap10.XmlMimeEntityHandler;

import chap12.simplesoap.util.EnvelopeUtil;
import chap12.simplesoap.MessageConsumer;

public class HttpTransportSender implements MessageConsumer {
    public static String CONTENT_TYPE_VALUE=
                            "text/xml; charset=UTF-8";
    private String soapAction = "\"\"";
    private URL url;

    public HttpTransportSender(URL url) {
        this.url = url;
    }
    public String getSoapAction() {
        return soapAction;
    }
    public Document invoke(Document request) throws Exception {
        HttpURLConnection con =
            (HttpURLConnection)url.openConnection();
        con.setRequestMethod("POST");
        con.setRequestProperty("Content-Type", CONTENT_TYPE_VALUE);
        con.setRequestProperty("SOAPAction", soapAction) ;
        con.setDoOutput(true);

        // Serialize and send the request message
        OutputFormat formatter =
            new OutputFormat(request, "utf-8", false);
        formatter.setPreserveSpace(true);
        OutputStream out = con.getOutputStream() ;
        XMLSerializer serializer =
            new XMLSerializer(out, formatter);
        serializer.serialize(request);
```

```
            if (con.getResponseCode() != HttpURLConnection.HTTP_OK)
                throw
                    new Exception(
                        "HttpURLConnection received a response: " +
                        con.getResponseMessage()) ;

            // Receive response message
            DocumentBuilderFactory factory =
                DocumentBuilderFactory.newInstance();
            factory.setNamespaceAware(true);

            InputStream in = con.getInputStream();
            InputSource input =
                XmlMimeEntityHandler
                    .getInputSource(con.getContentType(), in);
            Document resp = factory.newDocumentBuilder().parse(input);
            return resp;
        }
        public void setSoapAction(String newSoapAction) {
            soapAction = newSoapAction;
        }
        public void setProperties(java.util.Properties props)
            throws java.lang.Exception {}
    }
```

Listing 12.15 shows `SOAPHttpRequestor`, which is rewritten based on
`SOAPHttpRequestor0`. More specifically, the HTTP-specific portion is replaced
with `new HttpTransportSender(new URL(args[1]))`, so the whole code is
cleaned up.

**Listing 12.15** Modified SOAP-over-HTTP requestor with `HttpTransportSender`,
`chap12/travel/requestor/SOAPHttpRequestor.java`

```
    package chap12.travel.requestor;

    import java.io.FileReader;
    import java.io.InputStream;
    import java.io.OutputStream;
    import java.net.URL;
    import javax.xml.parsers.DocumentBuilder;
    import javax.xml.parsers.DocumentBuilderFactory;
    import org.w3c.dom.Document;
    import org.xml.sax.InputSource;
    import org.apache.xml.serialize.OutputFormat;
    import org.apache.xml.serialize.XMLSerializer;

    import chap10.XmlMimeEntityHandler;
    import chap12.simplesoap.MessageConsumer;
```

```java
import chap12.simplesoap.transport.HttpTransportSender;
import chap12.simplesoap.util.EnvelopeUtil;

public class SOAPHttpRequestor {
    public static String SOAP_ENV="SOAP-ENV:Envelope";

    public static void main(java.lang.String[] args)
        throws Exception {
        Document doc;

        // Parses the request XML with the specified charset
        // (utf-8)
        DocumentBuilderFactory factory =
            DocumentBuilderFactory.newInstance();
        factory.setNamespaceAware(true);
        InputSource input =
            new InputSource(new FileReader(args[0]));
        doc = factory.newDocumentBuilder().parse(input);
        OutputFormat formatter =
            new OutputFormat(doc, "utf-8", false);
        formatter.setPreserveSpace(true);

        // SOAP-ENV:Envelope is added if needed
        if (!doc.getDocumentElement().
                getTagName().equals(SOAP_ENV))
        {
            Document env = EnvelopeUtil.createEmptyEnvelope();
            doc = EnvelopeUtil.addBodyEntry(env, doc);
        }

        // Print out the request message
        System.out.println("******* Request Message *******");
        XMLSerializer serializer =
            new XMLSerializer(System.out, formatter);
        serializer.serialize(doc);

        MessageConsumer sender =
            new HttpTransportSender(new URL(args[1]));

        Document resp = sender.invoke(doc);

        System.out.println("\n\n******* Response Message *******");
        formatter = new OutputFormat();
        formatter.setPreserveSpace(true);
        serializer = new XMLSerializer(System.out, formatter);
        serializer.serialize(resp);
        System.out.println("\n\n******* Succeeded *******");

    }
}
```

`SOAPHttpRequestor` can be executed as follows:

```
R:\samples>java chap12.travel.requestor.SOAPHttpRequestor
           chap12\travel\requestor\request0.xml
           http://demohost:8080/xmlbook2/chap12/servlet/
           SOAPTravelServlet
```

Listing 12.16 shows `JMSTransportSender`, which sends and receives SOAP messages over JMS. As in `JMSTransportListener`, this class also creates the `QueueSender` and `QueueReceiver` objects to put and get JMS messages on and from the queues. One of the big differences here is that a temporary queue is created, and it is set to an outgoing JMS message that includes a request SOAP message. Because the provider puts a JMS message for response on the temporary queue, the requestor monitors only the temporary queue.

**Listing 12.16** Program to send SOAP messages over JMS, `chap12/simplesoap/ transport/JMSTransportSender.java`

```java
package chap12.simplesoap.transport;

import java.io.StringReader;

import javax.jms.JMSException;
import javax.jms.Queue;
import javax.jms.QueueConnection;
import javax.jms.QueueConnectionFactory;
import javax.jms.QueueSession;
import javax.jms.QueueSender;
import javax.jms.QueueReceiver;
import javax.jms.Session;
import javax.jms.TemporaryQueue;
import javax.jms.TextMessage;
import javax.naming.InitialContext;

import org.w3c.dom.Document;
import org.apache.soap.util.xml.DOM2Writer;

import chap12.simplesoap.util.EnvelopeUtil;
import chap12.simplesoap.MessageConsumer;

public class JMSTransportSender
    implements chap12.simplesoap.MessageConsumer
{
    private QueueConnection connection = null;
    private java.lang.String queueName;
    public JMSTransportSender() {}

    public JMSTransportSender(String queueName) {
        this.queueName = queueName;
```

```
    }

    public void setProperties(java.util.Properties props)
        throws Exception
    {
        this.queueName = props.getProperty(JMSConstants.QUEUE_NAME);
    }

    public void initializeConnection() {
        try {
            InitialContext jndiContext = new InitialContext();
            QueueConnectionFactory factory =
                (QueueConnectionFactory)
                    jndiContext.lookup("QueueConnectionFactory");
            this.connection = factory.createQueueConnection();
            this.connection.start();
        } catch (JMSException je) {
            je.printStackTrace();
        } catch(Exception e) {
            e.printStackTrace();
        }
    }

    public org.w3c.dom.Document invoke(org.w3c.dom.Document request)
        throws Exception
    {
        QueueSession session = null;
        try {
            if (connection == null)
                initializeConnection();
            session =
                connection
                    .createQueueSession(false,
                                        Session.AUTO_ACKNOWLEDGE);
            return send(session, request);
        } catch (JMSException je) {
            je.printStackTrace();
            throw je;
        }
    }
    private Document send(QueueSession session, Document request)
        throws Exception
    {
        QueueSender sender = null;
        QueueReceiver qRec = null;
        TemporaryQueue replyTo = null;
        try {
```

```
                Queue queue = session.createQueue(queueName);
                sender = session.createSender(queue);
                TextMessage outMessage = session.createTextMessage();
                String content = DOM2Writer.nodeToString(request);
                outMessage.setText(content);

                replyTo = session.createTemporaryQueue();
                outMessage.setJMSReplyTo(replyTo);
                sender.send(outMessage);
                qRec = session.createReceiver(replyTo);
                javax.jms.Message replyMessage = qRec.receive();
                String replyString =
                    ((TextMessage) replyMessage).getText();
                Document resp =
                    EnvelopeUtil.createDOM(
                        new StringReader(replyString));
                return resp;
            } catch (JMSException je) {
                je.printStackTrace();
                throw je;
            } finally {
                try {
                    if (sender != null)
                        sender.close();
                } catch (JMSException ex) {}
                try {
                    if (qRec != null)
                        qRec.close();
                } catch (JMSException ex) {};
                try {
                    if (replyTo != null) {
                        replyTo.delete();
                    }
                } catch (JMSException je) {};
                try {
                    if (session != null)
                        session.close();
                } catch (JMSException ex) {};
            }
        }
    }
}
```

We can modify SOAPHttpRequestor using JMSTransportSender instead of
HttpTransportSender, as in Listing 12.17. As you can see, the difference is only
one instruction, in which SOAPJmsRequestor creates a JMSTransportSender
object.

**Listing 12.17** SOAP-over-JMS requestor, `chap12/travel/requestor/`
`SOAPJmsRequestor.java`

```java
package chap12.travel.requestor;

import java.io.FileReader;
import java.io.InputStream;
import java.io.OutputStream;
import javax.xml.parsers.DocumentBuilder;
import javax.xml.parsers.DocumentBuilderFactory;
import org.w3c.dom.Document;
import org.xml.sax.InputSource;
import org.apache.xml.serialize.OutputFormat;
import org.apache.xml.serialize.XMLSerializer;

import chap10.XmlMimeEntityHandler;
import chap12.simplesoap.MessageConsumer;
import chap12.simplesoap.transport.JMSTransportSender;
import chap12.simplesoap.util.EnvelopeUtil;

public class SOAPJmsRequestor {
    public static String SOAP_ENV="SOAP-ENV:Envelope";

    public static void main(java.lang.String[] args)
        throws Exception
    {
        Document doc;

        // Parses the request XML with the specified charset (utf-8)
        DocumentBuilderFactory factory =
            DocumentBuilderFactory.newInstance();
        factory.setNamespaceAware(true);
        InputSource input =
            new InputSource(new FileReader(args[0]));
        doc = factory.newDocumentBuilder().parse(input);
        OutputFormat formatter =
            new OutputFormat(doc, "utf-8", false);
        formatter.setPreserveSpace(true);

        // SOAP-ENV:Envelope is added if needed
        if (!doc.getDocumentElement().
                getTagName().equals(SOAP_ENV))
        {
            Document env = EnvelopeUtil.createEmptyEnvelope();
            doc = EnvelopeUtil.addBodyEntry(env, doc);
        }

        // Print out the request message
        System.out.println("******* Request Message *******");
```

```
            XMLSerializer serializer =
                new XMLSerializer(System.out, formatter);
            serializer.serialize(doc);

            MessageConsumer sender =
                new JMSTransportSender(args[1]);

            Document resp = sender.invoke(doc);

            formatter = new OutputFormat();
            formatter.setPreserveSpace(true);
            serializer = new XMLSerializer(System.out, formatter);
            serializer.serialize(resp);
            System.out.println("\n\n******** Succeeded *******");
        }
    }
```

To execute SOAPJmsRequestor and SOAPJmsListener, we need a queue manager that supports JMS. Because the JMS examples in this section are based on
Sun's Java 2 Software Development Kit, Enterprise Edition (J2EE SDK) version 1.3,
you have to start up the J2EE server and configure a queue. Refer to the CD-ROM
to learn how to use the J2EE SDK to execute our examples. After starting up J2EE
SDK, you should start up JMSTransportListener as follows:

```
R:\samples>java
        -Djms.properties=%J2EE_HOME%\config\jms_client.properties
        chap12.simplesoap.transport.JMSTransportListener
        chap12.travel.provider.TravelServiceSOAP MyQueue
```

Then you can execute SOAPJmsRequestor with the following command:

```
R:\samples>java
        -Djms.properties=%J2EE_HOME%\config\jms_client.properties
        chap12.travel.requestor.SOAPJmsRequestor
        chap12\travel\requestor\request0.xml MyQueue
```

Now we have abstracted transport layers and developed two transport supports:
HTTP and JMS.

### Intermediary Support

Because we have two transports, HTTP and JMS, supported in our SOAP engine,
we now combine them to implement an intermediary, which is one of the most
interesting concepts in SOAP. Figure 12.7 illustrates the improved architecture.
SOAPHttpRequestor sends a request SOAP message to an intermediary node
via HTTP. At the intermediary node, the incoming SOAP message is dispatched to
HeaderCheckerIntermediary, which processes a header entry, removes it, and

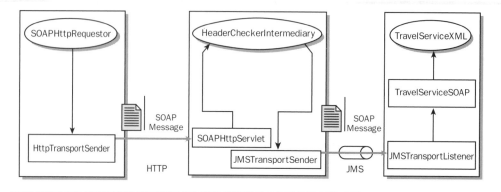

**Figure 12.7** Supporting intermediaries in a SOAP engine

feeds the message to `JMSTransportSender`. `JMSTransportSender` sends the SOAP message via JMS. At the final destination node, the SOAP message is received by `JMSTransportListener` and dispatched to `TravelServiceXML` via `TravelServiceSOAP`. A response SOAP message is returned to the requestor node along the request path in the opposite direction.

### Header Processing

With SOAP header entries, you can add any facets that are not specialized for applications. If you use header entries properly, you can plug in various functions without impacting existing requestor and provider applications. As an example, we assume that a requestor is required to show a *letter of introduction* in our travel reservation scenario. An immediate approach is to embed the introduction letter in an XML document of the travel reservation request. However, you have to modify both requestor and provider applications. Using a header entry, you can easily extract the introduction letter from a SOAP message; you do not have to modify applications.

Listing 12.18 shows a SOAP message for a travel reservation request with an introduction header. We assume that the requestor acquires the introduction letter from a third party such as a travel association. Then the requestor embeds it in SOAP message to get a 5% discount.

**Listing 12.18** SOAP message with an introduction header entry

```
<SOAP-ENV:Envelope
    xmlns:SOAP-ENV="http://schemas.xmlsoap.org/soap/envelope/">
    <SOAP-ENV:Header>
        <intro:Introduction
```

```
                  xmlns:intro="http://example.com/introduction"
                  SOAP-ENV:mustUnderstand="1"
                  SOAP-ENV:actor="http://xmlbook/inter2">
                  <intro:issuer>Japan Travel Association</intro:issuer>
                  <intro:description>5% discount</intro:description>
              </intro:Introduction>
          </SOAP-ENV:Header>
          <SOAP-ENV:Body>
              <ns1:reserve xmlns:ns1="urn:reserve-tour-msg">
                  <ns1:user>nakamury</ns1:user>
                  <ns1:tourId>hawaii55</ns1:tourId>
                  <ns1:departure>
                      <ns1:year>2001</ns1:year>
                      <ns1:month>9</ns1:month>
                      <ns1:day>15</ns1:day>
                  </ns1:departure>
              </ns1:reserve>
          </SOAP-ENV:Body>
      </SOAP-ENV:Envelope>
```

Listing 12.19 shows a program of the SOAP intermediary. The member variables `myActorURI` and `handler` are set to specify what header entries are processed here. As in the `invoke` method, this program is concerned only with header entries whose `actorURI` is equal to `myActorURI` and whose namespace is one to be processed by `handler`. After invoking a header handler, this program dispatches the incoming SOAP message to the next node by using the `Transport Sender` object specified by the member variable `sender`.

Listing 12.20 shows the handler for checking the introduction header entry. Although it should check the validity of the introduction, here it just prints an "ok" message on the screen for simplicity. Note that when `IntroductionHeader Handler` has an error while processing, it has to generate a SOAP Fault to return. Such error handling is also omitted here.

**Listing 12.19** Program of the SOAP intermediary, `chap12/travel/intermediary/HeaderCheckerIntermediary.java`

```
package chap12.travel.intermediary;

import java.util.Vector;

import org.w3c.dom.Node;
import org.w3c.dom.Element;
import org.w3c.dom.NodeList;
import org.w3c.dom.Attr;
import org.w3c.dom.NamedNodeMap;
```

```java
import chap12.simplesoap.transport.JMSTransportSender;
import chap12.simplesoap.MessageConsumer;
import chap12.simplesoap.util.EnvelopeUtil;

public class HeaderCheckerIntermediary implements MessageConsumer {
    private MessageConsumer sender;
    private String myActorURI="http://xmlbook/inter2";
    private IntroductionHeaderHandler handler =
        new IntroductionHeaderHandler();

    public void setProperties(java.util.Properties props)
        throws java.lang.Exception
    {
        this.sender = new JMSTransportSender();
        this.sender.setProperties(props);
    }

    public org.w3c.dom.Document invoke(org.w3c.dom.Document request)
        throws Exception
    {
        // Extract header entries
        Vector headers = EnvelopeUtil.getHeaderEntries(request);
        Vector list = new Vector();
        for(int i=0; i<headers.size(); i++) {
            Element el = (Element)headers.elementAt(i);
            if (getActor(el).equals(this.myActorURI)) {
                String ns1=this.handler.getNamespace();
                String ns2=getNamespace(el);
                if(ns1.equals(ns2)) {
                    this.handler.process(request, el);
                    list.addElement(el);
                } else {
                    throw new Exception("MUST Understand Fault");
                }
            }
        }
        removeHeaderEntries(list);
        System.out.println("Removed Processed Header Entry(s)");
        return this.sender.invoke(request);
    }
    private String getActor(Element header) {
        return header.getAttribute("SOAP-ENV:actor");
    }
    private void removeHeaderEntries(Vector list) {
        for(int i=0; i<list.size(); i++) {
            Element el = (Element)list.elementAt(i);
```

```
                    Node node = el.getParentNode();
                    node.removeChild(el);
                }
            }
            private String getNamespace(Element header) {
                NodeList list = header.getChildNodes();
                NamedNodeMap attrs = header.getAttributes();
                for(int i=0; i<attrs.getLength(); i++) {
                    Attr attr=(Attr)attrs.item(i);
                    String name = attr.getName();
                    if (name.startsWith("xmlns:"))
                        return attr.getValue();
                }

                return null;
            }

        }
```

**Listing 12.20** Header handler for introduction header entries, `chap12/travel/` `intermediary/IntroductionHeaderHandler.java`

```
        package chap12.travel.intermediary;

        import org.w3c.dom.Document;
        import org.w3c.dom.Element;

        public class IntroductionHeaderHandler {
            private String namespace="http://example.com/introduction";
            public void process(Document msg, Element header) {
                System.out.println("Processing " + header.getTagName() );
                System.out.println("Any introduction is ok" );
                System.out.println("Done.");
            }
            public String getNamespace() {
                return this.namespace;
            }
        }
```

Let us look at the Tomcat configuration file for setting up `HeaderChecker` `Intermediary` at the intermediary node (see Listing 12.21). This time, the initial parameter `ConsumerClass` specifies `HeaderCheckerIntermediary`, and then request SOAP messages received by the servlet are dispatched to the object of this class. Although the queue name specified by `JMS.QUEUE` is also fed to the `Header` `CheckerIntermediary` object, it is passed to `JMSTransportSender` via the `setProperties` method.

**Listing 12.21**  Excerpt from the Tomcat `web.xml` file for configuring the intermediary

```
<web-app>
  <display-name>XML and Java Edition 2</display-name>

  <servlet>
    <servlet-name>SOAPServlet3</servlet-name>
    <display-name>Travel SOAP Servlet with Introduction Checking
    </display-name>
    <servlet-class>
        chap12.simplesoap.transport.SOAPHttpServlet
    </servlet-class>
    <init-param>
      <param-name>ConsumerClass</param-name>
      <param-value>chap12.travel.intermediary.HeaderChecker
      Intermediary</param-value>
    </init-param>
    <init-param>
      <param-name>JMS.QUEUE_NAME</param-name>
      <param-value>MyQueue</param-value>
    </init-param>
  </servlet>

  <servlet-mapping>
    <servlet-name>SOAPServlet3</servlet-name>
    <url-pattern>/servlet/SOAPTravelServlet3</url-pattern>
  </servlet-mapping>

</web-app>
```

As in previous examples, you can execute the program as follows, only specifying another servlet URL.

```
R:\samples>java
chap12.travel.requestor.SOAPHttpRequestor
chap12\travel\requestor\request-intro.xml
http://demohost:8080/xmlbook2/chap12/servlet/SOAPTravelServlet3
```

You can make sure that the header handler is invoked by looking at the Tomcat running command-line screen. You will see the following message:

```
chap12.travel.intermediary.HeaderCheckerIntermediary@617189
Removed Processed Header Entry(s)
Java(TM) Message Service 1.0.2 Reference Implementation (build b13)
Processing intro:Introduction
Any introduction is ok
Done.
Removed Processed Header Entry(s)
```

The processing here is only to find the header entry, but of course you can insert any program there. The important point is that you can add any functions by defining header entries and adding handlers to process them. Such modification can be carried out without modifying the original requestor and provider applications. Furthermore, the new functions can be located on an intermediary node.

## 12.3.2 SOAP Engine Products

In Section 12.3.1, we explained some basic concepts of SOAP in greater detail, prototyping a SOAP engine. Here, we examine two SOAP engine products: Apache SOAP and Axis. First we look at Apache SOAP to consider what is required to use it realistically. Then we overview Apache Axis, a successor to Apache SOAP.

### Apache SOAP

In our prototype, a `TransportListener` object is tightly coupled with a particular application, `TravelServiceSOAP`. However, what should we do when we have fairly large number of applications on the provider side? Apache SOAP introduces the concept of a "router," with which SOAP messages are routed to an appropriate application. Figure 12.8 illustrates the architecture of Apache SOAP in terms of the router concept, incorporating our travel reservation scenario. We assume that a travel agency hosts a provider node on which Apache SOAP is running. Let us include a travel search service in our scenario, in addition to the travel reservation service we have discussed. Because the travel agency node receives both travel search and travel reservation request messages, the router must dispatch the messages to the proper application. In addition, Apache SOAP provides two kinds of routers: one for RPC and the other for document-centric messaging. Because DCM is just called *messaging* in Apache SOAP, the latter router is called a message router in the figure.

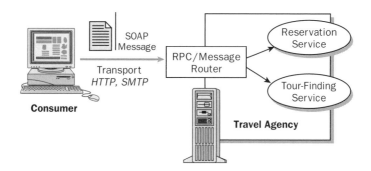

**Figure 12.8** Message routing in Apache SOAP

Now you may ask, how can we route messages? Apache SOAP performs routing based on the namespace specified in the first body entry. Accordingly, each application is registered to the router with an identifier represented in a namespace URI. Configuration information, such as identifier/application mappings, is described in an XML document called a *deployment descriptor*. Listing 12.22 shows a deployment descriptor for `TravelServiceRPC`.

**Listing 12.22** A deployment descriptor for Apache SOAP, `DeploymentDescriptor.xml`

```
<isd:service xmlns:isd="http://xml.apache.org/xml-soap/deployment"
             id="urn:reserve-tour-rpc">
    <isd:provider type="java"
                  scope="Application"
                  methods="reserve">
        <isd:java
            class="chap12.travel.provider.TravelServiceRPC"
            static="false"/>
    </isd:provider>

    <isd:faultListener>org.apache.soap.server.DOMFaultListener
    </isd:faultListener>

    <isd:mappings>
        <isd:map encodingStyle=
                    "http://schemas.xmlsoap.org/soap/encoding/"
            xmlns:x="urn:xml-soap-travel-demo"
            qname="x:reservation"
            javaType="chap12.travel.Reservation"
            java2XMLClassName=
                "org.apache.soap.encoding.soapenc.BeanSerializer"
            xml2JavaClassName=
                "org.apache.soap.encoding.soapenc.BeanSerializer"/>
    </isd:mappings>
</isd:service>
```

First, we want to describe that the `reserve` method of the `TravelServiceRPC` class should be used, and the identifier of this service is `urn:reserve-tour-msg`. In Listing 12.22, the class name is specified in the `class` attribute of the `isd:java` element, the method name is specified in the `methods` attribute of the `id:provider` element, and the identifier is specified in the `id` attribute of the `isd:service` element.

The rest of Listing 12.22 specifies how to encode Java objects in XML (see `isd:mappings`). Let us look at Listings 12.7 and 12.8 again. Listing 12.7 is an encoding of the method invocation for the `reserve` method of the `TravelServiceRPC` class. The types of the parameters of the methods are basic Java types, such as String and Date, and Apache SOAP can encode them without any extra configuration. On the other hand, the type of the return value is the `Reservation` class, which is an application-specific class; therefore, we need to specify how to encode the objects of this class. Fortunately, Apache SOAP provides a utility class, called `BeanSerializer`, which serializes objects of JavaBeans classes. More specifically, `Reservation` has getter/setter methods for its properties and conforms to the JavaBeans specification. Therefore, we can specify such information with the `javaType` and `java2XMLClassName` attributes of the `isd:map` element so that `BeanSerializer` can serialize the objects of the `Reservation` class. `Bean Serializer` itself can deserialize, and we can specify it in the `xml2JavaClass Name` attributes of the `isd:map` element.

So far, we have reviewed the provider side of Apache SOAP. Now we move on to the requestor side, concerning how to perform RPC. Listing 12.23 is an example that invokes the `reserve` method of the `TravelServiceRPC` class with Apache SOAP. The `Call` class plays a central role here. An object of the `Call` class is created; the namespace URI of the target service (`urn:reserve-tour-rpc`), the method name (`reserve`), and the parameters (user ID, tour ID, and date) are fed to the object; and then you can perform RPC by using the `invoke` method of the `Call` class. Note that you have to specify how to serialize and deserialize the `Reservation` objects as on the provider side. In this example, we configure programmatically with the `SOAPMappingRegistry` class.

**Listing 12.23** SOAP-over-HTTP requestor based on Apache SOAP, `chap12/apachesoap/ApacheSOAPRequestor.java`

```
package chap12.apachesoap;

import java.net.URL;
import java.util.Calendar;
import java.util.Date;
import java.util.Vector;

import org.apache.soap.util.xml.QName;
import org.apache.soap.Constants;
import org.apache.soap.Fault;
import org.apache.soap.rpc.Call;
import org.apache.soap.rpc.Parameter;
import org.apache.soap.rpc.Response;
import org.apache.soap.encoding.SOAPMappingRegistry;
import org.apache.soap.encoding.soapenc.BeanSerializer;

import chap12.travel.Reservation;
```

```
public class ApacheSOAPRequestor {
    public static void main(String[] args) throws Exception {
        if (args.length != 6
            && (args.length != 7 || !args[0].startsWith ("-"))) {
            System.err.println (
                "Usage: java " +
                ApacheSOAPRequestor.class.getName () +
                " [-encodingStyleURI] SOAP-router-URL user " +
                "tourId yy mm dd");
            System.exit (1);
        }

        int offset = 7 - args.length;
        String encodingStyleURI = args.length == 3
                                ? args[0].substring(1)
                                : Constants.NS_URI_SOAP_ENC;
        URL url = new URL (args[1 - offset]);
        String user = args[2 - offset];
        String tourId = args[3 - offset];
        String year = args[4 - offset];
        String month= args[5 - offset];
        String day = args[6 - offset];
        Calendar cal=Calendar.getInstance();
        cal.clear();
        cal.set(Integer.parseInt(year),
                Integer.parseInt(month)-1,
                Integer.parseInt(day));
        Date departure = cal.getTime();

        SOAPMappingRegistry smr = new SOAPMappingRegistry();
        BeanSerializer beanSer = new BeanSerializer();

        smr.mapTypes(Constants.NS_URI_SOAP_ENC,
                     new QName("urn:xml-soap-travel-demo",
                               "reservation"),
                     Reservation.class, beanSer, beanSer);

        Call call = new Call ();
        call.setSOAPMappingRegistry(smr);
        call.setTargetObjectURI ("urn:reserve-tour-rpc");
        call.setMethodName ("reserve");
        call.setEncodingStyleURI(encodingStyleURI);

        Vector params = new Vector ();
        params.addElement(
            new Parameter("user", String.class, user, null));
        params.addElement(
```

```
                    new Parameter("tourId", String.class, tourId, null));
            params.addElement(
                new Parameter("departure", Date.class,
                              departure, null));
            call.setParams (params);

            // make the call: note that the action URI is empty
            // because the
            // XML-SOAP rpc router does not need this. This may change
            // in the
            // future.
            Response resp = call.invoke (url, "");

            if (resp.generatedFault ()) {
                Fault fault = resp.getFault ();
                System.out.println ("Ouch, the call failed: ");
                System.out.println ("  Fault Code   = " +
                                    fault.getFaultCode ());
                System.out.println ("  Fault String = " +
                                    fault.getFaultString ());
            } else {
                Parameter result = resp.getReturnValue ();
                System.out.println (""+result.getValue ());
            }
        }
    }
}
```

Let us execute Apache SOAP. First you have to configure the provider side, sending
the deployment descriptor shown in Listing 12.22 so that the `reserve` method of
the `TravelServiceRPC` class can be accessible. Apache SOAP provides a utility
class, `ServiceManagerClient`, and you can deploy the service as follows:

```
R:\samples>java org.apache.soap.server.ServiceManagerClient
        http://demohost:8080/soap/servlet/rpcrouter deploy
        chap12/travel/DeploymentDescriptor.xml
```

Now let us execute RPC with Apache SOAP. `ApacheSOAPRequestor` can be executed as follows:

```
R:\samples>java chap12.apachesoap.ApacheSOAPRequestor
        http://demohost:8080/soap/servlet/rpcrouter
        nakamury hawaii55 2002 5 10
```

The program in Listing 12.23 seems too complicated for performing RPC because
you have to construct the method invocation by yourself. From a programmer's
point of view, a proxy class for `TravelServiceRPC` should be provided so that

we can just invoke its reserve method. We discuss how to generate such a proxy class in greater detail in Chapter 13.

In this section, we reviewed Apache SOAP, paying attention to its routing function and RPC encoding mechanism. In addition, Apache SOAP provides the following advanced functions to achieve product-level quality:

- EJB and COM support in addition to Java
- Secure Sockets Layer (SSL) and HTTP Basic Authentication
- SOAP attachments support

### Apache Axis

Apache SOAP is useful for performing SOAP messaging as a first step in the sense that functions like routing, encoding, and security are stable enough for production. However, the most interesting portions of SOAP—that is, header processing and intermediary support—are not fully implemented. That situation leads some developers of Apache SOAP to a new project called Apache Axis. As for routing and encoding, Axis takes over the idea of Apache SOAP. Therefore, Figure 12.8 is still valid in Axis except that Axis processes both RPC and document-centric messaging with a single router.

Figure 12.9 depicts the handler-chaining architecture of Axis, which is introduced for header handling. With Axis, you can flexibly configure handlers, such as our introduction header handler. On the provider side, you have a pivot handler, which invokes an application, such as our `TravelServiceRPC` and `TravelService SOAP`, and can add preprocessing and postprocessing handlers, as in the figure, to construct a handler chain. In the same manner, on the requestor side, you can configure a handler chain, viewing `TransportSender` as a pivot handler. With this architecture, you can add new functions without modifying the requestor and provider applications, as we demonstrated in our prototype SOAP engine. For example, our introduction header handler can be placed in a preprocessing chain

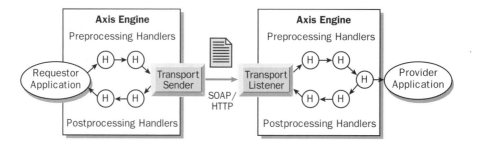

**Figure 12.9** Handler-chaining architecture of Axis

on the provider side, and you can develop a handler for inserting an introduction header to place at the preprocessing chain on the requestor side. In this way, you do not have to modify both applications, but you can add new functions.

Axis is at the alpha-3 level as we write this book, so we have only overviewed its architecture here. However, because some major software vendors are joining in the development, Axis will be adopted for their products instead of Apache SOAP.

### 12.3.3 Java API for SOAP

Although there are a number of SOAP engine implementations, they are not inter-operable. From a developer's point of view, applications developed for one engine should run on others. To define a Java standard API for a SOAP engine, two specifi-cations are being developed in JSR processes: Java API for XML Messaging (JAXM) and Java API for XML RPC (JAX-RPC). Let us look at Figure 12.1, shown at the beginning of this chapter. We classified the application layer into two categories: document-centric messaging and RCP. Approximately, JAXM handles DCM, and JAX-RPC handles RPC. Because JAX-RPC depends heavily on the Web Services Description Language (WSDL), introduced in the next chapter, here we review mainly JAXM.

The conceptual model of JAXM is close to that of our prototype, so we can explain it in terms of Figure 12.6. For example, a requestor application constructs a SOAP message and transmits it with a transport sender. One big difference is that our prototype operates directly on DOM; JAXM, on the other hand, provides an abstract API that is not specialized for an XML data model such as DOM. Listing 12.24 shows sample code for a JAXM client. SOAPConnection is an abstract class for various transports such as HTTP and SMTP. By invoking the call method, you can transmit SOAP messages. So far, SOAPConnection is extremely similar to our TransportSender.

**Listing 12.24** A sample program for JAXM

```
public class JAXMClient {
    public void sendMessage() throws Exception {
        // Create connection to send message
        SOAPConnection con = SOAPConnection.newInstance();
        // Create a message factory
        MessageFactory mf = MessageFactory.newInstance();
        // Create a message
        SOAPMessage msg = mf.createMessage();
        SOAPPart sp = msg.getSOAPPart();
        SOAPEnvelope envelope = sp.getEnvelope();
        // Create a soap body from the envelope.
```

```
SOAPBody bdy = envelope.getBody();
// Add a soap body element to the soap body
SOAPBodyElement gltp =
    bdy.addBodyElement(
        envelope.createName("GetLastTradePrice",
                            "ztrade",
                            "http://wombat.ztrade.com"));
gltp.addChildElement(
    envelope.createName("symbol",
                        "ztrade",
                        "http://wombat.ztrade.com"))
    .addTextNode("SUNW");

// Creating attachment
URL url = new URL(data); // e.g. data=location of the data
Attachment art ap =
    msg.createAttachment art(new DataHandler(url));
ap.setContentType("text/html");
// Add the attachment part to the message.
msg.addAttachment art(ap);
//Send the message
URLEndpoint urlEndpoint = new URLEndpoint(to);
SOAPMessage reply = con.call(msg, urlEndpoint);
.....
}
```

On the other hand, classes for SOAP messages are much different from ours. Although we operated on DOM objects, JAXM provides a DOM-independent API. More specifically, there are SOAP-specific classes such as SOAPEnvelope, SOAPBody and SOAPBodyElement, and you can act through these classes without being concerned about the DOM API. For example, the createName method of the SOAPEnvelope class is used to create an XML element from an element name, its prefix, and its namespace URI. With the abstract API, SOAP engine developers would choose other effective implementations. For instance, you would only manage text on the requestor side because you would be only required to transmit an XML document as text. Apache Axis records SAX events instead of creating DOM objects to abstract the SOAP Envelope API, and support of the envelope API of JAXM is being developed.

As in the sample code, JAXM provides a SOAPMessage class to support the "SOAP with Attachment" specification. A SOAPMessage object can manage multiple Part objects, and you can access a particular Part object with SOAPMessage methods. As such a class is added to JAXM, it seems to be a common agreement that SOAP engines should support SOAP attachments in addition to SOAP.

## 12.4 Summary

In this chapter, we have discussed XML messaging. First we showed the XML messaging stack to give an overview of XML messaging. The messaging stack defines the following three layers:

- Application
- Messaging
- Transport

In addition, we provided a distinction between RPC and document-centric messaging, emphasizing the importance of both.

We also discussed SOAP, addressing some important concepts such as the Envelope, header processing, the intermediary, and SOAP encoding. We also developed a prototype SOAP engine to understand how easy it is to develop a SOAP engine. As product-level SOAP engines, we described Apache SOAP and Axis. We believe that experience with the prototype can help you better understand the products.

XML messaging is expected to play a central role in future B2B collaborations. Especially, SOAP is considered a key technology because it has been widely accepted, and therefore interoperability can be achieved to some extent. On the other hand, a number of problems must be solved for real business use. At the least, support for security and transactions is mandatory. As we discuss in Chapter 14, security for XML and SOAP is proceeding well. An XML digital signature has been submitted to W3C and recently became a Recommendation. On the other hand, there is no active standardization for transactions, but you should keep your eyes on it.

In Chapter 13, we extend our perspective from XML messaging to Web services. As we will show there, you should know three basic technologies for Web services: SOAP, Web Services Description Language (WSDL), and Universal Description, Discovery, and Integration (UDDI). We have already explained one of them, and applications accessible via SOAP are Web services by definition. When we explain the other two technologies, you will see the big picture of Web services.

# Web Services

## 13.1 Emergence of Web Services

In Chapter 12, we described XML messaging, especially addressing the Simple Object Access Protocol (SOAP). With SOAP, you can integrate applications distributed on the network in a decentralized manner because no particular platforms are assumed for SOAP. This indicates that you can integrate applications on the Internet with SOAP. However, SOAP alone is not sufficient for such integration. When you want to access an application, you have to know what the application is. You may not even know about the existence of the application on the Internet. The concept of Web services is proposed to solve such issues.

The key technologies of Web services are SOAP, Web Services Description Language (WSDL), and Universal Description, Discovery, and Integration (UDDI). Because we have already covered SOAP, in this chapter we cover WSDL and UDDI, showing example programs. Before discussing them, we describe why the Web services concept is necessary and provide a conceptual architecture of Web services.

### 13.1.1 Publishing, Finding, and Integration

While the Web has been growing for connecting computers and humans, it is not strange for someone to start thinking about using the same technology background and infrastructure for connecting computers by simply replacing HTML with XML. This concept is called Web services. More exactly, in contrast with a Web server accepting an HTTP GET/POST message as input and returning an HTML document as output, a Web services server accepts and returns XML messages. In this sense, XML messaging, described in Chapter 12, plays an important role in Web services. Note that Web services do not require HTTP as their network transport protocol even though the term "Web services" seems to imply HTTP as the transport protocol. Rather, being transport protocol–agnostic is an important feature of Web services. For example, a Web services server can accept the same XML message via more than one transport protocol, such as HTTP and SMTP.

There is another important feature of Web services that we have not yet described. Before we explain this feature, let's consider the fact that the Web exists for reference. What do you want to do first when you create your home page? You will not hesitate to submit the URL of your home page to search sites like Yahoo if you want people to visit your home page as often as possible. Otherwise, no one will know about your home page, and only a few people will visit it.

The same thing happens for Web services. For example, suppose that you create a Web service to provide hotel reservations, and you plan to offer a special travel package as an opening sale. Your Web service accepts and returns XML messages as a request and its response. Naturally, you also create a home page and submit its URL to many search sites. Is that enough?

Even if someone finds your home page by chance and becomes interested in your service, that person might be upset with it because it requires an XML message as a request form. That reaction is natural because your service is not tailored for humans. How can you deal with that?

The answer is simple. You need a search site for Web services that is also a Web service. You can register your Web service with the site so that other computers can find it. You may feel that the answer is so simple and nothing seems new about it. It is, however, very new and revolutionary for traditional intercompany business deals, which are usually closed and static. For example, when you ask a travel agency for a vacation plan, the agency usually selects possibilities only from the list of hotels and flights that have a business contract with the agency, and the list does not change frequently. As a result, the vacation plan offered by the agency may not be the best for you.

You may go to a travel search site, such as Yahoo Travel, to find a list of hotels that match your preferences (such as place, date, and cost), choose one or more hotels from the search result, and go to their home pages to get more detailed information. You may get the best deal, but it takes long time. Web services allow you to automate such time-consuming manual operations. You can create a simple program by dynamically integrating Web services available on the Internet, such as hotel- and flight-finding services and their reservation services. If this scenario became true, Web services would change the traditional closed and static business environment. If so, it would become the second explosion of the Internet.

## 13.1.2 What Are Web Services?

In 2000 and 2001, major vendors announced their support for Web services. IBM announced its Web services architecture and Microsoft announced Microsoft .NET in 2000. Sun Microsystems announced Sun One in 2001. It is interesting that the overall objectives in their announcements are very similar. They seem to share the same view for Web services but try to differentiate them by providing different tools and programming languages.

We'll describe the architectural detail of Web services based on IBM's Web services architecture. Figure 13.1 illustrates the three important roles in the Web services architecture (service provider, service requestor, and service broker) and three operations between the roles (publish, find, and bind). We explain each role in more detail.

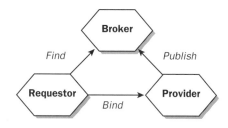

**Figure 13.1**  Web services architecture

*Service provider*

A service provider describes its service based on the specification prepared by a service broker and registers it with the service broker for searching (*publish* operation). A service provider defines its API (for example, network protocol and data format). The API is also registered with the service broker so that a service requestor can connect to invoke the service (*bind* operation). The hotel reservation service described in the previous subsection can be regarded as a service provider.

*Service requestor*

A service requestor creates a new service by integrating services provided by service providers. The travel agency is an example of a service requestor. A service requestor invokes a service broker to get a list of service providers it is interested in (*find* operation), selects one or more service providers from the list, and then invokes the selected service providers (*bind* operation). Note that a service requestor is not just client software such as a Web browser. It becomes a new service provider if it registers itself with a service broker.

*Service broker*

A service broker registers service descriptions submitted by service providers (*publish* operation) and executes a search based on a request from a service requestor (*find* operation). The search site for the Web services described in the previous subsection can be regarded as a service broker. A service broker defines a service description format and an API for registering and searching services. Unlike existing search sites for humans, this format and API must be defined as strictly as possible so that a service provider and a service requestor can use it without human intervention. In Figure 13.1, a service broker is shown as an independent role because it plays an important role in the Web services architecture, but it is also a service provider.

Because this architecture only summaries the concept of Web services, the data formats and APIs still need to be defined to make it real. For that purpose, IBM and Microsoft jointly defined the following three XML-based specifications: SOAP, UDDI, and WSDL. SOAP is designed as a network transport–agnostic envelope to convey XML messages. UDDI corresponds to a service broker. It defines a service description format and an API to invoke its registry. WSDL corresponds to CORBA's IDL for describing the API of a service provider. The following sections explain the details of UDDI and WSDL with programming examples. SOAP is described in Chapter 12.

## 13.1.3  Status of Web Services

Before we cover the technologies of Web services, you may want to know how mature this technology area is. For now, we only have some basic specifications, such as SOAP, WSDL, and UDDI, and it is often insufficient to build real applications with them. For instance, in the security area, we only have SOAP Digital Signature as a W3C Note, and we do not yet have other technologies such as SOAP encryption. In addition, for Web services composition, IBM and Microsoft have each proposed their own specifications, but they have not reached an agreement.

There is also a big question about Web services: How can we integrate Web services technologies into existing enterprise systems? J2EE is a good vehicle for performing Enterprise Application Integration (EAI) with Java. This indicates that we may need a means to integrate Web services into the J2EE architecture. To address this issue, Java Specification Request (JSR) 109 has been formed to come up with an enterprise Web services architecture (we describe it in greater detail in Section 13.5.). Although it is one of the most promising directions, no final specification has been published.

In summary, the technology basis of Web services is not mature enough. However, many software vendors are actively investing in this area because it is likely to drastically change system development in the near future. From a developer's point of view, you may want to know how long you should wait. Unfortunately, we expect that for a while a large number of technologies will be proposed but will go away. Accordingly, you have to judge whether each technology will survive. From this perspective, it is not enough for you to know how to use the basic Web services technologies such as SOAP, WSDL, and UDDI. Rather, you should be comfortable with discussing their technical details, including the implementation aspects. In the previous chapter, we looked at the implementation details of SOAP by means of a prototype. In the same manner, we review a fairly large number of programs here. Through the examples shown here, you should be able to make sense of Web services technologies. As a result, you can consider which standardization activities and proposals are promising, and see the direction of this area.

## 13.2 Web Services Description

In Chapter 12, we showed examples of SOAP messaging with the travel reservation scenario. According to the Web services architecture (see Figure 13.1), the travel agency should be able to publish its service on a service broker. But how can we describe the necessary information on the service? In this section, we explain WSDL. We first discuss the syntax and semantics of WSDL. Then we examine WSDL tools that can help in application development. Finally, we develop a prototype of a WSDL compiler so that you can understand further details of WSDL in terms of programming.

### 13.2.1 Overview of WSDL

Let us begin by looking at an example of SOAP messaging. Listings 13.1and 13.2 show request and response messages in our travel reservation example developed in Chapter 12. In addition to SOAP messages, we include HTTP headers for our discussion. The question here is, what should requestors know to perform such message exchange? At first glance, we can come up with the following items based on Listings 13.1 and 13.2.

- The format of request and response messages is explicitly represented.
- The messages are combined to organize request/response messaging.
- Each message is wrapped by a SOAP Envelope.
- HTTP is used for transport, and its access point URL is `http://demohost:8080/xmlbook2/chap12/servlet/SOAPTravelServlet`.

The previous information is described with WSDL.

**Listing 13.1** Example of SOAP messaging over HTTP (request message)

```
POST /xmlbook2/chap12/servlet/SOAPTravelServlet HTTP/1.1
Content-Type: text/xml; charset=UTF-8
SOAPAction: ""
User-Agent: Java1.3.0
Host: demohost:2020
Accept: text/html, image/gif, image/jpeg, *; q=.2, */*; q=.2
Connection: keep-alive
Content-length: 373

<?xml version="1.0"?>
<SOAP-ENV:Envelope
    xmlns:SOAP-ENV="http://schemas.xmlsoap.org/soap/envelope/">
    <SOAP-ENV:Body>
        <ns1:reserve xmlns:ns1="urn:reserve-tour-msg">
            <user>nakamury</user>
            <tourId>hawaii55</tourId>
            <departure>
                <year>2002</year>
                <month>9</month>
                <day>15</day>
            </departure>
        </ns1:reserve>
    </SOAP-ENV:Body>
</SOAP-ENV:Envelope>
```

**Listing 13.2** Example of SOAP messaging over HTTP (response message)

```
HTTP/1.0 200 OK
Content-Type: text/xml; charset=UTF-8
Servlet-Engine: Tomcat Web Server/3.2.1
(JSP 1.1; Servlet 2.2; Java 1.3.0;
 Windows 2000 5.0 x86; java.vendor=Sun Microsystems Inc.)

<?xml version="1.0"?>
<SOAP-ENV:Envelope
    xmlns:SOAP-ENV="http://schemas.xmlsoap.org/soap/envelope/">
    <SOAP-ENV:Body>
        <ns1:accepted xmlns:ns1="urn:reserve-tour-msg">
            <user>nakamury</user>
            <tourId>hawaii55</tourId>
            <departure>
                <year>2002</year>
                <month>9</month>
                <day>15</day>
```

```
                    </departure>
                    <reservation-id>hawaii551000144683336</reservation-id>
                </ns1:accepted>
            </SOAP-ENV:Body>
        </SOAP-ENV:Envelope>
```

Listing 13.3 shows a WSDL document for a document-centric messaging (DCM) version of our travel reservation example. In other words, this document describes how to access the `TravelServiceSOAP` class (refer to Listing 12.12 in Chapter 12) via SOAP. The root element of WSDL is `definitions`, and it has five types of child elements: `types`, `message`, `portType`, `binding`, and `service`. Let us briefly map our examples to the elements.

**Listing 13.3**  WSDL for document-centric messaging over SOAP

```
<?xml version="1.0"?>
<definitions name="TravelServiceMessaging"
    targetNamespace="http://example.com/travel-msg.wsdl"
        xmlns:tns="http://example.com/travel-msg.wsdl"
        xmlns:xsd1="http://example.com/travel-msg.xsd"
        xmlns:soap="http://schemas.xmlsoap.org/wsdl/soap/"
        xmlns="http://schemas.xmlsoap.org/wsdl/"
        xmlns:xsd="http://www.w3.org/2000/10/XMLSchema">

    <types>
        <schema targetNamespace="http://example.com/travel-msg.xsd"
            xmlns="http://www.w3.org/2000/10/XMLSchema">
            <element name="reserve" type="reserveType"/>
            <complexType name="reserveType">
                <element name="user" type="xsd:string"/>
                <element name="tourId" type="xsd:string"/>
                <element name="departure" type="dateType"/>
            </complexType>
            <complexType name="dateType">
                <element name="year" type="xsd:int"/>
                <element name="month" type="xsd:int"/>
                <element name="date" type="xsd:int"/>
            </complexType>
            <elementname="accepted"type="acceptedType"/>
            <complexType name="acceptedType">
            <element name="user" type="xsd:string"/>
            <element name="tourId" type="xsd:string"/>
            <element name="date" type="dateType"/>
                <element name="reservation_id" type="xsd:string"/>
            </complexType>
            </schema>
        </types>
```

```
<message name="ReserveRequest">
    <part name="body" element="xsd1:reserve"/>
</message>

<message name="ReserveResponse">
    <part name="body" element="xsd1:Reservation"/>
</message>

<portType name="ReservePortType">
    <operation name="ReserveOperation">
        <input message="tns:ReserveRequest"/>
        <output message="tns:ReserveResponse"/>
    </operation>
</portType>

<binding name="ReserveSoapBinding" type="tns:ReservePortType">
    <soap:binding style="document"
        transport="http://schemas.xmlsoap.org/soap/http"/>
    <operation name="ReserveOperation">
        <soap:operation soapAction="http://example.com/reserve"/>
        <input>
            <soap:body use="literal"/>
        </input>
        <output>
            <soap:body use="literal"/>
        </output>
    </operation>
</binding>

<service name="ReserveService">
    <documentation>Travel Reservation Service</documentation>
    <port name="ReservePort" binding="tns:ReserveSoapBinding">
        <soap:address
            location=
"http://demohost:8080/xmlbook2/chap12/servlet/SOAPTravelServlet"/>
<!-- Indentation is broken for printing -->
    </port>
</service>

</definitions>
```

### message and types

The message section specifies an abstract typed definition of messages. In our example, we have two types of messages: a travel reservation request and a reservation acceptance response. These two message types are defined in Listing 13.3. The message sections do not specify the actual type definition for the messages. Such information is defined in the types section. Here, the types are defined with XML

Schema, and the names of the types are referred to in the `message` section. For example, a reservation request is defined as `ReserveType` and is given `reserve` as an element name, and the `message` section named `ReserveRequest` specifies `reserve` in the `element` attribute in the `part` element.

*portType*

We want to define that two message types for a travel reservation are combined in a request/response manner. The `operation` element in this section provides a means for combining with `input` and `output` elements. The `portType` section can be defined as a collection of operations. We would have a travel search operation in this `portType` in addition to the reservation operation.

*binding*

This section specifies how to bind `portType` to a particular protocol. The example here takes SOAP over HTTP as the protocol, as shown in the `transport` attribute in the `soap:binding` element.[1] The `operation` element in this section specifies how each operation in `portType` is bound to the protocol in more detail. The `soap:body` element and the value `literal` of the attribute `use` indicates that the message defined in the `message` section is included in the SOAP body as it is.

*service*

The `port` element in this section describes how the `portType` bound to a particular protocol can be accessed. The only missing information for that purpose is the access point, and it is specified by the `location` attribute of the `soap:address` element. A service itself is considered as a collection of ports.

Figure 13.2 illustrates the structure of WSDL documents. In the figure, solid lines indicate parent-child relationships between elements. Such relationships are clearly represented in XML, but WSDL defines additional relationships, shown in dashed lines in the figure. As an example, let us understand the relationship between `binding` and `portType` (indicated by a dashed line labeled "type") more precisely, referring to Listing 13.3. You can see `ReservePortType` in the attribute `name` of the `portType` element. On the other hand, the `type` attribute of the `binding` element is `tns:ReservePortType`. This indicates that the binding is a decoration of the `ReservePortType` port type. In the same manner, WSDL defines other relationships between elements, as shown in the figure.

---

[1] In WSDL, the core portion and the extensions are clearly separated. In the example, constructs qualified by `wsdl` belong to the core part, and the ones qualified by `soap` belong to the SOAP extension. Although HTTP and MIME bindings are defined in the WSDL specification in addition to SOAP binding, you can define your own bindings.

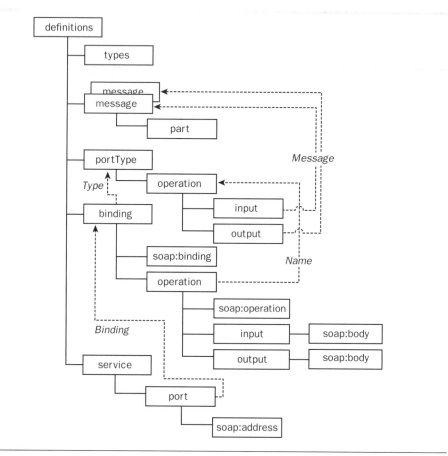

**Figure 13.2** Relationships between WSDL elements

Now we shift our focus to RPC. Listing 13.4 shows a WSDL document for RPC for the `TravelServiceRPC` class (refer to Listing 12.1) developed in Chapter 12. The key difference from Listing 13.3 is that the `part` elements in `message` sections correspond to parameters of the method `reserve` in the `TravelServiceRPC` class. For example, three parts of the first `message` element are parameters of `reserve`, while the part in Listing 13.3 is just an XML document. This indicates that the `part` element is intended to be a flexible mechanism for describing the logical abstract content of a message.

The difference in the parts affects the `binding` section. Let us look at the `soap:binding` element where the `style` attribute is `rpc`. This indicates that the message is used for RPC. Furthermore, in the `soap:binding` element, the message is defined to be encoded (`use="encoded"`), and the encoding style is specified in the `encodingStyle` attribute (SOAP encoding is specified here). Also, as we discussed in Chapter 12 (see Listings 12.7 and 12.8), we have to specify a namespace URI to indicate a resource that can process messages. The `namespace` attribute here indicates `urn:reserve-tour-rpc` as in the RPC examples in Chapter 12.

**Listing 13.4** WSDL for SOAP-RPC

```
<?xml version="1.0" ?>

<definitions name="TravelServiceRPC"
             targetNamespace="http://example.com/travel-rpc.wsdl"
             xmlns:tns="http://example.com/travel-rpc.wsdl"
             xmlns:typens="http://xmlbook2/chap13/wsdl/types"
             xmlns:xsd="http://www.w3.org/1999/XMLSchema"
             xmlns:soap="http://schemas.xmlsoap.org/wsdl/soap/"
             xmlns:java="http://schemas.xmlsoap.org/wsdl/java/"
             xmlns="http://schemas.xmlsoap.org/wsdl/">

  <!-- type defs -->
  <types>
    <xsd:schema
      targetNamespace="http://xmlbook2/chap13/wsdl/types"
                 xmlns:xsd="http://www.w3.org/1999/XMLSchema">
      <xsd:complexType name="ReservationType">
        <xsd:element name="user" type="xsd:string"/>
        <xsd:element name="tourId" type="xsd:string"/>
        <xsd:element name="date" type="xsd:timeInstant"/>
        <xsd:element name="reservationId" type="xsd:string"/>
      </xsd:complexType>
    </xsd:schema>
  </types>

  <!-- message declns -->
  <message name="ReserveRequest">
    <part name="user" type="xsd:string"/>
    <part name="tourId" type="xsd:string"/>
    <part name="date" type="xsd:timeInstant"/>
  </message>

  <message name="ReserveResponse">
    <part name="reservation" type="typens:ReservationType"/>
  </message>

  <!-- port type declns -->
  <portType name="TravelServiceRPCPortType">
    <operation name="ReserveOperation">
      <input message="tns:ReserveRequest"/>
      <output message="tns:ReserveResponse"/>
```

```
        </operation>
      </portType>

      <!-- binding declns -->
      <binding name="SOAPBinding" type="tns:TravelServiceRPCPortType">
        <soap:binding style="rpc"
                      transport="http://schemas.xmlsoap.org/soap/http"/>
        <operation name="ReserveOperation">
          <soap:operation soapAction=""/>
          <input>
            <soap:body use="encoded"
                       namespace="urn:reserve-tour-rpc"
                       encodingStyle=
                            "http://schemas.xmlsoap.org/soap/encoding/"/>
          </input>
          <output>
            <soap:body use="encoded"
                       namespace="urn:reserve-tour-rpc"
                       encodingStyle=
                            "http://schemas.xmlsoap.org/soap/encoding/"/>
          </output>
        </operation>
      </binding>

      <!-- service decln -->
      <service name="TravelServiceRPCService">
        <port name="SOAPPort" binding="tns:SOAPBinding">
          <soap:address
              location="http://demohost:8080/soap/servlet/rpcrouter"/>
        </port>
      </service>

    </definitions>
```

We have overviewed WSDL using our travel reservation examples: document-centric messaging and RPC. We have not covered all the features of WSDL or discussed them word by word because this book focuses on the programming aspects of XML. As for the details of WSDL, refer to the specification. The rest of this section further discusses how to use WSDL.

## 13.2.2 WSDL as an Interface Definition Language

The main purpose of WSDL is to provide a basis on which service providers can communicate with service requestors about information on the service. However, if you only want to do that, you may not have to use such a formal description as WSDL, but you may want to use a natural language description. Although WSDL is human-readable, it is also machine-readable so that programs can process it to automate some tasks. For example, a requestor program may process a WSDL document and automatically invoke the service without human intervention. In this sense, we can consider WSDL documents as specifications for enabling requestor and provider programs to interact with each other.

If WSDL is machine-readable, we can immediately come up with an idea for supporting program development. In the distributed object area, such as with CORBA, there is a concept of an Interface Definition Language (IDL). In the same manner, we can consider WSDL as an IDL in Web services. A number of WSDL tools exist, and most of them are based on IDL technologies.

With an IDL perspective in mind, we can illustrate the relationship between WSDL and programs, as shown in Figure 13.3. If we consider WSDL as an IDL, we can compile a WSDL document to generate client stub code and a server skeleton. As in an IDL, the client stub serves as a proxy of the server application, so a client application can invoke the server application by invoking the client stub locally. As a result, the client application does not have to care about complicated pre- and postprocessing for remote invocation. On the other hand, service providers can develop a server application by filling in some codes in the server skeleton, ensuring that the completed application conforms to the WSDL document.

Furthermore, apart from IDL concepts, when you already have a server application, you may want to automatically or semiautomatically generate a WSDL document. Especially when the application is written in Java, you can use the Java reflection API. Therefore, there are a number of WSDL generation tools for Java (see Section 13.2.3).

The perspective in Figure 13.3 indicates that we can define a mapping between a WSDL document and programs. Let us go into the details of the mapping with

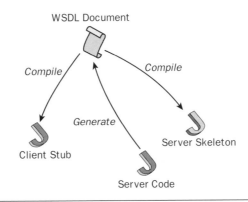

**Figure 13.3** Relationships between WSDL and programs

examples. Listing 13.5 shows an example of a server skeleton, which is an abstraction of our `TravelServiceRPC` class (see Listing 12.1), and would be generated from the WSDL in Listing 13.4. The interface name is based on the `name` attribute of the `portType` type element. Note that we introduce a convention so that `PortType` is viewed as a *suffix* added to the interface name. For example, we remove `PortType` from `TravelServiceRPCPortType` to get the interface name.

**Listing 13.5** Server skeleton example

```
package chap13.generated;

public interface TravelServiceRPC {
    public chap12.travel.Reservation
        reserve(java.lang.String user,
                java.lang.String tourId,
                java.util.Date date);
}
```

The method name `reserve` comes from the `name` attribute of the `operation` element in `portType`. We remove `Operation` from `ReserveOperation` and make the first character a lowercase (R->r). As for parameters, we traverse `operation`, `input`, `message`, and `part`, as shown in Figure 13.2. As for the first part, the `name` attribute is `user`, and the `type` attribute is `xsd:string`. Therefore, we can generate a definition of the parameter, such as `java.lang.String user`.

As for the return value, we traverse `operation`, `output`, `message`, and `part`. Because the `type` attribute of the part is `typens:ReservationType`, we could place `chap12.travel.Reservation` as a return type for the `reserve` method. Note that we have to provide the mapping between `ReservationType` and `chap12.travel.Reservation` somewhere else, although the definition of `Reservation` can be automatically generated based on the JavaBeans convention of setter/getter. The package name `chap13.generated` should also be provided.

So far, we have discussed the relationship between a WSDL document and a server skeleton. When we have conventions such as removing `PortType` from the interface name and providing a small amount of information such as a package name, the mapping can be performed automatically. We can reuse that idea here when considering the client stub, described next.

Listing 13.6 shows the client stub code that would be generated from the WSDL document. The target platform for this code is Apache SOAP, and the code for another platform such as Apache Axis could be quite different from Listing 13.6. Let us compare Listing 13.6 with `ApacheSOAPRequestor` in Listing 12.23 in Chapter 12. As you can see, we extract a typical pattern of RPC invocation for requestor programs and fill in information extracted from a WSDL document in

the pattern. For example, the class name `TravelServiceRPCPrxoy` is based
on the `name` attribute of the `portType` element. More specifically, we remove
`PortType` from `TravelServiceRPCPortType` and add `Proxy` to create the
class name. The construction of the method interface is exactly the same as for the
server skeleton. The definition of the `reserve` method consists of the instantiation of the `Call` class, the parameter setup for the object, and the invocation of
the object. The pattern here is typical, and you can find the necessary parameters
from the WSDL document.

**Listing 13.6**  Client stub example

```
package chap13.generated;

import java.net.URL;
import java.util.*;
import org.apache.soap.util.xml.*;
import org.apache.soap.*;
import org.apache.soap.rpc.*;
import org.apache.soap.encoding.*;
import org.apache.soap.encoding.soapenc.*;

import chap12.travel.Reservation;

public class TravelServiceRPCProxy {
    private URL url;
    private SOAPMappingRegistry smr = new SOAPMappingRegistry();
    public TravelServiceRPCProxy(URL url){
        this.url = url;
        BeanSerializer beanSer = new BeanSerializer();
        smr.mapTypes(Constants.NS_URI_SOAP_ENC,
                    new QName("urn:xml-soap-travel-demo",
                            "reservation"),
                            chap12.travel.Reservation.class,
                            beanSer, beanSer);
    }
    public chap12.travel.Reservation
        reserve(java.lang.String user,
                    java.lang.String tourId,
                    java.util.Date date)
        throws Exception
    {
        Call call = new Call ();
        call.setSOAPMappingRegistry(smr);
        call.setTargetObjectURI(
            "urn:reserve-tour-rpc");
        call.setMethodName ("reserve");
        call.setEncodingStyleURI(Constants.NS_URI_SOAP_ENC);
```

```
            Vector params = new Vector ();
            params.addElement(
                new Parameter("user", java.lang.String.class,
                              user, null));
            params.addElement(
                new Parameter("tourId", java.lang.String.class,
                              tourId, null));
            params.addElement(
                new Parameter("date", java.util.Date.class,
                              date, null));
            call.setParams (params);
            Response resp = call.invoke (this.url, "");
            if (resp.generatedFault ()) {
                Fault fault = resp.getFault ();
                throw new Exception(fault.toString());
            } else {
                Parameter result = resp.getReturnValue ();
                return (chap12.travel.Reservation)result.getValue ();
            }
        }
    }
```

In this section, we described the relationship between WSDL documents and programs in greater detail. You have already seen the basic principle for WSDL compilation and code generation shown in Figure 13.3. Next we cover the existing
WSDL tools that are applications of the principle we explained here.

## 13.2.3 WSDL Tools

Tools for the three operations shown in Figure 13.3 are provided in Web Services
Toolkit (WSTK) 2.4, included on the CD-ROM.[2] Some good articles on how to
use the WSDL tools are already available (such as Graham Grass's article on IBM
developerWorks).[3] Here, we only briefly overview the tools to see how they map
WSDL and Java programs.

Before executing the tools, you need to install and set up WSTK 2.4. You should
find wstk4.zip under the tools directory on the CD-ROM. Unzip the zip file
under "R:\", and then you can see the R:\wstk-2.4 directory. In the chap12
directory, we have the modified TravelServiceRPC and Reservation classes.

---

[2] As we write this book, WSTK 3.01 is the latest version, and you cannot get WSTK 2.4 at its
Web page (http://www.alphaworks.ibm.com/tech/webservicestoolkit). Therefore, we
extracted the WSDL tools from WSTK 2.4 and included them on the CD-ROM.

[3] See the Web page at http://www-106.ibm.com/developerworks/webservices/library/
ws-peer4/. The article is based on WSTK 2.1, but the basic steps are the same.

Because the WSDL tools in WSTK 2.4 cannot handle the Java `Date` class properly, we changed `Date` to `String`. The necessary jar files are placed under the `lib` directory. You need to add these jar files (`wstk.jar`, `xerces.jar`, `wsdl4j.jar`, and `soap.jar`) and `tools.jar` to the class path, provided with the Java Development Tools.

### WSDL Generation from Server Code

You can generate a WSDL document from your requestor application. Let's try out the WSDL generation tool with our `TravelServiceRPC`. Execute the following command:

```
R:\wstk-2.4\wsdlegen>java com.ibm.wstk.swrapper.ui.WizardMain
```

Then the GUI shown in Figure 13.4 appears. In the GUI, specify the class name `chap12.travel.provider.TravelServiceRPC` and its `classpath`.[4] When you specify the class name, default values for Service Name, Service URN, and so on are automatically generated based on a convention. Then press the Next

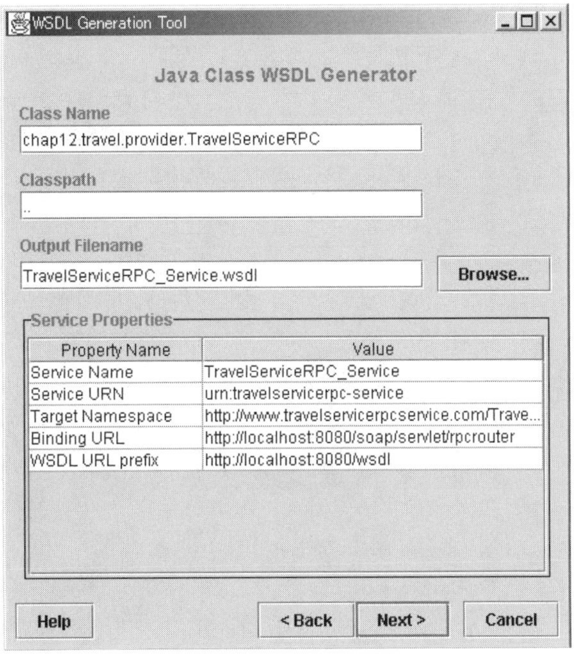

**Figure 13.4** WSDL Generation Tool GUI, screen 1

---

[4] To execute this, we have modified the `TravelServiceRPC` and `Reservation` classes, changing `Date` to `String`. They are different from the ones provided in Chapter 11.

button. In the next GUI, shown in Figure 13.5, select the `reserve` method to publish the method as a service, and press the Next button. Finally, you are required to select a complex type to wrap in the WSDL document, as shown in Figure 13.6. Select `Reservation` and press the Next button. After you press Finish in a confirmation window, two WSDL documents are generated: one for the interface, the other for the implementation. We will discuss the distinction later.

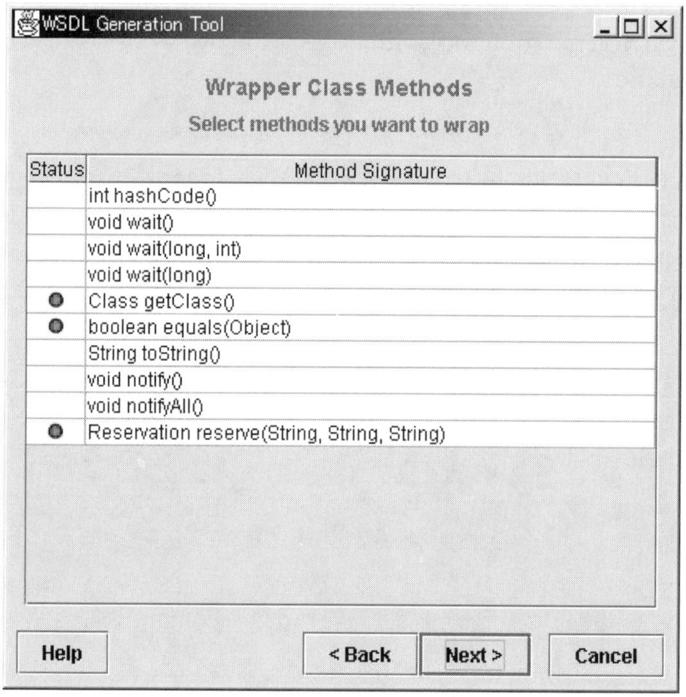

**Figure 13.5** WSDL Generation Tool GUI, screen 2

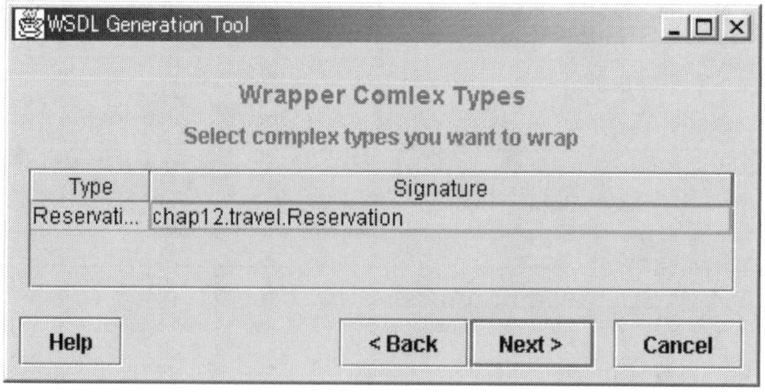

**Figure 13.6** WSDL Generation Tool GUI, screen 3

### Generating a Server Skeleton from WSDL

Next we generate a server skeleton from the generated WSDL document. Issue the following command:

```
R:\wstk-2.4\servicegen>java com.ibm.wstk.tools.gen.ui.Main -target server
        ..\wsdlgen\TravelServiceRPC_Service-interface.wsdl
```

In addition to the server skeleton, a `Reservation` class is also generated. These classes are found in the `com\travelservicerpcservice\www\Travel ServiceRPC_interface` directory and its subdirectory (the `types` directory).

### Generating a Client Stub from WSDL

Furthermore, you can generate a client stub from the WSDL document. Issue the following command:

```
R:\wstk-2.4\proxygen>java com.ibm.wstk.tools.gen.ui.Main -target client
        ..\wsdlgen\TravelServiceRPC_Service-interface.wsdl
```

Although the generated code looks complicated, the core idea is the same as in our client stub example in Listing 13.6.

In this section, we explained how to use the WSDL tools provided by WSTK 2.4. If you compare the generated WSDL document, server skeleton, and client stub, you may notice that there is a convention to relate them. In other words, once you define such a convention, you can easily develop WSDL tools. In the next section, we develop a prototype of a WSDL tool.

## 13.2.4  Programming with WSDL4J

The WSDL tools provided by WSTK 2.4 are enough for many cases. However, you may want to operate on a WSDL document directly or develop your own WSDL tools. For that, you need to work with a lower-level API for WSDL. Such an API is being developed through the JSR process (JSR 110), and there is an open source project called WSDL for Java (WSDL4J). The goal here is to understand WSDL in terms of programming, using WSDL4J. Although you may feel that working with WSDL is too much detail, we encourage you to walk through the WSDL4J API because WSDL is becoming a central entity in Web services (see Sections 13.2.5 and 13.5, for example).

The basic idea of WSDL4J is simply to prepare a Java class for each WSDL element and to prepare operations on the class. For example, a `Definition` class is prepared for the `definitions` element, a `Binding` class is prepared for the `binding` element, and so on. Table 13.1 summarizes the main classes.

To show how to use WSDL4J, we develop a prototype of the WSDL compiler. Because the prototype is too big to include in the book, we only show some excerpts from it. You can find the complete source code in `chap13.wsdl.WSDLCompiler.java`. Our `WSDLCompiler` generates a server skeleton and a client stub from a WSDL document. You can execute it as follows:

```
R:\samples>java chap13.wsdl.WSDLCompiler
              chap13\wsdl\travel-rpc.wsdl
-----  Generating Server Skeleton ------
package chap13.generated;

 public interface TravelServiceRPC {
      public chap12.travel.Reservation reserve(java.lang.String user,
java.lang.St
```

**Table 13.1**   WSDL Elements and WSDL4J Classes

| WSDL ELEMENT | WSDL4J CLASS | HOW TO ACCESS THE OBJECT |
| --- | --- | --- |
| definitions | Definition | Created by `WSDLReader.readWSDL` |
| types | N/A | You can get a DOM element only by using `Definition.getTypesElement` at this moment. |
| message | Message | `Definition.getMessage/getMessages` |
| part | Part | `Message.getPart/getParts/getOrderdParts` |
| portType | PortType | `Definition.getPortType/getPortTypes` |
| operation | Operation | `PortType.getOperation/getOperations` |
| input | Input | `Operation.getInput` |
| output | Output | `Operation.getOutput` |
| binding | Binding | `Definition.getBinding/getBindings` |
| soap:binding | SOAPBinding | Use `Binding.getExtensibilityElements`, and then check the type of each of the returned elements. |
| operation | BindingOperation | `Binding.getBindingOperation/ getBindingOperations` |
| soap:operation | SOAPOperation | Use `BindingOperation.getExtensibility Elements()`, and then check the type of each of the returned elements. |
| input | BindingInput | `BindingOperation.getInput` |
| output | BindingOutput | `BindingOperation.getOutput` |
| soap:body | SOAPBody | Use `BindingInput/BIndingOutput. getExtensibilityElements`, and then check the type of each of the returned elements. |

```
ring tourId, java.util.Date date) throws Exception;
}
-----  Generating Client Stub ------
package chap13.generated;
................
```

When you specify WSDL for the RPC travel service (see Listing 13.4), the server skeleton as in Listing 13.5 and the client stub as in Listing 13.6 are generated. Note that the current code just prints the server and client code on the screen, but you can easily modify it to save the generated code in files.

Let us walk through WSDLCompiler. Listing 13.7 shows an excerpt from WSDLCompiler.java. The listing includes a class definition, member variables, a constructor, and the main() method. The member variable mappingXsdJava is a mapping table from types used in WSDL to Java classes. Although we should register all basic types in XML Schema, we only added String and Date classes for now, as you can see in the constructor. The member variable mappingQnameClass is a mapping table from qualified names to Java classes. Apache SOAP requires this mapping table. The main method loads a WSDL document to create a Definition object and creates a WSDLCompiler object. Then it sets up travel service–specific information (setTravelInfo), generates the server skeleton (printServerSkeletons), and generates the client stub (printClientStubs).

**Listing 13.7** Part of WSDLCompiler (constructor and main() method)

```
public class WSDLCompiler {
    private Definition def;
    static public String PORT_TYPE="PortType";
    static public String OPERATION="Operation";
    static public String XSD_NAMESPACE=
        "http://www.w3.org/1999/XMLSchema";
    private Hashtable mappingXsdJava = new Hashtable();
    private Hashtable mappingQnameClass = new Hashtable();

    public WSDLCompiler(Definition def) {
        this.def = def;
        mappingXsdJava.put(new QName(XSD_NAMESPACE,"string"),
                           "java.lang.String");
        mappingXsdJava.put(new QName(XSD_NAMESPACE,"timeInstant"),
                           "java.util.Date");
    }
    public static void main(java.lang.String[] args) {
        try {
            InputSource src =
                new InputSource(new FileReader(args[0]));
```

```
                    Definition def =
                        WSDLReader.readWSDL(
                            new URL("http://example.com/wsdlhome/"), src);
                    WSDLCompiler comp = new WSDLCompiler(def);
                    comp.setTravelInfo();
                    System.out.println(
                        "-----  Generating Server Skeleton ------");
                    comp.printServerSkeletons(new PrintWriter(System.out));
                    System.out.println(
                        "-----  Generating Client Stub ------");
                    comp.printClientStubs(new PrintWriter(System.out));
                } catch(Exception ex) {
                    ex.printStackTrace();
                }
            }
```

Although we can develop a complete compiler, some portion of the compiler
depends on our travel service example for simplicity. Listing 13.8 shows
member variables and a method specialized for the travel service. The method
setTravelInfo first registers the Reservation class to the mapping tables
and then prepares a package definition and import declarations for the server
and client programs. Ideally, such information should be separated to describe
in other files. However, as shown in Table 13.1, because the implementation for
types is not available for now, we could not work on types. Except for this portion, WSDLCompiler is not dependent on the travel service.

**Listing 13.8**  Method and member variables for setting up travel-specific information

```
private String serverHeader = "";
public String clientHeader = "";
static public String SOAP_CLIENT_CLASS_CONST_DEF =
    "(URL url){\n" +
    "        this.url = url;\n" +
    "     }\n";
static public String SOAP_CLIENT_CLASS_DEF_HEADER =
    "     private URL url;\n";

public void setTravelInfo() throws Exception {
    // Register Java classes for compiler and Apache SOAP
    String travelType="http://xmlbook2/chap13/wsdl/types";
    mappingXsdJava.put(
        new QName(travelType,"ReservationType"),
                "chap12.travel.Reservation");
    mappingQnameClass.put(
        new QName("urn:xml-soap-travel-demo", "reservation"),
                "chap12.travel.Reservation");
```

```
          // Prepare headers for client and server
          serverHeader =
              "package chap13.generated;\n\n";
          clientHeader =
              "package chap13.generated;\n\n";
          clientHeader += "import java.net.URL;"+"\n";
          clientHeader += "import java.util.*;"+"\n";
          clientHeader += "import org.apache.soap.util.xml.*;"+"\n";
          clientHeader += "import org.apache.soap.*;"+"\n";
          clientHeader += "import org.apache.soap.rpc.*;"+"\n";
          clientHeader += "import org.apache.soap.encoding.*;"+"\n";
          clientHeader +=
              "import org.apache.soap.encoding.soapenc.*;"+"\n\n";
          clientHeader += "import chap12.travel.Reservation;\n\n";
      }
```

Listing 13.9 shows the methods for generating a server skeleton. The `print
ServerSkeletons` method invokes the `printServerSkeleton` method
for each `binding`, and a Java interface is created for each `portType`. Each
method is generated by `getMethodSignature`. To understand this method,
refer to Figure 13.2 and Table 13.1. For example, the method name is found in
the `operation` element, which is traversed via `binding` and `operation` under
`binding`.

**Listing 13.9**  Methods for generating server skeletons

```
  public void printServerSkeletons(Writer wrt) throws Exception {
      Map map = def.getBindings();
      Iterator itr = map.keySet().iterator();
      while(itr.hasNext()){
          Binding binding = (Binding)map.get(itr.next());
          printServerSkeleton(wrt, binding);
      }
      wrt.flush();
  }
  public void printServerSkeleton(Writer wrt, Binding binding)
      throws Exception
  {
      QName name = binding.getQName();
      PortType portType = binding.getPortType();
      wrt.write(serverHeader);
      wrt.write("public interface " +
              removeSuffix(portType.getQName()
                  .getLocalPart(),PORT_TYPE) +
              " {\n");
      SOAPBinding soapBinding = getSOAPBinding(binding);
```

```
        if (soapBinding==null){
            throw new Exception(
                "No SOAP binding is defined under "+ name);
        }
        Iterator bindingOps =
            binding.getBindingOperations().iterator();
        while(bindingOps.hasNext()){
            BindingOperation bindingOp =
                (BindingOperation)bindingOps.next();
            SOAPOperation soapOp = getSOAPOperation(bindingOp);
            if (soapOp==null){
                throw new Exception(
                    "No SOAP operation is defined under "+
                    name + "/" + bindingOp.getName());
            }
            wrt.write("    " + getMethodSignature(bindingOp) +
                    ";\n");
        }
        wrt.write("}\n");
    }
    private String getMethodSignature(BindingOperation bindingOp)
        throws Exception
    {
        String resp="";
        SOAPBody inputSOAPBody =
            getSOAPBody(bindingOp.getBindingInput());
        SOAPBody outputSOAPBody =
            getSOAPBody(bindingOp.getBindingOutput());
        Operation op=bindingOp.getOperation();
        Message inputMessage=op.getInput().getMessage();
        Message outputMessage=op.getOutput().getMessage();
        resp += "public ";
        Part outputPart =
            (Part)outputMessage.getOrderedParts(null).get(0);
        String returnType =
            (String)mappingXsdJava.get(outputPart.getTypeName());
        if(returnType==null)
            throw new Exception(
                "No Java type for " +
                outputPart.getTypeName().toString());
        resp += returnType + " ";
        resp +=
            removeSuffix(op.getName(),OPERATION).toLowerCase()+"(";
        Iterator parts =
            inputMessage.getOrderedParts(null).iterator();
        while(parts.hasNext()){
```

```
            Part part = (Part)parts.next();
            String javaType =
                (String)mappingXsdJava.get(part.getTypeName());
            if(javaType==null)
                throw new Exception("No Java type for " +
                                    part.getTypeName().toString());
            resp += javaType + " " + part.getName();
            if (parts.hasNext())
                resp += ", ";
        }
        resp += ") throws Exception";
        return resp;
    }
```

As shown in Table 13.1, SOAP-specific elements cannot be gotten directly from core element (qualified by `wsdl`) classes. Rather, extensions like SOAP are accessed in a different way. The `getSOAPBinding` method invoked in `printServer Skeleton` shows how to get SOAP-specific elements (see Listing 13.10). As you can see, `Binding` provides a method for getting extensibility elements, and `SOAPBinding` objects could be included in the elements. Therefore, we check whether each element is an object of the `SOAPBinding` class.

**Listing 13.10** Method for finding `SOAPBinding`

```
    public SOAPBinding getSOAPBinding(Binding binding) {
        Iterator exEls =
            binding.getExtensibilityElements().iterator();
        SOAPBinding soapBinding=null;
        while(exEls.hasNext()){
            Object ex=exEls.next();
            if (ex instanceof SOAPBinding) {
                soapBinding = (SOAPBinding)ex;
                break;
            }
        }
        return soapBinding;
    }
```

As for client stub generation, we only show the `writeMethodStub` method in Listing 13.11. As in server skeleton generation, the `printClientStubs` method is invoked first, then `printClientStub` is invoked for each binding, and finally `writeMethodStub` is invoked for each operation. In the method, first the signature is generated, as in server skeleton generation. Because the target platform is Apache SOAP, the main task is to pick up the necessary information from the WSDL document to fill it in in a typical pattern for Apache SOAP requestors.

**Listing 13.11** Method for generating client stub code

```
private void writeMethodStub(Writer wrt,
                             BindingOperation bindingOp)
    throws Exception
{
    String signature = getMethodSignature(bindingOp);
    wrt.write("    " + signature + "{\n");
    wrt.write("        " +
            "SOAPMappingRegistry smr = " +
            "new SOAPMappingRegistry();\n");
    wrt.write("        " +
            "BeanSerializer beanSer = " +
            "new BeanSerializer();\n");
    for (Enumeration keys = mappingQnameClass.keys();
        keys.hasMoreElements() ;)
    {
        QName qname=(QName)keys.nextElement();
        wrt.write("        " +
                "smr.mapTypes(Constants.NS_URI_SOAP_ENC,\n");
        wrt.write("        " + "            new QName(\"" +
                qname.getNamespaceURI() + "\", \"" +
                qname.getLocalPart() + "\"), \n");
        wrt.write("        " + "                    " +
                mappingQnameClass.get(qname) +
                ".class, beanSer, beanSer);\n");
    }
    wrt.write("        " + "Call call = new Call ();\n");
    wrt.write("        " +
            "call.setSOAPMappingRegistry(smr);\n");

    SOAPBody inputSOAPBody =
        getSOAPBody(bindingOp.getBindingInput());
    SOAPBody outputSOAPBody =
        getSOAPBody(bindingOp.getBindingOutput());
    Operation op=bindingOp.getOperation();

    wrt.write("        " + "call.setTargetObjectURI (\"" +
            inputSOAPBody.getNamespaceURI() + "\");\n");
    wrt.write("        " + "call.setMethodName (\"" +
            removeSuffix(op.getName(),OPERATION).toLowerCase()
            +"\");\n");
    wrt.write("        " + "call.setEncodingStyleURI" +
            "(Constants.NS_URI_SOAP_ENC);\n\n");
    wrt.write("        " + "Vector params = new Vector ();\n");

    Message inputMessage=op.getInput().getMessage();
    Message outputMessage=op.getOutput().getMessage();
```

```
            Iterator parts =
                inputMessage.getOrderedParts(null).iterator();

        while(parts.hasNext()){
            Part part = (Part)parts.next();
            String javaType =
                (String)mappingXsdJava.get(part.getTypeName());
            if(javaType==null)
                throw new Exception(
                    "No Java type for " +
                    part.getTypeName().toString());
            wrt.write("        " +
                    "params.addElement (new Parameter(\"" +
                    part.getName() + "\", " + javaType +
                    ".class, " + part.getName() +", null));\n");
        }
        wrt.write("        " + "call.setParams (params);\n");
        SOAPOperation soapOp = getSOAPOperation(bindingOp);
        wrt.write("        " +
                "Response resp = call.invoke (this.url, \"" +
                soapOp.getSoapActionURI()  + "\");\n");

        Part outputPart =
            (Part)outputMessage.getOrderedParts(null).get(0);
        String returnType =
            (String)mappingXsdJava.get(outputPart.getTypeName());
        if(returnType==null)
            throw new Exception("No Java type for " +
                outputPart.getTypeName().toString());

        wrt.write("        " + "if (resp.generatedFault ()) {\n");
        wrt.write("        " +
                "    Fault fault = resp.getFault ();\n");
        wrt.write("        " +
                "    throw new Exception(fault.toString());\n");
        wrt.write("        " + "} else {\n");
        wrt.write("        " +
                "    Parameter result = " +
                "resp.getReturnValue ();\n");
        wrt.write("        " + "    return (" + returnType +
                ")result.getValue ();\n");
        wrt.write("        " + "}\n");
        wrt.write("    " + "}\n");
    }
```

In this section, we examined WSDL4J, developing a prototype of a WSDL compiler. Although we briefly walked through the code, we encourage you to look at the code on the CD-ROM and play with it. We are sure that programming with WSDL4J will improve your understanding of WSDL.

## 13.2.5 JAX-RPC

So far, we have shown how to compile WSDL documents to generate client stub and server skeleton code in greater detail. As shown in Listing 13.6, the client stub tends to depend on a particular SOAP engine. For instance, our stub code is based on Apache SOAP and invokes an object of the `Call` class to perform RPC. This indicates that it is advantageous to define a standard API for RPC because client stub code generated from WSDL documents can be executed on any SOAP engine. Java API for XML RPC (JAX-RPC) defines an API for XML-based RPC and how to compile WSDL documents.

Figure 13.7 illustrates the JAX-RPC architecture from a requestor point of view. First, client stub code like that in Listing 13.6 is generated from a WSDL document. The requestor application can invoke a remote method via SOAP over HTTP using the stub code. The JAX-RPC runtime is a SOAP engine that implements the JAX-RPC API, and the client stub must invoke the API by definition.

`Call` is a central class of the client-side core API in JAX-RPC and is similar to the `Call` class in Apache SOAP. Here is an example to show how to use the `Call` class:

```
javax.xml.rpc.Service service = //... get a Service instance
javax.xml.rpc.Call call =
    service.createCall(portName, ?<operationName>?);
Object[] params = new Object[] {?<SomeString>?};
Integer ret = (Integer) call.invoke(params);
```

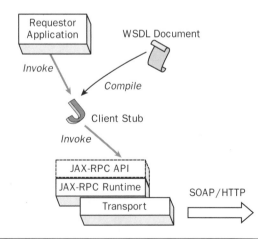

**Figure 13.7** JAX-RPC client architecture

The `Service` class (in the first line) indicates the `service` section in WSDL, and a `Call` object is created by feeding the port name and operation name to a `Service` object. Actual RPC invocation is performed by the `invoke` method, giving the method parameters as an array of `Object` objects. As you can see, in spite of the API difference, the basic concept of the `Call` class is similar to one in Apache SOAP. On the other hand, note that JAX-RPC has introduced WSDL-specific classes such as `Service`. This indicates that JAX-RPC can go beyond the API for SOAP engines to invoke non-SOAP services. In other words, non-SOAP services are described with WSDL, considering WSDL as an IDL of Web services. Such a direction has been shown in enterprise Web services (JSR 109), described in Section 13.5.

We also have to carefully consider the relationship between Java API for XML Messaging (JAXM) and JAX-RPC. In theory, we can provide the DCM capability with JAXM and can provide the RPC capability with JAX-RPC. Accordingly, we should be able to develop a JAX-RPC runtime on top of JAXM. However, JAX-RPC depends only on the `javax.xml.soap` package of JAXM and does not rely on the transport packages of JAXM. Furthermore, JAX-RPC itself can perform DCM with SOAP.[5] This implies that JAX-RPC may do anything we want, including SOAP-RPC and SOAP-DCM, without JAXM.

For now, Apache Axis (mentioned in Chapter 12, Section 12.3.2) partially supports JAX-RPC, and we expect that it will become fully compliant with JAX-RPC. Also, Axis developers are intentionally working on WSDL support. We encourage you to check the latest status of Axis.

## 13.3  Service Registration and Discovery

Once you have described the information about the Web services, you must be concerned with how to provide requestors with it. According to the Web services architecture (see Figure 13.1), you can employ a service broker for publishing, and requestors can access your service information on a service broker by using find operations. Universal Description, Discovery, and Integration (UDDI) is a specification of an XML-based API for publish and find operations, with which service requestors and service providers can access service brokers. On the service broker, a UDDI server called the *UDDI registry* is running to manage registered information.

In this section, we overview the basic concepts of UDDI and develop a program to access the UDDI registry with UDDI for Java (UDDI4J). UDDI itself is not

---

[5] However, when DCM is included in WSDL as in Listing 13.3, its processing seems unclear in JAX-RPC (as long as we are concerned with JAX-RPC 0.7).

specialized for WSDL; any format of service information can be registered. We describe a best practice to register WSDL on the UDDI registry.

### 13.3.1  Overview of UDDI

Through UDDI, you can register information about your Web services. Although our ultimate goal here is to register WSDL, UDDI takes into account a broader perspective—you can register businesses in addition to services. Figure 13.8 illustrates the key constructs of UDDI and the relationships among them.

A *business entity* indicates information about the business that may provide some services. For example, business names and their contact information are included. A *business service* contains only descriptive information about services. For example, service names and their narrative descriptions are included. Implementation-specific information on the services is described in a *binding template*. Typically, the access point of the service is included here, but more details, such as message formats, are included in *technology model* (tModel).

tModel is one of the most important (and difficult) concepts in UDDI. UDDI does not define standard ways to describe the details of a business entity, business service, and binding template, because such detailed descriptions are provided by standardization bodies, industry associations, and software vendors. This indicates that we need a mechanism to refer to such detailed information described by those other than UDDI. tModel is viewed as metadata on such non-UDDI information. We will discuss tModel using concrete examples soon.

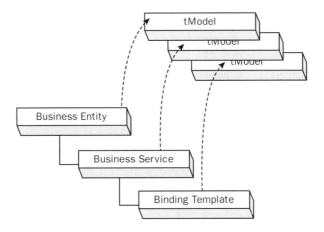

**Figure 13.8** Key constructs of UDDI

Listing 13.12 shows an example of UDDI data for a business entity, business service, and binding template, using our travel service example. The `businessEntity` element represents the business that provides the services. The name and a narrative description of the business are included here. Note that all constructs of UDDI are assigned unique keys represented as a Universal Unique Identifier (UUID). As for `businessEntity`, its `businessKey` attribute indicates the key. Also, because a business can provide multiple services, there is a container element called `businessServices`.

The `categoryBag` element at the end of the listing shows which category this business belongs to. However, to specify such a category, we need a taxonomy in advance. NAICS in the `keyName` attribute of `keyedReference` is the name of the taxonomy, and the `ModelKey` attribute is the ID of the taxonomy.[6] The `keyValue` attribute indicates a particular category in the NAICS taxonomy. The value 56151 indicates a category of "Travel agency."

The `businessService` element represents a particular service. A business service is described with a name and a description and potentially includes `binding Templates`. For example, if the service is provided via telephone and fax, no `bindingTemplate` is required. Like business entities, services can be mapped to categories. The `categoryBag` element in the `businessService` element shows that this service belongs to a category of 901215 in the UNSPSC taxonomy.[7] The value 901215 is a category of "Travel reservation service" in UNSPSC.

The `bindingTemplate` element represents implementation-specific information to access the service. The `accessPoint` element specifies the physical location of the service—the URL. However, there is no information on how to format messages to access the service. Such service interface information is referred via a tModel that is pointed to by the `tModelInstanceInfo` element.

**Listing 13.12** UDDI data: business entity, business service, and binding template

```
<businessEntity authorizedName="nakamury1"
    businessKey="0D0976E0-B4FC-11D5-84EB-AAA81F9305C3"
    operator="kbaba2.trl.ibm.com:80/services/uddi">
  <discoveryURLs>
    <discoveryURL useType="businessEntity">
      http://kbaba2.trl.ibm.com:80/uddi/get?
        businessKey=0D0976E0-B4FC-11D5-84EB-AAA81F9305C3
```

---

[6] See the Web page for the North American Industry Classification System (NAICS) Association at `www.naics.com`.

[7] See the Web page for Universal Standard Products and Services Classification (UNSPSC) at `www.unspsc.org`.

```
        </discoveryURL>
      </discoveryURLs>
      <name>XMLBook2 Travel Agency</name>
      <description xml:lang="en">
        Wonderful travels to Hawaii and Neighbor Islands
      </description>
      <businessServices>
        <businessService
            businessKey="0D0976E0-B4FC-11D5-84EB-AAA81F9305C3"
            serviceKey="0E0D5250-B4FC-11D5-84EB-AAA81F9305C3">
          <name>TravelReservationService</name>
          <bindingTemplates>
            <bindingTemplate
                bindingKey="0EF96000-B4FC-11D5-84EB-AAA81F9305C3"
                serviceKey="0E0D5250-B4FC-11D5-84EB-AAA81F9305C3">
              <accessPoint URLType="http">
                http://demohost:8080/soap/servlet/rpcrouter
              </accessPoint>
              <tModelInstanceDetails>
                <tModelInstanceInfo
                    tModelKey=
                        "UUID:0C0F1150-B4FC-11D5-84EB-AAA81F9305C3"/>
              </tModelInstanceDetails>
            </bindingTemplate>
          </bindingTemplates>
          <categoryBag>
            <keyedReference
                keyName="UNSPSC" keyValue="901215"
                tModelKey=
                    "UUID:DB77450D-9FA8-45D4-A7BC-04411D14E384"/>
          </categoryBag>
        </businessService>
      </businessServices>
      <categoryBag>
        <keyedReference keyName="NAICS" keyValue="56151"
            ModelKey="UUID:C0B9FE13-179F-413D-8A5B-5004DB8E5BB2"/>
      </categoryBag>
    </businessEntity>
```

Listing 13.13 is an example of a tModel for our travel reservation. Its key is specified by the tModelKey attribute of the tModel element and is referred to by the tModelKey attribute of the tModelInstanceInfo element in Listing 13.12. The tModel is metadata for the actual description—a WSDL document, in our example. The overviewURL element specifies the WSDL document, and the categoryBag element specifies that its format is WSDL.

**Listing 13.13** UDDI data: tModel

```
<tModel authorizedName="nakamury1"
    operator="kbaba2.trl.ibm.com:80/services/uddi"
    tModelKey="UUID:0C0F1150-B4FC-11D5-84EB-AAA81F9305C3">
  <name>
      XMLBOOK2 Travel Reservation Service Interface Definition
  </name>
  <description xml:lang="en">
      This tModel defines the service interface definition
      for travel reservation
  </description>
  <overviewDoc>
    <overviewURL>
        http://demohost:8080/soap/wsdl/travel-iface.wsdl
    </overviewURL>
  </overviewDoc>
  <categoryBag>
    <keyedReference keyName="uddi-org:types"
        keyValue="wsdlSpec"
        tModelKey="UUID:C1ACF26D-9672-4404-9D70-39B756E62AB4"/>
  </categoryBag>
</tModel>
```

So far we have seen four key constructs of UDDI: business entity, business service, binding template, and tModel. UDDI defines operations on the constructs to provide publish and find operations, shown in Figure 13.1. Four operation types are defined as follows:

- *Find*: Find elements
- *Get*: Find elements including their details
- *Save*: Register elements
- *Delete*: Delete elements

These operation types can be combined with the constructs we described to define a complete set of operations—that is, `find_business`, `save_tModel`, `delete_service`, and so on. Also, note that the actual operation is represented in XML and is transmitted over SOAP.

## 13.3.2 Programming with UDDI4J

Here, we develop a program to access the UDDI registry with UDDI for Java. Like WSDL4J, UDDI4J is an open source project, so you can find the source code at IBM developerWorks. First we show how to access the UDDI registry and then show the program.

### Accessing the UDDI Registry

Multiple public UDDI registries exist on the Internet, including those from IBM, Microsoft, and HP. Here we explain how to access one of them. With a Web browser, access the IBM Test Registry at `http://www.ibm.com/services/uddi/testregistry/protect/registry.html`. You will see a home page as shown in Figure 13.9. Then go to "Search UDDI Business Test Registry" in the lower-right portion of the screen. On the page "IBM UDDI Inquiry," specify "S" in the "Starting with" field, which gives you businesses that start with "S," as shown in Figure 13.10.

We can perform the same operation with a Java client. In other words, we can send a SOAP message that includes an XML document for a find operation. Listing 13.14 shows such a SOAP message. With `SOAPHttpRequestor`, developed in Chapter 12, you can issue the find command as follows:[8]

```
R:\samples>java chap12.travel.requestor.SOAPHttpRequestor
          chap13\uddi\uddi-find.xml
          http://www.ibm.com/services/uddi/servlet/uddi
```

**Listing 13.14** SOAP message for finding a business

```
<SOAP-ENV:Envelope
    xmlns:SOAP-ENV="http://schemas.xmlsoap.org/soap/envelope/"
  <SOAP-ENV:Body>
    <find_business generic="1.0" xmlns="urn:uddi-org:api" >
      <name>S</name>
    </find_business>
  </SOAP-ENV:Body>
</SOAP-ENV:Envelope>
```

Unlike find operations, update operations, such as save and delete, require user registration in advance. Go to "First Time?" at the middle-right of the screen shown in Figure 13.9, and you will be navigated to register your ID and set up a password. (You need to keep a record of your ID and password.)

Alternatively, you can install the IBM UDDI Registry server included on the CD-ROM. We encourage you to install it because accessing a public registry may cause some problems. First, you may have to set up a proxy for invoking the program shown later. Second, SSL settings can be difficult. Finally, public registries can be down.

---

[8] Within an intranet, you may have to set up a proxy for invoking the command with the `socksProxy` system property in Java.

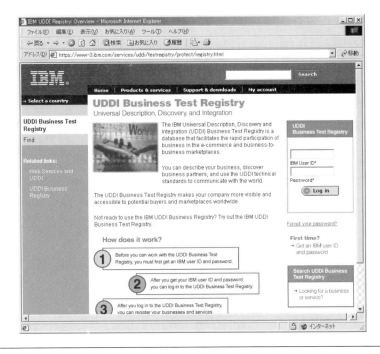

**Figure 13.9** IBM UDDI Test Registry

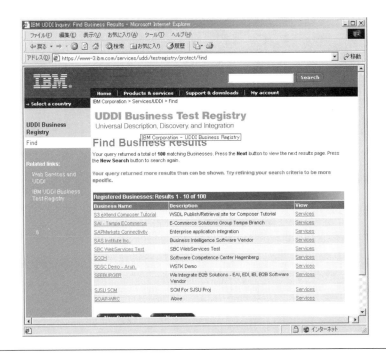

**Figure 13.10** Business entities found at the Test Registry

### The UDDIClient Program

The design concept for UDDI4J is similar to WSDL4J; that is, it provides Java classes that correspond to UDDI constructs. With these classes, you can perform find, get, save, and delete operations on UDDI constructs. Here we develop a program with UDDI4J called UDDIClient. It constructs UDDI data, as in Listings 13.12 and 13.13, saves it to the UDDI registry, searches for information, and deletes it.

Listing 13.15 shows the top-level functions of UDDIClient. As you can see in the main method, you can perform one of three operations by specifying an option (-create, -search, and -clear).

**Listing 13.15** A portion of UDDIClient.java (main() method, member variables, and constructor)

```
public class UDDIClient {
    private UDDIProxy proxy;
    private String userid;
    private String password;
    private static final String DUMMY_XML =
        "<d:Dummy xmlns:d=\"http://example.com//dummy\">\n" +
        "</d:Dummy>\n";
    public static void main (String args[]) {
        if (args[0].equals("-search") && args.length == 3) {
            UDDIClient app = new UDDIClient(args[1], args[2]);
            app.search();
        } else if ((args[0].equals("-create")||
                    args[0].equals("-clear")) &&
                   args.length == 5) {
            // for updating, ssl setup is required
            System.setProperty(
                "java.protocol.handler.pkgs",
                "com.sun.net.ssl.internal.www.protocol");
            java.security.Security.addProvider(
                new com.sun.net.ssl.internal.ssl.Provider());

            // main processing start here
            UDDIClient app = new UDDIClient(args[1], args[2]);
            app.setAuthInfo(args[3], args[4]);
            if (args[0].equals("-create")) {
                app.create();
                System.out.println("Created successfully!!");
            } else if (args[0].equals("-clear")) {
                app.clear();
                System.out.println("Cleared successfully!!");
            }
```

```
        } else {
            System.out.println("Wrong parameters");
        }
    }
    public UDDIClient(String inquiryURL, String publishURL){
        proxy = new UDDIProxy();
        try {
            proxy.setInquiryURL(inquiryURL);
            proxy.setPublishURL(publishURL);
        } catch (Exception e) {
            e.printStackTrace();
        }
    }
    public void setAuthInfo(String userid, String password) {
        this.userid = userid;
        this.password = password;
    }
```

This class defines three member variables. The `proxy` variable refers to a `UDDIProxy` object that is used for accessing a UDDI registry and provides utility methods such as `find_Business` and `save_tModel`. The `userid` and `password` variables are required for performing update operations, such as save and delete. They are set up by the `setAuthInfo` method. Note that you have to register an ID with the UDDI registry in advance. The constructor takes two parameters because a UDDI registry ordinarily provides two different URLs for search and update.

In the `main` method, the `search`, `create`, or `clear` method is invoked, according to the option given. Because `create` and `clear` are required for access via SSL and HTTP Basic Authentication (see Chapter 14 for more details), the code for such secure access is embedded. Next, we look at each method (`create`, `search`, and `clear`) in turn.

Listing 13.16 shows the `create` method with which the UDDI data in Listings 13.12 and 13.13 is registered in the UDDI registry. We prepare four creation methods for `businessEntity`, `businessServices`, `bindingTemplates`, and `tModel`, and they are invoked in the `create` method. When creating `bindingTemplates`, you need a key of a tModel. Therefore, in the method, we invoke `createTModel` first. Note that `UDDIProxy.getAuthToken()` returns a *token* that is required when you invoke update operations.

**Listing 13.16** Method for registering information

```
public void create() {
    try {
        AuthToken token = proxy.get_authToken(userid, password);
        TModelDetail td = createTModel(token);
```

```
              BusinessDetail bd = createBusiness(token);
              ServiceDetail sd = createService(token, bd);
              BindingDetail bndDetail = createBinding(token, sd, td);
        } catch (UDDIException e) {
              DispositionReport dr = e.getDispositionReport();
              if (dr!=null) {
                  System.out.println(
                      "UDDIException faultCode:" + e.getFaultCode() +
                      "\n operator:" + dr.getOperator() +
                      "\n generic:"  + dr.getGeneric() +
                      "\n errno:"     + dr.getErrno() +
                      "\n errCode:"  + dr.getErrCode() +
                      "\n errInfoText:" + dr.getErrInfoText());
              }
              e.printStackTrace();
        } catch (Exception e) {
              e.printStackTrace();
        }
    }
```

Listing 13.17 shows `createTModel`. Within the method, we first create a
`TModel` object, set properties on it, and register it by invoking `UDDIProxy`.
`save_tModel()`. You can specify a key of the tModel with the first parameter of
the `TModel` constructor. As shown in the code, when you specify an empty string
(`""`), the key is assigned by the UDDI registry. We create the `OverviewDoc` and
`OverviewURL` objects to add the `overviewDoc` and `overviewURL` elements. As
you can see from Listing 13.13, you can specify the location of a WSDL document.
Although `KeyedReference` is obvious, note that you have to create a `Vector`
object and add a `KeyedReference` object because `categoryBag` can contain
more than one `KeyedReference` object. The return value here is almost the same
as for `tModels` in the method. The key difference is that the `TModel` object is now
assigned a key in UUID.

**Listing 13.17** Method for registering a tModel

```
public TModelDetail createTModel(AuthToken token)
    throws Exception
{
    TModel tmodel =
        new TModel("",
                    "XMLBOOK2 Travel Reservation Service " +
                    "Interface Definition") ;
    tmodel.setDefaultDescriptionString(
        "This tModel defines the service interface definition "
          + "for travel reservation");
```

```
    OverviewDoc ovDoc = new OverviewDoc();
    ovDoc.setOverviewURL(
        new OverviewURL(
            "http://demohost:8080/"+
                "xmlbook2/chap13/travel-rpc-iface.wsdl"));
    tmodel.setOverviewDoc(ovDoc);
    CategoryBag cBag = new CategoryBag();
    Vector keyRefVector = new Vector();
    KeyedReference keyRef =
        new KeyedReference("uddi-org:types", "wsdlSpec");
    keyRef.setTModelKey(
        "UUID:C1ACF26D-9672-4404-9D70-39B756E62AB4");
    keyRefVector.addElement(keyRef);
    cBag.setKeyedReferenceVector(keyRefVector);
    tmodel.setCategoryBag(cBag);
    Vector tModels = new Vector();
    tModels.addElement(tmodel);
    return proxy.save_tModel(
                        token.getAuthInfoString(),
                        tModels);
}
```

Listing 13.18 shows the `createBusiness` method. First, we create a `BusinessEntity` object and register it with `UDDIProxy.save_business()`. As in `TModel`, the constructor of `BusinessEntity` takes an empty string in its first parameter, and the UDDI registry assigns a key. Because `save_business` is intended for registering multiple businesses, we need to create a `Vector` object to add the business entity. Also, `CategoryBag` is created to specify "Travel agency," which is referred to as 56151 in the NAICS taxonomy.

**Listing 13.18** Method for registering a business entity

```
public BusinessDetail createBusiness(AuthToken token)
    throws Exception
{
    Vector entities = new Vector();
    BusinessEntity be =
        new BusinessEntity("", "XMLBook2 Travel Agency");
    be.setDefaultDescriptionString(
        "Wonderful travels to Hawaii and Neighbor Islands");
    entities.addElement(be);
    CategoryBag cBag = new CategoryBag();
    Vector keyRefVector = new Vector();
    KeyedReference keyRef =
        new KeyedReference("NAICS", "56151");
    keyRef.setTModelKey(
```

```
                    "UUID:C0B9FE13-179F-413D-8A5B-5004DB8E5BB2");
        keyRefVector.addElement(keyRef);
        cBag.setKeyedReferenceVector(keyRefVector);
        be.setCategoryBag(cBag);
        return proxy.save_business(token.getAuthInfoString(),
                                entities);
    }
```

Listing 13.19 shows the `createService` method. Here we create a `Business Service` object, set up properties, and register it with the UDDI registry. Because `BusinessService` requires a key of the business entity, `BusinessEntity.getBusinessKey()` is invoked. `CategoryBag` is created to specify "Travel reservation service," which is referred to as 901215 in the UNSPSC taxonomy.

**Listing 13.19** Method for registering a business service

```
    public ServiceDetail createService(AuthToken token,
                                    BusinessDetail bd)
        throws Exception
    {
        Vector businessEntities = bd.getBusinessEntityVector();
        BusinessEntity be =
            (BusinessEntity)(businessEntities.elementAt(0));

        BusinessServices bSvcs=new BusinessServices() ;
        Vector bsVector = new Vector();
        BusinessService bSvc =
            new BusinessService("",
                            "TravelReservationService",
                            new BindingTemplates());
        bSvc.setBusinessKey(be.getBusinessKey());
        bsVector.addElement(bSvc);
        bSvcs.setBusinessServiceVector(bsVector);
        CategoryBag cBag = new CategoryBag();
        Vector keyRefVector = new Vector();
        KeyedReference keyRef =
            new KeyedReference("UNSPSC", "901215");
        keyRef.setTModelKey(
            "UUID:DB77450D-9FA8-45D4-A7BC-04411D14E384");
        keyRefVector.addElement(keyRef);
        cBag.setKeyedReferenceVector(keyRefVector);
        bSvc.setCategoryBag(cBag);
        return proxy.save_service(token.getAuthInfoString(),
                                bsVector);
    }
```

Listing 13.20 shows `createBinding`, where we create a `BindingTemplate` object, set properties, and register it with the UDDI registry. `BindingTemplate` requires the keys of the business service and the `TModel`, and they are extracted. `AccessPoint` is also created to specify the access point of the service.

**Listing 13.20**  Method for registering a binding template

```
public BindingDetail createBinding(AuthToken token,
                                   ServiceDetail sd,
                                   TModelDetail tModelDetail)
    throws Exception
{
    BusinessService bSvc =
        (BusinessService)
            sd.getBusinessServiceVector().elementAt(0);
    BindingTemplates bTmps = bSvc.getBindingTemplates();
    BindingTemplate bTmp = new BindingTemplate("", null);
    bTmp.setAccessPoint(
        new AccessPoint(
            "http://demohost:8080/soap/servlet/rpcrouter",
            "http"));
    bSvc =
    (BusinessService)sd.
        getBusinessServiceVector().elementAt(0);
    bTmp.setServiceKey(bSvc.getServiceKey());
    TModel tmodel =
        (TModel)tModelDetail.getTModelVector().elementAt(0);
    Vector tModelInfoVector = new Vector();
    tModelInfoVector.addElement(
        new TModelInstanceInfo(tmodel.getTModelKey()));
    TModelInstanceDetails tModelDetails
        = new TModelInstanceDetails();
    tModelDetails.setTModelInstanceInfoVector(tModelInfoVector);
    bTmp.setTModelInstanceDetails(tModelDetails);

    Vector btVector = new Vector();
    btVector.addElement(bTmp);
    bTmps.setBindingTemplateVector(btVector);
    return proxy.save_binding(token.getAuthInfoString(),
                              btVector);
}
```

You can execute the `create` method as follows:

```
R:\samples>java chap13.uddi.UDDIClient -create
        http://demohost/services/uddi/servlet/uddi
        http://demohost/services/uddi/servlet/uddi
        userid password
```

Listing 13.21 shows the `search` method, which finds the information we have registered so far. We first find `BusinessInfo` by a business name, get its business, and finally get `BusinessDetail`. `BusinessDetail` is a container that can include all the information in Listing 13.12. Information on `TModel` can be found in the same manner, and the result is contained in `TModelDetail`.

**Listing 13.21** Method for searching business and tModel information

```
public void search() {
    try {
        BusinessList bizList =
            proxy.find_business(
                "XMLBook2 Travel Agency", null, 100);
        BusinessInfos bizInfos = bizList.getBusinessInfos();
        BusinessInfo bizInfo =
            (BusinessInfo)
                bizInfos.getBusinessInfoVector().elementAt(0);
        BusinessDetail bd =
            proxy.get_businessDetail(bizInfo.getBusinessKey());
        System.out.println("---- Business Detail ----");
        printDetail((UDDIElement)bd);

        TModelList tmodelList =
            proxy.find_tModel(
                "XMLBOOK2 Travel Reservation Service "+
                    "Interface Definition",
                null, 100);
        TModelInfos tmodelInfos = tmodelList.getTModelInfos();
        TModelInfo tmodelInfo =
            (TModelInfo)
                tmodelInfos.getTModelInfoVector().elementAt(0);
        TModelDetail td =
            proxy.get_tModelDetail(tmodelInfo.getTModelKey());
        System.out.println("\n\n---- tModel Detail ----");
        printDetail((UDDIElement)td);
    } catch (UDDIException e) {
        DispositionReport dr = e.getDispositionReport();
        if (dr!=null) {
            System.out.println(
                "UDDIException faultCode:" + e.getFaultCode() +
                "\n operator:" + dr.getOperator() +
                "\n generic:"  + dr.getGeneric() +
                "\n errno:"    + dr.getErrno() +
                "\n errCode:"  + dr.getErrCode() +
                "\n errInfoText:" + dr.getErrInfoText());
        }
        e.printStackTrace();
```

```
    } catch (Exception e) {
        e.printStackTrace();
    }
}
```

You can search as follows:

```
R:\samples>java chap13.uddi.UDDIClient -search
        http://demohost/services/uddi/servlet/uddi
        http://demohost/services/uddi/servlet/uddi
```

Removal of the registered information can be performed with the `clear` method, as shown in Listing 13.22. As for both the business and the tModel, keys are retrieved by name, and we can delete entries with the keys by invoking `UDDIProxy.delete_business` and `UDDIProxy.delete_tModel`.

**Listing 13.22**  Method for removing business and tModel information

```java
public void clear() {
    try {
        AuthToken token =
            proxy.get_authToken(userid, password);
        BusinessList bizList =
            proxy.find_business("XMLBook2 Travel Agency",
                                 null, 100);
        BusinessInfos bizInfos = bizList.getBusinessInfos();
        Vector bizInfoVector =
            bizInfos.getBusinessInfoVector();
        Vector bizKeyVector = new Vector();
        for(int i=0; i<bizInfoVector.size(); i++) {
            BusinessInfo bizInfo =
                (BusinessInfo)bizInfoVector.elementAt(i);
            bizKeyVector.addElement(bizInfo.getBusinessKey());
        }
        proxy.delete_business(
            token.getAuthInfoString(), bizKeyVector);

        TModelList tmodelList =
        proxy.find_tModel(
        "XMLBOOK2 Travel Reservation Service"+
            " Interface Definition", null, 100);
        TModelInfos tmodelInfos = tmodelList.getTModelInfos();
        Vector tmodelInfoVector =
            tmodelInfos.getTModelInfoVector();
        Vector tmodelKeyVector = new Vector();
        for(int i=0; i<tmodelInfoVector.size(); i++) {
            TModelInfo tmodelInfo =
                (TModelInfo)tmodelInfoVector.elementAt(i);
```

```
                    tmodelKeyVector.addElement(
                        tmodelInfo.getTModelKey());
        }
        proxy.delete_tModel(
            token.getAuthInfoString(), tmodelKeyVector);
    } catch (UDDIException e) {
        DispositionReport dr = e.getDispositionReport();
        if (dr!=null) {
            System.out.println(
                "UDDIException faultCode:"
                + e.getFaultCode() +
                "\n operator:" + dr.getOperator() +
                "\n generic:"  + dr.getGeneric() +
                "\n errno:"    + dr.getErrno() +
                "\n errCode:"  + dr.getErrCode() +
                "\n errInfoText:" + dr.getErrInfoText());
        }
        e.printStackTrace();
    } catch (Exception e) {
        e.printStackTrace();
    }
}
```

You can delete the information as follows:

```
R:\samples>java chap13.uddi.UDDIClient -clear
    http://demohost/services/uddi/servlet/uddi
    http://demohost/services/uddi/servlet/uddi userid password
```

We have demonstrated programming with UDDI4J, showing how to register, search, and delete information in the UDDI registry. Further information can be found on the UDDI4J home page (http://www.uddi.org).

### 13.3.3 Registering WSDL with the UDDI Registry

How can we register WSDL with the UDDI registry? UDDI aims at a generic means to publish and find information on services. This indicates that UDDI is independent of any particular protocols, such as SOAP, and any services description language, such as WSDL. Accordingly, there is no description of the registration of WSDL. Instead, we show an approach as a best practice.

During the client stub generation in Section 13.2.4, we did not use the service section of the WSDL document. As you can see in Listing 13.6, the access point specified in WSDL (see Listing 13.4) is not embedded in the code. Rather, it is provided as a parameter of the constructor. The motivation here is that the service provider may want to change the URL address without changing contents of the service. Or other companies could provide the travel service in the exact same way, except by publishing through a different URL.

On the basis of such a motivation, WSDL tends to be divided into two parts: interface and implementation. As we mentioned, the `wsdlgen` tool of WSTK generates two WSDL documents along this concept. Figure 13.11 illustrates the separation of WSDL documents. The service implementation contains the `service` section, and the service interface contains the remaining sections. There is an interesting question about this separation: Shouldn't we put the `binding` section in the service implementation? In some sense, this is reasonable because this section is specialized for a particular underlying protocol, such as SOAP and CORBA. At this moment, there is no specification to prescribe the separation. Rather, some activities implicitly assume the separation shown in Figure 13.11. One example is the WSDL tools in WSTK; another is the best practices document for UDDI.

Figure 13.12 shows how the interface and implementation parts of WSDL documents are integrated into UDDI. The implementation part refers to the interface part with the `import` element on the WSDL side. On the UDDI side, `Binding Template` refers to `TModel` with the tModel key, as in the UDDI specification.

In the best practices document, the location of the service interface is represented as a URL, and `overviewURL` in the tModel can specify the location. Also, the access point of the service is specified in the `accessPoint` element in the binding template. With these instructions, we can provide the minimum information to invoke the service.

However, there is no documented instruction on how to register the service implementation with the UDDI registry. One idea is to specify the location URL of the implementation in the `tModelInstanceInfo` element of the binding template. You can find such a convention when looking at entries in the IBM UDDI Registry. However, there is no agreement on this approach. For now, we encourage you to use `accessPoint` only.

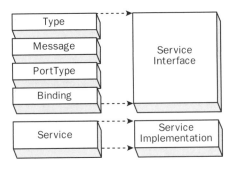

**Figure 13.11** Separation of WSDL

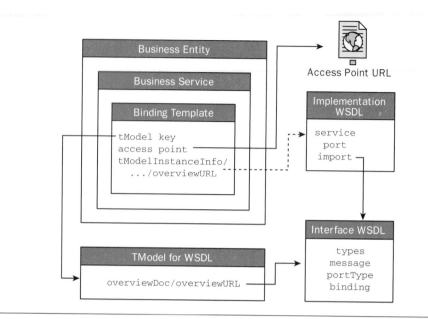

**Figure 13.12** Relationship between UDDI and WSDL

# 13.4  Application to Dynamic e-Business

So far, we have discussed WSDL and UDDI and the relationship between them. The UDDI registry can store information on businesses and services in an orderly fashion as well as implementation-specific information such as access points. Also, WSDL documents can be retrieved via tModels in the UDDI registry. In principle, you can get all the information needed to invoke services. In this sense, we have already obtained a basis to perform dynamic e-business, in which a requestor finds a particular service provided by a business and invokes it, referring an access point and a WSDL document. In this section, we show a dynamic e-business scenario with the travel service example and implement some portions of the scenario.

## 13.4.1  Application Scenario

Figure 13.13 illustrates a dynamic e-business scenario. A travel agency publishes in advance the tModel for its WSDL and business details that include business, service, and binding information. The following are the typical steps a requestor can take to retrieve all the necessary information and invoke services:

1.  Find businesses based on a category code of NAICS
2.  Filter services provided by the businesses based on a category code of UNSPSC

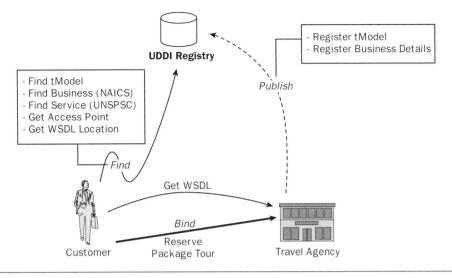

**Figure 13.13** Dynamic e-business scenario

3. Find access points from binding templates in the filtered services

4. Find tModels by using the tModel key provided in the binding templates

5. Find the locations of WSDL documents from the tModels

6. Retrieve WSDL documents from the locations

7. Invoke services by referring to the access points and the WSDL documents

The ultimate dynamic e-business would automate all the steps without human intervention. However, there are at least two obstacles to complete automation. First, it is often risky for the requestor to trust the retrieved businesses. In UDDI 2.0, the `validate_values` element has been added to ensure accurate values for taxonomies such as NAICS and UNSPSC. With this extension, the requestor can trust the retrieved businesses and services to some extent. Although this is still insufficient for real trading, it is a good first step toward solving the first problem. Second and more important, even if you can get the WSDL documents, your programs cannot always invoke the services properly. Generally, any program cannot *understand* the semantics defined in the WSDL documents. You can develop a program that finds a mapping from a known WSDL document to the unfamiliar document based on the similarity of words—for example, "travel" is similar to "trip." However, it is almost impossible to develop a complete inference engine. What we can do for the second problem is provide human users with some tools to help the mapping.

In Section 13.4.2, we show an example of finding a business, service, and access point dynamically, assuming that the requestor knows the WSDL document. In

Section 13.4.3, we improve the example, adding dynamic binding. More specifically, we process the WSDL document on the fly to invoke a service. The second example is still far from the ultimate dynamic e-business but can help you consider semiautomating service invocations.

## 13.4.2 Discovering Businesses on the Fly

Here, we show a typical use of the UDDI registry with a program called `DynamicTravelRequestor`. Listing 13.23 shows the `main` method of the class. We assume that the requestor knows a WSDL document and the tModel for a travel service. However, you have your own tModel key if you performed the instructions in this chapter. Therefore, we check the tModel with its WSDL location URL (line 74). In the program, first we find businesses with a NAICS code and then find services with a UNSPSC code. Next we retrieve binding templates, checking whether they include the tModel key. We can get access points from the binding templates. So far, we have all the necessary information for the target services. Next, we create a `TravelServiceRPCProxy` object (see Listing 13.6), specifying the access point we have found. Finally, we invoke the `reserve` method of the proxy to reserve a package tour.

**Listing 13.23** The `main()` method in `DynamicTravelRequestor.java`

```
public static void main(java.lang.String[] args) {
    // args[0]: UDDI Registry access point url
    // args[1]: User ID for travel reservation
    // args[2]: Tour ID
    // args[3]: year of the departure (e.g. 2002)
    // args[4]: month of the departure (e.g. 5 for May)
    // args[5]: date of the departure (e.g. 15 for 15th)
    try {
        DynamicTravelRequestor req =
            new DynamicTravelRequestor(args[0]);
        // looking for tModel
        System.out.println("Looking for tModel " +
                            "for the travel service");
        TModelInfo tmodelInfo = req.getTravelServiceTModel();

        // get location of the WSDL
        TModel tmodel = req.getTModel(tmodelInfo);
        String wsdlLocationURL =
            tmodel.getOverviewDoc().getOverviewURL().getText();
        String wsdlLocation =
            "http://demohost:8080/xmlbook2/chap13/" +
            "travel-rpc-iface.wsdl";
```

```
[74]          if (!wsdlLocationURL.equals(wsdlLocation)) {
                  System.out.println("I am not familiar to " +
                              wsdlLocationURL);
                  System.exit(1);
              } else {
                  System.out.println("I am familiar to " +
                              wsdlLocationURL);
              }

              // find business by NAICS,  "56151"
              System.out.println("Looking for travel agencies");
              BusinessInfos bizInfos = req.getTravelAgencies();

              // find service by "UNSPSC", "901215"
              System.out.println("Looking for "+
                              "travel reservation service");
              BusinessInfo bizInfo =
                  (BusinessInfo)
                      bizInfos.getBusinessInfoVector().elementAt(0);
              ServiceInfos svcInfos = req.getTravelSerivces(bizInfo);

              // find binding template
              // which matches against our TModel
              System.out.println("Looking for a binding template");
              ServiceInfo svcInfo =
                  (ServiceInfo)
                      svcInfos.getServiceInfoVector().elementAt(0);
              BindingTemplate bTmp =
                  req.findBindingTemplate(tmodelInfo, svcInfo);

              // get access point
              AccessPoint accessPoint = bTmp.getAccessPoint();
              String accessPointURL = accessPoint.getText();
              System.out.println("Access point is " +
                              accessPointURL);

              // instantiate proxy object
              TravelServiceRPCProxy proxy=
                  new TravelServiceRPCProxy(new URL(accessPointURL));
              Calendar cal=Calendar.getInstance();
              cal.clear();
              cal.set(Integer.parseInt(args[3]),
                      Integer.parseInt(args[4])-1,
                      Integer.parseInt(args[5]));
              Date departure = cal.getTime();
              // invoke the service
              Reservation rsv =
                  proxy.reserve(args[1], args[2], departure);
```

```
// print out the given reservationId
System.out.println("The reservation id is: " +
```

You can execute the program as follows:

```
R:\samples>java chap13.demo.DynamicTravelRequestor
        http://demohost/services/uddi/servlet/uddi
        nakamury hawaii55 2002 8 21
Looking for tModel for the travel service
I am familiar to http://demohost:8080/xmlbook2/chap13/travel-rpc-
iface.wsdl
Looking for travel agencies
Looking for travel reservation service
Looking for a binding template
Access point is http://demohost:8080/soap/servlet/rpcrouter
The reservation id is: hawaii551002540004508
```

`DynamicTravelRequestor` defines a collection of utility methods for searching the UDDI registry, such as `getTravelServiceTModel`, `getTModel`, `get TravelAgencies`, `getTravelServices`, and `findBindingTemplate`. Here we examine only `getTravelAgencies` to see how we can use category IDs for the search.

Listing 13.24 is a method to find travel agencies by using an NAICS category ID. The idea is to create a `KeyedReference` object setting an NAICS tModel key and an NAICS category ID (56151). The `KeyedReference` object is contained in a `CategoryBag` object to invoke the `UDDIProxy.find_business` method. The result should be a collection of businesses that have the NAICS category ID.

**Listing 13.24** Finding businesses by using an NAICS category ID

```
public BusinessInfos getTravelAgencies() throws Exception {
    CategoryBag cBag = new CategoryBag();
    Vector keyRefVector = new Vector();
    KeyedReference keyRef =
        new KeyedReference("NAICS", "56151");
    keyRef.setTModelKey(
        "UUID:C0B9FE13-179F-413D-8A5B-5004DB8E5BB2");
    keyRefVector.addElement(keyRef);
    cBag.setKeyedReferenceVector(keyRefVector);
    BusinessList bizList =
        proxy.find_business(cBag, null, 0);
    BusinessInfos bizInfos = bizList.getBusinessInfos();
    return bizInfos;
}
```

We have shown a program that dynamically finds a business, service, and access point and invokes services with the client stub code shown in Listing 13.6. This is the most typical use of the UDDI registry. Although we have reviewed only a small portion of the program, the complete code for `DynamicTravelRequestor` is provided on the CD-ROM.

### 13.4.3 Dynamic Binding

Now we extend the previous program, adding dynamic processing of WSDL. The `main` method of the new program, called `DynamicTravelRequestor1`, is shown in Listing 13.25. The key difference from the previous program is that the `WSDLServiceProxy` class is used to invoke the service.

**Listing 13.25** The `main()` method in `DynamicTravelRequestor1.java`

```
public static void main(java.lang.String[] args) {
    // args[0]: UDDI Registry access point url
    // args[1]: User ID for travel resrvation
    // args[2]: Tour ID
    // args[3]: year of the departure (e.g. 2002)
    // args[4]: month of the departure (e.g. 5 for May)
    // args[5]: date of the departure (e.g. 15 for 15th)
    try {
        DynamicTravelRequestor1 req =
            new DynamicTravelRequestor1(args[0]);
        // looking for tModel
        System.out.println("Looking for tModel " +
                        "for the travel service");
        TModelInfo tmodelInfo = req.getTravelServiceTModel();

        // get location of the WSDL
        TModel tmodel = req.getTModel(tmodelInfo);
        String wsdlLocationURL =
            tmodel.getOverviewDoc().getOverviewURL().getText();
        System.out.println("WSDL is located at " +
                        wsdlLocationURL);

        // find business by NAICS,  "56151"
        System.out.println("Looking for travel agencies");
        BusinessInfos bizInfos = req.getTravelAgencies();

        // find service by "UNSPSC", "901215"
        System.out.println("Looking for "+
                        "travel reservation service");
        BusinessInfo bizInfo =
            (BusinessInfo)
```

```
            bizInfos.getBusinessInfoVector().elementAt(0);
ServiceInfos svcInfos = req.getTravelSerivces(bizInfo);

// find binding template
// which matches against our TModel
System.out.println("Looking for a binding template");
ServiceInfo svcInfo =
    (ServiceInfo)
        svcInfos.getServiceInfoVector().elementAt(0);
BindingTemplate bTmp =
    req.findBindingTemplate(tmodelInfo, svcInfo);

// get access point
AccessPoint accessPoint = bTmp.getAccessPoint();
String accessPointURL = accessPoint.getText();
System.out.println("Access point is " +
                    accessPointURL);

// create WSDLServiceProxy object
System.out.println("creating WSDLServiceProxy object");
URL objURL = new URL(wsdlLocationURL);
HttpURLConnection
    con = (HttpURLConnection)objURL.openConnection();
con.getInputStream();
InputSource src =
    new InputSource(
        new InputStreamReader(con.getInputStream()));
WSDLServiceProxy proxy = new WSDLServiceProxy(src);

// set up travel-specific information
proxy.setTravelInfo();

// prepare parameters
Object params[] = new Object[3];
params[0] = args[1];
params[1] = args[2];
Calendar cal=Calendar.getInstance();
cal.clear();
cal.set(Integer.parseInt(args[3]),
        Integer.parseInt(args[4])-1,
        Integer.parseInt(args[5]));
Date departure = cal.getTime();
params[2] = departure;

// invoke service, feeding the access point
System.out.println("invoking the service");
URL url = new URL(accessPointURL);
ServiceResponse resp = // Reservation object
    proxy.invoke(url, "reserve", params);
```

```
                 // print out the given reservationId
                 System.out.println("The reservation id is: " +
                                    resp.getValue("reservationId"));

        } catch(Exception ex) {
            ex.printStackTrace();
        }
    }
}
```

Before going into the details of the program, let us see how it works. You can execute the program as follows:

```
R:\samples>java chap13.demo.DynamicTravelRequestor
          http://demohost/services/uddi/servlet/uddi
          nakamury hawaii55 2002 8 21
Looking for tModel for the travel service
WSDL is located at
    http://demohost:8080/xmlbook2/chap13/travel-rpc-iface.wsdl
Looking for travel agencies
Looking for travel reservation service
Looking for a binding template
Access point is http://demohost:8080/soap/servlet/rpcrouter
creating WSDLServiceProxy object
invoking the service
The reservation id is: hawaii551001820780320
```

The output message is similar to that of the previous program. But you may notice that a WSDLServiceProxy object is created and used.

Let us look at the WSDLServiceProxy class in more detail. This class takes a WSDL document as a parameter of the constructor and uses it to perform SOAP RPC. In Section 13.2, we compiled a WSDL document to generate client stub code, but this program does the same thing on the fly. Listing 13.26 shows its key method, invoke. In the method, we retrieve the information from the WSDL document necessary for constructing a Call object of Apache SOAP. For example, the target object URI is extracted from the soap:body element in the binding section (see Listing 13.4 also). The types and names of parameters are also retrieved so that given parameter values are properly set on the Call object. Because of such careful analysis of the WSDL document, the service invocation can be performed properly.

**Listing 13.26**  The invoke() method in WSDLServiceProxy.java

```
public ServiceResponse invoke(
    URL url, String op, Object paramArray[])
    throws Exception
{
```

```
// construct call object
Call call = new Call ();
call.setSOAPMappingRegistry(smr);

BindingOperation bindingOp = getBindingOperation(op);
SOAPOperation soapOp = getSOAPOperation(bindingOp);

SOAPBody inputSOAPBody =
    getSOAPBody(bindingOp.getBindingInput());
call.setTargetObjectURI (inputSOAPBody.getNamespaceURI());
call.setMethodName (op);
call.setEncodingStyleURI(Constants.NS_URI_SOAP_ENC);

Vector params = new Vector ();
for(int i=0; i<paramArray.length; i++) {
    Part part = getPart(bindingOp, i);
    QName qname =
        new QName(part.getTypeName().getNamespaceURI(),
                  part.getTypeName().getLocalPart());
    String javaType = (String)mappingWsdlJava.get(qname);
    params.addElement(
        new Parameter(
            part.getName(),
            Class.forName(javaType),
            paramArray[i], null));
}
call.setParams (params);

Response resp =
    call.invoke(url, soapOp.getSoapActionURI());
if (resp.generatedFault ()) {
    org.apache.soap.Fault fault = resp.getFault ();
    throw new Exception(fault.toString());
} else {
    Parameter result = resp.getReturnValue ();
    return new ServiceResponse(result.getValue());
}
}
}
```

The program shown here seems flexible enough. However, as you can see in
Listing 13.25, you have to embed the semantics of the service. In other words,
DynamicTravelRequestor1 knows the travel service reservation precisely. In
this sense, this program does not provide any value by dynamically analyzing the
WSDL document. However, if you want to semiautomate the dynamic binding,
the program should be a good starting point.

## 13.5 Enterprise Web Services

How can we incorporate Web services into EAI? JSR 109 addresses *enterprise Web services* and attempts to develop a specification for a *Web services container* that sits on top of J2EE platforms.[9] A core construct is the Service-Enabled EAR, which is an extension of the J2EE Enterprise Application Archive (EAR) for Web services. The Service-Enabled EAR includes a brand-new deployment descriptor called `webservice.xml` in addition to Java classes for implementing Web services. Listing 13.27 shows an example for a stock quote service. The `webservice.xml` deployment descriptor basically includes the source for generating WSDL documents and implementation-specific information. As for this particular example, the `message` and `operation` sections for a WSDL document are generated by looking up the specified Java class with Java reflection, and the `binding` and `service` sections are also generated to include in the WSDL document. The Web services container is responsible for creating such WSDL documents from Service-Enabled EAR files and is even responsible for publishing the WSDL documents to UDDI registries. On the other hand, a requestor finds the WSDL document via a UDDI registry, generates a client stub, and invokes the service with the JAX-RPC runtime.

**Listing 13.27** The deployment descriptor `webservice.xml`

```
<?xml version="1.0" encoding="UTF-8"?>
<Web-Services>
  <WSDL>
    <portType>
      <implementation-link>
        examples.stockservice.jar#stockquote
      </implementation-link>
      <binding>
        <soap><transport>http</transport></soap>
      </binding>
    </portType>
  </WSDL>
</Web-Services>
```

One of the important goals of JSR 109 is to integrate SOAP-based RPC and RMI seamlessly, as shown in Figure 13.14. Assume that a service is implemented as an Enterprise JavaBeans (EJB) component. The easiest way to access the service is to

---

[9] The discussion here is based on a Java community draft specification and thus may be obsolete when a draft is released.

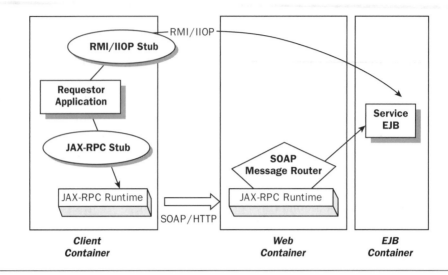

**Figure 13.14** Invoking a service EJB via JAX-RPC and RMI/IIOP

use RMI/IIOP stub code generated by the EJB platform. On the other hand, you can publish a WSDL document via a Web services container so that a requestor can generate client stub code—a JAX-RPC stub. At runtime, the requestor application invokes the stub code to perform SOAP-RPC (typically over HTTP) by the JAX-RPC runtime. Once the server receives the SOAP-RPC message, the JAX-RPC runtime decodes the message to invoke the service EJB via RMI/IIOP. Note that the stub code for both RMI/IIOP and JAX-RPC has an identical API, so the requestor application does not have to be concerned with the difference between them. In other words, the actual means for remote invocation can be determined at runtime.

JSR 109 indicates an important change to the Web services definition. In this chapter and the previous one, we have had the following definition in mind (see Section 12.1.1).

> Web services are applications that can be accessed via standard technologies such as XML and HTTP.

However, JSR 109 defines Web services this way.

> A Web service is implemented by a J2EE-compliant component that implements an interface that is describable by WSDL and supported by JAX-RPC.

The key difference here is, the former emphasizes XML messaging, such as SOAP, and the latter emphasizes WSDL. From another perspective, the former addresses B2B collaboration on the Internet, and the latter addresses enterprise application integration within an intranet in addition to the Internet. For now, although we do not know which definition will be broadly accepted, major software vendors, such as Sun and IBM, seem to be moving toward the latter.

## 13.6 Summary

In this chapter, we covered many concepts and technologies for Web services. First, we discussed why Web services are important and how they have emerged. We described WSDL and UDDI as technology bases. We did not walk through all the constructs of WSDL and UDDI because they are too complicated to cover here. Rather, we showed how to use them in greater detail, providing running examples. We also showed programs geared toward dynamic e-business to demonstrate how to use UDDI and WSDL in an integrated manner. Finally, we described the enterprise Web services discussed in JSR 109 as a future direction.

The concept of Web services emerged only one year ago. Its technology basis is still not solid for starting a serious e-business. In Chapters 14 and 15, we cover security and data binding, each of which can contribute to making *real* Web services. Despite their immaturity, Web services are expected to make current B2B collaboration more dynamic. There is no doubt that we are moving toward such a dynamic e-business. Keep your eyes on this promising arena.

# CHAPTER 14

# Security

## 14.1 Introduction

In Chapter 12, we discussed how XML could be used for data exchange and remote procedure calls. Further, in Chapter 13, we showed the new idea of combining such XML-based services to dynamically build new applications. These services can reside in a single company's intranet, but the biggest value of using XML is gained when doing data exchange between different companies over the Internet.

One of the major concerns about doing B2B data exchange over the Internet is security. The Internet is an open network, and any data flowing through it can be monitored or altered.[1] You need to make sure that the party at the other end of the communication line is the one you believe it is. In addition, you should build some form of trust relationship with your business partners.

In this chapter, we show you what kinds of security technologies are available for you to improve the security of your Java-based B2B system that exchanges XML data on the Internet. In Section 14.2, we cover the security requirements of such a system. Then in Section 14.3, we show how Secure Sockets Layer/Transport Layer Security (SSL/TLS) can be employed to secure your communication channel on the Internet. Section 14.4 discusses XML Digital Signature—why you need it and how you use it. Various access control mechanisms in Java applications are discussed in Section 14.5. Before concluding the chapter, we describe a brief list of upcoming technologies in Section 14.6 that will enhance the security of our systems.

---

[1] Some network appliances, such as a Network Address Translation (NAT) box, modify IP packets on purpose.

## 14.1.1 IT System Security in General

There is one disclaimer. Although we show you the available security options for B2B systems based on XML and Java, these technologies cannot secure your entire system by themselves. Security is like a chain and can be broken at its weakest link. This means *every* security aspect of your system, including, but not limited to, controlling physical access to your system, patching and updating your operating systems and server software as soon as any security vulnerability is found, properly configuring and monitoring your networks (firewalls, routers, intrusion detection systems, and so on), and educating end users about managing their passwords properly and not opening any unknown e-mail attachments, and so on. Without such very broad precautions, the technologies introduced in this chapter could become meaningless.

Please understand that no information system is 100% secure. Your operating system may have security vulnerabilities that have not yet been found. Some of your employees may be using weak passwords. The network administrator may not be able to respond to intrusions quickly enough on Friday nights. Even the cryptographic algorithms that we use in this chapter are not proven to be 100% secure. They are merely *believed* to be secure because no one has broken them yet. It is completely possible, although unlikely, that somebody will break the RSA algorithm tomorrow.

So you need to do two things. First, define your *security policy*. Assess the possible losses if your system's security is broken and the cost of introducing each security countermeasure. The cost may include inconvenience to the end users because of complicated security procedures. Then decide what risks you will take, and what risks you will eliminate.

Second, not only must you implement countermeasures in your system according to the defined policy, you also need to design procedures for detecting attacks and reacting to them. We recommend that you read the book titled *Secrets and Lies* (John Wiley & Son, ISBN 0-471-25311-1), written by a well-known cryptographer, Bruce Schneier, which gives general ideas of what information system security is and what it is not.

Enough about the disclaimer. Now let us move on to security requirements.

## 14.2 Security Requirements on B2B Systems

The first thing you need to do when planning to secure your system is to determine your *security requirements*—that is, what you need to protect from what kinds of attacks, based on your security policy. We review two types of the most common security requirements seen in B2B systems.

## 14.2.1 Security of Communication

First, let us consider the security requirements for network communication.

Historically, Internet technology has been weak in security because in its early days, the Internet was used by a small group of cooperating, trusted people. Ethernet packets are visible to anyone who has a locally attached machine because Ethernet is essentially a broadcast medium. If sensitive information is sent over the Internet, it must be protected against eavesdropping.

Internet packets are also vulnerable to alteration. Anybody who can access network cables or routers can modify the contents of a communication. You cannot know whether any changes have been made to the contents since the sender created the message.

Even when you are confident that the contents of a message are protected against eavesdropping and forgery, your communication is vulnerable if your communication peer is not who it claims to be. In a TCP/IP connection, the sender of a packet is identified by the sender's IP address and the port number in the packet header, and these fields are easy to modify, as we discussed. So we must have proof of the identity of the message sender.

In real businesses, exchanging data or documents between companies often constitutes a step or steps of an agreement or a contract. Sending a purchase order to a supplier is a good example. In these cases, the business must keep an audit log that can be used as evidence of the transaction. A simple communication log does not make good evidence, because it is fairly easy to modify the contents of a communication log without being noticed.

In summary, there are four security requirements in B2B communication.

- Confidentiality—Message contents cannot be monitored or copied by an unauthorized entity.
- Integrity—Message contents cannot be altered by an unauthorized entity.
- Authentication—No one can disguise themselves as the legitimate communication party.
- Nonrepudiation—The message sender cannot deny the fact of sending a message and the contents of the message.

The recent development of cryptography technologies makes it possible to satisfy these security requirements at a reasonable level. For example, SSL (more recently known as TLS) satisfies the first three security requirements. In Section 14.3, we show you how you can use SSL/TLS in your Java-based B2B applications. The fourth requirement, nonrepudiation, can be achieved by using digital signature technology. In Section 14.4, we discuss the XML Digital Signature specification and how you can use it in your XML applications.

## 14.2.2  Access Control

We have covered the security requirements of B2B communication. Once a message is received from a secured communication channel, you need to determine what kinds of operations are allowed to process the message based on your security policy and the identity of the requester. Suppose that you received a message from a company named XYZ Corp. requesting access to your purchase order database to review its purchase order history. Because this message came from a secure communication channel with a proper authentication mechanism, you can be sure that the sender of the message is in fact XYZ Corp. Should you allow this company to access your database and return the requested information?

The answer to this question depends on your policy. For example, you may have an access control policy for your purchase order application as follows.

- All properly authenticated companies can access the product catalog database.
- All companies in the "trusted" category can submit a new purchase order.
- A company can review the history of a purchase order that has been issued by the same company.

As you can see from this example, an access control policy determines who can do what operation on what data.

Access control is sometimes confused with authentication. This is understandable because in many cases, an access control mechanism and an authentication mechanism are integrated into a single mechanism. For example, you can access the password-protected Web pages of the Apache Web Server only when you are properly authenticated. However, in general cases, you should distinguish access control from authentication. Authentication is used to prove the identity of your communication peer. In a large system, the authentication database sometimes contains the userids and passwords of many users, but only a subset of this population is allowed to access a particular component.[2] Therefore, access control should be discussed separately from authentication. In Section 14.5, we discuss the available options in Java-based B2B systems.

---

[2] In UNIX, authentication is logging in to the operating system. Access control is done through protection bits associated with files.

# 14.3 SSL/TLS

Secure Sockets Layer is defined by Netscape Communications Corporation for securing HTTP connections. Because SSL is implemented in Netscape's browsers, it has become a de facto standard for secure HTTP connection. Today, virtually all browsers and HTTP servers support SSL. The current version of SSL is 3. Based on SSL version 3, the Internet Engineering Task Force (IETF, `http://www.ietf.org/`) defined Transport Layer Security 1.0. TLS 1.0 is almost identical to SSL version 3, so in this book we use the expression SSL/TLS to refer to both of them. These protocols use X.509 certificates for authentication.

As we discussed earlier, SSL/TLS provides solutions to three security requirements: confidentiality, integrity, and authentication. Confidentiality is achieved by using a symmetric cryptosystem, such as these.

- Data Encryption Standard (DES), which has a 56-bit key.
- RC4, or Ron's Code, which was developed by the famous cryptographer Ron Rivest. Its key length is variable but is normally 40 to 128 bits.

Integrity is guaranteed by using a message authentication code (MAC) based on a secure hash function, such as Message Digest 5 (MD5) and Secure Hash Algorithm 1 (SHA-1).

Client authentication is optional in an SSL/TLS connection, but server authentication is mandatory. In other words, the client always knows the server's identity, but in many cases the server does not know the client's.

## 14.3.1 Server Authentication

Figure 14.1 depicts how SSL/TLS works for authentication. To use SSL, a Web server must acquire a server's digital certificate from a certification authority (CA), a third-party organization that issues digital certificates. A digital certificate guarantees that the public key contained in it belongs to its owner so that the receiver of a digitally signed message can verify the authenticity of the signature. The digital certificate format used in SSL/TLS is X.509, defined by the International Telecommunications Union-Telecommunication Standardization Sector (ITU-T).

When a client connects to a server using SSL/TLS, the client and server first look for the strongest common cryptographic algorithm and agree on it. Then they exchange a symmetric key that is used in the encryption of the message body. The key exchange is done by using public-key cryptography as follows.

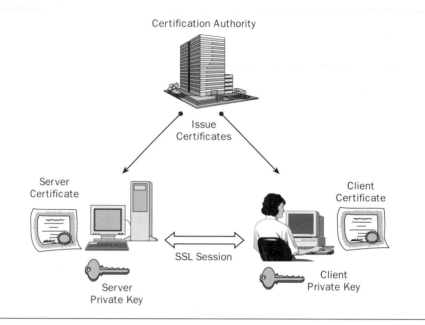

**Figure 14.1** Authentication in SSL/TLS

1. The server sends its X.509 certificate containing the server's public key.
2. The client generates a 48-byte random number, a *premaster secret,* and encrypts the number using the server's public key. It then sends the encrypted premaster secret to the server.
3. The server decrypts the encrypted premaster secret using its private key.
4. The server and the client, sharing the same premaster secret, which cannot be obtained by anybody else, generate symmetric keys for message encryption from the premaster secret and start communicating using the generated keys.

Because only the server that owns the proper private key can decrypt the encrypted premaster secret (and thus generate the proper symmetric keys), the client knows, by decrypting the first encrypted message from the server, that it is in fact talking to the correct server.

## 14.3.2  Client Authentication

Client authentication is optional in SSL/TLS. Although it is often reasonable for a client to stay anonymous in a communication between a browser and a Web server, in many B2B situations client authentication is critical. Two client authentication methods are popularly used with HTTP.

- HTTP basic authentication (RFC 2617) combined with SSL/TLS without client authentication
- SSL/TLS certificate-based client authentication

We discuss both of these in the following two subsections.

### Combining HTTP Basic Authentication with SSL/TLS

HTTP basic authentication (RFC 2617) is part of the HTTP protocol specification and is based on userids and passwords. Because both are sent without encryption (they are Base64-encoded but are not encrypted), this is not a secure method of authentication. So it must be combined with SSL/TLS, which provides confidentiality.

When basic authentication with SSL/TLS occurs, the following takes place (see Figure 14.2).

1. The client connects to the Web server using a URL—for example, `https://www.powerwarning.com/`. Note that the protocol used is not `http:` but `https:`, which refers to HTTP over SSL/TLS.

2. When the SSL connection is established, the client knows the server's identity with confidence because of the server's X.509 certificate. However, the server does not know the client's identity, so it replies with a return code of 401, thereby requesting that the client authenticate itself.

3. The client sends its Base64-encoded userid and password in the HTTP header.

Now, all the data is going through the SSL/TLS connection, so it cannot be stolen during transmission. Also, no malicious server can successfully disguise itself as the original Web server in an attempt to steal the user's password.

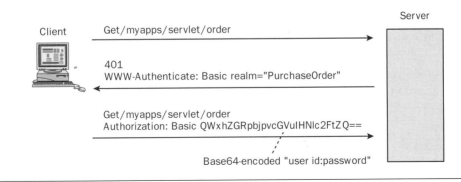

**Figure 14.2** HTTP basic authentication

### Certificate-Based Client Authentication in SSL/TLS

Using SSL/TLS certificate-based client authentication requires that the client obtain an appropriate digital certificate before connecting to a server. To obtain a client certificate, a client must generate a public key/private key pair in its client software. The private key is kept secret in a keystore, and it is usually protected by a pass-phrase. Then the public key is sent to a CA, and a signed certificate is returned.

The advantage of using certificate-based client authentication over HTTP basic authentication with SSL/TLS is that with the former, it is possible to separate the application and the authentication. That is, the application does not need to maintain a userid/password database. It only needs to verify that the certificate presented by the client is indeed signed by a trusted CA.

Consider the following situation. Suppose our power warning service presented in Chapter 1 cannot attract enough customers by itself, so we decide to partner with nine other companies that provide similar services on the Internet. As a group of service providers, we offer a package deal to our common customers. A customer pays a fixed monthly fee to a designated billing company for accessing ten different services operated by the ten independent companies.

In this case, HTTP basic authentication with SSL/TLS has some drawbacks.

- Each application must maintain its own copy of the userid/password database. This entails associated security risks.

- The billing company must notify each company of the addition and deletion of new customers and changes to customers' payment status. In addition, this communication must be secure.

- The customer must manage ten different passwords (if the same password is used, a dishonest employee of, for example, company A can use your password to access, for example, company B's service in your name).

By contrast, when certificate-based authentication is used, applications do not need to do user administration. Figure 14.3 shows the user presenting its certificate to companies A, B, and C. Because this certificate is issued by the CA, the companies can trust that the user is in fact a legitimate user. Thus they are freed from the burden of the complex and possibly human-intensive task of registering and charging customers.

## 14.3.3 Selecting a Public-Key Infrastructure

For a server or a client to be authenticated in SSL/TLS, it must have an X.509 certificate issued by some CA. Issuing certificates involves a set of policies, procedures, and mechanisms for receiving a certificate request, verifying the identity of a

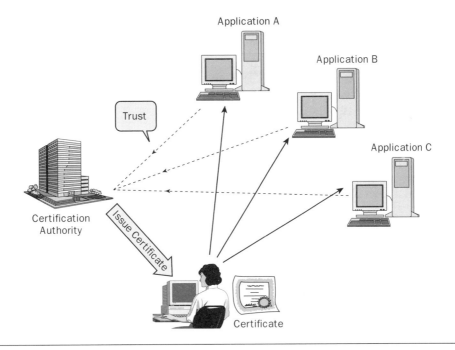

**Figure 14.3** Use of client certificates

requester, signing a certificate, revoking a certificate, and so on. These are collectively called the *public-key infrastructure,* or *PKI.* You must decide what PKI to use with SSL/TLS. PKI can be any of the following.

- Commercial CAs issue certificates for general Internet use. For example, Verisign issues certificates for e-mail and software signing and even provides free, 60-day trial Class 1 certificates for individual users. Anyone who has access to an Internet e-mail address can obtain a Verisign Class 1 certificate. When using this certificate, however, you must be sure that the level of security it provides is sufficient to meet your needs. A Class 1 certificate guarantees that the e-mail address of the certificate owner is unique but does not guarantee anything about the true identity of the certificate owner. Although this level of security might be enough for casual e-mail exchange, it certainly is not for serious e-business uses. Verisign offers other classes of certificates of higher security levels. Class 3 certificates are the ones used in ordinary SSL/TLS Web servers.

- Outsource PKI to outside vendors. Operating a CA properly is not easy. It requires a highly secure hardware and software installation that is professionally maintained, as well as security policies and auditing rules, among other requirements. Therefore, it is reasonable to outsource the CA operation.

- Although *operating* a CA properly is not an easy task, it is relatively easy to set up your own CA using one of the CA software packages. This might be a good choice for trial and educational purposes because you can learn various issues in issuing and revoking certificates. Running a private CA also is a possible choice if your organization is serious about setting up its own PKI that will be used across many different applications.

In any case, it is very important that you document your certification policy that dictates the condition of issuing and revoking certificates.

## 14.3.4 Configuring a Server and a Client for SSL/TLS

Now, let us show you how SSL/TLS can be deployed in a Java-based B2B application. Because software supporting SSL/TLS is becoming popular, most of what you need to do to secure your Web application using SSL/TLS is to configure your software correctly according to your policy.

### Configuring a Server

Because certificate-based server authentication is mandatory in SSL/TLS, the first thing you need to do in configuring a server for SSL/TLS is to obtain a server certificate. We assume that you have already decided which PKI to use. To obtain a server certificate, you follow these steps.

1. Generate a private key/public key pair in the server's key-management software.
2. Send the public key along with the identity information of the server owner (or operator) to the CA. You might be required to send an official document verifying this identity.
3. Once the CA is satisfied with the requester's identity and the fact that the key was generated by the requester, it creates a certificate that binds the requester's distinguished name (DN) to the public key by signing the certificate. The signed certificate is sent back to the requester.
4. The server administrator installs the certificate in the server software.

Next, depending on the client authentication method, you need to do one of the following:

- Configure the server's basic authentication.
- Install the trusted CA's certificate that is used for verifying client certificates for certificate-based client authentication.

In the case of using HTTP basic authentication for client authentication, the same authentication mechanism that is used for controlling access to Web pages can be used for authenticating requesters to B2B applications. In Apache Web Server, the most popular HTTP server and also an HTTP frontend of many popular application servers, an access control file named .htaccess contains a reference to an authentication database. In the Tomcat application server we introduced in Chapter 10, a file named conf/tomcat-users.xml is used as the authentication database. An authentication database can be a flat file if the number of users is small, but you need to use a more efficient database when the number of users is large or the same database needs to be shared by multiple servers. Apache Web Server provides a few options with respect to the authentication database. The module mod_auth_dbm allows a large database by means of UNIX's standard database API. The module mod_auth_ldap, although available only in Apache Web Server version 2, can be used for centralizing many authenticating databases into a single directory.

When you use SSL/TLS certificate-based client authentication, no authentication database is necessary. Instead, the server needs to be configured so that only client certificates that are issued by a trusted CA are accepted. This is done by installing the certificate of the trusted CA in the server's keystore.

### Configuring a Client

To configure a client for SSL/TLS, first you need to install the certificate of the CA that issues the certificates of the servers to which you intend to connect.

When HTTP basic authentication is used for client authentication, no additional configuration is necessary, but the client program has to explicitly embed a userid and password into an HTTP header.

When SSL/TLS certificate-based client authentication is used, you need to create a public key/private key pair and, in the same process for obtaining the server certificate, ask your CA to issue a certificate for the key and install the certificate into your keystore.

### Preparing Keys for the Samples in This Chapter

As we have seen, using SSL/TLS requires processes such as generating a key pair, requesting a certificate, and installing a certificate. Unfortunately, there is no standard tool for performing these tasks. The way these tasks are performed is largely dependent on your server software, client middleware, and the PKI you use. For the reader's convenience, we created a set of keys and certificates that are used in the sample programs in this chapter. The tools we used are keytool, which comes with Java 2 SDK, and OpenSSL, a popular, open source cryptography package. Figure 14.4 shows the relationships between these keys and certificates along with the filenames where these keys and certificates are stored.

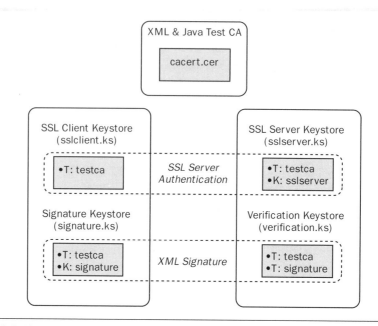

**Figure 14.4** Keystores used in this chapter

For the selection of PKI, we take the third approach (operating a private CA) that we discussed in Section 14.3.3. XML & Java Test CA is the name (more precisely, the distinguished name, or DN) of our CA that issues all the certificates used in our samples. (This is a private CA that we created specifically for evaluating the sample programs in this book and should never be used for production.) All the keystores have the certificate of this CA as a trusted entry. We used OpenSSL for creating the CA key pair and its certificate. The CA key is in the file `chap14/keystore/cakey.pem`, while the CA certificate is in the file `chap14/keystore/cacert.cer`.

In Section 14.3.5, we show you a sample client program for making an SSL/TLS connection with HTTP basic authentication. In this connection, the server will be authenticated via an X.509 certificate. For this purpose, the client keystore, `chap14/keystore/sslclient.ks`, must have the CA certificate as a trusted entry.[3] On the server side, we created a server public key/private key pair (we gave it the key alias `sslserver`) in the server keystore, `chap14/keystore/sslserver.ks`. Then we had our CA issue a certificate for this key, and we stored the issued certificate back into the keystore. During these processes, we used OpenSSL for

---

[3] In Sun's implementation of JSSE, which we use in Section 14.3.5, the default keystore is located at `$JAVA_HOME/jre/lib/security/cacerts`. Instead of having a separate keystore for your application, you can install the CA certificate into this default keystore. By default, it contains a set of root CA certificates that are commonly used for Web servers.

issuing certificates, while using `keytool` to manage both the client and the server keystores.

We also prepared keys for executing the sample programs for XML Digital Signature, which we cover in Section 14.4. We created keys for signature and verification, which are stored in the keystores `chap14/keystore/signature.ks` and `chap14/keystore/verification.ks`, respectively.

The accompanying CD-ROM contains all the keys ready for use. We also included on the CD-ROM a detailed explanation of how you can build these keys from scratch using OpenSSL and `keytool`.

## 14.3.5  SSL/TLS Programming in Java

Now let us look at how we can use SSL/TLS from our Java programs.

### Java 2 Cryptography Architecture

First, let us briefly touch on the Java 2 cryptography packages. Collectively, they provide application programs with a very flexible way to select and use cryptographic algorithms. We review three such packages.

- Java Cryptography Architecture (JCA) is a basis for Java 2's cryptography functions. It defines the architecture of separating the API and specific implementations as well as the API for the digital signature and digest function. JCA has no encryption API, so it is not subject to the export regulations of the United States.

- Java Cryptography Extension (JCE) is an optional package that provides encryption APIs.

- Java Secure Socket Extension (JSEE) is an optional package that implements SSL/TLS using JCA and JCE.

The latter two packages may be missing in a standard distribution of Java 2. If so, you need to obtain these packages and install them into `$JAVA_HOME/jre/lib/ext`.

The use of cryptography technologies is sometimes restricted by government policies. For example, the United States poses certain restrictions on exporting strong encryption technologies (for example, symmetric cipher cryptosystems with a key length of 128 bits or more). To minimize the impact of such policies on application programs, Java 2 employs a *provider architecture*, which provides a common set of APIs with pluggable implementation modules, called *crypto service providers*. Usually, an application does not need to specify which crypto service provider is to be used. Instead, available providers are registered in a configuration file,

$JAVA_HOME/jre/lib/security/java.security, as shown next, and the Java cryptography library will select from these the most appropriate provider for a given request.[4] In this example, a JCA provider called sun.security.provider. Sun, a JCE provider called com.sun.crypto.provider.SunJCE, and a JSSE provider called com.sun.net.ssl.internal.ssl.Provider are configured.

```
    :
security.provider.1=sun.security.provider.Sun
security.provider.2=com.sun.crypto.provider.SunJCE
security.provider.3=com.sun.net.ssl.internal.ssl.Provider
    :
```

You can also configure other providers. If you want to use IBM's implementations, the configuration file will look like this. The number after security.provider. represents the priority of the provider when the library selects one.

```
    :
security.provider.1=sun.security.provider.Sun
security.provider.2=com.ibm.crypto.provider.IBMJCE
security.provider.3=com.ibm.jsse.JSSEProvider
    :
```

A provider can also be dynamically added at runtime by executing the java. security.Security.addProvider() method like this.

```
java.security.Security.addProvider(new com.ibm.jsse.JSSEProvider());
```

However, this technique should not be used unless there is a good reason to do so, because hardcoding a crypto service provider will constrain the environments in which your application can be executed.

## Using Java Secure Socket Extension

JSSE provides a socket-equivalent API for SSL/TLS. Therefore, once an appropriate keystore is properly configured, using JSSE is fairly straightforward. The following is a snippet of Java code for calling JSSE.

```
import javax.net.ssl.*;
    :
SSLSocketFactory factory
        =(SSLSocketFactory)SSLSocketFactory.getDefault();
SSLSocket socket = (SSLSocket)factory.createSocket("demohost", 8443);
```

---

[4] In Windows, the configuration file is %JAVA_HOME%\jre\lib\security\java.security.

The class `SSLSocket` is a subclass of `java.net.Socket`, so a socket created this way can be used as if it is an ordinary socket.

If the protocol being used is HTTPS—that is, an HTTP protocol over SSL/TLS—it is simpler to specify `https` as the protocol in a URL. When creating a `URLConnection` object, instead of calling the following:

```
URLConnection uc = new URL("http://www.abc.com/").openConnection();
```

you can call this:

```
URLConnection uc = new URL("https://www.abc.com/").openConnection();
```

One catch is that this feature is not part of the JSSE specification. But most implementations, including Sun's reference implementation, support this feature. When you run a program using this feature, you need to set a special protocol handler to the system property `java.protocol.handler.pkgs`. You can do this by adding the following option in a command line when executing the `java` command.

```
-Djava.protocol.handler.pkgs=com.sun.net.ssl.internal.www.protocol
```

You also need to specify what keystore you want to use in the command line. The option you need is as follows. The keystore password, `changeit` in our prefabricated keystores, should be changed to the password of your keystore.

```
-Djavax.net.ssl.trustStore=./chap14/keystore/sslclient.ks
-DtrustStorePassword=changeit
```

Listing 14.1 shows a simple client program that sends an HTTP GET request to a server using an SSL/TLS connection with HTTP basic authentication. The use of SSL/TLS is specified by using a URL starting with `https:`. For HTTP basic authentication, the supplied userid and the password are concatenated using a colon (:) as a separator; then the concatenated string is Base-64 encoded and added as an HTTP header named `Authorization`.

**Listing 14.1** Client using HTTP basic authentication with SSL/TLS, chap14/
SSLClientWithHTTPBasicAuth.java

```java
package chap14;
import java.net.URL;
import java.net.URLConnection;
import java.io.BufferedReader;
import java.io.InputStreamReader;

public class SSLClientWithHTTPBasicAuth {
    public static void main(String[] args) throws Exception {
```

```
                    String url = "https://demohost:8443/xmlbook2/chap14/index.html";
                    if (args.length > 0) url = args[0];
                    String userid = "tomcat";
                    if (args.length > 1) userid = args[1];
                    String passwd = "tomcat";
                    if (args.length > 2) passwd = args[2];
                    URLConnection uc = new URL(url).openConnection();
                    sun.misc.BASE64Encoder base64enc = new sun.misc.BASE64Encoder();
                    String auth =base64enc.encodeBuffer(
                                (userid+":"+passwd).getBytes("UTF-8")).trim();
                    uc.setRequestProperty("Authorization","Basic "+auth);
                    BufferedReader ins = new BufferedReader(
                                        new InputStreamReader(uc.getInputStream()));
                    String line;
                    while ((line = ins.readLine()) != null) {
                        System.out.println(line);
                    }
                    ins.close();
            }
    }
```

To run this program, you must include the system properties that we mentioned earlier in the command line as follows. Note that the command line is broken into multiple lines for readability, but they must be typed in a single line.

```
    R:\samples>java
 -Djava.protocol.handler.pkgs=com.sun.net.ssl.internal.www.protocol
            -Djavax.net.ssl.trustStore=./chap14/keystore/sslclient.ks
            -DtrustStorePassword=changeit
            chap14.SSLClientWithHTTPBasicAuth
```

## 14.3.6  Firewall Considerations

When SSL/TLS is used for B2B communication, you should consider how your firewalls are configured, as your server is probably located behind the firewall that restricts TCP connections in a certain way. A typical firewall configuration is depicted in Figure 14.5, where the SSL/TLS server is sitting in a network segment bracketed by a pair of firewalls. This network segment, which is isolated from both the Internet and the intranet, is called the Demilitarized Zone (DMZ).

One firewall of the DMZ is facing the Internet and accepts certain connections from the Internet to a selected set of servers in the DMZ. The other firewall, facing the intranet, usually blocks all the inbound connections. Both of the firewalls

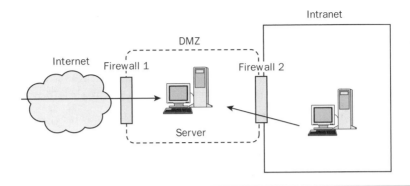

**Figure 14.5**  SSL server located in the DMZ

allow outbound connections for popular Internet applications, such as HTTP for Web browsing. This configuration implements the policy "Selected DMZ hosts are accessible from the Internet, but no hosts in the intranet are accessible from the Internet, even if some host in the DMZ is compromised." With this configuration, all the SSL/TLS connections must terminate at the SSL/TLS server in the DMZ. If the server needs to communicate further with some host in the intranet, a separate connection needs to be established.

There are two ways to connect the SSL/TLS server in the DMZ with a host in the intranet. One is to allow inbound connections from the SSL/TLS server to the intranet host by carefully configuring the inner firewall so that it only allows connections between the specific pairs of hosts on a specific port. The other way is to prohibit all the inbound connections and let the intranet host make an outbound connection every time the connection is required.

### 14.3.7  Summary of Using SSL/TLS

We have looked at how we can use SSL/TLS for securing our B2B communications. Most of the task involves understanding the available options, selecting the ones that satisfy your security policy, and configuring the software accordingly. The programming part is very small.

Because SSL/TLS-enabled Web sites are very popular, many companies let their firewalls allow HTTPS (port 443) connections. Therefore, an application sitting inside a company's firewall can have a direct secure connection to another company's server using SSL/TLS. It is said that in the United States, more than 50% of network crimes are committed from inside a firewall. Given this fact, the end-to-end security achieved by SSL/TLS has a large value.

# 14.4 XML Digital Signature

In the previous section, we discussed how SSL/TLS can be used for satisfying the first three communication security requirements: confidentiality, integrity, and authentication. What about the last of the four, nonrepudiation?

Suppose that you receive a purchase order for a $2,000 PC from company X. This order came via an SSL/TLS connection with certificate-based client authentication, and the client X.509 certificate verified flawlessly according to your trusted CA. Satisfied, you process the order and ship the PC. But you do not receive payment. What can you do? Even if you kept all the communication logs, including the X.509 certificate itself, you cannot prove that you actually received the order from company X, because you cannot deny the possibility that you forged the log.

Here is where a digital signature plays a key role. A digitally signed order form can be used as undeniable evidence of the order because only the person who has the private key can create the signature bit string (normally 512 to 2,048 bits). This technology is mature enough that some governments, such as those of Singapore, Japan, and the United States, have passed legislation that gives digitally signed business contracts the same legal standing as contracts signed by humans.

There are several standard digital signature formats. The most widely used is Public-Key Cryptography Standard (PKCS) #7 (http://www.rsasecurity. com/rsalabs/pkcs/index.html), whose syntax is based on Abstract Syntax Notation One (ASN.1, ITU-T Rec. X.680 (1997) | ISO/IEC 8824-1:1998). It takes a binary bit string as the data to be signed. The type of the data is irrelevant as far as the signature's validity is concerned. Any signature algorithm is expensive to apply directly to a large amount of data, so first a *hash* (or *digest*) value (typically 128 bits or 160 bits) is calculated for the entire data, and then the hash value is signed. Even a single bit change in the bit string always results in a completely different hash value, so any modification of the data invalidates the signature.

For signing XML documents, a joint working group between IETF and W3C has defined XML Digital Signature. In this section, we discuss how we can use XML Digital Signature in B2B applications using IBM's XML Security Suite for Java (XSS4J) as an implementation of XML Digital Signature.

## 14.4.1 XML Canonicalization

To digitally sign an XML document, you first must calculate the hash value of the document. It is possible to take an XML document as a character string (and thus a bit string) and compute its hash value. The problem with this approach is that logically the same XML document can be represented in many different ways because of XML's flexibility in character encoding, whitespace handling, and so on. If a purchase order signed by one company is processed through several applications equipped with different implementations of XML processors, the surface character string—that is, an octet string representing the XML document—might be changed during the process without the content being changed, thereby resulting in an invalid signature.

The surface string can vary without changing the content in any of several ways, including the following.

### Character Encoding

The character set in an XML document is defined in the XML 1.0 Recommendation as Unicode, which is a subset of ISO/IEC 10646. However, the Recommendation allows considerable freedom in encoding. Thus the same document can be represented in different ways, depending on the character encoding used—for example, ISO 8859-1, UTF-16, UTF-8, US-ASCII, and Shift-JIS.

### Handling Whitespace

The number of whitespace characters between attributes is insignificant in XML. XML processors are not required to preserve the number of spaces. Thus, the following two lines of code are treated as being exactly the same.

```
<order    id="C763" date="1998-11-17">
<order id="C763" date="1998-11-17">
```

Also, #x0D, #x0A, and #x0D#x0A are all converted into a single newline character (#0x0A).

### Empty Elements

An empty element may be expressed by using either an empty tag or a pair of start and end tags—for example, `<book></book>` or `<book/>`.

### Order of Attributes

The order of attributes is insignificant. For example, the following are the same:

```
<order id="C763" date="1998-11-17">
<order date="1998-11-17" id="C763">
```

To alleviate the problem of surface string deviation, the joint working group of XML Digital Signature defined XML Canonicalization (it is often abbreviated as C14N because there are 14 characters between C and N in the word "canonicalization"). XML Canonicalization (C14N) became a Recommendation in March 2001.

C14N defines a set of rules for how XML documents are represented as a character string in a standard way so that the same XML documents have exactly the same C14N representation, and different XML documents have different C14N representations.

## 14.4.2  XML Digital Signature Sample

Suppose company A wants to purchase a PC from company B. The order document would look like what is shown in Listing 14.2.

**Listing 14.2** Purchase order document, `chap14/po.xml`

```
<?xml version="1.0" encoding="UTF-8"?>
<PurchaseOrder xmlns="urn:purchase-order">
  <Customer>
    <Name>Robert Smith</Name>
    <CustomerId>788335</CustomerId>
  </Customer>
  <Item partNum="C763">
    <ProductId>6883-JF3</ProductId>
    <Quantity>3</Quantity>
    <ShipDate>2002-09-03</ShipDate>
    <Name>ThinkPad X20</Name>
  </Item>
</PurchaseOrder>
```

Before sending this order to company B, company A digitally signs it with its private key so that company B can use it as an undeniable proof of the order. This is depicted in Figure 14.6.

An XML Signature can be embedded in an XML document, or it can contain a signed body within the signature, or it can sign an external resource pointed to by a URL, or it can combine these. Here, we embed a signature in a document that

**Figure 14.6** Digital signature and verification

also contains the order document. The signed document that we generate with our sample program looks like that shown in Listing 14.3.

**Listing 14.3** The signed document, `chap14/signed_po.xml`

```xml
<?xml version='1.0' encoding='UTF-8'?>
<SignedPurchaseOrder>
<PurchaseOrder id="id0" xmlns="urn:purchase-order">
  <Customer>
    <Name>Robert Smith</Name>
    <CustomerId>788335</CustomerId>
  </Customer>
  <Item partNum="C763">
    <ProductId>6883-JF3</ProductId>
    <Quantity>3</Quantity>
    <ShipDate>2002-09-03</ShipDate>
    <Name>ThinkPad X20</Name>
  </Item>
</PurchaseOrder>
```

```xml
[15]    <Signature xmlns="http://www.w3.org/2000/09/xmldsig#">
[16]       <SignedInfo>
[17]          <CanonicalizationMethod Algorithm="http://www.w3.org/TR/2001/
                 REC-xml-c14n-20010315"/>
[18]          <SignatureMethod Algorithm="http://www.w3.org/2000/09/
                 xmldsig#rsa-sha1"/>
[19]          <Reference URI="#id0">
[20]             <DigestMethod Algorithm="http://www.w3.org/2000/09/
                    xmldsig#sha1"/>
[21]             <DigestValue>UfeiscUCL7QkhZtRDLWDPWLpVlA=</DigestValue>
[22]          </Reference>
[23]       </SignedInfo>
[24]       <SignatureValue>
[25]          Ptysg8WdHI2mxwryOOt5I9r9qZm/2gNFNOJyH1Wak4nCUegRpe72tWnsigAKZ
                 yopmgUSH3TG
[26]          aGGQF1BTSvk3JUUY/ljrw+5FpTpf3hgZBi7GSWf6WtXqZvMYGUKIlvR/
                 421MZg7P9XRUyy37
[27]          ZUzQHtmCYkBorEkEx1J4CYB0G2c=
[28]       </SignatureValue>
[29]       <KeyInfo>
[30]          <X509Data>
[31]             <X509Certificate>
[32]     MIIDGjCCAoOgAwIBAgICAQAwDQYJKo ... LMAkGA1UEBhMCS1AxETAPBgNVBAgT
[33]     CEthbmFnYXdhMQ8wDQYDVQQHEwZZYW ... TA0lCTTEMMAoGA1UECxMDVFJMMRAw
[34]     DgYDVQQDEwdUZXN0IENBMB4XDTAxMT ... xMTAwMTA3MTYxMFowUDELMAkGA1UE
[35]     BhMCS1AxETAPBgNVBAgTCEthbmFnMQww ... JQk0xDDAKBgNVBAsTA1RSTDESMBAG
[36]     A1UEAxMJU2lnbmF0dXJlMIGfMA0GCS ... NADCBiQKBgQCvnFQiPEJnUZnkmzoc
[37]     MjsseD8ms9HBgasZR0VOAvsbytB18d ... jBdprX+epfF4SLNP5ankfphhr9QXA
```

```
[38]    NJdCKpyF3jPoydckle7E7gI9w3Q4NO ... 7OVPqiXIDVlCH4u6GbIoJEpJ57yzx
[39]    dQIDAQABo4HzMIHwMUdEwQCMAAYDVR ... gMCwGCWCGSAGG+EIBDQQfFh1PcGVu
[40]    U1NMIEdlbmVyYXRlZCBDZXJ00ZTAdB ... UYapFv9MvQ9NNn1Q7zgzqka4XORsw
[41]    gYgGA1UdIwSBgDB+gBR7FuT9bLBzIe ... FjpGEwXzELMAkGA1UEBhMCSlAxETA
[42]    BgNVBAgTCEthbmFnYXdhMQ8wDQYDVQ ... AKBgNVBAoTA01CTTEMMAoGA1UECxM
[43]    VFJMMRAwDgYDVQQDEwdUZXN0IENBgg ... BBQUAA4GBALFzGDXMzxJvOnCdJCMZ
[44]    2NsZdz1+wmoYyejB5J6Ch2ygdPeibM ... qr1BN1gSVqA6nyvjHsVIvgBfwx37D
[45]    hJ5hz4azpWu1X22XqyU9fUqoQUtEAd ... JXTFzzvm/3DoEiBkX/BT78YdM8eq0
[46]          </X509Certificate>
[47]        </X509Data>
[48]      </KeyInfo>
[49]    </Signature>

        </SignedPurchaseOrder>
```

The document has a `<Signature>` element in the namespace `http://www.w3.org/2000/09/xmldsig#` (lines 15–49). The signed order is also in this document, with an additional `id` attribute that is used for referring to this element (lines 3–14). This is referred to by the `<Reference>` element at line 19.

```
[19]    <Reference URI="#id0">
[20]      <DigestMethod Algorithm="http://www.w3.org/2000/09/xmldsig#sha1"/>
[21]      <DigestValue>UfeiscUCL7QkhZtRDLWDPWLpVlA=</DigestValue>
[22]    </Reference>
```

This `<Reference>` element means that the hash value of the canonicalized form of the XML fragment referred to by identifier `id0` is `UfeiscUCL7Qk . . . .`

The signature algorithm is applied to the canonicalized form of the `<SignedInfo>` element (lines 16–23). The signature value is in the `<SignatureValue>` element (lines 24–28). Because the hash value of the `<PurchaseOrder>` element is in the signature scope, any change in the contents of the `<PurchaseOrder>` element results in a change in the C14N form of `<SignedInfo>`, thus invalidating the signature.

## 14.4.3  Signing XML Documents with XML Security Suite for Java

XSS4J is a Java library available from IBM's alphaWorks Web site (see `http://www.alphaworks.ibm.com`). It contains an implementation of XML Digital Signature. We use this library to implement our signature and verification samples.[5]

---

[5] In this section, we use XSS4J dated 2001-10-29. This version is dependent on Xerces 1.4 and Xalan 2.1. These jar files must be in the CLASSPATH, along with `xss4j.jar`. At the time of writing, Java Community Process is defining an API for XML Digital Signature as JSR 105. When this work is finished, the API may be different from the one described here.

Listing 14.4 shows the entire program to create an XML Digital Signature document that contains the signed XML fragment.

**Listing 14.4**  Digitally signing an XML document, `chap14/EnvelopedSignature.java`

```java
package chap14;

import share.util.MyErrorHandler;
import com.ibm.xml.dsig.TemplateGenerator;
import com.ibm.xml.dsig.SignatureContext;
import com.ibm.xml.dsig.XSignature;
import com.ibm.xml.dsig.util.AdHocIDResolver;
import com.ibm.xml.dsig.Reference;
import com.ibm.xml.dsig.Transform;
import com.ibm.xml.dsig.KeyInfo;
import com.ibm.xml.dsig.SignatureMethod;
import com.ibm.xml.dsig.Canonicalizer;
import com.ibm.xml.dsig.TransformException;
import com.ibm.xml.dsig.XSignatureException;
import com.ibm.xml.dsig.SignatureStructureException;

import com.ibm.dom.util.ToXMLVisitor;
import org.w3c.dom.Document;
import org.w3c.dom.Element;
import javax.xml.parsers.DocumentBuilder;
import javax.xml.parsers.DocumentBuilderFactory;
import java.security.Key;
import java.security.KeyStore;
import java.security.KeyStoreException;
import java.security.NoSuchAlgorithmException;
import java.security.NoSuchProviderException;
import java.security.InvalidKeyException;
import java.security.UnrecoverableKeyException;
import java.security.cert.CertificateException;
import java.security.cert.X509Certificate;
import java.io.FileInputStream;
import java.io.Writer;
import java.io.OutputStreamWriter;
import java.io.IOException;
import java.util.Hashtable;

public class EnvelopedSignature {

    private static DocumentBuilderFactory factory;
    private static DocumentBuilder builder;

    public static Element signIt(Document doc,
                                 String id2sign,
```

```
                                     String keystorepath,
                                     char[] storepass,
                                     String alias,
                                     char[] keypass)
                      throws IOException, KeyStoreException,
                             NoSuchAlgorithmException,
                      SignatureStructureException, CertificateException,
                      UnrecoverableKeyException, NoSuchProviderException,
                      InvalidKeyException, XSignatureException, TransformException {

                          // 1. Prepare key
[55]                      KeyStore keystore = KeyStore.getInstance("JKS");
[56]                      keystore.load(new
                                  FileInputStream(keystorepath), storepass);
[57]                      X509Certificate cert = (X509Certificate)keystore.
                          getCertificate(alias);
[58]                      Key key =
                                  keystore.getKey(alias, keypass); // a private key
[59]                      if (key == null) {
[60]                          System.err.println("Could not get a key: "+alias);
[61]                          System.exit(1);
[62]                      }
[63]
[64]                      String signatureMethod = "";
[65]                      if (key.getAlgorithm().equals("RSA")) {
[66]                          signatureMethod = SignatureMethod.RSA;
[67]                      } else if (key.getAlgorithm().equals("DSA")) {
[68]                          signatureMethod = SignatureMethod.DSA;
[69]                      } else {
[70]                          System.err.println(
                                  "Unknown key algorithm"+key.getAlgorithm());
[71]                          System.exit(1);
[72]                      }

                          //
                          // 2. Prepare Signature element
                          //
                          TemplateGenerator
                              signatureGen = new TemplateGenerator(doc,
                              XSignature.SHA1,
                                          Canonicalizer.W3C2,
                                          signatureMethod);
                          Reference ref = signatureGen.createReference(id2sign);
                          signatureGen.addReference(ref);

                          Element signatureElement =
                                  signatureGen.getSignatureElement();
```

```
                    KeyInfo keyInfo = new KeyInfo();
                    KeyInfo.X509Data x509data = new KeyInfo.X509Data();
                    x509data.setCertificate(cert);
                    x509data.setParameters(cert, false, false, false);
                    keyInfo.setX509Data(new KeyInfo.X509Data[] { x509data });
                    keyInfo.insertTo(signatureElement);

                    //
                    // 3. Sign
                    //
[96]                SignatureContext sigContext = new SignatureContext();
[97]                sigContext.setIDResolver(new AdHocIDResolver(doc));
[98]                sigContext.sign(signatureElement, key);
                    return signatureElement;
            }

        public static void main(String[] argv) throws Exception {
            if (argv.length < 5) {
                System.err.println("Usage: chap15.EnvelopedSignature
                keystore storepass keyalias  keypass file");
                System.exit(1);
            }
            String keystorepath = argv[0];
            char[] storepass = argv[1].toCharArray();
            String alias = argv[2];
            char[] keypass = argv[3].toCharArray();

            factory = DocumentBuilderFactory.newInstance();
            factory.setNamespaceAware(true);
            builder = factory.newDocumentBuilder();
            builder.setErrorHandler(new MyErrorHandler());
            Document doc = builder.parse(argv[4]);
            //
            // Wrap the root element with <SignedPurchaseOrder>
            //
            Element root = doc.getDocumentElement();
            doc.removeChild(root);
            Element signedRoot =
                    doc.createElementNS(root.getNamespaceURI(),
                                        "Signed"+root.getNodeName());
            doc.appendChild(signedRoot);
            signedRoot.appendChild(root);
            root.setAttribute("id","id0");
            Element signature =
                signIt(doc,"#id0",keystorepath,storepass,alias,keypass);
            signedRoot.appendChild(signature);
            //
```

```
                    // Output
                    //
                    try {
                        Writer wr = new OutputStreamWriter(System.out, "UTF-8");
                        wr.write("<?xml version='1.0' encoding='UTF-8'?>\n");
                        new ToXMLVisitor(wr).traverse(signedRoot);
                        wr.close();
                    } catch (Exception ex) {
                        ex.printStackTrace();
                    }
                }
            }
```

The heart of this program is the following three lines. Line 96 creates a signature context, an object responsible for generating a signature. The invocation of the method `sign(signatureElement, Key)` in line 97 performs the signing operation.

```
[96]    SignatureContext sigContext = new SignatureContext();
[97]    sigContext.setIDResolver(new AdHocIDResolver(doc));
[98]    sigContext.sign(signatureElement, key);
```

All the necessary parameters are included in the `signatureElement` variable. This is a skeleton DOM structure that represents a complete `<Signature>` structure except for the values of the `<DigestValue>` element and `<SignatureValue>` element. This structure, before signing, looks like this.

```
<Signature xmlns="http://www.w3.org/2000/09/xmldsig#">
  <SignedInfo>
    <CanonicalizationMethod Algorithm="http://www.w3.org/TR/2001/
    REC-xml-c14n-20010315"/>
    <SignatureMethod Algorithm="http://www.w3.org/2000/09/
    xmldsig#dsa-sha1"/>
    <Reference URI="#Res0">
      <DigestMethod Algorithm="http://www.w3.org/2000/09/
      xmldsig#sha1"/>
      <DigestValue/>
    </Reference>
  </SignedInfo>
  <SignatureValue/>
  <KeyInfo>
    <X509Data>
      <X509Certificate>
         :
      </X509Certificate>
```

```
        </X509Data>
      </KeyInfo>
   </Signature>
```

Thus, numerous parameters necessary for XML Digital Signature can be passed as a single DOM structure. To assist in creating this structure, a helper class, `TemplateGenerator`, is provided. Parameters appearing in `SignedInfo`, such as the signature algorithm, references to the resources to be signed, and information appearing in `<KeyInfo>`, are all set to a `TemplateGenerator` object.

Alternatively, the template DOM structure can be read from an external XML file. The program would have been simpler in that case.

Since a `<Reference>` element uses an intradocument reference in the form of `#id`, we need to provide a way to resolve such a reference to yield an element reference. The interface `IDResolver` is provided for this purpose. We used `AdHocIDResolver`, which is provided as a utility class in XSS4J.

To use the private key that we have prepared for this sample program, we need to retrieve it from the keystore. Lines 55–72 retrieve the key specified by a keystore filename and a key alias, and then extract the pertinent information, such as the key algorithm and the associated certificate.

To run this program for signing the file `po.xml`, execute the following command.

```
R:\samples>java chap14/EnvelopedSignature chap14/keystore/signature.
ks changeit signature changeit chap14/po.xml
```

The result should look like Listing 14.3.[6]

## 14.4.4 Verifying XML Digital Signature with XML Security Suite for Java

When a company receives a signed document, it must verify the signature to determine whether it is authentic. Let us develop a Java program to verify an XML Signature. To verify a signature, we should obtain the signer's certificate issued by a trusted CA. Usually, this is done by accessing a certificate directory published by a CA. In our private PKI, however, we assume that the signer certificate is already installed in the keystore of the verifier. This configuration is practical as long as the number of certificates you need to manage is small.

---

[6] We inserted a few new lines for readability.

Listing 14.5 shows a verification program using XSS4J.

**Listing 14.5** A signature-verification program, `chap14/VerifySignature.java`

```java
package chap14;

import share.util.MyErrorHandler;
import com.ibm.xml.dsig.SignatureContext;
import com.ibm.xml.dsig.XSignature;
import com.ibm.xml.dsig.Validity;
import com.ibm.xml.dsig.SignatureStructureException;
import com.ibm.xml.dsig.TransformException;
import com.ibm.xml.dsig.util.AdHocIDResolver;

import javax.xml.parsers.DocumentBuilder;
import javax.xml.parsers.DocumentBuilderFactory;
import org.w3c.dom.Document;
import org.w3c.dom.Element;
import org.w3c.dom.NodeList;
import java.io.FileInputStream;
import java.io.IOException;
import java.security.Key;
import java.security.KeyStore;
import java.security.KeyStoreException;
import java.security.NoSuchAlgorithmException;
import java.security.NoSuchProviderException;
import java.security.UnrecoverableKeyException;
import java.security.SignatureException;
import java.security.InvalidKeyException;
import java.security.cert.X509Certificate;
import java.security.cert.CertificateException;

public class VerifySignature {

    static boolean verifyIt(Document doc,
                            Element e,
                            String keystorepath,
                            char[] storepass,
                            String alias)
        throws IOException, KeyStoreException, NoSuchAlgorithmException,
        SignatureStructureException, CertificateException,
        UnrecoverableKeyException, NoSuchProviderException,
        InvalidKeyException, SignatureException, TransformException {

            // 1. Prepare key
            KeyStore keystore = KeyStore.getInstance("JKS");
            keystore.load(new FileInputStream(keystorepath), storepass);
            X509Certificate cert = (X509Certificate)keystore.
            getCertificate(alias);
```

```
                          Key key = cert.getPublicKey(); // a private key
                          if (key == null) {
                              System.err.println("Could not get a key: "+alias);
                              System.exit(1);
                          }
[51]                      SignatureContext sigContext = new SignatureContext();
[52]                      sigContext.setIDResolver(new AdHocIDResolver(doc));
[53]                      Validity validity = sigContext.verify(e,key);
[54]
[55]                      return validity.getCoreValidity();
                  }

          public static void main(String[] argv) throws Exception {
              DocumentBuilderFactory factory;
              DocumentBuilder builder;

              if (argv.length < 4) {
                  System.err.println("Usage: VerifySignature keystore
                  storepass keyalias file");
                  System.exit(1);
              }
              String keystorepath = argv[0];
              char[] storepass = argv[1].toCharArray();
              String alias = argv[2];
              factory = DocumentBuilderFactory.newInstance();
              factory.setNamespaceAware(true);
              builder = factory.newDocumentBuilder();
              builder.setErrorHandler(new MyErrorHandler());
              Document doc = builder.parse(argv[3]);

              NodeList nodeList = doc.getElementsByTagNameNS(XSignature.
              XMLDSIG_NAMESPACE, "Signature");
              if (nodeList.getLength() == 0) {
                  System.err.println("The specified document has no
                  Signature element.");
                  System.exit(1);
              }
              Element signature = (Element)nodeList.item(0);

              if (verifyIt(doc, signature, keystorepath, storepass, alias)) {
                  System.out.println("Signature verify");
              } else {
                  System.out.println("Signature does not verify");
              }

          }

      }
```

The focus of this program is lines 51–55. In a similar way to the signing program, we create a `SignatureContext` object and let it validate a `<Signature>` element by calling the `verify()` method. This method returns a `Validity` object, which contains the information on the verification. To know whether the verification was successful, we need to call the `getCoreValidity()` method.

```
[51]    SignatureContext sigContext = new SignatureContext();
[52]    sigContext.setIDResolver(new AdHocIDResolver(doc));
[53]    Validity validity = sigContext.verify(e,key);
[54]
[55]    return validity.getCoreValidity();
```

To run this program for verifying the signature in the file `signed_po.xml` using our prefabricated keystore, `chap14/keystore/verification.ks`, enter the following command.

```
R:\samples>java chap14/VerifySignature chap14/keystore/verification.
ks changeit signature chap14/signed_po.xml
```

Try slightly modifying `signed_po.xml` and see whether the signature verifies. If you change any content in the `<PurchaseOrder>` element, such as modifying the quantity from 3 to 4, you will notice that the signature no longer verifies. On the other hand, nonessential changes, such as adding extra whitespace between attributes, do not affect the verifiability of the signature.

## 14.5  Access Control in Java

In Sections 14.3 and 14.4, we examined the security options against threats associated with communications over the Internet. In this section, we study the technologies that satisfy the other category of security requirement—access control.

### 14.5.1  Declarative Access Control and Programmatic Access Control

Suppose that our purchase order application receives an XML request. This request has been authenticated by using one of the methods that we described in Section 14.3, so we are confident about the identity of the requester. We consider how we can impose our access control policy on this request. We assume the access control policy we mentioned in Section 14.2.2, which we repeat here for your convenience.

- All properly authenticated companies can access the product catalog database.
- All companies in the "trusted" category can submit a new purchase order.

- A company can review the history of a purchase order that has been issued by the same company.

Assume that our application has three operations—(1) browse the product catalog database, (2) submit a new purchase order, and (3) review the purchase order database—and that these operations are implemented as three servlets, each of which has a distinct URL. How can we implement our access control policy?

One important concept in access control is to use a *choke point*. A choke point in a system is a position where all the requests must go through. A choke point is a logical place to impose an access control policy. In our system, the two obvious choke points are as follows:

- When the servlet container authenticates a request
- When the application accesses a database

In many cases, access control at authentication time is achieved by statically configuring the platform software, such as the servlet container. This is called *declarative access control* (see Figure 14.7). In this case, there is no need for the application program to take care of access control. On the other hand, some policy requires that the application itself be involved in access control decisions. In such a case, it is natural that the access control occurs when the application tries to access a protected resource. This is called *programmatic access control* (see Figure 14.7).

We show how we can implement our policy in each case.

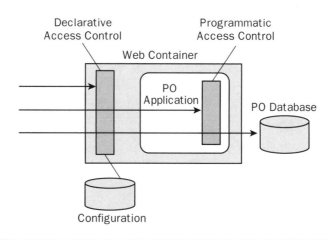

**Figure 14.7** Two strategies of access control

## 14.5.2 Declarative Access Control

Our first policy, "All properly authenticated companies can access the product catalog database," is best implemented as declarative access control because all that is needed to make an access control decision is authentication. In this case, we can use the access control mechanism associated with HTTP basic authentication.

To do this, we need to configure the Web server that is a frontend of our servlet container. If the frontend Web server is Apache Web Server, this configuration can be done by placing an appropriate `.htaccess` file in the directory that corresponds to our servlet.

### Role-Based Access Control

What about our second policy, "All companies in the 'trusted' category can submit a new purchase order"?

One straightforward way to enforce this policy would be to prepare another authentication database specifically for the purchase order operation and to register all the "trusted" customers in this database. This is not, however, a desirable solution from a management point of view. For example, when a new customer is registered, you would need to update both databases. In general, the following three items should be separately managed in a corporation:

- How to authenticate a requester
- What role the requester is to play
- Which application should accept what categories of requester

The idea of categorizing subjects and assigning *roles* to them for separating authentication from declarative access control is called *role-based access control* (RBAC). Subjects (in our case, requesters) are assigned their roles when authenticated, and our application should make access control decisions based on the roles, not on the identity of the individual.

Apache Tomcat, which we introduced in Chapter 10, has a primitive mechanism to assign roles to a requester. In its authentication database, `$TOMCAT_HOME/conf/tomcat-users`, we can assign a set of roles to each user, as shown in Listing 14.6.

**Listing 14.6** Assigning roles to users, `$TOMCAT_HOME/conf/tomcat-users.xml`

```
<tomcat-users>
  <user name="maruyama" password="montelac" roles="none" />
  <user name="kosaka"  password="ymt03" roles="trustedCustomer"  />
  <user name="murata" password="frtnct" roles="administrator,
  trustedCustomer"/>
</tomcat-users>
```

For each application deployed on a Tomcat Server, the deployment descriptor of the application can specify the roles into which the requesters to the application must be categorized. For example, the deployment descriptor shown in Listing 14.7 requires that any requester to this application must have the `trustedCustomer` role.

**Listing 14.7**  Deployment descriptor, `webapps/chap14/WEB-INF/web.xml`

```
<?xml version="1.0" encoding="ISO-8859-1"?>

<!DOCTYPE web-app
    PUBLIC "-//Sun Microsystems, Inc.//DTD Web Application 2.2//EN"
    "http://java.sun.com/j2ee/dtds/web-app_2_2.dtd">

<web-app>

    <security-constraint>
      <web-resource-collection>
        <web-resource-name>Protected Area</web-resource-name>
        <url-pattern>/*</url-pattern>
        <http-method>DELETE</http-method>
        <http-method>GET</http-method>
        <http-method>POST</http-method>
        <http-method>PUT</http-method>
      </web-resource-collection>
      <auth-constraint>
        <role-name>tomcat</role-name>
      </auth-constraint>
    </security-constraint>

    <login-config>
      <auth-method>BASIC</auth-method>
      <realm-name>XMLJAVA</realm-name>
    </login-config>

</web-app>
```

Thus, in many cases access control policies can be enforced declaratively by configuring the servlet container. Whenever the policy to implement can be enforced this way, the declarative access control method should be used to clearly separate the enforcement of the access control policies from the application development.

## 14.5.3  Programmatic Access Control

However, some access control policies require information that is available only after executing the application. Consider our third access control policy, "A company can review the history of a purchase order that has been issued by the same company." To implement this policy, the application would need to access the database first, and based on the retrieved data, it would need to make an access control decision. This type of access control cannot be realized in a declarative way.

To make access control decisions within an application, the application must know the identity or the role of the requester. It is desirable that the application be able to obtain this information regardless of whether the authentication method is HTTP basic authentication, SSL/TLS certificate-based client authentication, or any other authentication method. J2EE provides two methods, `getUserPrincipal()` and `isUserInRole()`, for `HTTPServletRequest` objects.

### Security Architecture in Java

As long as the application can access the `HTTPServletRequest` object that represents the current request, it can use `getUserPrincipal()` and `isUser InRole()` to make access control decisions. However, this is not always possible at all the choke points where the access control policies are to be enforced. Therefore, the application must pass around the `HTTPServletRequest` object or the information of the subject either in an additional parameter in many methods or in a global variable. Neither of them is desirable from the application development and maintenance point of view. Therefore, it would be beneficial if a Java thread could be associated with the subject, and an application could query the subject information at any time.

In addition, because Java programs usually run in a single userid of the platform operating system, the built-in access control mechanism to OS-managed resources such as local files and network connections cannot be used directly. Again, if the subject could be used for controlling access to these resources, it would be useful for ensuring that unauthorized requesters could not gain access to these resources accidentally or intentionally.

Java 2 SDK 1.3 provides Java Authentication and Authorization Services (JAAS) as a solution to these requirements. Figure 14.8 shows Java's security architecture. All the libraries that access protected resources (for example, local file systems) call the `checkPermission()` method of the class `java.security. SecurityManager`.

The security manager decides, according to the policies, whether the access is allowed based on the following.

- Who wrote the classes that are making the call (this information is called the *code source principal*).
- Who is the subject associated with the current execution context (called the *subject principal*).

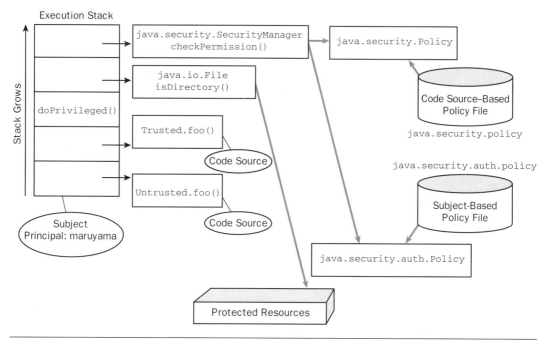

**Figure 14.8** Java security architecture

If the access is denied, the security manager throws an exception.

The reason Java attaches importance to the code source principal is that Java allows programs to be downloaded from the network. The security manager prevents malicious download programs from accessing protected resources via the system libraries by inspecting all the class files that constitute the calling chain up to the `checkPermission()` call.[7] The security policy for code source principal is managed by the class `java.security.Policy`, which by default reads a policy file located at `$JAVA_HOME/jre/lib/security/java.policy`.

A subject principal is created by a user-supplied class called a *login module*. The created subject is added to the current execution context by calling `javax.security.auth.Subject.doAs()`. The following code fragment illustrates how a login module is called to create a subject principal and how the created principal is added to the current execution context.

---

[7] If the call chain includes `java.security.SecurityManager.doPrivileged()`, the security manager does not check the code source principals from the stack bottom to that point. This mechanism allows a trusted library to provide a service to untrusted programs with limited access to the protected resources.

```
    . . .
LoginContext lc = new LoginContext("loginModuleFoo");
try {
    lc.login();
} catch (LoginException le) {
    System.out.println("authentication unsuccessful"+le.
    printStackTrace());
}
Subject.doAs(lc.getSubject(), new PrivilegedAction() {
    public Object run() {
        //
        // Run under the authenticated subject
        //
        . . .
        return null;
    }
});
    . . .
```

The login module used here (referred to by the name "loginModuleFoo") must be configured in a JVM configuration file. Both creating a subject principal and attaching it to the current execution are protected operations. Therefore, both the login module and the class containing this code fragment must be given permissions for these operations under their code source principal.

Once a subject principal is added to an execution context, an application program does not need to explicitly propagate the information on the subject. At any time, an application program can test whether the current subject is allowed access to protected resources by calling checkPermission(), or it can obtain the subject information with the following code.

```
AccessControlContext acc = AccessController.getContext();
Subject subj = Subject.getSubject(acc);
```

In addition, by configuring your JVM through the class java.security.auth. Policy, you can also control access to the standard protected resources, such as local file systems and network connections.

These access control features can be used only when the security manager is enabled. By default, JVM runs without the security manager enabled. To enable the security manager, the java command line must have the following option:[8]

```
-Djava.security.manager=
```

---

[8] To run Tomcat Server with the security manager enabled, you must add the -security option to the startup.cmd command.

### 14.5.4  Security Architecture of EJB

Enterprise JavaBeans (EJB), which we introduced in Chapter 11, also has its own security model, which is consistent with the other pieces in the J2EE framework. Let us briefly touch on it. EJB allows both declarative access control and programmatic access control.

When an EJB component is called from a Web container or from another EJB container, it receives the information of the original requester. For each method of a component, declarative access control policies can be configured based on the subject's role propagated from the caller. For example, if the caller is a Web container, it passes the information on the subject that is obtained by one of the methods described in Section 14.2.2 (for example, HTTP basic authentication) to the called EJB component.

JAAS provides a mechanism for propagating subject information within a Java execution context (that is, a thread). Unfortunately, this mechanism cannot be used for EJB, because EJB components are able to call other EJB components running in other JVMs. Instead, properly configured EJB containers allow called components to share the same *context* as the caller component. A context may contain the subject information of the original requester.

EJB components manage contexts by means of `EJBContext` objects. The following two methods are provided so that an EJB component can examine the identity and the role of the subject:

- `getCallerPrincipal()`
- `isCallerInRole()`

EJB is a large specification, and there are a lot of features related to security. Most of these security features are related to the configuration of EJB containers and are dependent on the implementation of EJB containers. For example, your EJB container may have an ability to map a Kerberos identity to an EJB principal.[9] See the documentation of your EJB container for the details.

## 14.6  Security in Web Services

In Chapter 13, we introduced the concept of Web services, exemplified by technologies such as SOAP, WSDL, and UDDI. The security techniques described in this chapter can also be applied to Web services. An idea that is the other way around is to use the Web services technologies to provide security services such as

---

[9] Kerberos is a distributed authentication mechanism widely used in intranet installations.

authentication and authorization. These are hot topics at the time of writing, and nothing is concrete today, but we will look at some of them in order to show the future possibilities.

## 14.6.1 Using SSL/TLS and XML Digital Signature in SOAP

We can apply SSL/TLS (see Section 14.3) and XML Digital Signature (see Section 14.4) to SOAP messaging to achieve a secure messaging that satisfies the four security requirements—confidentiality, integrity, authentication, and nonrepudiation. How can we combine these technologies with SOAP?

If your SOAP middleware supports HTTPS connections, using SSL/TLS should be no problem. Just follow the steps described in Section 14.3. For example, Apache SOAP supports HTTPS.

Because the body of a SOAP message is XML, it should be possible to embed an XML digital signature in the message body. Alternatively, an XML Signature can be carried as a header entry of a SOAP Envelope. In this case, extensible SOAP middleware, such as Apache SOAP, that allows adding new header handlers can be used for adding and verifying a signature. The W3C Note "SOAP Security: Signature" is a proposal to add such a header entry to a SOAP Envelope.

## 14.6.2 Access Control in SOAP Applications

Access control in a SOAP application is also possible by using the methods described in this chapter. For Apache SOAP, declarative access control can be done by configuring the servlet container. There is one limitation, however. In Apache SOAP, all the operations deployed on a single server share the same URL (for example, `http://demohost/soap/servlet/rpcrouter/`), so it is not possible to apply different access policies to different operations. In such a case, you may need to use one of the programmatic access control methods mentioned in Section 14.5.4.

## 14.6.3 Partial Encryption of XML

SSL/TLS encrypts all the transmitted data. This is enough for achieving confidential communication between two parties. However, if a communication involves more than two parties, and an access control policy requires different levels of confidentiality for different portions of data (for example, a credit card number cannot be viewed by a merchant, but a credit card company should be able to read it), SSL/TLS does not provide enough flexibility. This situation occurs when a SOAP message is relayed through one or more intermediaries, which may or may not have access rights to either header entries or the message body. SSL/TLS does not provide protection of stored data, either.

These requirements triggered a new W3C Working Group in February 2001 for defining XML encryption in. The goal is to define a standard syntax for encrypting part or all of an XML document. A sample encrypted document, according to the Candidate Recommendation dated March 2002, follows.

```
<EncryptedData xmlns="http://www.w3.org/2001/04/xmlenc#"
Type="http://www.w3.org/2001/04/xmlenc#Element">
  <EncryptionMethod Algorithm="http://www.w3.org/2001/04/
  xmlenc#tripledes-cbc"/>
  <ds:KeyInfo xmlns:ds="http://www.w3.org/2000/09/xmldsig#">
    <EncryptedKey>
      <EncryptionMethod Algorithm="http://www.w3.org/2001/04/
      xmlenc#rsa-1_5"/>
      <ds:KeyInfo>
        <ds:X509Data>
          <ds:X509IssuerSerial>
            <ds:X509IssuerName>CN=Hiroshi Maruyama, O=IBM,
            C=JP</ds:X509IssuerName>
            <ds:X509SerialNumber>378261448</ds:X509SerialNumber>
          </ds:X509IssuerSerial>
        </ds:X509Data>
      </ds:KeyInfo>
      <CipherData>
        <CipherValue>k3453rvEPO0vKtMup4NbeVu8nk=</CipherValue>
      </CipherData>
    </EncryptedKey>
  </ds:KeyInfo>
  <CipherData>
    <CipherValue>j6lwx3rvEPO0vKtMup4NbeVu8nk=</CipherValue>
  </CipherData>
</EncryptedData>
```

You may notice that the same `<KeyInfo>` structure defined in XML Digital Signature is used here.

## 14.6.4 Security Service as Web Services

As the specifications for XML Signature and encryption are becoming ready for use and the idea of Web services is getting popular, a new idea of providing security functions—such as key management, certificate management, authentication, and authorization—as Web services is emerging. The public-key cryptosystem is a very powerful technology but at the same time a difficult technology to use. The technologies we described in this chapter are useful to achieve a reasonable level of security, but there is a danger of introducing new security vulnerabilities if these technologies are not configured correctly or they are not managed properly.

The idea behind providing security functions as Web services is to delegate these security functions to Web services that are professionally configured and managed, thus freeing application developers and administrators from these tasks that require highly specialized skills.

At the time of this writing, two such specifications are being discussed: XML Key Management Specification (XKMS), which provides key and certificate management services, and Security Assertion Markup Language (SAML), which can be used for implementing authentication and authorization services. We can expect that more services—such as signature services, encryption services, and timestamping services—will be defined in the future.

## 14.7 Summary

In this chapter, we discussed how SSL/TLS, HTTP basic authentication, and XML Digital Signature can be used to achieve four communication security requirements: confidentiality, integrity, authentication, and nonrepudiation.

We also discussed ways to implement declarative access control and programmatic access control in Java programs.

Remember that security must be considered for every aspect of an information system. The technologies shown in this chapter will add very little to the security of an information system if the network, operating system, or any other software has a vulnerability, or the system is poorly managed or monitored.

# Data Binding

## 15.1 Introduction

In Chapter 8, we discussed the fact that there are certain patterns in mappings between XML documents and application data. In particular, we touched upon the possibility of mechanizing the mapping if the application data structure is isomorphic to the XML document structure. If we use a software tool to automatically generate the mapping, we can significantly reduce the programming burden of XML processing. The technique to automate these mappings is called *data binding*.

There are two major approaches to data binding; one is to deduce a Java data structure from a given XML schema, and the other is to deduce an XML structure from a given Java program (possibly through reflection). These two approaches are complementary. Both have their respective advantages and limitations, and neither is superior to the other. If an XML schema is given and you are required to write a program to read XML data according to the schema, a data binding tool of the former type is useful. On the other hand, if you already have your application program and you are requested to externalize the application data in some XML format, one of the reflection-based tools is a better choice.

In this chapter, we examine several available data binding tools in these two categories. In Section 15.2, we look at two technologies that fall in the first category: Java Architecture for XML Binding (JAXB) and Relaxer. In Section 15.3, we discuss generating XML from a Java program using Castor XML and SOAP encoding as our examples. Each section briefly discusses when these tools are most useful.

## 15.2 Generating Java Classes from a Schema

The structural constraints that a class of XML documents (for example, purchase order documents) should satisfy are given as some form of a schema language. In addition, contemporary schema languages, such as W3C XML Schema, allow you to specify the data types of elements. Therefore, once a schema of input XML documents is given, an application programmer knows the data structures and data types needed in the application program that works on XML documents of the given schema. Some data binding tools follow this idea—that is, generating Java classes from a given schema. In this section, we look at two of these tools: JAXB, which is being discussed as Java Community Process JSR 31, and Relaxer, which is based on the schema language RELAX, described in Chapter 9.[1]

## 15.2.1 JAXB

JAXB[2] is a data binding specification that is being defined by Java Community Process JSR 31. The goal of JSR 31 is to support Java class generation from W3C XML Schema, but at the time of writing, the specification supports only DTD, not XML Schema. Because DTD has no data type support, we must supply data type information in a separate file called a binding schema. JAXB's schema compiler (a program named `xjc` in Sun's technology preview version of JAXB) takes both a DTD and a binding schema as input and generates a set of Java source files (see Figure 15.1).

Let us use JAXB with our purchase order example. First, we need a DTD, `PurchaseOrder.dtd`, shown in Listing 15.1, which describes the syntax of the purchase order documents.

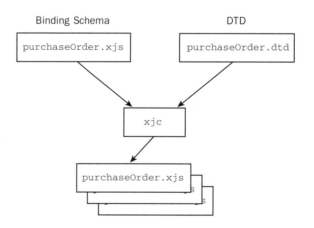

**Figure 15.1** JAXB schema compiler

---

[1] Generating Java classes from a WSDL document, as explained in Chapter 13, Section 13.2, can also be considered as data binding. See Section 15.3.3 for further discussion.

[2] The description of JAXB in this section is based on Sun's Early Access Implementation 1.0. You are urged to check for any updates on the technology.

**Listing 15.1**  DTD for the purchase order documents, `chap15/jaxb/`
`PurchaseOrder.dtd`

```
<?xml version="1.0" encoding="us-ascii"?>
<!ELEMENT purchaseOrder (customer, comment?, items)>
<!ELEMENT customer (name, customerId?, address)>
<!ELEMENT name (#PCDATA)>
<!ELEMENT customerId (#PCDATA)>
<!ELEMENT address (#PCDATA)>
<!ELEMENT comment (#PCDATA)>
<!ELEMENT items (item+)>
<!ELEMENT item (productName, quantity, USPrice, shipDate)>
<!ATTLIST item partNum CDATA #REQUIRED>
<!ELEMENT productName (#PCDATA)>
<!ELEMENT quantity (#PCDATA)>
<!ELEMENT USPrice (#PCDATA)>
<!ELEMENT shipDate (#PCDATA)>
```

We can generate a Java program from this DTD alone, but if we do so, the data
types of all the elements and attributes, including the `<quantity>` element and
the `<USPrice>` element, will be `String`. To map these elements to the appropriate data types, we need the mapping schema `purchaseOrder.xjs`, shown in
Listing 15.2.

**Listing 15.2**  A mapping schema, `chap15/jaxb/PurchaseOrder.xjs`

```
       <?xml version="1.0" encoding="UTF-8"?>
       <!DOCTYPE xml-java-binding-schema SYSTEM "xjs.dtd">
       <xml-java-binding-schema version="1.0-ea">
[4]       <options package="chap15.jaxb"/>

          <element name="purchaseOrder" type="class" root="true"/>

          <element name="productName" type="value"/>
[9]       <element name="quantity" type="value" convert="int"/>
[10]      <element name="USPrice" type="value" convert="float"/>
          <element name="shipDate" type="value"/>

          <element name="item" type="class">
            <content>
              <element-ref name="productName"/>
              <element-ref name="quantity"/>
              <element-ref name="USPrice"/>
              <element-ref name="shipDate"/>
            </content>
            <attribute name="partNum"/>
          </element>
       </xml-java-binding-schema>
```

In this mapping file, lines 9 and line 10 specify that the data types of `<quantity>` and `<USPrice>` are `int` and `float`, respectively. If we want to have a Java class instead of a base data type, we can also specify it as follows:[3]

```
<element name="quantity" type="class" .../>
```

Let us look at the generated Java program. From the DTD and the schema mapping file that we provided as the input, the schema compiler generates four classes— `PurchaseOrder.java`, `Customer.java`, `Items.java`, and `Item.java`— each of which corresponds to one of the four element types that have a complex content type. Because it is clear from the DTD that the `<productName>` and `<shipDate>` elements have no complex content model, the schema compiler maps these elements to a simple type of `String`.

How are the names of the generated Java classes determined? Element type names, such as `purchaseOrder` and `customer`, are mapped to `PurchaseOrder` and `Customer` by capitalizing the first letter, following the standard Java coding style. JAXB has a set of rules to derive a Java name from an XML element type name or an attribute name. These rules absorb the differences between the naming rules of XML and the naming rules of Java programs.

Listing 15.3 shows part of `PurchaseOrder.java`, which is generated by the JAXB schema compiler.

**Listing 15.3** A generated Java class, `chap15/jaxb/PurchaseOrder.java`

```
       public class PurchaseOrder
           extends MarshallableRootElement
           implements RootElement
       {

[29]         private Customer _Customer;
[30]         private String _Comment;
[31]         private Items _Items;

             public Customer getCustomer() {
                 return _Customer;
             }
           ...
       }
```

As you can see, three fields, `_Customer`, `_Comment`, and `_Items`, are generated according to the content model of the element type `purchaseOrder` (lines 29–31). Also, you may notice that this class extends the parent class

---

[3] This mapping file also contains other parameters that are pertinent to the code generation. For example, the `<options>` element in line 4 specifies the package name of the generated classes.

`MarshallableRootElement`. `MarashallableRootElement` is in turn a subclass of `ValidatableObject`, which signifies that its subclasses are derived from
a schema, and thus they have a `validate()` method to test whether the current
contents of the object conform to the schema.

Next, we examine how the generated code parses (that is, unmarshals) an XML
document. The pertinent portion of the generated `PurchaseOrder.java` class is
shown in Listing 15.4.

**Listing 15.4** Continuation of the generated class, `chap15/jaxb/`
`PurchaseOrder.java`

```
        public void unmarshal(Unmarshaller u)
            throws UnmarshalException
        {
            XMLScanner xs = u.scanner();
            Validator v = u.validator();
[102]       xs.takeStart("purchaseOrder");
            while (xs.atAttribute()) {
                String an = xs.takeAttributeName();
                throw new InvalidAttributeException(an);
            }
[107]       _Customer = ((Customer) u.unmarshal());
[108]       if (xs.atStart("comment")) {
[109]           xs.takeStart("comment");
[110]           String s;
[111]           if (xs.atChars(XMLScanner.WS_COLLAPSE)) {
[112]               s = xs.takeChars(XMLScanner.WS_COLLAPSE);
[113]           } else {
[114]               s = "";
[115]           }
[116]           try {
[117]               _Comment = String.valueOf(s);
[118]           } catch (Exception x) {
[119]               throw new ConversionException("comment", x);
[120]           }
[121]           xs.takeEnd("comment");
[122]       }
            _Items = ((Items) u.unmarshal());
[124]       xs.takeEnd("purchaseOrder");
        }
```

The statements `xs.takeStart("purchaseOrder")` in line 102 and
`xs.takeEnd("purchaseOrder")` in line 124 are responsible for parsing a start
tag and an end tag of a `<purchaseOrder>` element. After consuming a start tag,
this code parses a `<customer>` element by calling the `unmarshal()` method of

the class `Unmarshaller` (line 107). This method returns a Java object corresponding to the next element in the input XML document. If the returned object is not
of the class `Customer`, a `ClassCastException` is thrown.

Next, this method looks for a `<comment>` element, parses it if it is present
(lines 108–122), and then moves on to parsing an `<Items>` element. This parsing technique is well known as the *recursive descent* method and is used in various
compiler generation tools, such as JavaCC. In other words, JAXB can be considered
as a compiler-compiler that generates a parser program from a grammar.

Similarly, an `unmarshal()` method is generated for the other three classes:
`Customer`, `Items`, and `Item`.

Now the parsing can be done by calling the `unmarshal()` method of the top-
level class, `PurchaseOrder`. The main program that needs to be written by an
application programmer is therefore as simple as `ProcessOrder.java`, shown
in Listing 15.5.

**Listing 15.5** The main program for purchase orders, JAXB version, `chap15/jaxb/`
`ProcessOrder.java`

```
package chap15.jaxb;

import java.io.FileInputStream;
import java.util.List;
import java.util.Iterator;

public class ProcessOrder {

    public static void main(String[] args) throws Exception {
        if (args.length < 1) {
            System.err.println("Usage: java chap15.jaxb.ProcessOrder
            file");
            System.exit(1);
        }
        PurchaseOrder po = PurchaseOrder.unmarshal(new
        FileInputStream(args[0]));
        Customer co = po.getCustomer();
        System.out.println("*********** Invoice ************* ");
        System.out.println("Date:"+ new java.util.Date());
        System.out.println("");
        System.out.println("To: "+co.getName());
        System.out.println("     "+co.getAddress());
        System.out.println("     Customer#:"+co.getCustomerId());
        System.out.println("");
        System.out.println("-----------------------------------------");
```
[14]

```
List items = po.getItems().getItem();
float total = (float)0.0;
int i=0;
for (Iterator itr=items.iterator(); itr.hasNext(); i++) {
    Item item = (Item)itr.next();
    System.out.println("Item #"+i+" : "+item.getPartNum()+
                        ", Quantity="+item.getQuantity()+
                        ", UnitPrice="+item.getUSPrice()+
                        ", ShipDate="+item.getShipDate());

    total += item.getUSPrice();
}
System.out.println("-------------------------------------");
System.out.println("total = $"+total);
    }
}
```

At line 14, this program executes the following instruction to parse the input XML document:[4]

```
[14]    PurchaseOrder po = PurchaseOrder.unmarshal(new
        FileInputStream(args[0]));
```

This program is almost identical to the main program that we developed in Chapter 8, Section 8.2. However, the difference is that this is the *only* code that the application programmer needs to write. The rest of the program that does mapping from an XML document into Java data structure is taken care of by the JAXB schema compiler. Do you understand how the idea of data binding is powerful?

## 15.2.2 Relaxer[5]

As another example of a data binding tool, we pick up Relaxer, which tries to generate a Java program that is as faithful to a given schema as possible. Relaxer is based on RELAX, a schema language described in Chapter 9. Because RELAX supports data types defined in "XML Schema Part 2: Datatypes" and has a simple but powerful grammatical model, it serves as a good basis for a data binding tool. Let us consider writing our purchase order application using Relaxer. First, we need to convert our purchase order schema into RELAX. Listing 15.6 shows this schema, `PurchaseOrder.rlx`. The syntax differs somewhat from W3C XML Schema (and more from DTD), but in this simple example, you should have no problem

---

[4] Here, we assumed that the root element is `<purchaseOrder>`. In general, however, we do not know the root element before looking at the root element itself. JAXB provides a class called `Dispatcher` that calls the `unmarshal()` method of the appropriate class, depending on the root element type.

[5] This description of Relaxer is based on Relaxer 0.14.2.

understanding the semantics.[6] Informally, the grammar is the same as `PurchaseOrder.dtd`, which we used in the JAXB example, except that this RELAX grammar also specifies the data type of each element and attribute.

**Listing 15.6** Purchase order schema in RELAX, `chap15/relaxer/PurchaseOrder.rlx`

```
<?xml version="1.0" encoding="UTF-8"?>
<!DOCTYPE module SYSTEM "relaxCore.dtd">
<module relaxCoreVersion="1.0">

  <interface>
    <export label="purchaseOrder"/>
  </interface>

  <elementRule label="purchaseOrder">
    <tag/>
    <sequence>
      <ref label="customer"/>
      <element name="comment" occurs="?" type="string" />
      <ref label="items"/>
    </sequence>
  </elementRule>

  <elementRule label="customer">
    <tag/>
    <sequence>
      <element name="name" type="string" />
      <element name="customerId" occurs="?" type="string" />
      <element name="address" type="string" />
    </sequence>
  </elementRule>

  <elementRule label="items">
    <tag/>
    <ref label="item" occurs="+"/>
  </elementRule>

  <elementRule label="item">
    <tag>
      <attribute name="partNum" type="token" required="true"/>
    </tag>
    <sequence>
      <element name="productName" type="string"/>
```

---

[6] Theoretically, RELAX can generate a larger class of tree languages than XML Schema. However, we confine ourselves to the simple example in this chapter.

```
        <element name="quantity" type="integer"/>
        <element name="USPrice" type="float"/>
        <element name="shipDate" type="string"/>
      </sequence>
    </elementRule>

  </module>
```

Relaxer converts any element types that have a complex content model into a Java class with an automatically derived name, using similar name-conversion rules that we have seen in JAXB. Relaxer does not, however, take a binding schema, so it is not good at mapping an element to a Java class with a completely different name. On the other hand, Relaxer automatically decides the optimum form of Java representation of each XML construct; for example, attributes and element types with a simple content model are mapped to fields of the parent objects. Therefore, when the application data structure reflects the structure of the XML documents, Relaxer is a very powerful tool indeed.

The following Relaxer command generates four Java classes: `PurchaseOrder.java`, `Customer.java`, `Items.java`, and `Item.java`.

```
R:\samples>relaxer -verbose -package:chap15.relaxer
chap15/relaxer/PurchaseOrder.rlx
```

As is the case in JAXB, the classes generated by Relaxer have a set of accessor methods for accessing their fields based on the standard design pattern, such as `setXX()` and `getXX()`. These generated classes provide a few constructors that can be used for a parser. For example, the following code parses the input URL given as *x* and creates a `PurchaseOrder` instance.

```
PurchaseOrder po = new PurchaseOrder(x);
```

The main program that calls the generated code, shown in Listing 15.7, is almost the same as the main program for JAXB.

**Listing 15.7** The main program for purchase orders, Relaxer version, `chap15/relaxer/ProcessOrder.java`

```
package chap15.relaxer;

public class ProcessOrder {

    public static void main(String[] args) throws Exception {
        if (args.length < 1) {
            System.err.println("Usage: java chap15.jaxb.ProcessOrder
            file");
            System.exit(1);
```

```
    }
    PurchaseOrder po = new PurchaseOrder(args[0]);
    Customer co = po.getCustomer();
    System.out.println("*********** Invoice *************   ");
    System.out.println("Date:"+ new java.util.Date());
    System.out.println("");
    System.out.println("To: "+co.getName());
    System.out.println("     "+co.getAddress());
    System.out.println("    Customer#:"+co.getCustomerId());
    System.out.println("");
    System.out.println("-----------------------------------");
    Item[] items = po.getItems().getItem();
    float total = (float)0.0;
    for (int i=0; i<items.length; i++) {
        System.out.println("Item #"+i+" : "+items[i].getPartNum()+
                           ", Quantity="+items[i].getQuantity()+
                           ", UnitPrice="+items[i].getUSPrice()+
                           ", ShipDate="+items[i].getShipDate());

        total += items[i].getUSPrice();
    }
    System.out.println("-----------------------------------");
    System.out.println("total = $"+total);
    }

}
```

Instances of the classes generated by JAXB and Relaxer are essentially passive data objects (although they have marshaling and unmarshaling methods) and contain no application-specific logic. However, application programmers may want to add new methods to these classes to do some application-specific tasks. For example, you may want to add a `bill()` method to the generated `Customer` class to implement a billing process for this customer. One obvious way to do this is to modify the generated Java source files, but it is not desirable for source code maintenance, because every time you run a schema compiler, you must add your code to the generated Java source files.

Relaxer provides two solutions for this problem. Both of them are based on well-known design pattern techniques.

### Abstract Factory

One solution is to subclass the class generated by Relaxer. The subclass contains application-specific logic, while all the data mappings are handled in the parent class. For example, you can write a `MyCustomer` class as a subclass of `Customer`. Then the `bill()` method is implemented in your `MyCustomer` class. There is one catch in this approach, though. In the generated code, all the instance creations are hardcoded by default as follows:

```
new Customer()
```

Relaxer provides the -factory option to address this issue. If this option is specified when the schema compiler is executed, all the instance creations are replaced by a call to a factory class called AbstractPurchaseOrderFactory. As shown in the following code fragment, you can subclass this abstract factory class with your own factory class, which creates instances of your MyCustomer class instead of Customer.

```
public class MyPurchaseOrderFactory extends
AbstractPurchaseOrderFactory {
    public Customer createCustomer() {
        return new MyCustomer();
    }
}
```

This factory class can be registered to the parser as follows:

```
PurchaseOrderFactory.setFactory(new MyPurchaseOrderFactory());
PurchaseOrder po = new PurchaseOrder(args[0]);
```

With this code, the parsing results will have your MyCustomer instances instead of Customer instances, so you can call your methods as in the following:

```
MyCustomer co = (MyCustomer) po.getCustomer();
co.bill();
```

### Visitor

The other option is to use the *visitor* pattern. The visitor pattern is a technique to separate (1) codes for scanning a data structure and (2) codes for processing each node in the structure (see Figure 15.2).

The -visitor option of the Relaxer schema compiler, shown in the following example, generates the necessary files for the visitor pattern.

```
R:\samples>relaxer -composite -visitor -package:chap15.relaxer
chap15/relaxer/PurchaseOrder.rlx
```

When this option is specified, a class called URVisitor is generated. This class has a traverse() method that is responsible for scanning the structure in a depth-first, left-to-right manner.

You can write a class for an application-specific process as shown in the following example. You need to subclass the abstract class RVisitorBase that is

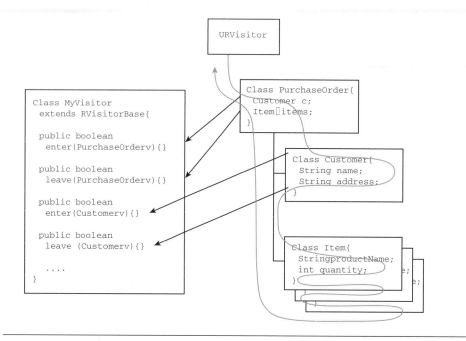

**Figure 15.2** Visitor pattern

automatically generated by Relaxer for you. Your MyVisitor class has a set of enter() and leave() method pairs that are called during the traversal of an object tree.

```
public class MyVisitor extends RVisitorBase {

    public boolean enter(PurchaseOrder v) {
        // Do whatever necessary when entered
        return true;
    }

    public boolean leave(PurchaseOrder v) {
        return true;
    }

    public boolean enter(Customer v) {
        // Do whatever necessary when entered
        return true;
    }

    public boolean leave(Customer v) {
        return true;
    }

    ...

}
```

You can now instruct URVisitor to traverse a tree, with your MyVisitor being called every time the traversal enters and leaves each object, as follows:

```
PurchaseOrder po = new PurchaseOrder(args[0]);
MyVisitor visitor = new MyVisitor();
URVisitor.traverse(po, visitor);
```

Figure 15.2 illustrates the execution of this program. As you can see, whenever your application logic requires scanning the entire object tree, this pattern is very useful.

Relaxer even allows you to combine these two design patterns. Generally, a program with a lot of design patterns in it is easy to maintain, but often it is very tedious to write manually because the code tends to have a lot of similar code fragments. If tools can generate this code from simple and clean specifications, developers will be more motivated to use design patterns, resulting in more maintainable code.

### 15.2.3 Pros and Cons of Generating a Java Program from a Schema

We have examined data binding tools that generate a Java program from a given schema. In what situations are these tools most useful? Of course, we need a schema to use such tools; therefore, they are most useful when a schema is given before the application development.

In addition, as we have seen in the visitor pattern example, these tools are most useful when the natural data structure and the accessing patterns to the data are essentially isomorphic to the structure defined by the schema; that is, the data can be naturally represented as a tree, and the application tasks can be implemented by traversing the tree.

This book was written using a document processing tool called SmartDoc. The draft was prepared as a set of XML documents that conform to a schema named SmartDoc.rlx. This system uses Relaxer as a data binding tool to process input XML documents. The internal structures of documents in this application are exactly the same as the ones represented by the schema. In such cases, schema-driven data binding tools are most useful.

## 15.3 Generating an XML Document from Java Classes

Data binding is also an attempt to represent Java data in XML so that the data can be exchanged on a network. Java has a *reflection* capability that allows a running program to know the fields, methods, and method signatures of the class of a given instance if the class is defined using a certain design pattern. Using this functionality, a Java program can marshal an internal data structure into an XML document. The structure of the generated XML documents is, therefore, determined by the internal data structure of the Java program. This is the opposite approach to the one we studied in Section 15.2, where the data structure of the Java program is determined by the schema of the input XML documents. Castor XML is a data binding tool that marshals Java data in XML. In this section, we use Castor XML as an example of data binding tools that generate XML documents from internal Java data structures and read the generated XML documents into other Java programs.[7]

### 15.3.1 Castor XML[8]

Castor XML started as a data binding tool that supported the JSR 31 (JAXB) specification, but later it became an independent tool. Let us look at this tool using our purchase order example. This time we start with an application program, not with a schema. Assume that in our purchase order application we have the three Java classes shown in Listings 15.8, 15.9, and 15.10.

**Listing 15.8** The `PurchaseOrder` class, `chap15/castor/PurchaseOrder.java`

```
package chap15.castor;
import java.util.Vector;
import java.util.Iterator;

public class PurchaseOrder implements java.io.Serializable {

    Customer customer;
    String comment;
    Vector items = new Vector();

    public Customer getCustomer() {
        return customer;
    }

    public void setCustomer(Customer c) {
        this.customer = c;
    }

    public String getComment() {
        return comment;
    }

    public void setComment(String c) {
        this.comment = c;
    }
```

---

[7] Castor XML is a data binding tool that is based on reflection, but it also has a tool called Castor Sourcegen that does schema-based code generation. In this section, we discuss Castor XML only.

[8] The description here is based on Castor 0.9.3.

```java
    public Vector getItem() {
        return this.items;
    }

    public void setItem(Vector v) {
        this.items = v;
    }

    public Item getItem(int i) {
        return (Item) items.get(i);
    }

    public void setItem(int ix,Item i) {
        if (this.items.size() <= ix) {
            this.items.setSize(ix+1);
        }
        this.items.set(ix, i);
    }

}
```

**Listing 15.9**  The `Customer` class, `chap15/castor/Customer.java`

```java
package chap15.castor;

public class Customer implements java.io.Serializable {

    String name;
    int customerId;
    String address;

    public String getName() {
        return this.name;
    }

    public void setName(String n) {
        this.name = n;
    }

    public int getCustomerId() {
        return this.customerId;
    }

    public void setCustomerId(int id) {
        this.customerId = id;
    }

    public String getAddress() {
        return this.address;
    }
```

```
        public void setAddress(String z) {
            this.address = z;
        }

    }
```

**Listing 15.10**  The Item class, chap15/castor/Item.java

```
package chap15.castor;

public class Item implements java.io.Serializable {
    String partNum;
    String productName;
    int quantity;
    double usPrice;
    String shipDate;

    public String getPartNum() {
        return this.partNum;
    }

    public void setPartNum(String p) {
        this.partNum = p;
    }

    public String getProductName() {
        return this.productName;
    }

    public void setProductName(String n) {
        this.productName = n;
    }

    public int getQuantity() {
        return this.quantity;
    }

    public void setQuantity(int q) {
        this.quantity = q;
    }

    public double getUSPrice() {
        return this.usPrice;
    }

    public void setUSPrice(double p) {
        this.usPrice = p;
    }

    public String getShipDate() {
        return this.shipDate;
    }
```

```
        public void setShipDate(String d) {
            this.shipDate = d;
        }
    }
```

These classes have getters and setters, such as `getXX()` and `setXX()`, based on the standard design pattern. Castor XML needs no more information to generate XML documents from these objects. If your application already created a `PurchaseOrder` instance in memory, you only need to call the `org.exolab.castor.xml.Marshaller.marshal()` method, as shown in the following code fragment:[9]

```
    import org.exolab.castor.xml.Marshaller;
        :
    PurchaseOrder po = new PurchaseOrder();
        :
    FileWriter writer = new FileWriter("newpo.xml");
    Marshaller.marshal(po,writer);
    writer.close();
```

The Castor XML library examines what fields and methods the object `po` has using Java's reflection capability and determines the XML structure, including element names and attribute names. A sample XML document generated from a `PurchaseOrder` instance is shown in Listing 15.11.[10]

**Listing 15.11** Generated XML document

```
    <?xml version="1.0"?>
    <purchase-order>
      <customer customer-id="788335">
        <name>Robert Smith</name>
        <address>8 Oak Avenue, New York, US</address>
      </customer>
      <comment>Hurry, my lawn is going wild!</comment>
      <item quantity="1"
            USPrice="148.95"
            xmlns:xsi="http://www.w3.org/2001/XMLSchema-instance"
            xsi:type="java:chap15.castor.Item">
        <part-num>872-AA</part-num>
        <product-name>Lawnmower</product-name>
        <ship-date>2002-09-03</ship-date>
      </item>
```

---

[9] Unlike the previous two data binding tools, Castor XML does not have an offline tool that is used at design time. All the data binding operations are performed at runtime.

[10] For readability, this list is indented appropriately. However, real generated documents do not have any extra whitespace.

```
<item quantity="3"
      USPrice="32.22"
      xmlns:xsi="http://www.w3.org/2001/XMLSchema-instance"
      xsi:type="java:chap15.castor.Item">
  <part-num>ABC-123</part-num>
  <product-name>Hyper Toothbrush Turbo</product-name>
  <ship-date>2002-08-21</ship-date>
</item>
</purchase-order>
```

A closer look at this generated XML document reveals the mapping rules of Castor XML, as shown in Table 15.1. Class names and field names are converted to element type names and attribute names using Castor XML's name mapping rules. If fields are of Java primitive types such as `int` and `double`, they are mapped to attributes. If they are not primitive types (including `String`), new elements are created for them.

**Table 15.1**  Mapping Rules of Castor XML

| JAVA CLASS NAME OR FIELD NAME | XML ELEMENT NAME OR ATTRIBUTE NAME |
| --- | --- |
| class PurchaseOrder | purchase-order (element) |
| class Customer | customer (element) |
| int customerId | customer-id (attribute) |
| String comment | comment (element) |
| : | : |

This XML document can be read (that is, unmarshaled) into another Java program by calling the `org.exolab.castor.xml.Unmarshaller.unmarshal()` method, as shown in the following code fragment.

```
import org.exolab.castor.xml.Unmarshaller;
   :
  FileReader reader = new FileReader("newpo.xml");
  PurchaseOrder po = (PurchaseOrder) Unmarshaller.unmarshal
  (Purchase.class, reader);
```

Note that you need to pass the class object of `Item` as a parameter, because when looking at the root element `<purchase-order>`, the unmarshaler cannot determine the class to be mapped. There may be more than one class that could be mapped to this element name. For example, there may be other `PurchaseOrder` classes in different packages, or there may be a `purchaseOrder` class (with the uncapitalized "p"). For a similar reason, the XML document contains the following type information in the `<item>` elements.

```
xmlns:xsi="http://www.w3.org/2001/XMLSchema-instance"
xsi:type="java:chap15.castor.Item"
```

These attributes tell the unmarshaler that the `items` field of a `PurchaseOrder` instance should have `Item` instances. If this information is omitted, Castor XML creates `Vector` objects for the `<item>` elements instead of `Item` instances.

### 15.3.2 Pros and Cons of Generating XML Documents from Java Classes

In what situations are these data binding tools based on Java reflection most useful? Let us consider this question by contrasting these tools with the schema-driven tools that we studied in Section 15.2. The biggest difference is that reflection-driven data binding tools can be used without having a schema before the application development. So the obvious answer is, when the application program is already designed or implemented, and the program needs to exchange its application data with other applications.

Data exchange between distributed applications has been studied for many years in the form of remote procedure calls and distributed objects. In Java, the Java language provides Java object serialization, which is used for implementing Java's Remote Method Invocation (RMI). How are the reflection-based XML data binding tools different from Java object serialization?

Java object serialization is a specification of encoding Java objects in an octet stream so that the object can be exchanged over a network. Therefore, *serialization* in Java object serialization has the same meaning as the marshaling we have described in this chapter.

To use Java object serialization, classes to be serialized must implement the `Serializable` interface. This interface is used for marking the implementation classes that are subject to the serialization and deserialization operations and has no required methods to be implemented. When a serializable object is written to a `java.io.ObjectOutputStream`, the object is converted into an octet string. For example, if you want to serialize an object referenced by the variable `po`, the following code fragment does it for you.

```
ObjectOutputStream os = new ObjectOutputStream(new FileOutputStream
(args[1]));
os.writeObject(po);
os.close();
```

The object referred to by the variable `po` and all the objects referenced by the fields of the object are serialized into a single octet stream. As an example, in Listing 15.12 we show a serialized purchase order that we created in Section 15.3.1.

**Listing 15.12** Serialized purchase order

```
00000000: aced 0005 7372 001b 6368 6170 3135 2e63   ....sr..chap15.c
00000010: 6173 746f 722e 5075 7263 6861 7365 4f72   astor.PurchaseOr
00000020: 6465 7207 41d6 ba16 4616 5602 0003 4c00   der.A...F.V...L.
00000030: 0763 6f6d 6d65 6e74 7400 124c 6a61 7661   .commentt..Ljava
00000040: 2f6c 616e 672f 5374 7269 6e67 3b4c 0008   /lang/String;L..
00000050: 6375 7374 6f6d 6572 7400 184c 6368 6170   customert..Lchap
00000060: 3135 2f63 6173 746f 722f 4375 7374 6f6d   15/castor/Custom
00000070: 6572 3b4c 0005 6974 656d 7374 0012 4c6a   er;L..itemst..Lj
00000080: 6176 612f 7574 696c 2f56 6563 746f 723b   ava/util/Vector;
00000090: 7870 7400 1d48 7572 7279 2c20 6d79 206c   xpt..Hurry, my l
000000a0: 6177 6e20 6973 2067 6f69 6e67 2077 696c   awn is going wil
000000b0: 6421 7372 0016 6368 6170 3135 2e63 6173   d!sr..chap15.cas
000000c0: 746f 722e 4375 7374 6f6d 6572 4574 8df5   tor.CustomerEt..
000000d0: 5b62 39e3 0200 0349 000a 6375 7374 6f6d   [b9....I..custom
000000e0: 6572 4964 4c00 0761 6464 7265 7373 7100   erIdL..addressq.
000000f0: 7e00 014c 0004 6e61 6d65 7100 7e00 0178   ~..L..nameq.~..x
    ...
```

This octet stream can be deserialized by a receiving Java program by using `java.io.ObjectInputStream` as follows:

```
ObjectInputStream is = new ObjectInputStream(new FileInputStream
(args[1]));
po = (PurchaseOrder) is.readObject();
is.close();
```

So from its functionality, Java object serialization looks very similar to the data binding of Castor XML. Why would we want to use a separate library when the Java language provides a built-in function that does the same task? There are several reasons.

### Data Exchange between Different Implementations

The first limitation of Java object serialization is that it requires exactly the same class implementations on the sending side (the marshaling or serializing side) and on the receiving side (the unmarshaling or deserializing side). Java has a dynamic class loading capability, so it is technically possible to share the same class implementations across a network, but for management and security, it is sometimes not feasible or not desirable.[11]

---

[11] Executing downloaded programs without an extensive sanity check is not generally recommended for security reasons.

## Exchanging Data with Applications Written in a Non-Java Language

A more serious limitation for B2B communication is that the use of Java object serialization as the standard data exchange format requires all the communication parties to use Java as the implementation language. In B2B environments, we cannot make any assumptions about the platform, operating systems, programming languages, and middleware to be used by the communicating parties.

Reflection-based data binding tools serialize Java objects to an XML format that is a widely accepted data format for B2B data exchange. Therefore, it is easier for other companies to receive data expressed as an XML document and process it in any programming language.

We have seen that data binding tools have interoperability advantages over Java object serialization. It also has some drawbacks.

## Handling Shared Structures

One such drawback is handling shared data structures. When marshaling a graph structure, Java object serialization keeps its topology in the serialized form, but the current data binding tools, at least the ones examined in this chapter, are not capable of preserving the shared structure information.[12] The XML 1.0 Specification defines attributes of type ID and IDREF that could be used for representing data sharing information, so it appears to be one of the ways to handle shared structures in data binding, but it is not widely supported today.[13]

## Size and Speed

Another possible limitation of data binding is the size of serialized data and the execution speed of the marshaling and unmarshaling operations. As we have seen, Java object serialization has a binary format, which is generally more efficient than the text representation of XML. One of the biggest time-consuming parts of XML parsing and generation is the tight loop of scanning characters, so the performance is largely affected by the size of XML documents. Therefore, it is a common belief that XML data binding is less efficient than Java object serialization. There is, however, no decisive evidence that supports this belief. Different benchmarks have shown different results. In many cases, existing implementations of Java object serialization are not as efficient as applications need. Therefore, if the performance of serialization is absolutely critical in your application, you may need to write your own specialized marshaler and unmarshaler anyway.

---

[12] We discussed graph structures in more detail in Chapter 8, Section 8.6.

[13] The SOAP Encoding specification we discussed in Chapter 12 specifies a way of referring to shared data by using the `id` attributes of the type ID and the `href` attributes of the type anyURI.

## 15.3.3  SOAP Encoding

In Chapter 12, we discussed the use of SOAP for remote procedure calls. SOAP has its encoding rule, which allows you to express a program internal data structure in XML. In this sense, the SOAP encoding rule can be considered as marshaling. How is it different from the data binding tools that we have looked at in this chapter?

### Encoding from Java Classes

The SOAP encoding rule has a simple type system that tries to capture the common ingredients found in the type systems of various programming languages. The primitive types of the SOAP encoding rule are those of W3C XML Schema (see Chapter 9 for the details of XML Schema primitive types). When the programming language in use has a type system consistent with the SOAP encoding rule, it should be possible to create an XML schema from the application data model. In this book, the programming language in question is Java, and Java's primitive data types have almost straightforward mappings to XML Schema's primitive data types, so we should be able to create XML structures from Java object instances as we did with Castor XML. Do existing SOAP implementations have this capability?

The answer is yes. For example, remember Apache SOAP programming, introduced in Chapter 12? In Listing 12.23, we called the `mapType()` method of the `SOAPMappingRegistry` class to specify how a particular Java class should be mapped to an XML element. Using our purchase order example, the mapping could be specified as in the following fragment of `ProcessOrderClient.java`.

```
[47]    SOAPMappingRegistry smr = new SOAPMappingRegistry();
[48]    BeanSerializer beanSer = new BeanSerializer();
[49]
[50]    // Map the types.
[51]    smr.mapTypes(Constants.NS_URI_SOAP_ENC,
[52]                 new QName("urn:purchaseOrder", "purchaseOrder"),
[53]                 PurchaseOrder.class, beanSer, beanSer);
```

The `smr.mapTypes()` call in line 51 says that a `PurchaseOrder` instance should be mapped to an XML element with the namespace URI `urn:purchaseOrder` and the local name `purchaseOrder`, and the marshaling and unmarshaling algorithms are provided in the class `BeanSerializer`. Unlike the data binding tools we have shown in this chapter, the SOAP encoding rule has no default name conversion rules between XML elements and attribute names and Java names. This is because the SOAP encoding rule does not assume any particular programming language. Therefore, we have to supply such rules. In addition, by supplying your own marshaling and unmarshaling algorithms, you can also control the structure of your XML document—for example, the order of child elements of the `<purchaseOrder>` element. Apache SOAP provides a built-in marshaling and unmarshaling algorithm called `org.apache.soap.encoding.soapenc.BeanSerializer`.

On the accompanying CD-ROM, you can find a complete set of source files for the Apache SOAP version of our purchase order application. Part of a SOAP message generated by this program is shown in Listing 15.13. It shows the SOAP encoding of our `PurchaseOrder` object.

**Listing 15.13** Part of a generated SOAP message

```
<purchaseOrder xmlns:ns2="urn:purchaseOrder"
xsi:type="ns2:purchaseOrder">
  <item xmlns:ns3="http://xml.apache.org/xml-soap" xsi:type="ns3:
  Vector">
    <item xsi:type="ns2:item">
      <shipDate xsi:type="xsd:string">2002-09-03</shipDate>
      <partNum xsi:type="xsd:string">872-AA</partNum>
      <productName xsi:type="xsd:string">Lawnmower</productName>
      <USPrice xsi:type="xsd:double">148.95</USPrice>
      <quantity xsi:type="xsd:int">1</quantity>
    </item>
    <item xsi:type="ns2:item">
      <shipDate xsi:type="xsd:string">2002-08-21</shipDate>
      <partNum xsi:type="xsd:string">ABC-123</partNum>
      <productName xsi:type="xsd:string">Hyper Toothbrush Turbo
      </productName>
      <USPrice xsi:type="xsd:double">32.22</USPrice>
      <quantity xsi:type="xsd:int">3</quantity>
    </item>
  </item>
  <customer xsi:type="ns2:customer">
    <address xsi:type="xsd:string">8 Oak Avenue, New York, US
    </address>
    <name xsi:type="xsd:string">Robert Smith</name>
    <customerId xsi:type="xsd:int">788335</customerId>
  </customer>
  <comment xsi:type="xsd:string">Hurry, my lawn is going wild!
  </comment>
</purchaseOrder>
```

As you may notice, SOAP encoding by `BeanSerializer` inserts type information into every element generated.

### Generating Java Classes from WSDL

Although XML documents created by Apache SOAP using `BeanSerializer` have an `xsi:type` attribute to designate the data type of the element, this information is optional in the SOAP Encoding specification. If both the sender and the receiver agree on the schema of the messages and the data types are clear from the schema, you can omit the type information from individual XML documents.

WSDL, introduced in Chapter 13, is designed so that it can be used as a schema language for SOAP messaging. This means that we can consider a data binding tool that generates Java codes from a WSDL document. In fact, the WSDL compiler we developed in Chapter 13 is a sort of data binding tool. Also, most WSDL tools (for example, the WSDL Toolkit contained in IBM's Web Services Toolkit) have a similar schema compiler that generates a set of Java classes for data binding. Using such a schema compiler, you can generate Java classes from a WSDL document.

It should be clear now that the SOAP encoding rule is a specification that enables both schema-driven and reflection-driven data binding tools. However, the specification poses certain limitations on generated XML documents. For example, in the SOAP encoding rule all application data must be represented as element content, not as attribute values. Therefore, data binding tools based on the SOAP encoding rule cannot be used for dealing with general XML documents. These tools are most useful when a schema is represented as a WSDL document.

## 15.4  Summary

In this chapter, we looked at a few open source data binding tools currently available and compared them using the same purchase order application. As we can see, these tools have their own advantages and disadvantages. It does not look likely at this moment that any one of these tools will become dominant in the near future. Instead, these tools can be most effective when they fit the specific needs of your application. Data binding technologies are still in their infancy, and we can expect a lot of advances in this field—more flexible mapping, support for nonisomorphic data structures such as tables and graphs, increased performance, and standardization, to name a few.

# 16

# Principles of Schema Languages

## 16.1 Introduction

Schema languages play critical roles in XML. In Chapter 9, we provided a quick overview of W3C XML Schema and RELAX NG. In this chapter, we reconsider schema languages in the bigger picture.

W3C XML Schema is a complicated language, and Chapter 9 covers only a small subset of it. Perhaps because of its complexity, adoption of W3C XML Schema has been slower than that of XML 1.0 (including DTDs). On the other hand, new schema languages, such as RELAX NG of OASIS and ISO/IEC JTC1 as well as Rick Jelliffe's Schematron, have appeared. Some people believe that W3C XML Schema will not succeed because of its complexity and that it will eventually be replaced by these new languages. Many others believe that W3C XML Schema, which is supported by W3C, will survive and that other schema languages will not be accepted by the market. This turmoil confuses developers of Web applications. Which schema language should they adopt?

We could even question whether *any* schema languages will be accepted by the market. Ever since SGML, the predecessor of XML, arrived, DTDs have annoyed users. Although use of DTDs does provide some advantages, the cost of DTD authoring and maintenance is excessive. Some people believe that it is the DTD language that has prevented widespread use of SGML. The same observation may apply to schema languages for XML. If the cost of schema authoring and maintenance outweighs the advantages of using schemas, schema languages might fail to become widespread. In fact, it is not unusual for XML application programmers not to use DTDs or schemas.

The goal of this chapter is to reconsider schema languages in the bigger picture. Rather than comparing the features of schema languages, we consider the roles of schema languages in application development. We hope that this approach will clarify the principles behind each schema language and show which is more promising.

The rest of this chapter is organized as follows. In Section 16.2, we reconfirm why schema languages are required. In Section 16.3, we show the data models of XML documents and study the use of schemas as data models. In Section 16.4, we discuss the relationship between schema languages and other software technologies for constructing Web applications. In Section 16.5, we study four schema languages: DTD, W3C XML Schema, RELAX NG, and Schematron. In Section 16.6, we consider special-purpose schema languages, such as RDF Schema, and then study a framework (RELAX Namespace) for combining multiple schema languages. We conclude this chapter in Section 16.7.

## 16.2  Schemas as Syntactic Constraints

In this section, we show one important reason for creating schemas. Schemas allow us to focus on documents that satisfy our assumptions about documents.

### 16.2.1  Checking Unexpected Documents

In Chapter 1, we constructed our PowerWarning application using XML. We obtained the current temperature by using the strategy *The current temperature is shown by the* `<CurrTemp>` *tag*. We observed that use of XML keeps programs independent from the way the Web page is displayed for human users.

Now, suppose that the XML document, shown in Listing 16.1, is received as weather information. Although this document appears to correctly represent weather information, it differs from our expectations in three points.

- The element `Temperature` (line 7) is introduced as a parent of `Current` (line 8), `High` (line 9), and `Low` (line 10).
- The tag name is `Current` (line 8) rather than `CurrTemp`.
- The content of the element `Current` (line 8) is "seventy" rather than "70".

**Listing 16.1**  Unexpected XML document

```
<?xml version="1.0" encoding="utf-8"?>
<WeatherReport>
  <City>White Plains</City>
  <State>NY</State>
```

```
            <Date>1998-07-25</Date>
            <Time>11:00:00-04:00</Time>
[7]         <Temperature>
[8]            <Current unit="Fahrenheit">seventy</Current>
[9]            <High unit="Fahrenheit">82</High>
[10]           <Low unit="Fahrenheit">62</Low>
            </Temperature>
         </WeatherReport>
```

Our PowerWarning application does not work properly when it receives this document. First, it fails to obtain the element `Current`. Second, even if it could obtain the element `Current`, it would fail to obtain the integer 70 from the string "seventy".

Let us make sure that it fails to obtain the element `Current`. If we used SAX to construct our PowerWarning application, we have tested that the start tag received by the method `startElement` contains the name `CurrTemp`. If we used DOM, we have used either `getElementsByTagName`/`getElementsByTagNameNS` or a combination of the methods `getChildNodes` and `getLocalName`. In both cases, it is fatal that the tag name is `Current` rather than `CurrTemp`. When we combine `getChildNodes` and `getLocalName`, we even fail to obtain the element `Current` from the root element `WeatherReport` by `getChildNodes` because of the intervening element `Temperature`; even if the tag name were `CurrTemp` rather than `Current`, our PowerWarning application would not work properly.

In general, when we develop an application program for handling XML documents, we make some assumptions about target documents and deal with only those documents that satisfy these assumptions. The application program works properly when it receives documents satisfying these assumptions but does not work when it receives documents not satisfying these assumptions. It is a schema that ensures that a given document satisfies such assumptions. A *schema* is a formal description written in some schema language, and it precisely specifies permissible XML documents. If we have a validator for the schema language, we can *validate* a given XML document against a schema; that is, we can determine whether the document is permitted by the schema (see Figure 16.1).

A schema declares names for tags and attributes. For example, consider a schema for our PowerWarning application. That example schema declares `CurrTemp` as a permissible tag name. A schema further declares permissible structural relationships among elements and attributes. Our example schema declares that a `CurrTemp` element is allowed as a child element of a `WeatherReport` element. A schema further declares datatypes to which the character contents of elements or values of attributes belong. Our example schema declares that the character content of `CurrTemp` is of the datatype `integer`.

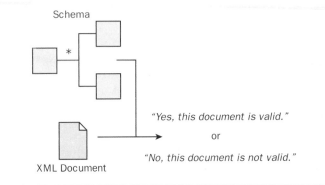

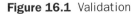

**Figure 16.1** Validation

The DTD shown in Chapter 1, Section 1.4, provides an example of schemas. It specifies which XML document is permitted as a proper representation of weather information as far as possible in the DTD language. Because it is not equipped with rich datatypes, the DTD does not specify that the content of `CurrTemp` is an integer.

## 16.2.2  What Happens If We Neglect Schemas?

Now, let us reconsider the criticism that schemas are hard to create. Although the DTD in Section 1.4 is simple, its creation is not cost-free. Creating a huge DTD sometimes requires several years. What would happen if we do not create schemas to eliminate the burden of schema authoring and maintenance?

Neglecting schemas implies that we cannot use validators to determine whether a given document satisfies our assumptions. Rather, our application programs have to perform the required check. In the PowerWarning application example, the application program is forced to examine the following conditions.

- Is the root element a `WeatherReport` element?
- Does the root `WeatherReport` element have any attributes?
- Is the first child element of the `WeatherReport` element a `City` element?
- Does the `City` element have any attributes?
- Is the content of the `City` element a character string?

Although there are many other things to check, these conditions already require a long Java program, as shown in Listing 16.2. If we try to capture all the conditions specified in the DTD, this program will become significantly longer. Such long programs for validation are hard to create and maintain.

**Listing 16.2**  Part of the Java program `HandWrittenValidator.java`

```java
package chap16;
/**
 *        HandWrittenValidator.java
 **/
import java.io.IOException;
import org.xml.sax.SAXException;
import org.w3c.dom.*;
import javax.xml.parsers.*;
import share.util.MyErrorHandler;

public class HandWrittenValidator {

    public HandWrittenValidator() {
    }

    public void validateWeatherReport(Element element) {

        //Does the root element have a tag name "WeatherReport"?
        if (!(element.getTagName().equals("WeatherReport"))) {
            System.err.println(
                "[Invalid] Incorrect root");
            return;
        }

        //Does the WeatherReport element have any attributes?
        if (element.getAttributes().getLength() != 0) {
            System.err.println(
                "[Invalid] WeatherReport has illegal attributes.");
            return;
        }

        //Validate children
        Node child;

        for (child = element.getFirstChild();
             child != null;
             child = child.getNextSibling()){

            if ((child instanceof Text)
                 && (((Text)child).getData().trim().length() != 0)) {
                System.err.println(
                    "[Invalid] WeatherReport cannot have a text
                     child.");
                return;
            }
            else if (child.getNodeType() == Node.ELEMENT_NODE) {
                break;
            }
```

```
        }
        if (child == null) {
            System.err.println(
                "[Invalid] WeatherReport has no child elements.");
            return;
        }
        else {
            validateCity((Element)child);
        }
    }

    public void validateCity(Element element) {
        //Does this element have a tag name "City"?

        if (!(element.getTagName().equals("City"))) {
            System.err.println("[Invalid] City is missing.");
            return;
        }

        //Does the City element have any attributes?

        if (element.getAttributes().getLength() != 0) {
            System.err.println(
                "[Invalid] City has illegal attributes.");
            return;

        }

        //Does the City element have character contents?

        for (Node child = element.getFirstChild();
             child != null;
             child = child.getNextSibling()) {

            if (child.getNodeType() == Node.ELEMENT_NODE) {
                System.err.println(
                    "[Invalid] City cannot have a text child.");
                return;
            }
        }
    }
...
```

Checking by schemas and validators is more effective than checking by application programs. For application programs to check documents, programmers have to write lengthy programs, as in Listing 16.1. When many application programs use these documents, such checking programs have to be written many times (possibly in different programming languages). On the other hand, once a schema is created, validation can be easily repeated many times. Application programmers only have to invoke their favorite validators.

Furthermore, a fundamental problem of not creating schemas is that assumptions about XML documents become unclear. If different programmers have different understandings of these assumptions, application programs that should interwork thorough XML documents fail to interwork. For example, suppose that a programmer thinks that the attribute `unit` is optional and creates a program that does not output this attribute. The XML documents created by this program cannot be correctly handled by other programs that rely on this attribute.

Put another way, we can dispense with schemas only when we can clearly specify permissible XML documents with prose and we are willing to write programs for the required checks (possibly several times). Otherwise, we have to create schemas and validate documents with validators. The cost of schema authoring and maintenance is a problem, but we cannot completely avoid it. All we can do is choose good schema languages, which minimize the cost of schema authoring and maintenance while taking advantage of schemas to the maximum.

### 16.2.3  Desiderata for Schema Languages

Discussion in this section leads to some desiderata for schema languages. They are basic and indispensable for making Web application development easier by using schemas. In other words, if a schema language fails to satisfy these desiderata, that schema language should be strongly avoided.

- Desideratum 1: A schema language should be easy to learn.
- Desideratum 2: A schema language should make it easy to write, read, and maintain schemas.
- Desideratum 3: A schema language should be able to capture assumptions about documents for Web applications.
- Desideratum 4: A schema language should provide rigorous validation against such assumptions.

Although these desiderata are important, we do not discuss whether each schema language satisfies these desiderata. The reason is that such discussion can easily become subjective and unpersuasive. Readers are encouraged to read schema examples in this book and other resources and draw their own conclusion. In particular, the report of the schema language comparison panel at XML 2001 is helpful.

## 16.3 Schemas as Data Models

In Section 16.2, we considered schemas as mechanisms for examining whether a document satisfies assumptions by Web application designers. However, schemas can also be considered as mechanisms for enabling easy access to documents. In other words, a schema provides a *data model*, which describes the structures of and access methods for XML documents in an abstract manner.

In this section, we present four data models (see Figure 16.2) having different abstraction levels, and we consider schemas as data models. The first three data models coexist, and we can choose the one most appropriate for the task at hand. The last data model is specific to some application area and is not always implementable.

- Data model 1: character strings
- Data model 2: trees comprising elements and text
- Data model 3: data compliant with schemas
- Data model 4: information for Web applications

### 16.3.1 Documents as Character Strings

*Data model 1*: An XML document is a character string.

The lowest data model for XML documents provides primitive operations for handling character strings only. This data model does not rely on the XML parser. Raw XML documents are directly manipulated as character strings (see Figure 16.3).

Figure 16.4 depicts information flow among programs. In this model, we have application programs and character strings only.

Model 4        70 Fahrenheit

Model 3    `int WeatherReport.Temperature.Current=70;`
           `...`

Model 2    `<WeatherReport>`
              `└─ <City> "White Plains"`

Model 1    `<` `x` `m` `l` ...

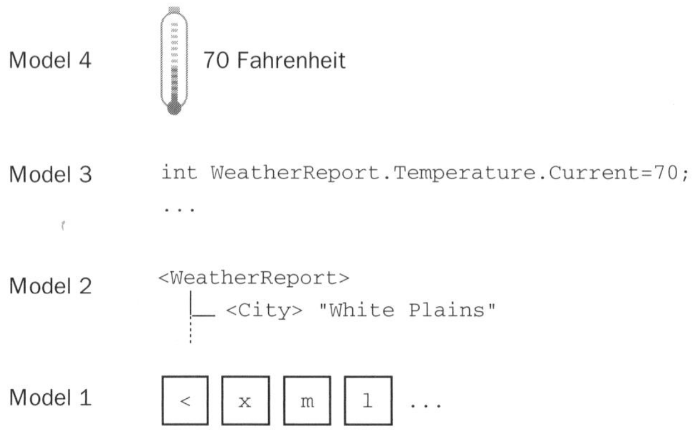

**Figure 16.2** Four data models

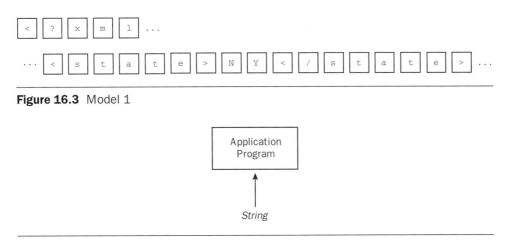

**Figure 16.3** Model 1

**Figure 16.4** Layering in model 1

Text-processing tools handle XML documents as strings. We can read and modify XML documents with text editors. We can also write scripts in text-processing languages (Perl, sed, awk, Ruby, and so on). In fact, to execute very simple tasks, text-processing languages are often as useful as general-purpose languages such as Java.

For example, to replace the tag name `currTemp` with `currentTemp`, we only have to write small scripts that replace the strings `"<currTemp"` and `"</currTemp"` with `"<currentTemp"` and `"</currentTemp"`, respectively. The following is an example script in Perl.

```
while (<>) {
  s/<currTemp/<currentTemp/g;
  s/<\/currTemp/<\/currentTemp/g;
  print;
}
```

As another example, suppose that we want to obtain the value of the attribute `unit` of `High` elements. The following simple Perl script does the job.

```
while (<>) {
  if (/<High\s+unit\s*=\s*"([^"]+)"/) {
    print $1, "\n";
  }
  elsif (/<High\s+unit\s*=\s*'([^']+)'/) {
    print $1, "\n";
  }

}
```

However, the abstraction level of this data model is often too low to handle XML documents. In fact, the previous Perl scripts are not quite right. The first one cannot correctly handle occurrences of `"<currTemp"` and `"</currTemp"` within CDATA sections. On top of this problem, the second script cannot handle start tags that do not fit into single lines, and it cannot handle attribute values containing entity references or character references. To fix these problems, we have to more or less analyze the XML syntax. More elaborate tasks for real applications do require programmers to implement syntactical analysis of a good portion of the XML syntax. To free programmers from this burden, we need a data model of a higher abstraction level.

## 16.3.2 Documents as Trees

*Data model 2*: An XML document is a tree of elements and text.

The next data model makes syntactical analysis of XML documents unnecessary. This data model relies on the XML parser. Parsing an XML document yields a tree of attributed elements and text (see Figure 16.5). Application programs access this tree through APIs such as DOM and SAX. Because the XML parser performs syntactical analysis, application programs are liberated from it.

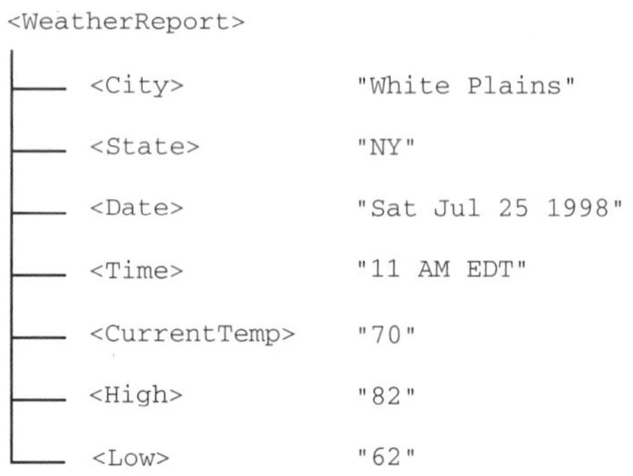

```
<WeatherReport>
    |___  <City>           "White Plains"
    |___  <State>          "NY"
    |___  <Date>           "Sat Jul 25 1998"
    |___  <Time>           "11 AM EDT"
    |___  <CurrentTemp>    "70"
    |___  <High>           "82"
    |___  <Low>            "62"
```

**Figure 16.5** Model 2

Figure 16.6 depicts information flow among programs when documents are not validated. Programs are application programs and XML parsers, while information is strings and trees.

When documents are validated, validators also receive trees from XML parsers and report the validation result to application programs (see Figure 16.7). The validation result may by true ("Yes, this document is valid.") or false ("No, this document is not valid."). It may contain a further diagnostic message or even show which element/attribute in the given XML document matches which description

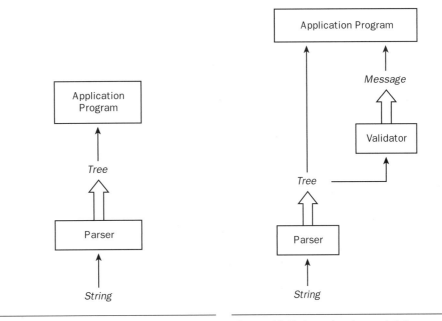

**Figure 16.6** Layering in model 2 (without validation)

**Figure 16.7** Layering in model 2 (with validation)

in the given schema. Although application programs may use such validation results, the trees returned by XML parsers are still the primary information.

Recall that in our previous example, we want to obtain the value of the attribute `unit` of `High` elements. To do so, we use the SAX method `startElement` to find elements of the tag name `High` and then get the value of the attribute `unit`. Alternatively, we can use the DOM method `getElementsByTagName(NS)` and then get the value of the attribute `unit`, as shown in Listing 16.3. The fact that XML parsers create trees from XML documents is a significant advantage of XML for programmers.

**Listing 16.3** Getting element values by using the tag name, part of `chap 16/Model2.java`

```
package chap16;
/**
 *        Model2.java
 **/
import java.io.IOException;
import org.xml.sax.SAXException;
import org.w3c.dom.*;
import javax.xml.parsers.*;
import share.util.MyErrorHandler;
```

```
public class Model2 {

    public Model2() {
    }

    public void printTime(Document doc) {

        NodeList nl = doc.getElementsByTagName("Time");

        Element time = (Element)(nl.item(0));

        String timeContent ="";

        for (Node child = time.getFirstChild();
             child != null;
             child = child.getNextSibling()) {

            if (child instanceof Text) {
                timeContent += ((Text)child).getData();
            }
        }
        java.sql.Time t = java.sql.Time.valueOf(timeContent);
        System.out.println(t);
    }
    ...
```

Furthermore, this data model allows application programs (rather than APIs) that are applicable to any well-formed XML document. As long as the XML parser can create trees, these programs always work. Here are some examples of such application programs.

- Some XML document editors allow editing based on tree structures and ensure that start and end tags are balanced.
- Some XML database systems provide XML-aware full-text retrieval.
- Some XML viewers graphically represent the tree structures of XML documents.
- Some XML database systems and XML viewers support XPath (described in Chapter 7), which provides structure-sensitive access to documents.

However, we could argue that this data model does not provide enough abstraction yet. Programmers require information for Web applications rather than attributes, elements, or strings. In the PowerWarning application example, programs need the fact that the current temperature in Fahrenheit is integer 82 rather than the element <CurrTemp unit="Fahrenheit">82</CurrTemp>. In fact, many programmers convert trees of attributed elements and text to some internal representation and then perform the task for Web applications using this internal representation. Such conversion (discussed in Chapter 8) reveals that this data model is insufficient. A data model of a high-level abstraction is desirable to make development of Web applications even easier.

### 16.3.3  Documents as Data Compliant with Schemas

*Data model 3*: An XML document is a collection of data compliant with a schema.

The motivation for this data model is to use schemas for easily accessing XML documents. First, this data model allows access to data of the specified datatypes. Because schemas specify datatypes for the character contents of elements or attributes, it is possible to convert the character contents to data of the specified datatypes. In the PowerWarning application example, the current temperature (in Fahrenheit) is made available to programmers after the string "70" is converted to integer 70. Programmers do not have to perform this conversion themselves.

Second, schemas also allow easy access to the tree structures of elements. In the example of weather information, the schema ensures that WeatherReport contains CurrTemp only once. Thus, access to the content of CurrTemp of WeatherReport is guaranteed to return a single integer. Programmers do not have to worry about zero or multiple return values.

The following program, written in an imaginary programming language, shows that an XML document provides a structure representing weather information. For example, line 3 shows the date of this weather report. If this program can be generated from a schema, it becomes significantly easier to develop our PowerWarning application.

```
      string WeatherReport.City      = "White Plains";
      string WeatherReport.State     = "NY";
[3]   date   WeatherReport.Date      = 1998-07-25;
      time   WeatherReport.Time      = 11:00:00-04:00;
      int    WeatherReport.CurrTemp  = 70;
      int    WeatherReport.High      = 82;
      int    WeatherReport.Low       = 62;
```

There are two approaches to using schemas for document access. One approach is data binding by generating programs from schemas, and the other is post-schema-validation infosets (PSVI).

*Data binding by generating programs from schemas*

As we discussed in Chapters 8 and 15, some data binding tools generate programs from schemas and further convert XML documents to data (and vice versa). In this approach, validators are not required to change the output of XML parsers. Data binding tools receive trees returned by XML parsers (possibly accompanied with validation results from validators) and then pass data to application programs (see Figure 16.8). In other words, data binding tools form another layer between application programs and XML parsers.

This approach does not complicate validators. Validators and data binding tools can be independently built, possibly in different programming languages and platforms. Moreover, it is possible to perform validation without performing data binding, and it is also possible to perform data binding without validation (when documents are known to be valid).

*PSVI*

Validators for W3C XML Schema augment the output of XML parsers by adding data to them. The result is called PSVI. In this approach, validators are required to change the output of XML parsers (see Figure 16.9).

This approach complicates validators. On the other hand, it has also been argued that this approach is more efficient because validation (for example, testing whether "1" represents an integer) and data binding (for example, converting

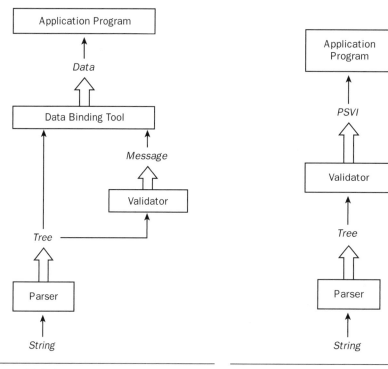

**Figure 16.8** Layering in model 3 with data binding

**Figure 16.9** Layering in model 3 with PSVI

"1" to integer 1) are not separated. It has been also argued that PSVI is programming-language neutral and is thus applicable to many programming languages.

There is no consensus about which approach is better. In Section 16.5, we consider the approach taken by W3C XML Schema and that taken by RELAX NG.

### 16.3.4 Documents as Information for Web Applications

*Data model 4:* An XML document provides information about the real world handled by Web applications.

The three data models we have seen so far are generic, but this one is specific to some application area. Furthermore, it is not always implementable.

Web applications usually relate to the real world. XML documents used by such Web applications are representations of information about the real world. However, seemingly small changes to such documents can easily make them meaningless. For XML documents to sensibly represent real-world information, they are required to satisfy many conditions, which are sometimes called *business rules*.

In the case of our PowerWarning application, an XML document specifies the temperature in a city at a certain date and time. The example document shows that the temperature in White Plains is 70 degrees Fahrenheit at 11 A.M. on July 25, 1998. On the other hand, the XML document shown in Listing 16.4 is meaningless, because there are no cities named "foo" (line 3) in New York and also because the temperature in New York (line 4) is not likely to be 100 degrees Fahrenheit (line 7) in January (line 5). Here, one business rule is that the specified city must exist in the specified state, and another is that the temperature be realistic for the specified date, time, and location.

**Listing 16.4** An XML document not representing real-world information

```
        <?xml version="1.0" encoding="utf-8"?>
        <WeatherReport>
[3]       <City>foo</City>
[4]       <State>NY</State>
[5]       <Date>2002-01-01</Date>
          <Time>11:00:00-04:00</Time>
[7]       <CurrTemp unit="Fahrenheit">100</CurrTemp>
          <High unit="Fahrenheit">82</High>
          <Low unit="Fahrenheit">62</Low>
        </WeatherReport>
```

As another example, consider online shopping. A seller in an online shop provides products to a consumer, and the consumer pays the seller. The seller then reports the profit to the tax office and pays the tax. XML documents used in such online shopping are required to satisfy many business rules. First, an order document from a consumer must indicate the name of a product that is for sale. Second, a receipt document must show the price and sales tax of the product. Third, the receipt XML document must be consistent with a tax report document. If some of these business rules are not satisfied, these XML documents are no longer meaningful representations of online shopping.

If some data model guarantees that business rules are satisfied, it becomes much easier to develop Web applications. Programmers are liberated from programming for ensuring business rules. For example, if some data model directly supported the technology model (tModel) of UDDI (see Chapter 13), programming would become very easy.

However, such data models are obviously dependent on particular Web applications. Even if we limit our concern to online shopping, different companies selling different goods in different ways have different business rules. Thus, such a data model cannot be constructed in advance but should be constructed per each Web application on demand. Rather, what is needed is a base layer upon which such data models can be constructed easily. Data models 2 and 3 provide such base layers.

### 16.3.5  Desiderata for Schema Languages

It is not clear which design of schema language better serves the data models presented in this section. However, it is not difficult to agree on the following desideratum. In fact, all the general-purpose schema languages covered in this chapter satisfy it.

- Desideratum 5: Schema languages should provide no mechanisms for data model 4.

If we incorporate mechanisms for one particular business application, we also have to accept mechanisms for other business applications. As a result, schema languages will become extremely complicated.

The following desideratum is debatable, but it deserves consideration at least.

- Desideratum 6: Schema languages should not change trees created by XML parsers.

Validation is an expensive process. In particular, with the addition of datatypes and rich syntactical constraints, schema-based validation can be very expensive. Thus, it should be possible to omit validation when documents are guaranteed to be valid. However, if a schema changes trees created by XML parsers, we cannot safely omit validation. This desideratum ensures that there are no such changes.

This desideratum is debatable because it does not allow validators to embed default values and also because it is in conflict with PSVI. We revisit this issue in Section 16.5.3.

## 16.4 Interworking with Other Software

A Web application is constructed from not only XML technologies but also other technologies, most notably programming languages and relational database management systems (RDBMSs). In this section, we consider the gaps between schema languages and these technologies.

### 16.4.1 Interworking with Programming Languages

This book concentrates on Java, but other programming languages, such as Visual Basic, C++, C#, Perl, Python, and Ruby, are also widely used. We certainly would like to handle XML documents from these languages. Here, we consider the similarities and differences between schema languages and such programming languages.

First, the data structures of XML and those in programming languages exhibit different characteristics.

- XML documents provide ordered trees. For example, in a document containing `<root><first/><second/></root>`, the `first` element precedes the `second` element. `NodeList`s of DOM represent such ordered lists of elements; sequentially reported SAX events also represent such ordered lists. On the other hand, instance variables in a Java class are not intended to be ordered.

- Although XML documents are trees, a collection of Java objects may form arbitrary graph structures.

- Content models for XML can easily represent rich conditions (that is, regular expressions) on sequences, but class definitions in programming languages have to use lists (or arrays) and intermediate classes to capture such rich conditions.

There are no standard ways to bridge these gaps. Some features of schema languages can be considered as mechanisms for narrowing the gaps (for example, `all` of W3C XML Schema and `interleave` of RELAX NG). However, the gaps are still large, and they are patched by data binding tools.

Second, inheritance is a controversial issue. Many programming languages provide inheritance, but different languages have different styles. Java has single inheritance, interfaces, and inner classes. On the other hand, C++ does not have interfaces but provides multiple inheritance and inner classes. Features of other languages are also different from Java or C++. To make XML programming easier (possibly by using data binding tools), should a schema language support inheritance? If so, which style of inheritance should be adopted, and how should inheritance be integrated with content models? W3C XML Schema and RELAX NG have very different answers, and we consider them in Section 16.5.

Third, both schema languages and programming languages need datatypes. It is obviously useful to share datatypes. In fact, many datatypes of W3C XML Schema are borrowed from Java, and other schema languages in turn use datatypes of W3C XML Schema. We have already shown correspondences between W3C XML Schema and Java in Chapter 9, Section 9.2.2.

### 16.4.2 Relational Databases

The structures of RDBMSs are flatter than those of XML documents. The former are basically collections of tables, while the latter are ordered trees without any upper bound on the height or width.

There have been many attempts to bridge this gap. However, it is still difficult to convert arbitrary XML documents to RDBMS data. Chapter 10 gives design guidelines for implementing such a conversion but does not provide automatic conversion. On the other hand, if an XML document already has a tabular structure, it is easy to store it in RDBMS. It is also easy to output the contents of an RDBMS as XML documents.

Again, it is useful to share datatypes between XML and RDBMS. W3C XML Schema borrows date-time-related datatypes from SQL, and other schema languages further borrow these datatypes. We have already seen correspondences between W3C XML Schema and SQL in Section 9.2.2.

### 16.4.3 Desiderata for Schema Languages

We have observed that data models of programming languages and RDBMSs differ significantly from schema languages. We have also observed that data binding tools patch the gaps.

Can and should schema languages fill the gaps? Some people (including the designers of W3C XML Schema) believe that schema languages should borrow mechanisms from programming languages and RDBMS to narrow the gaps. This approach may facilitate conversion from other technologies to schema languages, but may complicate schema languages and hamper conversion in the other direction.

Others (including the designers of RELAX NG) believe that schema languages should stay neutral from programming languages and RDBMSs by not incorporating any mechanisms specific to some of them. This approach makes schema languages simpler. However, the gaps have to be filled by data binding tools. We revisit this issue in sections 16.5.2 and 16.5.3.

## 16.5  General-Purpose Schema Languages

In this section, we consider four notable schema languages: DTD, W3C XML Schema, RELAX NG, and Schematron. We study whether these languages satisfy the desiderata shown in this chapter.

### 16.5.1  DTD

The DTD language does not satisfy desideratum 6: Schema languages should not change trees created by XML parsers. The reason is that default values, entity declarations, and notation declarations specified in DTDs affect the result of parsing. As a result, nonvalidating parsers do not always behave the same as validating ones. This lack of interoperability has caused problems in application development.

### 16.5.2  W3C XML Schema

W3C XML Schema does not satisfy desideratum 6. The reason is PSVI: Much information (including default values) specified in schemas is introduced into trees created by parsing. As a result, we cannot safely omit validation even when documents are guaranteed to be valid.

PSVI is intended to support data model 3 (An XML document is a collection of data compliant with a schema). PSVI contains diagnostic messages, data (for example, integer 1) of some datatypes, and references to declarations in schemas. Default values are also contained by PSVI. However, PSVI is defined only in an abstract manner as of this writing. Neither DOM nor SAX can handle PSVI, and there are no standards for concretely representing PSVI. This author believes that PSVI complicates W3C XML Schema and that data model 3 should be supported by data binding tools rather than PSVI.

W3C XML Schema provides derivation by addition, derivation by restriction, and substitution groups. These mechanisms support one style of inheritance. Some people believe that they narrow the gaps between XML and programs or databases.

However, these mechanisms complicate W3C XML Schema significantly.[1] This author believes that these mechanisms make data model 3 difficult because the inheritance of W3C XML Schema is very different from the inheritance of programming languages.

By mimicking `NULL` of SQL, `xsi:nil` is intended to narrow the gaps between W3C XML Schema and RDBMS. Although this attribute does not complicate W3C XML Schema, it is specific to one particular type of application. This author believes that an independent specification should be created for this attribute, if it is really necessary.

In summary, W3C XML Schema attempts to solve problems by incorporating many mechanisms from other technologies. However, opponents (including this author) believe that these mechanisms complicate W3C XML Schema and do not help in interworking with other technologies.

## 16.5.3 RELAX NG

RELAX NG satisfies desideratum 6 because it does not change trees created by XML parsers. We can thus safely omit validation when documents are guaranteed to be valid. On the other hand, desideratum 6 implies that RELAX NG and its validators do not provide default values. However, to help migration from DTDs to RELAX NG, annotations in RELAX NG schemas can represent default values. Without performing validation, programs can use such default values to transform trees created by XML parsers. In other words, RELAX NG separates validation and default values.

RELAX NG does not provide any mechanisms specific to particular programming languages or RDBMSs. It does not have inheritance and does not have anything like `xsi:nil`.

The absence of inheritance in RELAX NG is certainly debatable. James Clark has argued that modeling languages such as Unified Modeling Language (UML) should be used for representing inheritance and that RELAX NG schemas generated from UML do not have to provide inheritance. It is also possible to create syntax sugar, which mimics inheritance, and to convert schemas using such syntax sugar to RELAX NG schemas. Because we can introduce different sets of syntax sugar for different styles of inheritance, this approach can narrow the gap between RELAX NG and any programming language.[2]

---

[1] "W3C XML Schema Made Simple," by Kohsuke Kawaguchi, at XML.com (`http://www.xml.com/pub/a/2001/06/06/schemasimple.html`) discusses the disadvantages of these mechanisms.

[2] One set of such syntax sugar is presented in "Shorthand for Mimicking Inheritance in RELAX NG," by Makoto Murata (available at `http://www.asahi-net.or.jp/~eb2m-mrt/oo.html`).

Data binding tools for RELAX NG can support data model 3. Two data binding tools have been developed for RELAX NG: Relaxer (introduced in Chapter 15) and RelaxNGCC. Relaxer generates Java programs from schemas and provides bidirectional mapping between XML documents and Java objects. Although Relaxer was originally designed for RELAX Core, it can also handle RELAX NG. The absence of inheritance in RELAX Core and RELAX NG allows Relaxer to take full advantage of the inheritance of Java (see Section 15.2.2). Intuitively speaking, RelaxNGCC is yacc or JavaCC for RELAX NG. To manipulate XML documents that are valid against a RELAX NG schema, programmers insert Java code fragments in this schema. Then, RelaxNGCC generates a main program that executes these code fragments during parsing. By invoking this main program, programmers can easily handle XML documents with Java programs. Although RelaxNGCC supports the creation of Java objects from XML documents, it does not support the creation of XML documents from Java objects. Both Relaxer and RelaxNGCC are on the accompanying CD-ROM.

RELAX NG has a mathematical foundation, which is the tree or hedge automaton theory. This foundation provides a solid basis for implementing validators for RELAX NG. Furthermore, query languages (such as XQuery) and programming languages (such as XDuce) are based on the same foundation.[3]

In summary, RELAX NG concentrates on validation and lets data binding tools provide data model 3. By doing so, RELAX NG has become simple yet powerful.[4]

## 16.5.4 Schematron

Schematron is a schema language designed by Rick Jelliffe. Unlike other schema languages, such as W3C XML Schema or RELAX NG, schemas in Schematron are collections of rules using XPath expressions.

The Schematron schema in Listing 16.5 references an XML document (`source1.xml`) that provides a list of authors.[5] This schema ensures that each author in an instance document exists in the author list.

---

[3] For more about this theory, see "Taxonomy of XML Schema Languages Using Formal Language Theory," by Murata, Lee, and Mani, presented at Extreme 2001 and available at `http://citeseer.nj.nec.com/murata00taxonomy.html`.

[4] Each mechanism of RELAX NG is discussed in "The Design of RELAX NG," by James Clark, available at `http://www.thaiopensource.com/relaxng/design.html`.

[5] This example is borrowed from "Schematron Tutorial," by Nic Miloslav, available at `http://www.zvon.org/xxl/SchematronTutorial/General/contents.html`.

**Listing 16.5**  Schematron example

```
<?xml version="1.0" encoding="utf-8"?>
<schema xmlns="http://www.ascc.net/xml/schematron" >
  <pattern name="Compare with the database">
    <rule context="author">
      <assert
        test="document('source1.xml')//author[@id=current()/@id]">The
        author is not in the database.
      </assert>
    </rule>
  </pattern>
</schema>
```

Schematron satisfies desideratum 6 because it does not change trees created by XML parsers. Just like RELAX NG, Schematron does not provide default values.

Schematron has been used for validation but has not been used as a data model. No data binding tools for Schematron have appeared. In other words, Schematron has not been used to support data model 3 (An XML document is a collection of data compliant with a schema).

The use of XPath allows Schematron to capture what other schema languages cannot capture. In particular, only Schematron can capture constraints among multiple documents. For this reason, Schematron is expected to be used in conjunction with other schema languages such as W3C XML Schema and RELAX NG.

## 16.6  Special-Purpose Schema Languages

We have until now considered general-purpose schema languages, which can be used for XML documents of any kind. However, some schema languages are dedicated to particular kinds of XML documents. Furthermore, a framework for combining multiple schema languages has been proposed.

### 16.6.1  RDF Schema

RDF Schema is a schema language for XML documents representing Resource Description Framework (RDF) metadata. The basic constructs in the data model of RDF are resources, properties, and statements. To represent RDF metadata with an XML document, such basic constructs are represented by elements or attributes. Applications for handling RDF metadata are concerned about the basic constructs of RDF metadata rather than elements or attributes.

Schemas written in RDF Schema (see Listing 16.6) describe permissible basic constructs and their structural relationships. They do not directly handle elements or attributes. As far as RDF metadata is concerned, RDF Schema provides higher abstraction than general-purpose schema languages, and is thus expected to make schema authoring and metadata access easier.

**Listing 16.6** RDF Schema example borrowed from the W3C Candidate Recommendation for RDF Schema.

```
<?xml version="1.0" encoding="utf-8"?>
<rdf:RDF xml:lang="en"
  xmlns:rdf="http://www.w3.org/1999/02/22-rdf-syntax-ns#"
  xmlns:rdfs="http://www.w3.org/2000/01/rdf-schema#">

 <rdf:Description ID="registeredTo">
  <rdf:type resource="http://www.w3.org/1999/02/22-rdf-syntax-ns#
  Property"/>
  <rdfs:domain rdf:resource="#MotorVehicle"/>
  <rdfs:range rdf:resource="#Person"/>
 </rdf:Description>

 <rdf:Description ID="rearSeatLegRoom">
  <rdf:type resource="http://www.w3.org/1999/02/22-rdf-syntax-ns#
  Property"/>
  <rdfs:domain rdf:resource="#PassengerVehicle"/>
  <rdfs:domain rdf:resource="#Minivan"/>
  <rdfs:range
      rdf:resource="http://www.w3.org/2000/03/example/
      classes#Number"/>
 </rdf:Description>

</rdf:RDF>
```

In general, although a special-purpose schema language has a limited use, it provides features tailored to that use and also provides higher abstraction. Therefore, special-purpose schema languages are easier to understand and enable easy access to particular types of documents, as long as the market is big enough to justify tool development for special-purpose schema languages.

Besides RDF Schema, other special-purpose schema languages may emerge. For example, the Topic Map Constraint Language, already in progress at ISO/IEC JTC SC34, is a special-purpose schema language for XML documents representing topic maps. WSDL, explained in Chapter 13, can be seen as another special-purpose schema language.

## 16.6.2 RELAX Namespace

It is highly unlikely that a single general-purpose schema language will over-shadow all other schema languages. Although only a single general-purpose one may survive, some special-purpose ones are likely to provide more advantages and thus also survive.

Different schema languages have different target documents. If the targets of schema languages do not overlap, we only have to use the schema language most appropriate for the task at hand.

However, different parts of a single XML document may require different schema languages. An example is an XHTML document containing RDF metadata. RDF Schema is appropriate for the RDF metadata, while general-purpose schema languages such as RELAX NG are appropriate for the body of the XHTML document. To create a schema for such an XHTML document, we need a framework so that RELAX NG and RDF Schema can be combined.

RELAX Namespace has been designed as such a framework. For a single multi-namespace XML document, we can use different schema languages for different namespaces and combine them by using RELAX Namespace. In the XHTML+RDF example, we create a schema for the XHTML namespace in RELAX NG or RELAX Core and create another schema for the metadata namespace in RDF Schema. We then combine these schemas by writing a RELAX Namespace framework, as shown in Listing 16.7.

**Listing 16.7** RELAX Namespace example

```
        <?xml version="1.0" encoding="utf-8"?>
[2]     <framework xmlns="http://www.xml.gr.jp/xmlns/relaxNamespace"
            relaxNamespaceVersion="1.0">

[5]         <namespace name="http://www.example.net/document"
                moduleLocation="doc.rxm"/>

[8]         <namespace name="http://www.example.net/metadata"
                moduleLocation="meta.rdfs"
                language="http://www.w3.org/2000/01/rdf-schema#"/>

[12]        <topLevel>
              <ref name="doc" namespace="http://www.example.net/document"
                  xmlns="http://www.xml.gr.jp/xmlns/relaxCore"/>
            </topLevel>

        </framework>
```

This RELAX Namespace schema combines two schemas for two namespaces. The root element of this schema is a `framework` element (line 2). It has two namespace elements (lines 5 and 8) and one topLevel element (line 12). The first namespace associates a RELAX Core schema, doc.rxm, with the namespace http://www.example.net/document, and the second namespace associates an RDF Schema, schema meta.rdfs, with the namespace http://www.w3.org/2000/01/rdf-syntax. The topLevel element specifies that the root of an instance document is a doc element of the first namespace.

RELAX Namespace was designed together with RELAX Core in Japan. As of this writing, RELAX Namespace is a Draft Technical Report of ISO/IEC (ISO/IEC DTR 22250-2).

## 16.7  Summary

In this chapter, we have reconsidered schema languages. A schema is useful as a mechanism for checking documents and can also be used as a data model for accessing valid documents.

A number of mechanisms have been introduced to W3C XML Schema to provide powerful data models and help interworking with Java and RDBMS. However, one could argue that such mechanisms have complicated W3C XML Schema and have actually made it difficult to use schemas as data models and to map W3C XML Schema to Java, RDBMS, and other programming languages.

On the other hand, RELAX NG is a simple schema language. The reason is that RELAX NG validators are not intended to solve all problems. Rather, data binding tools for RELAX NG provide easy access to valid documents and mapping from RELAX NG to Java or RDBMS.

Special-purpose schema languages such as RDF Schema are useful for particular types of XML documents. They provide higher abstraction and make data binding easier. RELAX Namespace allows special-purpose and general-purpose schema languages to be combined to collectively form a single schema.

# About the CD-ROM

A CD-ROM comes with this book, and it contains all the source code, resource files, and some useful XML tools. In addition, the CD-ROM has the trial versions of these two IBM products:

- IBM WebSphere Application Server 4.0, which can be used to run the sample Web applications in Chapters 10 through 15

- IBM DB2 Universal Database 7.2, which can be used as the backend database of the sample programs described in Chapter 11

The following is an overview of the directory structure of the CD-ROM. See `readme_en.html` in the root directory to browse the content. Also, every directory contains a `readme_en.html` file to describe the content.

```
</>                         : Root directory
  + readme_en.html          : The Readme file describing the CD-ROM
                              contents
  + <alphaWorks>            : Software packages from IBM alphaWorks
  + <appendixB>             : Online version of Useful Links and Books
                              (Appendix B)
  + <appendixC>             : Online version of XML-Related
                              Standardization Activities (Appendix C)
  + <samples>               : Source code, XML documents, and other files
                              used in each chapter
  + <tools>                 : Tools such as Xerces and Xalan
  + <trial>                 : Trial versions of IBM products
```

# Useful Links and Books

This appendix is a compilation of useful links and books on the subjects mentioned in this book. See Appendix C for XML-related standards activities and standards documents.

## B.1 XML

### B.1.1 General

- The SGML/XML Web page by Robin Cover: `http://www.oasis-open.org/cover/xml.html`

  Comprehensive links to XML and SGML, including articles, books, XML data, and tools.

- Annotated XML Specification by Tim Bray: `http://www.xml.com/axml/axml.html`

- XML.com: `http://www.xml.com`

  This site has a rich mix of information for developers and beginners.

- XML.org: `http://www.xml.org`

  A portal site hosted by OASIS.

- xmlhack: `http://www.xmlhack.com`

  A news site for XML developers.

- xml-dev mailing list: `http://www.xml.org/xml/xmldev.shtml`

  Very active mailing list for discussing XML specifications. Participants include people in W3C Working Groups, tool developers, and so on.

- IBM developerWorks (XML zone): `http://www.ibm.com/developerworks/xml/`

  This site has a lot of articles.

- Microsoft MSDN (XML page): `http://msdn.microsoft.com/xml`
  This site has a lot of articles.

- James Clark's Web page: `http://www.jclark.com`
  James Clark is the author of XP, a highly conformant XML parser in Java. His page contains a set of XML test cases for testing the conformance of XML parsers.

- ID Alliance: `http://www.idealliance.org`
  ID Alliance organizes many conferences and seminars on XML.

## B.1.2  Software

There are a lot of downloadable tools.

- The following pages provide many software packages:
  - Apache XML project: `http://xml.apache.org/`
  - IBM alphaWorks: `http://www.alphaworks.ibm.com/`
  - IBM developerWorks open source projects: `http://www.ibm.com/developerworks/oss/`
  - XML Software.com: `http://www.xmlsoftware.com`
- XML parsers:
  - Java API for XML Processing (JAXP): `http://java.sun.com/xml/jaxp/`
  - Xerces Java 1: `http://xml.apache.org/xerces-j/`
  - Xerces Java 2: `http://xml.apache.org/xerces2-j/`
  - Crimson: `http://xml.apache.org/crimson`
- XPath and XSLT tools:
  - Xalan Java 2: `http://xml.apache.org/xalan-j/`
  - Cocoon 1: `http://xml.apache.org/cocoon/`
  - Cocoon 2: `http://xml.apache.org/cocoon2/`
- Data binding tools:
  - Castor: `http://castor.exolab.org`
  - Java Architecture for XML Binding (JAXB): `http://java.sun.com/xml/jaxb/`
  - Relaxer: `http://www.relaxer.org/`
  - RelaxNGCC: `http://homepage2.nifty.com/okajima/relaxngcc/index_en.htm`
- Schema validation tools:
  - Jing: `http://www.thaiopensource.com/relaxng/jing.html`

- Sun Multi-Schema XML Validator: `http://www.sun.com/software/xml/developers/multischema/`
- VBRELAXNG: `http://www.geocities.co.jp/SiliconValley-Bay/4639/vbrelaxng/vbrelaxng.html`
- Other software:
  - DTDinst: `http://www.thaiopensource.com/dtdinst/`
  - SmartDoc: `http://www.asahi-net.or.jp/~dp8t-asm/java/tools/SmartDoc/`

# B.2  Java

## B.2.1  Platform and SDK

- Sun Java 2 Platform Standard Edition: `http://java.sun.com/j2se/`
- Sun Java 2 Platform Enterprise Edition (J2EE): `http://java.sun.com/j2ee/`
- Sun J2EE Tutorial: `http://java.sun.com/j2ee/tutorial/1_3-fcs/index.html`
- Sun Java 2 SDK, Standard Edition, Version 1.2: `http://java.sun.com/products/jdk/1.2/`
- Sun Java 2 SDK, Standard Edition, Version 1.3: `http://java.sun.com/j2se/1.3/`
- IBM Java technology: Tools and products: Developer kits: `http://www.ibm.com/java/jdk/`

## B.2.2  Web Applications

- JavaServer Pages (JSP): `http://java.sun.com/products/jsp/`
- Java Servlet: `http://java.sun.com/products/servlet/`
- JavaBeans: `http://java.sun.com/products/javabeans/`
- Enterprise JavaBeans: `http://java.sun.com/products/ejb/`
- Tomcat: `http://jakarta.apache.org/tomcat/`

## B.2.3  Database

- JDBC Data Access API: `http://java.sun.com/products/jdbc/`
- JDBC-enabled drivers: `http://industry.java.sun.com/products/jdbc/drivers`

## B.2.4  Messaging

- Java Message Service API: `http://java.sun.com/products/jms/`

### B.2.5 Security

- Java Authentication and Authorization Service (JAAS): `http://java.sun.com/products/jaas/`

- Java Cryptography Extension (JCE): `http://java.sun.com/products/jce/`

- Java Secure Socket Extension (JSSE): `http://java.sun.com/products/jsse/`

# B.3 Web Services

## B.3.1 General

- Articles:
    - IBM developerWorks (Web services zone): `http://www.ibm.com/developerworks/webservices/`
    - Microsoft MSDN (Web services page): `http://www.microsoft.com/webservices/`
- Specifications (see also Appendix C):
    - Simple Object Access Protocol (SOAP) 1.1: `http://www.w3.org/TR/SOAP/`
    - Simple Object Access Protocol (SOAP) 1.2: `http://www.w3.org/TR/soap12/`
    - Universal Description, Discovery, and Integration (UDDI): `http://www.uddi.org/`
    - Web Services Description Language (WSDL) 1.1: `http://www.w3.org/TR/wsdl`

## B.3.2 Software

- Apache SOAP: `http://xml.apache.org/soap/`

- Apache Axis: `http://xml.apache.org/axis/`

- IBM Web Services Toolkit: `http://www.alphaworks.ibm.com/tech/webservicestoolkit`

- Java API for XML Messaging (JAXM): `http://java.sun.com/xml/jaxm/`

- Java API for XML Registries (JAXR): `http://java.sun.com/xml/jaxr/`

- Java API for XML-Based RPC (JAXRPC): `http://java.sun.com/xml/jaxrpc/`

- UDDI4J Project: `http://www-124.ibm.com/developerworks/projects/uddi4j/`

- WSDL4J Project: `http://www-124.ibm.com/developerworks/projects/wsdl4j/`

# B.4 Standards

See also Appendix C for XML-related standards activities and standards documents.

- Standards bodies:
  - Internet Engineering Task Force (IETF): `http://www.ietf.org`
  - International Organization for Standardization (ISO): `http://www.iso.ch/`
  - Object Management Group (OMG): `http://www.omg.org/`
  - Organization for the Advancement of Structured Information Standards (OASIS): `http://www.oasis-open.org/`
  - World Wide Web Consortium (W3C): `http://www.w3.org`
- Common Object Request Broker Architecture (CORBA): `http://www.corba.org/`
- Hypertext Markup Language (HTML) home page: `http://www.w3.org/MarkUp/`
- Hypertext Transfer Protocol (HTTP): `http://www.w3.org/Protocols/`
- IP Security Protocol (IPSec): `http://www.ietf.org/html.charters/ipsec-charter.html`
- Java Community Process (JCP): `http://www.jcp.org/`
- Public-Key Cryptography Standards (PKCS): `http://www.rsasecurity.com/rsalabs/pkcs/`
- Resource Description Framework (RDF) home page: `http://www.w3.org/RDF/`
- Secure Sockets Layer 3.0 (SSL 3.0) home page: `http://home.netscape.com/eng/ssl3/`
- Security Assertion Markup Language (SAML) home page: `http://www.oasis-open.org/committees/security/`
- Transport Layer Security (TLS): `http://www.ietf.org/html.charters/tls-charter.html`
- Unicode: `http://www.unicode.org/`
- XML Media Types (RFC 3023): `http://www.ietf.org/rfc/rfc3023.txt`

# B.5  Books

There are many books that cover Java or XML. These are only some of them.

### B.5.1  Java

1. The Java Series, Addison-Wesley: Reading, Mass. In particular:
   1. Arnold, Ken and James Gosling, *"The Java Programming Language, Third Edition,"* Addison-Wesley, 2000. ISBN: 0-201-70433-1

2.  Campione, Mary and Kathy Walrath, *"The Java Tutorial, Second Edition,"* Addison-Wesley, 1998. ISBN: 0-201-31007-4

3.  Chan, Patrick and Rosanna Lee, *"The Java Class Libraries, Second Edition, Volume 1,"* Addison-Wesley, 1998. ISBN: 0-201-31002-3

4.  Chan, Patrick, Rosanna Lee, and Doug Kramer, *"The Java Class Libraries, Second Edition, Volume 2,"* Addison-Wesley, 1998. ISBN: 0-201-31003-1

5.  Hamilton, Graham, Rick Cattell, and Maydene Fisher, *"JDBC Database Access with Java: A Tutorial and Annotated Reference,"* Addison-Wesley, 1997. ISBN: 0-201-30995-5

6.  Joy, Bill, Guy Steele, James Gosling, and Gilad Bracha, *"The Java Language Specification, Second Edition,"* Addison-Wesley, 2000. ISBN: 0-201-31008-2

7.  Kassem, Nicholas and Enterprise Team, *"Designing Enterprise Applications with the Java 2 Platform, Enterprise Edition,"* Addison-Wesley, 2000. ISBN: 0-201-70277-0

8.  White, Seth, Maydene Fisher, Rick Cattell, Graham Hamilton, and Mark Hapner, *"JDBC API Tutorial and Reference: Universal Data Access for the Java 2 Platform,"* Addison-Wesley, 1999. ISBN: 0-201-43328-1

2.  Englander, Robert and Mike Loukides, *"Developing Java Beans,"* O'Reilly, 1997. ISBN: 1-565-92289-1

3.  Flanagan, David, *"Java in a Nutshell: A Desktop Quick Reference, 3rd Edition,"* O'Reilly, 1999. ISBN: 1-565-92487-8

4.  Horstmann, Cay and Gray Cornel, *"Core Java 2 Volume I—Fundamentals,"* Prentice Hall, 2000. ISBN: 0-130-89468-0

5.  Horstmann, Cay and Gray Cornel, *"Core Java 2 Volume II—Advanced Features,"* Prentice Hall, 2001. ISBN: 0-130-92738-4

6.  Hunter, Jason and William Crawford, *"Java Servlet Programming,"* O'Reilly, 2001. ISBN: 0-596-00040-5

7.  Monson-Haefel, Richard, *"Enterprise JavaBeans,"* O'Reilly, 2001. ISBN: 0-596-00226-2

8.  Patel, Pratik and Karl Moss, *"Java Database Programming with JDBC,"* The Coriolis Group, 1997. ISBN: 1-576-10159-2

9.  Reese, George, *"Database Programming with JDBC and Java,"* O'Reilly, 2000. ISBN: 1-565-92616-1

## B.5.2  XML/SGML

1.  Bradley, Neil, *"The XML Companion,"* Prentice Hall Computer Books, 1998. ISBN: 0-130-81152-1

2.  Fung, Khun Yee, *"XSLT: Working with XML and HTML,"* Addison-Wesley, 2001. ISBN: 0-201-71103-6

3. Harold, Elliotte Rusty, *"XML: Extensible Markup Language,"* IDG Books Worldwide, 1998. ISBN: 0-764-53199-9

4. Harold, Elliotte Rusty and W. Scott Means, *"XML in a Nutshell: A Desktop Quick Reference,"* O'Reilly, 2001. ISBN: 0-596-00058-8

5. Hunter, David, Jeff Rafter, Jon Pinnock, Chris Dix, Kurt Cagle, and Roger Kovack, *"Beginning XML,"* Wrox Press, 2001: ISBN: 1-861-00559-8

6. Jelliffe, Rick, *"The XML and SGML Cookbook: Recipes for Structured Information,"* Prentice Hall, 1998. ISBN: 0-136-14223-0

7. Kay, Michael H., *"XSLT Programmer's Reference, 2nd Edition,"* Wrox Press, 2001. ISBN: 1-861-00506-7

8. Ray, Erik T., *"Learning XML,"* O'Reilly, 2001. ISBN: 0-596-00046-4

9. Simpson, John E., *"Just XML,"* Prentice Hall Computer Books, 1998. ISBN: 0-139-43417-8

10. St. Laurent, Simon, *"XML: A Primer,"* Hungry Minds, 1999. ISBN: 0-764-54777-1

11. St. Laurent, Simon, *"XML Elements of Style,"* McGraw-Hill Professional Publishing, 1999. ISBN: 0-072-12220-X

12. Williams, Kevin, et al., *"Professional XML Databases,"* Wrox Press, 2000. ISBN: 1-861-00358-7

## B.5.3 Web Services

1. Graham, Steve, Simeon Simeonov, Toufic Boubez, Glen Daniels, Doug Davis, Yuichi Nakamura, and Ryo Neyama, *"Building Web Services with Java: Making Sense of XML, SOAP, WSDL and UDDI,"* Sams, 2001. ISBN: 0-672-32181-5

2. Snell, James, Doug Tidwell, and Pavel Kulchenko, *"Programming Web Services with SOAP, "* O'Reilly, 2001. ISBN: 0-596-00095-2

## B.5.4 Other Topics

1. Gamma, Erich, Richard Helm, Ralph Johnson, and John Vlissides, *"Design Patterns,"* Addison-Wesley, 1995. ISBN: 0-201-63361-2

2. Garfinkel, Simson and Gene Spafford, *"Web Security & Commerce,"* O'Reilly, 1997. ISBN: 1-565-92269-7

3. Schneier, Bruce, *"Secrets and Lies,"* John Wiley & Sons, 2000. ISBN: 0-471-25311-1

# XML-Related Standardization Activities

Since the XML 1.0 Recommendation was issued in February 1998, a lot of related standard activities have begun. This appendix describes some of these activities, including the ones mentioned in this book. Almost all the activities belong to one of the following standardization bodies, and some of them are joint works.

- World Wide Web Consortium (W3C): `http://www.w3.org`

  List of all the documents submitted/published by W3C: `http://www.w3.org/TR`

- Internet Engineering Task Force (IETF): `http://www.ietf.org`

- International Organization for Standardization (ISO): `http://www.iso.ch/`

- Organization for the Advancement of Structured Information Standards (OASIS): `http://www.oasis-open.org/`

Note that the status of these standards documents is as of March 2002 and may have been changed after that. Please check the standard body's home pages for the latest information.

Also, this appendix contains a list of Java Specification Requests (JSRs) related to this book.

| NAME | URL | STATUS | BODY |
|------|-----|--------|------|
| Extensible Markup Language (XML) 1.0 | `http://www.w3.org/TR/1998/REC-xml-19980210` | Recommendation (February 10, 1998) | W3C |
| Extensible Markup Language (XML) 1.0 (Second Edition) | `http://www.w3.org/TR/REC-xml` | Recommendation (October 6, 2000) | W3C |

## C.1 XML Core

### C.1.1 Namespace

XML namespaces provide a simple method for qualifying element and attribute names used in XML documents by associating them with namespaces identified by URI references. In the following example, the <book> tag and the <price> tag have the namespace prefixes order and edi, respectively. This means that they are associated with the namespaces identified by http://ecommerce.org/order and http://ecommerce.org/edi, respectively.

```
<?xml version="1.0"?>
<order:book
  xmlns:order='http://ecommerce.org/order'
  xmlns:edi='http://ecommerce.org/edi'>
    <edi:price>14.95</edi:price>
</order:book>
```

XML namespaces envision applications of XML where a single XML document may contain elements and attributes that are defined for and used by multiple software modules. In the previous example, the <book> tag and the <price> tag may be processed by different software modules.

The namespace specification is a W3C Recommendation and is widely used in a lot of standards.

| NAME | URL | STATUS | BODY |
|------|-----|--------|------|
| Namespaces in XML | http://www.w3.org/TR/ REC-xml-names/ | Recommendation (January 14, 1999) | W3C |

### C.1.2 XML Fragment Interchange

The XML standard supports logical documents composed of possibly several entities. An application is often required to view or edit one or more of the entities or parts of entities rather than the entire document. The problem is how to provide to the application of such a fragment the appropriate information about the context that fragment had in the larger document that is not available to the application. XML Fragment Interchange addresses this issue.

For example, assume that an application needs to view and edit the second <book> element from the following document but has no interest in viewing and editing the first <book> element.

```
<?xml version='1.0'?>
<list>
  <book>
    <author>H. Maruyama, K. Tamura, and N. Uramoto</author>
    <title>XML and Java: Developing Web Applications</title>
  </book>
  <book>
    <author>IBM TRL XML Team</author>
    <title>XML and Java, 2nd Edition</title>
  </book>
</list>
```

Here is a fragment representing the second <book> element from the previous document:

```
<?xml version='1.0'?>
<p:package xmlns:p="http://www.w3.org/2001/02/xml-package">
  <p:fcs xmlns:f="http://www.w3.org/2001/02/xml-fragment">
    <list>
      <book/>
      <p:fragbody/>
    </list>
  </p:fcs>

  <p:body>
    <book>
      <author>IBM TRL XML Team</author>
      <title>XML and Java, 2nd Edition</title>
    </book>
  </p:body>
</p:package>
```

| NAME | URL | STATUS | BODY |
|---|---|---|---|
| XML Fragment Interchange Requirements Version 1.0 | http://www.w3.org/TR/ NOTE-XML-FRAG-REQ | Note (November 23, 1998) | W3C |
| XML Fragment Interchange | http://www.w3.org/TR/ xml-fragment | Candidate Recommendation (February 12, 2001) | W3C |

## C.1.3  XML Inclusions

Many programming languages provide an inclusion mechanism to facilitate modularity. XML also often needs such a mechanism. XML Inclusions introduces a generic mechanism for merging XML documents (as represented by their information sets) for use by applications that need such a facility.

In the following example, an XML document contains an `<xi:include>` element that points to an external document named `external.xml`.

```
<?xml version='1.0'?>
<document xmlns:xi="http://www.w3.org/1999/XML/xinclude">
  <p>This is a document</p>
  <xi:include href="external.xml"/>
</document>
```

Assume that the external document is the following:

```
<?xml version='1.0'?>
<external>
  <p>This is an external document.</p>
</external>
```

Then the XML document resulting from resolving inclusions on the previous document is the following document:

```
<?xml version='1.0'?>
<document xmlns:xi="http://www.w3.org/1999/XML/xinclude">
  <p>This is a document</p>
  <external>
    <p>This is an external document.</p>
  </external>
</document>
```

| NAME | URL | STATUS | BODY |
|------|-----|--------|------|
| XML Inclusions (XInclude) Version 1.0 | http://www.w3.org/TR/ xinclude/ | Candidate Recommendation (February 21, 2002) | W3C |

## C.1.4 XML Infoset

The XML 1.0 Recommendation describes the physical representation of XML documents. However, XML-based standards are usually defined at a higher, logical level: in other words, standards tend to refer to abstract objects like element or data rather than to the physical sequences of characters that match the XML 1.0 Recommendation's syntactic productions. XML Information Set describes these abstract XML objects and their properties.

| NAME | URL | STATUS | BODY |
|------|-----|--------|------|
| XML Information Set Requirements | http://www.w3.org/TR/ NOTE-xml-infoset-req. html | Note (February 18, 1999) | W3C |
| XML Information Set | http://www.w3.org/TR/ xml-infoset/ | Recommendation (October 24, 2001) | W3C |

## C.2  XML Tools

### C.2.1  XPath

XPath is the result of an effort to provide a common syntax and semantics for functionality shared between XSL Transformations and XPointer. The primary purpose of XPath is to address parts of an XML document. XPath uses a compact, non-XML syntax to facilitate use of XPath within URIs and XML attribute values. See Chapter 7.

| NAME | URL | STATUS | BODY |
|---|---|---|---|
| XML Path Language (XPath) Version 1.0 | `http://www.w3.org/TR/xpath` | Recommendation (November 16, 1999) | W3C |
| XPath Requirements Version 2.0 | `http://www.w3.org/TR/xpath20req` | Working Draft (February 14, 2001) | W3C |

### C.2.2  XML Pointer, XML Base, and XML Linking

XML Pointer Language (XPointer) is the language to be used as the basis for a fragment identifier for any URI reference that locates a resource whose Internet media type is one of text/xml, application/xml, text/xml-external-parsed-entity, or application/xml-external-parsed-entity. XPointer is based on the XML Path Language (XPath) and supports addressing into the internal structures of XML documents and external parsed entities.

The following example locates the element with an ID attribute whose value is "chap1" in the XML document specified by `http://www.foo.com/doc.xml`.

```
http://www.foo.com/doc.xml#xpointer(id("chap1"))
```

XLink provides a framework for creating both basic unidirectional links and more complex linking structures. It allows XML documents to:

- Assert linking relationships among more than two resources
- Associate metadata with a link
- Express links that reside in a location separate from the linked resources

One of the stated requirements for XLink is to support HTML linking constructs in a generic way.

Specifically, XLink defines several global attributes for use on elements that are in any arbitrary namespace. The global attributes are `type`, `href`, `role`, `arcrole`, `title`, `show`, `actuate`, `label`, `from`, and `to`. Document creators use the XLink global attributes to make the elements recognizable as XLink elements. The following is an example taken from the XLink specification. The `type` attribute indicates the XLink element type (simple, extended, locator, arc, resource, or title). In this example, the type is simple, which means that this link associates exactly two resources, one is a local resource and the other is a remote resource (or resource fragment). The local resource is `<my:crossReference>` itself, and the remote resource is specified in the `href` attribute (`students.xml`). XPointer may be used to specify the remote resource fragment. The `role` and `title` attributes are used to describe the meaning of the resources. The value of the `role` attribute must be a URI reference (`http://www.example.com/linkprops/studentlist`). On the other hand, the value of `title` can be used to describe the meaning in a human-readable fashion (Student List). See the XLink specification for more details.

```
<my:crossReference
   xmlns:my="http://example.com/"
   xmlns:xlink="http://www.w3.org/1999/xlink"
   xlink:type="simple"
   xlink:href="students.xml"
   xlink:role="http://www.example.com/linkprops/studentlist"
   xlink:title="Student List"
   xlink:show="new"
   xlink:actuate="onRequest">
Current List of Students
</my:crossReference>
```

XML Base provides a mechanism for providing base URI services to XLink, but as a modular specification so that other XML applications benefiting from additional control over relative URIs but not built upon XLink can also make use of it. The syntax consists of a single XML attribute named `xml:base`.

W3C's home page for XML Pointer, XML Base, and XML Linking is `http://www.w3.org/XML/Linking`.

| NAME | URL | STATUS | BODY |
|---|---|---|---|
| XML Linking Language (XLink) Version 1.0 | http://www.w3.org/TR/ xlink/ | Recommendation (June 27, 2001) | W3C |
| XML Base | http://www.w3.org/TR/ xmlbase/ | Recommendation (June 27, 2001) | W3C |
| XML Pointer Language (XPointer) Version 1.0 | http://www.w3.org/TR/ xptr/ | Candidate Recommendation (September 11, 2001) | W3C |

## C.2.3 Extensible Stylesheet Language

Because XML only defines syntax, a program does not know how to format an XML document without having explicit instructions on styles. For example, what typeface and font size should be used for displaying text in an element? How can a program lay it out on the screen? Extensible Stylesheet Language (XSL) is a language for expressing stylesheets. An XSL stylesheet is a file that describes how to display an XML document of a given class. It consists of two parts:

- A language for transforming XML documents
- An XML vocabulary for specifying formatting semantics

An XSL stylesheet specifies the presentation of a class of XML documents by describing how an instance of the class is transformed into an XML document that uses the formatting vocabulary.

In particular, the first part is separately standardized as XSL Transformations (XSLT). Originally intended to perform complex styling operations, like generating tables of contents and indexes, it is now used as a general-purpose XML processing language. XSLT is thus widely used for purposes other than XSL, like generating HTML Web pages from XML data. See Chapter 7 for more details.

W3C's home page for XSL is `http://www.w3.org/Style/XSL/`.

| NAME | URL | STATUS | BODY |
|---|---|---|---|
| XSL Transformations (XSLT) Version 1.0 | `http://www.w3.org/TR/xslt` | Recommendation (November 16, 1999) | W3C |
| XSL Transformations (XSLT) Version 1.1 | `http://www.w3.org/TR/xslt11/` | Working Draft (August 24, 2001) | W3C |
| Extensible Stylesheet Language (XSL) | `http://www.w3.org/TR/xsl/` | Recommendation (October 15, 2001) | W3C |
| Associating Style Sheets with XML Documents Version 1.0 | `http://www.w3.org/TR/xml-stylesheet/` | Recommendation (June 29, 1999) | W3C |

# C.3  Schema Languages

## C.3.1  XML Schema

While the XML 1.0 Recommendation supplies a mechanism, the Document Type Definition (DTD), for declaring constraints on the use of markup, the DTD is often not sufficient. For example, the DTD does not support namespaces, and it supports only a few datatypes. To overcome these problems of DTDs, W3C formed the XML Schema Working Group in 1998, and XML Schema was published as a W3C Recommendation in May 2001. See Chapters 9 and 16 for more details.

W3C's home page for XML Schema is `http://www.w3.org/XML/Schema`.

| NAME | URL | STATUS | BODY |
|---|---|---|---|
| XML Schema Requirements | `http://www.w3.org/TR/NOTE-xml-schema-req` | Note (February 15, 1999) | W3C |
| XML Schema Part 0: Primer | `http://www.w3.org/TR/xmlschema-0/` | Recommendation (May 2, 2001) | W3C |
| XML Schema Part 1: Structures | `http://www.w3.org/TR/xmlschema-1/` | Recommendation (May 2, 2001) | W3C |
| XML Schema Part 2: Datatypes | `http://www.w3.org/TR/xmlschema-2/` | Recommendation (May 2, 2001) | W3C |

## C.3.2  RELAX NG

RELAX NG is another schema and has been developed by OASIS. It is a unification of two schema languages: TREX and RELAX Core. Visit `http://www.thaiopensource.com/trex/` and `http://www.xml.gr.jp/relax/` for TREX and RELAX, respectively. See Chapter 16 for more details.

The official site of RELAX NG is `http://www.oasis-open.org/committees/relax-ng/`. The working drafts are available there.

| NAME | URL | STATUS | BODY |
|---|---|---|---|
| RELAX NG Tutorial | `http://www.oasis-open.org/committees/relax-ng/tutorial-20011203.html` | Committee Specification (December 3, 2001) | OASIS |
| RELAX NG Specification | `http://www.oasis-open.org/committees/relax-ng/spec-20011203.html` | Committee Specification (December 3, 2001) | OASIS |
| RELAX NG DTD Compatibility | `http://www.oasis-open.org/committees/relax-ng/compatibility-20011203.html` | Committee Specification (December 3, 2001) | OASIS |
| Guidelines for Using W3C XML Schema Datatypes with RELAX NG | `http://www.oasis-open.org/committees/relax-ng/xsd-20010907.html` | Committee Specification (September 7, 2001) | OASIS |

### C.3.3 Schematron

Schematron is yet another schema language. See Chapter 16 for more details.

The official site of Schematron is `http://www.ascc.net/xml/resource/schematron/schematron.html`.

| NAME | URL | VERSION | EDITOR |
|------|-----|---------|--------|
| Schematron 1.5 | `http://www.ascc.net/xml/schematron/` | 1.5 | Rick Jelliffe |

## C.4 APIs

### C.4.1 Document Object Model

The Document Object Model (DOM) is a platform- and language-neutral interface that allows programs and scripts to dynamically access and update the content, structure, and style of XML documents. To provide a precise, language-independent specification of the DOM interfaces, it defines the specifications in OMG IDL, as defined in the CORBA 2.2 specification. In addition to the OMG IDL specification, it defines language bindings for Java and ECMAScript (an industry-standard scripting language based on JavaScript and JScript). See Chapter 4 for more about the Java binding.

There are a lot of DOM-related specifications. See `http://www.w3.org/DOM/DOMTR` for the list of specifications. The following tables list the specifications related to this book.

DOM Level 1

| NAME | URL | STATUS | BODY |
|------|-----|--------|------|
| Document Object Model (DOM) Level 1 Specification | `http://www.w3.org/TR/REC-DOM-Level-1/` | Recommendation (October 1, 1998) | W3C |

DOM Level 2

| NAME | URL | STATUS | BODY |
|------|-----|--------|------|
| Document Object Model (DOM) Level 2 Core Specification | `http://www.w3.org/TR/DOM-Level-2-Core/` | Recommendation (November 13, 2000) | W3C |
| Document Object Model (DOM) Level 2 Views Specification | `http://www.w3.org/TR/DOM-Level-2-Views/` | Recommendation (November 13, 2000) | W3C |

| | | | |
|---|---|---|---|
| Document Object Model (DOM) Level 2 Events Specification | `http://www.w3.org/TR/DOM-Level-2-Events/` | Recommendation (November 13, 2000) | W3C |
| Document Object Model (DOM) Level 2 Style Specification | `http://www.w3.org/TR/DOM-Level-2-Style/` | Recommendation (November 13, 2000) | W3C |
| Document Object Model (DOM) Level 2 Traversal and Range Specification | `http://www.w3.org/TR/DOM-Level-2-Traversal-Range/` | Recommendation (November 13, 2000) | W3C |

DOM Level 3

| NAME | URL | STATUS | BODY |
|---|---|---|---|
| Document Object Model (DOM) Level 3 Core Specification | `http://www.w3.org/TR/REC-DOM-Level-1/` | Working Draft (January 14, 2002) | W3C |
| Document Object Model (DOM) Level 3 Abstract Schemas and Load and Save Specification | `http://www.w3.org/TR/DOM-Level-3-ASLS/` | Working Draft (January 14, 2002) | W3C |
| Document Object Model (DOM) Level 3 Events Specification | `http://www.w3.org/TR/DOM-Level-3-Events/` | Working Draft (February 8, 2002) | W3C |
| Document Object Model (DOM) Level 3 XPath Specification | `http://www.w3.org/TR/DOM-Level-3-XPath/` | Working Draft (March 28, 2002) | W3C |

## C.4.2  Simple API for XML

The Simple API for XML (SAX) is another interface that allows programs and scripts to dynamically access and update the content, structure, and style of XML documents. See Chapter 5 for more details. Unlike DOM and other specifications, it is not from W3C. Instead, David Megginson and the xml-dev mailing list (currently hosted by OASIS) collaboratively developed the SAX 1.0 specification. SAX is now hosted from SourceForge at `http://sax.sourceforge.net/`.

| NAME | URL | BODY |
|---|---|---|
| SAX 1.0: The Simple API for XML | `http://www.saxproject.org/` | SourceForge |
| SAX 2.0: The Simple API for XML | `http://www.saxproject.org/` | SourceForge |

## C.5  XML Security

### C.5.1  XML Signature

The purpose of XML Signature is to digitally sign digital content (including XML documents and portions thereof). An XML Signature may be applied to the content of one or more resources. The XML Signature specifications define XML syntax and processing rules for creating and representing digital signatures. See Chapter 14 for an implementation.

W3C's home page for XML Signature is `http://www.w3.org/Signature/`.

| NAME | URL | STATUS | BODY |
|---|---|---|---|
| Canonical XML | `http://www.w3.org/ TR/xml-c14n` | Recommendation (March 15, 2001) and RFC 3076 (March 2001) | W3C and IETF |
| XML Signature Requirements | `TR/http://www.w3. org/xmldsig- requirements` | Working Draft (October 14, 1999) and RFC 2087 (July 2000) | W3C and IETF |
| XML Signature Syntax and Processing | `http://www.w3.org/ TR/xmldsig-core/` | Recommendation (February 12, 2002) | W3C and IETF |
| XML Key Management Specification (XKMS) | `http://www.w3.org/ TR/xkms/` | Note (March 30, 2001) | W3C |
| SOAP Security Extensions: Digital Signature | `http://www.w3.org/ TR/SOAP-dsig/` | Note (February 6, 2001) | W3C |

### C.5.2  XML Encryption

The purpose of XML Encryption is to define a process for encrypting/decrypting digital content (including XML documents and portions thereof) and an XML syntax used to represent the (1) encrypted content and (2) information that enables an intended recipient to decrypt it.

W3C's home page for XML Encryption is `http://www.w3.org/Encryption/2001/`.

| NAME | URL | STATUS | BODY |
|---|---|---|---|
| XML Encryption Requirements | `http://www.w3.org/TR/ xml-encryption-req` | Working Draft (March 4, 2002) | W3C |
| XML Encryption Syntax and Processing | `http://www.w3.org/TR/ xmlenc-core/` | Working Draft (March 4, 2002) | W3C |
| Decryption Transform for XML Signature | `http://www.w3.org/TR/ xmlenc-decrypt` | Working Draft (March 4, 2002) | W3C |

## C.5.3  Platform for Privacy Preferences Project

The Platform for Privacy Preferences Project (P3P) provides a simple, automated way for users to gain more control over the use of personal information on Web sites they visit. P3P defines an XML syntax to describe how a Web site handles personal information about its users. P3P-enabled browsers can "read" such a policy automatically and compare it with the consumer's own set of privacy preferences. The following is an example taken from the P3P 1.0 specification.

```
<POLICY xmlns="http://www.w3.org/2000/12/P3Pv1"
    discuri="http://www.catalog.example.com/PrivacyPracticeBrowsing.
    html">
 <ENTITY>
  <DATA-GROUP>
   <DATA ref="#business.name">CatalogExample</DATA>
   <DATA ref="#business.contact-info.postal.street">4000 Lincoln
   Ave.</DATA>
   <DATA ref="#business.contact-info.postal.city">Birmingham</DATA>
   <DATA ref="#business.contact-info.postal.stateprov">MI</DATA>
   <DATA ref="#business.contact-info.postal.postalcode">48009
   </DATA>
   <DATA ref="#business.contact-info.postal.country">USA</DATA>
   <DATA ref="#business.contact-info.online.email">catalog@example.
   com</DATA>
   <DATA ref="#business.contact-info.telecom.telephone.intcode">
   1</DATA>
   <DATA ref="#business.contact-info.telecom.telephone.loccode">
   248</DATA>
   <DATA ref="#business.contact-info.telecom.telephone.number">
   3926753</DATA>
  </DATA-GROUP>
 </ENTITY>
 <ACCESS><nonident/></ACCESS>
 <DISPUTES-GROUP>
  <DISPUTES resolution-type="independent"
    service="http://www.PrivacySeal.example.org"
    short-description="PrivacySeal.example.org">
   <IMG src="http://www.PrivacySeal.example.org/Logo.gif"
   alt="PrivacySeal's logo"/>
   <REMEDIES><correct/></REMEDIES>
  </DISPUTES>
 </DISPUTES-GROUP>
 <STATEMENT>
  <PURPOSE><admin/><develop/></PURPOSE>
  <RECIPIENT><ours/></RECIPIENT>
```

```
<RETENTION><stated-purpose/></RETENTION> <!-- Note also that the
site's human-readable privacy policy MUST mention that data is
purged every two weeks, or provide a link to this information. -->
<DATA-GROUP>
 <DATA ref="#dynamic.clickstream"/>
 <DATA ref="#dynamic.http"/>
</DATA-GROUP>
</STATEMENT>
</POLICY>
```

W3C's home page for P3P is `http://www.w3.org/P3P/`.

| NAME | URL | STATUS | BODY |
|---|---|---|---|
| The Platform for Privacy Preferences 1.0 (P3P 1.0) Specification | `http://www.w3.org/TR/ P3P/` | Proposed Recommendation (January 28, 2002) | W3C |
| A P3P Preference Exchange Language 1.0 (APPEL 1.0) | `http://www.w3.org/TR/ P3P-preferences` | Working Draft (February 26, 2001) | W3C |

# C.6  Web Services

This section describes standards activities for Web services (see Chapter 13).

## C.6.1  XML Protocol (SOAP)

The goal of XML Protocol is to develop technologies that allow two or more peers to communicate in a distributed environment, using XML as the encapsulation language. Solutions developed by this activity allow a layered architecture on top of an extensible and simple messaging format, which provides robustness, simplicity, reusability, and interoperability. The specification of Simple Object Access Protocol (SOAP) will be updated in this activity.

W3C's home page for XML Protocol is `http://www.w3.org/2000/xp/`.

| NAME | URL | STATUS | BODY |
|---|---|---|---|
| XML Protocol Abstract Model | `http://www.w3.org/TR/ xmlp-am/` | Working Draft (July 9, 2001) | W3C |
| XML Protocol (XMLP) Requirements | `http://www.w3.org/TR/ xmlp-reqs/` | Working Draft (March 19, 2001) | W3C |
| Simple Object Access Protocol (SOAP) 1.1 | `http://www.w3.org/TR/ SOAP/` | Note (May 8, 2000) | W3C |

| | | | |
|---|---|---|---|
| SOAP Version 1.2 Part 1: Messaging Framework | `http://www.w3.org/TR/ soap12-part1/` | Working Draft (December 17, 2001) | W3C |
| SOAP Version 1.2 Part 2: Adjuncts | `http://www.w3.org/TR/ soap12-part2/` | Working Draft (December 17, 2001) | W3C |

### C.6.2  Web Services Description Language

Web Services Description Language (WSDL) is an XML format for describing network services as a set of endpoints operating on messages containing either document-oriented or procedure-oriented information. The operations and messages are described abstractly and then bound to a concrete network protocol and message format to define an endpoint. Related concrete endpoints are combined into abstract endpoints (services).

| NAME | URL | STATUS | BODY |
|---|---|---|---|
| Web Services Description Language (WSDL) 1.1 | `http://www.w3.org/TR/ wsdl` | Note (March 15, 2001) | W3C |

### C.6.3  Universal Description, Discovery, and Integration

The Universal Description, Discovery, and Integration (UDDI) project is a sweeping industry initiative. The project creates a platform-independent, open framework for describing services, discovering businesses, and integrating business services using the Internet as well as an operational registry.

The UDDI specification documents are available at `http://www.uddi.org/`.

## C.7  Java Specification Requests

The following table is a list of Java Specification Requests (JSRs) related to this book.

| NUMBER | TITLE | URL | DESCRIPTION |
|---|---|---|---|
| 5 | XML Parsing Specification | `http://www.jcp.org/ jsr/detail/5.jsp` | The Java API for XML Parsing (JAXP) allows developers to easily use XML Parsers in their applications via the industry-standard SAX and DOM APIs. |
| 31 | XML Data Binding Specification | `http://www.jcp.org/ jsr/detail/31.jsp` | This JSR is a facility for compiling an XML schema into one or more Java classes that can parse, generate, and validate documents that follow the schema. |

| 53 | Java Servlet 2.3 and JavaServer Pages 1.2 Specifications | http://www.jcp.org/jsr/detail/53.jsp | The title says it all. |
|---|---|---|---|
| 63 | Java API for XML Processing (JAXP) 1.1 | http://www.jcp.org/jsr/detail/63.jsp | The proposed specification will define a set of implementation-independent portable APIs supporting XML processing. |
| 67 | Java APIs for XML Messaging (JAXM) 1.0 | http://www.jcp.org/jsr/detail/67.jsp | JAXM provides an API for packaging and transporting business transactions using on-the-wire protocols being defined by ebXML.org, OASIS, W3C, and IETF. |
| 74 | Public Key Cryptography Standards (PKCS) 1.0 | http://www.jcp.org/jsr/detail/74.jsp | This JSR defines a standard set of APIs for a subset of the Public Key Cryptography Standards (PKCS #1, #5, #7, #8, #9, #10, and #12). |
| 93 | Java API for XML Registries 1.0 (JAXR) | http://www.jcp.org/jsr/detail/93.jsp | JAXR provides an API for a set of distributed Registry Services that enable business-to-business integration between business enterprises, using the protocols being defined by ebXML.org, OASIS, and ISO 11179. |
| 101 | Java APIs for XML based RPC (JAX-RPC) | http://www.jcp.org/jsr/detail/101.jsp | These are Java APIs to support emerging industry XML-based RPC standards. |
| 102 | JDOM 1.0 | http://www.jcp.org/jsr/detail/102.jsp | JDOM is a way to represent an XML document for easy and efficient reading, manipulation, and writing. |
| 104 | XML Trust Service APIs | http://www.jcp.org/jsr/detail/104.jsp | This JSR defines a standard set of APIs and a protocol for a "trust service." A key objective of the protocol design is to minimize the complexity of applications using XML Signature. By becoming a client of the trust service, the application is relieved of the complexity and syntax of the underlying PKI used to establish trust relationships, which may be based on a different specification, such as X.509/PKIX, SPKI, or PGP. |

| 105 | XML Digital Signature APIs | http://www.jcp.org/jsr/detail/105.jsp | This JSR defines a standard set of APIs for XML digital signature services. The XML Digital Signature specification is defined by W3C. This proposal defines and incorporates the high-level implementation-independent Java APIs. |
| --- | --- | --- | --- |
| 106 | XML Encryption APIs | http://www.jcp.org/jsr/detail/106.jsp | This JSR defines a standard set of APIs for XML digital encryption services. This proposal defines and incorporates the high-level implementation-independent Java APIs. |
| 109 | Implementing Enterprise Web Services | http://www.jcp.org/jsr/detail/109.jsp | This specification defines the programming model and runtime architecture for implementing Web services in Java. |
| 110 | Java APIs for WSDL | http://www.jcp.org/jsr/detail/110.jsp | This JSR provides a standard set of APIs for representing and manipulating services described by WSDL documents. These APIs define a way to construct and manipulate models of service descriptions. |
| 152 | JavaServer Pages 1.3 Specification | http://www.jcp.org/jsr/detail/152.jsp | The title says it all. |
| 153 | Enterprise JavaBeans 2.1 | http://www.jcp.org/jsr/detail/153.jsp | The Enterprise JavaBeans 2.1 specification extends the existing Enterprise JavaBeans 2.0 specification with new features, including support for JAXM message-driven beans, enhancements to EJB QL to support aggregate and other operations, support for linking of messaging destinations, support for Web services uses within EJB, and a container-managed timer service. |
| 154 | Java Servlet 2.4 Specification | http://www.jcp.org/jsr/detail/154.jsp | This specification builds on Servlet Specification version 2.3 by enhancing existing features and adding new and reasonably small facilities. |
| 155 | Web Services Security Assertions | http://www.jcp.org/jsr/detail/155.jsp | This JSR provides a set of APIs for securely exchanging assertions between Web services based on OASIS SAML. |

| 156 | XML Trans-actioning API for Java (JAXTX) | http://www.jcp.org/jsr/detail/156.jsp | JAXTX provides an API for packaging and transporting ACID transactions (as in JTA) and extended transactions (for example, the BTP from OASIS) using the protocols being defined by OASIS and W3C. |
| 157 | ebXML CPP/A APIs for Java | http://www.jcp.org/jsr/detail/157.jsp | This JSR provides a standard set of APIs for representing and manipulating Collaboration Profile and Agreement information described by ebXML Collaboration Protocol Profile/Agreement (CPP/A) documents. |

# C.8 Other Topics

## C.8.1 Web Distributed Authoring and Versioning

HTTP is good for distributing contents to clients. For publishing to a Web server, on the other hand, more primitive protocols such as FTP are usually used. Web Distributed Authoring and Versioning (WebDAV), being defined by IETF, tries to address this issue by extending the existing HTTP protocol. This set of extensions to the HTTP protocol allows users to collaboratively edit and manage files on remote Web servers. For example, WebDAV supports locking and versioning for distributed authoring. XML is used as the data format for exchanging complex queries and responses on such properties as authors, versions, and locks. The following example shows a simple query in XML along with the extended HTTP header.

```
PROPFIND /container/ HTTP/1.1
Host: www.foo.bar
Depth: 1
Content-Type: text/xml; charset="utf-8"
Content-Length: xxxx

<?xml version="1.0" encoding="utf-8" ?>
<D:propfind xmlns:D="DAV:">
 <D:allprop/>
</D:propfind>
```

| NAME | URL | STATUS | BODY |
| --- | --- | --- | --- |
| HTTP Extensions for Distributed Authoring—WEBDAV | http://www.ietf.org/rfc/rfc2518.txt | RFC 2518 (February 1999) | IETF |

## C.8.2 Wireless Markup Language

Wireless Markup Language (WML) is a markup language based on XML that is intended for use in specifying content and user interfaces for narrowband devices, including cellular phones and pagers. It is being defined by the Wireless Application Protocol Forum (WAP Forum). A single WML document is known as a *deck*. A deck consists of multiple primitive pages called *cards*. Thus, no communication is necessary as long as the user is navigating within a deck. The following simple example shows a deck consisting of two cards.

```
<?xml version='1.0'?>
<!DOCTYPE wml PUBLIC "-//WAPFORUM//DTD WML 1.1//EN"
"http://www.wapforum.org/DTD/wml_1.1.xml">
<wml>
  <card>
    <do type="accept">
      <go href="#card2"/>
    </do>
    Hello world! This is the first card...
  </card>
  <card name="card2">
    This is the second card. Goodbye.
  </card>
</wml>
```

| NAME | URL | BODY |
| --- | --- | --- |
| Wireless Markup Language Specification | http://www.wapforum.org/what/technical.htm | WAP Forum |

## C.8.3 XHTML

XHTML is a reformulation of HTML 4 as an XML 1.0 application. It provides three DTDs corresponding to the ones defined by HTML 4. The semantics of the elements and their attributes are defined in the W3C Recommendation for HTML 4.

W3C's home page for HTML is http://www.w3.org/MarkUp/.

| NAME | URL | STATUS | BODY |
| --- | --- | --- | --- |
| XHTML 1.0: The Extensible HyperText Markup Language | http://www.w3.org/TR/xhtml1/ | Recommendation (January 26, 2000) | W3C |
| XHTML Basic | http://www.w3.org/TR/xhtml-basic/ | Recommendation (December 19, 2000) | W3C |
| Modularization of XHTML | http://www.w3.org/TR/xhtml-modularization/ | Recommendation (April 10, 2001) | W3C |

| XHTML 1.1—Module-based XHTML | `http://www.w3.org/TR/xhtml11/` | Recommendation (May 31, 2001) | W3C |

## C.8.4  XML Query

This activity is relatively new. The mission statement says that XML Query provides flexible query facilities to extract data from real and virtual documents on the Web, therefore finally providing the needed interaction between the Web world and the database world. Ultimately, collections of XML files will be accessed like databases.

W3C's home page for XML Query is `http://www.w3.org/XML/Query`.

| NAME | URL | STATUS | BODY |
| --- | --- | --- | --- |
| XML Query Requirements | `http://www.w3.org/TR/xmlquery-req` | Working Draft (February 15, 2001) | W3C |
| XQuery 1.0 and XPath 2.0 Data Model | `http://www.w3.org/TR/query-datamodel/` | Working Draft (December 20, 2001) | W3C |
| XQuery 1.0 Formal Semantics | `http://www.w3.org/TR/query-semantics/` | Working Draft (March 26, 2002) | W3C |
| XQuery 1.0: An XML Query Language | `http://www.w3.org/TR/xquery/` | Working Draft (December 20, 2001) | W3C |
| XML Syntax for XQuery 1.0 (XQueryX) | `http://www.w3.org/TR/xqueryx` | Working Draft (June 7, 2001) | W3C |
| XQuery 1.0 and XPath 2.0 Functions and Operators Version 1.0 | `http://www.w3.org/TR/xquery-operators/` | Working Draft (December 20, 2001) | W3C |

APPENDIX **D**

# JDBC Primer

## D.1 Introduction

Java Database Connectivity (JDBC) is a standard database access interface with SQL. It provides programmers with a uniform interface to various relational database systems regardless of differences in implementations. JDBC is part of Java 2 (the `java.sql` package). We use JDBC version 2.0 in this book (a proposal of JDBC 3.0 is available at the time we are writing this book). Database vendors ship JDBC drivers that enable accessing their databases from Java program through JDBC.

For example, DB2, IBM's RDBMS, provides a JDBC driver class, `COM.ibm.db2.jdbc.app.DB2Driver`, that translates JDBC calls into native DB2 calls and converts the DB2 results into a JDBC data structure. The class `COM.ibm.db2.jdbc.net.DB2Driver` is used for remote access of the database. Thus application programs that use JDBC can run with different RDBMSs without modification. A list of more than 150 JDBC drivers supplied by database vendors is maintained at Sun's Web site (`http://industry.java.sun.com/products/jdbc/drivers`).[1]

In this book (in particular, in Chapter 11), we use DB2 Universal Database (DB2) as the DBMS implementation, but the example programs should run with any other implementations by using an appropriate JDBC driver. The accompanying CD-ROM contains a trial version of DB2 you can use. Or you can download the latest trial version of DB2 from `http://www.ibm.com/software/data/`. See the documentation on the CD-ROM to find out how to install DB2.

In this section, assume there is a `sample` database that contains a table named `employee`. The `employee` table has the schema shown in Table D.1. The `sample`

---

[1] If you want to use Open Database Connectivity (ODBC), a standard API for accessing a database, to connect Java applications to Microsoft Access or Excel, you can use the JDBC-ODBC bridge, but describing the details exceeds the scope of this book.

database and the `employee` table are included in DB2 as a sample, so you do not have to create them.

**Table D.1**   Schema for the `employee` Table

| COLUMN NAME | DATA TYPE |
| --- | --- |
| EMPNO | CHARACTER(6) |
| FIRSTNME | VARCHAR(12) |
| LASTNAME | VARCHAR(15) |
| JOB | CHARACTER(8) |
| EDLEVEL | SMALLINT |
| SEX | CHARACTER(1) |
| BIRTHDATE | DATE |
| SALARY | DECIMAL |
| BONUS | DECIMAL |

Symbols such as CHARACTER and DATE show the data types of each column. For example, the data type CHARACTER(6) represents a six-letter character string, while VARCHAR(12) represents the data type of a character string that is at most 12 characters long. We use the data in this table as shown in Table D.2, which is based on the schema in Table D.1.

**Table D.2**   Content of the `employee` Table

| EMPNO | FIRSTNME | LASTNAME | PHONENO | JOB | SEX | BIRTHDATE | SALARY | BONUS |
| --- | --- | --- | --- | --- | --- | --- | --- | --- |
| 000010 | SHILI | HAAS | 3978 | PRES | F | 1933-08-24 | 52750.00 | 1000.00 |
| 000020 | MICHAEL | THOMPSON | 3476 | MANAGER | M | 1948-02-02 | 41250.00 | 800.00 |
| 000030 | SALLY | KWAN | 4738 | MANAGER | F | 1941-05-11 | 38250.00 | 800.00 |
| 000050 | JOHN | GEYER | 6789 | MANAGER | M | 1925-09-15 | 40175.00 | 800.00 |
| 000060 | IRVING | STERN | 6423 | MANAGER | M | 1945-07-07 | 32250.00 | 500.00 |
| 000070 | EVA | PULASKI | 7831 | MANAGER | F | 1953-05-26 | 36170.00 | 700.00 |
| 000090 | EILEEN | HENDERSON | 5498 | MANAGER | F | 1941-05-15 | 29750.00 | 600.00 |
| 000100 | THEODORE | SPENSER | 0972 | MANAGER | M | 1956-12-18 | 26150.00 | 500.00 |
| 000110 | VINCENZO | LUCCHESSI | 3490 | SALESREP | M | 1929-11-05 | 46500.00 | 900.00 |
| 000120 | SEAN | O'CONNELL | 2167 | CLERK | M | 1942-10-18 | 29250.00 | 600.00 |

Before creating a sample program that accesses the `employee` table by using JDBC, let's look at the functions of JDBC.

## D.2  JDBC Package

JDBC 2.0 is provided by the `java.sql` package. Tables D.3, D.4, and D.5 show lists of classes, interfaces, and exceptions, respectively.

**Table D.3**   Classes in the `java.sql` Package

| CLASS NAME | DESCRIPTION |
| --- | --- |
| Date | A subclass of `java.util.Date` and a thin wrapper of the SQL DATE value |
| DriverManager | A class that provides basic services for managing multiple JDBC drivers, such as loading drivers and logging on |
| DriverPropertyInfo | A class for accessing the properties of loading drivers |
| SQLPermission | A class used when Security Manager inspects an applet that calls the `setLogWriter()` method |
| Time | A subclass of `java.util.Date` and a thin wrapper of the SQL TIME value |
| Timestamp | A subclass of `java.util.Date` and a thin wrapper of the SQL TIMESTAMP value |
| Types | A class that defines SQL data types such as INTEGER and VARCHAR |

**Table D.4**   Interfaces in the `java.sql` Package

| INTERFACE NAME | DESCRIPTION |
| --- | --- |
| Array | An interface that represents the SQL ARRAY type |
| BLOB | An interface that represents the Binary Large Object (BLOB) type |
| CLOB | An Interface that represents the SQL Character Large Object (CLOB) type |
| CallableStatement | An interface used for executing a stored procedure of SQL |
| Connection | An interface that represents a session with a specific database. It is created by calling the `Driver#connection()` method. |
| DatabaseMetaData | An interface used for accessing the properties of a database as a whole |
| Driver | This is the main body of a JDBC driver. An implementation-specific driver must implement this interface. |
| Ref | An interface used to access the SQL structured type |
| PreparedStatement | A subinterface of `Statement` that represents a compiled query for efficiently executing the same query many times |
| ResultSet | An interface that provides access to a table of data generated by executing an SQL query using a `Statement` object |
| ResultSetMetaData | An interface used for accessing the properties of query results, such as data types and column names |
| SQLData | An interface used to access an SQL user-defined type |
| SQLInput | An interface that represents an input stream to get an SQL user-defined type stored in database |
| SQLOutput | An interface that represents an output stream to write attributes of a user-defined data type to the database |
| Statement | An interface used for executing an SQL statement |
| Struct | An interface that represents an SQL structured type |

**Table D.5** Exceptions in the `java.sql` Package

| EXCEPTION NAME | DESCRIPTION |
|---|---|
| SQLException | An exception that provides information on a database access error |
| SQLWarning | An exception that provides information on a database access warning |
| BatchUpdateException | An exception that occurs during a batch update operation |
| DataTruncation | An exception that occurs when JDBC unexpectedly truncates data |

Let us write a sample program by using JDBC. First, we need to import the JDBC package as follows:

```
import java.sql.Connection;
import java.sql.Statement;
import java.sql.PreparedStatement;
import java.sql.ResultSet;
import java.sql.DriverManager;
import java.sql.SQLException;
```

# D.3 Loading a JDBC Driver

The second step in writing our sample program is to load a JDBC driver. We do this by telling `DriverManager`, which manages JDBC drivers and provides an appropriate driver for the database. There are a few different ways to achieve this, but the simplest is to use the `Class.forName()` method as follows:

```
Class.forName("COM.ibm.db2.jdbc.app.DB2Driver");
```

In this case, we used the JDBC driver for DB2. The class name must be replaced when you use other database implementations. The coding style is something strange. What happens when the method is called?

The static method `forName()`, defined in the class `Class`, generates a class object of the specified class. How is the JDBC driver object registered with `DriverManager`? Any JDBC driver has to have a static initialization part that is executed when the class is loaded, as shown next. As soon as the class loader loads this class, the static initialization is executed, which automatically registers it as a JDBC driver with `DriverManager`.

```
public class DB2Driver {

  public DB2Driver() {
    ...
  }
```

```
static {
   try  {
           DriverManager.registerDriver(new DB2Driver());
           return;
   } catch(SQLException sqlexception)
 }
}
```

Some drivers do not automatically create an instance when the class is loaded. If `forName()` alone does not create a driver instance for you, you may need to explicitly create an instance as follows:

```
Class.forName("COM.ibm.db2.jdbc.app.DB2Driver").newInstance();
```

## D.4  Connecting to a Database

With the driver in place, we next need to specify the data source we want to access. In JDBC, a data source is specified by a URL with a scheme `jdbc`. The syntax of the URL is as follows:

```
jdbc:<subprotocol>:<subname>
```

`Subprotocol` represents the type of the data source, which is normally the name of the database system, such as `db2` and `oracle`. `Subname` is used to specify information for the database. The contents and syntax of `subname` depend on the subprotocol.

For example, to access a table named `sample` stored in IBM's DB2 on a local machine, you need to create a URL as follows:

```
String url = "jdbc:db2:sample";
```

If the database is on a remote machine, the URL would look like this:

```
String url = "jdbc:db2:monet.trl.ibm.com/sample";
```

You connect the database using this URL by calling the `getConnection()` method.

```
// Userid and password are specified as
// System properties
String userid = System.getProperty("chap11.userid");
String password =System.getProperty("chap11.password");
// Connects with default username and password
Connection con = DriverManager.getConnection(url,
                                        userid,
                                        password);
```

Often databases are protected by a user name and password for proper access control. With JDBC, you can specify your user name and password when connecting to a database as follows. If a user name and password are not specified (see the previous code fragment), a default user (login user) name and password are used.

```
// Default username is used
Connection con = DriverManager.getConnection(url);
```

## D.5  Submitting a Query

Once a connection is established, we can submit queries to the database. However, we first need to create a `Statement` object by calling the `createStatement()` method of the `Connection` object:

```
Statement stmt = con.createStatement();
```

Now we are ready to submit an SQL query. You may need to be familiar with SQL to do this. Call the `executeQuery()` method with an SQL statement as its only argument, and you get the `Resultset` object that contains the result. In this case, all records in the `employee` database are returned.

```
String SQLquery = "SELECT * FROM EMPLOYEE";
// Gets result of the query
ResultSet rs = stmt.executeQuery(SQLquery);
```

The class `ResultSet` defines a number of methods for accessing the result. The result set is basically a sequence of rows, over which we can iterate using the `next()` method. The result set maintains a `cursor` to remember the current row in the result set. A call of the `next()` method advances this cursor to the next row until the end of data, where `next()` returns `null`. Within the cursor row, you can access the value of each column by specifying either the index number of the column or the name of the column. The get*XX* methods, where *XX* represents data types such as `Int` and `String`, can be used to access each column.

The following code fragment shows how to retrieve the first column (`EMPNO`) and second column (`FIRSTNAME`) of the result set.

```
while (rs.next()) {
    String firstColumn  = rs.getString(1);
    String secondColumn = rs.getString(2);
    System.out.print(firstColumn);
    System.out.print(" " + secondColumn);
    System.out.print("\n");
}
```

Listing D.1 shows a sample program that accesses the `employee` table in the `sample` table.

**Listing D.1** Program to access the `employee` table, `appendixD/JDBCSample.java`

```java
package appendixD;

import java.sql.Connection;
import java.sql.Statement;
import java.sql.PreparedStatement;
import java.sql.ResultSet;
import java.sql.DriverManager;
import java.sql.SQLException;

class JDBCSample {
    static {
        try {
            // Register the driver with DriverManager
            Class.forName("COM.ibm.db2.jdbc.app.DB2Driver");
        } catch (Exception e) {
            e.printStackTrace();
        }
    }

    public static void main(String argv[]) {
        try {
            // URL is jdbc:db2:dbname
            String url = "jdbc:db2:sample";
            // Userid and password are specified as
            // System properties
            String userid = System.getProperty("appendixD.userid");
            String password =
                        System.getProperty("appendixD.password");
            // Connects with default username and password
            Connection con = DriverManager.getConnection(url,
                                                    userid,
                                                    password);

            // Creates statement
            Statement stmt = con.createStatement();
            String SQLquery = "SELECT * FROM EMPLOYEE";
            // Gets result of the query
            ResultSet rs = stmt.executeQuery(SQLquery);
            // Displays Result
            while (rs.next()) {
                String firstColumn  = rs.getString(1);
                String secondColumn = rs.getString(2);
                System.out.print(firstColumn);
                System.out.print(" " + secondColumn);
```

```
                        System.out.print("\n");
                    }
                    rs.close();
                    stmt.close();
                } catch(SQLException e) {
                    e.printStackTrace();
                }
            }
        }
```

Executing this program generates the following output.

```
R:\samples>java -DappendixD.userid="db2admin" -DappendixD.
password="db2admin" appendixD.JDBCSample
000010 SHILI
000020 MICHAEL
000030 SALLY
000050 JOHN
000060 IRVING
000070 EVA
000090 EILEEN
000100 THEODORE
000110 VINCENZO
000120 SEAN
```

This section introduced a program using JDBC. This program is quite simple but shows a typical pattern appearing in large applications. The next section describes other functions of JDBC by using more complex programs.

## D.6  Using a Connection Pool

We showed how to connect to a database in the previous section. However, connecting to a database is expensive work for most Web applications. Therefore, application servers provide various ways for managing database connections and reducing the overhead for the connections. However, the implementation is vendor-specific, and it is an obstacle to developing vendor-independent systems.

To resolve this issue, JDBC supports the `javax.sql.DataSource` and `javax.sql.ConnectionPoolDataSource` classes, which abstract low-level connection information. These classes are distributed separately as an optional package of JDBC 2.0.

By using the connection pool, you do not need to specify the database URI in a program. Instead, you use the Java Naming and Directory Interface (JNDI) to bind a declared name to a database. It makes a program more robust for changing database settings. The connection pool also provides a way to control the number of connections. We recommend that you use the connection pool if it is available in your middleware, such as an application server.

However, the detailed setting of connection information still depends on implementations of JDBC drivers. The function is now supported mainly by J2EE-compliant application servers, so it may be available when you are developing applications on an application server. In the other sections in this appendix, we use sample programs that connect to database without using the connection pool, as shown in Listing D.1.

On the server side, we should bind an actual database name with a JNDI name. If we are using DB2, the code for the binding looks like this.

```
import javax.naming.Context;
import javax.naming.InitialContext;
import COM.ibm.db2.jdbc.DB2DataSource;

// Connects with default username and password
DataSource ds = (DataSource)Class.forName(
                "COM.ibm.db2.jdbc.DB2DataSource").newInstance();
// Sets database-specific info. It depends on JDBC driver
// implementations
(DB2DataSource)ds).setDatabaseName("sample");

Context ctx = new InitialContext();
// Binds JNDI name and DataSource instance
ctx.bind("jdbc/SampleDataSource", ds);
...
```

The `Context` interface is used to specify a name context. A JNDI name is managed by the context. The `Context` object is initiated by calling a constructor of the `InitContext` class. An implementation of JNDI is provided as a `provider`. There are some implementations of the JNDI provider based on Lightweight Directory Access Protocol (LDAP), an ordinal file system, and so on.

The class `COM.ibm.db2.jdbc.DB2DataSource` is an implementation of `DataSource` and provides some (implementation-specific) methods to set database information. After setting the information, you register a JNDI name by using the `bind()` method. To learn the details of the connection pool, please consult the vendor-specific APIs for the `DataSource` implementation, or consult the manuals for the application server you are using.

The following is a code fragment for the client side to get a database connection.

```
import javax.naming.Context;          // JNDI
import javax.naming.InitialContext;
```

```
import java.sql.Conncection;            // JDBC 2.0 Core
import javax.sql.DataSource;            // JDBC 2.0 Optional
import COM.ibm.db2.jdbc.DB2DataSource;  // DB2 specific
...

// Connects with default username and password
Context ctx = new InitialContext();

DataSource ds = (DataSource)ctx.lookup("jdbc/SampleDataSource");
Connection con = ds.getConnection("db2admin", "db2admin");
...
```

You can get a `DataSource` object with the JNDI API, and it supplies a
`Connection` object. You can see there is no database URL like `jdbc:db2:`
`sample` in the previous code fragment. The string `jdbc/SampleDataSource`
shows a JNDI name for the database, and it is used to address the database instead
of the database URL.

# Index

# Also from Addison-Wesley

**Building Scalable and High-Performance Java™ Web Applications Using J2EE Technology**
By Greg Barish
0-201-72956-3
Paperback
416 pages with CD-ROM
© 2002

The concise roadmap Java developers and Web engineers need to build high-performance and scalable enterprise Web applications.

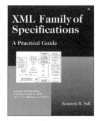

**XML Family of Specifications**
A Practical Guide
By Kenneth B. Sall
0-201-70359-9
Paperback
1072 pages with CD-ROM
© 2002

*XML Family of Specifications* provides a complete roadmap for understanding how XML, XSL, XML Schema, and related specifications interlink to create powerful, real-world applications.

**Inside Servlets, Second Edition**
By Dustin R. Callaway
0-201-70906-6
Paperback
912 pages with CD-ROM
© 2001

This book offers important background information on Web technologies, an inside look at Java servlet technology, a hands-on servlet tutorial, and a guide to advanced servlet programming for creating sophisticated, high-performance Web sites.

**XML and SQL**
Developing Web Applications
By Daniel K. Appelquist
0-201-65796-1
Paperback
256 pages
© 2002

*XML and SQL: Developing Web Applications* is a guide for Web developers and database programmers interested in building robust XML applications backed by SQL databases.

**Enterprise Java™ Servlets**
By Jeff M. Genender
0-201-70921-X
Paperback
464 pages with CD-ROM
© 2002

Learn to design and build a base enterprise servlet; create an architecture that makes your enterprise applications run faster and more reliably.

**The XML Companion, Third Edition**
By Neil Bradley
0-201-77059-8
Paperback
864 pages
© 2002

Building on the success of the first and second editions of *The XML Companion*, Neil Bradley has updated this accessible, in-depth reference to cover many of the new supporting standards that have emerged since XML was released in 1998.

# Register
## Your Book
at www.aw.com/cseng/register

You may be eligible to receive:
- Advance notice of forthcoming editions of the book
- Related book recommendations
- Chapter excerpts and supplements of forthcoming titles
- Information about special contests and promotions throughout the year
- Notices and reminders about author appearances, tradeshows, and online chats with special guests

## Contact us

If you are interested in writing a book or reviewing manuscripts prior to publication, please write to us at:

Editorial Department
Addison-Wesley Professional
75 Arlington Street, Suite 300
Boston, MA 02116 USA
Email: AWPro@aw.com

Addison-Wesley

Visit us on the Web: http://www.aw.com/cseng

## CD-ROM Warranty

Addison-Wesley warrants the enclosed disc to be free of defects in materials and faulty work-manship under normal use for a period of ninety days after purchase. If a defect is discovered in the disc during this warranty period, a replacement disc can be obtained at no charge by sending the defective disc, postage prepaid, with proof of purchase to:

Editorial Department
Addison-Wesley Professional
Pearson Technology Group
75 Arlington Street, Suite 300
Boston, MA 02116
Email: AWPro@awl.com

Addison-Wesley makes no warranty or representation, either expressed or implied, with respect to this software, its quality, performance, merchantability, or fitness for a particular purpose. In no event will Addison-Wesley, its distributors, or dealers be liable for direct, indirect, special, incidental, or consequential damages arising out of the use or inability to use the software. The exclusion of implied royalties is not permitted in some states. Therefore, the above exclusion may not apply to you. This warranty provides you with specific legal rights. There may be other rights that you may have that vary from state to state. The contents of this CD-ROM are intended for non-commercial use only.

More information and updates are available at:
http://www.awl.com/cseng/titles/0-201-77004-0